P9-DFY-002

Fodor's

WHERE SHOULD WE TAKE THE KIDS?

CALIFORNIA
by Clark Norton

Fodor's Travel Publications, Inc.

New York • Toronto • London • Sydney • Auckland

www.fodors.com

Special Sales

About the Writer

Clark Norton and his wife, Catharine, raised their children in San Francisco. Clark knows California from the far northern redwoods to the far southern deserts and from coastal cities and resorts to remote mountain passes. Recipient of several major travel-writing awards, Clark has written about traveling with children for *Parenting, Family Fun, Hemispheres, California Travel Ideas, Baby Talk, Discovery,* and the *San Francisco Examiner,* among other publications.

Dedication

To Catharine, Grael, and Lia, my companions on all trails; there would be no book without you.

Author's Acknowledgments

Among many people who have offered their assistance and guidance in preparing this book, the author would like to thank Fred Sater of the California Office of Tourism and numerous representatives of visitors bureaus, attractions, and parklands around the state, including: Kathleen Gordon-Burke, Cammie Conlon, Sharon Rooney, Karen Whitaker, Phil Weidinger, Pettit Gilwee, Keith Walklet, Dana Hartshorn, Laurie Armstrong, Amy Herzog, Ken Peterson, Katrina Paz, Koleen Hamblin, Carol Martinez, Monica Poling, Elaine Cali, Julien Foreman, Joe Timko, Anne North, Jamie Wolcott, Gary Sherwin, Carolyn Patten, and Diane Strachan. Special thanks go to Catharine, Grael, and Lia Norton for vital editorial and emotional support, and to Daniel Mangin, my ever-supportive editor at Fodor's.

Contents

Part I Openers

Part II Pleasures

Part III Places

How to Use this Book

Where Should We Take the Kids? California is divided into three parts. Part I, **Openers,** contains information and tips on packing, resources, transportation, lodging, restaurants, tours, climate, and other essentials about traveling with children in the Golden State.

Part II, **Pleasures,** provides detailed descriptions and evaluations of top family activities and destinations in a variety of categories, with suggested age ranges for each individual listing. Many activities are suitable for all ages, which means that you can comfortably bring children from infants to teenagers there. This book rates activities for children up to age 15, but older teens will probably enjoy most of the activities appropriate for 15 year olds. Parents should use these age ranges mostly as rough guidelines; only you know your children well enough to determine if they would appreciate a ballet at age 4 or a historic site at age 6.

Northern Forests and Lakes includes the expansive, scenic, and sparsely populated land of redwoods, lakes, and volcanoes that lies north of the San Francisco Bay Area and the Sierra Nevada mountain range. **Sierra and the Gold Country** combines the colorful, historic region where the Gold Rush began (including the state's capital city, Sacramento) with the adjoining Sierra Nevada mountain areas and their world-famous national parks: Yosemite, Sequoia, and Kings Canyon. **San Francisco and the Bay Area** includes cosmopolitan San Francisco plus nearby Oakland and San Jose, and the Napa/Sonoma Wine Country to the north. **Central Coast and Valley** covers family-favorite central Pacific resort towns such as Santa Cruz, Monterey, and Santa Barbara, along with the state's heartland, the Central Valley. **Los Angeles and Environs** spans the enormous urban complex ranging from Malibu to Orange County, Santa Mon-

ica to Riverside, along with L.A.'s nearby mountain resort areas. **San Diego and the Southern Deserts** extends from the beautiful oceanside city of San Diego through vast stretches of desert north and east to Palm Springs and Death Valley.

Part III, **Places,** provides a detailed overview of California's major cities—San Francisco, Los Angeles, and San Diego—plus the best family-friendly resort areas throughout the state (both by the sea and mountain/inland). You'll find recommended family activities and sights, plus places to stay and eat and play, for each place. Price information for lodgings and restaurants is grouped into three categories: Expensive ($$$: hotels, over $150; restaurants, over $50), Moderate ($$: hotels, $100–$150; restaurants, $25–$50), and Inexpensive ($: hotels, up to $100; restaurants, up to $25), based on a standard hotel room for four people (two adults and two children) or a typical breakfast, lunch, or dinner bill for a family of four (not including drinks, tax, and tip).

If you have difficulty locating any specific site, destination, or activity, check the general Index or the Directory of Attractions, which will also provide useful lists of places of interest and activities arranged by age group and location.

Now gather up the kids, grab some toys and snacks for the road, and get ready to explore the Golden State, family style.

Icons and Abbreviations

(👫) Recommended ages
🏠 Address, telephone number, cost, opening times

Credit card abbreviations: AE, American Express; D, Discover; DC, Diners Club; MC, MasterCard; V, Visa.

Please Write to Us

You can use this book in the confidence that all prices and opening times are based on information supplied to Fodor's at press time; Fodor's cannot accept responsibility for any errors. Time inevitably brings changes, so always confirm information when it matters—especially if you're making a detour to visit a specific place—and have a wonderful trip!

Were the restaurants recommended in the book as described? Did you find a recommended museum a waste of time? If you have complaints, Fodor's will look into them and ask the writer to revise the entries when the facts warrant it. If you've discovered a special place that hasn't been included, we'll pass the information along to the writer and ask him to check it out. So send your feedback, positive and negative, to the *Where Should We Take the Kids? California* Editor at 201 East 50th Street, New York, NY 10022. Also check out Fodor's Web site (www.fodors.com), where you'll find travel information on major destinations around the world and an ever-changing array of travel-savvy interactive features.

Karen Cure
Editorial Director

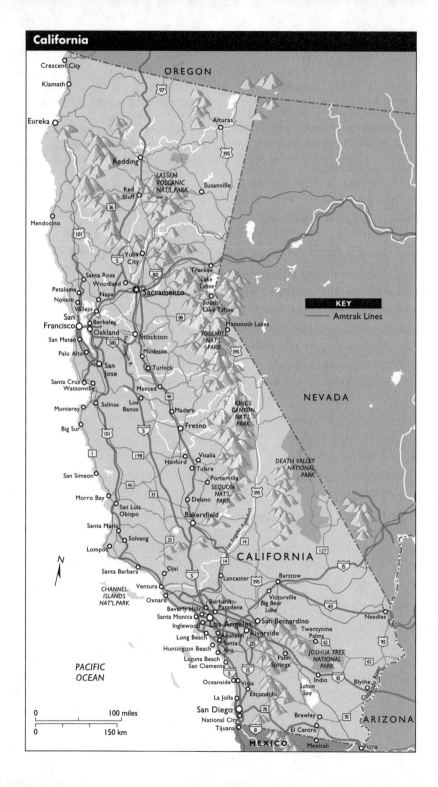

PART I

OPENERS

ARE WE THERE YET?   I
GETTING STARTED IN THE GOLDEN STATE

When I was growing up in the Midwest my parents piled my sister and me into the family car every summer and set off to explore the country. My favorite destination was California, where I cornered TV stars for autographs (in Los Angeles), downed my first taco (in San Diego) and crab cocktail (in San Francisco), posed for snapshots next to the world's largest trees (in Sequoia National Park), and careened down the Matterhorn (at Disneyland). So when I moved to San Francisco as an adult and became a father, I couldn't wait to show my son, Grael, some of the wonders of his native state. Our first big trip was to Lake Tahoe, where we went hiking. Gazing out over the alpine lake's deep blue waters, I asked Grael if he had ever seen anything so beautiful. Hearing no reply, I looked down at him—sleeping peacefully in his front pack. All that fresh air and exercise were too much for a boy of three weeks, I guess.

Grael is now a teenager, and has traveled in 40 states and 11 foreign countries. His sister, Lia, three years younger, had logged 15,000 vacation miles in the car before she was out of diapers and has joined Grael on numerous cross-country trips as well as journeys abroad. Along with their parents, they've gone horseback riding in the New Mexico wilderness, river-rafting in the California Gold Country, hot-air ballooning over the Napa Valley, cruising along the Alaska coast, RVing in Australia, snorkeling in Fiji, pyramid-climbing in Mexico, camping in Death Valley, skiing in the Sierra Nevada—and yes, taco-tasting in San Diego, picture-snapping in Sequoia National Park, and thrill-seeking at Disneyland.

Not all our family travels, to be sure, have been as peaceful as that moment overlooking Lake Tahoe when Grael was an infant. We've had our share of squalling and bickering, our lifelong quota of "Are we there yet?" and vast experience with the crankies, grumpies, and moodies (the kids have been pretty cranky at times, too).

And every chance we get, we keep coming back for more.

The main reason is that, for all the annoyances that may crop up along the way, traveling with children is ultimately a wondrous voyage of discovery, filled with potential excitement and adventure for every member of the family above the gurgling stage (and I'm convinced those early gurgling trips were somehow imprinted on our kids as well). Travel teaches children about the world—its cultures, foods, languages, natural wonders, history—with vivid immediacy. Travel-related activities can provide a lifetime of memories, whether it's catching close-up views of whales in the Pacific, the Rose Parade in Pasadena, learning to swim and canoe at a family camp in the Sequoias, descending deep into a limestone cavern at Lake Shasta, or ascending by cable car to a mountain peak above Lake Tahoe. Not every moment is enriching or thrilling or smile-inducing, of course—traveling with children is often rife with hard work and, at times, sheer frustration. But then, so is staying home with children.

No matter what the destination or activity, travel helps bring families closer by providing shared experiences. Even when Grael's responses to our questions about school and friends range from a teenager's shrug to a grunt, he invariably opens up when we reminisce about the time we hiked to the top of a volcano (in Lassen National Park) or the day he finally convinced his dad to ride "Top Gun" at Great America near San Jose. Lia loves to be the first in the family to recite the names of all five swimming pools at the San Diego Paradise Point Resort (which she sampled in one chlorine-soaked afternoon) or to debate which of us first spotted the mother bear and her cubs in Yosemite.

Traveling sometimes offers children unexpected challenges they would never encounter at home. Grael was just 7 and on horseback for the first time when his mount was stung by a hornet and bolted off at a full gallop; shouting "Whoa, Chico!" all the way, Grael held on for several hundred yards before the little pinto finally drew to a halt. Lia was 11 when she, her brother, and I went white-water rafting together; at a swirling, churning stretch of rapids known as Troublemaker, Grael and I (along with our burly guide) were washed from the raft by a sudden gush of water. Lia screamed but managed to keep her seat, as the raft spun like a top in the rapids before finally plunging downriver—where she helped rescue us wet, bedraggled males. In both cases, the kids walked a little taller after surviving their "awesome" adventures.

Having traveled with infants through teenagers, I'm convinced there's no single "good" or "bad" age to take kids on a trip; each stage of childhood offers both pluses and minuses for traveling families. Infants, for instance, are highly portable, never talk back, and may actually sleep in restaurants; on the other hand, they often require bulky equipment, always require diapers, and may cry in restaurants. Toddlers, meanwhile, need less equipment, but they often insist on toddling in inappropriate circumstances (hold off on those concert tickets), almost always talk back, and may throw tantrums in restaurants.

Preschoolers can usually stay seated longer than toddlers, and will pay attention to at least some of the sights you point out to them. They may still tire easily, though—unless it's bedtime. Grade-schoolers are likely to take an active interest in the trip—but the active interest may be quite different from yours. Junior high (middle school) students are often excellent travelers, reflecting their growing maturity; alas, they've outgrown most children's discounts. Older teens can walk long distances, behave beautifully in restaurants, and truly appreciate cultural experiences—they just don't want to do any of that with their parents.

All kidding aside, traveling with children of significantly different ages can indeed present practical problems; it's unrealistic to expect a teenager and a preschooler, or a toddler and a grade-schooler, to enjoy all the same activities. Resorts, guest ranches, or family camps that offer organized age-appropriate programs for kids (see Chapters 12 and 13) are one popular solution. Theme and amusement parks (see Chapter 9) often have separate sections for young and older children. In any event, make sure to include activities suitable for each child every day. If feasible, try splitting up duties: One parent can take a toddler to Oakland's Children's Fairyland, for instance, while the other takes the 10-year-old to visit the Oakland Museum of California. In this book you'll find suggested age ranges for many of the activities described.

Whatever their age, children can absorb a surprising amount. Years after a trip Lia will astonish me by piping up, "Dad, you know those two lizardy-type things we saw that time in Death Valley? I found a picture in a book that looks just like them." (I consider myself lucky to remember what day it is, much less the lizardy-type things in Death Valley.) Like many kids, Grael and Lia became mini-experts on dinosaurs and assorted marine mammals by age 4 or 5. Early on, I learned to let them lead me through natural history museums—their confidence soared, and I got a crash course in Pinniped 101.

In fact, I soon discovered that my children were helping me become a better traveler—more flexible, more receptive, more relaxed. Part of the transformation was from necessity: For years Lia and Grael never knowingly passed up a playground or park, and regardless of our itinerary I invariably spent some of every day watching my kids play and the grass grow. (As one parent put it, "The perfect time to stop and smell the roses is right after you've kept your kids from trampling on them.") Children can also be great "icebreakers" on the road, forging instant friendships with other kids, parents, hotel and restaurant workers, even various types of officials; for all the times kids "slow you down," they can also help speed you onto airplanes and through lines of any type.

Young travelers also serve to remind us that many of nature's most compelling sights are all around us, simply waiting to be discovered. For creatures who never seem to notice an unmade bed or chocolate-stained shirt, kids have remarkable powers of observation. They may not see the redwood forest for the trees, but they'll spot a robin's egg at 50 paces; they may not care much about that mountain vista in the distance, but the pretty pebbles they find at their feet are future prizes for "show and tell." During a visit to the San Diego Zoo I watched as a father tried to steer his 4-year-old daughter in the direction of a Chinese lesser panda. She wouldn't budge, her attention completely focused on another animal. And what exotic species was the object of her fascination? A common gray squirrel burying an acorn.

Parents miss an opportunity, I believe, when they assume that kids can be happy only at Disneyland, enchanting though it may be. Most children have an innate and nearly boundless sense of curiosity. It never hurts to stretch their horizons, and they'll often surprise you with what interests and excites them—and what doesn't. Lia's first great travel food discovery wasn't the hamburger but fried squid, tentacles and all. Grael's first carousel ride, on the other hand, was an occasion for tears rather than smiles (his "horsey" didn't go up and down). The best approach, I've discovered, is simply to introduce kids to a wide range of travel experiences and not to let adult expectations get too much in the way of their finding a good time.

All this said, few children are "born" travelers; most need to be guided, starting in the days or weeks before a trip. Talking about your upcoming destination—what type of place it is, how you'll get there, how you expect your kids to behave en route, and what sorts of problems you may encounter once you arrive—can help relieve any anxieties and prepare them for unfamiliar situations.

If you're traveling to a place where your child's favorite food may not be available, for instance, mention that—then be sure to bring along a familiar snack to help ease the withdrawal. If you're planning a trip to Universal Studios Hollywood in the summertime, be sure to point out that riding "Jurassic Park" could mean a long wait in line. (A good way to pass the time while waiting, when that time arrives, is to make up some games: naming nearby objects that begin with the letters "A," "B," "C," and so on; counting the number of people in line wearing blue shirts, dangling earrings, or brown shoes; playing "I Spy"—"something red," "something round," etc.—about objects you can see while in line, with others having to guess what they are.)

Children's interest in a trip will usually grow in direct proportion to their involvement in the planning. School-age kids can write away for brochures, look at maps, and perhaps read a book or watch a film about the destination. If you're heading for Hearst Castle at San Simeon, the movie *Citizen Kane* (a thinly veiled bio of the castle's owner, newspaper tycoon William Randolph Hearst) would help set the scene; it's available on video. If you're visiting Point Lobos State Reserve near Monterey, the novel *Treasure Island* would make ideal reading; Point Lobos's rugged, beautiful landscape is said to have inspired the Robert Louis Stevenson classic.

Parents, meanwhile, need to do their own preparation; the last thing you want to encounter with tired kids in tow are transportation snafus or a string of "no vacancy" signs. Start by asking questions. If you're flying, quiz the airline about the availability of special meals (such as hamburgers or spaghetti) your child might like, or about the possibility of reserving bulkhead seats, which provide more room, and, on some carriers, bassinets. (See Chapter 2 for more information and tips on air travel.)

If you're planning to stay at a resort or big hotel, ask if it has a children's program and, if so, about the specifics (see Chapter 12 for evaluating children's programs). Inquire about the sizes and number of beds in the room. If your child needs a crib, make sure to reserve one when you call; just because a hotel says it has cribs doesn't mean one will be available when you arrive. (One basic rule when traveling is never to assume anything.) You may also want to check on the size and depth of the swimming pool (if any), whether there's a separate children's pool, and whether a lifeguard is on duty. Above all, make sure the hotel, resort, lodge—or any accommodation you're reserving—is child friendly. Fortunately for families, the trend these days is toward making children feel welcome, even at some of the fanciest resorts.

When you're nearing the start of your trip, check and double-check as much as possible. Make lists for yourself and your child; you don't want to leave home without the traveler's checks—or those disposable diapers.

Here are some more tips for traveling with kids that our family has gleaned from countless miles on the highway, numerous nights in hotel and motel rooms, and more road food than we might care to think about:

• When planning your departure, keep in mind your child's "best" and "worst" times of day, if any. A 7 AM start may work beautifully for early risers, not so well with kids who tend to be cranky in the mornings; a late-night flight may find your kids either sleeping peacefully or wide awake and overly tired.

• Unless you're riding in a van with unlimited space, pack only the minimum clothes you think you'll wear—then try to pare that down by half. A good rule of thumb is to "bring everything you need—but as little as possible." Always leave space in a suitcase or a vehicle for items acquired while on the road. Overcrowding is neither comfortable nor safe, and cramped kids tend to be crabby kids.

Bring a backpack for every child old enough to carry one, and let him pack it with things that provide some of the comforts of home. Make sure, however, that it includes the essentials: art supplies, a few books, and a favorite stuffed animal or doll (but perhaps not the one, indispensable "lovey," which, if lost, could ruin a trip; Lia was devastated when she left her cherished toy seal in a hotel room at age 5).

• When you're flying, always carry hard-to-replace or nonreplaceable items (medicines, any valuables, a child's favorite toy) with you in flight bags in case checked luggage is lost or delayed. Also, carry some emergency backup items you may need, such as extra underwear, socks, swimsuits, light nylon jackets, toothbrushes—and, for babies, extra formula and pacifier if appropriate, plus plenty of disposable diapers. (Never rely on the airlines to have diapers or other baby supplies on hand.)

• When you're carrying luggage through crowded airports, make sure you have at least one free hand to hold onto a small child. That's one reason to bring backpacks for kids and bags with shoulder straps for parents.

• Always dress the kids comfortably for travel; no one will care if they aren't wearing that Armani jumpsuit on the interstate. Stick to simple, color-coordinated, mix-and-match cotton outfits. To avoid fights, let kids who are old enough pick out their clothes themselves—including some favorite T-shirts, jeans, and shorts, and one out-to-dinner outfit. Two bathing suits, a pair of sneakers, sunglasses and sandals (in summertime), a windbreaker, and a hat are other essential items.

• Bring snacks, whether in a car, airplane, or out sightseeing. A hungry kid is generally an unhappy one, and restaurants, snack bars, and airline meals seldom seem to appear when you need them most. Avoid snacks that melt, crumble, stick, or dribble down chins. Instead, fill zip-top plastic bags with unsalted pretzels, crackers, and bite-size pieces of cheese. For children older than 4, add choices such as trail mix, dried fruit, or easy-to-eat fresh fruit, popcorn, and raw vegetable sticks. Water is the best car drink, because it doesn't stain or stick when spilled; refillable bottles with straws or squirt attachments are handy and easy to use.

• If appropriate, don't forget to pack: a night-light for a child afraid of the dark; extra prescription medications; a basic first-aid kit and manual; waterproof sunscreen; premoistened towelettes; lots of resealable plastic bags (for wet diapers and miscellaneous messy things); electrical outlet covers and safety gates for toddlers; a molded plastic bib for babies; a lightweight, collapsible stroller or a front pack; a portable bottle warmer that plugs into an automobile cigarette lighter; and, above all, your sense of humor.

• Some suggested travel toys and games: magnetic drawing slates, action figures, toy animals and vehicles, sticker books, coloring books, a book of car games.

Some things that might be better left at home: toys with small parts that can get lost; any toy that makes loud noises; any toy that can double as a backseat weapon. Try to limit the number of toys to a total that will fit in a shoe box.

• Bring a surprise toy or surprise package. The toy(s), games, books, treats and the like should be new and different enough to distract your children when the whining and bickering reach eardrum-popping levels—but try to hold off at least until you pull out of the driveway.

• Give the kids road maps and have them help navigate during a drive. They can estimate distances and learn some geography. Generally speaking, the more involved children are in a trip, the less antsy they'll be. And if they hold the maps, the less likely you'll hear, "Are we there yet?"

• If your children are subject to car sickness, bring along an over-the-counter nausea-quelling medication such as Dramamine (for ages 2 and up only), which has the added benefit of making kids drowsy. Meanwhile, keep fresh air circulating in the car, avoid curvy roads if possible, boost your children so they can easily see out the window (facing front in the front seat is best, facing rear in the backseat the worst), and don't let queasy types overeat or overdrink. And always keep a small container with a lid on hand.

• While traveling in a car, especially, make things as handy as possible for the kids to reach themselves—whether it's snacks, water, toys, art supplies, books, tapes, or pillows. This will save you from having to turn around every few seconds to pour your children drinks or hand them toys. A shoe box or pocketed organizer that fits over the backs of the front seats serves as a convenient container.

• Portable tape or CD players with headphones are worth their weight in gold. Both music and story tapes (these can be as simple as mom or dad reading a book) can provide hours of entertainment on the road. Don't forget extra batteries. The headphones are essential for peace and quiet; before we acquired some for our kids, my wife and I endured the Chipmunks' rendition of "Beat It" hundreds of times during one cross-country car trip.

If you have more than one child, bring two tape players and two of anything else that they might possibly squabble over; if feasible, label each item with their names.

• If you have two children who tend to quarrel in the backseat, keep them separated by placing pillows or toy boxes between them. Make a hard and fast rule: no touching each other. If you have three children, place the most mild-mannered in the middle between the other two.

• If kids squabble over who gets to sit in what seat, who gets to choose a campsite, or who gets to play the Mariah Carey tape first, put their names on a list and rotate the top name each day to decide who gets first choice when.

• Make picnicking a regular occurrence while on a driving trip. Find a local park, picnic table, or playground, and pull over for an alfresco meal. It will save money and allow the kids a chance to run around.

• Even if you aren't picnicking, take a break from driving every two hours or so. Kids need to let off steam; you may want to bring along a Frisbee, inflatable beach ball, softball and gloves, or other portable play equipment.

• Hotel room service makes for a nice indulgence. Kids love the ordering, the "special" delivery, and the eating in—think of it as an indoor picnic. And if they're feeling homesick, a hotel room may seem a bit more like home than a restaurant.

• If you have young children, try to arrive early in restaurants to avoid the most crowded dining times; you'll probably receive faster and more attentive service, and chances are the kids will be in a better mood.

• When you're planning a daily itinerary, make sure to include a mix of activities: indoor and outdoor, quiet and active, and things that appeal to both kids and adults. Flexibility is crucial; if the kids start to get cranky in the art museum, for instance, cut the visit short and head for the park.

• When scheduling a day's activities with an infant, try to stick to your baby's normal schedule for naps, feedings, and alert times; if you fly cross-country, keep in mind the time difference.

• Consider switching off child-care duties so that each parent can spend some time alone, if desired. Mom could take the kids for one afternoon, dad the next. And use baby-sitters so parents can have an occasional night out together.

• Don't try to cram too much into any one day. Leave plenty of time both for rest breaks and for those unexpected "surprises" that kids will scope out like radar, whether it's a playground or a frog pond.

• When in doubt about things to do, think: parks (playing, hiking, picnicking); water (swimming, boating, fishing, water slides); animals (zoos, aquariums, wildlife refuges); and unusual, fun-filled rides (roller coasters, cable cars, steam trains, flying teacups).

ESSENTIALS

Gearing Up to Go

Visitor Services

Write or call the **California Division of Tourism** (Box 1499, Department 200, Sacramento 95812, tel. 916/322–2881 or 800/862–2543, from the United States and Canada only, fax 916/322–3402 or 916/322–0501) to receive a free *California Visitor's Guide*. It contains listings and descriptions of attractions around the state plus discount coupons for some of them. You'll also receive information about special events and a map. **California Welcome Centers** can be found in the North Coast town of Arcata; Kingsburg, along Highway 99 in the Central Valley; Rohnert Park (Sonoma County) on Highway 101; Oakhurst (14 miles south of Yosemite National Park) on Highway 41; Anderson (Shasta County) on I–5 about 160 miles north of Sacramento; and San Francisco at Pier 39.

Other good sources of information include city, county, and regional visitors' bureaus and chambers of commerce. You'll find many of these addresses and phone numbers in Part III of this book. Some important regional offices not included in Part III are the **Shasta Cascade Wonderland Association** (1699 Hwy. 273, Anderson 96007, tel. 530/365–7500 or 800/326–6944), which dispenses information about seven northern California counties (Lassen, Modoc, Plumas, Shasta, Siskiyou, Tehama, and Trinity); the **Redwood Empire Association** (The Cannery, 2801 Leavenworth, 2nd floor, San Francisco 94133, tel. 415/394–5991 or 888/678–8502), which provides

guides to California's North Coast from San Francisco to Oregon; the **Sacramento Convention & Visitors Bureau** (1421 K St., Dept. 100, Sacramento 95814, tel. 916/264–7777); the **Central Coast Tourism Council** (Box 14011, San Luis Obispo 93406, tel. 805/544–0241), which covers coastal destinations from Santa Cruz south to Ventura; and the **California Deserts Tourism Association** (Box 364, Rancho Mirage 92270, tel. 760/328–9256), which provides information about six desert counties covering such areas as Death Valley, Palm Springs, Joshua Tree, and Anza-Borrego.

Information about national parks is available from the **National Park Service** (Western Region Information Center, Fort Mason, Bldg. 201, San Francisco 94123, tel. 415/556–0560). For maps and written information about state parks, contact the **California Department of Parks and Recreation** (Box 942896, Sacramento 94296, tel. 916/653–4000; 916/653-6995 for recorded information); the *Official Guide to California State Parks* costs $2. *California Escapes,* which provides thumbnail sketches of California's 275 state park lands and a calendar of special events and programs, is free. Most campgrounds can be reserved (up to seven months in advance) by calling 800/444–7275. For more information on outstanding state and national parks in California, see Chapter 8.

For information about outdoor activities such as fishing, hunting, and wildlife viewing, contact the **California Department of Fish and Game** (3211 S St., Sacramento 95816, tel. 916/227–2244). See Chapter 10 for details about outdoor sports.

Family-Oriented Tour Agencies

Family Adventure Tours (1164 Alvira St., Los Angeles 90035, tel. 323/939–2819) takes families on three-day group camping trips to Yosemite National Park, Anza-Borrego Desert State Park, Montana de Oro State Park, and other park lands in southern and central California. Trips include escorted nature walks, meals, and campground fees.

Grandtravel (6900 Wisconsin Ave., Suite 706, Chevy Chase, MD 20815, tel. 301/986–0790 or 800/247–7651) offers tours for people traveling with their grandchildren, in a catalog as charmingly written and illustrated as a children's book.

Rascals in Paradise (650 5th St., Suite 505, San Francisco 94107, tel. 415/978–9800 or 800/872–7225) arranges family trips in San Francisco, the Napa Valley Wine Country, the Monterey Peninsula, Los Angeles, and San Diego, among other California destinations.

Travel Wizards (200 Park Rd., Burlingame 94010, tel. 650/696–6900 or 800/446–0046) is a full-service travel agency. Ask for family-vacation specialist Andrea DeGraff.

Travelling with Children (2313 Valley St., Berkeley 94702, tel. 510/848–0929 or 800/499–0929) provides consultation services and makes reservations for California guest ranches, house rentals, and Disneyland packages, among other family vacations.

Additional Resources

Family Travel Times (40 5th Ave., New York, NY 10011, tel. 212/477–5524 or 888/822–4388; $39 per year) is a bimonthly national newsletter with a wealth of tips and up-to-date advice on traveling with children, including periodic features on California destinations. On Wednesday, you can call the editor and ask questions.

Specialty Travel Index (305 San Anselmo Ave., Suite 313, San Anselmo, CA 94960, tel. 415/459–4900; $10 per year for 2 issues) lists a number of specialized family vacation offerings in California, including hot-air balloon rides, guest ranches, and white-water rafting trips.

When to Go

If your children are not yet school age, consider traveling in the off-season (from September to May excluding holidays) when crowds are lighter and prices are often lower. A day at blockbuster attractions such as Disneyland or Universal Studios can be a much more relaxed experience in late fall than in mid-summer. On the other hand, many attractions limit their hours or close altogether during the off-season, so if a particular site is important to your family, call ahead to avoid disappointment. Many attractions close on major holidays such as Thanksgiving, Christmas, and New Year's; call ahead if you're traveling at one of these times.

Hotels and airlines sometimes lower rates in summer to attract families, but if you travel then, reserve accommodations (including park campsites) and transportation well in advance. The same goes for the winter and spring holiday periods.

Almost any weekend in the year finds a delightful outdoor festival, fair, or other special event somewhere in the state. To coordinate your visit with a special event, see Chapter 3.

California may not have the extreme seasonal contrasts of much of the rest of the country, but it's not all sun, sand, and surf, despite popular images. San Francisco, for instance, is often foggy and quite chilly in summer; long pants and sweatshirts are usually more suitable than shorts and T-shirts (it's best to dress in layers). Winter is the Bay Area's rainy season. The coast from San Diego north to San Luis Obispo tends to be mild year-round, with most rain falling in winter. The inland desert regions are among the hottest on earth in summer; try to time your visits here for the fall through spring. Deserts can turn quite cool at night, however, so be sure to bring jackets. The state's mountain areas often see snow from November until April, sometimes even into late spring and early summer, yet much of the Sierra Nevada averages 300 days of sunshine annually, and even winter days can be pleasantly mild.

What to Pack

Necessities like film and sunscreen lotion are available almost anywhere, but as a traveler you may end up buying them at shops on the tourist track, where prices can be high; stock up in advance to save money. If your kids are still in diapers, buy them (along with wipes) at local supermarkets—hotel sundry shops usually don't sell them, though they do sell toothpaste, aspirin, and other adult toiletry needs. Bring an extra pair of your glasses, contact lenses, or prescription sunglasses, and pack any prescription medications you need regularly. And be sure everyone in the family takes comfortable walking shoes—nothing ruins the fun of sightseeing like blistered feet.

On airlines, the adult baggage allowance applies for children paying half or more of the adult fare. In general, you are entitled to check two bags—neither exceeding 62 inches (length + width + height) or weighing more than 70 pounds. A third piece may be brought aboard as a carry-on; its total dimensions are generally limited to less than 45 inches; it must fit easily under the seat in front of you or in the overhead compartment. Diaper bags, like purses, are allowed in addition to carry-ons; strollers can be checked at the boarding gate and retrieved immediately upon arrival. You can bring an FAA-approved car seat aboard for your baby and hope to find an unoccupied seat for it (check with your airline to see if they accept your car seat and charge for this use).

Money for the Road

Traveler's checks are preferable in metropolitan centers; the most widely recognized are American Express, Citicorp, Diners Club, Thomas Cook, and Visa, which are sold by major commercial banks. Both American Express and Thomas Cook issue checks that can be countersigned and used by you or your companion. Typically, the issuing company or the bank at which you make your purchase charges 1% to 3% of the checks' face value as a fee. Record the numbers of checks as you spend them, and keep this list separate from the checks.

Many automated-teller machines **(ATMs)** are tied to international networks such as Cirrus and Plus. You can use your bank card at ATMs away from home to withdraw money from your accounts, or to get cash advances on a credit-card account (if your card has been programmed with a personal identification number, or PIN). There's usually a limit to how much you can get; check in advance. On cash advances you are charged interest from the day you receive the money. Transaction fees for ATM withdrawals outside your home turf may be higher than for withdrawals at home. For specific locations, call Cirrus (tel. 800/424–7787, for locations in the United States and Canada) or Plus (tel. 800/843–7587, for U.S. locations), and press the area code and first three digits of the number you're calling from (or of the calling area where you want an ATM).

Getting There

By Plane

California has seven international airports: San Francisco, Oakland, San Jose, Sacramento, Los Angeles, Ontario, and San Diego. When flying into the San Francisco Bay Area, you may find the Oakland and San Jose international airports more convenient, less crowded, and less of a hassle than San Francisco International; San Jose has one of the few airports in the country with a children's play area, the Kidport, which has a "runway" slide, aerial maps with blinking lights, and little air traffic control towers. In the Los Angeles area consider using Ontario, Burbank, or John Wayne/Orange County airports as alternatives to busy Los Angeles International. Regional airports provide access to the more remote parts of the state, including mountain ski resorts in the Sierra.

Major domestic airlines serving California include **Alaska** (tel. 800/426–0333); **American** (tel. 800/433–7300); **Continental** (tel. 800/525–0280); **Delta** (tel. 800/221–1212), **Northwest** (tel. 800/225–2525); **Southwest** (tel. 800/435–9792); **TWA** (tel. 800/221–2000); **United** (tel. 800/241–6522); and **US Airways** (tel. 800/428–4322). Internationally, **Virgin Atlantic Airways** (tel. 800/862–8621), which flies from London to Los Angeles and San Francisco, is one of the most family-friendly airlines, providing a backpack full of goodies for kids and video screens at every seat.

Most airlines provide special meals if requested in advance of the flight; a few offer hamburgers for kids, and almost all can provide fruit plates or meals to suit special diets. Don't count on domestic airlines to carry baby formula, though. A biannual issue of *Family Travel Times* details children's services on dozens of airlines (see Additional Resources, *above*).

KID DISCOUNTS. When you make plane reservations, be sure to state the ages of your children and ask about discounts and special packages available for families. Though it's no longer the norm, some airlines still offer children's discounts on certain flights, and infants under 2 generally fly free on domestic flights when held on a parent's lap. (A seat with belt is safer, though.) In recent years, the best family deals have been periodic "Kids Fly Free" promotions offered by several major airlines; these typically require an accompanying paying adult for each child. Southwest, Delta, and Alaska airlines have all featured special packages to Los Angeles (including flight, Disneyland or other theme park tickets, hotel, and rental car); call the airlines or ask a travel agent about offerings.

BABY ON BOARD. If you'd like a bassinet—not available on all airlines—be sure to request one when you make a reservation. You'll need a bulkhead seat for a bassinet, and be warned—the seat trays in the bulkhead usually fold out of your chair arm, which makes them impossible to use with a child on your lap.

By Train

With room for fidgety kids to roam about, train travel can be a great alternative for vacationing families—as long as you have the time and the trains go where you need to go. Snack bars, rest rooms, and water fountains help kids fend off travel boredom; reclining seats, overhead luggage racks, and even sleeping compartments and showers on long-distance routes make travel hours relatively comfortable. On **Amtrak** (tel. 800/872–7245 for information and reservations), kids' meals are served in dining cars, and children's activity books are available on long-distance trains.

Amtrak service in California includes segments of four major national trains: the *California Zephyr* (connecting Chicago and Oakland/San Francisco via Denver), the *Southwest Chief* (linking Chicago and Los Angeles), the *Sunset Limited* (connecting Miami and Los Angeles via New Orleans), and the *Coast Starlight* (running from Los Angeles to Seattle). Frequent daily in-state service includes the *Capitols* (linking San Jose, Oakland, and Sacramento); the *San Joaquins* (linking Bakersfield and Oakland); and the *San Diegans* (linking San Diego, Los Angeles, and Santa Barbara). Each of the in-state trains is also linked to Amtrak Thruway bus service to subsequent destinations, and to transit lines within the large cities.

Children ages 2 to 15 ride for half-fare on Amtrak, when accompanied by an adult paying full fare. Children under 2 ride free. For frequent train travelers, 15- and 30-day regional passes are a good value, allowing unlimited stopovers en route. Peak season, when fares are highest, is from June through August. While reservations are not required for some Amtrak trains, they are necessary for long-distance overnight coach seats, sleeping-car accommodations, and for certain special trains and services; it's a good idea to make reservations in any event, as many trains fill up, and you may be able to get advance-purchase discounts. You may also want to ask about special Amtrak packages to Disneyland, Hearst Castle, San Francisco, and San Diego. For an Amtrak Travel Planner, call 800/321–8684.

By Car

From scenic coastal and mountain highways to busy urban freeways, travel in California has become almost synonymous with the automobile. But keep in mind that California is the nation's third-largest state—that can add up to a lot of miles on the highway, and too much time spent in a car could prove tiring for children (and their parents). Consider using public transportation when convenient and available.

Major interstate highways in California include **I–5**, which bisects the state from north to south; **I–80**, which runs from the San Francisco Bay Area to the Lake Tahoe area and Reno; and **I–15**, which heads north and east from San Diego through the Mojave Desert toward Las Vegas.

CAR SEATS. California law requires that children under age 4 or weighing less than 40 pounds (regardless of age) must be secured in a child safety seat, and everyone age 4 or older must wear seat belts. If you're renting a car, be sure to reserve a safety seat if needed when you make your reservation.

RENTAL CARS. All major rental-car agencies serve California. When you call, ask about seasonal promotions, discounts, and possible tie-ins with hotels, airlines, and family attractions. Here are toll-free numbers for some of the top agencies: **Alamo** (tel. 800/327–9633); **Avis** (tel. 800/331–1212); **Budget** (tel. 800/527–0700); **Dollar** (tel. 800/800–4000); **Enterprise** (tel. 800/325–8007); **Hertz** (tel. 800/654–3131); **National** (tel. 800/227–7368); and **Thrifty** (tel. 800/367–2277).

Major international companies have programs that discount their standard rates by 15% to 30% if you make the reservation before departure (anywhere from 24 hours to 14 days), rent for a minimum number of days (typically three or four), and prepay the rental. More economical rentals may come as part of fly/drive or other packages.

Be aware that picking up the car in one city and leaving it in another may entail substantial drop-off charges or one-way service fees. Some rental agencies will charge you extra if you return the car before the time specified on your contract, too—ask before making unscheduled drop-offs. Many companies offer a prepaid gas option, where for a reasonable extra fee you can return the car with an empty gas tank; otherwise, fill the tank when you turn in the vehicle to avoid being charged for refueling at what you'll swear is the most expensive pump in town.

In general, if you have an accident, you are responsible for the automobile. Car-rental companies may offer a collision damage waiver (CDW), which can cost as much as $14 a day. You should decline the CDW only if you are certain you are covered through your personal insurer or credit-card company.

ROAD CONDITIONS. Call **Caltrans** (tel. 800/427–7623) from a touch-tone phone for information about California road conditions. For Northern California only, call 916/445–7623; for Southern California, call 213/628–7623. From a rotary phone call 916/445–1534 for statewide information.

Once You're Here

Special Family Programs

The **California Department of Parks and Recreation** (tel. 916/653–6995) sponsors programs and special events of interest to families. Many parks have family campfire programs and Junior Ranger programs for children (see Chapter 8). Recent events in state park areas have included a "Mother's Day Breakfast" at Henry W. Coe State Park (tel. 408/779–2728) southeast of San Jose; a Kids' Fishing Derby in June at Brannan Island State Recreation Area (tel. 916/777–7701) in the Sacramento Delta; an "Underwater Treasure Dive/Children's Treasure Hunt" at Malibu's Leo Carrillo State Beach (tel. 818/880–0350) in June; and an August "Family Day" at Calaveras Big Trees State Park (tel. 209/795–2334) near Arnold, highlighted by wagon rides, nature hikes, and crafts.

For hotel chains' family discounts, see *below*. Some cities and resort areas offer special discount coupon books; see Part III for details.

In Case of Sickness

Before leaving home, ask your pediatrician for any prescriptions you think your children may need. Also check with your insurance company to see whether you are covered for hospital emergency room or doctor visits while in California, and remember to bring insurance cards and forms for every family member.

If you're staying in a hotel, resort, or family camp, especially in a rural area, ask about the availability of health care there, including the location of the nearest hospital. Some resorts and camps have medical personnel on staff. Most hotels can furnish lists of local pediatricians and doctors or contact one for you.

To call for an **ambulance** or in the event of other medical emergencies, dial 911.

Places to Eat

California restaurants offer virtually every type of cuisine in the world, including "California cuisine," which emphasizes fresh ingredients and inventive combinations. Although gourmets may love this food, kids may turn up their noses at hot dogs with fennel-seed rolls or goat-cheese burgers. Ask questions before ordering to save a lot of grief. Tried-and-true casual options for families include '50s-era diners, "family-style" eateries, pizza parlors, and taco stands, as well as the ubiquitous national fast-food chains, but there's no need to limit yourself to these. Ethnic restaurants provide great food, often at bargain prices—try Italian, Mexican, Chinese, Vietnamese, and Basque restaurants, which tend to have child-friendly food and atmosphere. Introduce your children to fried calamari, *carne asada* burritos, Hakka salt-baked chicken, Vietnamese spring rolls (*cha gio*), or multicourse Basque feasts.

Many restaurants have special children's menus (usually limited to children ages 10 or 12 and under), and some allow children to order from the adult menu for half price. Some hotels (see *below*) allow young guests to eat free from children's menus, though convincing a preteen to order from a "small fry" selection may be tough. Anyway, children's menus are often limited to the burger/hot dog/fried chicken/grilled cheese school of cuisine. If they find that boring, ask your server if kids can share an adult portion—most restaurants that welcome families will try to accommodate smaller appetites—or try ordering appetizers instead of entrées.

Places to Stay

Many hotels and resorts now actively court family business, offering special deals such as allowing kids to stay free in a room with their parents. Others let families rent adjoining rooms at discounts, which is a great way for mom and dad to have some privacy. You can get the same effect, often for less money, by staying at an all-suites hotel.

Here are some prominent chains with California properties that have recently offered children's programs and discounts. Some of these deals are strictly seasonal or aren't available at all sites, however, so be sure to call for current information:

Best Western (tel. 800/528–1234) allows kids to stay free in their parents' room in most locations, though the maximum age to qualify varies widely, from 2 to 20. Some locations let kids eat free from children's menus.

Choice Hotels (tel. 800/424–6423)—which includes Comfort, Clarion, Quality, Sleep, Rodeway, EconoLodge, and Friendship Inns—allows kids 18 and under to stay free with parents at most locations.

Doubletree and **Red Lion Inns** (tel. 800/733–5466) allow kids 12 or 18 (varying by location) and under to stay free with parents.

Embassy Suites (tel. 800/362–2779) lets children 18 and under stay free with their parents, and everyone gets a complimentary cooked-to-order breakfast. Some locations offer "Family Friendly" suites—baby- and child-proofed suites that come stocked with emergency baby supplies. Some also have on-site day care.

Four Seasons Hotels and Resorts (tel. 800/332–3442) has children's programs such as Kids for All Seasons, which includes amenity bags filled with goodies, milk, and cookies upon arrival, and other perks. Video games, toys, children's movies, baby supplies—even child-size furniture—are all available. Guest rooms can be child-proofed upon request. At most hotels, kids under 18 stay free with parents.

Hilton Hotels (tel. 800/445–8667) offers the summertime Vacation Station, where kids can borrow classic games and toys for free, and receive a Family Fun Kit advising of

family activities in the area. Some locations have supervised kids' programs.

Holiday Inn (tel. 800/465–4329) allows kids 19 and under to stay free in their parents' room.

Howard Johnson Hotels (tel. 800/446–4656) lets kids under 18 stay free with parents. The free summertime Fun Packs contain crayons, puzzles, stickers, and comic books; in recent years, some locations have offered free video-game rentals.

Hyatt (tel. 800/233–1234) doesn't charge extra for kids under 18 staying in their parents' room and offers 50% discounts on second rooms most of the year, based on availability. During summers and on weekends, Hyatt resorts offer Camp Hyatt—supervised arts and crafts, cookie baking, puppet shows, and sing-alongs—for kids ages 3 to 12. At most Hyatt hotels, kids are handed a welcoming pack at check-in. "Frequent stay" kids can earn prizes.

Marriott (tel. 800/228–9290) lets kids 17 and under stay free at most locations. Some properties run supervised children's activities, such as nature hikes, fishing trips, treasure hunts, and pizza parties.

Radisson Hotels (tel. 800/333–3333) lets kids 14, 17, or 18 and under (varying by location) stay free. "Family Magic" offers families lower than regular rates, including discounts on second rooms, plus free breakfasts and activity kits for ages 6 to 12. The chain's designated "Family Approved" hotels (ask when making reservations) offer child-proofing kits, children's menus and books, playpens, and other family-oriented perks.

Ramada (tel. 800/272–6232) lets kids 18 and under stay free, and in some locations kids 10, 12, or 18 and under (varying by hotel) eat free.

Ritz-Carlton Hotels (tel. 800/241–3333) allows kids (age 12 or 18 and under, depending on location) to stay free, and offers discounted second rooms in some locations. The Ritz Kids program for ages 4 to 12 offers supervised nature walks, arts and crafts, sing-alongs, storytelling, and other activities, and lends out books, movies, and games. Some hotels have Christmas season "Teddy Bear Teas."

Sheraton (tel. 800/325–3535) lets kids 17 and under stay free in their parents' room.

Vagabond Inns (tel. 800/522–1555) are free for kids 18 and under when staying in their parents' room.

Westin (tel. 800/228–3000) offers at most resort locations the year-round Westin Kids Club with planned activities for kids age 12 and under. When families arrive in their rooms, they'll find them equipped with cribs, bed rails, night-lights, and potty seats. Jogging strollers, high chairs, and bottle warmers are available at no extra cost.

Wyndham Hotels and Resorts (tel. 800/822–4200) allows kids under 18 to stay free and offers second-room discounts at most locations. The supervised Kids Klub program for ages 5 to 8 and 9 to 12 provides activities—sing-alongs and scavenger hunts for younger kids, arts and crafts and sports for preteens.

For ski resorts offering special kids' programs, see Chapter 11; for individual resorts, lodges, and guest ranches with special kids' programs, see Chapter 12.

To obtain hotel reservations throughout California, often at a discount, try **Hotel Reservations Network** (tel. 800/964–6835), **Quickbook** (tel. 800/789–9887), or **Room Finders USA** (tel. 800/473–7829).

Finding B&Bs that welcome young children can be difficult. Many are filled with fragile antiques, serve communal breakfasts of fruit, bran muffins, and yogurt (not necessarily child-pleasers), and seldom have TV in the rooms. A Guide to California Bed and Breakfast Inns ($4) is published by the California Association of Bed and Breakfast Innkeepers (2715 Porter St., Soquel 95073, tel. 831/462–9191); it doesn't tell whether an inn is child-friendly, however. **Bed & Breakfast California** (tel. 650/696–1690 or 800/872–4500)— a reservations service ($10 fee) that represents 450 B&Bs, guest houses, and homes—will match families with accommodations that fit their needs.

Telephone Area Codes

During 1999 and 2000, watch for area code splits in the 619 (San Diego), 310 (coastal Los Angeles), 415 (San Francisco and Marin County), 408 (San Jose), and 909 (east of Los Angeles) regions, even though most of these experienced a previous split in 1997 or 1998. The 310 region will receive an "overlay" in July 1999, meaning that no existing 310 numbers will have to change; new numbers will receive a new 424 area code. If you dial a 310 number from another 310 number, however, you must dial 1 plus the area code first.

PART II

PLEASURES

Top Family Activities and Destinations by Category

DRAGON PARADES, WORM RACES, AND JUMPING FROGS
HOLIDAYS, FESTIVALS, AND SEASONAL EVENTS

3

Blessed by a near-perfect temperate climate, Californians enjoy an abundance of outdoor festivals, jubilees, fairs, and parades throughout the year. Pageantry, ethnic foods, live music, arts and crafts—plus some of the world's wackiest contests and competitions—are all part of the fun, and kids are drawn to such events like flies to cotton candy. In this chapter, events are listed in chronological order within each region of the state.

Long holiday weekends, of course, are prime time for any kind of celebration. The state of California observes all national holidays. If a holiday falls on a Saturday, the preceding Friday becomes a holiday; if a holiday falls on a Sunday, the following Monday generally becomes the holiday. Here are California state holidays: New Year's Day (**January 1**); Martin Luther King Day (**third Monday in January**); Presidents Day (**third Monday in February**); Memorial Day (**last Monday in May**); Independence Day (**July 4**); Labor Day (**first Monday in September**); Columbus Day (**second Monday in October**); Veterans' Day (**November 11**); Thanksgiving Day (**fourth Thursday in November and following Friday**); and Christmas (**December 25**).

For a comprehensive calendar of festivals and other special events in California, send for a copy of "California Celebrations" from the California Division of Tourism (Box 1499, Dept. 60, Sacramento, CA 95812, tel. 800/462–2543 or 800/862–2543). City and county visitors bureaus often compile listings of local events, which they will send on request.

Northern Forests and Lakes

Crustacean Festival and World Championship Crab Races

(🏃 3 – 15) Part of the fun of this event is watching the humans cajole the often-reluc-tant crustaceans into skittering down a race ramp to victory; winning bettors collect scrip for use in local stores. Smallish rock crabs are used for racing, while meatier (but slower) Dungeness crabs are the focal point of the crab feast that follows. (Hot dogs are on the menu for those who don't eat crab.) Children's games and entertainments and a Little Miss Mermaid Contest are also featured, along with arts and crafts and 5K and 10K runs (humans only).

🏛 *Del Norte County Fairgrounds, Hwy. 101, Crescent City, tel. 707/464–3174 or 800/ 343–8300. Sun. of Presidents Day weekend. Admission free.*

Whale Festivals

(🕺 6–15) To celebrate the gray whales' annual Pacific migrations, the North Coast resort towns of Mendocino and Fort Bragg each hold a Whale Festival (Mendocino's is on the first weekend of March, Fort Bragg's on the third). During the festivals the Point Cabrillo Lightstation, usually closed to the public, is opened for whale viewing. Families can also join 1½-hour whale-watching boat trips out of Fort Bragg's Noyo Harbor (offered by several charter companies) or go whale-watching on horseback at Ricochet Ridge Ranch (tel. 707/964–7669). MacKerricher State Park, 3 miles north of Fort Bragg, also has excellent vantage points. In town, you can sample seafood chowder or whale-size hot dogs, take a horse-drawn carriage ride (tel. 800/399–1454), listen to live jazz, and visit sportscard, gem, and doll shows.

🏛 *Fort Bragg–Mendocino Coast Chamber of Commerce, 332 N. Main St., Box 1141, Fort Bragg 95437, tel. 707/961–6300 or 800/ 726–2780. 1st and 3rd weekends in Mar. Admission free.*

World Championship Great Arcata to Ferndale Cross-Country Kinetic Sculpture Race

(🕺 3–15) Made of old bicycle, motorcycle, and power lawnmower parts, and shaped like giant crabs, iguanas, castles, bananas, or spaceships, these human-powered works of art run a zany 38-mile, three-day race "for the glory," as the motto goes. It all began in 1969 when a Ferndale artist transformed his son's tricycle into a five-wheeled "pentacycle"; other local artists were similarly inspired and a race down Main Street ensued. Today the race is inter-

nationally known, but the emphasis is still on fun; awards are given for speed, costumes, sound effects, and even finishing in the "dead middle." Children who enter the race—and there are many—must have parental approval. Write in advance for the amusing official souvenir rules booklet ($2).

🏛 *Kinetic Sculpture Race, Box 916, Ferndale 95536, tel. 707/786–9259. Memorial Day weekend. Admission free. Entry fee: $20 pilot, $15 pit crew.*

Clearlake International Worm Races

(🕺 ALL) The tension is high. Some of the world's speediest night crawlers and red worms are placed in the bull's-eye at the center of a circle 2 feet across, which in turn is drawn on a 4-foot-square racing board. Spectators whoop and holler as the worms inch toward the outer edges of the circle. The first worm completely out of the circle wins first prize, as much as $250 for its human sponsor or trainer. With stakes this high, contestants come from all over the world to compete at this highlight of Clearlake's Fourth of July festivities, held since 1966. Contestants can dig, name, and train their own worms or rent a fully trained one for 50¢. Though cheering is encouraged, no artificial help is allowed—including worm steroids or grease applications. (The boards are kept moist for the worms' comfort, however.) The fun starts at noon in Clearlake's Redbud Park. Other festivities that day include a parade, a barbecue, music, children's games, and fireworks.

🏛 *Clear Lake Chamber of Commerce, 4700 Golf Ave., Clearlake 95411, tel. 707/994–3600. July 4. Admission free. Race entry fee: $2 per worm ages 13 and over, $1 ages 12 and under.*

Bigfoot Days

(🕺 ALL) Willow Creek—known as the "Gateway to Bigfoot Country"—holds a three-day festival over Labor Day weekend to celebrate the legend of the "large hairy creature" said to roam these northern woods. While tales of Bigfoot sightings go way back in these parts—Native American tribes had their own version known as "Oh Mah"—Bigfoot Days has its roots in the 1958 discovery of some really big apelike footprints about 40 miles north of here. The festivities kick off with a Bigfoot-theme downtown parade, followed by an ice-cream social, barbecue, horseshoe and softball tournaments, food booths, and an arts and crafts fair. Labor Day itself is Kids Day, complete with games and contests: sack races, ball throws, and bike races.

🏠 *Willow Creek Chamber of Commerce, Box 704, Willow Creek 95573, tel. 530/629–2693. Labor Day weekend. Admission free.*

Paul Bunyan Days

(👫 **ALL**) Fort Bragg (see Chapter 17) is logging country, and during Paul Bunyan Days loggers here get to show off their strength and skills at events such as ax throwing and power-saw bucking. Most kids, though, come for the hilarious Fire Department Water Fight, where volunteer firefighters wage a drenched battle, and the Paul Bunyan Kiddie Games, featuring three-legged, egg-and-spoon, and tricycle races. Other events include a fiddlers' contest, a crafts fair, and an old-fashioned dress review. The Paul Bunyan Parade caps the weekend.

🏠 *Paul Bunyan Days Association, Box 2282, Fort Bragg 95437, tel. 707/964–8687. Labor Day weekend. Admission free.*

Sierra and the Gold Country

Snowfest

(👫 **ALL**) Lake Tahoe's Snowfest, the largest winter carnival in the western United States, packs more than 120 events into 10 days. Typical events may include a dress-up-your-dog contest, a snow sculpture contest,

an ice-cream eating contest, a pizza-dough throwing contest, snowshoe races, snowmobile rides for kids, a children's parade, children's theater productions, and a penny carnival. Snowfest kicks off with a torchlight ski parade, a laser light show, and a fireworks display, followed by ski races, a community parade, ice carving, various zany contests, a costume party, a Hawaiian luau, and a "polar bear" swim in the icy waters of Lake Tahoe.

🏠 *Snowfest, Box 7590, Tahoe City 96145, tel. 530/583–7625; lodging information, 800/824–6348. 10 days in late Feb./early Mar.–mid-Mar. Admission free to many events.*

Festival de la Familia

(👫 **ALL**) Old Sacramento is transformed into a lively *mercado* (open-air market) as people from throughout Latin America—and anyone who enjoys the sights, sounds, and aromas of Latino culture—celebrate Sacramento's "Festival of the Family." More than two dozen Latin American nations are represented, and—attracting 150,000 people—the festival has become one of Northern California's most popular one-day events. Besides entertainment, food booths, and arts and crafts sales for all, there are activities designed for children: puppet shows, games, and Latin American stories and songs.

🏠 *Festival de la Familia, Box 162845, Sacramento 95816, tel. 916/552–5252, ext. 4127 or 916/264–7777. Last Sun. in Apr. Admission free. Open 10–5.*

Calaveras County Fair and Jumping Frog Jubilee

(👫 **ALL**) During a visit to his Gold Country cabin in 1860, author Mark Twain heard tales of a local jumping frog, which he later immortalized in his story, "The Celebrated Jumping Frog of Calaveras County." Since the late 1920s the historic town of Angels Camp has held an amphibian Olympics in Twain's honor, and today it draws spring-legged entrants from all over the world. The stakes are high—a winning frog who sets a world's record nets his human sponsor $5,000. (The record frog-jump of 21 feet was set here in 1986 by "Rosie the Ribiter.") Any fair-goer can enter up to 10 frogs per day in the four-day event; you can either catch your own or have them provided for $2 per frog. Kids under 12 have their own competitions. The fair also includes carnival rides, rodeo and livestock shows, street performers, a demolition derby, a petting zoo, pig races, a children's parade, and a Kids Place for games.

🏠 *Calaveras County Fair and Jumping Frog Jubilee, Box 489, Angels Camp 95222, tel. 209/736–2561 or 800/225–3764. 3rd weekend in May. Admission: $8–$10 adults, $6–$8 ages 6–12, 5 and under free; 4-day pass $25 adults, $23 ages 6–12. Frog entry fee: $3 adults, $1 ages 6–12 (free on Thurs.). Open Thurs.–Sun. 8 AM–10 PM.*

Mule Days Celebration

(👫 **6–15**) Here in the Mule Capital of the World, as the Eastern Sierra town of Bishop is known, your kids can learn exactly what that expression "stubborn as a mule" is all about. Take them to the "Packers' Scramble," the highlight of Bishop's four-day celebration of all things mule. Packers—they're the pros who pack mules for high-country trail trips and the like—compete to see who can round up, pack, and then ride their mules around an arena the fastest. With some 90 mules running loose and amok at the start, this is one wild and woolly competition. All told, there are more than 100 competitions starring nearly 1,000 mules: racing, riding, jumping, driving; the chariot races are especially exciting. Also on the docket are country music and dances, barbecues, and a parade.

🏠 *Bishop Mule Days, Box 815, Bishop 93515, tel. 760/872–4263. Memorial Day weekend (Wed.–Sun.). Admission: $10 per show; all-show pass $45 (reserved grandstand seating extra); ages 12 and under free (except grandstand) with paid adult. Open 8 AM–9 PM.*

Cherries Jubilee and West Coast Cherry Pit–Spitting Championships

(👫 **ALL**) The time-honored picnic tradition of cherry-pit spitting, a normally unrewarded talent, can lead to fame and glory if you celebrate Father's Day at Goldbud Farm's Cherries Jubilee—two days of food, music, and family activities in the Gold Country. You also cheer on competitors in cherry-pie eating, speed-pitting, and stem-tying contests. The West Coast Cherry Pit–Spitting Championships are open to the public, free (except for practice fruit), with separate competitions for boys, girls, men, and women. After warming up on sweet cherries, contestants compete with sour ones; the pucker is said to propel the pits farther—up to 70 feet and beyond for champions.

🏠 *Goldbud Farms, 2501 Carson Rd., Placerville 95667, tel. 530/626–6521. Schnell School Rd. exit off U.S. 50, north to Carson Rd., east 2 mi. Father's Day weekend. Admission free. Open Sat.–Sun. 10–5.*

Fourth of July at Mammoth

(👫 **ALL**) Up to 30,000 people pour into the eastern Sierra resort town of Mammoth Lakes (see Chapter 18) to celebrate an old-fashioned Fourth of July, with a parade that features horses, clowns, custom cars, floats, Dixieland and mariachi bands, plus offbeat "doo dah" entries—a marching chain-saw drill team, perhaps, or men in deer costumes driving a car with a human strapped to the roof. It's the center of a three-or-more-day blowout that also includes fireworks over Crowley Lake (gate fee $10 per car), a chili cook-off, a pancake breakfast, a volleyball tournament, a footrace, art and auto shows, and Old West Days, a Western theme festival held at Sierra Meadows Ranch (tel. 760/934–6161).

🏠 *Mammoth Lakes Visitors Bureau, Box 48, Mammoth Lakes 93546, tel. 760/934–2712 or 800/367–6572. Early July. Parade admission free.*

California State Fair

(**ŤŤ ALL**) One of the largest agricultural fairs in the United States, the California State Fair, held at Sacramento's Cal Expo grounds, runs for 2½ weeks, concluding on Labor Day. Besides livestock exhibits (including a nursery) and horse and pig racing, the fair offers plenty of carnival rides and games, rodeo riding, demolition derbies, food booths, live music, fireworks, and activities for children at Kids Park, where youngsters can make masks or have their faces painted.
🏛 *California State Fair, Box 15649, Sacramento 95852, tel. 916/263–3247. Late Aug.–early Sept. Admission: $7 adults, $4 ages 5–12. Parking: $4. Open Fri.–Mon. 10–10, Tues.–Thurs. noon–10.*

Black Bart Days

(**ŤŤ 3 – 15**) Black Bart was the most notorious stagecoach bandit in the Gold Country, thought to have held up 30 stages between 1877 and 1883 (when finally unmasked, the outlaw turned out to be a respected San Francisco businessman who never even loaded his shotgun!). Black Bart Days celebrates his legend with festivities on San Andreas's historic Main Street including food and crafts booths, a barbecue dinner at night, a street dance (for adults), and, of course, a man dressed as Black Bart. Highlights for kids include a parade, a tug-of-war, footraces, face painting, and clowns. At some point during the day—even though it's called "Days," it's traditionally been only one—visit the old jail cell where the outlaw was held after his arrest.
🏛 *San Andreas Chamber of Commerce, Box 115, San Andreas 95249, tel. 209/754–4009. Usually 1st or 2nd Sat. in Sept. Admission free.*

Kokanee Salmon Festival

(**ŤŤ 3 – 15**) The official mascot, "Sammy Salmon," welcomes kids to this two-day festival based at the U.S. Forest Service Visitors Center along Highway 89 on the south shore of Lake Tahoe (see Chapter 18). It's a tribute to the dramatic natural spectacle of kokanee salmon swimming upstream to their mating grounds; you can follow the Rainbow Trail to the Taylor Creek Stream Profile Chamber to get a fascinating below-the-surface view of the salmon in the stream. Naturalists are along the trail to help answer questions. Children's events include a ½-mile Tadpole Trot race (ages 10 and under; call 530/573–2629 for registration) and a fishing booth where kids can cast lines for prizes. Festivities include a salmon barbecue on both days—Pacific variety, not kokanee.
🏛 *Lake Tahoe Basin Management Unit, U.S. Forest Service, 870 Emerald Bay Rd., Suite 1, South Lake Tahoe 96150, tel. 530/573–2600 or 530/573–2674. Early Oct. weekend. Admission free.*

San Francisco and the Bay Area

Chinese New Year Festival and Parade

(**ŤŤ ALL**) San Francisco's Chinese New Year Parade may be the most colorful and exciting parade in the state. A half million spectators line the streets of the Financial District and Chinatown to watch marching bands, drum and bugle corps, brightly lighted floats, lion dancers, martial artists, acrobats, and towering Chinese deities. The highlight is the arrival of Gum Lum, a 200-foot-long Golden Dragon propelled by 35 dancers inside. Two warnings: Exploding firecrackers, an integral part of the celebration, may frighten young children; and rain often dampens this parade (February is San Francisco's wettest month). The Chinatown Street Fair is held the same weekend; kite-making, lion dancing, fortune-telling, and food booths are among the draws.
🏛 *Chinese New Year Festival and Parade, 809 Montgomery St., 2nd Fl., San Francisco*

94133, tel. 415/391–9680. Sat. in Feb. or early Mar. (dates vary with lunar calendar). Admission free.

Cherry Blossom Festival

ᛉᛉ ALL The grace of traditional Japanese dancing, along with the excitement of martial arts demonstrations, keep families flocking to San Francisco's Cherry Blossom Festival, a two-weekend spring-greeting extravaganza at the Japan Center and in surrounding Japantown. The flower-arranging demonstrations and tea ceremonies are too staid for most kids; head instead to the outdoor stage to watch judo, aikido, or folk dancing—often by kids in colorful kimonos. A Children's Village is set up with arts, crafts, and games, too. A dazzling 2½-hour parade caps the second weekend, starring dancers, floats, samurai warriors, taiko drummers, shrine bearers, and the festival queen; it runs 15 blocks from City Hall to the Japan Center, located at Post and Buchanan streets.

Cherry Blossom Festival, Box 15147, San Francisco 94115, tel. 415/563–2313. 2 weekends in Apr. Admission free to most events.

Cinco de Mayo Parade and Festival

ᛉᛉ ALL San Jose's one-day Cinco de Mayo fiesta has become Northern California's premier celebration of the Mexican holiday. More than 250,000 people of all ethnic backgrounds gather downtown to enjoy Latin music, dancing, entertainment, food, arts and crafts, and a 90-minute parade that includes bands, floats, and equestrians. (The parade route winds from San Jose Arena to Cesar Chavez Park, ending near the Children's Discovery Museum.) Guadalupe River Park is transformed into the Centro de Nuestra Cultura for the day, hosting dancing, contests, and children's art shows. Food and crafts booths operate both in the park and along a three-block stretch of Almaden Avenue, between Santa Clara and San Carlos streets.

Cinco de Mayo Celebration, 1680 Alum Rock Ave., San Jose 95116, tel. 408/258–0663. 1st Sun. in May. Admission free. Open 9–5.

Bay to Breakers

ᛉᛉ 3–15 In a city known for wacky spectacles, the *San Francisco Examiner's* Bay to Breakers race tops them all. The most thunderous herd of runners since the great buffalo stampedes of the 19th century takes off on a 7½-mile course from San Francisco Bay over the hills to Ocean Beach. An elite group of athletes gets prime starting positions; the rest of the 100,000 participants are "fun runners" of all ages (infant to elderly) who run, jog, walk, run backwards, or ride in wheelchairs or strollers. Many runners come in costume—dressed as alligators, chocolate kisses, the Golden Gate Bridge—or, occasionally, in no dress at all. Most impressive are the "centipedes"—groups of costumed runners tied together (dentists disguised as teeth, swarms of attorneys dressed as killer bees). Spectators line the route much of the way, but we like the views along John F. Kennedy Drive in Golden Gate Park, near the finish line. A post-race festival (Footstock) is held in the park's Polo Field, beginning at 8:30 AM.

San Francisco Examiner Bay to Breakers, Box 429200, San Francisco 94142, tel. 415/777–7773; Breakers hot line, 415/808–5000, ext. 2222. Sun. (8 AM) in mid-May. Admission free. Race-entry fee: $15–$20.

Carnaval

ᛉᛉ 6–15 San Francisco stages its version of Carnaval not in February like Rio, but in late spring, in hopes of warmer weather. It's one of the nation's largest Carnaval celebrations—three nightly balls, a two-day outdoor festival, and the Carnaval Grand Parade, with extravagant floats, glittering dance contingents, lively bands, and massive masked figures. The event is Latino in spirit, but the dance troupes represent cultures from Bolivia to Polynesia, West Africa to East Asia. The dancers are resplendent in feathered and sparkled costumes (often scanty). Starting at 10 AM the Sunday before Memorial Day, the parade runs down 24th Street between Bryant and Mission streets, and then on Mission from 24th to 14th streets; find a spot near the beginning, as kids (and parents, too) may fade before the usually slow-moving spectacle is over. The free accompanying outdoor festival (held on Harrison Street between 16th and 21st streets) presents live music—salsa, calypso, steel drum, world beat, reggae—plus food and crafts booths.

🏛 *Mission Economic Cultural Association, 2899 24th St., San Francisco 94110, tel. 415/ 826–1401. Memorial Day weekend. Parade and festival admission free. For reserved grandstand seating tickets, call 415/206–7747.*

Ugly Dog Contest

(👫 **ALL**) Does your family have an ugly dog? (Crooked legs, bulgy eyes, overbites, underbites, and droopy ears all qualify.) Then consider turning those endearing traits into doggie glory by entering your pooch in this event held on the final day of the Sonoma-Marin Fair in Petaluma. The ugliest of the purebreds faces off against the ugliest mutt, then the overall champ competes against past winners for a trophy. About 25 dogs are entered each year. The rest of the fair includes a junior livestock show, a carnival, live entertainment, and kids' competitions in photography, baked goods, and arts and crafts.

🏛 *Sonoma-Marin Fair, Box 182, Petaluma 94953, tel. 707/763–0931. 3rd wk in June. Fair admission: $7 adults, $3 ages 6–12. Dog entry fee: $3.*

Fourth of July Waterfront Festival

(👫 **3 – 15**) Although the fog over San Francisco Bay is sometimes so thick you can't see the fireworks, the city's Fourth of July celebration always draws huge crowds. Before the 9 PM fireworks in the sky over Alcatraz, there's an afternoon and evening's

worth of live music, stage entertainment, and ethnic food booths along the waterfront between Aquatic Park and Pier 39.

🏛 *San Francisco Chronicle 4th of July Celebration Promotion Dept., 901 Mission St., San Francisco 94103, tel. 415/777–7120 or 415/ 777–8498. July 4. Admission free.*

World Championship Pillow Fights

(👫 **ALL**) Two combatants sit astride a metal pole above a mud pit, armed only with feather pillows. Without grabbing on to the pole for support, they must swing their pillows—and only their pillows—at their opponents. The first contestant to land in the yucky brown mud below loses. The contestants must be at least 14, but all ages enjoy watching. The World Championship Pillow Fights have been raging for more than 25 years, as part of Kenwood's Fourth of July Celebration, drawing upward of 15,000 spectators to this Wine Country town of 1,200. After the fight champions have been crowned, celebrants can watch Kenwood's Hometown Parade and sample the offerings at the Not Yet World Famous Chili Cookoff. Games, food booths, live music, a children's play area, a footrace, and a raffle round out the festivities, which are held at Kenwood Plaza Park on Warm Springs Road.

🏛 *Kenwood Firemen's Association, Box 249, Kenwood 95452, tel. 707/833–2042. July 4. Admission: $3. Entry fee: $10.*

À la Carte, à la Park

(👫 **3 – 15**) At this three-day food fair in San Francisco's Golden Gate Park, 50 of the city's top restaurants set up booths to serve samplings of their most popular dishes (small portions, just right for kids) at prices ranging from 50¢ to $5 per dish. Because it's set in grassy Sharon Meadow, the kids can run around and make as much noise as they want, while live music is played on stage. More than 50,000 people per year attend; proceeds benefit the San Francisco Shakespeare Festival.

🏠 *Events West, 99 E. Blithedale, Mill Valley 94941, tel. 415/383–9378. Labor Day weekend. Admission: $8.50 adults, under 12 free. Open Sat.–Mon. 11–6.*

Renaissance Pleasure Faire

(👫 **3 – 15**) The Bay Area's Renaissance Pleasure Faire is an enormously entertaining history lesson—our kids think it's like hopping into a time machine. You'll "travel" to a 16th-century English village where costumed players—jesters, jugglers, jousters, shepherds, merchants, farmers, and revelers—roam the grounds, discoursing in convincing Elizabethan English. You may also meet such celebrities as Queen Elizabeth I, Shakespeare, and Sir Francis Drake. (Fairgoers are encouraged to come in period costume themselves, and many do.) Join in games ranging from archery to catapults or watch knights battle on horseback, then feast on shepherd's pie, beef ribs, "toad-in-the-hole," bangers, and Cornish pasties. Marketplaces (crafts booths), music, dancing, parades, and pageantry appear throughout. The longtime site at Black Point, in Novato, has changed, so call for the latest location and dates.

🏠 *Renaissance Pleasure Faire, 2501 E. 28th St., Suite 110, Signal Hill 90806, tel. 800/ 523–2473. Labor Day weekend–mid-Oct. (6 weekends). Admission: $17.50 adults, $15.50 students, $7.50 ages 5–11, under 5 free. Discounts available for advance-purchase and season tickets. Parking: $6. Open 10–6.*

Art and Pumpkin Festival

(👫 **ALL**) Every year in the weeks preceding Halloween the fields around the coastal town of Half Moon Bay become a sea of orange pumpkins, drawing flocks of children in search of the perfect jack-o-lantern-to-be. This celebration includes pumpkin pie-eating, Halloween costume contests, pumpkin-carving demonstrations, the Great Pumpkin Parade, and the Great Pumpkin Weigh-Off, a growers competition that stars gigantic pumpkins (some weighing

more than 700 pounds). Traffic heading down Highway 1 from San Francisco for the festival can heat up, bumper-to-bumper, so try to arrive early in the day.

🏠 *Art and Pumpkin Festival, Box 274, Half Moon Bay 94019, tel. 650/726–9652. Sat.–Sun. in mid-Oct. Admission free. Open daily 10–5.*

Central Coast and Valley

Flying Leap Storytelling Festival

(👫 **3 – 12**) Solvang's Danish immigrant founders wanted to keep their heritage alive; today this town near Santa Barbara is almost more of a Danish theme park than a real village, with windmills, cobbled walkways, thatched roofs, gas streetlights, and Scandinavian restaurants, bakeries, and chocolate shops. During the Storytelling Festival professional yarn-spinners from around the region and the country entertain with fairy tales, animal tales, and ghost and ethnic stories. Story sessions are held in Solvang's Santa Ynez Mission and several other locations in the Santa Ynez Valley. Members of the public swap stories at a free session.

🏠 *Arts Outreach, Box 755, Los Olivos 93441, tel. 805/688–9533. Fri.–Sat. of 3rd weekend in Feb. (call for times). Admission: $5–$10 per session; family pass (4 people) $60 for Sat. sessions.*

Oakdale Chocolate Festival

(👫 **ALL**) The Central Valley town of Oakdale is home to Hershey Chocolate U.S.A. (120 S. Sierra Ave., near the corner of Yosemite Ave. and F St., tel. 209/848–8126), a plant that manufactures candy bars and other treats. And each year Oakdale holds a two-day weekend Chocolate Festival that for many kids may be the festival closest to their hearts and tummies. Here they can stroll down Chocolate Avenue (in

Wood Park, at the intersection of Highways 108 and 120) and feast on chocolate delights ranging from kisses to truffles. Other activities include a kids playland, a classic car show, entertainment, arts and crafts, and a 5K fun run. Though you can't tour the chocolate plant during the festival, you can tour it throughout the year weekdays from 8:30 to 3, except holidays.

🏠 *Oakdale Chamber of Commerce, 590 N. Yosemite Ave., Oakdale, tel. 209/847–2244. 3rd weekend in May. Admission: $2; ages 12 and under free. Open Sat. 9–6, Sun. 9–5.*

California Strawberry Festival

(👪 **ALL**) One-fifth of the state's crop of strawberries grows in the Oxnard area, between Santa Barbara and Los Angeles. Held at Strawberry Meadows in College Park (3250 S. Rose Ave. in Oxnard), the Strawberry Festival is a tribute to all things strawberry. Sampling the berries is, of course, at the top of the list, and dozens of booths dish out delights such as strawberry shortcake, strawberry cheesecake, strawberry funnel cake, strawberry crepes and blintzes, strawberry kabobs, chocolate-dipped strawberries—did we leave out strawberry pizza? You'll also find games such as a strawberry shortcake–eating contest, a strawberry tart toss, and a strawberry relay and limbo contest. The Strawberryland area for kids has music and magic acts, clowns, puppet shows, jugglers, a petting zoo, train rides, and crafts activities. There are also four stages of live music and arts and crafts—some of which, remarkably, are not made from strawberries.

🏠 *1621 Pacific Ave., Suite. 127, Oxnard 93033, tel. 805/385–7578 or 888/288–9242. Sat.–Sun. in mid-May. Admission: $7 adults, $4 ages 2–12, under 2 free. Open 10–6:30.*

California Rodeo

(👪 **6–15**) Relive the Old West at the California Rodeo in Salinas, a four-day festival of cowboy contests, races, parades, and horse shows. Top cowboys and cowgirls compete in the world's largest rodeo arena in events like bull-riding, bareback bronc-riding, steer-wrestling, calf-roping, barrel-racing, and "exceptional rodeo" (which pairs professional cowboys with children with disabilities). Barbecues, carnival rides, cowboy poetry and ballad performances, square dances, and pow-wow dancing round out the festivities. Keep in mind that young children may be frightened or upset to see calf-roping or to watch a rodeo clown being chased by a bull. The Professional Rodeo Cowboys Association, however, maintains that it respects the welfare of the animals.

🏠 *California Rodeo, Box 1648, Salinas 93902, tel. 831/775–3100 or 800/771–8807. Thurs.–Sun. in July. Admission per session: $10–$17 adults, $6 ages 12 and under Sat.–Sun., $2 Thurs.–Fri. Order tickets by phone or mail.*

Pushem-Pullem Parade

(👪 **ALL**) This children's parade, a highlight of Ventura's July 4 Street Fair, is perfectly described by its name, Pushem-Pullem. There's nothing motorized here. Hundreds of local kids decorate their trikes, bikes, wagons, and skateboards, dress up in costumes, and then at 10:30 AM parade for five blocks down Main Street pushing—or pulling—their vehicles. Meanwhile, the nine-block street fair presents live entertainment, children's crafts booths, magicians, clowns, puppet shows, and food.

🏠 *City of Ventura Special Events, Box 99, Ventura 93002, tel. 805/654–7830 or 800/333–2989. July 4. Admission free.*

Gilroy Garlic Festival

(👪 **3–15**) Depending on your feelings about garlic, this three-day celebration of the "stinking rose" will either attract you to or repel you from the town of Gilroy, 30 miles south of San Jose. Count our family among the 135,000 visitors drawn each July to the wafting aromas of 8 tons of garlic sizzling in Gourmet Alley pans, as cooks turn out mountains of grilled garlic bread, barbecued chicken, flaming calamari, marinated sirloin, sautéed scampi, stir-fried local vegetables, even garlic ice cream. If your kids aren't enamored of garlic (or just want to have some fun), steer them toward Herbie and Friends, a Place for Kids, where they can make assorted garlic craft items and be entertained by game booths, clowns, magicians, marionettes, and music. The festival is held in Christmas Hill Park (follow the signs from U.S. Highway 101).

🏫 *Gilroy Garlic Festival, Box 2311, Gilroy 95021, tel. 408/842–1625. Last full weekend in July. Admission: $10 adults, $5 ages 6–12. Open 10–7.*

Old Spanish Days Fiesta

(👫 **ALL**) At this popular five-day fiesta, El Desfile de los Niños (the Children's Parade) is said to be the most photographed children's event in the country: *Niñas* (girls) and *charritos* (little cowboys) ride down Santa Barbara's Main Street in traditional costumes, on floats they've made and decorated themselves, pulled by dad, big brother, or even the family dog. The grown-ups' version is El Desfile Historico (the Old Spanish Parade), with costumed dancers and equestrians, antique carriages, and flower-studded floats. Two Spanish-style marketplaces—one with contemporary and mariachi music and dancing, another focusing on children's entertainment and Mexican food—are open from 11 AM to midnight. Free Latin-flavored variety shows (including one starring only children), miniature train rides, and rodeo competitions are among the other events.

🏫 *Old Spanish Days, Box 21557, Santa Barbara 93121, tel. 805/962–8101 or 800/ 927–4688. 5 days in early Aug. Admission free to many events; events that require tickets, call 805/963–4408.*

California Beach Festival

(👫 **ALL**) This may be the ultimate California festival, at least if your view of the

state is rooted in Frankie Avalon and Annette Funicello movies—a California-lifestyle theme party that bops along a mile-long stretch of the Beachfront Promenade between Ventura Pier and Surfers Point. Live surfing-style music provides the backdrop, while beach volleyball, canine Frisbee-catching contests, surfing, a body-building contest, a swimwear fashion show, arts and crafts, seafood, and a children's entertainment area (with game booths, bubble-making, and crafts) make for fun in the sun.

🏫 *City of Ventura Special Events Office, Box 99, Ventura 93002, tel. 805/654–7830 or 800/333–2989. Mid.-Sept. weekend. Admission: $6 adults, under 12 free.*

Great Sand Castle Contest

(👫 **ALL**) Contestants start arriving by 5 AM on the appointed day to sculpt fabulous creations at Carmel Beach. Judging begins at noon. Among the 60 or so yearly entrants are children and adults, including professional architects who take this contest seriously—judge-bribing is a long and good-humored tradition here (among the prizes awarded is the "sour grapes" award for least-rewarded bribe). Most kids who enter receive a prize. The highlight for some kids comes afterward, when they jump on the castles and reduce them to glorified sand piles—an unsanctioned part of the contest. The exact date is announced only two weeks ahead of time; it's all dependent on the tides.

🏫 *Carmel Beach (foot of Ocean Ave.), Carmel-by-the-Sea, tel. 408/624–2522. Sept. or Oct. Admission free.*

Morro Bay Harbor Festival

(👫 **ALL**) Seafood, fishing, and Morro Bay marine life are showcased at this Central Coast waterfront weekend, with lots of activities geared to kids and families. At Kids Cove youngsters work on marine-oriented crafts, making fish-print or kelp-print T-shirts, and then get even more hands-on at a touch tank filled with abalone, mollusks, starfish, urchins, and crabs. Around the harbor you can tour a historic tall ship, a Coast Guard cutter, or a fishing boat. In Chess Live games, costumed performers (playing kings, queens, knights, etc.) make their moves around a giant board. Surfing, oyster-eating, boat races, rides and games, sand sculptures, and Hawaiian-shirt contests round out the action, along with live entertainment, giant sand sculptures, and arts and crafts.

🏨 *Morro Bay Harbor Festival, Box 1869, Morro Bay, CA 93443, tel. 805/772–1155 or 800/366–6043. 1st full weekend in Oct. Admission: $6 adults, 12 and under free.*

Butterfly Parade

(👭 **ALL**) Elementary schoolchildren in Pacific Grove, the seaside community near Monterey that prides itself as "Butterfly Town USA," annually welcome migrating monarch butterflies with this colorful parade, now 60 years old. While high school bands play, more than 1,000 students march in costumes based on a theme such as butterflies, sea animals, space creatures—even tourists. The 45-minute parade starts at 10:30 AM at Robert H. Down Elementary School on Pine Street and proceeds along Lighthouse Avenue; it's followed by a bazaar with games, food, and booths behind the elementary school.

🏨 *Robert H. Down Elementary School, 485 Pine St., Pacific Grove 93950, tel. 408/646–6540. 1st or 2nd Sat. in Oct. Admission free.*

Pismo Beach Clam Festival

(👭 **ALL**) Pismo Beach, known as the Clam Capital of the World, celebrates that distinction for a weekend each October in its long-running Clam Festival. Downtown, the Clam Festival Parade presents marching bands, floats, and antique cars. Local restaurants compete to create the "World's Best Clam Chowder," and visitors get to sample the goods and then cast ballots. Other activities include contests for sand sculpture,

bodyboarding, and the "World's Worst Poetry"; the Rubber Duckie Regatta; the popular Clam Dig, open to competitors of all ages; and carnival rides and booths. Food booths offer up barbecued clams and clam cakes (along with chowder). All events except the parade take place at the pier.

🏨 *Pismo Beach Chamber of Commerce, 581 Dolliver St., Pismo Beach 93449, tel. 805/773–4382. Mid-Oct. Admission: $2/day, $3/weekend.*

Los Angeles and Environs

Tournament of Roses Parade

(👭 **3–15**) Nearly a half billion viewers in 90 countries tune in every New Year's to watch this parade's fabulous floral floats and marching bands under typically sunny skies. If you want to see the world's most famous parade in person, you'll have to get up early—some people camp out on Pasadena's Colorado Boulevard starting shortly after Christmas. You'll see 60 extravagantly designed floats adorned with 6 million flowers and 60 million petals (put together by hundreds of volunteers working around-the-clock shifts in the days leading up to the parade), as well as 21 top-rated marching bands and 300 equestrians. The route is 5 miles long and the parade takes about two hours to pass any one point. You can inspect the floats close-up after the parade at a site adjacent to Pasadena High School at Sierra Madre and Washington boulevards; admission is $2. The parade is never held on Sunday, so if January 1 falls on that day, the show goes on January 2. The Rose Bowl football game, the "granddaddy of all bowl games," always follows the afternoon of the parade.

🏨 *Pasadena Tournament of Roses, 391 S. Orange Grove Blvd., Pasadena 91184, tel. 626/449–7673. Jan. 1 or 2. Admission free.*

Blessing of the Animals

(**ALL**) A colorful procession of domestic animals and pets—dogs, cats, turtles, rabbits, parakeets, cows, sheep—arrives to be blessed by a bishop in this pre-Easter tradition on Olvera Street. The procession takes place at the top of the street from around 1 to 4 PM, and live entertainment is usually offered on Olvera Street at the same time.

🏠 *Olvera St., Los Angeles, tel. 213/628–3562 or 213/628–7833. Day before Easter. Admission free.*

Renaissance Pleasure Faire

(**3 – 15**) Similar to and staged by the same organization as the Renaissance Pleasure Faire in the San Francisco Bay Area, (see *above*), this thoroughly entertaining event runs for nine weekends in Glen Helen Regional Park (2555 Glen Helen Pkwy., San Bernardino).

🏠 *Renaissance Pleasure Faire, 2501 E. 28th St., Suite 110, Signal Hill 90806, tel. 800/523–2473. Mid-Apr.–early June (9 weekends). Admission: $17.50 adults, $15.50 students, $7.50 ages 5–11, under 5 free. Discount advance-purchase and season tickets available. Parking: $6. Open 10–6.*

Fiesta Broadway

(**ALL**) Held one week before the Mexican holiday Cinco de Mayo, the Fiesta Broadway is a giant Latin-flavored street party—the country's largest Cinco de Mayo celebration. The fiesta stretches along 36 city blocks, including Broadway between First Street and Olympic Boulevard, as well as parts of nearby streets. Latino music, dancing, and foods are highlights of the one-day event, and there's an area ("*Los Niños*" Play Park) for kids' games and activities.

🏠 *Fiesta Broadway, 2130 Sawtelle Blvd., Suite 304, Los Angeles 90025, tel. 310/914–0015. Sun. before Cinco de Mayo; usually late Apr. Admission free. Open 11–6.*

Children's Day Celebration

(**ALL**) In Japan, Children's Day is a family-oriented celebration with activities such as kite-flying and doll-making; in L.A.'s Little Tokyo, this delightful event has been transplanted as a two-day outdoor festival that includes dance and performing arts groups, arts-and-crafts activities for kids, games, food, films, and martial arts demonstrations. Early on Sunday morning, children ages 4 to 12 participate in a fun run through the streets of Little Tokyo; a race registration fee includes T-shirt, pancake breakfast, and goody bag.

🏠 *Japanese American Cultural and Community Center, 244 S. San Pedro St., Los Angeles 90012, tel. 213/628–2725. Weekend in mid-May. Admission free. Open 10–4.*

Huntington Beach Fourth of July Parade and Fireworks

(**ALL**) Huntington Beach celebrated its first Fourth of July Parade in 1904; today it draws 300,000 visitors and is said to be the largest Independence Day parade west of the Mississippi. Along with marching bands, floats, horses, antique cars, and clowns, this parade showcases a variety of celebrities including movie, TV, and sports stars. The parade starts at 10 AM; best views are along Main Street, between 6th Street and Clay Avenue, in downtown Huntington Beach. Evening brings a fireworks spectacular at Huntington Beach High School.

🏠 *Huntington Beach Conference and Visitors Bureau, 417 Main St., Huntington Beach 92648, tel. 714/969–3492. July 4. Parade admission free.*

Old Miners' Days

(**ALL**) Each summer since the 1950s Big Bear Lake has celebrated its 19th-century mining and Western heritage with a blowout known as Old Miners' Days. To get into the spirit of Big Bear Valley's colorful frontier days—before speedboats and

Jet Skis added a new type of color to the lake—residents and visitors are encouraged to wear Western dress. Participants in the Miss Clementine Pageant wear period costumes—the pageant's 14 categories include a baby Clementine. Also part of the lineup are a chili cook-off, cowboy music, a wacky doo-dah parade, a quick-draw contest, mounted cowboy shoot-outs, stagecoach "robberies," a boat parade of lights on the lake, and a 5K/10K run-walk. Free all-day activities for children ages 5 to 13 begin at 10 AM on the final Saturday in Meadow Park. Capping the festivities on the final Sunday are floats, bands, and horses in the Old Miners' Days Parade, which runs along Big Bear Boulevard.

🏠 *Big Bear Village Visitor Center, Box 1936, Big Bear Lake 92315, tel. 909/866–4607 or 800/424–4232. 3 weekends in mid-July to early Aug. Admission: $1 for general admission button, $1 for most events. Open: Sat.–Sun. (3 weekends), usually 9–5; call for events schedule.*

Los Angeles African Marketplace & Cultural Faire

(👫 **ALL**) Now in its second decade, this fair has grown into the largest African cultural celebration in the United States. For three weekends families can visit a 10-acre "global village" representing African culture as it has dispersed around the world—in more than 40 cultures and 70 countries from Africa to the Caribbean and throughout the Americas. The Children's Village includes multicultural music and dance performances, storytellers, clowns, amusement and pony rides, and a petting zoo. There are live stage performances of music and dance (reggae, blues, jazz, salsa, world beat), sports and games, 350 arts and crafts vendors, multiethnic food booths, and a business expo. The event takes place in Rancho Cienega Park on Rodeo Road in Los Angeles.

🏠 *African Marketplace & Cultural Faire, 2520 West View St., Los Angeles 90016, tel. 213/734–1164 or 213/237–1540. 3 weekends in late Aug. and early Sept. Admission: $3, ages 10 and under free.*

Los Angeles County Fair

(👫 **ALL**) Established in 1927, the country's largest county fair draws around 1½ million people for 24 days and nights of carnival rides and games, horse and livestock shows, horse and pig races, live entertainment, contests, monorail rides, and exhibits of everything from gems to miniature trains. The Fairplex grounds are about 30 miles east of downtown L.A. (Fairplex Dr. exit from I–10, 2 blocks north).

🏠 *Los Angeles County Fair, Box 2250, Pomona 91769, tel. 909/623–3111. Early Sept.–late Sept. or early Oct. Admission: $9 adults, $5 ages 6–12 (children free Mon.–Fri.); discounted 2-day passes available. Parking: $4. Open Mon.–Thurs. 11–10, Fri. 11–11, Sat. 9 AM–11 PM, Sun. 9 AM–10 PM.*

Hollywood Christmas Parade

(👫 **ALL**) This being a Hollywood parade, you can be certain that dozens of TV, film, and music stars will add extra glamour to the pageantry of bands, equestrian units, floats, and antique cars. But the ultimate star of the show is Santa Claus, who has made nearly 70 visits to Tinseltown for this parade. The Christmas Parade starts at 6 PM and runs 3½ miles from Melrose Avenue (in front of Paramount Pictures) to Hollywood Boulevard; some of the best vantage points are along Sunset Boulevard between Vine Street and Highland Avenue.

🏠 *Hollywood Christmas Parade, 7018 Hollywood Blvd., Hollywood 90028, tel. 323/469–2337. Sun. after Thanksgiving. Admission free; reserved grandstand tickets available for $18–$25 (call 626/795–0896).*

Rose Bud Parade

(👫 **1–9**) A miniature version of Pasadena's Tournament of Roses Parade (see above), the Rose Bud Parade stars hundreds of children—some still in diapers—riding in wagons or on bikes, trikes, scooters, and skateboards decorated with flowers and balloons. Others march or toddle down

Pasadena's Lake Avenue (between California and Del Mar boulevards) as bands play and parents and other spectators cheer them on. Professional float builders and staff members from Kidspace Museum (see Chapter 5) help kids create their own floats using fresh flowers, seeds, and greenery donated by local florists. A Rose Bud king and queen are selected by drawing. The registration fee includes the float-making workshop.

🏛 *Kidspace Museum, 390 S. El Molino Ave., Pasadena 91101, tel. 626/449–9144. Mid-Nov.; call for date. Parade registration: $5 per child.*

Christmas Boat Parade

(👫 3–15) Southern California's oldest and largest lighted boat parade began in 1908 with a gondola and eight canoes lighted by Japanese lanterns. Since then, the Newport Harbor Christmas Boat Parade has grown to a spectacular two-hour procession of up to 200 illuminated boats, lasting seven nights just prior to Christmas Day. It begins and ends at Collins Island, winding past Balboa Island and numerous beachfront restaurants and clubs from 6:30 to 8:30 PM; you can pick up a schedule predicting when it will pass different viewing areas.

🏛 *Newport Beach Chamber of Commerce, 1470 Jamboree Rd., Newport Beach 92660, tel. 949/729–4400. Dec. 17–23. Admission free.*

San Diego and the Southern Deserts

Riverside County Fair and National Date Festival

(👫 ALL) This 10-day desert festival, more than a half-century old, draws a quarter-million people to celebrate the not-always-appreciated date (the fruit is appreciated here, though—the surrounding Coachella Valley grows 97% of the entire

U.S. crop). Daily ostrich and camel races and a lavish Arabian Nights Pageant add an exotic note; a Presidents Day Parade through downtown Indio continues the Arabian Nights theme. Other events may include a Wild West rodeo, Aztec dancers, Mexican music and dancing, camel and elephant rides, a petting zoo with exotic animals, a talent contest (with dancers age 5 and above competing), carnival rides and games, a junior fair and livestock show, and food (including date shakes). The festival is held at the Riverside County Fairgrounds about 12 minutes east of Palm Desert; follow Highway 111 south from I–10. Anyone who comes in complete Arabian Nights costume is admitted free.

🏛 *Riverside County Fair and National Date Festival, 46-350 Arabia St., Indio 92201, tel. 760/863–8247 or 800/811–3247. Ten days in mid- to late Feb. Admission: $6 ages 13–54, $5 ages 55 and up, $4 ages 5–12, under 5 free. Parking: $3. Open daily 10–10.*

Indian Fair

(👫 ALL) Native Americans from the Sioux, Hopi, Zuni, Navajo, Cherokee, and 25 other tribes from across the country gather each year at this two-day celebration held at the San Diego Museum of Man in Balboa Park (see Chapter 5). Traditional stories, legends, and ceremonies are brought to life as tribal members in full costume dance, sing, and drum; traditional Native American foods such as hot fry bread, posole, piki bread, Hopi stew, and parched corn are sold (Mexican and American foods are available as well). At the Crafts Corner kids can string beads and feathers, paint clay pots, and create other Indian crafts, while in the museum's own Indian Market artisans demonstrate their craftsmanship and sell jewelry, beadwork, baskets, pottery, and kachina carvings.

🏛 *San Diego Museum of Man, 1350 El Prado, Balboa Park, San Diego 92101, tel. 619/239–2001. 2nd or 3rd weekend in June. Admission (including museum): $5 adults, $3 ages 6–17, 5 and under free. Open 10–4:30.*

Huck Finn's Jubilee

(👭 **ALL**) The roster of old-time contests and games here may outdo that of any other festival in the state. The jubilee is three days of 1880s-era fun, with events such as a Tom Sawyer fence-painting contest, a Huck Finn look-alike contest, a searching-for-nickels-in-a-haystack contest, and the Great Western Cow Chip Throwing Championships—plus an egg toss, treasure hunt, river-raft building, greased-pole climbing, and catfish derby. A liar's contest is open to ages 16 and up. Bluegrass and country music, clogging, line dancing, hot-air balloon rides, a circus, a petting zoo, hayrides, arts and crafts, food booths, and mountain men demonstrations complete the festivities. It's held in Mojave Narrows Regional Park south of Victorville from Friday through Sunday of Father's Day weekend; family camping (starting as early as Thursday night) is encouraged amid the park's trees and meadows.

🏠 *Huck Finn's Jubilee, Box 56419, Riverside 92517, tel. 909/780–8810. Father's Day weekend in June. Admission: $10 per day adults, $5 per day ages 6–11; weekend admission package (includes camping) $35–45 adults, $15 ages 6–11. Open Fri. 1 PM–10:30 PM, Sat. 9 AM–10 PM, Sun. 9–7.*

Pioneer Days Celebration

(👭 **ALL**) The fair's highlight is a raucous event: the Outhouse Race, with a "sitter" (in the obvious place) and four pushers tearing wildly along, competing for the prize of hand-painted toilet seats. There's plenty more going on, too—a carnival, a parade, a rodeo, food and game booths, dances, and competitions such as horseshoe pitching and arm wrestling. A "best legs" contest—for men—and a beard-growing contest (also for men) are other popular events. One day is designated as Children's Day, with a petting zoo, fire trucks to look at, face painting, and pony rides. Kids dress up in Western attire, with a girl and boy chosen "Little Miss" and "Little Master" respectively; they get to ride in the parade. Activities are held in various locations, so call for a schedule. You might want to combine a visit here with one to nearby Joshua Tree National Park (see Chapter 8).

🏠 *Twentynine Palms Chamber of Commerce, 6455-A Mesquite Ave., Twentynine Palms 92277, tel. 760/367–3445. 3rd weekend in Oct. and other days throughout month. Admission free for most events.*

Mother Goose Parade

(👭 **1–9**) After more than a half century, this event has blossomed into one of the state's largest parades, drawing close to half a million spectators to see bands, equestrians, clowns, cartoon characters, antique cars, and floats representing Mother Goose rhymes and fairy tales and celebrating children. Each year's parade has a theme, such as "Mother Goose Visits Oz," "Mother Goose Goes to a Ballgame," or "Mother Goose and Dr. Seuss." The one-hour, 180-unit parade begins at 12:30 PM and follows a 3½-mile route down Main Street in suburban El Cajon.

🏠 *Mother Goose Parade Association, 480 N. Magnolia, Suite 106, El Cajon 92020, tel. 619/444–8712. Sun. before Thanksgiving. Admission free.*

FORTS, LIGHTHOUSES, GHOST TOWNS, CASTLES, AND OTHER HISTORIC HOUSES AND SITES

4

The spanking newness of California's cities and attractions often overshadows the landmarks of its historic past. But they are here, and they are fascinating—sure to give your kids a history lesson they won't forget. You can journey from prehistory (La Brea Tar Pits) to the Spanish mission era (San Juan Capistrano and others) to the rough-and-tumble frontier times (Fort Sutter), the feverish Gold Rush years (Columbia and Bodie state historic parks), and the Victorian seafaring age (Battery Point Lighthouse). The 20th century has also been colorful, from the days of Jack London (Jack London State Historic Park) to those of John Steinbeck (Monterey's Cannery Row), from the wealthy excesses of moguls like William Randolph Hearst (Hearst Castle) to the glamour of early Hollywood (Mann's Chinese Theatre and the Hollywood Walk of Fame).

Some preparation can help your kids get the most out of these visits. Screen the classic Western *High Noon,* filmed at Columbia State Historic Park, or read London's *Call of the Wild.* For younger kids it's best to take the history and culture in small doses, combining it with plenty of time to relax or run off steam. But even small children can surprise you with what catches their imaginations. "Cool!" a 6-year-old boy proclaimed when he spotted a 19th-century hand loom at Fort Ross State Historic Park. "Don't you wish we had one of those, Mom?"

Northern Forests and Lakes

Battery Point Lighthouse

(**👫 3–15**) Of all the state's old lighthouses this one is my favorite to visit with children. It's an adventure just getting here: At high tide it's on an island surrounded by water, so you must wait for low tide. Built in 1856, this is still a real working lighthouse, where the lightkeeper and his wife live from April through September. They're glad to show visitors around, as long as they don't sit on the furniture; ask the lightkeeper about the legends of local ghosts, dragons, and mermaids. The tiny Lighthouse Museum downstairs displays such wonders as an 1856 banjo clock (still running), a 1909 Victrola, and an old lens containing a 40-watt lightbulb that was actually visible for 14 miles. Then you'll go upstairs on a narrow ladder to look out of the lantern room itself, with its panoramic ocean views. Kids can then peek into "Captain Hook's treasure chest," which contains a surprise for them. 🏠 *Foot of A St., Crescent City, tel. 707/464–3089. Admission: $2 adults, 50¢ children under 12. Open Apr.–Sept., Wed.–Sun. 10–4, tides permitting.*

Carson Mansion

(**ALL**) Along with countless other sightseers, my kids like snapping pictures of this three-story green Gothic Victorian, which is said to be one of the most photographed houses in the country. And little wonder: Its ostentatious architecture—commissioned in 1885 by a pioneer lumber baron—almost defies description. (My son, Grael, had a word for it, though: "awesome.") You can't go inside (the mansion is a private club), but it's situated on a pleasant street ideal for strolling and gawking.

2nd and M Sts., Eureka, tel. 707/443–5097. No admission to house.

Ferndale

(**6–15**) This entire beautifully preserved Victorian village has been declared a State Historic Landmark for its restored 19th-century dwellings and stores. Though children aren't likely to appreciate its many antiques shops and art galleries, Ferndale is well worth a stop for a walking tour along Main Street and nearby blocks (pick up maps and information at the Kinetic Sculpture Race Museum Building, 580 Main St. at Shaw). Don't miss the stunning century-old Queen Anne known as the Gingerbread Mansion (400 Berding St., tel. 707/786–4000, now a bed-and-breakfast), painted in bright peach and yellow, festooned with gables and turrets.

5 mi west of Hwy. 101 at Fortuna, 17 mi south of Eureka, tel. 707/786–4477. Admission free. Open daily.

Fort Humboldt State Historic Park

(**6–15**) The rangers here seemed almost embarrassed when my family and I asked, "Where's the fort?" The long-abandoned U.S. Army garrison erected here in 1853 is slated for restoration eventually, but it may not be in our lifetimes. Meanwhile, the site, on a pretty bluff above Humboldt Bay, is great for picnicking, and older children

may enjoy the museum of Native American artifacts and the short trail leading past displays of cutting tools, redwood stumps, and steam "donkey engines" used to drag logs. The century-old locomotives steam up on the third Saturday of each month from April to September, and during "Steam Donkey Days," a celebration of the past held on a spring weekend.

3431 Fort Ave., Eureka, tel. 707/445–6567. Admission free. Open daily 9–5; exhibits open daily 9–4.

Fort Ross State Historic Park

(**3–15**) This picturesque fort—on a windswept bay a few hours' drive north of San Francisco—was once the most distant outpost in the Russian empire. A small group of Russian settlers and their native Alaskan crews ventured here in 1812 to hunt for sea otters, with hopes of establishing a permanent colony, but they abandoned the area in 1841 after hunting the otters nearly to extinction. The large redwood fort, meticulously restored in 1974, contains a Russian Orthodox chapel (kids love ringing its bell) and an octagonal blockhouse with cannons pointing toward the bay. There are picnic tables and lots of grass for running around within the compound. Costumed interpreters give presentations of the history nearly every day; call for times. Two caveats: The site can get very foggy and cold (especially in summer fog season), and the winding coastal highway may be rough on kids subject to car sickness.

19005 Hwy. 1 (11 mi north of Jenner), tel. 707/847–3286. Admission: $6 per car. Open daily 10–4:30.

Weaverville Joss House State Historic Park

(**6–15**) Built in 1874 by Chinese gold miners in this remote community near the Trinity Alps, the Weaverville Joss House is an exotic place for kids to see the Gold Rush era from an immigrant perspective. The Joss House, a Taoist temple that's still in use, may be visited on guided tours. Though the tours last 30 to 40 minutes, even young kids are often entranced by the ornately carved, brightly painted altar and colorful silk embroidered banners. The visitors center has exhibits on the miners and on Chinese astrology. The temple grounds, with a footbridge leading over a creek, are beautiful. **🏠** *Hwy. 299, Weaverville, tel. 530/623–5284. Tours: $2 adults, $1 ages 6–12. Open June–Aug., daily 10–5; Apr.–May and Sept.–Oct., Wed.–Sun. 10–5; Nov.–Mar., Sat. 10–5. Tours hourly 10–4.*

Sierra and the Gold Country

Bodie State Historic Park

(**👫 3–15**) In 1880 the rip-roaring Wild West town of Bodie had a population of 10,000, complete with gold miners, gunfighters, 65 saloons, and a reputation as one of the meanest places around. Today 150 buildings remain, all deserted when the gold veins dried up; it's the largest unrestored ghost town in the West. Much less commercial than restored towns like Calico (see below), Bodie is all the more compelling. Pick up a self-guided trail brochure ($1), then wander around the abandoned stores, schools, mines, mill, churches, and gallows, imagining what it was like when gold was plentiful and life was cheap. A museum on Main Street contains photos and artifacts, and rangers roam the streets to answer questions, but take heed: No food, drink, or lodging is available (there is a picnic area ½ mile away). Also note that the last 3 miles of the road leading here are unpaved and very rough. **🏠** *Rte. 270 (13 mi off Hwy. 395 and 8 mi south of Bridgeport), tel. 760/647–6445. Admission: $2 ages 6 and up, $1 ages 5 and under. Park open summer, daily 8–7; spring and fall, daily 8–5; winter, daily 8–4, weather and road conditions permitting; museum open summer, daily 10–5, closed most of rest of year.*

Capitol Building

(**👫 6–15**) Saved from demolition two decades ago, California's Capitol has been magnificently restored, with classical columns, a 120-foot-high, French Renaissance-style rotunda, mosaic-tiled floors, carved mahogany railings, and a golden globe atop the dome. The legislative chambers contain original desks from 1869 and authentically re-created chandeliers. You can visit re-creations of state offices as they were nearly a century ago. The bank vault in the 1906 State Treasurer's Office is where the state kept its entire $7 million reserves—in cash! Stop by the basement tour room for either self-guided tour brochures or free tickets for a one-hour guided tour. The 40-acre grounds surrounding the building are filled with trees and plants from around the world, providing a shady respite in summer. **🏠** *Capitol Ave. and 10th St., Sacramento, tel. 916/324–0333. Admission free. Tours daily on the hr from 9–4 (pick up tickets ½ hr in advance).*

Columbia State Historic Park

(**👫 3–15**) Columbia, a onetime boomtown known as the "Gem of the Southern Mines," is a must for families traveling in the Gold Country. Columbia boasted a population of 15,000 in the 1850s, fueled by a slew of breweries, saloons, and gambling and fandango halls. Shortly after gold was discovered here, it was said the average man could extract a pound of gold a day from the local rivers. Today you and your children can walk the streets where *High Noon* was filmed, ride a Wells Fargo stagecoach, visit working blacksmith and carpentry shops, and pan for gold. But the park also provides entertainment: You can stay at historic hotels, watch plays at a vintage theater, buy a treat at old-fashioned bakeries and candy stores, or down a sarsaparilla at one of two saloons advertising "Ladies and Minors Welcome." The shops, restaurants, and hotels have all been restored or reconstructed, and the workers wear period costume; it could be hokey, but it isn't. A museum (corner of Main and State Sts.) displays exhibits about the town's history, and at the Matelot Gulch Mine Supply Store (corner of Main and Washington Sts.) you can pan for gold ($5–$10) or book a 75-minute tour down into the nearby Hidden Treasure Gold Mine, the only active working hard-rock gold mine open to the public. When we brought Grael here at age 9, the guide's graphic descriptions of child labor in the mines in the 1880s made modern-day school look pretty good by comparison.

🏠 *Parrot's Ferry Rd., off Rte. 49, 5 mi north of Sonora, tel. 209/532–4301. Admission free. Town exhibits open daily 10–5:30; museum open daily 10–4:30. Gold-mine tours (tel. 209/532–9693) daily, Mar. 15–Labor Day, Wed.–Sun. rest of year, weather permitting; call for times; admission $8 ages 13 and up, $7 ages 12 and under; infants free.*

Empire Mine State Historic Park

(👫 6–15) Opened in 1850, the Empire Mine was once the biggest, deepest, richest hard-rock mine in the Gold Country. Miners descended each day into the dark shaft, toiling for long hours and short wages thousands of feet below the surface; mules were lowered into the mine when young, remaining to work their entire lives. For our children, peering into the shaft provided a bleak, poignant lesson in what went into building 19th-century America. Nearby, you can tour the Bourn Mansion, an English-style country lodge that the mine owner used as a vacation home; the contrasts are striking. The lodge is surrounded by lawns and formal gardens, and the park is honeycombed with hiking trails.

🏠 *10791 E. Empire St., Grass Valley, tel. 530/273–8522. Admission: $3 adults, $1 ages 6–12. Mine open Jan.–Apr. and Sept.–Dec., daily 10–5; May, daily 9–5; June–Aug., daily 9–6. Mansion hrs vary; guided tours daily.*

Fort Sutter State Historic Park

(👫 6–15) John Sutter, a pioneer land baron and industrialist, is best known as the owner of Sutter's Mill (see Marshall Gold Discovery State Historic Park *below*), where the Gold Rush began in 1848. But Sutter's main wealth came from the formidable business empire he ran from within this walled bastion a dozen blocks east of the State Capitol. The fort, built with the aid of a powerful private army of Native Americans, was abandoned during the Gold Rush but has been reconstructed; you can explore a cooperage, a blacksmith shop, and a cannon room. Many kids enjoy carrying the portable audio speakers that re-create Sutter's voice as he describes his triumphs and ultimate fall.

🏠 *2701 L St., Sacramento, tel. 916/445–4422. Admission: $6 adults, $3 ages 6–12. Open daily 10–5.*

Indian Grinding Rock State Historic Park

(👫 3–15) An enormous flat limestone slab, 175 feet by 82 feet, gives this Gold Country park its name. The Miwok Indians who once lived here (as long as 20 or 30 centuries ago) would gather acorns, then grind them into meal, using as mortars nearly 1,200 cuplike holes they had scooped out of the rock. Have your kids try to picture this scene, with dozens of Native American women kneeling at the rock, grinding, socializing, and watching their children. There are five smaller grinding rocks in the park as well, all fenced off to protect them from wear. Some also contain petroglyphs, ancient Indian rock carvings; rangers say these are more visible by lantern light at night than in the daytime. The park's Chaw'se Regional Indian Museum has interesting displays (some interactive) on the Miwok culture, and there's an attractively reconstructed Miwok Village of bark houses, as well as picnic areas, 23 no-reservation campsites ($12 per night), and nature trails.

🏠 *14881 Pine Grove–Volcano Rd., Pine Grove, tel. 209/296–7488. Admission: $5 per car. Park open daily sunrise–sunset. Museum open weekdays 11–3, weekends 10–4.*

Malakoff Diggins State Historic Park

(👫 6 – 15) Once the site of the largest hydraulic gold-mining operation in the world, the Malakoff Diggins are a testament to unbridled greed and environmental degradation. The mining company that owned the lands here in the 1860s to 1880s literally washed away entire hillsides in the search for gold. Eventually the mine was shut down when its techniques led to flooding of nearby communities. The site, North Bloomfield, is now a ghost town (some buildings have been restored), with guided tours at 1:30 PM daily in summer, weekends the rest of the year. Despite the area's checkered history, the park is a favorite of those who like to get away from it all—it's quiet and peaceful and still rich with gold; you and your kids may want to try gold panning in backcountry streams. (Seek out a ranger or old-timer for tips.) You can stay in cabins ($20 a night) or camp here, too; campsites are $10 per night. Note that the road to the park is steep and winding, much of it unpaved.

🏠 *23579 N. Bloomfield Rd., off of Hwy. 49, 29 mi northeast of Nevada City, tel. 530/265–2740. Admission: $5 per car. Park open daily. Visitors center and museum open Memorial Day–Labor Day, daily 10–5; rest of year, weekends 10–4.*

Marshall Gold Discovery State Historic Park

(👫 3 – 15) Along with Columbia State Historic Park (see *above*), this scenic site is one of the Gold Country's two indispensable stops. James Marshall discovered gold along the south fork of the American River in 1848, while building a sawmill for entrepreneur John Sutter; and the course of California history changed forever: A remote, little-populated territory soon boomed with tens of thousands of fortune seekers dredging through icy river beds with placer pans, hoping to trap little flakes of gold. (If your kids are like mine, they'll scan the waters for glimpses of the treasured golden particles.) A reconstruction of Sutter's Mill stands along the riverbank, with models of the miners' tiny cabins and a small museum nearby. An easy hike leads to the gold discovery site.

🏠 *Hwy. 49, Coloma, tel. 530/622–3470 (museum tel. 530/622–1116). Parking: $5 per car. Museum admission free. Park open daily 8:30–sunset. Museum open during daylight savings time, daily 10–5; during standard time, daily 10–4:30.*

Old Sacramento State Historic Park

(👫 ALL) This 28-acre site along the banks of the Sacramento River makes a thoroughly pleasant, if somewhat commercial, place to absorb the flavor of the Gold Rush era, with its restored Victorian buildings, wooden boardwalks, gas lamps, and cobbled streets. Your family can ride a horse-drawn carriage or a steam train (Central Pacific Freight Depot, Front St. between J and K Sts., tel. 916/445–6645; $6 adults, $3 ages 6–12) along the river from April till early December; take a paddle-wheeler cruise (L Street Landing, tel. 916/552–2933 or 800/433–0263); or stay overnight on a restored riverboat, the *Delta King* (1000 Front St., tel. 916/444–5464), Old Sacramento's only hotel. The world's largest train museum (see Chapter 5) is down near the hardware store where several tycoons met to plan the first transcontinental railroad. The Discovery Museum (101 I St., tel. 916/264–7057; $4 adults, $2 ages 6–12; open in summer, daily 10–5; in winter, Tues.–Sun. 10–5) presents a variety of hands-on exhibits for exploring local history, science, and technology, plus $1 million in gold specimens (sorry, no hands-on for this one). Other sights include the 1880s-era Old Sacramento Schoolhouse (1200 Front St., tel. 916/483–8818; open daily 10–4; admission free); the still-active Old Eagle Theater (925 Front St., tel. 916/323–6343), which dates from 1849; and the spot at 2nd and J streets where the fabled Pony Express began in 1860, marked by a monument and a small museum.

🏛 *Bounded by Sacramento River and 2nd St., I St., and Capitol Mall, tel. 916/442–7644. Admission free; some attractions charge fees. Visitors center (2nd and K Sts.) open Fri.–Tues. 9–5, Wed.–Thurs. 10–1.*

San Francisco and the Bay Area

Alcatraz Island

🚹 3–15 The former maximum-security prison here, closed in 1963, once held some of the nation's most incorrigible criminals— and though only a 10-minute boat ride from Fisherman's Wharf, the island still seems eerily isolated, its lighthouse tower often shrouded in mist. Its reputation as "America's Devil's Island," along with the gorgeous views it provides, are irresistible lures— Alcatraz is deservedly one of San Francisco's most popular tourist sites. Public transport is all via Blue & Gold Fleet ferries from Pier 41; boat reservations are strongly advised, and essential in summer. Once on The Rock, which is now a national park, kids can peer into tiny, spartan cells that once held the likes of Al Capone and Robert ("Birdman of Alcatraz") Stroud and visit the grim dark holes where disobedient prisoners were left to languish in solitary confinement. (No child I know who has visited these holes has ever robbed a bank.) You have your choice of tour methods here; you can take a ranger-led tour or guide yourself around using an audiocassette or a pamphlet. (The Cell House Audio Tour, with ex-inmates and guards describing their experiences, is riveting.) Wear comfortable shoes for climbing over rocky terrain, and bring some warm clothing; the island (and boat ride) may be

chilly. If the day is clear, however, island trails allow exceptional views of San Francisco and the Bay. Allow between 2 and 2½ hours for a visit.

🏛 *Pier 41, Fisherman's Wharf, San Francisco, tel. 415/773–1188 (boat schedules and information); 415/705–5555 or 800/426–8687 (credit-card ticket orders); 415/705–1042 (park information). Admission: $11 adults, $5.75 ages 5–11, under 5 free (without audio-cassette tour: $7.75 adults, $4.50 ages 5–11). Evening tours (including audiocassettes): $18.50 adults, $15.75 ages 12–17, $9.25 ages 5–11. Boats daily 9:30–4:15; Thurs.–Sun. also 6:15 PM and 7 PM.*

Cliff House

🚹 ALL Historic Cliff House, perched above the Pacific Ocean and Ocean Beach, offers knockout views of land and sea from its indoor eating places and outdoor observation deck. Especially appealing to kids are the views of sea lions basking and barking (from October to June) on offshore rocks. You can also gaze down at the ruins of the old Sutro Baths, once the world's largest indoor swimming pool. Built in 1909, Cliff House (the third on this site) has popular restaurants and bars, a visitors center (tel. 415/556–8642) with historical and natural history displays, and the Musée Mécanique (tel. 415/386–1170), a quirky, fascinating antique arcade, brimming with coin-operated player pianos, pinball machines old and new, and nickelodeons. The adjacent camera obscura (admission $1), a replica of an invention by Leonardo da Vinci, projects images from outside and displays them on a matte-finish dish inside. You might see people walking on the beach below, or, on a clear day, glimpse the Farallon Islands 30 or so miles offshore.

🏛 *1090 Point Lobos Ave., at Great Hwy., San Francisco, tel. 415/386–3330. Admission free. Museum open Memorial Day–Labor Day, daily 10–8; rest of year, Mon.–Fri. 11–7, weekends and holidays 10–7. Visitors center open daily 10–5 except major holidays.*

Coit Tower

(👫 ALL) One of San Francisco's most distinctive landmarks, 210-foot Coit Tower crowns the crest of 284-foot Telegraph Hill. The city's exciting panorama of hills, islands, bridges, and bay spreads out below. You can ride an elevator to the Observation Gallery on top for a 360° vista, or simply hang outside at the tower's base and soak in the free views. (Do go inside, though, for a peek at the ground-level, Depression-era murals painted in a style pioneered by Mexican artist Diego Rivera.) Built in 1933 as a monument to the city's volunteer firefighters, the tower was named after Lillie Coit, a wealthy eccentric and fire-engine buff. The easiest way to walk to the tower is via Lombard Street (not the famous crooked part) and up a flight of steps, but the climb can be tiring. The No. 39 Coit bus goes from Washington Square, or you can drive, though traffic often backs up and the parking lot at the top is often filled.

🏠 *Telegraph Hill Blvd., at Greenwich St. or Lombard St., Telegraph Hill, San Francisco, tel. 415/362–0808. Observation-gallery admission: $3, $1 ages 6–12. Observation gallery open daily 10–7.*

Golden Gate Bridge

(👫 ALL) It's San Francisco's most recognized landmark—the symbol of the city—and probably the most celebrated and photographed bridge in the world. Completed in 1937, after four years of construction, the Golden Gate Bridge is still one of the world's longest suspension bridges, stretching from San Francisco north to Marin County. Its two towers rise 750 feet into the air, and it uses enough cable wire to wrap around the Equator three times. More than 40 million vehicles cross it each year. You can drive across the bridge, too, of course, but the best ways to see it—and the views from it—are by walking or biking across. The reddish-orange (not golden!) bridge is nearly 2 miles long, but you don't have to cover the full distance to get the effect—

simply park your car in one of the lots (either on the south or north sides; bring quarters for the meters) and walk as far as you wish. The views—some 220 feet above the water—are unforgettable: Alcatraz, Angel Island, the San Francisco skyline, the Marin Headlands, and a parade of sailboats, windsurfers, and freighters. Our family's favorite time to walk here is when the fog begins to swirl across the bridge, lending an almost mystic element to its beauty. Be sure to dress warmly, whatever the weather. The Golden Gate Bridge toll plaza may also be reached by Muni buses No. 28 or 29. For details on biking across and beyond the bridge, see Chapter 14.

🏠 *Hwy. 101, San Francisco, tel. 415/921– 5858. Toll: $3 per car (southbound only); free for walkers, cyclists, and northbound drivers. Open daily, 24 hrs for cars and bikes, 5 AM–9 PM for pedestrians.*

Jack London State Historic Park

(👫 3 – 15) Writer Jack London, author of *The Call of the Wild* and *White Fang,* lived and worked the last years of his life in these magnificent wooded hills. He called this property his Beauty Ranch, and it's easy to see why. You can visit his wood-frame cottage (which is being restored), his horse barns, and, at the end of a moderate mile-long hike, the ruins of Wolf House, London's dream estate, which burned down before he could move in. There's also horseback riding (tel. 707/996–8566) on site and picnicking.

🏠 *2400 London Ranch Rd., Glen Ellen, off Hwy. 12, north of Sonoma, tel. 707/938– 5216. Admission: $6 per car. Open during daylight savings time, daily 9:30–7; during standard time, daily 9:30–5.*

Luther Burbank Home and Gardens

(👫 9 – 15) Renowned horticulturalist Luther Burbank (1849–1926) used this site as his working garden for more than 40 years, developing some 800 new plants—hybrid varieties of potatoes, cacti, fruit, flowers, and trees. Kids should be interested in seeing his "plumcot," a cross between a plum and an apricot that's so perishable, its fruit is edible for only one day. The guided 30- to 40-minute house tour consists mostly of historical detail; most kids would prefer to spend their time wandering the attractive gardens.

⋔ *Sonoma and Santa Rosa Aves., Santa Rosa, tel. 707/524–5445. Admission to garden free. House tour: $3 adults, ages 12 and under free. Gardens open Apr.–Oct., daily 8–7; Nov.–Mar., daily 8–5. House tours Apr.–Oct., Tues.–Sun. 10–3:30.*

Mission Dolores

(**⋔⋔ 6–15**) Mission Dolores, the sixth and one of the best preserved of California's 21 Spanish-era missions, is the oldest building in San Francisco, completed in 1791. (Don't mistake the humble historic mission for the multidomed basilica next door, built in 1913, where most local parishioners actually come to worship). The mission is small and can be toured quickly. When you go inside be sure to look up at the ceiling, where local Costanoan Indians hand-painted the Native American designs with vegetable dyes. The tiny chapel is decorated with frescoes and a hand-painted wooden altar; some artifacts were brought from Mexico by mule in the late 18th century. The old cemetery next to the chapel is the most intriguing sight. Here, dozens of early San Francisco pioneers and settlers are buried—many of them youngsters who died during the Gold Rush, a poignant reminder of the hardships of those times. And lying in unmarked graves in back are the remains of an estimated 5,000 Native Americans.

⋔ *16th and Dolores Sts., San Francisco, tel. 415/621–8203. Suggested donation: $2 adults, $1 ages 5–12; audio tour $5. Open daily 9–4.*

Sonoma State Historic Park

(**⋔⋔ 9–15**) This historic park includes both Sonoma Mission (known officially as Mission San Francisco Solano) and the home of General Mariano Vallejo, California's last Mexican governor. The mission is right on the plaza in downtown Sonoma (20 Spain St. E), which makes it a convenient, quick visit; it takes only a few minutes to walk through its largely reconstructed rooms and attractive chapel. Established in 1823, Sonoma's was the northernmost and last of California's 21 missions founded by Franciscan priests to bring Christianity to Native Americans, and to secure territory for Spain and Mexico. (One goal was to fend off Russian encroachment on the territory, which will interest kids who've visited Fort Ross; see Northern Forests and Lakes *above*.) The same ticket will admit you to General Vallejo's splendid 1852 Gothic-Victorian home, ½ mile west on Spain Street. There's a 20-minute guided tour of the beautifully furnished house; if your kids are too young to appreciate that, come here for a picnic at shaded tables looking out over cacti, flower gardens, grapevines, and ponds. My children did enjoy seeing Vallejo's son Napoleon's tiny hillside studio, where the boy painted and kept a menagerie of pets.

⋔ *Spain St., Sonoma, tel. 707/938–1519. Combined admission: $2 adults, $1 ages 6–12. Open daily 10–5.*

Winchester Mystery House

(**⋔⋔ 6–15**) Sarah Winchester's 160-room Victorian dwelling is touted as the world's "oddest historical mansion," and I won't argue with the description. Rifle heiress Winchester, a wealthy widow and devotee of the occult, began work on her house in 1884. Convinced by a spiritualist that continuous building would appease the spirits of those killed by Winchester firearms, she kept carpenters working on it 24 hours a day for the next 38 years, following no discernible blueprints. The results are both beautiful and bizarre: Rooms with Tiffany art-glass windows, gold and silver chandeliers, inlaid doors, and parquet floors are juxtaposed with stairways and chimneys that lead nowhere, doors that open to blank walls, and a layout so rambling and complex that our guide quipped, "If you get separated from the group, there's no guarantee you'll ever be found." The standard tour lasts one hour and goes through 110 rooms, a 1½-mile jaunt; my kids loved it, but a 3-year-old in our group was clearly restless. A new 55-minute "behind-the scenes tour" ($10.95 ages 13 and up) winds through previously unseen workings of the estate and is good for return visitors. Hard hats are required, and kids 12 and under aren't allowed for safety reasons. You can also tour the extensive gardens and firearms museum on your own. Special flashlight tours and trick-or-treating are offered during Halloween season.

🏠 *525 S. Winchester Blvd., San Jose, tel. 408/247–2101. Admission: $13.95 adults, $7.95 ages 6–12. Open daily at 9:30 AM; closing hrs vary, call for schedule.*

Central Coast and Valley

Cannery Row

(**👫 ALL**) When John Steinbeck's *Cannery Row* was published in 1945, this mile-long strip along the Monterey waterfront bustled with sardine canneries and processing plants. After the sardines were all but fished out in the late 1940s the area deteriorated. Now many of the old buildings have been renovated as hotels, restaurants, shops, and galleries; the site of the largest cannery has become the world-class Monterey Bay Aquarium (see Chapter 6). Steinbeck's hero, "Doc" Ricketts, kept his lab at No. 800, recently a private club. Other Steinbeck sites include Lee Chong's Heavenly Flower Grocery (No. 835), actually the Wing Chong Building, site of Alicia's Antiques store; and La Ida's Cafe (No. 851), now Kalisa's Cafe.

🏠 *Cannery Row, Monterey, tel. 831/373–1902. Admission free except to private attractions. Open daily.*

Carmel Mission

(**👫 6 – 15**) Formally known as Mission San Carlos Borromeo del Rio Carmelo, this restored Spanish-style adobe and stone complex is one of the most beautiful of all California missions. Established in 1770, it's the burial place of Father Junipero Serra, who founded the first nine Spanish missions, laying the foundations for modern-day California agriculture in the process. (Whether the Native Americans willingly came to work for the padres, as the mission brochure suggests, or were forced to lend their labors and convert to Christianity, is a matter of controversy.) My kids learned something about early California history through the exhibits here, and they enjoyed walking through the lovely central courtyard, past fountains and gardens. Lia was struck by the graves marked only with abalone shells in the old cemetery, where more than 3,000 Native Americans are buried—the result, mainly, of diseases contracted from Europeans at the mission.

🏠 *3080 Rio Rd., Carmel, tel. 831/624–3600. Suggested donation: $2 adults, $1 ages 6–15. Open Sept.–May, Mon.–Sat. 9:30–4:30, Sun. 10:30–4:30; June–Aug., Mon.–Sat. 9:30–7:30, Sun. 10:30–7:30.*

Colonel Allensworth State Historic Park

(**👫 6 – 15**) Founded in 1908 by African-American pioneer Col. Allen Allensworth, who escaped slavery to join the Union forces in the Civil War and rose to become the country's highest-ranking black officer, the Central Valley town of Allensworth became the only California town settled, governed, and financed by black Americans. After several years of prosperity, Allensworth came upon hard times and became a ghost town. Now it's a state historic park, with buildings rebuilt or restored to reflect the era when the town thrived. Special events are celebrated throughout the year; each October, for instance, three days of festivities—including hayrides, entertainment, and docent-guided tours—mark the town's "rededication."

🏚 *4129 Palmer Ave., Allensworth-Earlimart, along Hwy. 43, 45 mi north of Bakersfield, tel. 661/849–3433. Day use admission: $3 per car. Camping: $8 per night. Park open daily.*

Forestiere Underground Gardens

(👪 **3 – 15**) Yes, we too were mystified by the notion of an underground garden, but Sicilian immigrant Baldasare Forestiere, who arrived in Fresno in 1906 and died in 1946, carved out this remarkable subterranean world of tunnels, grottoes, and rooms by hand over the course of 40 years—an "obsession of love," as he called it. Kids can see where Forestiere lived below ground— his bedrooms (one with fireplace), kitchen, living room, bath, fishpond, and dozens of patios, alcoves, and arched passageways— along with the ground-level skylights that allow a variety of exotic, full-grown fruit trees to flourish as far as 22 feet below the surface. (One tree bears seven different kinds of citrus.) Rooms on view are only a tiny fraction of Forestiere's prodigious project, which spread out over 10 acres.

🏚 *5021 W. Shaw Ave., Fresno, tel. 559/ 271–0734. Admission: $6 adults, $5 teens, $4 ages 3–12. Open Memorial Day–Labor Day, Wed.–Sun. 10–4; Easter–Memorial Day and Labor Day–Thanksgiving (weather permitting), weekends noon–3.*

Hearst Castle

(👪 **6 – 15**) Newspaper czar William Randolph Hearst's fabulous hilltop estate, which he called "The Enchanted Hill" or simply "the ranch," is now officially known as Hearst San Simeon State Historical Monument, but is best known as Hearst Castle. No other American private residence of the time approached its splendor;

many of the top names in 1920s and 1930s Hollywood visited here, including Charlie Chaplin, Cary Grant, and Carole Lombard. Perched high above the Pacific Ocean, the estate includes 165 rooms—many furnished with valuable European antiques and art—and 127 acres of gardens, terraces, pools, and walkways. Construction began in the 1920s and took 28 years to complete. Four different tours cover the huge castle; all include a ½-mile walk, and at least 150 stairs, but tour No. 1 is the least strenuous and the best for first-time visitors. The entire tour time is 1¾ hours, including the bus ride up and back from the visitors center; the actual time at the castle is about 75 minutes. During our tour children younger than 6 got fidgety while the guide discussed the artwork. But my kids gaped and gawked as we passed through an ornate guest cottage larger than most mansions, a living room filled with priceless tapestries, a Gothic-style dining hall, and an indoor swimming pool area gilded with blue and gold tiles and decorated with Roman statues. (Docents outfitted in period costume help lend atmosphere along the way.) In spring and fall ask about special two-hour evening tours (at an additional charge).

🏚 *Hwy. 1, San Simeon, tel. 800/444–4445. Admission: $14 adults, $8 ages 6–12. Evening tours: $25 adults, $13 ages 6–12. Daytime tours from 8:20 AM daily; last tour leaves 3 PM in winter, later in summer. Reservations advised at least 48 hrs in advance.*

La Purisima Mission State Historic Park

(👪 **6 – 15**) La Purisima Mission is the most completely restored of the state's 21 Franciscan missions, but Grael found it the most interesting of all because "it's out in the middle of nowhere. You can really imagine what life was like back then." A self-guided tour of the mission complex runs ¾ mile and includes the church, a cemetery, soldiers' quarters, tallow vats, a garden, Indian barracks, and a livestock corral.

🏠 *2295 Purisima Rd., Lompoc, tel. 805/733–3713. Admission: $5 per car. Open daily 9–5.*

Mission Santa Barbara

(👫 6–15) Known as the "Queen of the Missions" for its beauty, Mission Santa Barbara, founded in 1786, has fountains, gardens, and some nicely displayed exhibits on mission history. Children may be most impressed by the missionaries' spartan bedrooms, with their wooden cots stretched with animal-hide mattresses.

🏠 *Laguna St., Santa Barbara, tel. 805/682–4713. Admission: $3 adults, ages 11 and under free. Open daily 9–5.*

Monterey State Historic Park

(👫 6–15) Monterey was California's first capital, and this historic section adjacent to Fisherman's Wharf contains several restored structures and houses from its glorious past—many still used as hotels, restaurants, government offices, and places of business. When our family took a 1½-hour guided walking tour of the area, led by a docent, our then 11-year-old daughter's eyes quickly began to glaze over; I'd recommend taking the history in smaller doses, selecting sites from the "Path of History" brochure (pick one up at the visitors center on Custom House Plaza). A good introduction is the free 15-minute film shown (daily 10–5) at the History Theater in the Maritime Museum at Stanton Center. Nearby is the adobe Custom House (admission free, open daily 10–5), the oldest standing public building in the state. Just outside it, in 1846, Commodore John Sloat of the U.S. Navy claimed California from Mexico. Inside, kids can view piles of untanned cowhides used in lieu of cash, dubbed "California banknotes." The Path of History continues for several downtown blocks, passing California's oldest brick house, a church built in 1794, a sidewalk made of whalebone vertebrae, California's first theater (where live melodramas are still staged), the hall where California's first constitutional convention was held in 1849, and a number of other adobe dwellings, including former homes of writers John Steinbeck and Robert Louis Stevenson. Some sites charge admission.

🏠 *Visitors center, Stanton Center, Custom House Plaza (foot of Fisherman's Wharf), tel. 831/649–7118. Many sites free. All-day admission to 4 sites (Casa Soberanes, Cooper-Molera Adobe, Larkin House, Stevenson House): $5 adults, $3 ages 13–17, $2 ages 6–12, including a selection of guided walking tours. Call for times for individual sites. Visitors center open daily 10–5.*

San Juan Bautista State Historic Park

(👫 6–15) Lining a large grassy plaza in a quiet town northeast of Monterey, this historic park offers neat glimpses of life in 19th-century California. The main attraction technically isn't part of the historic park: Mission San Juan Bautista, which still belongs to the Catholic Church. Unlike many California missions, it was never abandoned—it's been used continuously since 1797. You can view restored rooms from the early mission days, stroll among flower gardens, and go into the old cemetery, where 4,300 Native Americans and Spanish and pioneer settlers are buried in collective graves. Near the church, find the marker for the old El Camino Real, the 500-mile-long road that connected the 21 missions in the 19th century. My children were also intrigued with the San Andreas Fault exhibit (the great earthquake zone runs right through here), including a seismograph that records tremors in the area. Across the plaza, you can tour a 19th-century furnished home, a blacksmith shop, stables, a historic adobe, and (Lia's favorite) a carriage house with a surrey, an Amish buggy, and a stagecoach. Don't miss the tiny San Juan Jail down the street, with its posted warnings that "footpads, thieves and dance hall loungers must get out and stay out—otherwise hang!" The park presents living history programs, focusing on the 1860s, on the first Saturday of each month from noon to 4.

🏛 *2nd and Franklin Sts., San Juan Bautista, tel. 831/623–4881. Mission tel. 831/623–2127. Park admission: $2 adults, $1 ages 6–12. Suggested donation at mission: $2. Park open daily 10–4:30. Mission open Mon.–Sat. 9:30–5, Sun. 10–5.*

Los Angeles and Environs

El Pueblo de Los Angeles Historic Monument

(🧒🧒 **6–15**) Touring the place where Los Angeles was born (in 1781) proved an education for my kids, and they had some fun besides—especially at the colorful, pedestrian-only Olvera Street, with Mexican markets and outdoor restaurants that reminded them of their trip to Mexico City. We began our morning with an informative, free, hour-long guided walking tour of the area (offered Tues.–Sat. 10–1; meet next to the old firehouse on the south side of the Plaza de Los Angeles), but you can also pick up a brochure at the visitors center for a self-guided walking tour, which I recommend for families with young children. We visited the pleasant plaza, former site of bullfights and bear fights and now the site of Sunday folkloric performances; the city's first firehouse (admission free; open Tues.–Sun. 10–3), which dates from 1884; the Pico House, once known as Southern California's finest hotel; and the Avila Adobe on Olvera Street (free; open summer, daily 9–5, rest of year, daily 9–4), the oldest surviving house in Los Angeles, built in 1818. Cap your visit by browsing or munching your way along Olvera Street.

🏛 *Bounded by Alameda, Arcadia, Spring, and Macy Sts., downtown Los Angeles. Visitors center: Sepulveda House, 622 N. Main St., tel. 213/628–1274. Open Mon.–Sat. 10–3.*

Hollywood Walk of Fame

(🧒🧒 **ALL**) To view the Hollywood Walk of Fame, simply head for the corner of Hollywood Boulevard and Vine Street, stroll in any direction, and look down at your feet. You'll be stepping on terrazzo-and-brass stars honoring such Hollywood legends as Elvis Presley, Marilyn Monroe, Charlie Chaplin, Bette Davis, Clark Gable, and Rudolph Valentino. My kids drew blanks at many of the names, but then so did I—a number of the more than 2,000 figures "immortalized" here since 1958 have faded into obscurity. Keep an eye out for Chaplin, Monroe, and Elvis at 6751, 6774, and 6777 Hollywood Boulevard, respectively, and Mickey Mouse in front of Mann's Chinese Theatre (see *below*). Want to attend a Walk of Fame dedication ceremony? Call 323/469–8311 for a schedule of upcoming star additions. And by the way, if you're old enough to remember when the corner of Hollywood and Vine was a big deal, prepare for a disappointment: Whatever glamour this intersection once had is definitely a thing of the past.

🏛 *Hollywood Blvd., between Gower St. and Sycamore Ave., and Vine St., between Yucca and Sunset Blvd., Hollywood, tel. 323/469–8311 or 323/236–2331. Admission free. Open daily.*

La Brea Tar Pits

(🧒🧒 **ALL**) These oozing pools of asphalt in Hancock Park are the richest Ice Age fossil sites in the world. More than 100 tons of bones have been found here, representing hundreds of species of long-extinct animals, from 10,000 to 40,000 years old: American mastodons, imperial mammoths, huge ground sloths, California saber-toothed tigers. (Young dinosaur fans should be warned that these fossils date from millions of years after the dinosaur era.) In the big Lake Pit along Wilshire Boulevard, mastodon models show how the animals came to be so well preserved: Stopping for a drink at a prehistoric pond, they found themselves trapped in the gooey black asphalt, unable to escape, and laws of nature took it from there. Of the more than 100 pits here, several are open for observation, and you might even chance upon (as we did) some excavations in progress. Each July and August (from Wednesday to Sunday between 10 and 4), the public can watch paleontologists recover fossils from Pit 91. But beware: Oozing asphalt may be anywhere, even on the walkways; make sure your children step carefully. For essential bacground, go inside the excellent George C. Page Museum of La Brea Discoveries, also in Hancock Park (see Chapter 5; admission charged).

🏛 *5801 Wilshire Blvd., Los Angeles, tel. 323/ 934–7243. Admission free. Parking: $5. Open daily. Free tour Wed.–Sun. at 1 PM.*

Mann's Chinese Theatre

(**👫 ALL**) It's hard to miss Mann's Chinese Theatre: With its ornate pagoda entrance and garish lighting, it's the ultimate Hollywood statement. Mann's (formerly Grauman's) screens first-run movies, but the real draw is its famous front courtyard, where more than 160 celebrities have etched their signatures, handprints, or footprints in cement. My kids had a great time hunting up their favorites: Alfred Hitchcock, Houdini, Walt Disney, Eddie Murphy, Harrison Ford, Steven Spielberg. Others for kids to search for: young Shirley Temple's tiny hand- and footprints, Donald Duck's webprints, Roy Rogers's gun print (along with Trigger's hoofprint), and the not-quite-human signatures of Star Wars' C3PO, R2D2, and Darth Vader.

🏛 *6925 Hollywood Blvd., Hollywood, tel. 323/464–8111. Courtyard admission free. Open daily.*

Mission San Juan Capistrano

(**👫 6 – 15**) My daughter had never heard of the "swallows returning to Capistrano," but she was quickly intrigued to learn that faithfully each year on March 19 the birds

find their way back here to build their mud nests in and around the old mission. And just as faithfully, they depart annually on October 23. If you visit between these dates, your kids can buy birdseed within the mission walls to feed the swallows (when we were there, though, a swarm of insistent pigeons were the major beneficiaries). San Juan Capistrano, known as the "Jewel of the Missions," was established by Father Junipero Serra in 1776 and claims to have the oldest building (Serra's Chapel) still in use in California. The chapel's 300-year-old gilded Baroque altar is not to be missed. The mission's courtyards are filled with fountains, trees, and flowers.

🏛 *Camino Capistrano and Ortega Hwy., San Juan Capistrano, tel. 949/248–2048. Admission: $5 adults, $4 ages 3–12. Open daily 8:30–5.*

Queen Mary Seaport

(**👫 ALL**) My children have spent some time on cruise ships, but when they stepped aboard the *Queen Mary*, the largest passenger ship ever built, they were *impressed*. The luxurious 85,000-ton ocean liner, moored in Long Beach since completing its last transatlantic voyage in 1967, is now operated as a hotel (see Chapter 15). But much of it is open to the public on both guided and self-guided tours. As you stroll the upper decks of this Art Deco masterpiece, it's easy to imagine you're about to embark on a long romantic voyage. Staterooms on display are kept as they were in 1967, when a first-class suite cost a princely $5,000 for a nine-day Atlantic round-trip. Kids especially enjoy viewing the officers' quarters, the bridge, the wheelhouse, the enormous docking machinery on the bow, and the anti-aircraft guns dating from World War II, when the ship was used to transport troops (show the kids where Winston Churchill stood). There are several snack bars and restaurants on board. Until the year 2003 or so, you can also tour a one-time Russian submarine, the *Scorpion*, which is on display next to the ocean liner. You can ride the Metro Blue Line to Long Beach from downtown L.A., then catch a shuttle to the Queen.

🏨 *1126 Queen's Hwy., south end of Long Beach Fwy. (I–710), Long Beach, tel. 562/ 435–3511 or 800/437–2934. Admission: $13 adults, $8 ages 4–11; guided tours additional charge. Parking: $6. Open daily in summer 9–9, rest of year 10–6.*

Watts Towers

(👫 **6 – 15**) Though decidedly off the tourist track, the Watts Towers are worth hunting for, in their incongruous site on a quiet, dead-end residential street. At first, my children didn't know quite what to make of these odd folk-art sculptures, but they became fascinated as they learned about their eccentric but talented creator, Italian immigrant Simon Rodia. He worked single-handedly on the towers for 33 years, from 1921 to 1954, using only simple tools, buying or scavenging for the materials himself, and improvising their construction without plans or expert advice. He built these towers of structural steel (the two tallest are nearly 100 feet), covered them with mortar, and adorned them with seashells, colorful stones, pieces of pottery, broken china, tiles, and fragments of bottles. Rodia's creation also features his Ship of Marco Polo, with a 28-foot spire for a mast, a gazebo, and three birdbaths. Rodia's bungalow, which lies in ruins, was destroyed by fire one year after he moved away from the site; he never returned. The towers, under restoration for several years, are scheduled to reopen in 1999 or 2000; until then, you can only view them from outside the gates.

🏨 *1765 E. 107th St., Los Angeles, tel. 323/ 485–1795. Century Blvd. east to Central Ave.; turn south to 108th St. and follow signs. Admission (when open): $1 adults, under 17 free.*

San Diego and the Southern Deserts

Cabrillo National Monument and Old Point Loma Lighthouse

(👫 **3 – 15**) The tip of the Point Loma peninsula gets my vote as the most beautiful spot in San Diego, with commanding views of the city and harbor. A statue at a particularly scenic overlook here honors Portuguese explorer Juan Rodriguez Cabrillo, who landed in San Diego harbor in 1542, the first European to set foot on the West Coast. But kids will probably be more interested in the refurbished old lighthouse nearby, in use from 1855 to 1891, when this was a remote outpost. Climbing its narrow, winding stairs, peering into the living areas, kids can picture the lonely, simple existence of the lightkeeper and his family (including two young sons—don't miss their tiny bedroom, with their toys and washbasin on the floor). Point Loma is also popular for whale-watching and tidepooling (see Chapter 16).

🏨 *Point Loma, south on Catalina Blvd., San Diego, tel. 619/557–5450. Admission: $5 per car. Open daily 9–5:15; summer hrs may be extended.*

Calico Ghost Town

(👫 **3 – 15**) Calico Ghost Town was hopping with visitors the day our family went, and many appeared to be having a good time. But compared to Old West towns such as Columbia and Bodie (see *above*), Calico seemed more commercially than historically oriented. In its silver-mining heyday in the 1880s Calico had a population of 4,000, but it collapsed along with the price of silver near the turn of the century. Walter Knott (of Knott's Berry Farm fame) bought the site in 1950 for restoration; it has since been taken over as a county regional park. You pay to get in, and then you have to pay again for almost every interesting activity: a

1,000-foot tunnel of the Maggie Mine, train or horse-drawn wagon rides, panning for gold, a visit to the Mystery Shack ("House of Optical Illusions"), or a show at the Calibage Playhouse.

🏠 *Ghost Town Rd., 10 mi north of Barstow off of I–15, Yermo, tel. 760/254–2122. Admission: $6 adults, $3 ages 6–15; attractions charge extra fees. Open daily 9–5.*

Old Town State Historic Park

(👫 **3–15**) Each time we visit San Diego we find ourselves drawn to Old Town to enjoy the flavors of early California—or of a modern-day Mexican meal in restaurants adjacent to the historic park (see Chapter 16). This hugely successful civic restoration project has many historic buildings; there are some must-sees for families: the **Wells Fargo History Museum** (tel. 619/238–3929; admission free; open daily 10–5), with its 1868 stagecoach, gold samples, and telegraph; the **Mason Street School** (tel. 619/297–1183; admission free; open daily 10–4), built in 1865, where you can sit at the old wooden desks; and the **19th-century dentist and physician office** (eyeing the primitive dental tools, a young boy exclaimed, "My mouth is lucky they don't use those nowadays!"). Nearby, the historic **Whaley House Museum** (tel. 619/298–2482; $4 adults, $2 ages 5–17; open daily 10–5 except major holidays) has a collection of early California artifacts that isn't likely to thrill most youngsters. Pick up walking tour brochures ($2) at park headquarters in the Robinson-Rose House on Old Town Plaza,

or join a free guided tour. Living history presentations (working blacksmiths, tortilla-making, craft demonstrations) are held every Wednesday from 11 to 1 and the fourth Saturday of each month by costumed staff members.

🏠 *North of downtown San Diego at Juan St., near intersection of I–5 and I–8, tel. 619/220–5422. Admission free; some attractions adjacent to the park charge fee. Park open daily 10–5. Nearby shops and restaurants open daily 10–10. Free 1-hr guided tour daily at 10:30 and 2.*

Scotty's Castle

(👫 **6–15**) In Death Valley, an area filled with strange natural wonders, Scotty's Castle may be classified as a strange unnatural wonder. "Scotty" (full name Walter Scott) was a true Death Valley character who mooched off the real owner of this 1920s Moorish mansion, a Chicago millionaire who kept Scotty around because his tall tales were so entertaining. Though a considerable drive north of most of Death Valley's attractions (see Chapter 8), Scotty's Castle is well worth a look for its sheer improbability. But there's often a considerable wait for tours in high season. If that's the case, my suggestion is to skip the guided tour of the house (which contains artworks and imported carpets and furniture), and simply walk around the grounds.

🏠 *Hwy. 267, 3 mi northeast of Hwy. 190, Death Valley National Park, tel. 760/786–2392. Admission: $8 adults, $4 ages 6–11. Grounds open daily 8–6. House tours daily 9–5.*

DINOSAURS, COWBOYS, MUMMIES, AND OLD MASTERS

HISTORY, ART, AND SCIENCE MUSEUMS

When I was a child I thought most museums were stuffy and boring. But then, I'd never encountered places like the Exploratorium in San Francisco, the Los Angeles Children's Museum, the Tech Museum of Innovation in San Jose, or the Children's Museum of San Diego, where kids can make their own videos and record their own music, play with robots, put on their own theater productions, marvel at optical illusions, and experiment with their own shadows. Relying on a variety of innovative hands-on, interactive exhibits, the best children's museums help kids learn while having fun. One reason kids like them so much is that they explore not only the grand wonders of the world, but also the magic of the everyday—helping to transform the ordinary into the extraordinary. Besides those detailed here, you'll find children's museums in Carlsbad (see Chapter 16), Eureka (**Redwood Discovery Museum,** Bayshore Mall, tel. 707/443–9694), Lake Arrowhead (see Chapter 18), Oxnard (**Gull Wings Children's Museum,** 418 W. Fourth St., tel. 805/483–3005), Palo Alto (**Palo Alto Junior Museum,** 1451 Middlefield Rd., tel. 650/329–2111), Rancho Mirage (see Chapter 18), San Bernardino (see Chapter 15), San Luis Obispo (**San Luis Obispo Children's Museum,** 1010 Nipomo St., tel. 805/544–5437), Santa Ana (see Chapter 15), and Truckee (see Chapter 18).

Meanwhile, many "grown-up" museums, especially science museums, are also attracting children with new hands-on exhibits, plus special programs and classes. Art museums may be less kid-oriented, but after a few visits your children may surprise you.

Northern Forests and Lakes

Clarke Museum

6–15 Pioneers, Native Americans, lumberjacks, seafarers, hunters, shopkeepers: The folks who built rugged Humboldt County are all represented in this eclectic, eye-catching mix of exhibits. The prize is the museum's collection of Native American basketry, jewelry, and costumes; look for the elaborate ceremonial skirt made of deerskin, bear grass, and clam and abalone shells. Other items kids may like: a tiny gun (meant to be carried on a man's watch chain), a 1910 Edison phonograph, a collection of antique musical instruments, and a display of hummingbird eggs.

🏛 *240 E St., Eureka, tel. 707/443–1947. Admission free. Open Feb.–Dec., Tues.–Sat. noon–4. Closed Jan. and major holidays except July 4.*

End of the Trail Indian Museum

(★★ 6–15) A museum attached to the rear of a gift shop? I'd have been skeptical, too, until I wandered into the End of the Trail Indian Museum at the theme park Trees of Mystery (see Chapter 9), with its extensive—and exceptional—collection of Native American artifacts from tribal regions across the West. You'll be treated to elk-tooth dresses, bear-claw necklaces, whalebone masks, eagle-bone whistles, seal-intestine parkas, birch-bark and feather basketry, elaborate headdresses, kachina dolls, dentelia shells (used as money), argolite carvings, and a stunning series of original E. S. Curtis gold-tone photographs that document the people and scenes of the Old West.
🏠 15500 Hwy. 101, Klamath, tel. 707/ 482–2251 or 800/638–3389. Admission free. Open May–Sept., daily 8–8; Oct.–Apr., daily 9–5.

Turtle Bay Park and Museum

(★★ 6–15) Planned eventually to be an ambitious 60-acre combined museum park—with aquariums, exhibits, laboratories, and trails displaying the heritage of a living forest, a freshwater environment, and wildlife of the Sacramento River watershed—Turtle Bay has opened its first phase, called Paul Bunyan's Forest Camp. The camp has an exhibit building (resembling a turn-of-the-century lumber mill) along with an outdoor children's interactive center and play area with a forestry theme. A giant log slide transports kids from the second-floor indoor exhibits to the outside play area. The entire project, which is near I–5 and Highway 299 on a bend of the Sacramento River, is expected to be completed by 2000.
🏠 800 Auditorium Dr., Redding, tel. 530/ 243–8850 or 800/887–8532. Admission free. Open daily 10–4.

Sierra and the Gold Country

California State Mining and Mineral Museum

(★★ 6–15) If you want to be sure to see gold in the heart of the Gold Country, this museum in the historic gold-mining town of Mariposa is the place. Kids can "discover" gold in a variety of forms here: gold nuggets, leaf gold, wire gold, and crystallized gold. They can also explore an underground mine tunnel and see how a quartz mill works. Along with its permanent displays, the museum often has temporary exhibits of gold, gems, and minerals.
🏠 Mariposa County Fairgrounds, Hwy. 49, Mariposa, tel. 209/742–7625. Admission: $3.50 adults, $2.50 ages 15–18 and students, 14 and under free. Open May–Sept., Wed.– Mon. 10–6; Oct.–Apr., Wed.–Sun. 10–4.

California State Railroad Museum

(★★ 3–15) The largest interpretive museum of its kind in North America has 21 beautifully restored historic train cars and locomotives—dating from the 1860s to the 1960s—sharing the spotlight. Films, slide shows, and exhibits recount the role the trains played in history, including the birth of the first transcontinental railroad, engineered right here in Old Sacramento (see Chapter 4); and volunteers (many ex-railroad workers) are on hand to answer questions. My kids were in awe of the enormous 1944 Southern Pacific steam locomotive, one of the biggest ever built (it's 125 feet long and weighs more than a million pounds). They loved walking through the 1929 Canadian National Railways sleeper, the St. Hyacinthe, in which special light, sound, and rocking motion effects create the illusion of clattering down the rails during the night. And they were equally entranced by the "Dinner in the Diner" exhibit: a luxury passenger train

dining car set with china service and displaying a menu from 1937 (swordfish, salmon, or roast beef—all for under $1—and a kids' menu of full meals for 50¢). Upstairs you'll find exhibits on classic model trains, including ones used in the movies *E.T.* and *Throw Momma from the Train*. Tickets to the museum also include admission to the reconstructed Central Pacific Passenger Station (930 Front St., tel. 916/445–6645) nearby, a circa-1870 station with separate waiting rooms for ladies and children and a refreshment stand selling sarsaparilla.
🏫 *2nd and I Sts., Sacramento, tel. 916/445–7387. Admission: $6 adults, $3 ages 6–12. Open daily 10–5.*

Golden State Museum

(👫 6–15) This attractive museum, which opened in fall 1998, occupies the first two floors of the California State Archives building and tells the story of California's past, present, and future. The exhibit galleries make use of some of the archives' vast historical collections—from documents (including the state's constitutions) to newsreels—and include interactive exhibits geared toward kids and playful adults. The galleries are organized into four themes. "Place" looks at the state's differing landscapes and the connections between the land and its people—you'll see, for instance, how Indian trails eventually evolved into today's superhighways. Natural disasters—fires, floods, and earthquakes—get their due here, too, complete with dramatic film footage. The "People" gallery recounts the stories of immigrants' arrivals from all over the world—a vintage bus serves as a theater—and examines what it means to be "Californian" (something even longtime residents still ponder). Watch for the holographic image of the Chinese patriarch in the Gold Rush–era herbalist shop. "Promise" focuses on the allure that has drawn people to California since the Gold Rush, and illustrates the achievements and entrepreneurial spirit of the state's citizenry; Hollywood's take on the Golden State is

covered in this section. "Politics" looks at the beginnings of California statehood and contains catchy multimedia presentations of the political scene; don't miss the re-creation of Posey's Café, a onetime political hangout. Kids should enjoy the story of the 11-year-old who once introduced his own bill in the state Legislature. One particularly nice feature of the museum: The admission price includes headset audio guides geared to various age groups.
🏫 *1020 O St., Sacramento, tel. 916/653–7524. Admission: $6.50 adults, $3.50 ages 6–13, 5 and under free. Open Tues.–Sun. 10–5.*

San Francisco and the Bay Area

Bay Area Discovery Museum

(👫 1–10) Kids learn—and have fun—by doing here, in one of the top children's museums in the state. To learn more about the natural wonders of San Francisco Bay they can crawl through a tunnel "beneath" the sea or fish aboard their own Discovery Boat. The Maze of Illusions uses mirrors and holograms to challenge perceptions of color, dimension, and distance. At one of the newest exhibits, the Powerhouse, kids learn how that mysterious stuff called "energy" gets made. Other areas for exploration include a science lab that focuses on local plants and animals, an Architecture and Design section, and an interactive Media Lab, where kids can check out educational CD-ROMs and try out software. Toddlers have their own discovery area, the ToT SpoT, where they can enter a storybook cave with adjustable lighting and an echo chamber or sit on a waterbed and watch live fish in a tank above. And outdoors, there's a play area called Discovery Park, with bridges, trucks, and boats. The museum also runs morning workshops in creative movement, music, art; call for times and appropriate ages. The museum is housed in a collection of seven buildings that used to be part of

Fort Baker, a military installation at the entrance to San Francisco Bay. The site is now part of the Golden Gate National Recreation Area, making this the nation's only children's museum in a national park. A bonus for parents: The museum's location virtually beneath the Golden Gate Bridge offers some of the grandest views of the bay. **ᐁ** *Fort Baker, 557 E. McReynolds Rd., Sausalito, tel. 415/487–4398. Admission: $7 adults, $6 ages 1–18, under 1 free. Open school year, Tues.–Thurs. 9–4, Fri.–Sun. 10–5; summer vacation, Tues.–Sun. 10–5.*

Cable Car Museum

(**✦✦ 3–15**) Start out with a cable-car ride to or from Fisherman's Wharf, then head for this 1907 redbrick building at the corner of Washington and Mason streets (ask the conductor to call it out) to see how these amazing Victorian-age conveyances climb up and down some of the city's steepest streets—without engines! The ingenious secrets of cable power were developed more than 125 years ago. The method is simple, really. Four sets of cables (for the four streets on which cable cars operate) make a continuous 9½-mph circuit beneath city streets; the cars, which grip the cables, automatically travel along with them. The cable system, which you can view on the lower level here, is run by huge revolving wheels that pull and steer the cables as they enter and leave the powerhouse. (You can hear the whirring sounds as soon as you come in.) In the attractive mezzanine museum you can see the first cable car ever built, as well as a variety of other antique models. **ᐁ** *1201 Mason St., San Francisco, tel. 415/ 474–1887. Admission free. Open daily 10–5.*

California Academy of Sciences

(**✦✦ 3–15**) The California Academy of Sciences, a huge natural science complex in the heart of Golden Gate Park, is a three-in-one attraction for families. Founded in 1853, the Academy contains three museums that provide windows into the universes of land, space, and ocean: the Natural History Museum, the Morrison Planetarium, and the Steinhart Aquarium (see Chapter 6 for the aquarium, which can be viewed for the same admission price as the Natural History Museum). Start with the Natural History Museum, one of the largest in the world. At the multimedia Earthquake exhibit, visitors can experience several simulated quakes—complete with special effects—so California kids can get psyched for the Big One and out-of-staters can get a sense of what all the fuss is about. Wild California presents a life-like re-creation (complete with sound effects) of birds and marine mammals on the rocky offshore Farallon Islands. The exotic African Safari hall includes a Waterhole Diorama that's so realistic-looking you may feel like joining the (stuffed) animals for a drink. The Hall of Fossils displays dinosaur bones and a brontosaurus skull. You'll also find a gem and mineral hall; an insect room; a human cultures gallery; a Far Side of Science cartoons gallery; and Early Childhood, an open play-learning space for small children. Reached through the Natural History Museum, but requiring extra admission, is the Morrison Planetarium, Northern California's largest star show. Here you'll find daily multimedia shows presenting the night sky through the ages under a 55-foot dome, complete with special effects and music. Since whirling through galaxies, entering black holes, and other special effects can be "intimidating," the Planetarium staff urges caution in bringing preschoolers. Planetarium shows are given four times daily in summer (with two extra shows on weekends); the rest of the year they're given once daily (at 2) on weekdays, and six times daily on weekends and holidays. (Call 415/750–7141 for exact schedules.) Teens and preteens will gravitate to the Laserium programs, light shows played to rock music ($7 adults, $6 students, $4 ages 6–12; additional Academy admission not required; call 415/750–7138 for schedules). Laserium isn't recommended for kids under 6.

🏛 *Music Concourse, near 8th Ave. and Fulton St., Golden Gate Park, San Francisco, tel. 415/750–7145. Admission: $8.50 adults, $5.50 ages 12–17, $2.50 ages 4–11, ages 3 and under free; $1 discount with Muni transfer; free 1st Wed. of month. Planetarium: additional $2.50 adults, $1.25 ages 6–17. Open Memorial Day–Labor Day, daily 9–6; rest of year, daily 10–5. First Wed. of each month, closes at 8:45 PM.*

California Palace of the Legion of Honor

(👫 **6–15**) The California Palace of the Legion of Honor, one of the city's top fine arts museums, focuses on European paintings, sculpture, tapestries, and furniture. Works by the French Impressionists and the sculptor Rodin are highlights of the collection, but just as stunning are the gleaming palacelike structure itself and its splendid location in Lincoln Park, overlooking the Golden Gate. The museum offers special children's programs, tours, and workshops Saturdays at 2 for kids ages 3 to 6 and 7 to 12, respectively. Parents participate with the 3- to 6-year-olds.

🏛 *Legion of Honor Dr. at El Camino del Mar, Lincoln Park (enter at Clement St. and 34th Ave.), San Francisco, tel. 415/863–3330. Admission: $7 adults, $4 ages 12–17; free 2nd Wed. of month. Tickets are good for same-day admission to M. H. de Young and Asian Art museums (see below). Open Tues.–Sun. 9:30–5; 1st Sat. of month 10–8:45.*

Children's Discovery Museum of San Jose

(👫 **2–12**) The outside of this striking-looking complex is painted Easter-egg purple, setting the anything-goes tone of the place. One of the largest interactive children's museums in the country, it's designed for kids to "test, crank, listen, taste, prod, and tinker. Based on our visit here one summer morning, they take to it with gusto. Kids dashed excitedly from exhibit to exhibit as

they measured their heartbeats, sent messages through a pneumatic tube or via videophones, created art with recycled products, pumped water till their arms wore out, blew giant bubbles, and ground maize for their own tortillas. Some parents might find it joyous, others chaotic.

🏛 *180 Woz Way, San Jose, tel. 408/298–5437. Admission: $6 adults, $4 ages 2–18. Open Mon.–Sat. 10–5, Sun. noon–5.*

Exploratorium

(👫 **2–15**) Most kids' eyes light up as soon as they enter the Exploratorium. Set within the cavernous inner sanctum of the beaux-arts Palace of Fine Arts, it's one of the world's top science museums, with more than 650 hands-on exhibits inviting visitors to test and investigate mysteries of science and human perception—how we see, hear, smell, and feel the world around us. Light, color, sound, music, motion, language, electricity, and weather are among the subject areas. What's that cloud ring rising into the air? A 5-year-old boy made it in the Weather area. How did that 7-year-old girl leave her shadow on the wall? Your kids can capture their own shadows in the Shadow Box. Look at that 10-year-old—he's as tall as the ceiling! (But only in the Distorted Room.) How did that family make the Enchanted Tree light up? Just by clapping their hands. All these phenomena and many more are explained in easy-to-read text displayed near the exhibits; "Explainers"—often students on their days off from school—offer assistance and give demonstrations ("cow-eye dissection starting over here"). A separate area of the Exploratorium, the Tactile Dome, requires reservations, an additional fee, and a sense of adventure. The Tactile Dome is a pitch-black maze inside a geodesic dome; the challenge—and the fun—is to crawl, slide, and climb through it, relying entirely on your sense of touch. The dome takes about 15 minutes to work your way through once. It's not recommended for kids under 7, pregnant women, or the claustrophobic. For times and reservations, call 415/561–0362 from four to six weeks in advance; the $12 fee includes museum admission.

🏛 *3601 Lyon St. at Marina Blvd., San Francisco, tel. 415/561–0360. Admission: $9 ages 18–64, $7 university students, $5 ages 6–17, $2.50 ages 3–5; free 1st Wed. of month. Open Memorial Day–Labor Day, Thurs.–Tues. 10–6, Wed. 10–9:30; rest of year, Tues., Thurs.–Sun., and most Mon. holidays 10–5, Wed. 10–9:30.*

Lawrence Hall of Science

👫 **3 – 15** Like the Exploratorium, the University of California's Lawrence Hall of Science is a hands-on museum loaded with interactive displays that can entertain kids for hours. This is a more traditional museum, however, with big displays and flashy special exhibitions; the emphasis is on biology, chemistry, and astronomy. Once you've found the Lawrence Hall—nestled high in the Berkeley Hills—linger in the outer courtyard to let your kids clamber over the 60-foot-long model of DNA, while you enjoy panoramic views of San Francisco Bay. Or take a short walk up the nearby hillside to find the wind organ, a set of 36 long, slender pipes sticking out of the ground; you'll hear music if you walk among them when the wind is blowing. You can also play with their tones by turning one of six moveable pipes. Inside, permanent exhibitions include "Math Rules!" a collection of puzzles and hands-on challenges to show kids that math doesn't have to be dull; and "Within the Human Brain," which demonstrates how the brain works (you can even watch a video of a human brain dissection). The Earthquakes exhibit contains a working seismograph and tips on surviving the Big One. Just Build It allows budding young architects to construct with building blocks. On weekends, weekday holidays, and daily in summer, kids can enter the Biology Discovery Lab to pet a snake or hold a tarantula; on the same days, they can also attend a planetarium show (ages 6 and older only). On clear Sat-

urday evenings from 8 to 11, astronomers bring their telescopes to the Lawrence Hall of Science to give interested visitors a free peek at the moon, planets, star clusters, and galaxies; call the Hall's astronomy information line (tel. 510/642-5132) for details.

🏛 *Centennial Dr., near Grizzly Peak Blvd., Berkeley, tel. 510/642–5132. Follow signs up hill from Gayley Rd. on eastern end of Univ. of California campus. Admission: $6 adults, $4 ages 7–18, $2 ages 3–6, under 3 free. Open daily 10–5.*

Lindsay Museum

👫 **2 – 15** The centerpiece of this East Bay museum is the nation's oldest and largest wildlife rehabilitation center, which treats more than 8,000 injured wild animals per year. Birds and other creatures that can't be released back to the wild—including hawks, vultures, owls, bobcats, foxes, snakes, and rabbits—are displayed in creative models of their native habitats. Highlights include daily animal feedings. For kids there's also a petting zoo, as well as classes on animals. If you haven't visited the Lindsay since the early 1990s, you'll be pleasantly surprised by the sparkling expanded facility that opened in 1994.

🏛 *Larkey Park, 1931 1st Ave., Walnut Creek, tel. 925/935–1978. Admission: $4.50 adults, $2.50 ages 3–17, under 3 free. Open mid-June–early Sept., Tues.–Sun. 10–5; rest of year, Tues.–Fri. noon–5, Sat.–Sun. 10–5.*

M. H. de Young Memorial Museum/Asian Art Museum

👫 **3 – 15** In Golden Gate Park across from the Academy of Sciences, these two adjoining museums pack a double dose of fine art. The de Young focuses primarily on American art— paintings, sculpture, and decorative arts—and sometimes hosts blockbuster traveling exhibitions from around the world. Our kids, who've taken family and school trips here for years, recommend that you take your children to see Church's "Rainy Season in the Tropics"—a landscape with a particularly fabulous rainbow—and the Thomas Moran landscapes of the Grand Canyon of the Yellowstone. Kids might also enjoy the trompe l'oeil artworks by William Harnett and works by Whistler, Grant Wood, and Mary Cassatt. The museum's Gallery One is a year-round art area for children and their families; it includes exhibitions and guides to works from the permanent collections, as well as a computer station, a reading area, writing and drawing tables, and family drop-in art workshops. The museum sponsors free art classes for kids (divided into groups ages 3–6 and 7–12) most Saturdays at 10:30 AM (tel. 415/750-3658), with no advance registration necessary. The Asian Art Museum, meanwhile, displays art that spans more than 40 Asian countries and 6,000 years. To avoid overdosing, focus on a few sections. Lia likes to count how many ceramics and bronzes she can find with animal themes—a dragon-headed roof tile from China, or a duck-shape earthenware vessel from Korea. The Asian Art Museum plans to move to the old Main Library building in the Civic Center by the year 2001.

🏛 *North side of Music Concourse, off 8th Ave. and John F. Kennedy Dr., Golden Gate Park, San Francisco; de Young, tel. 415/863–3330 or 415/750–3600; Asian Art, tel. 415/379–8801. Admission: $7 adults, $4 ages 12–17; admission free 1st Wed. of month. Open Tues.–Sun. 9:30–5, 1st Wed. of month 9:30–8:45.*

Oakland Museum of California

(🎎 **6–15**) Probably because it's across San Francisco Bay in Oakland, this innovative museum near Lake Merritt doesn't get the publicity it deserves. But if you want a sense of California's history, ecology, art, and diversity, this is the place to find it. In the Cowell Hall of California History, kids can whisk their imaginations back to the days of Native Americans, missions and ranchos, the Gold Rush, the Victorian era, even the more recent

Californias of *American Graffiti* and the Summer of Love. In the Hall of California Ecology, your family can take a simulated walk across the state as it looked before Europeans arrived, from the coast to the Sierra to the desert. And in the Gallery of California Art, you'll find more than 500 paintings and crafts.
🏛 *Oak and 10th Sts., Oakland, tel. 510/238–2200 or 888/625–6873. Admission: $6 adults, $4 ages 6–17 or students, under 6 free; free for all Fri. 5–9 PM. Open Thurs. and Sat. 10–5, Fri. 10–9, Sun. noon–5.*

Rosicrucian Egyptian Museum

(🎎 **6–15**) Ancient Egyptian cultural and religious artifacts—with their animal deities, mysterious hieroglyphs, and, of course, mummies—hold a special fascination for many children, and the place to view them in the western United States is the Rosicrucian Egyptian Museum. It's housed in a dramatic building styled after an ancient temple, set in a lovely park. The mummies here were an immediate hit with my kids, especially the mummified animals: crocodiles, fish, hawks, a baboon, the head of a bull. You'll find human mummies here, too—don't miss Usermontu, a priest who lived more than 2,500 years ago, whom Lia described as "creepy—you could see his teeth and fingernails and he had no eyes!" (Translation: she loved it.) My kids also enjoyed a 15-minute guided tour going deep inside a recreated Egyptian rock tomb, where they could view wall paintings and hieroglyphs.
🏛 *1342 Naglee Ave., San Jose, tel. 408/947–3635 or 408/947–3636. Admission: $7 adults, $5 students, $3.50 ages 7–15, ages 6 and under free. Open daily 10–5 (last admission 4:30).*

San Francisco Museum of Modern Art

(🎎 **3–15**) It's true that few kids know abstract expressionism from analytical cubism, or surrealism from op art—and as for Dada, he's with Mama. But children are often drawn to the typically bright colors and often geometric shapes of modern and contemporary art. The San Francisco Museum of Modern Art (SFMOMA for short), which opened in 1995 across the street from the Yerba Buena Center for the Arts, is now the second-largest modern-art museum in the country. And the bright, airy six-story structure itself—topped by a 145-foot-tall skylight tower—is one of the main attractions. The focus of the permanent collections is painting and sculpture from 1900 to 1970—Picasso, Braque, Klee, Dali, Matisse, Diebenkorn, Pollock, de Kooning, Rivera, and Kahlo are all here. Architecture and design, 20th-century photography (Man Ray, Ansel Adams, many others), and special exhibits are also featured, along with video, audio, and interactive media installations, ranging from "weird" to "awesome" in the words of some young visitors. The museum puts strong emphasis on drawing kids and families into the world of modern art; call the museum for information on periodic weekend family art workshops (tel. 415/357–4097). Don't miss the attached bookstore, which has a wonderful section of children's art books and a small play area.

🏠 151 3rd St., San Francisco, tel. 415/357–4000. Admission: $8 adults, $4 students; ages 12 and under free; half-price Thurs. 6–9; free 1st Tues. of month. Open Memorial Day–Labor Day, Fri.–Tues. 10–6, Thurs. 10–9; rest of year, Fri.–Tues. 11–6, Thurs. 11–9.

Tech Museum of Innovation

(👫 6–15) Loaded with hundreds of custom-designed interactive exhibits, the all-new and greatly expanded Tech is devoted solely to technology—in particular the innovations in microelectronics, communications, robotics, and biotechnology that have emerged in Silicon Valley. While the description may be a mouthful, the museum does a great job in helping to demystify and make technology fun for kids

(and their parents). The Tech moved into a 132,000-square-foot mango-and-azure-color domed facility in the heart of downtown San Jose in fall 1998. Exhibits are arranged in four themed areas, and are meant not only to inform and entertain, but inspire visitors of all ages to be innovative themselves. Activities go beyond "hands-on" to "minds on," as museum staffers put it. In "Life Tech: The Human Machine," you can "drive" a simulated bobsled, use sound waves to "see" inside yourself, or enter images of a human body for an inside look. In "Innovation: Silicon Valley and Beyond," you can visit a cleanroom to see how actual microchips (the stuff of Silicon Valley) are made, create your own futuristic bike design, and take a portrait of yourself with a laser scanner. In "Communication: Global Connections," you and your kids can use teleconferencing equipment to communicate with each other on different floors of the museum, as well as experiment with the latest movie animation techniques: film yourself surfing, walking on the moon, or flying with Superman. And in "Exploration: New Frontiers," you can explore the ocean depths via an underwater, remote-controlled robot, test your ability to move around while weightless (as in a spaceship), and experience what it was like to shake through the 1906 and 1989 San Francisco earthquakes. The Hackworth IMAX Dome Theater, which requires separate admission or a combined admission ticket, has a hemispherical screen 82 feet in diameter and is the only one of its kind in Northern California.

🏠 201 S. Market St., San Jose, tel. 408/294–8324 or 408/795–6100. Tickets and reservations (including IMAX): 408/795–6101. Admission (exhibits or IMAX only): $8 adults, $6 ages 6–18. Combined admission: $13.50 adults, $10 ages 6–18. Open Memorial Day–Labor Day, daily 10–6 (until 8 Thurs); rest of year, Tues.–Sun. 10–5 (3rd Thurs. of month until 8).

Central Coast and Valley

Children's Museum of Stockton

(**†† 2 – 10**) This downtown facility contains an entire minicity, complete with a post office, a bank, a barbershop, a theater, a pet store, a fix-it shop, a grocery store, and a recycling center. Your kids can answer a call at the fire station, go on camera to deliver the news at the TV studio, drive a city bus, be a patient or doctor in an emergency room, even enter a cave inside the earth to find Indian drawings from the past. In the park, tiny tots and toddlers (ages 4 and under) can climb and play. 🏛 *402 W. Weber Ave., Stockton, tel. 209/ 465–4386. Admission: $4, ages 2 and under free. Open Oct.–May, Tues.–Sat. 9–4, Sun. noon–5; June–Sept., Mon.–Sat. 9–4.*

Discovery Center

(**†† 3 – 15**) This participatory museum, which has both indoor and outdoor exhibits, calls itself the "hands-on science center" of the Central San Joaquin Valley. Indoors, your kids can talk to each other across the room via "whisper cones," experiment in the electronic learning lab, view Native American basketry and artifacts, see animals such as turtles and lizards, and walk through a life-size human maze. Outdoors, they can explore a pond stocked with frogs and crayfish, peer into a Gemini space capsule, and watch desert tortoises. 🏛 *1944 N. Winery Ave., Fresno, tel. 559/ 251–5533. Admission: $4 adults, $2 ages 3– 16. Open Tues.–Sat. 10–4, Sun. noon–4, and some Mon. holidays.*

Kern County Museum/Lori Brock Children's Discovery Center

(**†† 3 – 15**) When gold was discovered in Kern County in the 1860s, settlers flocked to this huge region of central California, which encompasses high deserts, mountain ranges, wildlife refuges, oil fields, and fertile agricultural plains. The 16-acre Kern County Museum—highlighted by an open-air, walk-through historic village with 60 restored or re-created buildings—is a family-friendly place to learn about and relive the era of the 1860s–1940s in this region. You can visit a representation of the county's original courthouse (from an old gold-mining town), a jail, and a log cabin (all from the 1860s), plus a blacksmith shop, a one-room schoolhouse, a doctor's office, and settlers' homes, churches, and businesses. The main museum building holds more exhibits about the area's history, natural history, and culture. Be sure to leave time for the adjacent Lori Brock Children's Discovery Center, which offers permanent and changing hands-on displays and activities focusing on art, science, and technology, aimed at kids ages 3 to 8. 🏛 *3801 Chester Ave., Bakersfield, tel. 661/ 861–2132. Admission: $5 adults, $3 ages 3– 12. Open weekdays 8–5, Sat. 10–5, Sun. noon–5.*

Los Angeles and Environs

Autry Museum of Western Heritage

(**†† 3 – 15**) If your kids are like mine, they've only vaguely heard of the late old-time cowboy star Gene Autry, but this museum will quickly transport them to those thrilling days of yesteryear. The exhibits draw visitors into the life and spirit of the times, describing a colorful panoply of characters who helped forge the West: explorers, mountain men, Native Americans, cowboys, sheriffs, outlaws, Pony Express riders, pioneers, and show people. Several items are of historic importance, such as Wyatt Earp's pistol (used at the O.K. Corral shoot-out), General Custer's pistols, and Billy the Kid's rifle. Hollywood isn't neglected; the Lone Ranger's mask is on display, and videos show how stuntmen performed those wild stagecoach chases. At the Los Angeles Times Children's Discovery Center within the museum, kids can climb into a saddle, try on cowboy gear, twirl a lasso, and play pioneer family in a scaled-down Western ranch house.

🏛 *4700 Western Heritage Dr., adjacent to Los Angeles Zoo in Griffith Park, Los Angeles, tel. 323/667–2000. Admission: $7.50 adults, $5 ages 13–18, $3 ages 2–12. Open Tues.– Sun. and some Mon. holidays 10–5.*

Bowers Museum of Cultural Art and Kidseum

(👫 6 – 15) Orange County's largest museum offers a two-for-one experience for families (one admission fee permits entrance to both). The cultural art museum displays a first-class collection of artwork by indigenous peoples—ritual objects, sculpture, costume, carvings—from the Pacific Rim, Africa, and the Americas, with both permanent and changing exhibitions. The nearby Kidseum (included in the Bowers admission price) is billed as the nation's only hands-on cultural art museum for children; kids can create ethnic art from recycled materials, listen to tellings of folktales and legends, play musical instruments from other countries, help stage puppet shows and ethnic dances, try on costumes and masks, and embark on theme adventures complete with explorers' backpacks. Kidseum also hosts special events and family festivals throughout the year.

🏛 *1802–2002 N. Main St., Santa Ana, tel. 714/567–3600 (Bowers Museum), 714/ 480–1520 (Kidseum). Admission: $6 adults, $4 students, $2 ages 5–12, under 5 free. Bowers open Tues.–Wed. and Fri.–Sun. 10–4, Thurs. 10—9; Kidseum open Thurs.–Fri. 2–5, Sat.–Sun. 10–4.*

California Science Center

(👫 3 – 15) Years of renovations and the installation of state-of-the-art exhibits trans-

formed the former California Museum of Science and Industry into the California Science Center. High-tech halls focus on helping kids learn by doing. The eye-catching interactive "worlds" include the World of Life— how people, plants, animals, and even microbes use common means to survive— and "Creative World" (the world built and technology used by humans). You'll enter the World of Life through a 55-foot tunnel. Once inside, families can test their knowledge of animal brains by trying to guess which belongs to a salmon, and which to a monkey or cat; observe a termite colony through a magnifying lens; and, thanks to a 50-foot "dummy" named Tess, see how the organs in the human body work. At the World of Life Discovery Room, young kids can climb a tree house, create their own puppet shows, and see live plants and animals up close. In Creative World, kids and parents can have themselves superimposed on a computer screen to play virtual reality basketball; see crash-test dummies in action; and take part in a digital jam session. At the Creative World Discovery Room, young kids can test out a child-size TV studio, or build various contraptions at a "hardware store." Two more interactive "worlds"—the World of the Pacific (an aquarium spanning the Pacific Rim) and Worlds Beyond (an exploration of the universe and spacecraft)— won't open for several more years. A seven-story 3-D IMAX theater has replaced the previous five-story IMAX theater adjacent to the museum. (The spectacular IMAX movies cost $6.50–$7.50 adults, $5–$6 students 13 to 21, and $3.75–$4.75 ages 4 to 12; call 213/744–7400 for recorded show information and 213/744–2019 for tickets.)

🏛 *700 State Dr., Exposition Park, Los Angeles, tel. 213/744–2014 or 323/724–3623. Admission free. Parking: $5. Open daily 10–5.*

Children's Museum at La Habra

(👫 ALL) One of the first children's museums in California, this remains one of the best of its kind in the state, and a wing added to the original site, a renovated 1923 railroad depot, makes it one of the largest as well. Permanent exhibits include Preschool Playpark, with unusual climbing and crawling structures for kids up to age 5; Dino-Dig, where budding paleontologists can excavate fossil replicas of a velociraptor, a tyrannosaurus rex, and a saber-toothed cat; and Buster the Bus, a working section of an actual bus where kids can take over the roles of driver and passengers. There's also a minimarket, a shadow wall, a theater stage, a genuine railroad caboose, and a bee observatory. Parents are encouraged to participate and learn along with their kids. The museum is wheelchair accessible, and hands-on exhibits are designed to meet special needs of children with disabilities.

🏠 *301 S. Euclid St., La Habra, tel. 562/905–9693 or 562/905–9793. Admission: $4, under 2 free. Open Mon.–Sat. 10–5, Sun. 1–5.*

George C. Page Museum of La Brea Discoveries

(👫 **3 – 15**) No dinosaurs here, but you and your kids will find displays from the world's richest treasure trove of Ice Age fossils, the surrounding La Brea Tar Pits (see Chapter 4)—extinct species such as imperial mammoths, California saber-toothed cats, American camels, and giant ground sloths. I've been to this museum several times, and I've seldom seen a child who wasn't excited by it. Start by viewing the film that describes how thousands of animals were trapped and preserved in the oozing asphalt of the tar pits some 10,000 to 40,000 years ago. One exhibit challenges kids to pit their strength against the pull of asphalt; it's a graphic illustration of how the animals succumbed to the deadly gunk. Our kids also enjoyed looking at the bones of smaller creatures; a tiny mouse toe bone particularly fascinated Lia. The skeleton of the only human discovered at La Brea, a 9,000-year-old woman who apparently was murdered in her 20s, is also

on display; a fleshed-out image shows how she might have looked when alive. Guided tours are offered from Wednesday to Sunday, at 2:15.

🏠 *5801 Wilshire Blvd., Los Angeles, tel. 323/934–7243. Admission: $6 adults, $3.50 students, $2 ages 5–12, under 5 free; free to all 1st Tues. of month. Parking: $5.50. Open June.–Aug., daily 10-5; rest of year, Tues.–Sun. 10–5.*

Griffith Observatory Hall of Science

(👫 **3 – 15**) Perched high on a hill in Griffith Park with a great view of L.A. (on clear days), this observatory includes an interesting science museum and top-flight planetarium. In the Hall of Science, kids can test their knowledge of constellations and planets in interactive astronomy quizzes (younger kids just enjoy pressing the buttons), view the phases of the moon in a darkened chamber, stand inside a camera obscura (where they watch the unsuspecting people on the front lawn), and peer through a submarine periscope. Kids can also test their weight on earth versus what it would be on the moon, Mars, and Jupiter; one little girl was astonished to learn she would weigh 160 pounds on Jupiter. (If anyone in your family thinks they're overweight, however, send them to the "moon" scale, which registers one-sixth their weight on earth.) The Zeiss Telescope is open for public viewing every clear night except Monday, and the Planetarium has changing hour-long shows from Tuesday to Sunday ($4 adults, $2 ages 5–12). Children under 5 are admitted only to special weekend shows at 1:30. The planetarium also presents Laserium—light shows set to music—which are especially popular with teens and preteens (tel. 818/997–3624; admission $7 adults, $6 ages 5–12; no children under 5).

🏠 *2800 E. Observatory Rd., Los Angeles, tel. 323/664–1191. Admission free. Open mid-June–mid-Sept., daily 12:30–10; mid-Sept.–mid-June, Tues.–Fri. 2–10, weekends 12:30–10.*

Huntington Library, Art Collections, and Botanical Gardens

👫 3–15 The Huntington complex seems more like a baronial country estate than something you'd find in the metropolis. Art collections are housed in the late railroad tycoon Henry Huntington's mansion; the popular paintings *Blue Boy* and *Pinkie* are perennial children's favorites. In the less interesting upstairs galleries, head straight for the 17th-century miniature silver toys, which were intended for adults to play with. In the Huntington Library next door, kids old enough to have a sense of history may be awed by the priceless manuscripts—first printings of Shakespeare's plays, a Gutenberg Bible, the Dead Sea Scrolls, and original handwritten letters by Washington, Jefferson, and Lincoln.

With younger children concentrate on the fabulous Botanical Gardens, which reproduce a variety of garden environments from around the world. Within minutes you can walk from jungles with rushing waterfalls and tropical foliage (don't miss the Ombu tree from Argentina) to a Zen garden with its lovely bamboo groves, to an astonishingly rich desert garden, filled with colorful cacti and succulents. Be sure to walk through the Japanese area, with its replica of a 17th-century home, rock garden, and pools. Tea is served daily except Monday in the Rose Garden; call 626/683–8131 for reservations. 🏠 *1151 Oxford Rd., San Marino, tel. 626/405–2141. Admission: $8.50 adults, $5 students age 12 and over, under 12 free. Open Tues.–Fri. noon–4:30, weekends 10:30–4:30.*

J. Paul Getty Museum at the Getty Center

👫 6–15 Malibu's beautiful J. Paul Getty Museum, housed in a magnificent re-creation of a 1st-century Roman villa, closed for renovations in 1997 and will reopen in 2001 as the Getty Villa. All but the Greek and Roman antiquities collection was moved to the new J. Paul Getty Museum at the billion-dollar Getty Center in Brentwood, which opened in 1997. The new museum—which showcases European paintings, drawings, sculpture, photography, illuminated manuscripts, and decorative arts—stands on a 110-acre site on a rugged hilltop overlooking the Los Angeles basin, Santa Monica Mountains, and Pacific Ocean. (Kids should enjoy the five-minute electric tram ride from the parking structure up to the arrival plaza.) With 54 galleries occupying five two-story pavilions situated around a central courtyard, the new Getty has twice the exhibit space of the Malibu site, and it makes every effort to attract families. Before tackling the galleries, head for the Family Room, where you can ask for suggestions about which artworks kids might enjoy; you'll also find self-directed activity guides and game boxes to help make viewing art more fun. The Family Room also has puzzles and CD-ROMs, and an area where kids can don costumes for family portraits, as though they were posing for Velasquez or Rembrandt. Weekend family programs also encourage parents and their kids to enjoy art together; storytellers, for example, present tales related to the museum's collections. Families can also participate in hands-on studio projects. Space is provided outside for family picnicking, too; bring your own, or buy a box lunch at the museum. 🏠 *1200 Getty Center Dr., Brentwood, tel. 310/440–7300. Take I–405 to Getty Center Dr. Admission free. Parking: $5. Call for required parking reservations; arrivals via taxi, bus, or bicycle do not need reservations. Open Tues.–Wed 11–7, Thurs.–Fri 11–9, Sat.–Sun 10–6.*

Kidspace

👫 1–12 At this participatory museum, which draws 100,000 visitors a year, your kids can play disc jockey or star at their own TV studio, hang out at the Eco-Beach (with 4 tons of sand, a saltwater reef tank, live hermit crabs, and a wave machine), learn computers in the Mouse House, try their hands at construction in the Build It exhibit, put on their own costume dramas Back-stage, romp through Toddler Territory, or explore animal habitats high and low in Critter Caverns. Drop-in workshops, performances, and special events for children are a regular part of the program.

🏠 *390 S. El Molino Ave., Pasadena, tel. 626/449–9143. Admission: $5 ages 3–adult, $2.50 ages 1–2. Open Sept.–mid-June, Wed. 2–5, weekends 12:30–5; mid-June–Sept., Tues.–Fri. 1–5, weekends 12:30–5; also open last Mon. of month 5–8 PM with free admission.*

Los Angeles Children's Museum

(👬 3–12) As soon as I entered the Los Angeles Children's Museum I wished I were a kid again; this place looked like fun. With 15 hands-on exhibits, it packs a lot in to a comparatively small space, and the design is clever and appealing, with ramps connecting different areas. In the colorful City Streets section, filled with working traffic lights and real street signs, kids can steer a genuine cut-away county bus or ride in a fire truck. Elsewhere, preschoolers can toss giant multicolored foam shapes (with Velcro attached) to form tunnels, caves, and towers. Children 6 and up can write and record music in a sound studio, make videos, and create animated crayon cartoons in a Disney-designed facility. Special workshops and performances (in a theater built for young audiences) are announced throughout the day.

🏠 *310 N. Main St., Los Angeles Mall, Los Angeles, tel. 213/687–8800. Admission: $5, under 2 free. Open during school year, weekends 10–5 (Tues.–Fri. school groups only); summer vacation, Tues.–Sun. 11:30–5.*

Los Angeles County Museum of Art

(👬 6–15) Next to the La Brea Tar Pits in Hancock Park, this enormous complex—the largest art museum in the western United States—encompasses five buildings surrounding a central court. Our family's approach to big, eclectic museums like LACMA, as it's known, is to walk from room to room, waiting to see what catches our children's eyes; they've often surprised us with a sudden fascination for French Provincial furniture or Cambodian sculpture, and that's part of the fun. A good place to start is the Ahmanson Building, whose exhibits range from around the world and across the ages: Egyptian, Greek and Roman art; paintings and decorative art from Europe, America, and China; collections of glassware, silver, and mosaics; and one of the top Indian and Southeast Asian art collections in the Western world. The Pavilion for Japanese Art has a wonderful collection of painted screens, scrolls, and netsuke (small carvings of animals and deities). The Anderson Building displays 20th-century paintings and sculpture; the Hammer Building hosts special loan exhibitions; and the Bing Center contains a theater and auditorium. In 1998, two new facilities that should attract families opened at LACMA West, which is in the former May Company department store at the corner of Wilshire Boulevard and Fairfax Avenue, adjacent to the main museum. The Experimental Gallery is loaded with innovative and interactive elements—activity kits, an art-making station, a reading room, computer games, a video station—intended to make viewing art more engaging for children. A branch of the Southwest Museum (see *below*) is now here, too.

🏠 *5905 Wilshire Blvd., Los Angeles, tel. 323/857–6000. Admission: $7 adults, $5 students, $1 ages 6–17; free 2nd Tues. of month. Open Mon., Tues., Thurs. noon–8, Fri. noon–9, weekends 11–8.*

Museum of Tolerance

(👬 9–15) If your children are old enough to understand the concept of bigotry, bring them to the Simon Wiesenthal Center's Beit Hashoah Museum of Tolerance. In the Tolerancenter, interactive exhibits help them focus on major issues of intolerance. At the Point of View Diner, they can access a menu of controversial topics—such as hate speech—

on video jukeboxes. In the Holocaust Museum, visitors become witnesses to the horrors of the Nazi Holocaust. You can watch an outdoor café scene in prewar Berlin, where conversation focuses on the impending Nazi takeover of Germany, and view chilling reenactments of book burnings and Nazi rallies. Each visitor is handed a passport of a child whose life was altered forever by the Holocaust; the biographical information, including the fate of the child, is ultimately revealed. This can be heartbreaking—one passport we carried was of a child who died in a concentration camp—but it's an experience kids aren't likely to forget. Allow at least one hour for the Tolerancenter and another hour for the tour of the Holocaust Museum.

🏛 9786 W. Pico Blvd., Los Angeles, tel. 310/553–9036. Admission: $8 adults, $5 students, $3 ages 3–12. Open Mon.–Thurs. 10–4, Fri. 10–3 (10–1 Nov.–Mar.), Sun. 11–4.

Natural History Museum of Los Angeles County

(👫 2 – 15) This highly popular museum is loaded with first-class displays of dinosaurs, insects, butterflies, birds, reptiles, marine and land mammals, fish, fossils, gems, and plants—more than 35 million specimens in all. With young children you may want to start at the museum's hands-on Discovery Center (tel. 213/744–3559), where kids as young as 2 can stroke the teeth of a stuffed polar bear, examine a snake's X-ray, make crayon rubbings of fossils embedded in a rock wall, or dig for casts of dinosaur bones. The accompanying Insect Zoo allows kids to come face-to-face with a host of live tarantulas, emperor scorpions, hissing cockroaches, and giant walking sticks. Elsewhere, be sure to see the Dueling Dinosaurs, skeletons of a tyrannosaurus rex and a triceratops posed in battle, and the 14½-foot-long megamouth, the world's rarest shark and the only one of its kind on public display in the world. The Schreiber Hall of Birds exhibits animated bird habitats with real-life

sounds, while the Gem and Mineral Hall has a walk-through vault with diamonds, emeralds, rubies, and sapphires.

🏛 900 Exposition Blvd., Exposition Park, Los Angeles, tel. 213/763–3466. Admission: $8 adults, $5.50 students, $2 ages 5–12, under 5 free; free 1st Tues. of month. Open Mon.–Fri. 9:30–5, Sat.–Sun. 10–5. Discovery Center and Insect Zoo have abbreviated hrs; call for schedule.

Norton Simon Museum

(👫 6 – 15) The Norton Simon Museum showcases seven centuries of beautifully displayed European art, from the Renaissance to the 20th century. Because it has 30 galleries, it's best to pick and choose a bit. You might start with Old Masters like Rembrandt, Goya, and Raphael, then continue to the French Impressionists and post-Impressionists, especially the Monets, Van Goghs, and the Degas dancers. Finish off with 20th-century art, beginning with a roomful of colorful Picassos. The museum also has an impressive collection of Asian sculpture that spans 2,000 years. If your kids play chess (or even checkers), don't miss the fabulous 18th-century wood and ivory Indian chess set.

🏛 411 W. Colorado Blvd., Pasadena, tel. 626/449–6840. Admission: $4 adults, $2 students, under 12 free. Open Thurs.–Sun. noon–6.

Petersen Automotive Museum

(👫 3 – 15) If ever a museum were suited to its environment, it's this one—set along Wilshire's Miracle Mile (the first shopping area specifically designed for drivers) in Los Angeles, the only major city entirely shaped by the automobile. The fact that the Petersen, the world's largest automobile museum, is a branch of the L.A. County Natural History Museum only confirms that the automobile is as intrinsic to this vast, freeway-entwined metropolis as Hollywood or the beach. No mere showroom of cars, the Petersen displays its more than 200-strong collection of rare and classic autos, trucks, and motorcycles against imaginative backdrops depicting life and travel in various eras of 20th-century L.A. On the first floor, a 1911-vintage roadster is stuck in the mud in a canyon near Malibu; a 1922 Model T is crushed between two trolley cars (a re-creation of a scene from a Laurel and Hardy comedy); a California Highway Patrolman and his 1934 Harley motorcycle lurk behind an authentic billboard; and on through succeeding decades. On the second floor, cars of Hollywood celebrities—and "star cars" featured in films, such as Fred Flintstone's "sedan" from *The Flintstones* and James Bond's Aston Martin from *Goldfinger*—are the headliners. Don't miss the museum's May Family Discovery Center, intended to spark kids' interest in science through the workings of cars. They'll find a driver's education automobile simulator, a "gravitram" that demonstrates the principles of gravity and momentum, even a giant combustion engine where kids can become human spark plugs.

🏛 *6060 Wilshire Blvd., Los Angeles, tel. 323/930–2277. Admission: $7 adults, $5 students, $3 ages 5–12. Open Tues.–Sun. and Mon. holidays 10–6.*

Southwest Museum and Southwest Museum at LACMA West

(👫 **6 – 15**) The Southwest Museum—Los Angeles's oldest, founded in 1907—is dedicated to preserving Native American cultures, from Alaska to South America. The basketry collection is excellent. Kids might especially enjoy the Native American children's clothing, toys, and games; ceremonial costumes; and examples of rock art—prehistoric paintings by Native Americans who once lived in what is now California. In 1998 the museum began sharing space with the Los Angeles County Museum of Art (LACMA; see *above*) (Wilshire Blvd. and Fairfax Ave.), which enables the curators to display many items—such as a huge collection of Navajo textiles—that had been in

storage. For most visitors the LACMA location is more easily accessible than the museum's main one.

🏛 *Southwest Museum: 234 Museum Dr., Highland Park, Los Angeles, tel. 323/221–2164. Admission: $5 adults, $3 students, $2 ages 7–17. Open Tues.–Sun. 10–5. Southwest Museum at LACMA West: 6067 Wilshire Blvd., Los Angeles, tel. 323/933–4510. Admission: $5 adults, $3 students, free for ages 5 and under. Open Mon., Tues., and Thurs., noon–8, Fri. noon–9, Sat.–Sun. 11–8.*

San Diego and the Southern Deserts

Children's Museum of San Diego/Museo de los Niños

(👫 **2 – 12**) This is a boisterous "please touch" museum where kids and parents are invited to create their own art (including painting an old truck), put on their own plays, browse through a double-decker bus filled with books, play virtual-reality basketball, and learn with both hands-on and "minds-on" activities. Most exhibits change periodically, but you can be sure you'll find things that are fun and challenging. The museum, in an airy, brightly painted former warehouse with high ceilings, serves as the anchor for the nation's first planned "Kids' Block"—an entire downtown city block that will be devoted to educational, cultural, health, and commercial facilities for children and families.

🏛 *200 W. Island Ave., San Diego, tel. 619/233–5437. Admission: $5 ages 2–adult, under 2 free and free for all 4th Tues. of month. Open Tues.–Sun. 10–5.*

Palm Springs Desert Museum

(👫 **6 – 15**) Though this museum also contains artworks, the natural science wing is probably of most interest to kids, who can view live desert animals such as scorpions, sidewinders (snakes), and the tiny pocket mouse, a local critter that's said to be the world's smallest rodent. A diorama of the Coachella Valley includes re-created desert habitats, and an exhibit called The Desert: Night and Day shows how animals adapt to the intense local heat and aridity. The museum conducts nature field trips from October to April on Wednesday and Saturday mornings, involving hikes of 2 to 10 miles ($4 per person).

🏛 *101 Museum Dr., Palm Springs, tel. 760/ 325–7186 or 760/325–0189. Admission: $7.50 adults, $3.50 ages 6–17, free ages 5 and under and 1st Fri. of month. Open Tues.– Sat. 10–4, Sun. noon–5.*

Reuben H. Fleet Science Center

(👫 **ALL**) In Balboa Park, a short walk from the San Diego Zoo, this hands-on science museum has recently tripled in size, with five new galleries displaying a changing array of exhibits similar in style to those at San Francisco's Exploratorium (see *above*). Kids can try things like listening to their heartbeats, seeing their own faces appear on a friend's neck, and experimenting with lasers. We've seen tots as young as 2 testing the Bernoulli Effect—keeping a ball bouncing in space over an airstream—though I doubt they knew (or cared) about the scientific principle (they were having too much fun). The Omnimax Space Theater has a giant dome screen, a special camera, and 152 speakers that give viewers the sensation of traveling in a spaceship; the noise and special effects may frighten small children. Planetarium shows are also presented here. The Science Center has also added a motion-simulator ride called Sci Tours, which costs $2 extra.

🏛 *1875 El Prado, Balboa Park, San Diego, tel. 619/238–1233. Admission: $5 adults, $3 ages 3–12; free 1st Tues. of month. Omnimax Space Theater admission (includes entrance to Science Center): $8 adults, $5 ages 3–12. Museum open daily at 9:30; call for closing times.*

Roy Rogers and Dale Evans Museum

(👫 **3 – 15**) Housed in a replica of a frontier fort, this museum displays a host of colorful memorabilia of these two classic Western stars: wardrobes and saddles from their TV show, the late Roy Rogers's gun and car collection (one car has guns for door handles and a dashboard studded with silver dollars), and, yes, Roy's horse Trigger, mounted here in all his glory along with Dale's horse Buttermilk and their dog Bullet. Nellybelle, the Jeep of Roy's sidekick Pat Brady, is here, too. Two theaters show vintage Western films starring Roy, Dale, and a cast of their ever-loyal sidekicks, including Brady and Gabby Hayes. (Parents may find all this more fascinating than will their kids, who may never have heard of Roy and Dale, but a new generation of fans may be born.) RogersDale, a shopping, retail, and entertainment complex, is adjacent to the museum.

🏛 *15650 Seneca Rd., near I–15 off Roy Rogers Dr., Victorville, tel. 760/243–4547. Admission: $7 adults, $6 ages 13–16, $5 ages 6–12. Open daily 9–5.*

San Diego Aerospace Museum

(👫 **ALL**) At this museum in Balboa Park, families can see nearly 70 aircraft, spacecraft, and related exhibits—including a 1783 hot-air balloon, gliders from the 1890s, a reproduction of the Wright Brothers' first plane, World War I fighter planes, and the Apollo and Gemini space capsules. Kids can board a few of the craft, including the flight deck of a World War II Navy bomber. The adjacent International Aerospace Hall of Fame honors great men and women in aerospace history.

🏛 *2001 Pan American Plaza, Balboa Park, San Diego, tel. 619/234–8291. Admission: $6 adults, $2 ages 6–17, free 4th Tues. of month. Open daily 10–4:30.*

San Diego Museum of Man

(🏃🏻 3–15) Another in Balboa Park's outstanding parcel of museums, the Museum of Man focuses on anthropology: the history and culture of homo sapiens (and forebears). Kids and their parents can explore ancient cultures (such as ancient Egypt or Peru—both of which had mummies) at the new Children's Discovery Center. Grael's favorite area of the museum has life-size and lifelike depictions of early man, from our first ancestors in Africa to the Cro-Magnons who roamed Western Europe a mere 20,000 years ago. You'll also find Mayan costumes and Native American artifacts. From Wednesday to Sunday you can watch live demonstrations of Oaxacan weaving and traditional Mexican tortilla-making.

🏠 1350 El Prado, San Diego, tel. 619/239–2001. Admission: $5 adults, $3 ages 6–17, under 6 free; free for all 3rd Tues. of month. Open daily 10–4:30. Discovery center open Mon.–Fri. 1–4:30, Sat.–Sun. 10–4.

ANIMALS, ANIMALS
ZOOS, AQUARIUMS, AND WILDLIFE REFUGES

Most kids love to watch animals, and in California they can see loads of them, in the wild and in captivity. The state has a superb zoo (in San Diego), a state-of-the-art aquarium (in Monterey), and one of the finest wild animal parks in the world (also in San Diego). Two California theme parks specialize in marine and animal life; for details on these, see Chapter 9.

California also has a wealth of wildlife refuges. These don't offer the convenience or the guaranteed close-up views that zoos or wildlife theme parks do, but they can provide a thrill for everyone in the family, for this is genuine nature, not artificial display. To make sure your kids get the most out of visiting refuges, give them each a field guide—ideally one aimed at children, with big pictures and interesting facts highlighted—so that they can try to spot the wildlife themselves. In our family the kids are sharper-eyed than their parents. Grael was the one to spot our first bald eagle in the wild. Lia can spot bears even when they're motionless and blending in with the environment. Don't forget the binoculars, a camera with long lens, and comfortable old shoes for walking along marshy paths.

Northern Forests and Lakes

Klamath Basin National Wildlife Refuges

👫 6 – 15 These remote wildlife refuges take some effort to get to, but the rewards can be immense: views of bald eagles, golden eagles, great blue herons, and swarms of geese and ducks, the largest flocks of waterfowl in North America. Time your visit according to what you'd like to see most. In October and November, geese and ducks arrive by the millions on their southern migrations, along with pelicans, great blue herons, cormorants, gulls, terns, and grebes. From mid-December to February, some

500 bald eagles migrate from the north, the largest numbers of our national bird outside Alaska. Golden eagles, hawks, and owls are also frequently seen here in winter. In spring, you'll see waterfowl and shorebirds heading back north. In summer, you may see young birds being raised here. Mule deer, pronghorn, and coyotes also live on the marsh-laden land. The complex of refuges spreads out over 150,000 acres in far northern California and Oregon. Two "units" (both in California) are especially suited to public viewing—the Lower Klamath and Tule Lake refuges. Both have self-guided auto tour routes along generally good roads (winter travel can be snowy and difficult). The Tule Lake refuge also has a canoe trail, open July through September (bring your own canoe). Stop at the visitors center for exhibits and route information.

🏠 *Rte. 1, Box 74, Tulelake 96134, tel. 530/ 667–2231. From Hwy. 97, follow Rte. 161 east to Hill Rd., then Hill Rd. south 4 mi to Visitor Center. Or, from Tulelake, follow East-West Rd. 6 mi west to Hill Rd., then turn left. Admission $3 per car; $12 season pass. Refuges open sunrise–sunset; visitors center open weekdays 8–4:30, weekends 10–4.*

Ocean World

(👫 **3–15**) Don't expect high science or slick showmanship at this privately owned aquarium; like Crescent City itself, Ocean World is small and low-key, and for that reason it's just right for kids who get overwhelmed by crowds and spectacle. You wait in a gift shop for the guided tour, a 45-minute folksy ramble that heads first to tide pools populated with sea urchins, sea stars, sea anemones, and sea snails. (Our guide advised everyone that "you have to touch at least one wet and slimy thing, and that doesn't count the person next to you.") Next on the tour are underwater tanks, where you'll see bat rays, leopard sharks, wolf eels, and California sea lions. Everyone is then encouraged to pet an octopus, which is much like stroking a silk shirt. The finale is two sea lions balancing balls on their noses, catching rings around their necks, and giving kids kisses.

🏠 *304 Hwy. 101, Crescent City, tel. 707/ 464–3522. Admission: $5.95 adults, $3.95 ages 3–10. Open June–mid-Sept., daily 8–9; mid-Sept.–May, daily with shorter hrs; call for schedule.*

Sacramento National Wildlife Refuge Complex

(👫 **6–15**) More conveniently located than the Klamath Basin refuges (see *above*), the Sacramento National Wildlife Refuge complex also attracts millions of migrating waterfowl—ducks, geese, and swans—stopping on their way south from Arctic Alaska and Canada. Peak viewing season is from October to February, with 2 million or more birds likely to appear in December.

Water birds and shorebirds—pelicans, egrets, and herons—are especially prominent in the spring. The complex contains two refuges with separate entrances off I-5. The Sacramento Refuge visitors center (about 6 miles south of the town of Willows) has maps and information on good viewing points; the road leads to a 6-mile driving route and 2 miles of walking trails. The Colusa Refuge, the second part of the complex, east of Williams off I-5, has a 3-mile auto route and a 1-mile walking trail (but no visitors center).

🏠 *County Rd. 99W, Willows, tel. 530/934–2801. Norman-Princeton Rd. exit off I-5, about 70 mi north of Sacramento, 6 mi south of Willows. Admission: $3 during winter; annual pass $10. Refuge open sunrise–sunset. Visitors center open Oct.–Feb., daily 7:30–4; Mar.–Sept., weekdays 7:30–4.*

Sierra and the Gold Country

Sacramento Zoo

(👫 **ALL**) Set in an attractive botanical garden, complete with many rare and endangered plants, the Sacramento Zoo nurtures more than 350 mammals, birds, and reptiles, including 15 endangered or threatened species. Chimpanzees, orangutans, lions, tigers, cheetahs, zebras, polar bears, river otters, bat-eared foxes—and recently arrived snow leopards—are all here. The zoo's freshwater Lake Victoria is home to a variety of African and South American waterfowl. Another big hit is the fascinating Reptile House, where you can see gila monsters (some of them bred at the zoo) as well as more than 60 other species. Kids seem especially drawn to the snakes, which include spitting cobras, African gaboon vipers, reticulated pythons, and Dumeril's boas.

🏠 *3930 W. Land Park Dr. at Sutterville Rd., West Land Park, Sacramento, tel. 916/264–5166. Admission: weekdays, $4.50 adults, $3* *ages 3–12; weekends and holidays, 50¢ extra. Open June–Labor Day, daily 9–4; Labor Day–May, daily 10–4.*

San Francisco and the Bay Area

Año Nuevo State Reserve

(**✝✝ 6 – 15**) Año Nuevo State Reserve is home to one of America's great natural spectacles: the annual migration of more than 4,000 massive elephant seals, who come ashore here to rest, mate, and give birth. Once nearly extinct, these protected marine mammals are making a remarkable comeback; they've been breeding on Año Nuevo for the past four decades. The enormous males, weighing up to 5,000 pounds, are the first to return each December, battling each other for dominance in ferocious displays of raw power. The females, who only weigh up to a ton, show up near New Year's and give birth a few days later. Watching the newborn pups struggle to survive is a moving experience; we once witnessed a pup squirming to escape from the weight of a 2-ton bull, who had unknowingly rolled over on him. Meanwhile, the adults mate again, usually in less than a month, then head out to sea by mid-March, leaving the pups to learn to swim by themselves. By late April the pups—as many as 1,400 in recent years-

–head north to feed off the coast of British Columbia. The older elephant seals return to molt from April to August. The reserve covers a wild, undeveloped coastal point of windswept dunes and rocky offshore islands; you can also view a prolific assortment of sea lions, harbor seals, and shorebirds. From mid-December through March the reserve allows the public to visit the breeding grounds only on naturalist-led guided walks, which cover 3 miles and last about 2½ hours. Reservations are essential and can be made starting in late October, up to eight weeks in advance. From April through November free permits are issued daily at the reserve, with no reservations needed. Note that getting within 40 feet of the elephant seals is dangerous; they can bite, and, of course, crush anyone in their path. Carry very small children in a backpack and dress for possible cold and windy weather and muddy terrain; walks leave rain or shine.

🏛 *New Year's Creek Rd., Pescadero, tel. 650/879–0227 or 650/879–2025. Off Hwy. 1 about 55 mi south of San Francisco, 22 mi north of Santa Cruz. Admission: $5 per vehicle. Guided walks $4 per person plus service charge, ages 3 and under free; call 800/444–4445. Reserve open daily 8 AM–sunset; guided walks mid-Dec.–Mar. daily (except Christmas and New Year's Day) 8:45 AM–mid-afternoon. Seal area closed 1st 2 wks of Dec.*

Farallon National Wildlife Refuge

(**✝✝ 10 – 15**) The rocky slopes of the Farallon Islands, which jut up from the Pacific Ocean about 30 miles off San Francisco's Golden Gate, are home to an extraordinary display of wildlife. The seven islands' rocky slopes are home to thousands of harbor seals, California sea lions, Steller's sea lions, and Northern elephant seals. And up to 300,000 breeding seabirds visit the islands annually—making the Farallones the largest Pacific seabird rookery south of Alaska. The public isn't allowed to set foot in this fragile environment, but you can get close-up views from the deck of an Oceanic Society Expeditions boat, as our family did one foggy June day. It's an all-day cruise, lasting about eight hours, aboard a 63-foot Coast Guard-certified vessel. Kids must be 10 or older, and I can see why: the sea can get rough and the winds very cold. Be sure your child is seaworthy before embarking—there's no turning back. Naturalists are on board to point out wildlife and answer questions. As we set out past the Golden Gate, we saw gulls, murres, pelicans, double-crested cormorants, auklets, albatrosses, and tufted puffins; next, a half dozen Dall's porpoises joined our boat, darting around, past, and under the bow. Later we spotted humpback whales, their flukes shooting high in the air as they dived, and a migrating California gray whale. The granite islands themselves were alive with birds, their shrieking and squawking surrounding us, and barking sea lions provided the basso profundo. Dress warmly (and waterproofed), take seasickness precautions, and bring binoculars, sunglasses, sunscreen, lunch, and drinks. 🏠 *Oceanic Society Expeditions, Ft. Mason Center, Bldg. E, San Francisco 94123, tel. 415/ 474–3385 or 800/326–7491. Tickets: $60– $65 per person. Excursions run June–Nov., weekends and some Fri. and Mon. Reservations required.*

Oakland Zoo

(👫 **ALL**) Our family first visited here when the kids were tiny, and we were in no hurry to return—too many of the animal enclosures looked cramped and depressing. In fact, it was then known as one of the worst zoos in the country. But it has since embarked on a multiyear renovation program, and some of the areas are so attractive now that I was reminded of portions of the superb San Diego and Santa Barbara zoos (see *below*). The zoo now has 50 different exhibits on its 100 acres, harboring more than 300 native and exotic animals. At the entrance you're greeted by bright pink flamingos in Flamingo Plaza; head off to the right for the African Veldt area, with giraffes, gazelles, lions, and elephants. You can get a bird's-eye view of the African Veldt from the Sky Ride ($1.50); this 15-minute trip might scare young kids, as the open cars go very high. Our favorite area, straight ahead of Flamingo Plaza, holds the monkey, ape, and chimp habitats, including lush, tropical Siamang Island and Gibbon Island. Warthogs, hyenas, green monkeys, and meerkats scramble among the man-made rocks, a waterfall, and Kikuyu-style "mud and cowdung" (actually disguised concrete) structures at the African Savanna. Most kids enjoy climbing into a tube for a "meerkat's-eye view" of the savanna. Don't miss the Children's Zoo, where kids can watch alligators lie as still as logs and pet and feed domestic sheep and pygmy goats. To the right of the entrance, you can board the C.P. Huntington railroad ($1.50), a minitrain that circles part of the zoo; there is also a carousel among a number of small carnival-type rides here for kids age 3 and up (check the height limits). 🏠 *9777 Golf Links Rd., Knowland Park, Oakland, tel. 510/632–9525. Golf Links Rd. exit off I–580 and go ½ block east. Admission: $6 adults, $3 ages 2–14, under 2 free. Parking $3. Open (weather permitting) daily 10–4.*

San Francisco Bay National Wildlife Refuge

(👫 **6 – 15**) Directly north of San Jose on the southern reaches of San Francisco Bay, this was the country's first urban wildlife refuge, and it's still one of the most popular—

-with both wildlife and humans. Along 25 miles of shoreline, it has an extensive system of boardwalks and trails for hiking and cycling, where you can view wildlife in the salt ponds, salt marshes, and mudflats. During fall and spring migrations there are more than a million shorebirds, waterfowl, and wading birds: sandpipers, peregrine falcons, snowy egrets, great blue herons, canvasback ducks, mallards, kites, terns, and brown pelicans. Harbor seals also often hang around. Stop at the visitors center to see exhibits, use the observation deck, pick up trail information (several trailheads are nearby), and ask about weekend family programs. 🏠 *Box 524, Newark 94560, tel. 510/792– 0222. Entrance south of Dumbarton Bridge toll plaza in Fremont. Admission free. Refuge open daily 7 AM–sunset. Visitors center (1 Marshlands Rd., Fremont) open Tues.–Sat. 7 AM–sunset.*

San Francisco Zoo

(👫 **ALL**) The San Francisco Zoo, set on 125 acres in the fog belt near the ocean, is

Northern California's largest zoo. More than 1,000 birds and animals (220 species) reside here, and several habitats rank among the best in the state. One of the top sights is the 7-acre Children's Zoo, near the front entrance. Kids could easily spend an hour or more here, petting and feeding farm animals in the barnyard or peering at creepy-crawlies in the big indoor insect house. The Children's Zoo also has a deer park, a nature trail, and a nature theater, plus birds, mice, and a chick hatchery. Another don't-miss area of the zoo is the Primate Discovery Center, where 15 species of rare and endangered monkeys—including colobus monkeys, patas monkeys, white ruffed lemurs, and macaques—live and play in a spectacular bi-level setting. There are 23 interactive learning exhibits on the ground level. In the Kresge Nocturnal Gallery next door, careful searching will yield views (admittedly dim) of lemurs and other night creatures; children who are afraid of the dark may find this a bit spooky. A fair walk away, a family of lowland gorillas lives in spacious natural Gorilla World—one of the most luxurious such exhibits in the world. On Penguin Island, dozens of Magellanic penguins dive into a 200-foot-long pool; kangaroos and wallabies hop about in the Australian Walkabout; and koalas cling shyly to the trees in Koala Crossing. Fifty rainbow lorikeets occupy a walk-through aviary in the new Rainbow Landing. The South American Gateway exhibit contains 7 acres of rain forest where tapirs and howler monkeys roam. The zoo is home to rare and endangered species such as the black rhino, orangutan, Madagascar aye-aye, and, in the Feline Conservation Center, big cats such as the ocelot and jaguar. The usual complements of elephants, lions, tigers, bears, warthogs, and giraffes are on hand as well. Lions are fed daily (except Monday) at 2 PM; penguins are fed daily at 3 PM. The narrated Safari Train circles the zoo ($2.50; $1.50 ages 5 and under). You can also ride a carousel or miniature steam train (each $2), and there's a big children's playground near the front entrance. The Wildlife Theater

stages shows from late June to Labor Day daily except Monday.
🏠 *Sloat Blvd. at 45th Ave., San Francisco, tel. 415/753–7080. Admission: $9 adults, $6 ages 12–17, $3 ages 3–11, ages 2 and under free; free to all 1st Wed. of month. Stroller rental: $3–$7. Main zoo open daily 10–5; children's zoo daily 11–4.*

Steinhart Aquarium

(👀 **ALL**) Part of the prestigious California Academy of Sciences in Golden Gate Park (see Chapter 5), the Steinhart Aquarium is extremely popular with families, who stream here to view more than 15,000 fish and other aquatic creatures including sea mammals, reptiles, amphibians, and an incredibly cute parcel of black-footed penguins. Take the kids first to the Touch Tidepool, where they can pick up sea stars, anemones, and slimy sea cucumbers. Then head up the ramp to the riveting Fish Roundabout. Leopard sharks, sea bass, silver salmon, and pompano swim continually inside a huge circular tank. Elsewhere you'll find seals, dolphins, green sea turtles, piranhas, manatees, jellyfish, sea horses, eerie garden eels (who stick their heads menacingly out of sand), electric fish, and alligator gars (fish that resemble 'gators). Real alligators lie log-still at the alligator pond, surrounded by reptiles and amphibians in separate displays, including rattlesnakes, hairy scorpions, orange-kneed tarantulas, and red spitting cobras. On the living tropical coral reef, reef sharks and brilliantly colored fish swim around the equally colorful coral. Penguins are fed twice a day, at 11:30 AM and 4 PM. And at the Fish Roundabout you can watch the fish go into their feeding frenzy daily at 2 PM.
🏠 *Golden Gate Park, San Francisco, tel. 415/750–7145. Admission (to aquarium and Natural History Museum): $8.50 adults, $5.50 ages 12–17, $2.50 ages 4–11, ages 3 and under free; $1 discount with Muni transfer; free 1st Wed. of month. Open Memorial Day–Labor Day, daily 9–6; rest of year daily 10–5.*

UnderWater World at Pier 39

🕇🕇 3 – 15 Visitors to this "diver's-eye view" aquarium descend into clear acrylic tunnels to view an array of sharks (six species), bat rays, eels, sturgeon, sea stars, smelt, perch, and other creatures of San Francisco Bay. The concept is intriguing: people are, in effect, on the inside looking out into the tanks, while the marine life— swimming freely above and around the humans—are on the outside looking in. The two transparent tunnels are 400 feet long, and the two-story tank holds more than 700,000 gallons of water and 10,000 creatures, so there's a lot to see. Seeing a shark swimming directly over your head is an experience not easily forgotten. The narration—provided via headphones—is jaunty and informative. But there's a coordination problem between the length of the tape, which runs about 40 minutes, and the length of time it takes to ride the slow-moving walkways through the tunnels—only 20 to 30 minutes. So to get your money's worth, you really need to get off the moving walkway at times and stroll at your own pace, or linger at places on a parallel stationary platform. Still, many people in a "dive" reach the end in about a half-hour or so, missing some of the taped descriptions. It's also a bit awkward taking strollers on the moving walkway, and kids need to be age 6 or so to appreciate the headphone narration, though young kids can still admire the fish. The well-stocked gift shop (which you enter at the end when you "resurface") is almost bound to attract kids' eyes.

🏠 *Beach St. at The Embarcadero, tel. 415/623–5300; for reserved tickets, tel. 888/732–3483. Admission: $12.95 adults, $6.50 ages 3–11. Open daily 9–9.*

Central Coast and Valley

California Living Museum

🕇🕇 3 – 15 CALM, as it's known for short, is a combination zoo, botanical garden, and natural history museum, with all species— both animal and plant—native to the state. But the emphasis here is on "zoo." Most of the animals on its 88 acres couldn't be released in the wild; some have disabilities, some were raised as pets, and others come from zoos, wildlife refuges, and animal rehabilitation centers. CALM's Reptile House shelters every species of rattlesnake found in California. You'll also see a songbird aviary, tortoise and turtle exhibits, and mammals such as coyotes, mountain lions, and foxes. At the children's play area and the Children's Park little ones can pet sheep, goats, a burro, and other farm animals. Native California plants such as oaks, cacti, and chaparral provide the landscaping.

🏠 *14000 Alfred Harrell Hwy., Bakersfield, tel. 661/872–2256. Admission: $3.50 adults, $2 ages 3–12 and students. Open Tues.– Sun. 9–5.*

Chaffee Zoological Gardens

🕇🕇 ALL In tree-shaded Roeding Park, the Chaffee Zoological Gardens is best known for two state-of-the-art exhibits. The modern Reptile House, with computer-controlled temperature and light levels, displays geckos, chameleons, monitors, boas, rattlesnakes, and tortoises. From April through October you can "meet a reptile" each morning at 11:30, as a zookeeper presents a live lizard or snake at the entryway. The Tropical Rain Forest, landscaped with a waterfall and bridges, harbors exotic birds and butterflies. Elsewhere you'll find leopards, tigers, grizzly bears, sea lions, hippos, tapirs, elephants, and monkeys. Kids can pet baby animals at the Small Wonders exhibit

or watch the scheduled feedings of hippos, tapirs, and sea lions each afternoon.
🏠 *Roeding Park (between Olive and Belmont Aves.), Fresno, tel. 559/498–2671. Admission: $4.95 adults, $2.50 ages 2–11. Parking: $1. Open Mar.–Oct., daily 9–5; Nov.–Feb., daily 10–4.*

Charles Paddock Zoo

(👫 **ALL**) This is a small but interesting zoo, with a variety of exotic species exhibited in reasonably well-maintained habitats. It's worth a stop if you're traveling along U.S. Highway 101—especially because you can combine it with picnicking, paddleboating, or romping on the playground in adjacent Atascadero Lake Park. In the zoo itself we enjoyed seeing the two magnificent Bengal tigers, the Malayan sun bear, the meerkats, the spider monkeys, and the multicolored mandarin ducks in the aviary. Kids can feed goats, sheep, and llamas in the petting zoo.
🏠 *Hwy. 41, Atascadero, tel. 805/461–5080. From Hwy. 101 go west 1½ mi on Hwy. 41. Admission: $3 adults, $2 ages 3–15, $30 family season pass. Open Memorial Day–Labor Day, daily 10–6; rest of year, Mon.–Thurs. 10–4, Fri.–Sun. 10–5.*

Micke Grove Zoo

(👫 **ALL**) Micke Grove Park, between Stockton and Lodi, is among the Central Valley's most heavily visited recreation areas, and its compact zoo has two notable exhibits. Island Lost in Time displays endangered primates found only on the island of Madagascar. Paseo Pantera showcases mountain lions. The zoo also nurtures snow leopards, an African black leopard, and other animals on the endangered list. Before or after visiting the zoo, be sure to stop at Micke Grove's family amusement park, Funderwoods, which has 11 pay-as-you-go rides (most for kids age 2 to 10); it's open daily from 11 to 6 in summer, and on weekends only most of the rest of the year. The park also includes the San Joaquin County Histor-

ical Museum, California's only accredited agricultural museum ($2 adults, $1 ages 6–12; open Wed.–Sun., 1–4:45 PM); a Japanese garden; and picnic areas.
🏠 *Micke Grove Rd., Lodi (Eight Mile Rd. or Armstrong Rd. off Hwy. 99, go ½ mi west; or Eight Mile Rd. 3 mi east of I–5), tel. 209/331–7270 (zoo); 209/369–5437 (amusement park); 209/331–2055 (museum). Zoo admission: $1.50 adults, $1 ages 6–17. Zoo open May–Aug., weekdays 10–5, weekends 10–7; rest of year, daily 10–5. Park entry fee: $2 weekdays, $4 weekends, $5 holidays. Park open daily 8 AM–dusk.*

Monterey Bay Aquarium

(👫 **ALL**) A visit to this extraordinary facility is like exploring Monterey Bay without getting wet. Since it opened in the 1980s, the Monterey Bay Aquarium has been widely recognized as the country's finest and—with 1½ million visitors a year—most popular aquarium. On the site of a former sardine cannery along Monterey's historic Cannery Row (see Chapter 4), the aquarium has an innovative design that makes it almost seem part of the shoreline, and seawater helps nourish some of the exhibits. The open-air Great Tide Pool, where sea anemones and sea stars grow, is sometimes visited by wild sea otters and harbor seals. Several outdoor decks let visitors stop to drink in views of the bay. The Outer Bay wing showcases life in the open ocean on a scale found in no other aquarium. Here the world's largest window (15 feet high, 54 feet long) offers wide-angle views into a 1-million-gallon tank filled with sharks, ocean sunfish (which weigh up to 3,000 pounds), barracuda, and stingrays. The nearby tanks of jellyfish are another must-see; watching these delicate, opalescent creatures drift through the water is absolutely mesmerizing. A room overlooking the bay is devoted to interactive exhibits for kids ages 4 to 7; they'll discover how marine mammals eat, swim, and communicate—even hearing whales sing, dolphins squeak, and elephant seals bellow. In the original wing, our kids love the two-story Sea Otters exhibit, where these playful and endearing creatures (who came to the aquarium as orphaned pups) dive, tumble, chase, and groom each other, above and below water. Don't miss the three-times-daily feedings, when the bewhiskered otters swim on their backs and eat squid using their paws as utensils and their chests as "dinner plates." The three-story Kelp Forest, the tallest aquarium exhibit in the world, is another must-see. Kids can imagine themselves as deep-sea divers as they peer into a 335,000-gallon tank filled with thousands of fish. Leopard sharks are stars here—swimming amid towering, swaying kelp fronds. At the twice-daily feedings, divers enter the tank. At the Touch Pools, kids can fondle sea stars, stroke crabs, or reach out to pet the velvety skin of bat rays as they glide past. And at the Kelp Lab, they can touch or get close-up views of creatures who live in the Kelp Forest. In March 2000, the aquarium will open a children's gallery loaded with hands-on, climb on, and crawl-through exhibits (warning: kids may get wet!) designed to illustrate different ocean habitats. Penguins, moray eels, sharks, anemones, and coral will call the gallery home. As the aquarium draws huge crowds in summer and holiday periods, it's wise to call for advance tickets; many area hotels also sell them with no service charge.

🏠 *886 Cannery Row, Monterey, tel. 831/ 648–4888 or 800/756–3737 in CA (for advance tickets with $3 service charge). Admission: $14.95 adults, $11.95 students, $6.95 ages 3–12 and disabled. Open fall–spring, daily 10–6; summer and major holidays, daily 9:30–6.*

Santa Barbara Zoological Gardens

(👫 **ALL**) Santa Barbara, an idyllic resort for humans, has produced a zoo that resembles a resort for animals. "Zoological Gardens" is an apt description; the landscaping is magnificent, with lots of tropical vegetation and a wonderful overlook of the adjoining Andree Clark Bird Refuge, where seabirds congregate on a freshwater lake. A lot of care has been taken to provide the 600 animals open-air replications of their natural habitats, from the Amazon rain forest to the African veldt. Our favorite area runs from the sea lion pool to the nearby tropical aviary, where colorful macaws, cockatoos, and parrots hang out amid rushing waterfalls and lush foliage; in the distance, if you look up, you can spot Asian elephants. We also like the red panda (a raccoonlike relative of the giant panda), the gibbons (who have their own island where they can swing through the trees), the African lions (who rest majestically on rocks above the walkway), the ring-tailed lemurs from Madagascar, the rare Amur leopards, and the lowland gorillas. The zoo's 40 acres include a Discovery Area with a barn where kids can watch chicks hatching; a Miniature Train ($1; 50¢ ages 2–12) that runs around part of the park; and a playground.

🏠 *500 Niños Dr., Santa Barbara, tel. 805/ 962–5339. Admission: $6 adults, $4 ages 2– 12. Stroller rental: $2. Open daily 10–5.*

Los Angeles and Environs

Cabrillo Marine Aquarium

(👫 **2–15**) A combination aquarium and museum, the Cabrillo Marine Aquarium houses the world's largest collection of Southern California marine life, displayed in three dozen aquarium tanks, plus a touch tank and seawater laboratories. Though the tanks are smaller than those at some other aquariums, most of them are low to the ground and visible from all sides, making them easy for kids to look in. Exhibits are divided into five sections, highlighting different marine habitats. In Rocky Shores your kids can see a fascinating collection of sea animals that look exactly like plants, and others camouflaged to look like their surroundings. Children can also gently feel live prickly urchins or slimy sea hares in the big outdoor Touch Tank (open for 20 minutes each hour). The stars of the Sand and Mud sections are clams, crabs, and sand dollars. On display in the Open Ocean area are sharks, luminescent fish, and the skeletons of a dolphin and a California gray whale, as well as exhibits on whale migrations and Channel Islands seabirds. A 5,000-gallon tank showcases life in a kelp forest. Part of a planned expansion in 1999 are a 1-million-gallon tank for large fish, a two-story kelp forest, larger touch tanks, and a home for rescued but unreleasable sea otters.

🏛 *3720 Stephen White Dr., San Pedro, tel. 310/548–7562. Admission: $2 adults, $1 ages 12 and under. Parking: $6.50. Open Tues.–Fri. noon–5, weekends 10–5.*

Long Beach Aquarium of the Pacific

(👫 **ALL**) This striking aquarium that opened in 1998 occupies a site adjacent to Long Beach's Shoreline Lagoon, across the harbor from the *Queen Mary* (see Chapter 4), and makes good use of its seaside setting with outdoor exhibits and decks. With its wavelike ceiling and curving architecture, the building is designed to mirror the look of the nearby Pacific Ocean, which serves as its focus. More than 150,000 square feet of space and more than 1 million gallons of Pacific salt water accommodate the aquarium's 17 major habitats and 30 smaller exhibits, which hold some 10,000 ocean animals (550 species). You enter first into the Great Hall of the Pacific, where a full-scale model of a blue whale floats overhead and "sneak previews" entice you into the three main exhibit areas. In the Southern California/Baja region you can get close-up, indoor-outdoor, and below- and above-water views of once-injured or orphaned seals and sea lions of Santa Catalina Island; many cannot be released again in the wild. You can also

see a kelp forest, a collection of moon jellies, some endangered sea turtles from the Sea of Cortez, and a three-story-high predator exhibit that includes leopard sharks, giant sea bass, barracuda, and giant spined sea stars. The Northern Pacific section highlights the icy waters of the Bering Sea, where puffins nest and sea otters frolic. Also look for giant Pacific octopus, giant sea stars, and giant Japanese spider crabs. In the Tropical Pacific region you'll explore re-creations of the coral lagoons and deep reefs of Micronesia's Palau archipelago, which teems with creatures like stingrays, gray reef sharks, zebra sharks, giant groupers—and even some fish that change their gender when they mature. Scuba divers swim among the marine life and provide commentary through microphone masks. Be sure to visit Kids Cove, an outdoor area that's designed as a playground of the Pacific Ocean and is loaded with "please touch" exhibits. Kids can walk through a giant whale skeleton, nest on a giant sea bird egg, burrow in the sand like a hermit crab, or handle the critters in touch tanks.

🏛 *100 Aquarium Way, Long Beach, tel. 562/590–3100 or 888/826–7257. Admission: $13.95 adults, $6.95 ages 3–11. Open daily, 10–6.*

Los Angeles Zoo

(👫 **ALL**) Though the Los Angeles Zoo, located in sprawling Griffith Park, is overshadowed by the celebrated San Diego Zoo to the south, we thoroughly enjoyed it. Adventure Island, a children's zoo, presents animals of the American Southwest. A sign beckons "Explorers Welcome," and kids can enter a dark cave to search for bats and barn owls, stroll past mountain habitats looking for mountain lions, or stand by a waterfall to see seals. Truth be told, this is my favorite area of the zoo, and parents seem to have as much fun as their kids. Adventure Island is also the site of animal shows in the Zoorific Theater. Elsewhere you'll see more than 1,200 rare animals in natural settings, including meerkats, woolly monkeys, flamingos, alligators, koalas, kiwis, gorillas, black rhinos, tigers, lions, hippos, and giraffes. My kids were especially taken by the colobus monkeys, spectacular leapers with strikingly beautiful black and white fur; the huge prehistoric-looking Indian rhinos, whose hides suggest battle armor; and the entertaining siamang gibbons from Malaysia and Sumatra with their continual hooting cries. The zoo is in the process of expanding its primate areas. Chimpanzees recently moved into the state-of-the-art Chimpanzees of the Mahale Mountains exhibit, a spacious naturalistic setting with grass, palms, a waterfall, and logs; new orangutan and gorilla areas will follow. Other highlights include a reptile house and play and picnic areas. This zoo is big—80 acres. Get around on the Safari Shuttle ($3.50 adults, $1.50 ages 2–12), which stops at each of six locations every 30 minutes or so; you can board and reboard all day, but it doesn't go through exhibits—you'll need to get off to see most of the animals.

🏠 5333 Zoo Dr., Griffith Park, Los Angeles, tel. 323/644–6400. Admission: $8.25 adults, $3.25 ages 2–12, under 2 free. Stroller rental: $5. Open daily 10–5.

San Diego and the Southern Deserts

Birch Aquarium at Scripps

(👫 2–15) Run by the Scripps Institution of Oceanography, the sparkling Birch Aquarium at Scripps is San Diego's answer to the Monterey Bay Aquarium. Though not as spectacular, it occupies a dramatic perch on a hillside overlooking the Pacific, and it draws big crowds to view its more than 30 aquarium tanks. Start at the large outdoor tide pool on the front plaza, stocked with local marine creatures such as sea stars and sea urchins. Inside, see the sardine roundabout as well as some 3,700 fish and inver-

tebrates on display from the waters of the West Coast, Mexico, and the South Pacific. Our kids were transfixed watching big, menacing-looking wolf eels lurking in their caves, and eerie moon jellies floating past like parachutes (one little girl thought they looked like ghosts). A giant kelp tank teems with leopard sharks and other California coastal sea life. The coral reef tanks are dazzling, with bright tropical fish swimming amid equally colorful coral. Across the hall, a marine museum presents the history and study of oceanography in a series of interactive exhibits, Exploring the Blue Planet. The Submersible Ride is an enclosed, simulated submarine that takes 18 people at a time on a video "dive" to the depths of the ocean floor (expect a wait on crowded days). Kids under 4 may well be scared by the dark enclosure, and probably will enjoy the tide pool and fish tanks much more.

🏠 2300 Expedition Way, La Jolla, tel. 619/534–3474. Admission: $7.50 adults, $4 ages 3–17. Parking: $3. Open daily 9–5.

Living Desert Wildlife and Botanical Park

(👫 2–15) This outstanding 1,200-acre park has helped our family gain a new appreciation for the richness and diversity of the desert. Desert habitats from around the world are highlighted, in both botanical garden and wildlife displays; the animals (representing 130 desert species) will probably draw the kids' interest most. You'll see bighorn sheep climbing around their own rocky hill, the recently saved-from-extinction Arabian oryx (known as "the unicorn of the desert" for its distinctive horns), coyotes, gazelles, meerkats, Abyssinian hornbills, great horned owls, and rare desert pupfish that are relics of the Ice Age. At the dramatically designed Eagle Canyon, you enter through an aviary housing magnificent golden eagles (check out their 7-foot wingspans), then pass through a replica of a rugged desert canyon, populated with mountain lions, bobcats, kit foxes, badgers, and wolves.

The African Trade Village, with thatched huts and marketplace, also contains an aviary and African animals from warthogs to livestock. During the hot months try to get to the park early, when it's cooler, and you'll witness more activity among the animals. When we were here in early afternoon, the mountain lions were off sleeping in the shade somewhere. Take your kids to the Discovery Room (open 10–4), a hands-on nature exploration center. Fifty-minute tram tours ($4) give you a narrated spin around the park. There are also daily guided walking tours and weekend animal shows. Seven miles of self-guided hiking trails wind through the less-developed parts of the reserve.

🏦 47–900 Portola Ave., Palm Desert, tel. 760/346–5694. Admission: $7 adults, $3.50 ages 3–12. Stroller rental: $1. Open Oct.–June 15, daily 9–5; June 16–July and Sept., daily 8–noon. Closed Aug.

San Diego Wild Animal Park

👫 2 – 15   The perfect complement to the San Diego Zoo—you can even buy a discounted ticket to both—the Wild Animal Park may be the closest to a real safari experience you'll have this side of Kenya. Set in a valley 30 miles north of downtown San Diego, the 2,200-acre park has more than 3,000 mammals and birds, roaming freely in habitats resembling their homelands. The emphasis is on conservation, including saving and breeding endangered species; the largest captive rhino population in the world lives here. Unlike the typical zoo, the park is designed first for animals, and second for people. For humans, the bonus is views of animal behaviors normally seen only in the wild. You can walk through parts of the beautifully landscaped park; the 5-mile, 50-minute Wgasa Bush Line Monorail (included in the admission price) takes visitors through others. We usually start out with the monorail ride, as the long lines later in the day can be frustrating. If you can, position the kids on the monorail's right side for the best

views of the animals—African and Asian elephants, giraffes, and herds of antelopes and gazelles among them. The ride is fully narrated, and the guide will point out new baby animals, interesting natural behaviors, and tips on how everyone can help save the rain forests. (Toddlers may find the ride too long; when we first took Grael at age 2 he squirmed much of the time.) After your monorail ride, stroll through lush Nairobi Village, with its viewing areas of gorillas and lemurs and Petting Kraal (where kids can pet or feed baby deer, gazelles, and goats, most of which are being nursed to health in the nearby Animal Care Center). Nairobi Village also hosts animal shows (we recommend the Rare and Wild America Show). On one visit, Grael's favorite sight was the Hidden Jungle—an indoor greenhouse filled with hummingbirds, butterflies, bright green poison arrow frogs, and exotic insects and reptiles, where kid-height windows reveal giant black millipedes, Madagascar hissing cockroaches, rhinoceros beetles, orange-kneed tarantulas, and dead-leaf mantises. The Heart of Africa attraction is billed as the "Western Hemisphere's largest and most diverse safari experience." Here, you can take a walking safari through 30 acres of forest, wetland, savannah, and open-plains habitats, occupied by 260 animals including cheetahs, rhinos, and colobus monkeys. Later, while younger kids will happily slide and climb at the Samburu Jungle Gym, families with older children might consider taking a Photo Caravan into the heart of the preserve aboard an open-air truck; it may be your best chance to personally meet a herd of giraffe. For another memorable experience, reserve some spots in the Roar & Snore overnight camping program. (For either, call 760/738–5049 for information and reservations.)

🏦 15500 San Pasqual Valley Rd., Escondido, tel. 619/234–6541 or 760/747-8702. Hwy. 163 and I–15 30 mi north of downtown to Via Rancho Pkwy., then follow signs for 6 mi. Admission: $19.95 adults, $12.95 ages 3–11. Combined admission with San Diego Zoo *(within 5-day period): $33.55 adults, $19.95 ages 3–11. Parking: $3. Stroller rental: $5–$10. Open Mid-June–Labor Day, daily 9–8, rest of year, daily 9–4.*

San Diego Zoo

(👪 **ALL**) San Diego's top tourist attraction and indispensable stop for families sets the standard for zoos worldwide. It's a leader in the conservation and breeding of endangered species, showcases more than 4,000 animals (800 species), and has 100 acres of beautifully landscaped, mostly barless habitats that are a joy to behold. (The zoo is also a fully accredited botanical garden, with 6,500 species of exotic plants.) In Gorilla Tropics, with waterfalls, tropical pools, and lush foliage, and the nearby Pygmy Chimps at Bonobo Road you'll find gorillas, agile siamangs and colobus monkeys, orangutans (Lia went crazy over a baby orangutan with spiked orange hair), and bonobos (playful jungle gymnasts who like to play a simian version of blindman's bluff). Along Tiger River, a long, winding path takes you down into a canyon past Malayan tapirs, Chinese water dragons, tiny mouse deer, web-footed fishing cats, crocodiles, tree pythons, and Sumatran tigers. In Sun Bear Forest, playful lion-tailed macaques and sun bears frolic in a re-creation of an Asian rain forest. The multilevel Hippo Beach and Polar Bear Plunge areas provide underwater views of each creature—the latter re-creates an Arctic tundra environment, no mean feat in San Diego. The Giant Panda Research Sta-

tion harbors the country's only giant panda pair, who live in open-moated habitats lined with bamboo (call 888/697–2632 for viewing times). The zoo is hilly in parts, so a stroller is helpful for small children—but tough on parents to push. One solution may be the double-decker zoo bus ($4 adults, $3 ages 3–11), which takes a 40-minute, 3-mile narrated drive around the park, providing good views of some of the outlying canyons and mesas where Arabian oryx, elephants, camels, wild horses, and other big animals dwell. The narrated Kangaroo Bus Tours ($8 adults, $5 ages 3–11) follow the same route, but allow passengers to get off and reboard at eight different stops throughout the day. The Skyfari aerial tram ($1) offers wonderful bird's-eye views of the park from 180 feet above ground. Don't miss the Children's Zoo (no extra admission); it's the best of its kind, complete with a petting paddock and two baby animal nurseries where kids can meet meerkats, macaws, and pygmy falcons up close. Plan on spending at least half a day; in a full day you still won't cover it all. If you're here in summer, consider staying until evening; that's when the nocturnal animals (lions, leopards, and the largest koala colony outside Australia) are at their most active. 🏛 *2920 Zoo Dr., Balboa Park, San Diego, tel. 619/234–3153 or 619/231–1515. Admission: $16 adults, $7 ages 3–11. Combined admission with San Diego Wild Animal Park (within 5-day period, includes zoo bus and Skyfari): $33.55 adults, $19.95 ages 3–11. Stroller rental: $5–$10. Open late June–Labor Day, daily 9–9; rest of year, daily 9–4.*

REDWOODS, WATERFALLS, CAVERNS, AND OTHER NATURAL WONDERS

7

Although California is the nation's most populous state, with three sprawling metropolitan areas, its ultimate treasures lie beyond the cities. The world's biggest and oldest trees? They're all in California. The most spectacular coastline on earth? Many people would vote for California's Pacific coast. Mountains so beautiful that they inspired America's conservation movement? John Muir's Sierra Nevada, in California. Subterranean caverns where nature's artistry has sculpted amazing shapes? They're all over (well, actually under) the state.

Many of California's greatest natural wonders are in state or national parks, which are covered in Chapter 8. A few of those sites are also discussed in this chapter, along with numerous wonders found outside state and national park boundaries.

Northern Forests and Lakes

Avenue of the Giants

(✦✦ ALL) When I first told my then 4-year-old daughter, Lia, that we were driving to the Avenue of the Giants, she looked worried. No, I assured her, the road would not be lined with big, bad guys who lived in beanstalks; these were redwood trees, taller than a dozen of her storybook giants. She seemed both relieved and impressed. Parallel to U.S. 101, this 31-mile route in Humboldt County, which cuts through the heart of Humboldt Redwoods State Park (see Chapter 8), is essentially for sightseers. It can be driven at a relaxed speed in about an hour. From the south, the road begins at Phillipsville (it's well marked); from the north, at Pepperwood; it winds along the

Eel River past a steady procession of redwood groves. If you're heading north, the biggest giants begin to appear just beyond the town of Miranda. Dappled sunlight falls through the shade of the towering trees, many of which stand only feet away. Numerous pullovers allow for stops along the road, and hiking trails lead off into the trees. If the kids like their nature with a touch of sideshow, they'll find it along the Avenue of the Giants: Roadside attractions include The Chimney Tree (Phillipsville), a 1,500-year-old hollow, living redwood (tel. 707/923–2265); the Shrine Drive Thru Tree (Myers Flat), a living redwood you can walk or drive through ($1.50 per person, ages 9 and under free; tel. 707/943–3154); and The Immortal Tree (Redcrest), a 248-foot, 950-year-old redwood that has survived lightning, fire, and flood (tel. 707/722–4396). **🏚** *Tel. 707/946–2263. Reached via Hwy. 101, about 200 mi north of San Francisco. Admission free. Open daily.*

Castle Crags State Park

(👫 **ALL**) The soaring granite spires of the Castle Crags deserve a close look. Stop at the park's Vista Point for an excellent view of the ancient crags, which climb to nearly 7,000 feet; Castle Dome, at 5,000 feet, is the best known. Twenty-eight miles of hiking trails await if you have time. Only strong hikers should tackle the strenuous 5½-mile, five-hour round-trip trail to Castle Dome, a climb of 2,200 feet; if you make it, you'll find spectacular views of surrounding forests, the Sacramento River valley, and 14,000-foot Mount Shasta 15 miles north. For more gentle hiking, head for the Indian Creek nature trail, which forms a 1-mile loop. Pick up maps at the entrance station (staffed from mid-May to mid-September) or the visitors center. The park also offers picnicking, swimming, and fishing in and along rivers and creeks, plus camping at 76 developed sites.

🏠 *Box 80, Castella 96017, tel. 530/235–2684. Take Castle Crags exit off I–5 at Castella, 6 mi south of Dunsmuir. Day use fee: $5 per vehicle. Camping: $12–$16 per night; tel. 800/444–7275. Visitors center open mid-May–Oct., weekends 9–4; sporadic hrs on weekdays.*

Lake Shasta Caverns

(👫 **ALL**) Even the smallest child can enjoy the wondrous inner world of Lake Shasta Caverns, thanks to a tunnel entrance carved for public access in the 1960s. A visit to these beautiful limestone caverns begins with a scenic 15-minute catamaran ride across Lake Shasta, then a short—but curvy and steep—bus ride up a mountainside to the caverns. The outside views are surpassed only by those within the mountain chambers, where informative guides lead one-hour walks past a fairyland of multicolored formations: crystal-studded stalactites and stalagmites, marble "draperies" and columns, white flowstone waterfalls, and spaghetti-shape helictites (spiny stalactites). The names will especially delight young chil-

dren: "Snow White and the Seven Dwarfs," the "King and Queen and a Castle," and "Santa Claus." If things sometimes get a little spooky—such as when a brown bat flies past—well, even better! Stars of the show are the enormous, glittering Cathedral Room, with its 60-foot stalactites hanging from the ceiling like giant icicles; and the Crystal Room, which has both bacon-rind formations and the world's largest helictites, together forming a heaping subterranean version of spaghetti carbonara. The terrain is relatively easy, with guardrails, good lighting, paved walkways and stairs; strollers aren't feasible, but infants may be carried in front packs or backpacks (beware of low overhangs). The temperature is a cool but comfortable 58° year-round.

🏠 *Box 801, O'Brien 96070, tel. 530/238–2341. Shasta Caverns Rd. exit from I–5; go less than 2 mi to headquarters chalet. Admission: $14 adults, $7 ages 4–12. Open Memorial Day–Labor Day, daily 9–4; Apr.–May and Sept., daily 9–3; Oct.–Mar., daily 10–2 (weather permitting).*

Lava Beds National Monument

(👫 **6–15**) Though lacking the sheer volcanic sizzle of Yellowstone National Park or the island of Hawaii, Northern California has a long history of geothermal turbulence. And nowhere is it more dramatically displayed than at this remote and rugged park, pockmarked with cinder and spatter cones, blanketed with undulating beds of volcanic rock, and honeycombed with hundreds of lava tube caves. Some of these caves—formed by cooled ancient lava flows—are suitable for exploring. But this far northern park—it's a few miles south of Oregon—is decidedly remote: The nearest food, lodging, and gasoline services are in Tionesta, 14 miles southeast of park headquarters. (The park has 43 campsites, open from mid–May to mid–September.) The elevation ranges from 4,000 to 5,700 feet, so be prepared for cold weather almost any time of year, though summer temperatures can get hot. The visitors center lies toward the southern end of the park, where most of the explorable lava tube caves are. Mushpot Cave, adjacent to the center, is the only cave with lights installed. Cave Loop Road winds past a number of other tube caves, some of which have ladders or stairway access. For spelunking you'll need flashlights, hard-soled shoes, and protective headgear; ask about rentals at the visitors center. Some caves are hazardous, with low ceilings, steep trails, and uneven footing. Evaluate your young explorers carefully before embarking; adventurous school-age children will probably do fine. Wildlife viewing is especially good in the northern reaches of the park, which border the Tule Lake National Wildlife Refuge (see Klamath Basin National Wildlife Refuges *in* Chapter 6). Note: Rattlesnakes and other snakes are also present, as well as rodents that carry plague.

🏠 *Box 867, Tulelake 96134, tel. 530/667–2282. Entrance 28 mi southeast of Tulelake via Hwy. 139. Admission: $4 per car (good for 1 wk). Camping: $6–$10 per night. Open daily; visitors center open mid-May–mid-Sept., daily 9–6, mid-Sept.–mid-May, daily 8–5.*

McArthur-Burney Falls

🏃 ALL Theodore Roosevelt once called them the "Eighth Wonder of the World"; my son calls them "cool." Yet the McArthur-Burney Falls are relatively unknown, even in California, probably because they're off the beaten track, about 1½ hours from Redding and I–5. The drive, though, is scenic, and the falls themselves are exceptionally beautiful: Two thundering cascades of water, augmented by dozens of narrower falls streaming over the lichen-covered cliffs, plunge into a deep emerald pool below. The water hits with such force—at the rate of 100 million gallons a day—that rainbow-flecked mists rise from the pool, creating an ethereal scene. Because of erosion, the falls have actually moved more than 1 mile upstream since they were formed 3 million years ago. A pretty 1-mile-loop

nature trail, easy enough for young children (though not strollers) to negotiate, leads down to the foot of the falls and then along wooded Burney Creek before winding back to the top of the falls. Signs along the trail help kids identify lava layers from ancient volcanic eruptions, plus dogwood, fir, cedar, and alder trees. You can fish in the creek or follow another 1-mile trail to Lake Britton, where you can picnic at a sandy beach, rent canoes (tel. 530/335–4214), or go wading. The falls themselves are within a state park, which has 128 developed campsites.

🏠 *24898 Hwy. 89, Burney 96013, tel. 530/335–2777. 11 mi northeast of Burney off Hwy. 89. Day use: $5 per car. Camping: $12–$16 per night; tel. 800/444–7275. Open daily.*

Sierra and the Gold Country

Ancient Bristlecone Pine Forest

🏃 6–15 In our family's never-ending search for "things that are alive, but even older than Dad," as my son so cleverly puts it, I thought we had maxed out at 2,000-year-old giant sequoias. But then we came upon a living forest where some of the inhabitants are *twice* as old as sequoias. Now that, son, is ancient! And so the name: Ancient Bristlecone Pine Forest. At 4,300 years and counting, bristlecones are among the oldest living things. This protected 28,000-acre forest has survived remarkably in the harsh and arid soil of the White Mountains in far eastern California; it's about 100 miles southeast of Yosemite, in the Inyo National Forest. The eerily beautiful pines, with their spiky purplish-brown cones, are gnarled, polished, and sculpted by centuries of exposure to the elements. Unlike the sequoias, they grow extremely slowly, adding at most an inch of diameter per century and seldom reaching 25 feet in height. The two leading groves, usually accessible from late spring or early summer to early fall, are the Schulman Grove, at 10,100 feet elevation, and the Patriarch Grove, about 12 miles farther up the road at 11,200 feet. At Schulman Grove there is a 1-mile Discovery Trail and the 4½-mile Methuselah Trail; you can also take a short loop trail in the Patriarch Grove. The road is paved for the first 10 miles, then becomes dirt and gravel. This latter section is steep and not recommended for big RVs.

🏠 *White Mountain Ranger District, 798 N. Main St., Bishop 93514, tel. 760/873–2500. Take Hwy. 168, 13 mi east from Big Pine, then follow signs north. Admission free. Visitors center open Memorial Day–mid-Oct., daily, weather permitting.*

Boyden Cavern

(👫 **3–15**) Heading into the depths of Kings Canyon (see Chapter 8), you'll find this cavern right by the roadside, along the south fork of the King's River; you can take the guided tour through it and be back on the road within an hour or so. The first part's the hardest—after a steep five-minute climb up to the cavern entrance you pass through several rocky, narrow, low passageways. Don't try to maneuver a baby in a backpack through here. After that the going gets smoother, and the guide will lead you past ornate crystalline formations accented by colored electric lights. Adults marvel at formations dubbed the "Wedding Cake," "Crystal Cascade," and "Rainbow Room," and kids delight in those resembling taco shells, lasagna noodles, and pancakes (complete with a melting pat of butter and dripping syrup). At one point the guide played stalactites like chimes—he called it a "rock concert"—and at another (after asking if anyone objected) he turned out the lights to pitch us all briefly into total darkness. If any of your kids are afraid of the dark (or, for that matter, of cramped spaces), you may want to pass this one by. When the lights came back on kids watched for bats and spiders while parents snapped pictures. If there's water running through the stream in the cave, you may get

a little wet; the temperature is a constant 55°, so dress accordingly.

🏠 *Hwy. 180 (80 mi east of Fresno), Sequoia National Forest, tel. 559/736–2708. Admission: $6.50 adults, $3.25 ages 6–12. Open May– early Nov., daily 10–5. Tours leave on the hr.*

California Caverns

(👫 **3–15**) These were the state's first "show caverns," delighting the public as long ago as the Gold Rush days of 1850. Yet the California Caverns have yet to be fully explored—a good indication of their size and complexity. Within the caverns are miles of winding passages, several lakes (some more than 200 feet deep), and spectacular limestone and crystal formations. The basic 60- to 80-minute tours are the best for families with young children, a fairly easy 1-mile walk through 10 connecting underground chambers. Be prepared to negotiate some low ceilings ("bump caps" are provided) and narrow passageways (don't try to carry an infant in a backpack here, although a sling or front pack should be no problem). Wear old walking shoes if you can, because it can get a bit muddy, and dress for 55° temperatures. If your children are at least 8 years old you can take a two- to three-hour tour in spring and late fall; you'll be doing some crawling. In summer and early fall a more advanced tour takes place; children have to be at least 12, and you'll spend three to four hours crawling in mud. The longer tours are each $75 per person. Enjoy.

🏠 *Box 78, Vallecito 95251, tel. 209/736– 2708. 10 mi east of San Andreas via Mountain Ranch Rd. Admission: $7 adults, $4 ages 3–13. Open Memorial Day–Oct., daily 10–5; schedule varies rest of year (closed winter and spring when caverns flood).*

Daffodil Hill

(👫 **ALL**) During three seasons of the year you might not even give Daffodil Hill a second glance. But in spring wildflower season—from around mid-March until mid-

April—its 400,000 bulbs (in 300 different varieties) blossom in a dazzling display of Gold Country color. The 6-acre garden was first planted in the 1850s, and more bulbs (mostly daffodils, with some tulips) are added each year. The atmosphere is noncommercial, and you can walk the hill in an hour or less, or picnic as you enjoy the view.

🏠 *18310 Rams Horn Grade, Volcano, tel. 209/296–7048. Shake Ridge Rd. from Sutter Creek; garden is 3 mi north of Volcano. Contribution optional. Open daily in daffodil season, weather permitting.*

Devil's Postpile National Monument

(👫 **3 – 15**) Volcanic and glacial forces sculpted the striking geologic formation known as Devil's Postpile: a 60-foot-high rocky cliff whose upper reaches are covered with layers of smooth, vertical basalt columns. An easy 10-minute trail from the ranger station takes you to the base (inquire about ranger-led hikes for kids). For us, though, the highlight of our visit was a 2-mile hike past the Postpile to the national monument's second scenic wonder, Rainbow Falls, where the middle fork of the San Joaquin River plunges more than 100 feet over a cliff of volcanic rock. When the water hits the pool below, mists form a rainbow of color; walk down a bit from the top of the falls for the best viewing. The rangers can point you to a shorter though slightly more strenuous route to the falls; but whichever route you take, carry water and, at this high elevation (7,500 feet), stop to rest along the way. In summer you get to the monument via a shuttle bus ($9 adults, $5 ages 5–12), which starts operation as soon as the road opens after snow clearance—usually in June, but sometimes as late as July. The shuttle leaves from the Mammoth Mountain Inn every 20 minutes between 7:30 and 5:30. After Labor Day you can drive the 13 miles (the road is winding but paved) to the monument, until the snows come again, usually

around the first of November. Wonderfully scenic picnic spots dot the bank of the San Joaquin River, both near the parking lot and adjacent to Devil's Postpile itself.

🏠 *Box 501, Mammoth Lakes 93546, tel. in summer, 760/934–2289; in winter, 559/565–3341. Follow Minaret Rd. from Mammoth Lakes. Admission free; camping $12 per night. Open mid-June–late Oct., daily, weather permitting. Call for road conditions.*

General Grant Tree and General Sherman Tree

(👫 **ALL**) If your kids want to see the world's largest living things—bigger than blue whales or Shaquille O'Neal—take them to see the "Generals," who reign over the giant sequoia groves of Kings Canyon and Sequoia national parks (see Chapter 8 for more on these parks). The 2,000-year-old General Grant Tree, centerpiece of the Grant Grove in Kings Canyon (1 mile from Grant Village), has a trunk 40 feet around at the base, wider than a three-lane freeway. It has been proclaimed both the "Nation's Christmas Tree" and a living national shrine in honor of America's war dead. An easy, stroller-accessible ⅓-mile loop trail passes the General Grant as well as the Fallen Monarch, a huge fallen sequoia once used as a hotel, saloon, and horse stable; there's now a tunnel bored through it, which our kids loved to walk in. You'll also see the Centennial Stump, the remains of an enormous sequoia cut in 1875; its outer shell was reassembled and displayed on the East Coast, but folks there refused to believe a tree could be so big. Follow the General's Highway about 10 miles down into Sequoia National Park to see the General Sherman Tree, which is even bigger than the General Grant. Though some other trees are taller or are thicker at the base, the stout and straight General Sherman has the greatest volume of any tree, with 2.7 million pounds of wood—enough to build 40 five-room houses. It's estimated to be around 2,500 years of age, give or take a couple hundred. A 100-yard footpath from the highway takes you to the General Sherman.

🏠 *Kings Canyon/Sequoia National Parks, Three Rivers 93271, tel. 559/565–3134. Generals Hwy. (take Hwy. 180 east from Fresno). Day use: $10 per vehicle (good for both parks for 1 wk). Open daily.*

Mercer Caverns

(👫 3–15) Discovered by a prospector in 1885, Mercer Caverns proved you don't have to find actual nuggets to "strike gold." These caverns, in the thick of Gold Country, contain an array of dazzling and sometimes eerie underground formations, ranging from enormous stalactites and stalagmites to delicate crystalline curtains. Illuminated by colored lights, they go by names such as the "Organ Loft" (found in a vaulted churchlike chamber) and "Chinese Meat Market" (which at least vaguely resembles slabs of meat hanging in a butcher shop). Two children's favorites are "Angel Wings" and "Rapunzel"—the latter formation, naturally, looking very much like a girl with long hair. During the 45-minute tours the guides typically turn out the lights at one point to briefly plunge everyone into total darkness, which may delight—or frighten—small children. Otherwise the walkways are well lighted, though some of the steps are steep. The temperature is a constant 55° inside.

🏠 *Box 509, Murphys 95247, tel. 209/728–2101. Off Hwy. 4, 1 mi north of Murphys; follow Main St., Murphys, to Sheepranch Rd. Admission: $6–$7 adults, $3 ages 5–12. Open Memorial Day–Sept., daily 9–6; Oct.–May, weekends and school holidays 10–4.*

Moaning Cavern

(👫 ALL) Moaning Cavern may be the most spectacular of all the Gold Country's show caverns, boasting the largest underground room in the state; an archaeological site containing what are said to be the oldest human remains found in America; and a 100-foot descending spiral staircase. A 45-

minute tour takes visitors to see the fantastic crystalline formations and giant stalactites and stalagmites. Temperatures are in the low 60s. For an extra $35 you (kids must be at least age 12 and accompanied by an adult) can opt for a 170-foot rappel, a mountaineering-style rope descent into the depths of the cavern. The *truly* adventurous (minimum age 12) can sign up for a two- to three-hour guided trip into undeveloped and unlighted sections of the cavern, using lighted helmets and ropes through small rocky passages. That will cost you $75 a person, and reservations are required.

🏠 *Moaning Cave Rd., Vallecito 95251, tel. 209/736–2708. 7 mi east of Angels Camp off Hwy. 4 and Parrots Ferry Rd. Admission: $7.75 adults, $4 ages 3–17. Open Memorial Day– Oct., daily 9–6; Nov.–Memorial Day, weekdays 10–5, weekends 9–5.*

Mono Lake

(👫 ALL) Few sights in the state are as remarkable as the mysterious tufa towers of Mono Lake, about 8 miles east of Yosemite National Park. Geologists define tufa as porous rock deposits formed underwater, but that doesn't capture the wondrous essence of these white turretlike formations. The best description I've heard came from one excited little girl as she took her first look: "Daddy—there's castle towers floating on the lake!" By far the best vantage point is at the South Tufa area, 5 miles east of Highway 395, south of the town of Lee Vining. From the parking lot, follow the 1-mile Mark Twain Scenic Trail toward the lake. Along the way you'll pass numerous tufa towers that are now on dry land; for decades, Mono Lake has been slowly drying up as a result of Los Angeles's diversion of mountain stream water. This presents an excellent opportunity to help your kids understand the fragility of our natural world. The lake's rapid evaporation has created a crisis in an ecosystem that's a vital breeding ground for more than 70 species of migrating birds— though environmentalists have recently won key battles for the lake's protection and water is once again flowing into the lake. When you reach the lake, have your kids taste the water, which is three times as salty as the ocean (too salty for fish to survive) due to evaporation without enough fresh-water replenishment. Also, have them look closely along the shoreline for the tiny, feathery brine shrimp that inhabit the lake by the trillions, providing food for gulls, grebes, and other migrating birds. The Mono Basin Scenic Area Visitors Center, off Highway 395, north of Lee Vining, contains informative exhibits about the area as well as nice lake overviews and nature trails. Rangers lead 1½-hour interpretive walks in the South Tufa area three times daily in summer and once daily the rest of the year. But an even better way to see the lake is on a one-hour guided canoe tour from nearby Navy Beach ($15 adults, $6 ages 4–12, no children under 4; offered weekends, mid-June to mid-September; tel. 760/647–6595 for reservations). You can also swim at Navy Beach; the salty water is so buoyant that even kids who have never learned to float can bob on the surface—a memorable experience.

🏠 Box 429, Lee Vining 93541, tel. 760/647–3044. Off Hwy. 395. Admission: $2 (at visitors center). Park open daily; visitors center open summer, daily 8:30–5:30; fall–spring, Thurs.–Mon. 9:30–4:30.

San Francisco and the Bay Area

Muir Woods National Monument

(👫 **ALL**) Snuggled in a cool, often foggy redwood-lined canyon on the lower slopes of Mount Tamalpais, 12 miles north of the Golden Gate Bridge, Muir Woods National Monument is the world's most famous stand of old-growth redwoods—the last remnants of soaring trees that once covered the mountain and many parts of the Bay Area.

As California's most visited redwood park, this is definitely nature for the masses: The main hiking trails are paved, and the woods are a regular stop on tour-bus excursions. (Arrive by mid-morning or in late afternoon to avoid the crush.) But the virgin redwoods—accented with green ferns and colorful azaleas, the scents of moss and bay, and the sounds of splashing Redwood Creek—are so majestic that tranquillity still seems to prevail. You won't find the tallest redwoods here—those are farther north—but the trees in Muir Woods do soar to heights of up to 250 feet; many were already growing in the days of the Crusades. There are 6 miles of trails fully within the 560-acre park itself. The trails along the canyon floor are mostly level and suited for strollers, and four bridges spanning Redwood Creek allow you to make short loops. The tallest trees are found along the Main Trail in Bohemian Grove (a ½-mile loop from the parking lot) and Cathedral Grove (a mile loop). Venture a bit farther, along the unpaved trails (such as the 2½-mile round-trip Ben Johnson Trail) that lead up out of the canyon into Mount Tamalpais State Park (see Chapter 14), and you'll be surprised how few other folks you'll meet. No matter how sunny the day may be, bring jackets or sweatshirts; redwoods flourish in cool, foggy climates, and this is one of them. If you'd like to ride a ferry from San Francisco connecting by shuttle bus in Tiburon to Muir Woods, call the Red & White Fleet (tel. 415/447–0597 or 800/229–2784); the cost is $30 round-trip.

🏠 Muir Woods National Monument, Mill Valley 94941, tel. 415/388–2595 or 415/388–2596. U.S. 101 north to Hwy. 1, then Panoramic Hwy. to Muir Woods Rd. Admission: $2 ages 17 and up, 16 and under free. Open daily 8–sunset.

Old Faithful Geyser

(👫 **3 – 15**) This is the Bay Area's answer to Yellowstone: not as famous, to be sure, as that other Old Faithful, but one of only three geysers in the world considered regular enough to warrant the name. Typically, the geyser (in the crater of an extinct volcano) erupts at an average of every 40 minutes, shooting gushes of boiling water and steam as high as 150 feet into the air, for periods of 1 to 1½ minutes. Sometimes, though, it's faithful to a somewhat different clock, erupting anywhere from every 15 minutes to every two or three hours, for up to 14 minutes at a time. Whatever the schedule, it's still a great show—and not nearly as crowded as Yellowstone. (Trivia question for your kids: Where's the third "Old Faithful"? If they answer New Zealand, send them to the head of the class.)

M *1299 Tubbs La., Calistoga 94515, tel. 707/942–6463. 1 mi north of Calistoga. Admission: $6 adults, $2 ages 6–12. Open Apr.–Oct., daily 9–6; Nov.–Mar., daily 9–5.*

Petrified Forest

(**♥♥ ALL**) Calistoga's other natural wonder, the Petrified Forest, is a delight for the budding geologists in your family. How, exactly, does a living thing like a redwood turn to stone? Your kids can find out here, as well as wander among and touch trees that lived 3 *million* years ago. Short, easy-to-follow guided pathways lead past colorful petrified logs that sometimes reach 100 feet and longer. The redwoods were fossilized by being buried in the ashes of ancient volcanic eruptions; a small museum in the gift shop helps explain the process.

M *4100 Petrified Forest Rd., Calistoga 94515, tel. 707/942–6667. 5 mi west of Calistoga. Admission: $3 adults, $1 ages 4–11. Open daily 10–5.*

Central Coast and Valley

Big Sur

(**♥♥ 2–15**) If this landscape doesn't get your kids' attention, nothing in nature will. Winding for 93 miles along Highway 1, from just south of the Carmel Highlands to San Simeon, Big Sur is a continually unfolding panorama of sheer scenic wonder. You'll pass rocky bluffs that plunge precipitously to the ocean, lush green forests and valleys, dramatically bridged canyons, mountain cliffs that seem to rise right up out of the roadside—plus waterfalls, redwoods, secluded beaches, and perhaps sea otters frolicking along the shore or a whale spouting at sea. To best appreciate Big Sur with children, plan some stops along the way, starting with hiking at Pfeiffer Big Sur State Park (see Chapter 8). Next, exactly 1.1 miles south of the state park exit, look for a "Narrow Road" sign on the right side of the highway; drive 2½ miles down it to secluded Pfeiffer Beach, another longtime favorite of ours, for picnicking and sand play ($5 parking). Three other state parks along Big Sur, Garrapata, Andrew Molera, and Julia Pfeiffer Burns, also have beaches and hiking trails. (Don't miss the short Waterfall Trail at Julia Pfeiffer Burns.) Gas stations are few and far between in Big Sur, so fill your tank before setting off, and bring a picnic lunch—the scattered restaurants and lodgings along the route are often crowded in summer and on weekends. Try to complete your Big Sur drive before nightfall, when the winding roads get awfully dark.

M *Monterey Peninsula Chamber of Commerce and Visitors and Convention Bureau, Box 1770, 380 Alvarado St., Monterey 93942, tel. 831/649–1770. Admission free except $6 day use fee good for same-day admission to Pfeiffer Big Sur, Andrew Molera, and Julia Pfeiffer Burns state parks. Open daily.*

Carrizo Plain Natural Area

(**♥♥ 6–15**) It takes some effort to get to and explore the Carrizo Plain, a remote, treeless, largely arid basin nestled between the Temblor and Caliente mountain ranges, an hour's drive from both the coast and the Central Valley. Our family stumbled upon it by chance when taking a shortcut between I–5 and Highway 101. It's a glorious view of what the San Joaquin Valley looked like before civilization set in. If they look closely, kids may spot pronghorn antelope and tule elk, a tiny San Joaquin kit fox, or a blunt-nosed leopard lizard; this protected area contains many rare and endangered species, both animals and plants. You can also get a terrific view of the notorious San Andreas Fault, visible from an overlook, and some of the finest remaining examples of prehistoric Native American rock art (a 1½-mile round-trip walking trail leads from a parking area to Painted Rock); from mid-October till late February thousands of sandhill cranes congregate around Soda Lake, which is dry most of the rest of the year. Prime time to visit the Carrizo Plain is the spring, when wildflowers turn the grasslands into a sea of yellows, oranges, blues, magentas, russets, and golds against a background of deep green. Avoid this place in summer, though, when temperatures often soar to 100°F or more (with no root beer stands in sight). You'll find portable toilets at the Painted Rock parking area; bring your own drinking water—this is a primitive region. The northern part of Soda Lake Road is the only paved road, and dirt roads may be temporarily closed following winter rains.

🏛 *Soda Lake Rd., California Valley, tel. 661/ 475–2717. Hwy. 58 east from Hwy. 101, north of San Luis Obispo; at California Valley, take Soda Lake Rd. 8 mi south. Admission free. Open daily.*

Moreton Bay Fig Tree

(👫 **ALL**) Although our kids have seen the world's tallest and largest trees during their travels through the state, I don't think they've ever exclaimed so loudly as when they first beheld the gargantuan Moreton Bay Fig Tree in Santa Barbara. Its visual impact, I suspect, is increased by the fact that it stands alone in the middle of a city—an unexpected setting for a natural wonder. Planted in 1877, it's the United States' largest Moreton Bay fig (a species native to Australia), with branches that span 160 feet, equivalent to half a football field. The tree is said to be able to shade as many as 10,000 people on a sunny day. On the morning of our visit, however, we had the tree to ourselves, and the kids immediately took to scrambling over its huge roots, which extend like a giant's gnarled fingers over the ground.

🏛 *Chapala and Montecito Sts., Santa Barbara, tel. 805/965–3023. 1 block south of Hwy. 101. Admission free. Open daily.*

Morro Rock

(👫 **ALL**) This enormous dome-shape rock, which rises to a height of 576 feet, dominates the waterfront of the Mediterranean-style fishing village of Morro Bay. A State Historic Landmark, it's the most dramatically situated of a series of volcanic outcroppings that rise along this stretch of the Central Coast. Because the rock is connected to the mainland by a narrow isthmus, you can drive out to its base. Morro Rock is an ecological preserve; the whole area teems with bird life such as pelicans, egrets, blue herons, and endangered Peregrine falcons. There are plenty of distractions in the immediate vicinity: a sandy beach (with picnic tables and rest rooms), the Embarcadero along the Morro Bay harbor, and Morro Bay State Park (tel. 805/772–7434 or 805/772–9723) at the southern end of town, which has fishing, bird-watching, boating, and camping; day use admission for some areas is $6 per car. The park's Museum of Natural History (tel. 805/772–2694; $3 adults, $1 ages 6–12; open daily 10–5) occupies a perch overlooking the bay and has interesting exhibits on local wildlife.

🏛 *Waterfront, Morro Bay, tel. 805/772–4467. Follow Main St. to Embarcadero. Admission free. Open daily.*

Natural Bridges State Beach

(👫 **ALL**) The beaches of Santa Cruz are best known for surfing and sunning, but this prime stretch of sand holds two natural wonders. The first is the beach's namesake, a giant natural sandstone arch that stands regally in the water just offshore. Three of these natural bridges, sculpted by the swirling power of waves, stood here until around 1900; early residents of Santa Cruz used to picnic and even hold weddings on top of them. The other two fell down in this century, the victims of wave erosion and storms; the remaining one will eventually succumb to the same forces, so see it now (bring a picnic lunch, but eat it on the beach). It's not safe to try to swim through the natural bridge; the waves are powerful here. The second natural wonder is the Monarch Grove, site of one of the greatest annual migrations of monarch butterflies along the Pacific Coast. From mid-October through February, arriving from nesting grounds as far away as the northern Rocky Mountains, thousands of monarchs winter here in a grove of eucalyptus trees near the beach. Clustered in the trees they resemble big pine cones—until they start to fly around when the temperature warms. On the day of our visit on a late November afternoon some 30,000 monarchs were present, many fluttering madly about as they returned to the trees for the evening. An easy boardwalk trail leads from the beach parking lot to the Monarch Grove; a visitors center provides a trail map and fascinating exhibits on the life cycles of monarchs. Several generations of butterflies live and die before the next migration occurs—yet each year the latest generation returns like clockwork to the same sites.

🏛 *End of West Cliff Dr., Santa Cruz, tel. 831/ 423–4609. Parking: $6 per car. Open daily 8– sunset. Visitors center open mid-Oct.–Feb., daily 10–4; Mar.–mid-Oct., Fri.–Mon. 10–4.*

Pinnacles National Monument

(👫 3–15) The distinctive crags and spires of huge boulders, remnants of an ancient volcano, form the shapes that give this park its name; it's nature's version of a Gothic cathedral. Pinnacles is a bit off the main highways but well worth the drive if your children are old enough for moderate hiking. The park is divided into two sections—East Pinnacles and West Pinnacles—with completely separate entrances off two unconnected roads; most visitors choose one section or the other, though you can hike between the two. East Pinnacles is more woodsy, with some large shaded picnic areas; West Pinnacles lies in high desert country, with clearer vistas of the geologic formations. Both have non-reservable campgrounds (the East campground is privately owned and just outside the park), and each has its own visitors center: Bear Gulch in the East, Chaparral in the West. At both you can find maps, and, for kids 8 to 13, Junior Ranger Program activity books. In East Pinnacles our family enjoyed the easy trail to the Bear Gulch Caves, a one-hour round-trip hike from the visitors center. The caves have stone steps and handrails to ease passage, but you must do some maneuvering through narrow spaces in the dark (flashlights are essential!); in the spring the caves may also be wet. In West Pinnacles we liked the Balconies Caves trail, a 2-mile, 1½-hour round-trip. These caves, larger and longer than those at Bear Gulch (again, carry flashlights), were formed when long-ago earthquakes and erosion hurled a group of massive boulders onto each other. Returning from the caves, we took the alternate Balconies Cliffs route, which adds an extra ½ mile (almost all *up*), but provides dramatic scenery for energetic hikers. Hot and dry in summer, the Pinnacles are best in spring or fall, when temperatures are cooler; carry drinking water in any season, as none is available on the trails.

🏛 *5000 Hwy. 146, Paicines 95043, tel. 831/ 389–4485. East Pinnacles entrance: Hwy. 25 about 32 mi south of Hollister, turn right on Rte. 146 and drive west 5 mi. West Pinnacles entrance: Rte. 146 northeast 11 mi from Soledad. Admission: $4 per car (good for 1 wk). Camping: $10–$24 per night, 138 total sites; tel. 831/389–4485 (West) or 831/389– 4462 (East). Park open daily. Visitors centers open daily 9–5.*

San Diego and the Southern Deserts

Antelope Valley California Poppy Reserve

(ⵊ 3 – 15) In spring wildflower season this one is worth driving a bit out of your way to see. In the high desert near Lancaster, the reserve blooms with acres of golden poppies and other wildflowers following winter and spring rains—the best poppy displays in the state. Good viewing times range generally between mid-March and mid-May, but even in April one year we missed the peak blossoms by a week or so; in other words, call first or take your chances. Eight miles of trails loop through the rolling hills, and there's a nice visitors center where kids can pick up pictures of poppies to color.
🏠 15101 W. Lancaster Rd., Lancaster 93536, tel. 661/724–1180 or 661/942–0662. 13 mi west of Hwy. 14; from Lancaster follow Ave. I, which becomes Lancaster Rd. Admission: $5 per vehicle. Visitors center open mid-Mar.–mid-May, weekdays 9–4, weekends 9–5.

Mitchell Caverns

(ⵊ 6 – 15) You can take 1½-hour guided tours of Mitchell Caverns, a subterranean land—the only limestone caverns in the California state park system (others are run privately)—of stalagmites and stalactites, helictites and draperies, curtains and popcorn (as the geological formations are colorfully known). The caverns lie within the Providence Mountains State Recreation Area, 60 miles west of Needles off I–40. (If you're driving from the Grand Canyon to Los Angeles, you'll probably pass fairly close to it.) Because of the desert heat most visitors arrive from October to May, though the caverns themselves are a comfortable 65°F year-round. Expect to walk about 1½ miles total getting to and through the caves; wear sensible shoes for the cave surface. Call

before heading here to make sure you can get a spot on a tour.
🏠 Box 1, Essex 92332, tel. 661/942–0662. From I–40, follow Essex Rd. 17 mi north. Admission: $6 adults, $3 ages 6–12. Tours Labor Day–Memorial Day, daily; in summer, weekends. Call for times.

Red Rock Canyon State Park

(ⵊ 6 – 15) If young movie fans want to see where the desert (dinosaur-bone-digging) scenes in *Jurassic Park* were filmed—or parents want to view a scenic landscape used in many old Western films—head for isolated Red Rock Canyon, where colorful cliffs and rock formations attract a mix of Hollywood directors, geologists, and adventurous families. Layers of red, pink, white, and black sediment give the high-desert canyons a rainbow glow. The best times to visit are spring (when wildflowers may be abundant) and fall; summer can get broiling and winter quite cold. You can camp here at 50 primitive sites. Ask at the visitors center or call the park office for information about guided nature hikes and campfire programs.
🏠 1051 W. Ave. M, Suite 201, Lancaster 93534, tel. 661/942–0662. 25 mi northeast of Mojave along Hwy. 14. Day-use admission: $5 per vehicle. Camping (no reservations): $10 per night. Visitors center open spring and fall, Fri.–Sun. 10–4.

Salton Sea

(ⵊ 6 – 15) This natural wonder is certainly wonderful; whether it's natural is a subject of debate. Between 1905 and 1907, canals built to divert irrigation water from the Colorado River to the Imperial Valley flooded over, filling part of the huge, then-dry Salton Basin. Technically, that makes this an artificial lake. But the Salton Basin was filled with water many times in ancient ages—the last lake dried up only about 400 years ago—so geologists believe that, canals or no, the Colorado River would eventually have flooded the basin naturally. What we are left with is a remarkable inland sea about an hour's drive southeast from Palm Springs. At 234 feet below sea level, it's one of the lowest points in the country. And with 115 miles of shoreline, it's now the largest inland body of water west of the Rockies, growing ever larger through annual runoff of agricultural waters. This salty new water, added to the salt left from past evaporated lakes on the site, makes the name "Salton" Sea highly appropriate. The runoff has not occurred without ecological consequences, though much progress has been made in recent years repairing the damage. On the northeast shores, the Salton Sea State Recreation Area offers a total of 125 developed family campsites at two locations; an additional three primitive campgrounds with 1,450 sites are scattered around the lake. There's also fishing, boating, a nature trail, and good swimming at Mecca Beach. On the lake's southern shores, the marshes and freshwater ponds of the Salton Sea National Wildlife Refuge attract huge numbers of shorebirds and waterfowl: ducks, Canada geese, sandpipers, snowy egrets, great blue herons. Best viewing times are fall through spring (it's too hot in summer). Some hiking is required, as most refuge roads and trails are closed to visitors; get maps and suggestions from refuge headquarters.

🏕 *State Recreation Area: 100-225 State Park Rd., North Shore, tel. 760/393–3052. Hwy. 111 southeast from I–10. Day use: $5 per car. Camping: $10–$20 per night; tel. 800/ 444–7275. Visitors center open mid-Oct.–Apr., daily 9–4. Wildlife Refuge: 906 W. Sinclair Rd., Calipatria 92233, tel. 760/348–5278. Rte. 111, 4 mi south of Niland to Sinclair Rd., then west 7 mi. Admission free. Refuge open sunrise–sunset. Headquarters open daily 7–3:30.*

FROM YOSEMITE TO PATRICK'S POINT
STATE AND NATIONAL PARKS

8

When it's time to head for the great outdoors, California has a state or national park ideal for every family, ranging from world-famous destinations such as Yosemite and Sequoia national parks to little-known gems such as Patrick's Point and Montana de Oro state parks. Like to camp? Pitch your tent among towering redwoods, on a mountain lake, or along the Pacific Coast. (California state parks alone contain more than 17,500 campsites.) Only have time for a day hike? Take your kids on trails along wild rivers, through forests—even up a mountain. Like to fish, swim, or go boating? All of these activities, and much more, are available in some of the most beautiful settings imaginable.

With more than 300 state and national parks in California, it's impossible to detail all of them here. (You'll find others discussed in Chapters 4, 7, 10, and 14–18) For information about national parks in California, contact the National Park Service (Western Region Information Center, Fort Mason, Bldg. 201, San Francisco 94123, tel. 415/556–0560). For a concise guide to all California state parks, send for the *Official Guide to California State Parks* (California State Park Store, Box 942896, Sacramento 94296; enclose $2); the 120-page *Visitor's Guide to California State Parks* costs $14.95, from the same address). Or dial 916/653–6995 for general state park information. Unless otherwise noted, campground reservations may be made by calling (in the United States and Canada) 800/444–7275 for state parks and 800/365–2267 for selected national parks (Channel Islands, Death Valley, Joshua Tree, and Sequoia); for Yosemite, call 800/436–7275. If you're calling from outside the U.S. or Canada, call 916/638–5883 for state parks, and 310/722–1257 for national parks. For most parks, reservations are advised between Memorial Day and Labor Day and during major holiday weekends. For state parks, call up to seven months in advance but at least 48 hours before arrival; for national parks that require reservations, call up to five months in advance.

Fees for most state park campgrounds run from $7 to $28 per night (the average is $14), plus a $7.50 nonrefundable reservation charge if applicable; cancellation (tel. 800/695–2269) charges are $7, but you can book a new reservation within the same call for no additional fee. Fees for most national park campgrounds run between $6 and $16 per night, plus reservation charge if applicable. Day-use entrance fees for state and national parks range from $2 to $20 per vehicle. An annual day-use pass to the whole state park system, good for parking and picnicking, costs $75 for one family vehicle, plus $20 for a second vehicle; a permit for towing a boat behind your car costs $125. Senior citizens age 62 and up can get state park discounts on both camping and day-use fees. Golden Bear passes for certain limited-income state residents are $3.50 per year. An annual Golden Eagle pass ($50) allows free entrance to all national parks, as does a Golden Age pass ($10 for age 62 and over) and Golden Access pass (free for blind or permanently disabled citizens).

To get the most out of the parks you visit, stop by their ranger stations or visitors centers to pick up information and permits and view exhibits. While you're there, ask about programs for kids and families, which most parks offer during peak visiting periods. Unless otherwise noted, all these parks are open daily year-round. Opening times for visitors centers are also noted, but, because of continuing budget cuts at both state and national levels, they may have limited hours.

Northern Forests and Lakes

Humboldt Redwoods State Park

(👫 **ALL**) After Muir Woods, the most frequently visited redwoods in California are in Humboldt Redwoods State Park. Yet most travelers see only those trees along the Avenue of the Giants, the scenic roadway that cuts through the heart of the park (see Chapter 7). A bit off the highway, though, are groves of redwoods that have been called "the greatest spectacle of woodland on earth"—fully one-eighth of the world's old-growth redwood forests. These are trees that are at least 250 years old, soar to heights of 300 feet and above, and live as long as 2,000 years. Seven exits fan off from the Avenue of the Giants into the park, leading to nearly 100 miles of hiking trails. The visitors center, halfway along Avenue of the Giants, has information about ranger-led hikes and activities for kids, plus hands-on nature exhibits in the children's Discovery Corner. A few miles north is the Founders Grove, dedicated to those who founded the Save-the-Redwoods League in the 1920s, which helped rescue the state's

ancient trees from the logger's ax. The gentle ½-mile Founders Tree Trail, the park's most popular hike, leads to the 362-foot-high Founders Tree and the 500-ton Dyerville Giant, which was nearly 370 feet tall when it crashed to the ground in 1991. After viewing its massive roots, have your kids look straight up to where its huge canopy used to be; it seems to have left a hole in the sky. Nearby Mattole (Honeydew) Road leads about 5 miles west to the Rockefeller Forest, the world's largest grove of old-growth redwoods. Park in the "Big Trees Area" lot and take the short trail to the Giant Tree—363 feet high and 53.2 feet around—which has replaced the Dyerville Giant as the "champion coast redwood" (for combined height, circumference, and crown spread). Nearby you'll find the Tall Tree (nearly 360 feet high) and the Flatiron Tree (shaped like a flatiron). In season float along the Eel River on inner tubes, pick berries, view wildflowers, and fish for salmon or steelhead.

🏠 *Box 100, Weott 95571, tel. 707/946–2409. Off Hwy. 101, 200 mi north of San Francisco. Day use: $5 per vehicle collected only at Williams Grove and Woman's Federation Grove. 3 campgrounds (250 sites; $12–$16 per night) open year-round; rest rooms, showers. Visitors center open May–Sept., daily 9–5; Oct.–Apr., Thurs.–Sun. 10–4.*

Jedediah Smith Redwoods State Park

ALL   This is my favorite of California's 30 redwood parks. It has idyllic camping, hiking (20 miles of trails), picnicking, and fishing amid majestic trees and along the wild and scenic Smith River, the largest undammed river in California. Because it's tucked up in the state's far northwestern corner, 360 miles north of San Francisco, Jedediah Smith Redwoods gets far fewer visitors than many lesser parks to the south. But the locals are on such close terms with it, they call it "Jed." The visitors center hands out information about summertime ranger-led activities for children and families. Nearby, picnic tables rest in a grove of trees along the riverbank; there's a sandy beach, too, though swimming can be treacherous. An easy ½-mile self-guided nature trail threads through virgin redwoods, and the beautiful 2-mile Hiouchi Trail winds along the river. Alternatively, you can float down the Smith River in an inner tube, go canoeing, kayaking, or fish for salmon and steelhead (anyone age 16 or older requires a state sport fishing license). On summer evenings rangers lead campfire programs. A woodsy ½-mile trail encircles the Stout Memorial Grove, which many consider the single finest stand of virgin redwoods in the world. In summer you can reach it on a short hike from the campground across a footbridge; at other times of the year, however, you must drive by way of Howland Hill Road, a narrow and unpaved old stagecoach route that runs 6 miles from Crescent City, passing through an astonishingly beautiful stand of giant redwoods.

🏡 *1375 Elk Valley Rd., Crescent City 95531, tel. 707/464–6101. Hwy. 199, 9 mi northeast of Crescent City. Day use: $5 per vehicle (collected in developed area only). 1 campground (107 sites; $12–$16 per night) open year-round; rest rooms, showers. Visitors center open Memorial Day–Labor Day, daily 9–5.*

Lassen Volcanic National Park

3–15   Who says kids can't climb a mountain? At Lassen Volcanic National Park even some preschoolers can reach the summit of a 10,500-foot-high snowcapped peak. Lassen Peak, which last erupted in 1914, is the southernmost volcano in the Cascade Range and the centerpiece of this wonderfully scenic park, which also has lava pinnacles, cinder cones, boiling mud pots, glacier-carved canyons, pine forests, and alpine lakes and meadows. Much of it is wilderness and rivals Yosemite for beauty, yet it's far less crowded. One main road, state Highway 89, winds 29 miles through the more developed western half of the park; the visitors center is near the northwest entrance; an information station is at the other end of the road. Near the northwest entrance is Manzanita Lake, site of picnic areas and a level 1½-mile loop hike around the lake that's ideal for young children. From Manzanita Lake the road climbs another 1,000 feet to Summit Lake, site of two tree-shaded campgrounds. You'll find more picnicking in alpine surroundings at Kings Creek, where a popular 3-mile round-trip trail leads to Kings Creek Falls. Drive on to Lassen Peak, where you can park in a lot near rest rooms and picnic tables. The trail to the top does look daunting: The snowcapped summit is 2,000 feet above, reached via a series of 40 steep switchbacks. It's a 5-mile round-trip climb, which takes four or five hours; you'll need food, water, jackets, sunscreen, and sturdy walking shoes. Rest stops are essential (at this altitude we sometimes found ourselves gasping for air). The trail quickly passes beyond the tree line, and it borders an ice floe that sweeps down the eastern side of the peak. To reach the summit you'll cross over a glacier (where we had a brief snowball fight, though it was *summer*) and climb to the top of a craggy peak, where you can take pictures of each other like conquerors of a mini-Everest. The descent takes about 1½ hours.

A few minutes down the road from Lassen Peak trailhead is the Bumpass Hell parking lot, where a picturesque, moderately strenuous, 3-mile round-trip trail leads to the park's largest geothermal area. Bumpass Hell (named by its discoverer who lost his leg in the boiling waters) provides close-up looks—and smells—of hissing steam vents, bubbling fountains, roiling mud pots, and rumbling fumaroles. The area is safe as long as you stay on the boardwalks; a few visitors who've ventured off the paths have been severely burned, however, so watch kids closely. You can continue along the mountainous trail to Cold Boiling Lake, a four-hour round-trip hike. The alpine scenery is right out of Switzerland: spectacular views of snow-capped peaks, waterfalls, mountain lakes, and meadows blanketed with wildflowers. Another active geothermal area, Sulphur Works, lies just off Highway 89 about 5 miles south of Bumpass Hell. A bit farther down the road is the Lassen Chalet Café, where you can eat at outdoor tables with views of Lassen Peak. The southwest entrance station is nearby.

Prime time to visit Lassen Park is between mid-July and the end of September. Rangers lead nature programs and hikes from late June until Labor Day, and, from mid-January to early April, snowshoe hikes on the fringes of the park. Parts of Highway 89 are closed by November, usually not reopening until Memorial Day or even mid-June. Campground and visitors center opening and closing dates are dependent on weather and budgets. One lodge, Drakesbad Guest Ranch (see Chapter 12), is within park boundaries, but in the remote eastern section.

🏠 *Box 100, Mineral 96063, tel. 530/595–4444. Northwest entrance 1-hr drive from Redding on Hwy. 44; southwest entrance 1-hr drive from Red Bluff on Hwy. 36. Admission: $5 per vehicle (good for 1 wk). 7 nonreservation campgrounds (about 400 sites), open Memorial Day–Sept.; fees $8–$12 per night. (One campground open for snow camping in winter.) Visitors centers open June–Labor Day, daily 9–5.*

Patrick's Point State Park

(🚻 **2 – 15**) This is a "sleeper" that relatively few people know about, but those who do keep returning again and again. Patrick's Point State Park is small, off the beaten path in far Northern California, and overshadowed by the great redwood parks nearby. Yet it's a gem, blessed with an agate-studded beach, stunning views of the Pacific, picnic areas, bike trails, hiking trails through old-growth Sitka spruce trees, and opportunities to view California gray whales, sea lions, and harbor seals. Start by taking the short, steep (though not hazardous) hike down to Agate Beach, a wide, 2-mile-long strip of sand backed by sheer cliffs, where your kids can spend hours combing for water-polished semiprecious agates along the shore. (Riptides can be perilous, though, so don't enter the surf here.) At low tide—either at Agate Beach or at Palmer's Point or Abalone Point to the south—you can take your kids tidepooling, to observe (but not disturb) abundant sea life such as hermit crabs, anemones, even octopi. Next, follow the 2-mile-long Rim Trail, which connects to several short trails leading to rocky bluffs such as Patrick's Point and Wedding Rock, jutting out dramatically over the ocean. These are also excellent vantage points for watching sea lions on the offshore rocks and for spotting whales during their annual winter and spring migrations. Watch small children carefully along the bluffs; the cliffs are steep, the waves powerful. Away from the coastline, the Octopus Trees Trail leads to unusual trees named for their tentacle-like root formations. You can also visit the Yurok Village of Sumeg (open daily), consisting of dwellings and other redwood structures built in traditional style by local Native Americans. One weekend in June or July each year, there's a Yurok celebration (Sumek Village Days) involving traditional dancing and cultural ceremonies.

🏠 *4150 Patrick's Point Dr., Trinidad 95570, tel. 707/677–3570. 5 mi north of Trinidad, ½ mi west of Hwy. 101. Day use: $5 per vehicle.*

3 campgrounds (124 sites; $12–$16 per night) open year-round as needed; rest rooms. Information center open May–Sept. daily; hrs vary.

Prairie Creek Redwoods State Park

👫 ALL) Because of the routing for U.S. 101, you could unknowingly drive right past this beautiful state park, with its herds of grazing Roosevelt elk, giant redwoods, fern-blanketed canyon, and wild and remote beach. It's north of Redwood National Park (see *below*). Six miles north of Orick, pick up Newton B. Drury Parkway (formerly Elk Prairie Parkway), which roughly parallels 101 as it winds 8 miles through the redwoods before rejoining the highway. Tell the kids to watch for elk grazing along the roadway, though you should caution them never to approach these or any other wild animals. The parkway leads to the visitors center; behind the center, the Five Minute Trail leads past the Chimney Tree, left hollow by fire, and the slightly more strenuous 1½-mile Nature Trail heads off for an informative introduction to the redwoods. Along the parkway look for the Big Tree Wayside parking area, where you follow a very short paved trail to Big Tree, a majestic redwood 304 feet tall, 64 feet around, and 1,500 years old. If you have a few hours to spend in the park, find narrow, unpaved Davison Road (take the parkway south back to Highway 101 and go another 2 miles south), which leads to Gold Bluffs Beach—a 10-mile-long, wild, scenic stretch of coast where you can picnic and beachcomb. Fern Canyon, reached via the beach, is a steep, 50-foot walled canyon whose sides are covered by lush ferns; it's a magical sight, and there's a ¾-mile loop trail here easy enough for many 4-year-olds to handle.

🏠 *1375 Elk Valley Rd., Crescent City 95531, tel. 707/464–6101. Day use: $5 (collected at Gold Bluffs Beach only). 2 campgrounds (100 sites; $12–$16 per night) open year-round; rest rooms, showers. Visitors center open daily 9–5.*

Redwood National Park

👫 ALL) Along with the adjacent state parks (including Jedediah Smith and Prairie Creek, see *above*), Redwood National Park is like a shrine for nature's tallest living things, the coast redwoods. Hugging the northern coast of California for some 40 miles, it contains four out of five of the world's tallest known trees, although the 367.8-foot-high tree once considered the tallest lost its top, and probably its top ranking, in a storm a few years back. Though no one knows for sure, park rangers believe the new "tallest tree" stands about 364 feet. Families can hike among these ancient giants and along magnificent, often deserted beaches. If you're approaching from the south, stop at the Redwood information center, on Highway 101 east of Orick, to pick up maps and trail guides and watch for shorebirds along the wetlands boardwalk. This is also the place to get an access permit for the 20-mile drive to the Tall Trees Trail, running along Redwood Creek in a remote area of the park, where the most spectacular trees are. Permits are issued free daily from 9 to 1; get there early in summer. Trailers are prohibited. The Tall Trees Trail itself is 3 miles round-trip, including a very steep, difficult climb on the return; allow at least 4½ hours for the entire outing. The trail is sometimes closed because of storm damage, but if you're unable to make this excursion, don't despair—there's still plenty to see in the park. Go ½ mile north of Orick on Highway 101 to Bald Hills Road, which will take you to the 1-mile Lady Bird Johnson Grove Nature Loop Trail, one of the best family hiking spots. The easy self-guided interpretive trail (wheelchair accessible) follows an old logging road through an old-growth redwood forest; it was designated a national park in 1968. Or go north about 25 miles on 101 to the Lagoon Creek Rest Area to pick up the Yurok Loop Trail, a self-guided 1-mile walk around Native American territory. Several other trails lead to and along the beaches; one we liked was the Hidden Beach Trail, which starts across the highway from the Trees of Mystery theme park north of

Klamath (see Chapter 9). This round-trip trail through the woods is a bit longer than a mile, and the secluded beach it leads to is a drift-wood-strewn beauty on a bay. We also enjoyed a hike along gorgeous Crescent Beach, reached via Endert's Beach Road (turn south off of Highway 101 southeast of Crescent City); you can picnic here, watch sand-pipers, and build sand castles.

🏠 *1111 2nd St., Crescent City 95531, tel. 707/464–6101. Admission free. 3 primitive hike-in campgrounds (25 sites) open year-round. Information center open Memorial Day–Labor Day, daily 9–6; Labor Day–Memorial Day, daily 8–5.*

Sierra and the Gold Country

Calaveras Big Trees State Park

(👫 ALL) Back in the 1850s and '60s, after word of their "discovery" by a back-woods hunter spread around the world, the Calaveras Big Trees were the most cele-brated of all the giant sequoias, the largest things ever to have lived on earth. (Sequoias are cousins of the coastal redwoods, but tend to be thicker in the trunk, somewhat shorter, and longer lived—3,000 years old or more.) In those Gold Rush days the first thought was of economic exploitation, and the initially sighted "Discovery Tree," more than 300 feet tall and 24 feet in base diame-ter, was felled to create a traveling exhibit. The stump was then planed smooth and used as a dance floor. Near today's visitors center the Big Stump is the first stop on the 1-mile self-guiding North Grove Trail, a level, gentle, informative hike through the sequoias that's ideal for young children. (Lia's visit to the Big Stump at age 9 was one of her most memorable lessons in ecology.) Don't miss the special 600-foot-long Three Senses Trail, which starts in front of the Big Stump, letting kids touch, smell, and hear the

forest. The far larger but more remote South Grove is best for families with older children; hike in from the Beaver Creek Pic-nic Area parking lot to reach the South Grove Trail, a 3½-mile loop. You can also go wading in shallow Beaver Creek, or fish or swim in the Stanislaus River here. Ranger-guided hikes are available daily in summer in the North Grove and once or twice a week in the South Grove. In winter there are guided snowshoe hikes in the North Grove, as well as cross-country skiing.

🏠 *Box 120, Arnold 95223, tel. 209/795–2334. On Hwy. 4, 4 mi northeast of Arnold. Day use: $5 per vehicle. 2 campgrounds (129 sites; $12–$16 per night), some open year-round; rest rooms, showers. Visitors center (tel. 209/795–3840) open May–mid-June, daily 11–3; mid-June–Labor Day, daily 10–4; Labor Day–Apr., weekends 11–3, weather permitting.*

D. L. Bliss State Park

(👫 3 – 15) If I had to choose only one hike to take at Lake Tahoe, I'd pick the Rubicon Trail, which begins above Rubicon Bay in D. L. Bliss State Park. Winding along the rim of Tahoe's spectacular southwest shore, this immensely enjoyable trail has gorgeous scenery along with some moderately chal-lenging climbing—up and down hills, over roots and rocks, and around huge boulders. It's 4½ miles to Emerald Bay (see *below*), though you can get a good feel for the trail in a third of that. About a mile or so along, ask your kids to spot the old lighthouse (look above and to the right).

Even without tackling the Rubicon, D. L. Bliss should be a priority stop at Tahoe. It has sandy beaches with shallow waters suitable for swimming (though temperatures are pretty cold except, perhaps, in August and September); there are picnic tables near the beach, though be warned that the parking lots fill up early in summer. Or try the easy ½-mile self-guided Balancing Rock Nature Trail, which leads to a 130-ton eroded gran-ite boulder resting rather precariously on its foundation.

🏕 *Box 266, Tahoma 96142, tel. 530/525–7277. On Hwy. 89, 17 mi south of Tahoe City. Day use: $5 per vehicle. 168 campsites ($12–$21 per night), open Memorial Day–mid-Sept.; rest rooms, showers. Park open late May–mid-Oct., daily, weather permitting.*

Emerald Bay State Park

(👫 **3 – 15**)　Adjacent to and south of D. L. Bliss (see *above*), Emerald Bay State Park is set on Lake Tahoe's most scenic and photogenic shoreline, with justifiably famous views of shimmering blue-green Emerald Bay, rocky cliffs, pines, peaks, and tiny Fannette (Tahoe's only island). Every time we visit we can't resist taking more pictures. Park in the large parking lot at Emerald Bay Overlook (it fills up fast in summer), right off the dramatic curves of Highway 89, and let your kids scramble among the rocks while you soak in the views. Or take the steep, snaking 1-mile trail down to the bay and to Vikingsholm, a historic 38-room replica of a medieval Norse castle, which you can tour from June to September ($3 adults, $2 ages 5–12). Kids often like to wade at the small beach in front of the castle. Be prepared for a wicked climb back up. A much smaller parking lot across the highway provides access to a shaded picnic area and the Eagle Falls Trail, a steep ¼-mile climb (great exercise) to the lower cascades of Eagle Falls.

🏕 *Box 266, Tahoma 96142, tel. 530/525–7277. Hwy. 89, 22 mi south of Tahoe City. Day use: $5 per vehicle (no fee collected at Emerald Bay Overlook). 100 campsites ($12–$16 per night), open late May–Labor Day, weather permitting, plus boat camp (20 sites; $9 per night) accessible only by boat or on foot; rest rooms, showers.*

Kings Canyon National Park

(👫 **ALL**)　Only a small portion of Kings Canyon National Park is accessible by car, and many travelers miss much of that, stopping only at the celebrated Grant Grove of giant sequoias (see Chapter 7), and its visitors center (tel. 559/335–2856) for exhibits, information, and guided walks (ask about special kids' activities). But from late spring through October, when the road usually closes because of snow, you can make a dramatic descent by car into Kings Canyon itself—the deepest canyon in North America (yes, deeper than the Grand Canyon). The drive along Kings Canyon Highway (Highway 180) comes complete with vistas of wild rivers, waterfalls, and glacial rocks. Starting north of Grant Grove, the highway leaves the park for 30 miles, cutting across the Sequoia National Forest and winding down, down, and still farther down into the depths of the canyon, following the turbulent South Fork of the Kings River and passing Boyden Cavern (see Chapter 7). At Junction View, where the Middle and South Forks flow together, you'll see the deepest part of the canyon—nearly 8,000 feet—as well as distant peaks up to 13,000 feet high. You'll reenter the national park at Cedar Grove Village, where you'll find a visitors center (tel. 209/565–3793) with ranger programs (some just for kids), a lodge, a campground, a market, and a restaurant. There are several scenic stops along the road from here on. Roaring River Falls, reached on a short stroller-accessible trail, surges out of a mountainside and plunges into a deep, dark pool of water. Zumwalt Meadow Trail is an easy 1½-mile walk that winds along the Kings River. Canyon View marks the spot that inspired the great 19th-century naturalist John Muir to call Kings Canyon even grander than Yosemite Valley. At Road's End, 6 miles past Cedar Grove, longer trails lead off into the wilderness, or take the short trail to flat Muir Rock, where Muir once made conservationist speeches by the river; it's a nice scenic stroll for young kids. Then return up Highway 180 for 30 slow, winding uphill miles back to Grant Village, where you can swing south on the Generals Highway into Sequoia National Park (see *below*). You can stay in the park at either Grant Grove Lodge or, in season, at Cedar Grove Lodge; or camp at one of seven campgrounds with 720 sites, more than 100 open year-round. Horseback riding is available at Grant Grove Stables (tel. 209/565–3464), ½ mile north of the visitors center.

🏠 *Ash Mountain Headquarters, Three Rivers 93271; information, tel. 559/565–3134 or 559/565–3341; lodging reservations, tel. 559/561–3314 or 559/335–5500. Hwy. 180, 55 mi east of Fresno. Admission: $10 per vehicle (good for 1 wk; also valid for Sequoia National Park). Camping: $12 per night; no reservations. Visitors center open Memorial Day–Labor Day, daily 8–6, rest of year 8–5.*

Sequoia National Park

(👫 **ALL**) Sister park to adjacent Kings Canyon (see *above*), Sequoia National Park dates from 1890, which makes it the second-oldest U.S. national park after Yellowstone. As the name suggests, it's best known for its giant sequoias, the world's largest living things. Once dominating Northern Hemisphere forests, sequoias now survive in only 75 widely scattered groves along the western slopes of the Sierra Nevada; about a third of them are here, several within easy access of the scenic Generals Highway, which winds through the developed western reaches of the park. Arriving from Kings Canyon and the north, you'll find the Lodgepole visitors center (tel. 559/565–3782, open mid-Apr.–mid-Oct., daily 8–6), where there are a market, a gas station, a laundry, and a campground. Rangers lead hikes from here, and nature programs take place. A summertime shuttle bus service operates from here to many of the park's top attractions; the hours are from 8 to 6, and all-day passes cost $4 per person, $6 per family of four. Arriving from the south through the Ash Mountain entrance, you'll find the Foothills visitors center (tel. 559/565–3134, open daily 8–5), which sells some nice nature books for children. If you want to visit Crystal Cave (tel. 559/565–3759), one of the park's natural wonders, you'll need to purchase tickets ($5 adults, $2.50 ages 6–12) at one of these two visitors centers. Guided tours of the cave run from 10 to 3 from mid-May through September, weather permit-

ting; tours are daily from June to Labor Day, weekends only in May and September. You can also ask at the visitors centers about summertime horseback riding and wintertime cross-country skiing in the park.

Lodgepole is the gateway to the Giant Forest, where awesome sequoias dominate the landscape. About 5 miles north of Lodgepole is the Wuksachi Village, the first part of which opened in 1999; facilities include a 102-room lodge and a restaurant. About 3 miles south of Lodgepole stands the General Sherman Tree, the giant of giants (see Chapter 7). Farther south along the road you'll find two easy, gentle hiking trails ideal for young children—the ¾-mile Hazelwood Nature Trail, which runs through a majestic sequoia grove; and the Trail for All People, a ³⁄₁₀-mile self-guiding trail (stroller- and wheelchair-accessible) that crosses between a sequoia forest and a meadow. And a bit more to the south, be sure to take the turnoff to Moro Rock and Crescent Meadow. You'll come first to the corny but fun and photogenic Auto Log, where you can drive your car onto a fallen tree with a 21-foot base diameter. Next comes Moro Rock, an immense domed granite monolith that you can climb for spectacular views. But be forewarned: It's a steep and strenuous ¼-mile hike, almost straight up some 400 stone steps. To my mind, it's decidedly worth the climb, as long as your family members are in good hiking shape and aren't scared of heights (kids may do better than adults here). On a clear day you can see the towering mountain peaks of the Great Western Divide to one side, the vast expanses of the San Joaquin Valley to the other—and, nearly 4,000 feet straight down, the Kaweah River canyon. Beyond Moro Rock, the road leads to the Triple Tree (three trees growing from one trunk), the Buttress Tree (a fallen 2,300-year-old sequoia), and the Tunnel Log, a fallen tree you can drive through (the tunnel is 8 feet high, 17 feet wide). You'll then arrive at Crescent Meadow, which naturalist John Muir called the "Gem of the Sierra"—it's especially gemlike in early summer, when wildflowers bloom. Picnic here on big flat rocks near the parking lot, and hike the 1.8-mile loop trail around the sequoia-ringed meadow, which is even stroller-accessible part of the way. The High Sierra Trail leads off from here, too, toward Mount Whitney, but the peak is 71 wilderness miles away, on the far eastern edges of the park—not exactly an afternoon stroll. Returning to the Generals Highway and heading south, you can visit Crystal Cave (see *above*) if you've *already* bought tickets; watch for the Crystal Cave Road turnoff, then head 7 twisting miles west to the parking lot, where a 15-minute hike leads down to the cave, a wonderland of limestone and marble stalactites and stalagmites. Guided tours last 45 minutes, and temperatures in the cave are cool. Farther south on the Generals Highway, you'll pass right through Tunnel Rock, a huge bored-out chunk of granite. Stop here and gaze up at the mighty dome of Moro Rock; if you climbed it, you won't quite believe where you were.

⚡ *Ash Mountain Headquarters, Three Rivers 93271; information, tel. 559/565–3134 or 559/565–3341; lodging reservations, tel. 559/561–3314 or 888/252–5757; backcountry information, tel. 559/565–3708. Admission: $10 per vehicle (good for 1 wk; also valid for Kings Canyon National Park). Camping: $6–$14 per night. 7 campgrounds, 623 sites including 317 open year-round; all first-come, first-served except Lodgepole's 270 sites, by reservation only (tel. 559/565–3774 or 800/365–2267) mid-May–Labor Day.*

Yosemite National Park

👫 ALL Like many California families, we make at least one annual journey to Yosemite National Park. Theodore Roosevelt called it "the most beautiful place on earth," and it's hard to argue with that assessment. But the crowds can be so thick, especially in summer, that the valley sometimes resembles an enormous parking lot choked with cars and tour buses. In recent years, park officials have closed the gates to

drivers during peak hours of some holiday weekends, and long-range plans may result in eliminating most automobile traffic in the valley. Still, Yosemite remains one of the great natural wonders of the world. Come in spring, winter, or fall, or venture into the park's near-pristine backcountry, and your visit may be all the more enjoyable. (For information about wintertime cross-country skiing at Badger Pass here, see Chapter 11.) Yosemite is a 4½-hour drive from San Francisco, six hours from L.A.; Highways 120, 140, and 41 are the major arteries leading to it. The park has four entrances: two from the west, one from the south, and one from the east, via the nearly 10,000-foot-high Tioga Pass (closed during snow season, usually from November to late May).

Most visitors head first to Yosemite Valley, with its awesome 3,000-foot-high glacier-carved rock walls, accented by towering cliffs, waterfalls, and domed monoliths. On either road as you enter the valley you'll spot the park's two most famous landmarks: El Capitan, directly north of the road—put the kids on lookout for daredevil rock climbers on its sides—and, far off to the east, the majestic granite monolith Half Dome. The eastern portions of the valley are among the most heavily developed in the national park system, and there's a complimentary shuttle-bus service covering major stops in the eastern valley—I recommend taking it. The Yosemite Valley visitors center (shuttle stop No. 6) has maps and books; ask here about Family Discovery Walks led by ranger-naturalists. Get a copy of the park's weekly newspaper to find out about children's programs (such as summertime Junior and Senior Rangers for ages 8 to 12) that are scheduled at LeConte Memorial Lodge (shuttle stop No. 12), the Happy Isles Nature Center (shuttle stop No. 16; open daily spring–fall), and other locations. Near the visitors center are the Indian Cultural Exhibit at Yosemite Museum (open daily), with displays on the Miwok and Paiute peoples, and a re-creation of an Ahwahnichee Indian village. For family hiking in the valley, start with the easy ¼-mile trails leading to the bases of 620-foot Bridalveil Fall and 320-foot Lower Yosemite Fall (shuttle stop No. 7). For a longer hike, continue from Lower Yosemite Fall to Mirror Lake, a moderately easy 2-mile hike. Do it now: Mirror Lake is silting up and eventually will disappear entirely into a meadow. For a more challenging hike, tackle the superbly scenic, but strenuous, Mist Trail to 317-foot Vernal Fall, a three- to four-hour round-trip hike that climbs 1,000 feet in altitude. In the spring especially you'll feel the misty sprays of the falls as you negotiate the steep steps toward the top. When my son, Grael, reached age 12, he and I continued up the trail to Nevada Fall, another 1,000-foot climb with thrilling views. Allow most of a day for that hike.

Some of the park's most splendid attractions await outside the valley. If the access road isn't closed due to snow, don't miss 7,200-foot Glacier Point, which has some of Yosemite's finest views, notably of 4,425-foot Yosemite Falls (the highest waterfall in North America) and Half Dome. Our kids were thrilled to peer down a sheer rock cliff onto Yosemite Valley more than 3,000 feet below, spotting places they'd been. From here, the Panorama Trail leads all the way down to the valley, an 8-mile, four-hour trek. In the southern reaches of the park, 35 miles south of the valley, lies the Mariposa Grove, largest of three giant sequoia groves in Yosemite. We enjoyed hiking around the grove for two hours or so, encountering the massive-limbed Grizzly Giant, aged 2,700 years, and other mammoth trees, including a few the kids could walk through. Some uphill climbing is required, however, and many visitors opt for the one-hour Big Trees Tram ride ($6 adults, $3 ages 4–12, or $20 per family, available May–October). The beautiful old Wawona Hotel is also in this region of Yosemite (there's free shuttle service from the Wawona to the Mariposa Grove in summer.) And outside the park's south entrance is the Yosemite Mountain Sugar Pine R.R. depot, where you can take a narrated 4-mile scenic narrow-gauge railroad ride through a pine forest (56001 Hwy. 41, Fish Camp, tel. 209/683–7273; fare $11 adults and $6 ages 3–12 on steam train, $7 and $4, respectively, for jenny railcars; special summertime Saturday-night barbecue rides are $32.50 for adults, $18 for kids,). The vast northern regions of Yosemite reached by the Tioga Road are a rugged high-country world of their own, with lots of day hikes and backpacking opportunities. Many Yosemite aficionados now bypass the crowded valley entirely and head directly to stunning 8,600-foot-high Tuolomne Meadows, abounding with wildflowers and wildlife. The Tuolomne Meadows visitors center is open daily from 9 to 5 until the Tioga Road closes. Summertime shuttle bus service is available in Tuolomne Meadows during daylight hours.

More than 8 miles of bike paths crisscross the eastern valley (rent bikes at Curry Village, tel. 209/372–8319, in summer, or at Yosemite Lodge, tel. 209/372–1208 year-round); horseback rides (minimum age 7) depart daily from spring to autumn from stables in the valley, and in summer from Tuolomne Meadows and Wawona (call 209/372–1248 for reservations); rafts for the Merced River can be rented at Curry Village. The Yosemite Mountaineering School and Guide Service (tel. 209/372–1244) conducts rock climbing classes for all levels (minimum age 14, but younger kids can take group lessons), from spring to fall. Lodgings—more than 1,500 guest rooms—range from the inexpensive and rustic (unheated tent cabins in Curry Village, starting at $37) to the expensive and elegant (the famed Ahwahnee Hotel, up to $227); Yosemite Lodge and the Wawona Hotel provide a middle ground between the two. Yosemite Lodge and Curry Village have swimming pools, and Curry Village has ice-skating in winter. Eating places are at the various lodging facilities. It's a good idea to reserve lodging as far in advance as possible.

🏠 *Yosemite National Park, Box 577, 95389; information, tel. 209/372–0264 or 209/372–*

0265; lodging reservations, tel. 209/252–4848; camping reservations, tel. 800/436–7275; weather and road conditions, tel. 209/372–0200. Admission: $20 per vehicle (good for 1 wk); annual pass $40. Camping: $3–$15 per night. 15 campgrounds (1,840 sites); 377 sites open year-round. Valley visitors center open late spring–Aug., daily 8–8; Sept.–late spring, daily 9–5. Tuolomne Meadows visitors center open daily 9–5 while Tioga Rd. is open.

San Francisco and the Bay Area

Golden Gate National Recreation Area

(**ALL**) For sheer numbers of visitors, the Golden Gate National Recreation Area qualifies as "America's most popular national park." But many of the estimated 18.3 million people who use the GGNRA annually—visiting such tourist staples as Alcatraz, the Presidio, Fort Point, the Cliff House, and Muir Woods—probably aren't even aware they're in it. You'll find details on these attractions in Chapters 4, 7, and 14, but GGNRA encompasses much more. It extends from a few small areas south of San Francisco, north along the dunes and sands of Fort Funston and Ocean Beach, east to the San Francisco waterfront, across the Golden Gate to the Marin Headlands, and farther north in a ribbonlike swath to the mouth of Tomales Bay. World-renowned vistas, redwoods, wildlife, hiking, biking, camping, and historic sites are among the GGNRA's lures. One of the great delights for families is the 4-mile Golden Gate Promenade, winding from Aquatic Park near Fisherman's Wharf to the foot of the Golden Gate Bridge. At Fort Mason, a onetime military outpost that now houses offices, museums, and arts groups, stop at the GGNRA's Western Region information center (in Building 201). Then spend a couple of hours enjoying the sights along the promenade: historic ships, gleaming yachts, sailboats, joggers, kite fliers, windsurfers, fishing piers, and, the majestic Golden Gate Bridge. Mostly flat and partly paved, much of the route is stroller accessible. The San Francisco Headlands, also within the GGNRA, are among the great comparatively undiscovered areas of the city. One of our favorite hikes is the Coastal Trail, which traces nearly all of the coastline from the foot of the Golden Gate Bridge to Cliff House. It's 7 miles total, but we always take it in smaller portions. Our top choice is the stretch from the El Camino del Mar overlook, near the Palace of the Legion of Honor, past Lands End and Point Lobos to the ruins of the old Sutro Baths below the Cliff House. The trail cuts along wild, rugged cliffs, through groves of cypress trees, overlooking jagged rocks and deep blue Pacific waters; listen for the barking of sea lions and the bellow of fog horns. At the northern end of the Golden Gate Bridge, we like to drive on scenic Conzelman Road, which hugs the cliffs of the Marin Headlands for 5 miles to Point Bonita. Your kids will probably recognize these fabulous bird's-eye views of the bridge (and the city in the background) from TV commercials. At the end of the road, hike ½ mile to the picturesque Point Bonita Lighthouse. Then loop back to Highway 1, which, heading north along the coast, leads to Muir Beach and Stinson Beach, two of the Bay Area's most popular beaches.

∰ *Western Region Information Center, Fort Mason, Bldg. 201, San Francisco 94123, tel. 415/556–0560. Admission free (except Alcatraz and Muir Woods).*

Point Reyes National Seashore

(**ALL**) Point Reyes National Seashore, which borders the northern reaches of the GGNRA (see *above*), is our family's favorite natural region in the Bay Area, a great place for hiking to secluded beaches, viewing wildlife, and driving through rugged, rolling grasslands reminiscent of England or Wales. Within its 71,000 acres are 140 miles of hiking trails that lead through forests of pine and fir, across meadows thick with spring wildflowers, and past lakes and estuaries teeming with birds. Start at the Bear Valley visitors center, ½ mile off Highway 1 down Bear Valley Road; on our first few visits, when our kids were quite young, we found plenty to keep us busy in this area. A number of trails leave directly from here, too— the intriguing ½-mile loop Earthquake Trail, for instance, which follows the San Andreas Fault near the epicenter of the famed 1906 San Francisco quake. Ask the kids if they feel like they're moving: the land they're standing on is actually creeping along the Pacific plate toward Alaska at the rate of 2 inches a year (this peninsula was once in what is now *Southern* California. A nearby ¼-mile trail leads to Kule Lokto, a replica of a Coast Miwok Indian village. At the Morgan Horse Ranch, also near the visitors center, horses are trained for the National Park Service. The Bear Valley Trail is an easy 3-mile round-trip through a forest to a meadow and back; or you can make an 8-mile round-trip to one of a string of largely wild, uncrowded, golden sand beaches that line the coast. Our favorite "swimming" beaches—the water is cold, but some would-be polar bears find it refreshing—are Limantour Spit and Drakes Beach, both on sheltered Drakes Bay. Limantour has rolling dunes and seabirds, while Drakes is backed by high white cliffs and has picnic and snack bar facilities. Along a windswept 15-mile stretch of the Pacific Ocean, Point Reyes Beach North, Point Reyes Beach South, and McClures Beach are all hammered by surf that's too dangerous for swimming, but they're ideal for hiking, beachcombing, and picnicking. (McClures Beach is really a trip unto itself, requiring a ½-mile hike with a steep return climb.) Scenic Pierce Point Road leads to the McClures Beach trailhead, as well as to a trailhead leading 4 spectacular miles to Tomales Point, with views of a herd of tule elk along the way. We also like Sir Francis Drake Highway, a continuation of Bear Valley Road that winds a scenic 22 miles from

the visitors center to the tip of the peninsula and Point Reyes Light, an 1870 lighthouse dramatically perched over the Pacific Ocean. There are 300 steps leading down to the lighthouse, which means 300 steps to climb *up* on your way back. From mid-December to March the lighthouse is a popular whale-watching spot. On winter weekends cars are usually prevented from driving all the way to the end, and shuttle bus service is provided; call 415/669–1534 for schedules. Point Reyes is often fogbound in summer; you may want to call the park to check weather conditions before setting out. **⚓** *Point Reyes Station 94956, tel. 415/663–1092. Follow Hwy. 1 or 101 north from San Francisco to Bear Valley Rd. and then Sir Francis Drake Hwy. Admission free. Camping by permit only (tel. 415/663–8054) at 4 primitive hike-in campgrounds; $10 per night. Park open daily sunrise–sunset. Bear Valley visitors center open weekdays 9–5, weekends and holidays 8–5. Lighthouse visitors center (tel. 415/669–2534) open Thurs.–Mon. 10–5. Drakes Beach visitors center (tel. 415/669–1250) open Memorial Day–Labor Day, Fri.–Tues. 10–5; rest of year, weekends 10–5.*

Central Coast and Valley

Montana de Oro State Park

🏃 3–15 Before our last trip to Morro Bay, I had never heard of Montana de Oro State Park. But to Central Coast families it's no secret: More than half a million people visit here each year, drawn by 7 miles of magnificent ocean and bay shoreline. The highest point in the park, 1,347-foot Valencia Peak, reached by a 4-mile round-trip trail, provides wonderful panoramic views of the area. The Ranch House visitors center is perched above the park's finest beach, Spooner's Cove. Though swimming is dangerous here—watch the rip currents—the beach has golden sands, rocks to climb, and rich tide pools. (Check tide schedules at the visitors center; tidepooling is best within one hour of low tide). Nearby Corallina Cove, reached by a trail along the bluffs, also has teeming tide pools—look for sea stars, sea urchins, sea anemones, hermit crabs, periwinkles, barnacles, mussels, abalone, kelp, and algae. Also watch for harbor seals and sea otters offshore. Dune Trail extends north about 2 miles from Spooner's Cove to the southern edges of the Sand Spit, a 3½-mile-long natural preserve along Morro Bay that divides the estuary from the Pacific Ocean. From the trail, look north for wonderful views of Morro Rock (see Chapter 7). The most popular hike in the park is the easy 2-mile Bluff Trail, which follows the shoreline about 50 feet above the surf, with excellent vantage points for viewing harbor seals and, in winter and early spring, migrating gray whales.

ⓜ *Pecho Valley Rd., Los Osos 93402, tel. 805/528–0513 or 805/528–0513. 8 mi south of Morro Bay via Los Osos Valley Rd. Admission free. 50 primitive campsites ($7–$11 per night) open year-round; rest rooms. Visitors center open Memorial Day–Labor Day, daily 10–8; Labor Day–Memorial Day, Fri.–Sun. and holidays 11–3, dependent on staffing.*

Pfeiffer Big Sur State Park

(ⓜ 3–15) Nestled in a canyon thick with redwoods, sycamores, maples, oaks, and cottonwoods, Pfeiffer Big Sur is small and several miles away from the spectacular scenery of the Big Sur coast (see Chapter 7). But its inland location moderates the coastal fog, resulting in generally warm (though still well-shaded) summer days here. We love coming here to camp, using the park as a base for exploring the Big Sur region. Within the park, hiking's the major activity; our favorite trail is the one from the Big Sur Lodge (where rooms, food, and gifts are available; tel. 831/667–3100 or 800/424–4787) to Pfeiffer Falls, about a mile round-trip. Depending on the time of year, the falls may have dwindled to a trickle, but the trail itself is scenic, and our children got a big thrill once when we came upon five

black-tailed deer along the way. There's also hiking and picnicking along the Big Sur River, which cuts through the canyon. The main visitors center in Big Sur is ½ mile south of the Pfeiffer entrance at Big Sur Station; you can also get information there about two other Big Sur state parks: Andrew Molera, the region's largest state park, where rugged headlands overlook wild beaches; and Julia Pfeiffer Burns, site of a spectacular waterfall that pours into the Pacific. One fee per day allows entrance to all three parks.

ⓜ *Big Sur 93920, tel. 831/667–2315. Hwy. 1, 26 mi south of Carmel. Day use: $6 per vehicle. 218 campsites ($14–$20 per night), open year-round; rest rooms, showers. Visitors center open May–Oct., daily 8–6; Nov.–Apr., daily 9–5.*

Point Lobos State Reserve

(ⓜ 3–15) Count me among the many who consider Point Lobos State Reserve the "crown jewel" of the state park system: Its combination of pounding surf and rugged headlands has been called "the greatest meeting of land and water in the world," while its rich marine life and vegetation have made it a living museum. (The bulk of the park's acreage is actually underwater—it was America's first underwater marine preserve.) Hiking trails wind along the jagged shoreline to secluded coves and into forests of stately Monterey pine and gnarled Monterey cypress. Sea lions, harbor seals, sea otters, and seabirds throng along the shore, while California gray whales may pass in the distance. Rule No. 1 for visiting Point Lobos is to get here early in the day (before 10 if possible), especially in summer or on weekends. The number of automobiles is limited in the reserve, and the lineup of waiting cars can be long by afternoon. Once you're inside, head for the Sea Lion Point parking area, with its kiosk displaying pelts of sea lions, sea otters, and harbor seals, which kids can stroke. Then follow the ⅓-mile trail to Sea Lion Point itself, where you can watch sea lions cavorting and barking on the rocks offshore. The kids will no doubt want to scramble around the rocks in this area, but

Rule No. 2 is to keep a close eye on them: The cliffs and surf here can be dangerous. The reserve is dotted with numerous other scenic hiking trails. The ⅓-mile Cypress Grove Trail, which also leaves from the Sea Lion Point parking area, loops through one of the earth's last two surviving natural stands of Monterey cypress trees. Park in the Whaler's Cove area to take the 1.4-mile North Shore Trail, which winds along dramatic rugged sea cliffs. Or park at Piney Woods to follow the mile-long South Shore Trail, which leads along cliffs, rocks, and pebbly beaches; once again, watch kids on the slippery rocks and sometimes sheer cliffs. Picnicking in Point Lobos is permitted only in three areas: Piney Woods, Whaler's Cove, and Bird Island, in the reserve's southern reaches.

🏛 *Hwy. 1, tel. 831/624–4909. 3 mi south of Carmel. Admission: $6 per vehicle. No camping. Open May–Labor Day, daily 9–7; Labor Day–Apr., daily 9–5.*

Los Angeles and Environs

Channel Islands National Park

(👫 **6–15**) Only 20 miles from Los Angeles, the Channel Islands National Park seems a world away from the metropolis. Featuring rugged volcanic cliffs, gigantic sea caves, deep-blue waters, and teeming wildlife, its five unspoiled islands are accessible only by boat from Ventura Harbor, where cruises leave from next to the park visitors center. Boat tickets cost from $22 to $215 for adults, $15 to $195 for children 12 and under. These are *not* luxury cruises—the emphasis is on packing in small groups of nature-lovers. Seas are often rough, and if you plan to go ashore (most boats land, some do not), be in good physical condition and prepared for adventure—wear low-heeled, ribbed-soled shoes, for one thing. Before setting out with kids, check weather conditions and take seasick-

ness precautions. All this said, the rewards for going can be great. During the crossing you may see dolphins, flying fish, sea lions, whales, and blue sharks. Once there, you can hike, swim, picnic, kayak, snorkel, view more wildlife, and camp, though these primitive campsites are really for experienced campers. Call park headquarters (tel. 805/658–5711) for a free advance permit; you'll also need to carry in food, water, fuel, and other supplies. For most families the top island choice is Anacapa, actually three small islets only 90 minutes by boat from the mainland. (Trips cost $37 for adults, $20 for children 12 and under.) Most visitors disembark at East Anacapa, where a climb of more than 150 steps up an ocean bluff is required to reach the visitors center, picnic areas, and 2 miles of nature trails (guided walks are available). On summer weekends, snorkeling excursions go to a cove on West Anacapa; tidepooling trips come here from November to May. You can camp on the island year-round. Santa Cruz, the largest of the islands, is another good choice for families. Here, you'll find extensive wildlife and a coastline marked by steep cliffs, sea caves, and coves with sandy beaches. Once inhabited by the Chumash Indians, most of the island is now managed as a preserve. Island Packers runs all-day trips several days a week to the island's Scorpion Ranch, where you can lie on a beach, take a 2-mile nature walk, and picnic. Or you can join adventurous day trips to other parts of the island conducted by the Nature Conservancy (tel. 805/962–9111; Apr.–Nov., kids 10 and older only). Santa Cruz also has year-round camping. Santa Rosa, the second-largest island, has been open to the public only since 1987. One-day excursions are available from May through October; the boat trip lasts up to 3½ hours, with sometimes difficult landings. Once on the island, however, you'll find white sandy beaches and ranger-led hikes. San Miguel, the most distant island, is small, harsh, secluded, and a haven for seals, sea lions, and other wildlife. You can take a day trip here, but it's a five-hour boat ride—it makes sense to take a two-day excursion combining both Santa Rosa and San Miguel (you'll sleep aboard the boat, and all meals are included). Santa Barbara, a small isolated island far south of the others, is noted for sightings of marine mammals (elephant seals, dolphins, sea lions, whales) and birds, and for snorkeling, hiking, and swimming. Boat trips from the mainland to here (April–October) take about three hours. You can camp on the latter three islands from late spring to November.

🏠 *Visitors center, 1901 Spinnaker Dr., Ventura 93001, tel. 805/658–5730. Camping: 805/658–5711 or 800/365–2267. Park admission free. Visitors center open Memorial Day–Labor Day, daily 8–5; winter, weekdays 8:30–4:30, weekends 8–5. Island Packers (boat concession): 1867 Spinnaker Dr., Ventura; recorded information, tel. 805/642–7688; reservations, tel. 805/642–1393.*

Santa Monica Mountains National Recreation Area

(🏃 **ALL**)   Had it with seas of concrete? Then head for the Santa Monica Mountains, a refreshing splash of nature remarkably close to the L.A. urban sprawl. Parts of two counties lie within its boundaries, as do three state parks, a state historic park and several other sites of historic importance, plus various county parks, state and county beaches, preserves, and private recreation sites. Stop at the visitors information center in Agoura Hills for maps and brochures on the park areas. The National Park Service administers a number of old ranch sites here. At Paramount Ranch you can hike, picnic, and possibly watch a TV series being filmed. Peter Strauss Ranch, named for the actor who once lived here, has picnicking and hiking (try the easy ½-mile Peter Strauss Trail). Franklin Canyon Ranch, a few miles from the Ventura Freeway, also contains gentle hiking trails and nice picnic spots. The Circle X Ranch site includes Sandstone Peak, the highest point in the Santa Monica Mountains (3,111 feet), and has a number of hiking trails with excellent

views: the 2-mile Canyon View Loop is easy to moderate, and the Mishe Mokwa Trail, though nearly twice as long, is also good for kids. Circle X Ranch has hike-in camping as well; sites are first-come, first-served, and cost $6 per night. You can find wilderness experience in this parkland, too. Topanga State Park (tel. 310/455–2465; $5 day use) in Los Angeles, west of Santa Monica, contains 32 hiking trails within 9,000 acres of rugged mountain land. In Calabasas, Malibu Creek State Park (tel. 818/880–0350; $5 day use), a former setting for such 20th Century–Fox movie and TV productions as *M*A*S*H*, has mountain hiking, biking, horseback riding, fishing, and camping. Point Mugu State Park (tel. 818/880–0350, $6 day use), on Pacific Coast Highway in Ventura County, has hiking and biking through canyons and past meadows, plus camping and beaches. Will Rogers State Historic Park (tel. 310/454–8212, $5 day use) in Pacific Palisades, where the humorist once lived, includes Rogers's ranch house (which you can tour), polo fields, and hiking trails. A string of excellent beaches along the coastline is popular for surfing, skin-diving, whale-watching, bird-watching, sunbathing, and beachcombing. Among our favorites are Leo Carrillo, Topanga, and Will Rogers state beaches. (See Chapter 15 for more details on each.)

🏠 *30401 Agoura Rd., Suite 100, Agoura Hills 91301, tel. 818/597–9192 or 818/597–1036. Admission free to national-park lands; state and local parks charge separate fees. Most park sites open sunrise–sunset. Visitors center open weekdays 8–5, weekends and most holidays 9–5.*

San Diego and the Southern Deserts

Anza-Borrego Desert State Park

(🏃 **3–15**)   Though hardly a household name outside its region, Anza-Borrego

Desert State Park is California's largest state park, encompassing 600,000 acres of the Colorado Desert. San Diego families know it well; two hours northeast of the city, Anza-Borrego has desert canyons, badlands, mesas, nature trails, oases, cacti gardens, Native American rock art, and wildlife, all surrounded by rugged mountain ranges. One bonus to Anza-Borrego is that, unlike most state parks, almost all of it is open to camping (there are established camp- grounds as well). When visiting a vast desert area like this with children, take it slow and easy, stopping frequently along the way. Kids who may have little interest in the "big pic- ture" may delight in watching for lizards and beetles, or spotting tracks of coyotes and bighorn sheep. Stop first at the visitors cen- ter (closed weekdays in summer) near Bor- rego Palm Canyon; ask about the Junior Naturalist program, for children ages 7 to 12. This canyon, one of the park's top sights, includes its most popular trail, a 3-mile round-trip self-guided nature walk through a native palm grove, the state's third-largest palm oasis. (Watch for bighorn sheep.) A good, short hike for everyone in the family is the ¼-mile Narrows Earth Trail, which leads along an active fault line; kids can actu- ally reach down and touch the ruptured inner layers of the planet. The mile-long Ele- phant Trees Nature Trail leads to several rare trees. Another gentle 1-mile trail leads to a century-old boulder with red and yel- low ceremonial rock art. Ask at the visitors center for directions to these trails. Also check on road conditions for several self- guided driving tours: Erosion Road, with views of eroded, moonlike badlands; Font's Point, a viewpoint over the Borrego Bad- lands reached on a 4-mile dirt road; Split Mountain, where four-wheel-drive vehicles can wend their way through a 3-mile gorge; and Box Canyon, a long narrow chasm once traveled by gold seekers and stagecoaches. Due to searing summer heat (up to 125°) the ideal months to visit this park are from October to May; spring wildflower season (February–April) is especially beautiful. Call 760/767–4684 for recorded wildflower information at that time.

🏨 *200 Palm Canyon Dr., Borrego Springs 92004, tel. 760/767–5311. Visitors center, tel. 760/767–4205. Hwy. 78 east from I–15. Day use: $5 per vehicle. 12 campgrounds (173 developed sites, 200 primitive sites; $10–$22 per night); rest rooms, showers; open year- round; camping allowed in most of park. Visi- tors center open Oct.–May, daily 9–5; June– Sept., weekends and holidays 9–5.*

Death Valley National Park

(👫 **3 – 15**) Whenever we sing the praises of Death Valley National Park, friends who have never been there give us funny looks. Death Valley? What *is* with that morbid name? Well, around 1849 a group of pio- neers en route to the California goldfields took a fateful shortcut across the valley, suf- fering hardships and at least one death. That, however, was before automobiles, highways, campgrounds, and resorts. Today, in this remarkable landscape of rainbow- hued hills and canyons, graceful dunes, crusty salt flats, volcanic craters, and snow- capped peaks, you can see ghost towns and petroglyphs (Native American rock carv- ings). Yes, it's probably wise to avoid Death Valley in summer, when this is one of the hottest places on earth. But from October to April you'll also find days in the 80s, 70s, even 60s. Our favorite time here is spring, when the hillsides are blanketed with wild- flowers and blooming cacti.

Death Valley—the largest national park in the lower 48 states—is huge, but its major attractions are clustered in a few areas. In the center is the Furnace Creek region, where you'll find the Furnace Creek visitors center and Death Valley Museum, as well as lodgings at the stylish Furnace Creek Inn and Ranch (see Chapter 12). Furnace Creek Campground, the only campground in the park where sites can be reserved, is nearby; campers can use the pool at Furnace Creek Ranch for a small fee. South of Furnace

Creek, take state Highway 178 to the Golden Canyon Interpretive Trail, an easy 1-mile hike through a golden-hued canyon. Farther down the road, don't miss the fascinating Devil's Golf Course, a vast sea of bizarre salt formations carved by wind and rain. Grael, the young golfer in our family, walked among the crusty salt ridges, sharp spires, and shallow pools of salt water, imagining what it would be like to play 18 holes here. A few miles south comes Badwater, North America's lowest point at nearly 280 feet below sea level, where we removed our shoes to wade into the shallow, marshy waters. Incongruously, snowcapped 11,000-foot Telescope Peak looms 18 miles straight ahead. Heading back north to Furnace Creek, be sure to follow the detour loop called Artists Drive, where oxidation has colored the clay hills in shades of red, pink, purple, orange, yellow, brown, and green. A separate fork in the road south of Furnace Creek leads to three other not-to-be-missed sights. Zabriskie Point is Death Valley's most famous landmark, an ancient lake bed now composed of eroded hills shaded with yellows and browns that continually change in the light. Rousting the kids out of their tent before the sun came up one cool morning, we headed to Zabriskie Point for one of the most memorable sunrises of our lives. Right down the road is Twenty Mule Team Canyon, where a short one-way road winds through a wonderfully scenic badlands pocked with old borax mines. And 13 miles farther, where the road dead-ends, comes Dante's View, a panoramic perspective of salt flats and the Panamint Mountains from more than a mile above Badwater.

Other attractions line Highway 190 to the north of Furnace Creek. The Harmony Borax Works Interpretive Trail leads ¼ mile through desolate salt flats where Chinese laborers in the 1880s gathered borax to be hauled across the desert by 20-mule-team wagons. At nearby Mustard Canyon, you can drive through the middle of eerie mustard-colored salt cliffs. A few miles farther north, the ½-mile Salt Creek Interpretive Trail fol-

lows a boardwalk along a creek containing rare pupfish, remnants of the Ice Age. As Highway 190 turns west toward Stovepipe Wells Village (site of a motel, a store, and a gas station), you can see the Devil's Cornfield—clumps of bushes that resemble cornstalks—and the Sand Dunes, 14 square miles of rippling desert dunes where our kids enjoyed hunting for lizard trails in the sand. Scotty's Castle (see Chapter 4), a Moorish-style mansion and the major draw in the far northern reaches of the park, lies in a deep green valley that's a nice respite on a hot day. Eight miles west is the ½-mile-wide and 500-foot-deep Ubehebe Crater, formed by a volcanic eruption 1,000 years ago. We hiked (almost ran) down into the depths of the steep crater, then trudged slowly back up; if you have small children, stick to the ½-mile trail along the rim of the crater. If you have a full day for an adventurous side trip, venture into Titus Canyon (one-way Titus Canyon Road must be entered from Nevada, off Rte. 374). The rugged route (four-wheel drive is best for it) gives gorgeous views of high desert country, passes by the ghost town of Leadfield, and concludes by winding through a narrow, rocky, steep-sided gorge. You can also hike in to the lower gorge of the canyon, 3 miles round-trip from the Titus Canyon Mouth parking area off Scotty's Castle Road. A few tips: The valley's only gas stations are at Furnace Creek, Scotty's Castle, and Stovepipe Wells; fill up at every opportunity. Carry plenty of water, for both humans and the car. If your car breaks down, stay with it and wait for help. Wear hats and sunscreen, and avoid too much sun exposure.

🏠 *Death Valley 92328, tel. 760 /786–2331. From U.S. 395 from north, take Rte. 136 east to Rte. 190; from U.S. 395 from south, take Rte. 178 east to Rte. 190. Admission: $10 per vehicle. Camping: $10–$16; 9 campgrounds (more than 1,500 primitive sites with rest rooms); some sites open all year. Furnace Creek Campground reservations: tel. 800/ 365–2267.*

Joshua Tree National Park

(**†† ALL**) Visiting Joshua Tree National Park may change forever the way you and your children think of deserts. Vast stands of Joshua trees (named by early settlers who thought the tree's distinctive "arms" resembled the biblical figure Joshua in supplication before God) share the Mojave Desert with enormous granite rocks left behind by geological upheavals. In the southern reaches of the park, the Mojave and Colorado deserts meet and descend into lower elevations, marked by colorful cacti gardens and, in spring, a profusion of wildflowers. Sharp-eyed youngsters should keep a lookout for coyotes, bobcats, jackrabbits, roadrunners, lizards, even golden eagles. From the north entrance near the town of Twentynine Palms, stop at the Oasis visitors center, where there's a short nature walk to an oasis. If you have only a few hours to spend in the park, you can then drive the dramatic 31-mile Northern Loop to the west entrance. Our family's favorite stops along the way include the Jumbo Rocks area, where massive boulders sit near the road; Keys View, a 6-mile detour ending at panoramic views; and Hidden Valley, where a beautiful 1-mile loop nature trail winds through boulders toward an old-time cattle rustlers' hideout. If you have time, your family can seek out desert oases and abandoned gold mines, accessible by longer trails. Our top choice for hiking in the park is the Ryan Mountain Trail, a challenging 3-mile round-trip that leads up to a 5,400-foot summit with wonderful vistas; access is from the Ryan Mountain parking area. Nearby is Sheep Pass, our favorite camping area in the park; it's off the road a bit and has huge boulders for kids to climb on. The catch is that it's by reservation only for a minimum of 10 people; if you can round up that many friends or family, it's a find (most campgrounds at Joshua Tree are first-come, first-served). If you have additional time, the park's southern areas are well worth the drive; you'll pass a cholla cactus garden, a patch of red-flowered ocotillos, and acres of creosotes. Near the Cottonwood visitors center north of Joshua Tree's south entrance (which can also be reached on I–10 from Palm Springs), follow the rugged mile-long trail to Mastodon Peak; in spring there's a profusion of wildflowers and cacti in bloom here, like a desert garden. Remember that wherever you go in Joshua Tree, you should carry water; none is available in the park.

🏠 *74485 National Park Dr., Twentynine Palms 92277, tel. 760/367–5500. From I–10, west of Palm Springs, turn northeast onto Rte. 62; west entrance is south of the town of Joshua Tree, north entrance is south of Twentynine Palms. South entrance off I–10, east of Indio. Day use: $10 per vehicle. 9 campgrounds (535 sites), all year-round except White Tank (open Sept.–June); reservations only for Black Rock and Indian Cove, $10 per night (tel. 800/365–2267); others (except group campgrounds) all free and first-come, first-served; carry in water and firewood. Visitors centers open daily 8–5.*

FROM TOONTOWN TO THE ABYSS
THEME AND AMUSEMENT PARKS

Looking for surefire thrills for your kids? Then take them to ride monster roller coasters or whirling teacups; to meet Mickey Mouse or King Kong; to slide hundreds of feet into pools of water or watch dolphins jump dozens of feet into the air. California is unsurpassed in the range and quality of its theme and amusement parks. Some, like Disneyland, are so huge and so special that they are destinations in their own right, the focus of an entire family vacation.

As every traveling family knows, however, such parks come with high price tags. It's nothing for a family of four to drop $100 or more merely to get in the gate; add food, games, souvenirs, and other expenses, and the sky's the limit. But there are ways to blunt the bite. Discount coupons for Knott's Berry Farm, Universal Studios Hollywood, Sea World, and the Six Flags Marine World Theme Park are often available at hotels, tourist bureaus, and other outlets. Trim food costs by eating at restaurants outside the parks' gates or by bringing your own food and drink; though many parks don't permit picnicking on their grounds, they may provide lockers and picnic areas nearby. If you live near a particular park, consider buying season passes; often these cost less than two or three single visits. Some parks, notably Disneyland, also have multiday ticket deals and special packages that include hotel stays. None of these will make your family outing cheap, but they may help make it more feasible.

A generally less expensive alternative is water parks, which sunny California has in abundance. Free-fall water slides, wave pools with their own artificial surf, inner-tube rides on simulated white-water rapids, and water playgrounds for the younger set make for cool—and often exciting—recreation on a hot summer day. Surrounding the pools are food concessions, changing rooms, and usually decks, lounge chairs, or beaches where sunbathers can spread out. Most of these parks are open summers only. Though all have trained lifeguards on duty, adults should supervise their children prudently—and don't forget the sunscreen, beach towels, water sandals, hats, and extra T-shirts. Besides those detailed in this chapter, you'll find water parks in Antioch (**Antioch Waterpark,** 4701 Lone Tree Way, tel. 925/776–3070); Chula Vista (**White Water Canyon Park,** 2052 Otay Valley Rd., tel. 619/426-7275); Concord (**Waterworld USA,** 1950 Waterworld Pkwy., tel. 925/609–9283); Lake Elsinore (**Volcano Island,** tel. 909/676–1984); Manteca (**Manteca Waterslides,** Oakwood Lake Resort, 874 E. Woodward Ave., tel. 209/239–2500); Vista (**Wave Waterpark,** 161 Recreation Dr., tel.

760/940–9283); and Windsor (**Windsor Waterworks and Slides,** 8225 Conde La., tel. 707/838–7760).

Other less expensive options are "family fun centers," which offer combinations of miniature golf, batting cages, bumper cars or boats, minicar racing, rock climbing, arcade games, and water slides. You pay by the hour or by the ride or activity rather than one big fee at the gate, so these attractions give you more control over how much you spend. Among other locations, look for them in Anaheim (**Anaheim Family Fun Center,** 1041 N. Shepherd, tel. 714/630–7212); Cathedral City, near Palm Springs (**Camelot Park,** 67-700 E. Palm Canyon Dr., tel. 760/321–9893); Colton, near San Bernardino (**Fiesta Village,** 1405 E. Washington St., tel. 909/824–2944); Fairfield (**Scandia's Family Center,** I–80, tel. 707/864–8558); Fresno (**Blackbeard's Family Entertainment Center,** 4055 N. Chestnut St., tel. 559/292–4554); Irvine (**Palace Park,** 3405 Michelson Dr., tel. 949/559–8336); Lake Elsinore (**Haunted Galleon,** tel. 909/676–1984); Riverside (**Castle Amusement Park,** 3500 Polk St., tel. 909/785–4140); and Sacramento (**Paradise Family Fun Park,** Cal Expo, 1600 Exposition Blvd., tel. 916/924–3595).

Northern Forests and Lakes

Trees of Mystery

(★★ 3 – 15) Trees of Mystery is a throwback to the days when every highway featured at least one unusual "roadside attraction." It started back in 1928 as a small grove of redwoods and an idea. But like the redwoods themselves, Trees of Mystery has kept growing, attracting 300,000 visitors a year now. It's one part nature trail and two parts theme park, with a whale of a gift shop (selling crafts, candy, and redwood burls) and even a remarkable little Native American museum at the back of the shop (see Chapter 5). But you don't have to pay admission or even venture beyond the parking area to find the top draw here for most kids: a 49-foot-high, 30,000-pound talking figure of Paul Bunyan standing next to a 25,000-pound Babe the Blue Ox. Paul actually carries on personal conversations with the surprised and delighted children who pass by. How does he

do it? Ask him. Drag the kids away from Paul and Babe to enter the park, where you can tour the trees themselves. They're noted for their strange characteristics: The World's Largest Family Tree is 12 trees with only one trunk; Nature's Underpass is a crawl-through tree, popular with kids; the Upside-Down Tree is what the name promises. The enduring favorite, Cathedral Tree, is nine redwood trees growing in a half-circle, said to be the largest such formation in the world; some sappy recorded music plays right beside it. The path continues through the Trail of Tall Tales, with stories of Paul Bunyan and his friends sculpted in redwood and narrated on tape as you walk past.

🏠 *Hwy. 101, Klamath, tel. 707/482–2251 or 800/638–3389. Admission: $6.50 adults, $4 ages 6–12. Open daily, usually dawn–dusk. Call for exact times.*

Waterworks Park

(★★ 2 – 15) Though not as big as some of the state's water parks, this one will cool you off while providing fun for all ages, and what more could you ask? School-age kids (or daring preschoolers) can twist and turn on three giant serpentine water slides, as well as navigate the 400-foot Wild White-water Inner Tube River Ride. Two 300-foot slides here introduce a thrill called the Flash Flood: Sudden rushes of water release behind each slider, propelling him or her toward a pool below. Meanwhile, kids under 3 feet tall can cavort in the Kiddy Water Playground, which has its own 18-inch-deep pool, fountain, and miniature slides.

🏠 *151 N. Boulder Dr., Redding, tel. 530/246–9550. Admission: $13.50 adults, $11.50 ages 3–11, under 4 free. Discounts daily after 5 PM. Open Memorial Day–Labor Day, daily 10–8.*

speed slides. Shark Attack has five high-speed slides, and Cannonball Falls has a 30-foot-long dropout slide into a pool. Riders must be at least 4 feet tall; these are best for teens and brave preteens. Younger kids can have fun, though, at Treasure Island, a water play-ground complete with tamer slides, pools, and waterfalls. Super Surf Hill, a 100-foot slip-pery slide, is suited for kids ages 3 to 6.

🏠 *1600 Exposition Blvd. at I–80, Cal Expo, Sacramento, tel. 916/924–0556. Admission: $16.99 adults and children over 4 feet, $11.99 children 4 feet and under, under age 3 free. Parking: $4. Open Memorial Day weekend–Labor Day, daily 10:30–6. Food concessions.*

Sierra and the Gold Country

Fairytale Town

(👫 1–9) This 2-acre nursery-rhyme theme park, across from the Sacramento Zoo (see Chapter 6), is tailor-built for small children, with 14 different themed play sets: The Old Woman Who Lived in a Shoe is a 12-foot slide, Captain Hook's Ship is a climbing structure, and King Arthur's Castle and Sherwood Forest are sites popular for birthday parties. Kids can also attend puppet shows, meet farm animals, or participate in various special events.

🏠 *1501 Sutterville Rd., Sacramento, tel. 916/264–5233. Admission: $3.50 adults, $3 ages 3–12. Open daily 9–5.*

Waterworld USA

(👫 2–15) If you visit Sacramento in sum-mer, you'll quickly discover it gets *hot.* When everyone in the family starts to wilt, head for this 14-acre water park on the grounds of Cal Expo. Here you'll find Breaker Beach, said to be the largest wave pool in Northern Cali-fornia, where you can bodysurf on 3-foot-high waves. The park has some of the highest water slides in the state, including the six-story Cliff-Hanger, Cobra, and Hurricane

San Francisco and the Bay Area

Children's Fairyland

(👫 1–9) Was this charming little enchanted park on the shores of Lake Mer-ritt, founded in 1950, the inspiration for Dis-neyland? Maybe so: Walt Disney did visit here, a few years before he opened his own theme park in 1955 in Anaheim. There's even a "magic" connection here; a "Magic Key" ($1.65) unlocks "talking storybooks" so that the dozens of nursery rhyme and fairy-tale sets come to life. When our kids were young they loved to gaze through the window of Geppetto's Workshop, pass through Alice in Wonderland's Tunnel, enter the mouth of Willie the Whale, and view the Three Billy Goats Gruff—complete with live goats. At Play Island, based on the tale of the Swiss Family Robinson, there's sand, tropical-style huts with thatched roofs, and sound effects such as bongo drums. Puppet shows, a petting zoo, a maze, a children's art exhibit, slides, and minirides—a carousel, a Ferris wheel, and a train, which require small additional fees—provide more entertain-ment. As a safety measure, adults must be accompanied by kids and vice versa.

🏠 *Grand and Bellevue Aves., Lakeside Park, Oakland, tel. 510/238–6876. Admission:*

$3.25 adults, $2.75 ages 1–12. Parking: $2 (weekends and holidays). Open Mid-June–Aug., Mon.–Fri. 10–4, Sat.–Sun. 10–5; Sept.–mid-June, Wed.–Sun. 10–4, weather permitting.

Paramount's Great America

(👫 **3–15**) Tackling the roller coasters and other daredevil rides at this movie- and TV-theme park is nothing less than a rite of passage for many Bay Area youngsters. Ten-year-olds who board the Vortex for a heart-thumping stand-up roller coaster ride know they're growing up; 12-year-olds who brave a 22-story, 91-feet-per-second, open-air fall on The Drop Zone can claim bragging rights all winter over those who held back. Top Gun, a jet-coaster meant to simulate the sensations of flying an F-14 Tomcat jet fighter, provides short but intense thrills. When my son, Grael, graduated to being a teenager, he dared me to join him on it. We catapulted off into space at 50 mph, experiencing a 360° vertical loop, two 270° "afterburn turns," and a "zero-gravity barrel roll." One of the latest stomach-turners here, Invertigo, is the first suspended, inverted, face-to-face coaster in North America; it takes riders forward and backward at 55 mph through a boomerang and vertical loop. And James Bond 007: A License to Thrill is a new motion simulator ride that takes would-be Bonds on motorcycle and Jet-Ski chases and skydiving from a helicopter. There's plenty for younger kids, too. The Forest of Fun area is a scaled-down playland, while the Nicktoons Block Party show features characters from Rugrats and Angry Beavers. Lia loves the area called Nickelodeon Splat City, a 3-acre tribute to messiness, where everyone is guaranteed to get drenched with gallons of water and Green Slime; the Green Slime Mine Car Coaster is a kiddie-sized roller coaster. And don't miss the classic double-deck Carousel Columbia—the world's tallest—near the front entrance of the park. Great America also has mid-range rides that are exciting but less scary for squeamish youngsters or parents than Top Gun or Invertigo. Among these are The Grizzly, a classic wooden roller coaster, and three water rides including Rip Roaring Rapids, a river-rafting ride that's great for getting soaked on a hot day. Most of the scarier rides have minimum height requirements, and some of the kiddie rides have *maximum* height requirements. The park also has a number of stage shows that feature music, cartoon characters, and, in some cases, audience participation; there's also a seven-story IMAX theater.

🏠 *Great America Pkwy. between Hwys. 101 and 237, Santa Clara, tel. 408/988–1776. Admission (including rides and shows): $31.99 ages 7–54, $20.99 ages 55 and over, $18.50 ages 3–6 or under 48" tall, under 3 free. Parking: $6. Open June–Aug., daily at 10 AM, closing hrs vary; late Mar.–late May and Sept.–mid-Oct., most weekends and holiday periods (call for dates and hrs). Stroller rentals, food concessions, baby-care center.*

Raging Waters

(👫 **2–15**) Raging Waters is our daughter Lia's idea of heaven; it has more than 20 slides, pools, and attractions. The big draws here are the seven-story Serpentine slides, which are simply great fun for anyone who enjoys a combination of speed and splashing. I saw daredevil tots as young as 2 sliding down the Serpentines—though, frankly, I would have been nervous sending my own kids down them at that age. There's plenty for young kids, however, at the Wacky Water Works, which includes a combination jungle gym, wading pool, and playground (parents can relax on nearby chaise lounges). Most everyone can enjoy the Endless River inner-tube ride, though it may be a bit tame for teenagers, who tend to prefer the Rampage, a steep slide on a board, the White Lightning and Blue Thunder speed slides, and the new Barracuda Blaster, a four-person toboggan ride. The park also has a half-million-gallon wave pool.

🏠 *Tully Rd. and Capitol Expressway, in Lake Cunningham Park, San Jose, tel. 408/270–8000. Admission: $20.99 anyone 42" or taller, $16.99 anyone under 42", $10.99* *ages 60 and over, under 4 free, $14.99 for all after 3 PM. Parking: $3. Open mid-May–mid-June, and Labor Day–mid-Sept., weekends 10–6; mid-June–Labor Day, Mon.–Thurs. 10–6, Fri.–Sun. 10–7. Food concessions, diaper-changing station.*

Six Flags Marine World Theme Park

(👫 **ALL**) The former Marine World Africa USA packs the highlights of a wildlife park, an oceanarium, and an amusement park into 160 acres, about 35 miles northeast of San Francisco. If you want to feed a giraffe, ride an elephant, watch a waterski or other show, and ride a roller coaster, you can do it here. To make sure you cover the attractions and shows you want to see, plan your itinerary as soon as you arrive. The 20- to 25-minute shows, the park's mainstay, take place throughout the day, and on busy days good seats go early. Dolphin Harbor stadium provides a slick showcase for bottle-nosed dolphins, who can jump 20 feet out of the water and do tail walks, flips, air spins, and other "behaviors" (in the old days, we called them "tricks"). Acrylic panels allow the audience to watch the dolphins underwater, too. Killer whales jump, swim, and dive in rhythm in their own stadium. Most kids scramble down to sit in the first few rows of the stadium, where they're almost guaranteed to get wet—make that soaked—by the splashing whales. (Lia attended this show twice in one afternoon because she didn't get "wet enough" the first time.) You might also get chosen as a volunteer to get a kiss from a whale. Elsewhere, the Tiger Island Splash Attack provides an underwater view of a dozen Bengal tigers at play. In other shows, sea lions do high dives, elephants demonstrate their agility, birds swoop and squawk, and daring two-legged mammals perform stunts on waterskis and do 32-foot-high free falls. In all but the latter two shows, trainers lace the entertainment with learning, imparting lessons about how animals survive—and are endangered—in the wild. Other animal-

related exhibits include Shark Experience, which takes you on a moving ramp through a clear tunnel in a huge shark tank, while Walk-about! An Australian Adventure and the separate Walrus Experience provide close-up views of kangaroos, wallaroos, wallabies, koalas, and walruses. At Giraffe Dock kids can hand-feed the giraffes, and at Elephant Encounter you can ride an elephant or play tug-of-war with one. Scattered throughout the park are 16 amusement-park-style rides that range from a 150-foot-tall three-loop roller coaster (which travels forward and backward at 50 mph) to spinning teacups and a Ferris wheel. Others include a river rapids ride, a train, paddleboats, and a dinosaur-themed 3-D motion simulator ride. Looney Tunes Seaport is a fun zone with rides geared to kids 10 and under, including a carousel and a submarine. A scenic way to get to Marine World is on the Blue & Gold Ferry (tel. 415/705–5555) from Pier 39 in San Francisco. The boat trip is an hour each way and costs $40 for adults and $27.50 for ages 5 to 12; prices include park admission and the short shuttle-bus ride between the boat and the park. The only problem is that the boat may return to San Francisco before you want to leave (as early as 3 PM on weekdays).
🏛 *Marine World Pkwy., off I–80, Vallejo, tel. 707/643–6722 or 707/644–4000. Admission: $29.99 adults, $20.99 ages 4–12, ages 3 and under free. Discounts for 2-day tickets. Parking: $5–$6. Open Memorial Day–Labor Day and spring break wks, daily 10–10; late Mar.–Memorial Day and Labor Day–Nov. 1, Fri.–Sun. 10–8. Stroller rentals, food concessions.*

Central Coast and Valley

Santa Cruz Beach Boardwalk

(👫 **ALL**) A half-hour or so drive south of Paramount's Great America (see *above*) is its bohemian cousin, the Santa Cruz Beach Boardwalk, set alongside a wide,

sandy beach. Great America is squeaky clean, self contained, and one price fits all; the Beach Boardwalk is funky, where you can come and go as you please, and pay as you play for 27 rides and other attractions. The boardwalk is also considerably older; built in 1907 and declared a California Historic Landmark, it's the largest full-scale seaside amusement park on the Pacific Coast, drawing 3 million visitors annually. Though recent renovations have toned down the funkiness, it's still a nostalgic and refreshing alternative to more antiseptic modern theme parks. Our kids cut their amusement-park teeth on the tot rides here and now embrace the stronger, stomach-churning stuff. Grael heads for the Hurricane, an intense, high-tech metal roller coaster, as well as the park's enduring favorite, the 1924 wooden Giant Dipper. Lia prefers the Haunted Castle, where monsters pop out of the walls, and the Logger's Revenge, a water flume ride with a dramatic (and sometimes soaking) plunge at the end; I've seen kids as old as 10 who are positively terrified at the sight of it. We all like the Sky Glider, an overhead chairlift that travels high over the park (little kids might be scared at the height), and the ornate 1911 Looff Carousel, whose hand-carved horses have carried an estimated 50 million riders. The Boardwalk also has bumper cars, Ferris wheels, seven tot rides, four arcades, a Laser Tag arena, a virtual reality computer game, a new skateboard ride simulator called Top Skater (with 3-D graphics), various carnival-type games, shops, food stands selling corn dogs and cotton candy, and the fanciful Neptune's Kingdom Adventure Amusement Center, housed in the 1907 Plunge building, once an indoor bathing palace. Neptune's Kingdom includes a two-story minigolf course complete with talking pirates, firing cannons, and an erupting volcano.
🏠 *400 Beach St., Santa Cruz, tel. 831/426–7433 or 831/423–5590. Admission free; unlimited rides for 1 day $18.95 per person, 60-ticket strip $24.95 (can be shared among family; rides require 3–6 tickets each). Minia-*

ture golf $4. Boardwalk rides open Memorial Day–Labor Day, daily; fall–spring, most weekends and holidays; hrs vary seasonally (call for schedule). Closed Dec. Neptune's Kingdom and Casino Fun Center arcade open daily except Dec. 25.

Wild Water Adventures

(👫 2–15) To combat Central Valley summer heat, head for this 52-acre water park east of Fresno that combines rides and slides with lots of shady, grassy areas for lounging and picnicking. The Blue Wave is billed as the West's largest wave pool, where kids can rent boogie-boards to surf the 4-foot waves. "Wild" slides include the Banzai Pipeline, the Rampage, Vortex, Vertigo, Thunder Falls, and the Black Hole. (Some rides have a minimum height requirement of 48″, unless kids can pass a swim test.) For young kids the Adventure Bay water play area awaits, starring a 13-foot-high octopus slide. When kids want to take a break from sliding and splashing, they can head for the beach volleyball court, fishing lakes, or games arcade.
🏠 *11413 E. Shaw Ave., Clovis, tel. 559/299–9453 or 800/564–9453. Admission: $19.99 anyone 48″ and up, $15.99 anyone under 48″, ages 2 and under free. Open mid-June–late Aug., daily with varying hrs, call for schedule; late May–mid-June and late Aug.–early Sept., weekends and holidays with varying hrs, call for schedule. Food concessions, life jackets, sundries shop, changing rooms, showers.*

Los Angeles and Environs

Disneyland

(👫 ALL) Since it first opened in 1955 Disneyland has drawn 300 million visitors, most of them families, who pass through its gates into a land of make-believe and merriment like no other. No matter what else you do in the Los Angeles area, you should make at least one journey to the "Happiest Place on Earth" (not that your kids will give you much choice). The Magic Kingdom covers 85 acres, with several dozen attractions spread out in eight themed "lands." If you have young children, you may want to head directly from the entrance, at the foot of shop-lined **Main Street U.S.A.**, to **Mickey's Toontown,** which looks like a fanciful, rather wacky cartoon town come to life. The top attractions there are Mickey and Minnie Mouse's houses, Donald's boat *Miss Daisy,* Goofy's Bounce House, and an action-packed Roger Rabbit chase ride. Your preschooler can meet Mickey himself behind his house on the set of one of his famous cartoons, and ride the bouncy Jolly Trolley around town. The younger crowd also gravitates to **Fantasyland,** set right behind the Sleeping Beauty Castle and the Matterhorn, Disneyland's two most famous landmarks. (Fortunately, Fantasyland lines seem somewhat shorter now that Toontown is siphoning off many preschoolers.) When Grael and Lia were small we spent nearly an entire day on the delightful rides featuring storybook characters such as Peter Pan, Snow White, Pinocchio, Mr. Toad, Alice in Wonderland, and Dumbo. Lia was charmed by It's a Small World, where an international chorus of costumed, dancing dolls serenades you as you pass by on little boats. The famous Matterhorn Bobsleds was one of Grael's first "big" rides—it's an exciting but not overly scary roller coaster for kids 40 inches and taller. In later years Grael gravitated toward **Tomorrowland** and its extremely popular Space Mountain and Star Tours rides. Space Mountain is a darting roller coaster that races through pitch darkness; Grael loved it, but it scared the daylights out of his younger sister (think twice before bringing a child under age 7 on this one; no kids under 40 inches are allowed). Star Tours, a George Lucas creation that simulates an intergalactic journey, is a blast, though somewhat jarring; if your child is prone to motion sickness, this could set it

off. The rest of Tomorrowland was completely redesigned and updated in 1998. New attractions include the towering Astro Orbitor, where you can pilot your own spaceship; Rocket Rods XPR—high-speed "vehicles of the future" that zoom on an overhead track—and the 3-D film *Honey, I Shrunk the Audience.* After Tomorrowland, we all enjoyed a relaxing, oddly old-fashioned trip on the Disneyland Monorail to the adjacent Disneyland Resort (see Chapter 12). Even if you aren't staying there, I'd suggest taking a look around the resort and perhaps having a meal at Goofy's Kitchen, a restaurant where costumed Disney characters often stroll from table to table. Continuing around the park, **Frontierland**'s Old West motif appeals to all ages. We enjoy riding the rafts across the Rivers of America to Tom Sawyer's Island, where kids can explore secret caves and run around a bit. Frontierland's other main attraction is Big Thunder Mountain Railroad, a turbulent roller coaster in the form of a runaway mine train. Expect long lines, and kids must be at least 40 inches tall to get on. Tiny **Critter Country** is best known for Splash Mountain, a log flume ride that concludes with a very steep five-story plunge. Prepare to get wet, and to wait a long time for the privilege. (Minimum age 3, minimum height 40 inches.) Critter Country also contains Country Bear Playhouse, a 15-minute musical hoedown starring an assortment of joking "bear-itones"; sitting down to watch the show can give you an amusing break from standing in lines (though, ironically, you may have to stand in a line to get in). We've always been partial to nearby **New Orleans Square,** site of our family's all-time favorite ride: Pirates of the Caribbean, a rollicking underground boat trip along the old Spanish Main, with colorful sets and clever special effects. Long lines here tend to move quickly. The Haunted Mansion, another very amusing ride, takes you on a "doom buggy" ride through an old mansion filled with ghosts, ghouls, and holographic images. Some little ones could be scared by the effects on both these rides, but most will join in the fun. In **Adventureland,** which brings you back close to the main gates, the hot thrill ride is the Indiana Jones Adventure, an "archaeological expedition" gone haywire: While exploring the Temple of the Forbidden Eye in the jungles of India, you'll encounter a series of hair-raising perils such as a gigantic rolling boulder, a raining horde of insects, and a quivering suspension bridge. The Jungle Cruise, on the other hand, is pretty tame.

Evening entertainments at Disneyland change with the seasons, but all are loaded with glitz, tunes, talent, and pizzazz, not to mention beloved Disney characters. Fantasmic! is a not-to-be-missed outdoor show loaded with high-tech special effects: lasers, fog, water, pyrotechnics, and images of pink elephants, a whale, and a giant snake that seem to appear magically in the air.

Finally, here are some tips to help you avoid the crowds and up to two-hour-wait lines for the most popular rides. Order your "passports" (tickets) in advance (see *below*); call first to check the latest prices. If you're planning a multiday visit to Disneyland, by all means purchase a five-day "Flex Passport," available in advance (*not* at the park itself) through travel agents and tour operators; it's the same price as a regular two-day passport, and, along with unlimited entrance for five days, includes early park admission on most days. If you can, visit during the off-season (from September to May, excluding holidays and school vacations) or during midweek. If you're staying nearby, choose a hotel or motel that provides shuttle service (usually free) to the park; it'll eliminate having to deal with the immense parking area. Arrive early, preferably half an hour before official opening time (sometimes the gates open earlier than announced), and once you're in the park, head immediately for the rides you want to take most. Try to eat at off hours, eliminating the noontime and dinnertime crunches. In mid- to late-afternoon, get your hand stamped and leave the park

for a few hours' rest if possible, returning after dinner for evening rides, parades, and shows—then stay late, when lines for rides thin out again (Disneyland remains open daily till midnight in summer and on Saturdays the rest of the year). Parents may want to split up to take different-aged children on different rides. (Ask about "Child Switch Passes," too, allowing parents to trade off going on rides and staying with their small child.) It's wise to craft an itinerary before you get to the park, but keep in mind that few children will want to stick to a strict schedule and that surprises at Disneyland can pop up at every turn.

🏠 *1313 Harbor Blvd., Anaheim, tel. 714/781–4565 or 213/626–8605, ext. 4565. For advance tickets, send check or money order to Disneyland Admissions, Box 3232, Anaheim, CA 92803. Admission: $38 adults, $28 ages 3–11. Discounted 2-day, 3-day, and 5-day passports available. Parking: $7. Open daily. Hrs vary seasonally; call for schedule. Stroller rentals, wheelchair rentals, food concessions, baby-care station.*

Knott's Berry Farm

(👫 **ALL**) Though often viewed as the "poor relation" to the mouse empire down the road in Anaheim, Knott's Berry Farm has parlayed an eclectic combination of thrill rides, shows, and Old West history into a 5 million visitors-a-year attraction. Knott's is actually California's second-largest amusement park, with 150 acres and more than 165 rides, shows, shops, restaurants, and other diversions. Founded nearly 80 ago, it retains something of the rural, nostalgic flavor of its past, before the urban encroachments of Orange County wiped out the real berry farm for which it was named. But it's increasingly going the high-tech route with entertainments like Supreme Scream, the tallest descending thrill ride in the world (at 312 feet it's the highest structure in Orange County). Riders drop from the top to the ground in three seconds. The park is divided into six themed areas. **Camp Snoopy** appeals to the youngest generation, with more than 30 rides and attractions with a High Sierra theme. Some of its rides have maximum height requirements. When we came here with Lia at age 8, she was still young enough to appreciate the mini-roller coaster, mule-powered carousel, pint-size Ferris wheel, gentle plane and train rides, and wandering Peanuts characters. Woodstock's Airmail is a cute miniature (19 feet high) version of the Supreme Scream. At **Fiesta Village** you can ride on a restored handcrafted 1896 carousel populated with zebras, lions, and ostriches along with the usual steeds. The Jaguar, a mammoth coaster that begins at a "Mayan pyramid," swoops and swerves high above one-sixth of the entire park. Montezooma's Revenge loops upside down and backward at speeds of 55 mph (there's a 54-inch minimum height requirement). Knott's newest theme area is **The Boardwalk,** celebrating the southern California beach scene. Here you'll find the Windjammer Surf Racers, a dual-track steel racing coaster. Riders travel through a wavelike series of side-by-side loops, 60-foot drops, and twisting turns over water. Kingdom of the Dinosaurs, a "time machine" ride, is comparatively slow moving, but younger kids and their parents usually enjoy it. For more stomach-churning action test the Boomerang, which free-falls from 11 stories through three twisting, upside-down loops, and the HammerHead, which spins passengers up to heights of 80 feet. In **Wild Water Wilderness,** we all enjoy Bigfoot Rapids, an exciting replication of a white-water rapids rafting trip (minimum height 48 inches)—but it's best on hot days when you don't mind getting wet. This area is also the site of Mystery Lodge, a "sensory adventure" with a Native American theme combining lightning storms and other special effects with live actors. At the heart of the park is its original attraction, first built to occupy diners waiting to eat at Mrs. Knott's fried chicken restaurant (see Chapter 15): **Ghost Town,** modeled after the real Calico ghost town near Barstow

(see Chapter 4). Kids 9 to 12, too old for Camp Snoopy and too young for the Boomerang, come into their own here, riding the Timber Mountain Log Ride (you'll get wet during the exit) and the Calico Mine Train, which takes you into a reproduction of an actual mine. At age 8 Lia was scared by the former; the latter may be a bit dark for very young kids. You can also ride a real train—there's a surprise along the route—or walk through a Haunted Shack full of optical illusions. We enjoy the Wild West stunt shows here and the Bird Cage Theater, which presents intentionally corny old-time melodramas. The Ghostrider—billed as the West's tallest, longest, and fastest wooden roller coaster—races over Ghost Town. Finally, in the **Indian Trails** area, kids can learn tribal legends, dances, and crafts from Native Americans. California Marketplace, a collection of shops and restaurants just outside the gates, is a good place to relax and regroup. If you're in the park at night, watch for the new laser and pyrotechnic show over Reflection Lake.

🏠 *8039 Beach Blvd., Buena Park, tel. 714/ 220–5200 or 714/220–5220. Admission: $36 adults, $26 ages 3–11 and 60 and over, $16.95 for all after 4 PM. Parking: $7 (free 3-hr parking at California Marketplace). Open June–early Sept., daily 9–midnight; mid-Sept.– May, weekdays 10–6, Sat. 10–10, Sun. 10–7. Stroller rental, wheelchair rental, food concessions, diaper-changing station.*

Pacific Park

(👫 **ALL**) Pacific Park is the only West Coast amusement park right on an oceanfront pier—the famed Santa Monica Pier (see Chapter 15), which also has a vintage Looff carousel. Of Pacific Park's 12 rides the most dramatic is the West Coaster, a roller coaster that soars more than five stories above the pier deck; the ocean views are terrific, if fleeting. Somewhat more leisurely, and even higher views can be had from the Pacific Wheel, a Ferris wheel that carries riders more than 130 feet above Santa

Monica Beach at 2½ revolutions per minute. You can also board a swinging ship (the Sea Dragon), a spinning ride with pulsating music (the Rock and Roll), separate bumper car rides designed for kids and adults, and several tame rides for young children such as a mini–Ferris wheel and the Seaside Swing, a mini-swing ride. Kids can also perform in a live circus show or try out the Action Ride Theater, a motion-based simulator ride. And there are 11 amusement park–style midway games, a food plaza, and shops. Rides all have minimum height requirements (ranging from 24 to 48 inches) and everything here is pay as you go. The Pier is particularly colorful at night, though you may prefer to come in daytime with young kids, when it's less rowdy.
🏠 *380 Santa Monica Pier (Colorado Blvd. and Ocean Ave.), Santa Monica, tel. 310/260–8744. Admission: $1–$4 per ride; unlimited rides $15/day. Open daily; hrs vary by season (call for schedule). Selected rides only open Mon.–Thurs. from Labor Day–Memorial Day (full service on weekends). Food concessions.*

Raging Waters

(👫 2–15) With 50 million gallons of water in use, everything at this 50-acre water park is *big*. Splash Island Adventure, Raging Waters' largest attraction, contains five giant slides, plus crawl tunnels, water cannons, and swinging bridges. A thousand-gallon bucket atop a five-story tower pours water on all below. Thunder Rapids, where riders shoot down a 550-foot slide aboard six-person rafts, is the largest and widest flume ride in the western United States. El Niño: The Ride sends inner-tube riders turning and dipping 75 feet at speeds of up to 40 mph, with a final drop into a 3-foot-deep splash pool. High Extreme and High Extreme II are the nation's highest water toboggan and two-person tube rides, respectively. Other excitement comes from Drop Out, a seven-story drop slide; the Dark Hole, a two-person enclosed raft ride through a 450-foot fiberglass flume; Raging

Rivers, an inner-tube ride over man-made white-water cascades; and Vortex, a four-story tower with two enclosed 270-foot spiral body flumes. The million-gallon Wave Cove produces 3-foot oceanlike waves for bodysurfing or inner tubing. (Jet-Ski stunt shows take place in the wave pool daily from late June to early September.) For a mellower experience you can coast along a ¼-mile river in the Amazon Adventure. Kid's Kingdom, a 2,000-square-foot water playground for tykes, has slides, swings, a maze of plastic pipes, and waterfalls to stand under.
🏠 *111 Raging Waters Dr., Frank G. Bonelli Regional Park, San Dimas, tel. 909/592–8181 or 909/592–6453. Admission: $21.99 adults and children over 48", $14.99 children 42"–48", children under 42" free; discounts for adults aged 55 and over and for everyone after 5 PM. Open late May–mid-Sept., Mon.–Fri. 10–8, Sat.–Sun. 9:30–9; late Apr.–late May and mid-Sept.–mid Oct., weekends 10–6. Food concessions.*

Six Flags California

(👫 3–15) When your teens and pre-teens want the ultimate in thrills and chills, take them to Six Flags California, which combines **Magic Mountain** theme park and the **Hurricane Harbor** water park. A half hour north of Hollywood, this is Los Angeles County's only major amusement park, but it's a doozy: Magic Mountain alone covers 260 acres, with 10 landscaped theme areas. Magic Mountain is best known for its 11 "monster coasters." Several have movie themes. The Riddler's Revenge stand-up coaster soars more than 150 feet high and, while looping, twisting, and spiraling, reaches a speed of more than 63 mph. One 360-degree vertical loop is 124-feet high. Superman: The Escape, the world's first 100-mph coaster, rises 41 stories, then descends the same distance *backward*, resulting in more than six seconds of weightlessness. If that appeals to you and your family, well, have fun! Batman: The

Ride, a suspended coaster that spins riders over the outside of loops and corkscrews, is another high-tech favorite. A fourth intense coaster, called Flashback, provides an eight-story free-fall along six hairpin 180° dives, followed by a 540° upward spiral. Viper is the world's largest looping coaster, turning riders over seven times, at speeds of up to 70 mph. With nearly 2 miles of track, Colossus is one of the world's largest dual-track wooden coasters. Another "woodie," the Psyclone, propels you through a dark tunnel at 50 mph. Ninja is the West Coast's fastest suspended coaster, with swinging trains hanging from an overhead track. Revolution, another looping coaster, was the first steel coaster with a 360° loop. The oldest and tamest of the group, Gold Rusher, simulates a runaway mine train. Expect long waits; it's best to arrive when the park opens in the morning, especially on crowded summer weekends. The big coasters all require height minimums between 42 inches and 54 inches. For younger children there's the restored 1912 Grand Carousel, or, for kids under 54 inches, the 6-acre Bugs Bunny World, with rides like the Wile E. Coyote minicoaster or the Daffy Duners (racing dune buggies); Warner Bros. characters like Bugs and Daffy mingle with the kids here, and the area tends to be less crowded than other parts of the park. Nearby, you'll find a petting zoo and Yosemite Sam Sierra Falls, where you can splash down 760 feet of twisting, turning water slides aboard two-person rafts. Magic Mountain stages various shows, ranging from animals to stunts and fireworks.

Hurricane Harbor water park, adjacent to Magic Mountain and open in warm-weather months only, requires separate admission (adults and children over 48 inches can save a little by buying a combination ticket). Hurricane Harbor may be the most fancifully decorated water park around. The themes here are pirates, shipwrecks, tropical lagoons, sea creatures—and, of course,

plenty of water rides. Among the most exciting rides are the five speed slides at Black Snake Summit, including two of the tallest enclosed speed slides in the region; the five slides range from 300 to 650 feet long. The Lost Temple Rapids, in turn, are navigated by four-person rafts. Forgotten Sea is a wave pool for bodysurfers. The River Cruise is a 1,300-foot-long river for slow-moving rafts. And Castaway Cove—designed for kids under 54 inches tall—is a large water play area that includes slides, waterfalls, and plenty of places to splash around.

🏠 *26101 Magic Mountain Pkwy. exit off I–5, Valencia, tel. 661/255–4100 or 661/255–4111 or 818/367–5965. Magic Mountain admission: $36 adults and children 48" and over, $20 ages 55 and over, $18 children under 48", ages 2 and under free. Hurricane Harbor admission: $19 adults and children 48" and over, $12 children under 48"; ages 2 and under free. Two-park combo ticket: $46. Parking: $7. Magic Mountain open Apr.–Oct., daily at 10 AM, closing hrs vary; Nov.–Mar., weekends and most school holidays at 10 AM, closing hrs vary. Hurricane Harbor open Memorial Day–Labor Day, daily at 10 AM, closing hrs vary; mid-May and Sept., weekends at 10 AM, closing hrs vary. Stroller rentals, wheelchair rentals, food concessions.*

Universal Studios Hollywood

(👫 3–15) Nothing else in Tinseltown comes close to providing as entertaining a look at moviemaking as Universal Studios Hollywood does. If your kids are old enough to have watched a movie all the way through, they may be old enough to enjoy Universal Studios—though some of the attractions here can be frightening for tots. It used to be easy to see all of Universal Studios in a day, but on our family's last trip here in the peak summer season we were hard pressed to get onto all the major rides, much less take in the shows. The park is divided into three main areas: the Entertainment Center, the Studio Center, and the Back Lot. You enter through the **Entertainment Center,** site of several attractive movie-set streets and restaurants; various shows take place here. The shows are easier to get into than the rides, so consider leaving those till later in the day (it's also easier to watch a show when you're tired than to stand in another ride line). But before leaving the Entertainment Center, line up for Back to the Future—the Ride. Strapped into a "time travel" car, you'll feel you're in the middle of a 3-D movie—careening into the past in a dizzying chase scene, encountering avalanches, volcanoes, and a fierce tyrannosaurus rex along the way. The visual and sound effects are remarkable. There's a 40 inches minimum height requirement for kids, however, and pregnant women and people with certain health conditions are warned not to ride. Proceeding down the enormous Starway escalator, you'll reach **Studio Center.** Head directly for the blockbuster attraction, Jurassic Park: The Ride. Boarding a fast-moving river raft, you'll navigate through fog banks and tropical foliage until coming face-to-face with a pack of voracious velociraptors and an incredibly lifelike giant T-rex; prepare for an exciting (and for young kids, possibly terrifying) ride, with an 84-foot plunge and other thrills. After Jurassic Park, the long-time favorite Back Lot Tram Tour may seem positively tame, but don't miss it (keeping in mind that this, too, has some scary special effects). During the 50-minute tram ride through the studio's back lot, past facades of houses and streets used in many of the studio's movies and TV shows—from *Psycho* to *Leave It to Beaver*—you may see an actual show or commercial in production, complete with stars at work. Even if you don't, you'll still have some remarkable encounters: with King Kong, Jaws, a lava-spewing volcano, a collapsing bridge, a flash flood, and a simulated 8.3 earthquake. Once back at Studio Center, head for the E.T. Adventure, a visually dazzling interstel-

lar bike trip with everyone's favorite alien. Though this ride is fairly tame, no pregnant women or children under 2 are admitted. Backdraft, which features a host of fiery special effects, is decidedly not for young kids either; if you wait outside with the kids while your spouse stands in line for this, the ushers will let you in immediately once your partner finishes walking through the attraction, so couples can switch off on child care without waiting in line twice. The half-hour World of Cinemagic presentation tells you all about movie special effects; some of the scenes in the Hitchcock segment may be too bloody for the young or squeamish. Back at the Entertainment Center, you have your choice of several shows. Totally Nickelodeon, inspired by the cable TV channel, features lots of audience participation in stunts and games—including a chance to get drenched with green slime. Water-World, a "live sea war spectacular" complete with pyrotechnics, crams 60 stunts into 16 minutes, capped by a close-up seaplane crash. The Wild, Wild, Wild West stunt show, though a bit corny, does have some good action. The Animal Actors Stage, meanwhile, stars canine celebs such as Lassie and Beethoven. Summertime crowds can be overwhelming, with long lines at the most popular rides and attractions. Try to arrive early; the park opens at 8 AM. Another way to beat the crowds is to sign up for the "VIP Experience," which includes a behind-the-scenes tour and preferred entrance to rides and shows (that means you get to cut in line and collect angry stares from others); call 818/622–5120 for information and reservations. Restaurants, snack bars, and shops are scattered throughout the park, but consider getting your hand stamped and exiting for lunch or shopping at nearby **CityWalk** (see Chapter 15), where the food and merchandise are both better and less expensive. If you plan on spending more than one day at Universal Studios, buy a Celebrity Annual Pass, which is good for unlimited admission for a year and includes discounts at nearby hotels such as the Sheraton Universal (see Chapter 15).

🏨 *Universal City Plaza, Universal City, tel. 818/622–3801. Take Universal Center or Lankershim Blvd. exit off Hollywood Fwy. (Hwy. 101). Admission: $38 adults, $28 ages 3–11, under 3 free. Parking: $7. Open June–early Sept., daily 8–10; mid-Sept.–May, daily 9–7. Stroller rentals, wheelchair rentals, food concessions, diaper-changing stations.*

Wild Rivers

(**♈ 3–15**) Wild is right; this 20-acre Orange County water park has more than 40 rides and attractions, and they come with names guaranteed either to spark your sense of adventure or send you scurrying back to your hotel pool: The Edge, The Ledge, The Abyss, Bombay Blasters, The Cobras, Wipeout! and Chaos—the latter a tube ride through the dark complete with 360° turns, lightning, fog, and crashing timbers. The most intense action is centered around Wild Rivers Mountain, billed as Southern California's largest man-made earth mountain, complete with 25 rides. Here kids taller than 54 inches can slide the length of a football field or over a waterfall. At Thunder Cove you can try out two giant side-by-side wave action pools, one with gentle waves for bodysurfing, the other with strong waves for bodyboarding ($4 additional rental charge). Younger kids, meanwhile, can enjoy the adjacent two-headed Dinosaur Slide, or venture over to Explorers' Island and Typhoon Lagoon, where several of the Wild Rivers Mountain slides have been scaled down for smaller kids, alongside wading pools, activity pools and giant-sized whirlpools.

🏨 *8770 Irvine Center Dr., off I–405, Irvine, tel. 949/768–9453. Admission: $20.95 adults, $16.95 ages 3–9, $9.95 ages 55 and over and for all ages after 4 PM. Parking: $4. Open mid-June–mid-Sept., daily 10–8; mid-May–mid-June and mid-Sept.–late Sept., weekends and holidays 11–5. Food concessions.*

San Diego and the Southern Deserts

Legoland California

(**♈ 2–12**) If Grael were still 11, we might have to move to Carlsbad, a seaside town about ½-hour's drive north of San Diego, and home of the new Legoland California, which opened in 1999. Legoland is a theme park inspired by the Lego, the Danish-manufactured toy brick used for building castles, airplanes, even minicities—it was also Grael's all-time favorite toy, surpassing video games and that robot that used to wander all over the house screeching like a car alarm. Grael tells me even now that he would have liked to have grown up as close to Legoland as humanly possible; armed with a pass for the summer we could have dropped him off on the last day of school and picked him up around Labor Day. If your child is similarly afflicted, Legoland could become a must-see anytime you're in Southern California. (There are two Legolands in Europe; this is the first in the United States.) The park spreads out over 128 acres within sight of the Pacific. "Play is a child's most important work" is the guiding motto, which translates into plenty of opportunities to build and play with Legos, along with rides, shows, kid-friendly restaurants, and shops. The centerpiece of the park is called **Miniland,** a miniature landscape of five different North American landmarks—New York City, Washington, D.C., a New England harbor, New Orleans, and the California coast—all built with the trademark plastic blocks. (In all, 30 million Lego bricks are used in Miniland and other areas around the park.) Besides Miniland, there are five other themed areas. In the **Imagination Zone,** kids learn as they play in both structured workshops and free play areas. The medieval-themed **Castle Hill** houses a junior dragon coaster. **Fun Town** gives kids a chance to take part in producing Lego bricks at a Lego factory, as well as attend a miniature driving school with little cars, helicopters, and boats. The **Village Green** is a make-believe garden with a train ride, magic show, and interactive fountains. And **The Ridge** features a self-propelled ride to the top of a 30-foot lookout tower, plus an elaborate maze.

🏠 *One Lego Dr., Carlsbad, tel. 760/918–5300. Admission: $32 adults, $25 ages 3–16, under 3 free. Annual pass: $99 adults, $79 ages 3–16. Open daily 10–6; call for the latest schedules.*

Oasis Waterpark

(👬 **2–15**) What better spot for a water theme park than the desert? The aptly named Oasis Waterpark has the state's largest wave-action pool (suitable for older kids only), with 3-foot waves for bodyboard and bodysurfing. Add to this the 13 water slides, such as the twin 70-foot-tall Scorpion free-fall slides, the two 40-mph Rattlers, and the Black Widow—two-person inner-tubes ridden in 450 feet of complete darkness, leading to a 50-foot drop into a catch pool. Creature Fantasy, for 2- to 6-year-olds, features fanciful minislides—through a whale's mouth, along a giant frog's tongue, and out of a 6-foot-high shipwreck. Whitewater River is a leisurely inner-tube ride for all ages.

🏠 *1500 Gene Autry Trail, Palm Springs, tel. 760/325–7873. Admission: $18.95 anyone over 60″, $11.95 anyone 40″–60″, under 40″ free. Parking: $3. Open mid-Mar.–Labor Day, daily at 11 AM; closing hrs vary; Labor Day–Oct., weekends 11–6. Food concessions.*

Sea World

(👬 **ALL**) Our family has spent several days over the years at this lush, enormous aquatic theme park on Mission Bay, and we enjoy it more with each visit. Though we've been put off in the past by the cornier shows, the killer whale and dolphin shows here are truly spectacular, and the marine life exhibits keep getting better and better. The park's longtime top draw is the Killer Whale Show, presenting Shamu and a few of his orca pals in a 5 million-gallon tank. Shamu swims, Shamu jumps, Shamu dives, often with a trainer riding his back, stomach, nose, or even standing on his side; at one point, a lucky kid from the audience gets to sit on Shamu's back. Beware that those sitting in the first 14 rows will get soaked from Shamu's splashing; kids tend to love it, camera equipment doesn't. (Some families solve the problem by sitting in separate rows.) You can even visit Shamu Backstage—petting and helping to feed and "train" the killer whales (who may have a wet surprise for you). Other star Sea World performers include dolphins, birds, sea lions, sea otters, and walruses.

Next, head for Rocky Point Preserve, a big outdoor pool built to resemble the Pacific Coast, complete with rocks and waves. Grael thought this was one of the best marine exhibits he'd ever seen. You can stand or sit next to the pool as a half dozen dolphins swim playfully past you; you're so close you can actually get wet as they pass. Bewhiskered California sea otters frolic engagingly in a tank next to the dolphins. A second winner is the Penguin Encounter, where you ride a moving ramp past emperor, king, macaroni, and Gentoo penguins in a re-created Antarctic environment. Lia was fascinated by five king penguins standing in a circle "talking," much like tuxedoed waiters on their break. My third top recommendation is the Forbidden Reef, with an outdoor pool where you can pet bat rays (velvety on top, slimy underneath) and even feed them squid. Proceed indoors to the moray eel caverns, a riveting sight as dozens of the eerie, almost evil-looking eels stare out from their rock dwellings, their mouths agape. Sea World also has a Shark Encounter, said to be the world's largest shark display; you ride a moving stairway through a tunnel in the middle of a huge see-through tank, passing right beside a flotilla of leopard, hammerhead, and other sharks. The Manatee Rescue, a long-term care habitat for orphaned or ailing Florida manatees, is the only U.S. attraction outside of Florida to display these gentle aquatic mammals. There are also four aquariums, simulated tide pools, a Skytower ride ($2), and an "ocean dive" to the Bermuda Triangle. When the kids tire of shows and sights, take them to the new 2-acre tropical-theme play area Shamu's Happy Harbor, where everyone in the family—even parents—can climb, jump, and get wet.

🏠 *1720 S. Shores Rd., Mission Bay, San Diego, tel. 619/226–3901. Admission: $35.95 adults, $26.95 ages 3–11. 14-day pass: $68.95 adults, $50.95 ages 3–11. Parking: $6. Open daily; hrs vary by season (call for times). Stroller rentals, food concessions.*

GET WET, CLIMB HIGH, SPEED PAST, DRIFT BY
OUTDOOR ACTION

With California's generally mild weather year-round, kids can ride a wave, a wind current, a mountain bike, or a palomino somewhere in the state in every season. They can also help paddle a kayak, a canoe, or a raft; hike through a forest or along the seashore; cast a line into a lake; swim in the ocean; or join in almost any outdoor sport their ages and skills permit. Skiing and other winter sports are covered extensively in Chapter 11, and in Chapters 14 to 18 you can read about local options for golf, tennis, in-line skating, and certain other year-round sports. In this chapter you'll find information on where to go to pursue your family's other favorite sports.

Some sports are simple—slip on a swimsuit or some sneakers and hit the water or the hiking trail. Others require thought, planning, time, and expense, especially with children along. Safety is the first consideration. When biking, wear helmets and bright colors. When boating, wear life jackets. And when entrusting your safety to an adventure outfitter, check out whether the outfitter has experience, is reliable, and uses up-to-date equipment. Has the outfitter run previous family trips? (If the owner or guide is a parent, that can be a big plus.) Will other children be along? Is the adventure quotient "soft" enough for kids to handle? What's the pace of the trip—always on the go, or leaving time for play and rest?

Also ask yourself some tough questions: How well do your children cope with situations outside their regular routines—where bedrooms are tents, bathrooms may be the great outdoors, and trail dust may settle on the hot dogs? Are they old enough to always ride (stand, walk, hike) by themselves—or might you end up carrying them? And if you're thousands of feet in the air in a balloon, or miles downstream on a river, are you positive they won't suddenly panic and demand to turn around and go back? At that point, remember, it may not be an option.

There are ways to ease into a sport: short float trips on a river, perhaps, or a trail ride in a city park. But after a taste of the fun, most kids can't wait for more.

Biking

Mountain Biking

Mountain biking, one of the hottest sports in the country, originated in Northern California. Mountain bikes are built to challenge hilly, rocky, rugged terrain, with wide, knobby tires for extra traction, flat handlebars to let riders sit up comfortably, and 24 high-tech gears to provide climbing power. When Grael got his first mountain bike at age 12, he left his mom and me—still wheeling our old narrow-tired 10-speeds— literally in the dust on an off-road trail. Remember that it's mandatory in California for kids to wear safety helmets (parents should, too); gloves and goggles are also recommended for rough terrain.

The adventure travel company **Backroads** (801 Cedar St., Berkeley 74710, tel. 510/ 527–1555 or 800/462–2848) offers six-day Family Trips via bike in the Lake Tahoe area (see Chapter 18) in summer, with top-flight accommodations. These trips feature kid-size rental bikes, menus specially designed for children's tastes, and games and activities for kids. The minimum age is 10. The adult price is $1,798, with discounts for kids.

Top spots for mountain biking in the state include the sport's birthplace, Marin County's **Mount Tamalpais State Park** (see Chapter 14; take U.S. 101 north to Shoreline Hwy. [Hwy. 1]; exit at Panoramic Hwy. and follow signs; tel. 415/388–2070). The Old Railroad Grade climbs 6½ miles and 2,200 feet from the outskirts of Mill Valley to Mount Tam's East Peak parking lot; it also goes *down*, so take heart. **Sausalito Mountain Bike Rentals** (803 Bridgeway, Sausalito, tel. 415/331–4448) rents 24-speed mountain bikes for $10 per hour or $35 per day; seven-speed cruisers cost less.

The **Mammoth Lakes** area (see Chapter 18) has miles of paved and dirt roads, and bike lanes along mountain roads are popular with skaters, too. **Mammoth Mountain Bike Park**

(tel. 760/934–0706) at the Mammoth Mountain Ski Area, contains 70 miles of single-track trails ranging from easy to strenuous starting from atop the 11,000-foot peak; trails are usually open by July and close by the end of October. Chairlifts and bike shuttles ($18 adults, $10 ages 6–12 for two rides) provide easy, scenic access to the trails; if you'd like unlimited rides, the cost is $23 for adults, $12 for children per day. Midweek two-hour bike rental packages at the bike park, including two rides on chair lifts or bike shuttles, cost $23 for adults, $12 for kids. In town, rent mountain bikes at **Sandy's Ski & Sports** (Main St., tel. 760/934–7518) for $7 an hour or $28 per day, or at **Footloose** (Canyon St. and Minaret Rd., tel. 760/934–2400) for $8 an hour, $28 per day.

At **Lake Tahoe** (see Chapter 18), two ski resorts open their downhill slopes and cross-country trails to mountain bikers each summer. At **Northstar-at-Tahoe** (Hwy. 267, 6 mi north of Lake Tahoe, tel. 530/562–1010), chairlifts fitted with bike racks take riders up to two 7,000-foot-plus peaks where more than 100 miles of forested trails await. (Chairlifts cost $21 adults, $14 ages 5–12 for all day, 9:30–4.) Northstar's **Mountain Bike Park** (tel. 530/562–2268) rents mountain bikes from mid-June to mid-October, weather permitting. All-day bike rentals cost $32 for adult size, $24 for a junior bike, and $15 for a child's bike; helmets are included. Northstar also offers lodging/mountain biking packages; call 800/466–6784 for information. At Squaw Valley ski resort you can take your bike to the mountaintop via cable car for 25 miles of trails ($19 for one cable car ride, $26 for unlimited rides). The **Squaw Valley Mountain Bike Park** (1960 Squaw Valley Rd., Olympic Valley, tel. 530/583–3356 or 530/583–6985; open about June–Sept.) rents mountain bikes for $15 an hour, $35 all day. Other popular mountain biking spots at Tahoe include Blackwood Canyon on the west shore and the challenging Flume Trail on the east shore; rental shops include **Cyclepaths** (1785 W. Lake Blvd., Tahoe Park, tel. 530/581–1171; rentals $5 an hour, $21 per day) and **Porter's Ski and Sport** (501 N. Lake Blvd., Tahoe City, tel. 530/583–2314; rentals $10 for two hours, $20 per day). The season runs from about April to October.

In Southern California, **Big Bear Lake** (see Chapter 18) is the top spot for mountain biking. From May until snow season begins mountain bikers can ride the Sky Lift to the top of Snow Summit Mountain Resort (tel. 909/866–5766 or 909/866–4621; see Chapters 11 and 18) to test their skills on various types of mountain terrain. All-day passes for riders with bikes cost $19 for adults, $8 ages 7 to 12, ages 6 and under free; discounted half-day passes are also available. **Team Big Bear Mountain Shop** (tel. 909/866–4565), at the base of Snow Summit, rents bikes for $6.50 an hour or $32 all day. Helmets are included.

Road Biking

Road biking offers the exhilaration of pedaling along country lanes and past rivers, lakes, beaches, and marinas. Many cities have extensive bike-lane systems, and resort areas frequently provide scenic bike trails for miles of relatively flat, easy riding.

My vote for the top road biking in Northern California is on the **Monterey Peninsula** (see Chapter 17). The **Monterey Peninsula Recreation Trail** is a superb 5-mile bike trail along the shoreline from Pacific Grove's Asilomar State Beach to the Monterey waterfront and beyond. Along the way, you'll pass sea lions, surf-splashed rocks, fishing boats, Cannery Row, and the Monterey Bay Aquarium; there are plenty of places to stop for picnics or snacks. For a longer ride nearby, you can bike for free on Pebble Beach's famed 17-mile Drive (which charges $7.25 for cars); the first Pacific Grove entrance is 3½ miles from Lovers Point. **Bay Bikes** (640 Wave St. along Cannery Row, Monterey, tel. 831/646–9090; for delivery to hotels in Carmel, call 831/625–2453) rents 21-speed road and mountain bikes and four-wheel surreys, at rates from $10 for two

hours to $22 all day and $15 to $25 an hour for surreys. Children's sizes are available, and helmets and locks are provided. If you want to ride the whole 15 miles from Monterey to Carmel via Pebble Beach, you can pick up bikes in Monterey and drop them off in Carmel, or vice versa, for $2.50 extra. **Adventures by the Sea,** with three Monterey locations (299 Cannery Row, tel. 831/372–1807; the beach at Lovers Point in Pacific Grove; and 201 Alvarado Mall near Fisherman's Wharf, tel. 831/648–7235) rents hybrid bikes (crosses between mountain and road bikes), as well as kid's bikes and kiddie trailers, and offers free delivery to nearby hotels. Helmets, locks, and maps are provided. Rentals are $6 an hour, $18 for a half day, and $24 a day.

Elsewhere in Northern California, **Lake Tahoe** (see Chapter 18) contains extensive flat, scenic bike trails, **San Francisco** (see Chapter 14) has miles of relatively flat bike trails, and in **Sacramento** is the 32-mile **Jedediah Smith Memorial Bike Trail** along the American River Parkway, which connects Old Sacramento to Folsom Lake.

In Southern California, **Los Angeles** and **Huntington Beach** (see Chapter 15), **Palm Springs** (see Chapter 18), and **San Diego** (see Chapter 16) all offer great road biking. **Santa Barbara's** (see Chapter 17) palm-lined **Cabrillo Bike Lane** is as pretty as you'll find anywhere: a level, two-lane path running a little more than 3 miles along the waterfront, from the Andree Clark Bird Refuge to Leadbetter Beach. **Cycles-4-Rent** rents bikes ($7–$9 an hour), tandems ($9–$10 an hour), beach cruisers ($4–$6 an hour), and quadricycles ($10–$20 an hour) from three Santa Barbara locations: 101 State St., tel. 805/966–3804; Fess Parker's Doubletree Resort, 633 E. Cabrillo Blvd., tel. 805/564–4333; and the Santa Barbara Radisson Hotel, 1111 E. Cabrillo Blvd., tel. 805/963–0744. **Pedal and Paddle** (3949 Foothill Rd., #A, Santa Barbara, tel. 805/687–2912) offers customized bike tours that follow the waterfront and other gentle bike paths; in winter, you can watch for migrating birds and butterflies. The rates are $38 per person for two hours, $58 for a half day.

Boating

Lakes

Several full-service marinas at **Lake Tahoe** (see Chapter 18) rent boats, from paddleboats and sailboats to powerboats and Jet Skis. Among the best marinas are **Ski Run Marina** (tel. 530/544–0200) and **Tahoe Keys Marina** (tel. 530/541–2155) in South Lake Tahoe; **Camp Richardson Marina** (tel. 530/542–6570), on Hwy. 89 at Camp Richardson; **Sunnyside Marina** (tel. 530/583–7201) on the west shore; **North Tahoe Marina** (tel. 530/546–8248) in Tahoe Vista; and **Lighthouse Watersports Center** (tel. 530/583–6000) in Tahoe City.

Big Bear Lake (see Chapter 18) is another prime boating lake. For rentals of rowboats, paddleboats, pontoon boats, and sailboats, try these marinas: **Big Bear Marina** (corner of Paine Rd. and Lakeview Dr., Big Bear Lake Village, tel. 909/866–3218); **Holloway's Marina** (398 Edgemoor Rd., 1 mi west of Big Bear Lake Village, tel. 909/866–5706; **Pine Knot Landing** (north end of Pine Knot Blvd., Big Bear Lake Village, tel. 909/866–2628); or **Pleasure Point Landing** (603 Landlock Landing, at Metcalf Bay, tel. 909/866–2455). All are closed in winter.

Shasta Lake, California's largest man-made lake, has 11 marinas with all types of rentals, including an array of houseboats that combine lodging and transport in one craft—and allow kids to pretend they're Huck Finn. Houseboat rates vary widely based on season and amenities; except for the most luxurious, they range from around $450 to $700 for three days to $750 to $1,400 for a week (luxury houseboats could set you back from $2,500 to $3,000 or more). **Antlers Resort & Marina** (Box

140, Lakehead 96051, tel. 530/238–2553 or 800/238–3924) rents fishing boats, patio boats, ski boats, and houseboats year-round; **Bridge Bay Resort** (10300 Bridge Bay Rd., Redding, tel. 530/275–3021 or 800/752–9669) is a full-service year-round resort at Shasta Lake with ski boat, fishing boat, patio boat, and houseboat rentals; **Holiday Harbor** (Box 112, Shasta Caverns Rd., O'Brien 96070, tel. 530/238–2383 or 800/776–2628) is a full-service year-round houseboat resort and marina, where you can rent powerboats, canoes, Jet Skis, and waverunners; call for rates. For further information, contact the **Shasta Cascade Wonderland Association** (699 Hwy. 273, Anderson 96007, tel. 530/365–7500 or 800/474–2782). Also near Lake Shasta are **Trinity Lake** (also called Clair Engle Lake; tel. 530/623–6101), which has five marinas plus houseboat rentals; and **Whiskeytown Lake,** where **Oak Bottom Marina** (tel. 530/359–2269) has sailing, powerboating, and waterskiing.

Lake Oroville (tel. 530/538–2219), northeast of the Gold Country, has two marinas, waterskiing, and houseboat rentals. Northeast of Sacramento, **Folsom Lake State Recreation Area** (tel. 916/988–0205) has a full-service marina and is open to all types of boating. **Lake Isabella** (tel. 760/379–5646), which has three full-service marinas, is 45 miles northeast of Bakersfield.

Coastal Bays and Marinas

For a sheer boating wonderland, head to **San Diego** (see Chapter 16), where you can go sailing, paddleboating, and powerboating. Waters and breezes are generally ideal for sailing, and **Mission Bay** has a 1½-mile waterskiing course that's one of the most popular in Southern California. **Mission Bay Sportcenter** (1010 Santa Clara Pl., San Diego, tel. 619/488–1004) rents sailboats for $14 to $35 an hour, motorboats for $60–$85 an hour, and catamarans for $26 to $28 an hour. Instruction is also available; private lessons cost $25 an hour plus boat rental.

Seaforth Mission Bay Boat Rentals (1641 Quivira Rd., San Diego, tel. 619/223–1681) rents sailboats from $20 an hour, paddle-boats from $12 an hour, rowboats from $20 a day, and powerboats from $45 an hour, as well as waterskiing equipment.

San Francisco Bay (see Chapter 14) offers exceptional year-round sailing, though tricky currents can make it hazardous for the inex-perienced. Cass Marina (1702 Bridgeway, Sausalito, tel. 415/332–6789) has sailboats for rent to experienced sailors starting at $136 per day. For charters, try A Day on the Bay (San Francisco Marina, tel. 415/922–0227), which charges from $30 to $75 per hour and rents motorboats as well. The 55-foot catamaran Adventure Cat (Pier 39, Fish-erman's Wharf, tel. 415/777–1630 or 800/498–4228) offers 1½-hour sailing cruises for $25 adults, $12 ages 5 to 12, under 5 free.

Monterey Bay and Santa Barbara harbor (see Chapter 17) also offer sailing and boat-ing along the coast, as do Marina del Rey, Dana Point, Newport Beach, and other harbors and marinas in the greater Los Angeles area (see Chapter 15).

Canoeing

Canoe trips are usually leisurely meanders down gentle rivers or along quiet lakes, with time out for picnicking, swimming, playing in the sand, and enjoying the sun on shore. But canoeing does require effort and teamwork. Canoes can be stubborn craft, less maneu-verable than kayaks (see Kayaking, below), and less stable than rafts (see River Rafting, below). If partners aren't in synch with each other, or churning rapids or obstacles appear, there's always the chance the canoe will tip over or take on too much water. For these reasons, most canoeing outfitters require children to be at least 4 or 5 years old. Children up to age 10 or so can ride in the middle of a canoe between two parents, so young kids don't necessarily have to learn

to paddle (though many enjoy being part of the action). Everyone wears life jackets, so it's not essential for them to know how to swim, but any child who goes out on a canoe should at least be comfortable on—and in!—the water.

The most popular canoeing in California is along the redwood-lined Russian River in the Sonoma County Wine Country north of San Francisco (see Chapter 18). Kids can watch for otters, osprey, turtles, and great blue herons; on a summer weekend, alas, you're also likely to see lots of fellow humans in canoes (but then if your canoe tips over, you'll have plenty of potential res-cuers on hand). A good route for younger kids is the 5-mile stretch between Johnson's Beach in Guerneville and Monte Rio Beach, a two- to three-hour trip. Most routes run from 5 to 11 miles, so plan on spending about three to five hours paddling leisurely, and the rest of the day picnicking, swimming, or resting along shore on sunny beaches. All these trips are self-guided. Burke's Canoe Trips (8600 River Rd., Box 602, Forestville 95436, tel. 707/887–1222) offers one-day, 10-mile trips ($35 per canoe) from Forestville to Guerneville (at least a 3- to 3½-hour trip). Courtesy shuttle service will take you back to Burke's from Guerneville. Minimum age is 5; all adults should know how to swim. Trips run from May through September or October; call for reserva-tions. W. C. "Bob" Trowbridge Canoe Trips (20 Healdsburg Ave., Healdsburg, tel. 707/433–7247 or 800/640–1386) offers day trips that last from two to five hours and range from 5 to 11 miles. The half-day, 5-mile trips are $25 per canoe (each big enough for two adults and two kids age 6–12), and one-day 8- to 11-mile trips are $30 to $35 per canoe, with a number of routes along the river available. Two-day, 22-mile trips are $55, and three- to five-day trips are $75; minimum age is 6. Overnight camping on the banks of the river is $5 extra.

You can also find good, safe canoeing in Northern California along the Trinity River, which flows into Trinity Lake (see Boating, *above*)—try the sections from Junction City to the North Fork; South Fork to Willow Creek; and the Hoopa Valley. About ½ mile south of Mendocino (see Chapter 17) lies the Big River estuary, the longest unspoiled estuary in Northern California. The tidal stream winds quietly through a redwood canyon; watch for osprey, great blue herons, and harbor seals along the way. Rent a traditional or outrigger canoe from **Catch a Canoe & Bicycles, Too!** (Stanford Inn by the Sea, tel. 707/937–0273; $10–$18 an hour [2-hour minimum] and $30–$54 per day).

Lake Tahoe, Mammoth Lakes, and **Big Bear Lake** (see Chapter 18 for all three) also offer excellent canoeing.

Fishing

Fishing can be a wonderful family activity, a chance to spend time together and maybe even catch dinner. Bait, tackle, and a body of water are all you need—along with a little patience, of course, if the fish aren't biting right away. When Grael caught his first fish at age 5, a freshwater perch which he devoured for breakfast the next morning, it was one of the proudest moments of his young life.

California is dotted with freshwater lakes, reservoirs, and wild rivers teeming with trout, bass, and catfish. Along the ocean you can cast a line from many municipal piers or find a spot on shore to fish in the surf. You can also take half-day or full-day sportfishing trips out into the Pacific from several towns along the coast. If you take a trip with a fishing guide—especially if you're an inexperienced angler yourself—make sure the guide is willing to help kids learn to bait a hook or cast a line. With kids who've never fished before, you might consider visiting a trout farm or similar facility where catches are virtually guaranteed; although adults may enjoy the Zen of fishing, for most kids the name of the game is simply to reel 'em in.

Kids age 15 and under don't need a fishing license in California (anyone 16 and older does, except when fishing from municipal piers). Many bait-and-tackle shops sell licenses, or you can get one from an office of the State Department of Fish and Game (3211 S St., Sacramento 95816, tel. 916/227–2244). A one-day license is $9.45; a year's license costs $71.95 for nonresidents of the state and $26.50 for residents. Nonresidents can also buy a 10-day license for $26.50. Bait-and-tackle shops may charge a small additional fee.

Deep-Sea Fishing

Along the northern coast, head for **Noyo Harbor** in Fort Bragg (see Chapter 17), the largest fishing port between San Francisco and Eureka. Steelhead, ling cod, rockfish, and salmon are prime catches. **Tally Ho II Sportfishing** (Old Fish House, N. Harbor Dr., tel. 707/964–2079), offers daily five-hour trips in summer for $50 per person; the rest of the year, trips leave by reservation with a four-person minimum.

Dozens of sportfishing boats operate around **San Francisco** (see Chapter 14), leaving from Fisherman's Wharf, Sausalito, the Berkeley Marina, Emeryville, and Point San Pablo, in search of salmon, rockfish, halibut, striped bass, and giant sturgeon. Sometimes boats stay in the bay; other times they venture beyond the Golden Gate. Try **Caruso's Sportfishing Center** (Harbor Dr., Sausalito, tel. 415/332–1015; $55 for full day, $27.50 under 15); **Wacky Jacky** (Fisherman's Wharf, San Francisco, tel. 415/586–9800; $55 for full day, reduced rates for kids under 13); or **Emeryville Sport Fishing** (3310 Powell St., Emeryville, tel. 510/654–6040; $52 for full day, $26 under 12).

San Diego (see Chapter 16) is an ideal place to introduce kids to sportfishing, with generally warmer weather and calmer seas than the more northerly ports. Prime seasons are summer and fall, and catches include bass, bonita, barracuda, halibut, marlin, rock cod, snapper, and tuna. The city has one of the biggest sportfishing fleets in the world: some 70 large commercial vessels and more than 60 private charter luxury yachts. **Fisherman's Landing** (2838 Garrison St., tel. 619/221–8500) has daily full-day trips (including overnight travel), with tackle rentals and food service on board; cost is $108 adults, $78 for kids under 16. **Islandia Sportfishing** (1551 W. Mission Bay Dr., tel. 619/222–1164) offers morning and afternoon half-day departures, as well as summer twilight trips, with tackle rentals and sales and food service; rates are $25 adults, $18 for kids under 15. Half-day trips are preferable for younger kids. Or try **H&M Landing** (Emerson St. near Shelter Island, tel. 619/222–1144), where half-day trips cost $25 for adults, $18 for under 15.

On the central coast, charters go out from **Fisherman's Wharf** in Monterey (see Chapter 17) into Monterey Bay and Carmel Bay for rock cod and salmon; reserve with **Monterey Sport Fishing and Cruises** (tel. 831/372–2203); **Sam's Sportfishing** (tel. 831/372–0577); **Chris' Sportfishing** (tel. 831/375–5951); and **Randy's Fishing Trips** (tel. 831/372–7440). Rock cod trips average about $30 for adults and $20 for kids up to age 16; salmon trips average about $40 a person. Weekend prices are higher. Other harbors with sportfishing charters available include **Santa Barbara** (see Chapter 17) and, in the Los Angeles area, **Malibu, Marina Del Rey,** and **Dana Point** (see Chapter 15).

Lake Fishing

Several lakes in northern and central California offer world-class fishing. For sheer volume of great fishing opportunities, tops-in-the-state honors go to the **Mammoth Lakes** area in the eastern Sierra (see Chapter 18), where rainbow, brown, golden, cutthroat, and Eastern brook trout all thrive in the lakes, many of which are stocked by the state Fish and Game Department. Rainbow are the most prolific, but Eastern brook are considered the tastiest. **Crowley Lake** is the top trout-fishing spot in the area; **Convict Lake, June Lake,** and the lakes of the Mammoth Basin (where **Twin Lakes** is most popular and **Lake Mary** the largest) are other prime fishing spots. Fishing season runs from the last Saturday in April through October (though you may have to try ice fishing until May). **Kittredge Sports** (Main St. and Forest Trail, Mammoth Lakes, tel. 760/934–7566 or 800/441–3331 in Southern CA) rents fly rod and reel for $15 a day, trolling rod and reel for $10 a day, and spinning rod and reel for $8 a day, and operates guided trips for all experience levels for bait, spin, and fly-fishing at $150 for first person, $25 to $60 for each additional person. **The Trout Fitter** (Rte. 203 and Old Mammoth Rd., Mammoth Lakes, tel. 760/924–3676) rents spinning rod and reel for $8 a day, fly rod and reel for $15–$20 a day, and also runs half-day fly-fishing trips for $160 for two, $185 for three. Beginners' specials are $125 for a half day and $175 for a full day for two people; add $50 to each for a third person.

Another excellent spot is **Clear Lake State Park** (tel. 707/279–4293), about 130 miles north of San Francisco. Clear Lake, California's largest freshwater lake, is known as the "Bass Capital of the West." In the San Francisco Bay Area, **San Pablo Reservoir** offers great urban fishing (see Chapter 14). In Southern California, **Big Bear Lake** (see Chapter 18) offers trout, bass, bluegill, perch, and catfish; get licenses and permits and rent boats and equipment at several lakeside marinas, including **Pleasure Point Landing** (tel. 909/866–2455; half- to full-day rentals range from $30–$45). You can fish without a license at **Alpine Lakes Trout Fishing** (Catalina Rd., ¼ mi off Big Bear Blvd., tel. 909/866–4532), which is open except January (weather permitting) and charges $5 per family of six plus about $5 per pound (call for the exact price) for trout caught. The lake is stocked, so even young beginners are almost bound to reel one in, and there's no limit. You can rent equipment and get your fish cleaned for a small fee.

Pier Fishing

Several towns and cities along the coast offer excellent pier fishing, including **San Francisco** (see Chapter 14), **Santa Cruz, Monterey,** and **Santa Barbara** (see Chapter 17). But the pier-fishing capital of California has to be **San Diego** (see Chapter 16), where you can fish for free (no license required) off **Ocean Beach Pier, Crystal Pier** at Pacific Beach, and the piers at **Shelter Island,** the **Coronado Ferry Landing, Imperial Beach,** and **Oceanside.** Catches include yellowtail, perch, and bonito. Most piers have bait-and-tackle shops.

River and Stream Fishing

California has an abundance of rivers and streams ideal for bait or fly-fishing. One of the best trout rivers is the **San Joaquin** near Devil's Postpile National Monument in the Mammoth Lakes area (see Chapter 18). **Hot Creek,** a designated Wild Trout Stream also near Mammoth Lakes, is renowned for fly-fishing (catch and release only). But most of the prime fishing rivers and streams are in the northern reaches of the state. **Hat Creek** (tel. 530/335–2381) near Burney, with rainbow and brown trout, is one of the best fly-fishing streams in the western United States. The **Trinity River,** which winds past the gorgeous Trinity Alps Wilderness, provides an unbeatable combination: great fishing (for king salmon, trout, and steelhead), exceptional scenery, and relatively easy access (via Rte. 299, off either I–5 from Redding or Hwy. 101 from Arcata). You can fish here year-round, though spring through fall are the most popular seasons. Guided trips for both fly- and spin-fishing are available. **Bigfoot Campground Guide Service** (Box 98, Junction City 96048, tel. 530/623–6088) offers driftboat fishing trips on the Trinity, including all equipment; beginners are welcome. Rates are $250 per day. **God's Country Guide Service** (Box 35, Trinity Center 96091, tel. 530/266–3297) specializes in family fishing floats each summer; first-timers are welcome. The rates are

$150 for a half-day, $200 for a full day. **Trinity Alps Angling Experiences** (Box 176, Lewiston 96052, tel. 530/623–6757) conducts half-day and full-day guided float and walk-in fly-fishing trips year-round, for $215 to $275 for two people. Instruction is offered.

Hiking

Hiking is our family's favorite everyday outdoor activity, partly because we can do it on the spur of the moment. Put on a pair of hiking boots (or some comfortable old sneakers), pick a trail, and off you go—no lessons or high-tech equipment needed. Hiking's cheap, a great way to get fresh air and exercise, and the best way we know to get close to nature. On hikes, kids can find rocks to climb and pebbles to treasure, spot squirrels and butterflies and maybe even an elk, explore the mysteries of tide pools and fiddlehead ferns, discover the wonders of giant redwoods and volcanic mud pots. You don't have to be in the wilderness to find good hiking with kids; San Francisco and Los Angeles, for instance, both have excellent hiking trails within the city limits (see Chapters 14 and 15). Nor do hikes need to be sweaty, blister-raising ordeals; with young kids, in fact, a ¼- to ½-mile ramble along a flat trail could be just right. Of course, if your kids discover the fun of playing lead explorer, they may want to keep going.

Guided group hikes can be an excellent way for children to learn about nature and meet new friends. If you're visiting a state or national park (see Chapter 8), ask at the ranger station or visitors center about ranger-led family hikes. If you're interested in joining a hiking tour, **Sierra Club Outings** (85 2nd St., San Francisco 94105, tel. 415/977–5630) offers backpacking trips for families in Yosemite and other regions of the Sierra Nevada, as well as in the Santa Cruz Mountains, for ages 5 and up (some are best suited to ages 8 and up). Some trips include burros to carry gear; others are intended for grandparents and grandkids traveling together or for families with very young children.

For hikers, few places in the world can top **Yosemite National Park** (see Chapter 8), which combines incomparable beauty with hiking trails for every age and endurance level. Even toddlers on their first-ever hikes can reach some of Yosemite's towering waterfalls, its forests thick with pines and giant sequoias, its pastoral meadows shaded by enormous granite monoliths. Our favorite Yosemite hikes include the relatively easy 2-mile trail from Lower Yosemite Fall to Mirror Lake, the strenuous but superbly scenic Mist Trail to Vernal Fall, the trail in the Mariposa Grove of giant sequoias, and the high-country trails around Tuolomne Meadows. You can also ask at the Yosemite Valley visitors center about Family Discovery Walks led by ranger-naturalists.

California has far too many other outstanding hiking areas to list here, but some of our favorites include **Sequoia, Kings Canyon, Humboldt Redwoods,** and **Lassen** national parks, and **Point Reyes National Seashore,** all covered in Chapter 8. **Lake Tahoe, Mammoth Lakes,** and **Big Bear Lake** (see Chapter 18) and the **Mendocino** and **Monterey** areas (see Chapter 17) also have plenty of good hiking territory.

Horseback Riding

Grael's first horseback trip at age 7 was memorable, to say the least. Without ever having been on a horse before, he set off with me on a weeklong guided trek through the wilderness, where we encountered steep mountain passes, torrential rainstorms, and meadows thick with stinging hornets that sent his little pinto galloping off at full speed. Fortunately, Grael survived it all unscathed—and loved every minute of it. Looking back, I don't recommend starting kids off with something quite *that* ambitious.

For longer pack trips and the like, carefully assess your child's maturity and resilience before setting off; once you've reached the middle of the wilderness, there's no quick route back.

Tots as young as a year old can earn their spurs aboard ponies in San Francisco's **Golden Gate Park** (see Chapter 14) or Los Angeles's **Griffith Park** (see Chapter 15). As they gain comfort and confidence in the saddle, they work up to short guided trail rides atop gentle mounts. (Check with individual stables on age requirements; many set a minimum age of 7 or 8 years old for children with little or no riding experience.) Another good way to introduce your kids to horseback riding might be to stay at a ranch or resort (see Chapter 12) that offers trail rides for kids as part of its program; that way they can gain experience a bit at a time over the course of several days.

My pick for the top horseback riding area in California goes to the **Mammoth Lakes** region (see Chapter 18). This pristine, high-mountain lakeland has a number of stables that offer guided rides, from one-hour ambles to weeklong trips through the wilderness. Most stables set a minimum age of 7 for trail rides, with "walk and lead" rides available for younger kids. Mammoth Lakes is a high-altitude resort, with snow usually blanketing the ground from November to May, so stables in the area are typically open from June through September. **Mammoth Lakes Pack Outfit** (Lake Mary Rd., Box 61, Mammoth Lakes 93546, tel. 760/934–2434) offers one-hour ($27) to all-day ($75) trail rides in the Mammoth Lakes basin, as well as longer customized trips; children ages 3 to 6 can ride with leads ($14 for ½ hour). **McGee Creek Pack Station** (Rte. 1, Box 162, Mammoth Lakes 93546, tel. 760/935–4324) offers one-, two-, and four-hour guided trail rides through McGee Canyon (near Crowley Lake) plus all-day trail rides that can be combined with fishing, and customized pack trips; rates range from $22 for one hour to $70 for all day, and minimum age is 7 (kids

3–6 can ride with leads for ½ hour for $15). **Red's Meadow Pack Station** (Box 395, Mammoth Lakes 93546, tel. 760/934–2345), near Devil's Postpile National Monument on the San Joaquin River, runs fishing and scenic pack trips of all types; two-hour guided trail rides are $37, all-day rides $70, and minimum age is 3 (kids from 3 to 5 must ride with an adult). Five-day parent-child trips are $745 for adults, and $545 for children 16 and under. The **Sierra Meadows Ranch** (Sherwin Creek Rd., Mammoth Lakes, tel. 760/934–6161) conducts one- and two-hour, half-day and all-day guided trail rides for ages 7 and up, at rates ranging from $26 to $80, plus 15-minute "walk and lead" rides for kids ages 2 to 6 ($12).

Other top spots for family horseback riding are **MacKerricher State Park** near Mendocino and **Pebble Beach** near Monterey (see Chapter 17 for both), as well as **Lake Tahoe**, the **Wine Country** north of San Francisco, **Big Bear Lake** in the San Bernardino Mountains, and **Palm Springs** (see Chapter 18 for all four areas).

Hot-Air Ballooning

What child hasn't daydreamed of being carried up, up, and away in a multicolored storybook contraption, perhaps to drift toward a land of make-believe? For a brief but memorable time, kids can become like Phileas Fogg—if not going around the world in 80 days, at least sailing with the breezes for 80 minutes or so over vineyards, mountains, desert, or coastline far below. Hot-air ballooning provides an exhilarating but gentle family adventure: The giant balloons travel at only a few miles per hour (the same speed as air currents) and flights in good weather are soothing rather than jolting, with barely a feeling of motion. But there is an element of uncertainty: Pilots can only steer up and down (using propane burners to produce or reduce heat), though the actual direction of the journey is deter-

mined by prevailing breezes. Because breezes are generally lighter around dawn and sunset, most flights take place at those times.

We took our kids hot-air ballooning in the Napa Valley when they were ages 11 and 8, and we had a wonderful flight once Lia got used to the loud "whoosh!" of the propane burner (it scared her at first). Assess your children's readiness. If they're afraid of heights, do you really want to take them up 2,000 feet in an open-air basket? In general, kids should be big enough to stand on their own feet during the flight (not held), tall enough to see over the basket, old enough to follow safety instructions—and, for most flights, willing to get up before dawn. For all these reasons, some ballooning agencies set a minimum age of anywhere from 5 to 7. And remember, this is no cheap thrill: Figure on spending as much as $500 or more for a family of four for a 1- to 1¼-hour trip; at those prices, you'll want Junior to enjoy himself. Also, pregnant women should hold off on hot-air ballooning until another time. Finally, note that though accidents are rare, they can happen, especially if pilots misjudge wind conditions; winds should be no more than 5 mph to operate in complete safety and comfort.

California has some of the best hot-air ballooning in the world. You can float over mountains at **Lake Tahoe** or **Mammoth Lakes** (see Chapter 18), over the desert at **Palm Springs** (see Chapter 18), over the **Del Mar Coast** near San Diego (see Chapter 16), or over the **Central Valley** near Monterey (see Chapter 17). But the most popular spot is the **Napa Valley Wine Country** (see Chapter 18), where a combination of favorable wind currents and idyllic scenery (vineyards, rolling hills) creates an ideal year-round setting for the sport. If you're out on the road in early morning, you're almost certain to see dozens of colorful balloons drifting over the vineyards. Trips usually last from three to four hours (including shuttle service and brunch after;

actual air time is considerably shorter) and start at sunrise. These companies are long-established and reliable: **Adventures Aloft** (Box 2500 at Vintage 1870, Yountville 94599, tel. 707/944–4408 or 800/944–4408) charges $185 for adults, $150 ages 6 to 16; minimum age is 6. **Balloons Above the Valley** (5091 Solano Ave., Napa 94558, tel. 707/253–2222 or 800/464–6824) charges $175 for adults, $125 for children under 12, with no minimum age (but the company suggests that kids under 3 are too small). **Napa Valley Balloons** (6795 Washington St., Box 2860, Yountville 94599, tel. 707/944–0228 or, in Northern CA, 800/253–2224) charges $175 for adults, $90 for children 9 and under; minimum age is 5.

Kayaking

Kayaking is like no other form of boating. In a kayak you're as close to the water as you can be without getting wet; you feel like you're practically moving among the fish. Kayaks are generally so easy to control and so efficient—they don't require much power—that school-age kids can usually master the skills right along with their parents. But is your child ready? First, check with individual outfitters on their minimum age or height/weight requirements for kids. Then use your own judgment; although children don't need to be accomplished swimmers (everyone wears life jackets), they shouldn't be afraid of the water, and they should be old enough to float and to grab onto the side of the kayak if necessary. First-timers should probably stick to trips of half a day or less.

The most suitable kayaks for beginners are the open-deck kind (often called "sit-on-tops"), self-bailing kayaks that are easy to balance and maneuver. (The other major kind is the "closed" kayak, which requires more training.) Along with single-seaters, most outfitters rent tandem kayaks, which parents can share with a younger child. All reputable outfitters provide lessons in paddling and safety techniques along with

rentals. For a list of licensed outfitters who provide kayak instruction, guided trips, and rentals on various rivers, call the **California Outdoors Hotline** at 800/552–3625. For kids-only (ages 8 and up) sea-kayaking lessons in both open-deck and closed kayaks, call **California Canoe and Kayak** at 800/366–9804. The company has locations in Oakland (510/893–7833), Sacramento (tel. 916/353-1880), and Half Moon Bay (tel. 650/728–9616), and conducts trips throughout Northern California and along the Central Coast.

Among California's lakes, **Lake Tahoe** (see Chapter 18) is tops for kayaking. **Camp Richardson Marina** (tel. 530/542–6570) rents open-deck kayaks for exploring the south shore of the lake. Tandems cost $20 per hour. On the north shore, **Tahoe Paddle & Oar** (tel. 530/581–3029) at the North Tahoe Beach Center in Kings Beach rents sit-on-top and traditional sea kayaks. Rentals start at $10 an hour per person; tandems start at $20 an hour, sea kayaks at $25 an hour.

In the northern reaches of the state, the **Klamath** and **Trinity** rivers both offer good kayaking on easy-to-moderate white water; river kayaking is usually possible from spring to fall, depending on water levels. The Big River estuary, the longest unspoiled estuary in Northern California, lies about a half mile south of **Mendocino** (see Chapter 17). The tidal stream winds quietly through a redwood canyon; watch for osprey, great blue herons, and harbor seals along the way. Rent a kayak from **Catch a Canoe & Bicycles, Too!** (Stanford Inn by the Sea, tel. 707/937–0273) for $18 per hour (two-hour minimum) and $48 per day.

For sea kayaking, **Monterey Bay** is in a class by itself—and its often-gentle waves and spectacular scenery are especially well suited to children and families. Kayakers in Monterey Bay are virtually guaranteed close-up views of playful, barking sea lions; harbor seals; and lovable-looking sea otters, who like to snooze in the kelp beds. You can also kayak past Fisherman's Wharf, Cannery Row, and other parts of the Monterey waterfront. **Monterey Bay Kayaks** (693 Del Monte Ave., tel. 831/373–5357 or 800/649–5357) offers rentals, lessons, and guided natural history tours of Monterey Bay; for rentals, suggested minimum size is 4½ feet tall and 80 pounds (smaller kids can take the natural history tours). One- or two-seat kayaks rent for $25 per person per day; tours are $45. **Adventures by the Sea** (tel. 831/372–1807; see Road Biking, *above*) has locations on Cannery Row, Alvarado Mall near Fisherman's Wharf, and the beach at Lovers Point in Pacific Grove (where waters tend to be especially calm). Rentals are $25 per person per day, and the owners suggest that kids should be at least 6 (or older depending on water conditions). Younger kids, however, can go on guided tours ($45 per person). In Santa Cruz, on the northern end of Monterey Bay, contact **Kayak Connection** (413 Lake Ave., No. 4, tel. 831/479–1121), which offers rentals, classes (including one for kids ages 8–12), and guided tours along the bay and local estuaries and beaches.

The **San Francisco Bay Area** (see Chapter 14) offers great sea kayaking for families in the waters off Sausalito (part of San Francisco Bay) and Tomales Bay. Both have calm, sheltered waters; the Sausalito area also has sea lions, a bird refuge, and a community of houseboats, while Tomales Bay is in a wilderness setting and has sandy beaches where you can stop for picnics. **Sea Trek** (Schoonmaker Point Arena, Sausalito, tel. 415/488–1000 or 415/332–4465) is the premier local outfitter; besides Sausalito and Tomales Bay, Sea Trek offers guided paddles around Angel Island in San Francisco Bay, with great views of the Golden Gate, Alcatraz, and San Francisco. The company's guided trips run from $50 to $120, all-day classes cost from $95 to $110 per person, and open-deck double kayaks are available at $40 per two hours (or $70 per day) for small children to share with parents.

Farther south, you can kayak along the coast in **Santa Barbara** (see Chapter 17). Pedal and Paddle (3949 Foothill Rd., Santa Barbara, tel. 805/687–2912) arranges customized sea kayaking tours along the coastline and harbor, including instruction, for $38 per person for two hours, $58 for a half day. Minimum age is 10, and participants must know how to swim.

There's also good sea kayaking off **Catalina Island** (see Chapter 17). **Wet Spot Rentals** at the ferry dock (tel. 310/510–2229) operates half-day kayak trips (with sightseeing and snorkeling) aboard sit-on-top models for $65 to $95 a day; the latter price takes you to the other (windward) side of the island. Or you can rent a two-seat kayak here for $17 an hour. At Two Harbors the **West End Dive Center** (tel. 310/510–0303 ext. 272) offers sit-on-top models for beginners of any age at rates of $9 to $13 an hour (two-hour minimum), $30 to $40 for a half day, and $45 to $65 for a full day. A three-hour naturalist-guided tour costs $45 per person.

In **Malibu,** you can kayak off the coast with possible sightings of seals, dolphins, or whales. Contact **Malibu Ocean Sports** (across from Malibu Pier, tel. 310/456–6302), where tandems are $50 per day. In **Orange County,** call **Southwind Kayak Center** (tel. 800/768–8494), which has locations in Newport Beach, Irvine, and Dana Point. Besides instruction and tours, Southwind rents kayaks for $10 to $14 an hour or $40 to $55 per day.

River Rafting and Float Trips

You're floating gently down a river, basking in the sun, watching for moose along shore or gazing up at the steep cliffs of a rocky gorge. As you round a bend, a low, distant rumbling becomes a roar. You and your kids exchange knowing looks, then grab your oars tight. Your guide shouts, "Paddle left!" and everyone paddles furiously. You brace yourselves as the current plunges your raft into surging rapids, past boulders and over waves, water sprays your faces. Then, just as suddenly, you're drifting calmly again, perhaps toward a sandy beach where you'll stop to swim, have lunch, or camp overnight. Now it's time to exchange high fives: You've conquered "Satan's Cesspool," "Meatgrinder," or another of the many colorfully named rapids on California's free-flowing rivers.

River rafting is one of the most thrilling adventures a family can experience, and kids as young as 4 can join the fun. Several California outfitters actively court families by offering special trips complete with price discounts, relatively placid waters, and activities for kids on shore: arts and crafts, storytelling, nature hikes, and games. A free directory of 50 California river outfitters (for not only rafting but also kayaking and canoeing) is available from the **California Outdoors Hotline** (tel. 800/552–3625). When choosing a rafting trip, make sure that the company has experience with children, that the white water isn't too dangerous, and that there will be things to occupy the kids when you aren't on the river.

Most family rafting trips take place on easy-to-medium, Class II and III rivers. (Class II indicates easy rapids with waves that require some maneuvering; Class III means rapids with waves high enough to require complex maneuvering—and to possibly capsize a raft—and III+ is even more challenging.) For kids ages 4 to 6 Class II is as wild as you'll want to get. Kids may be ready for Class III beginning at age 7.

Because all passengers are required to wear life vests, it's not essential for children to know how to swim—but kids who are afraid of water or of getting wet are not ready for a Class III rafting trip. During our family's two-day trip on the Class III to III+ South Fork of the American River, for instance, almost everyone in the raft was sent "swimming"—

dumped or washed overboard—at one series of churning rapids. Though there were some scary moments before we were pulled out of the river, when it was over we all agreed it had been one of the most exciting adventures of our lives. How much danger is there? Well, the chance of serious injury is always there—we have an adult friend who broke her leg while rafting, and in high-water years there have been fatalities on Class V California rivers—but on Class II and III rivers, and under the guidance of experienced outfitters, the risk of serious injury is statistically very slight (about one in 25,000, according to one study). In the end, it's strictly each parent's call.

River rafting trips are usually available in California from around March to October, depending on water levels, which tend to be highest (and rapids strongest) in spring, so it's probably wise to wait till summer to raft with children. Most family rafting trips come in lengths of one, two, or three days, though you can find some as short as an hour or two and as long as five or six days. If you're on a "paddle" trip, everyone (including kids) joins in the paddling; if you're on an "oar" trip, the guide does all the work. Most outfitters offer both types, so state your preference in advance. Expect to spend about five hours on the river on a typical day—running rapids, floating, and challenging passing rafts to water fights. The rest of the time is spent on shore: eating, swimming, fishing, and sitting around the campfire (if it's a multiday trip).

Not sure whether you're ready? Then test the waters at a theme park such as **Paramount's Great America** in Santa Clara or **Six Flags California** in Valencia (see Chapter 9 for details on each). Both Great America's Rip-Roaring Rapids and Magic Mountain's Roaring Rapids are considered the equivalent of Class II white water.

For guided trips suitable for kids as young as 4, head for two beautiful mellow rivers in Northern California, at their best June through August. The **Trinity River,** which courses along the edges of the Trinity Alps Wilderness, is known for its mild waves, friendly swimming holes, and scenic surroundings. **Bigfoot Rafting** (Box 729, Hwy. 299 at Cinnabar Sam's Restaurant, Willow Creek 95573, tel. 530/629–2263 or 800/722–2223) offers half-day to three-day trips on the Trinity; rafting trips on the Class II Lower Trinity start at $43 adults, $33 under 17, with no minimum age. Rafts seating two to eight people can be rented starting at $38 a day, plus from $8 to $16 for shuttle service per group. **Aurora Adventures** (Box 938, 151 Kimtu Rd., Willow Creek 95573, tel. 530/629–3843 or 800/562–8475) runs gentle (Class I and II) river adventures on the Lower Trinity, open to kids as young as 4, as well as Class II and III runs on the Trinity and Klamath rivers for kids ages 7 and up. Trips range from one half to four days. Two-day Class II trips with a professional storyteller aboard, geared for kids age 4 to 12, are $168 for ages 11 and over, and $150 for ages 4 to 11. Aurora also offers three- and four-day Class II and III rafting trips on the isolated **Eel River,** at prices averaging around $360 a person, including a long car shuttle; kids as young as 4 may take these trips, though parents may not want to push it that young. Kids age 9 and up can join Aurora's exciting Class III trips on the Upper Trinity. The **Klamath River** has sandy beaches, warmish waters (great for swimming and water fights), and lots of wildlife. **Turtle River Rafting Co.** (Box 313, Mt. Shasta 96067, tel. 530/926–3223 or 800/726–3223) offers The Kids Klamath for children as young as 4—a two-day, 15-mile Class II+ splash down the river, with time for snacks and exploring side creeks. Rates are $195 adults, $145 ages 4 to 17. Turtle River also offers three- to five-day Class III trips on the Klamath, and one- to three-day Class III runs on the Trinity for kids at least 7 years old, at rates of $85 adults and $75 ages 7 to 17 (one day), $320 adults and $285 ages 7 to 17 (three days), and $540 adults and $485 ages 7 to 17 (five days). **River Dancers** (302 Terry Lynn, Mt. Shasta 96067, tel. 530/926–3517 or 800/926–5002) is another company that offers family-oriented trips on the Trinity and Klamath. One-day Class II trips on the Klamath suitable for kids as young as 3 are $50 for ages 17 and younger, $70 for adults, while slightly more difficult trips (minimum age 5) are $65 for kids and $85 for adults. Two-day trips with an age 3 minimum, meanwhile, are $120 for kids and $165 for adults, while the two-day trips with a minimum age of 5 are $155 for kids and $195 for adults. Three-day Class III trips on the Trinity are $235 for kids (age 5 minimum), and $295 for adults.

Families with kids ages 7 and up may be ready for California's most popular white water, the Class III to III+ **South Fork of the American River** in the Gold Country near Coloma. The typical South Fork rafting trip takes two days, with two nights spent camping along the riverbanks. There's easy access from Highway 49, magnificent scenery through granite canyons and past historic Gold Rush sites, and some 50 rapids that provide plenty of excitement, including Class III+ Troublemaker—the one that sent our family swimming. Among the many outfitters who run trips here, an excellent choice is **Adventure Connection** (Box 475, Coloma 95613, tel. 530/626–7385 or, in CA, 800/556–6060), which runs several midweek two-day family trips on the American for which each full-paying adult may bring a child age 7 to 15 for half price. Guides lead kids in crafts projects, on gold-panning trips, and on nature hikes. Rates are $185 to $229 adults; a one-day option (with lunch) is $85. Adventure Connection also offers a few family trips on weekends at regular rates, when kids age 15 and under receive a $10 discount. Another reliable company offering family rates on the South Fork American is **ARTA River Trips** (24000 Casa Loma Rd., Groveland 95321, tel. 209/962–7873 or 800/323–2782), whose two-day trips departing on Thursdays bring a special $160 rate for kids 8 to 17, while adults pay $199. ARTA also offers one-day trips for $99 to $109 adults and $10 off for kids. Minimum age is 8.

The **Lower Kern River,** which runs 18 miles downstream from Lake Isabella, near Kernville in the southern Sierra, is a Class III to IV river, more daring than the South Fork American; kids should be at least 12 to attempt this one. **Kern River Tours** (Box 3444, Lake Isabella 93240, tel. 760/379–4616 or 800/844–7238) offers two-day trips May–September; kids ages 12 to 18 get a 25% discount for trips that start on Tuesday. Pre-discount rates range from $235 to $275 per person.

Surfing and Boo-gieboarding

Though it originated in Hawaii, surfing is probably the sport most identified with California. (After all, the Beach Boys never sang about mountain biking or hot-air ballooning.) I wouldn't advise kids who've never surfed to try to ride a big wave the first time out, but beginners do have some options. You can take surfing lessons or rent a boogieboard and "hang 10" lying down and holding on.

California's quintessential Surf City is the town of **Santa Cruz** (see Chapter 17), at the north end of Monterey Bay, where the waves are gnarly and you can even visit a surfing museum. Experienced surfers flock to **Steamer's Lane** off Lighthouse Point and to **Pleasure Point** off East Cliff Drive. **Cowell Beach** near the Santa Cruz Boardwalk has more gentle surf (fine for boogieboarding and body surfing), as does **Twin Lakes Beach,** where waves break closer to shore. Wear wet suits—the water can be chilly. **Go Skate Surf and Sport** (601 Beach St., tel. 831/425–8578) rents surfboards and boogieboards for $3 an hour or $10 a day; rent wet suits for $5 an hour, $10 a day. **Club Ed** (tel. 831/459–9283 or 800/287–7873) at Cowell Beach rents boogieboards for $23 a day (including wet suit) and surfboards for $27 a day, including wet suit. Lessons are $70 including board and wet suit.

In the San Francisco area (see Chapter 14) experienced surfers head for **Ocean Beach,** but waves can be brutal. Marin County's Stinson Beach is another popular spot, often less risky; rent at the **Live Water Surf Shop** (3448 Shoreline Hwy., tel. 415/868–0333; $8 a day for boogieboards, $25 a day for surfboards, $10 a day for wet suits). There's also good—but sometimes treacherous (monster-waves)—surfing south of San Francisco at **Pacifica Beach** and in **Half Moon Bay**; rent at **Aqua Culture Surf and Beach Shop** (3032 N. Cabrillo Hwy., Half Moon Bay, tel. 650/726–6548; $8 a day for boogieboards, $15 a day for surfboards, $10 a day for wet suits).

Other top surfing spots are **Monterey** and **Santa Barbara** (see Chapter 17); **Malibu** and several **Orange County** beaches (see Chapter 15); and **La Jolla** (see Chapter 16).

Swimming

The main thing to remember when swimming in California (at least in the ocean) is that north is cold, south is warm—or at least warmer. In general, Pacific waters anywhere from San Francisco north appeal primarily to polar bear types. Admittedly, kids often fall into this category. But there's another caveat, one that applies to many southern waters as well: California beaches are often dangerous for swimming. Riptides, crashing waves, and strong undertow are common along the coast. Although prominent signs usually warn would-be swimmers of the threats, never let kids swim if there are any doubts about safety, and never turn your backs on small children near shore. Stick to swimming at beaches with lifeguards, and stay within easy sight.

The **San Francisco Bay Area** has several good swimming beaches, mostly at lakes away from the bay or ocean (see Chapter 14). You can even swim at 6,000-foot-high **Lake Tahoe** (see Chapter 18), most comfortably in August. Water-related theme parks—

complete with daring waterslides—provide another popular option (see Chapter 9).

The best swimming in California, though, is in the state's southern half. **Santa Barbara** (see Chapter 17) is an idyllic beach resort, and numerous beaches in the **Los Angeles** area (see Chapter 15) offer excellent swimming. But as with most water-related activities in the state, **San Diego** (see Chapter 16) sets the pace for family swimming. The San Diego area offers more than 70 miles of beaches, all open and free to the public. Those best for families include **Coronado Beach, Children's Pool Beach** in La Jolla, **La Jolla Shores Beach, Mission Beach,** and **Silver Strand State Beach.** See Chapter 16 for details on each.

Windsurfing

The fast-growing sport of windsurfing (also called sailboarding) is something like a combination of surfing and sailing. The sail is attached to a board much like a surfboard, which windsurfers stand atop to ride over the waves, adjusting the sails to catch the wind. Expert windsurfers love the rush of windy waters like San Francisco Bay, but beginners should head for inland lakes or quiet bays where winds are calmer. In warm-water lakes you probably won't need a wet suit, but in cooler waters near the coast or in the mountains you definitely will. Though windsurfing may look difficult at first, kids as young as 8 can learn the basics after one lesson; finesse is more vital than upper-body strength. Getting the right size equipment for body weight is important, too.

A good place for beginners to learn in the northern part of California is the **Benbow Lake State Recreation Area** (tel. 707/923-3238), a reservoir open from June to mid-September. **Folsom Lake State Recreation Area** (tel. 916/988-0205) northeast of

Sacramento can accommodate all skill levels during its windsurfing season, April through May. **Lake Tahoe** (see Chapter 18) offers good windsurfing throughout the summer. **San Francisco Bay** (especially off the Presidio's Crissy Field) offers world-class windsurfing for experienced sailboarders; **Lake Merced** and **Lake Del Valle** are good for beginners (see Chapter 14). Along the central coast **Santa Cruz** and **Santa Barbara** (see Chapter 17 for both) and **Morro Strand State Beach** (tel. 805/772-2560), north of Morro Bay, offer year-round windsurfing for all levels.

In the **Los Angeles** and **Orange County** areas head for **Marina del Rey, Malibu,** and **Dana Point** (see Chapter 15). Inland possibilities include **Big Bear Lake** in the San Bernardino Mountains (see Chapter 18), **Silverwood Lake State Recreation Area** (tel. 760/389-2303) north of San Bernardino, **Lake Isabella** (tel. 760/379-5646) northeast of Bakersfield, and the **Salton Sea State Recreation Area** (tel. 760/393-3052) in the southern deserts (see Chapter 7).

My top pick for a family-oriented windsurfing spot goes to **San Diego** (see Chapter 16), especially its water-sports mecca **Mission Bay.** The bay's smooth waters and light breezes are ideal for kids to learn the sport, and numerous outfitters rent sailboards and provide instruction for all levels. **Resort Water Sports** at the Bahia Resort Hotel (998 W. Mission Bay Dr., tel. 619/488-0551) rents sailboards at $20 an hour, $64 a day, and offers lessons at $35 per person for two people for two hours. **C. P. Watersports** (San Diego Hilton Hotel, tel. 619/276-4010) offers lessons as well as rental boards sized for all skill levels; rentals cost $20 an hour and from $50 to $70 a day. **Mission Bay Sportcenter** (1010 Santa Clara Pl., tel. 619/488-1004) rents sailboards at $16 per hour, $70 per day; the adjacent San Diego Sailing Center (tel. 619/488-0651) gives lessons.

ONLY IN WINTER
SKIING, SKATING, SNOWBOARDING

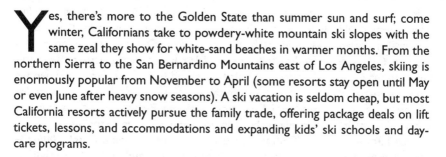

Yes, there's more to the Golden State than summer sun and surf; come winter, Californians take to powdery-white mountain ski slopes with the same zeal they show for white-sand beaches in warmer months. From the northern Sierra to the San Bernardino Mountains east of Los Angeles, skiing is enormously popular from November to April (some resorts stay open until May or even June after heavy snow seasons). A ski vacation is seldom cheap, but most California resorts actively pursue the family trade, offering package deals on lift tickets, lessons, and accommodations and expanding kids' ski schools and day-care programs.

Most downhill (alpine) ski areas permit snowboarding, an exciting cross between skateboarding and snow-surfing that's said to be the fastest-growing winter sport. Some resorts also offer ice-skating, sleigh rides, and cross-country (Nordic) skiing. Don't overlook the joys of cross-country: It's terrific exercise, generally costs less than downhill skiing, requires less equipment, and eliminates waiting in lift lines. Cross-country also tends to be less risky than either downhill skiing or snowboarding, and young children can pick it up fairly easily and stay with it throughout their lives. You can cross-country at well-groomed trails at major resorts or glide across a meadow for free.

California has five major skiing regions: Mount Shasta, Lake Tahoe, the central Sierra, the Mammoth Lakes area in the eastern Sierra, and the mountains of Southern California. North Lake Tahoe claims to have the largest concentration of snow skiing in the nation, and the North Lake Tahoe Resorts Association operates an excellent booking service (tel. 800/824–6348) for packages that include skiing, lodging, and air transportation from major U.S. cities; some packages offer midweek discounts and lift tickets interchangeable at several resorts. One such interchangeable ticket, the Ski Lake Tahoe ticket ($225), may be used at Alpine Meadows, Heavenly, Kirkwood, Sierra-at-Tahoe, Northstar, and Squaw Valley within a five-day period.

The state runs 19 cleared parking areas called Sno-Parks in northern and central California, which offer access to hills and meadows for cross-country skiing and snow play such as sledding and tobogganing. (Check out Echo Summit, on the south side of Highway 50, for great sledding.) Day permits are $5 per vehicle; season passes (good November–May) cost $25. Buy permits at many sporting goods stores or at selected Sno-Parks. For more information, call 916/324–1222 or write: Sno-Park program, Box 942896, Sacramento 94296.

All winter sports involve some risk of injury; everyone in the family should be properly grounded in fundamental skills and basic safety rules. A few hours in the company of a qualified instructor could save many weeks in the confines of a cast. Children should also wear protective gear where appropriate.

It generally snows only in the mountains in California, so few cars are equipped with snow tires, and highway snow-removal equipment may be slow in arriving, making travel difficult and hazardous during winter storms. It's essential to carry tire chains any time you drive to the mountains from October until as late as May or June. (We once headed to Yosemite on a drizzly but relatively warm fall morning without our chains, drove for four hours, and had to turn around when we encountered snow right at the gates of the park—which made for two very disappointed kids and two very frustrated parents.) Before setting out for the mountains, call the California Highway Information Network at the State Department of Transportation (Caltrans) for the latest road conditions: tel. 800/427–7623. For Northern California only, call 916/445–7623, and for Southern California only, call 213/628–7623. If you have rotary dial, call 916/445–1534 from anywhere in the state.

Besides the ski resorts detailed here, you'll find several other family-friendly ski areas in California, including: Donner Ski Ranch (Old Hwy. 40, Box 66, Norden 95724, tel. 530/426–3635), Sierra-at-Tahoe (1111 Sierra-at-Tahoe Rd., Twin Bridges 95735, tel. 530/659–7475), Ski Homewood (5145 West Lake Blvd., Box 165, Homewood 96141, tel. 530/525–2992), Sugar Bowl Ski Resort (Old Hwy. 40, Box 5, Norden 95724, tel. 530/426–3651), and Tahoe Donner (11509 Northwoods Blvd., Truckee 96161, tel. 530/587–9444), all in the Lake Tahoe area; Bear Valley Ski Area (Box 5038, Bear Valley 95223, tel. 209/753–2301), near the Gold Country; and Snow Valley (Box 2337, Running Springs 92382, tel. 909/867–2751 or 909/867–5151), near Lake Arrowhead, 20 miles north of San Bernardino in southern California.

Northern Forests and Lakes

Mount Shasta Board and Ski Park

(♔♔ 4 – 15) Mount Shasta Board and Ski Park is the only major ski resort in far Northern California. Still, with most San Francisco–area skiers heading to Tahoe or the central Sierra, Mount Shasta isn't terribly crowded, and it's easy to reach via I–5 (about an hour's drive north and east of Redding). It's also one of the least expensive ski areas in the state—lift tickets for ages 7 and under, for instance, are only $3—and the casual, low-key atmosphere makes the resort a great place to learn the sport. At the southern base (5,500 feet) of 14,162-foot Mount Shasta, with views of the Trinity Alps in the distance, the ski park offers downhill skiing, snowboarding, cross-country trails, night skiing, and a ski school. Some downhill runs are reasonably challenging, but

none is exceptionally steep, and one entire trail system (Marmot Ridge) is geared to beginners. Skiing and snowboarding lessons are available for everyone age 4 and above. The SKIwee program, for ages 4 to 7, includes two two-hour lessons, rental equipment, and a beginner ticket ($35; $25 for one lesson). A "First Time Beginner Package" (ages 7 and up for skiing, 9 and up for snowboarding) combines two 1½-hour lessons with equipment rentals and a beginner ticket for $40 ($30 for one lesson). The Ski Park's nearby Nordic Center (open daily in season, 9–4) provides 15 miles of trails and a groomed skating lane, plus lessons and rental packages. Trail passes cost $11 for adults, $7 for ages 8 to 12, and $3 for ages 7 and under. Lodgings, restaurants, and ski shops are in the towns of Mount Shasta and McCloud, both within 10 miles. The resort arranges economical weekday "Ski 'n' Stay" packages with local inns and motels.
🏔 *Mt. Shasta Board and Ski Park, 104 Siskiyou Ave., Mt. Shasta 96067, tel. 530/926–8610, snow phone 530/926–8686, fax 530/926–8607. 10 mi east of I–5 and town of Mt. Shasta via Hwy. 89. Facilities: 2 day lodges, rentals, lessons, children's program, food concessions. All-day lift tickets: $26–$31 adults, $16–$17 ages 8–12, $3 ages 4–7; half-day, night, day-night, Tues., and multiday discounts. AE, D, MC, V. Open early Dec.–mid-Apr., daily 9–4; night skiing Wed.–Sat. 4–10 PM.*

Sierra and the Gold Country

Alpine Meadows Ski Area

👪 **4 – 15** By almost any standard, Alpine Meadows is one of Lake Tahoe's top downhill ski resorts. Its 2,000 acres contain more than 100 runs catering to skiers of all abilities, with steep drops, gentle knolls, and open bowls; at elevations between 6,800 and 8,600 feet, the lake views are terrific. With the help of abundant snowfall and

snowmaking equipment when needed, Alpine usually has Tahoe's longest downhill ski season, running to the end of May and sometimes even into early July. New touches include a Family Ski Zone (a moderate slope for skiing at a relaxed pace), reduced-price teen tickets, a $48 interchangeable parent ticket so parents can trade off child-care and skiing throughout the day, and a parents' lounge with play area for young kids in the day lodge. In the past few years Alpine—one of the last holdouts—has opened its slopes to snowboarders and even embraced them, adding the Gravity Cavity half pipe and the Roo's Ride terrain park. Alpine's daily Junior Mountaineers Kids' Camp for children ages 7 to 12 ($72 all day, $46 half day) includes lesson, lift ticket, and rental equipment. Experienced skiers ages 7 to 12 can sign up for 2½-hour intermediate or advanced lessons for $32. Kids ages 4 to 6 can begin at the Little Mountaineers Kids' Camp ($46 half day, $72 full day). For reservations at the Kids' Camps, call 530/581–8240. For parents who plan to do a lot of skiing, Alpine 10-PAKs (of lift tickets) cost $400 (adults only). For information about ski-stay packages with various North Shore lodges, call 800/949–3296.
🏔 *2600 Alpine Meadows Rd., Box 5279, Tahoe City 96145, tel. 530/583–4232 or 800/441–4423, snow phone 530/581–8374, fax 530/583–0963. 6 mi northwest of Tahoe City off Hwy. 89. Facilities: day lodge, rentals, lessons, children's program, food concessions. All-day lift tickets: $48 adults, $36 ages 13–18, $10 ages 7–12, $6 ages 6 and under; afternoon, multiday, and early and late-season discounts. AE, D, MC, V. Open mid-Nov.–late May, June, or early July, daily 9–4 (late Apr.–end of season, 8:30–2).*

Badger Pass Ski Area

👪 **3 – 15** Badger Pass, the state's oldest operating ski area (opened in 1935), is one of the best budget choices for families in California and an ideal place to bring kids to learn to ski. For starters, it's fairly small—nine downhill runs, plus 90 miles of groomed cross-country trails—and the atmosphere is relaxed and uncrowded. Most of the runs are suitable for beginning and intermediate skiers. The prices are right, too, with economical downhill packages available and free cross-country skiing. Badger Pass is within Yosemite National Park (see Chapter 8), 23 miles from Yosemite Valley on Highway 41, with free shuttle buses from Valley lodgings to the ski area each morning. Its base elevation is 7,200 feet; it's 8,000 feet at the summit. Yosemite's a great place to visit in winter: Yosemite Valley is rid of the summer hordes, the snowcapped peaks are spectacular, wildlife is easier to spot, you can ice-skate on an outdoor rink at Curry Village (tel. 209/372–8341), and kids can earn Junior Snow Ranger certificates and patches by attending National Park Service programs. The downhill and cross-country ski schools here have excellent reputations and long experience; the Yosemite Ski School (for downhill) is the oldest in the West. The Badger Pups conducts classes for kids ages 4 to 6. The best deal for families (though you may have to take older kids out of school to take advantage of it) is the Midweek Ski Package ($25 per person a day, available Sunday–Thursday, except holiday periods) for those staying at Yosemite lodgings. The price includes an all-day lift ticket, two downhill or cross-country ski lessons, a pass to the ice rink, free ski area baby-sitting for kids 3 to 9, and evening activities such as movies and ranger programs. Packages are also available for skiers not staying in Yosemite, but why miss out on the fun?

🏠 *Badger Pass Ski Area, Yosemite National Park 95389, tel. 209/372–1446, snow phone 209/372–1000, room reservations 209/252–4848, fax 209/456–0542. Facilities: rentals, lessons, food concessions. Lift tickets: $26 adults, $13 under 13. Nordic-trail passes free. D, MC, V. Open Thanksgiving–Easter, daily 9–4:30.*

Boreal/Soda Springs Resorts

(👫 **ALL**) The theme at Boreal/Soda Springs these days is "making fun easy," and, in an attempt to do just that for families, the two ski resorts have simplified pricing, expanded kids' programs, and even allowed some free skiing opportunities. At 7,200-foot Donner Summit—which is some 40 miles closer to the Bay Area than Lake Tahoe resorts—Boreal usually opens its season earlier than other regional ski areas and, starting at Thanksgiving, stays open later at night. Kids ages 4 to 6 can attend Boreal's Animal Crackers Children's Snow School, while kids 7 to 12 learn at Snow Rangers. All-day price for each is $59, half-day is $45; the rate includes lift tickets, rental equipment, lesson, optional helmet, and, with the all-day program, lunch. If your kids (ages 3 to 10) are a bit timid for a group, they can also learn to ski—with your help if you're at least intermediate level—during one-hour private lessons; these cost $59 and include the child's equipment and lift ticket. Kids age 5 to 10 can get private snowboarding lessons for the same price. Call 530/426–3666, ext. 188 to reserve children's programs. Everyone in the family can ski for free any day of the week at Boreal's Nugget chairlift (open 9–4), which caters to beginners; kids can practice newly acquired skills on the gentle terrain. Beginners get free lessons at Boreal, which has other incentives for families: Two parents can buy one $28 interchangeable lift ticket, allowing them to trade off skiing and child-care duties (there's an unsupervised infant center where tiny ones can play). The first Sunday of each month (starting in December) brings a Kids Karnival with races, obstacle courses, and games, and there's a sledding area and a children's park. The Boreal Inn is a short walk from the slopes; economical "Stay and Play" packages are available (tel. 530/426–3666 ext. 123 for reservations). At Boreal's sister resort, Soda Springs, a small, relaxed ski and snowboarding area nearby, kids 7 and under ski free, and packages including lesson, equipment, and lift ticket are $35 for ages 8 and up. You can go tubing here for $16 a day or $10 for two hours.

🏠 *Boreal/Soda Springs Resorts, Box 39, Truckee 96160, tel. 530/426–3666, fax 530/*

426–3173. Boreal: off I–80 at Donner Summit, 10 mi west of Truckee. Facilities: lodging, rentals, lessons, children's program, snowboard park, food concessions. Lift tickets: $28 adults, $10 ages 5–12. AE, D, MC, V. Open Early Nov.–Thanksgiving, daily 9–4:30; Thanksgiving–Easter, daily 9–9. Soda Springs: Old Hwy. 40, take Soda Springs/Norden exit off I–80. Facilities: rentals, lessons, food concessions. Lift tickets: $16, ages 7 and under free. D, MC, V. Open Thanksgiving–Easter, daily 9–4:30.

Dodge Ridge

(†† 2–15) Dodge Ridge takes pride in being a family ski area, a place for low-key fun at low prices. At 6,600 feet (with an 8,200-foot summit) near Pinecrest Lake in the Gold Country, Dodge Ridge has none of the glamour or clamor of Lake Tahoe, but it's the closest ski area to the Central Valley and the San Francisco Bay Area. The majority of its skiers, in fact, come up for the day. When they arrive, they find an acclaimed children's instructional program, free skiing for kids 6 and under, snowboarding, 7 miles of free cross-country skiing trails, and downhill skiing. And visitors who do want to stay a while can find inexpensive stay-and-ski packages in the area (call 800/446–1333 for information on nearby motels, cabins, and condos). Kids' lessons are based in the Children's Center, which has its own practice area, so kids don't have to fear older skiers whizzing by while they're trying to learn. SKIwee, for ages 4 to 8, costs $65 all day, $50 half day. Trackers, a similarly priced program for kids ages 9 to 12, teaches environmental awareness along with skiing fundamentals; Trackers also explore nearby treasure sites as part of their lessons. Terrain Trackers, for ages 9 to 14, is for more advanced skiers; it's $65 for ages 9 to 12 and $75 for ages 13 to 14, including lunch. For ages 13 and up there are EZ Turns and EZ Riders packages for skiers and boarders, including lift ticket, rental equipment, and two hours of instruction for $45. First-time skiers, meanwhile, can get a free one hour lesson each afternoon.

🏠 Dodge Ridge Ski Area, Box 1188, Pinecrest 95364, tel. 209/965–3474 or 209/965–4444, fax 209/965–4437. Hwy. 108, 30 mi northeast of Sonora. Facilities: day lodge, equipment rentals, ski lessons, children's programs, food concessions. All-day lift tickets: $39 adults, $30 ages 13–19, $15 ages 7–12, 6 and under free. Weekday, half-day, multiday, season discounts. AE, D, MC, V. Open Nov.–Apr., weekdays 9–4, weekends and holidays 8:30–4.

Granlibakken

(†† ALL) Granlibakken, the oldest ski resort at Lake Tahoe, is ideal for families seeking a low-key, inexpensive introduction to the sport. Its lift tickets are among the least expensive in the area, a one-hour group lesson costs $20 for skiing, $25 for snowboarding, and a package of lesson, rentals, and lift tickets is $35 for skiing, $40 for boarding. The setting is quiet, the slopes are sheltered and uncrowded, and you can learn to ski without competition from "hot dog" skiers and other distractions. There's a 160-room bed-and-breakfast lodge (with one- to three-bedroom condos) and a small children's snow play area (admission $4) adjacent to the ski area; families staying here get half off on both lift ticket prices and admission to the snow play area. Keep in mind, however, that the ski area is only open from Friday to Sunday and on holidays, and it has limited facilities; one chairlift, a vertical drop of only 300 feet, and no expert-level runs. Hotel guests at Granlibakken, however, can take advantage of packages that allow skiing at nearby Alpine Meadows (see above) or Squaw Valley (see below).

🏠 Granlibakken Resort, Box 6329, Tahoe City 96145, tel. 530/583–4242 or 800/543–3221, fax 530/583–7641. End of Granlibakken Rd. off Hwy. 89, ½ mi south of Tahoe City. Facilities: lodge, rentals, lessons, snow play area, food concession. All-day lift tickets: $15 adults, $8 under 13. Half-day discounts. AE, D, MC, V. Open Nov.–Apr., Fri.–Sun. and holidays 9–4.

Heavenly Ski Resort

(**ii** 4–15) At the sprawling Heavenly Ski Resort, which anchors Lake Tahoe's South Shore, you can actually ski into another state and back (keep the kids away from the slot machines across the border). It has three full-service base day lodges, one in South Lake Tahoe, California, and two in adjoining Stateline, Nevada; mid-mountain day lodges on both California and Nevada sides; and 16 lifts in California and 11 in Nevada. Heavenly has the longest vertical drop of any Lake Tahoe ski resort (3,500 feet) and a mountain descent 5½ miles long; with a summit of more than 10,000 feet, it offers magnificent views of the lake and surrounding mountains. (You can "Ski with a Ranger" here, a free mountain tour led by U.S. Forest Service rangers that focuses on the mountain, Tahoe geology, and wildlife.) Other options include cross-country skiing, snowshoeing, sleigh rides, and snowmobiling. Add to that 82 runs on terrain for all abilities of skiers, as well as snowboarding across the entire mountain—including two new snowboard parks and two half pipes— Heavenly makes for an appealing package. But because of its enormous size and often huge crowds, I'd recommend taking preschoolers to a smaller ski area; wait to bring kids here until they're at least 6 or 7, unless they're already experienced skiers. Still, even the youngest kids can find a place here. The expanded Perfect Turn Children's Center, which has branches at both the California Base Lodge and the Boulder Base Lodge in Nevada, offers the Perfect Kids introductory package for skiing or snowboarding ($78 for five hours, $55 for 2½ hours) for kids ages 4 to 13 of all ability levels (kids' snowboard clinics are for ages 7 to 13). The prices include instruction, lift access, equipment rental, lunch or snacks, and snow play. And the California base lodge has a new day-care center for infants, toddlers, and preschoolers that includes snow play for little ones ages 6 months to 4 years. For ski vacation packages with area lodgings, call 800/243–2836.

** Å** Heavenly Ski Resort, Box 2180, Stateline, NV 89449, tel. 702/586–7000, ski conditions 530/541–7544, fax 702/588–5517. California base lodge at corner of Wildwood and Saddle off Ski Run Blvd., South Lake Tahoe. Facilities: 7 day lodges, rentals, lessons, children's program, day care, food concessions, aerial tramway. All-day lift tickets: $52 adults, $38 ages 13–15, $24 ages 6–12, under 6 free. Half-day and multiday discounts available. AE, MC, V. Open Nov.–early May, weekdays 9–4, weekends and holidays 8:30–4.

Kirkwood Ski Resort

(**ii** 3–15) Kirkwood is only 30 miles south of Lake Tahoe, but it seems like a world away from the hubbub; you can ski here in a beautiful alpine village setting, stay in a slope-side condominium (for packages, call 209/258–7000 or 800/967–7500), and take skiing or snowboarding lessons at reasonable rates. Kirkwood's base elevation of 7,800 feet is the highest of any Northern California ski resort, and in several recent years it has had the deepest snow base. Its 68 runs cover 2,300 skiable acres with wide trails, chutes, and vast open bowls. The vertical drop is 2,000 feet. Kirkwood also offers weekend sleigh rides ($10 adults, $5 under $13; tel. 209/258–7433) and 50 miles of groomed cross-country trails. Children ages 4 to 12 can sign up for the Mighty Mountain Children's Ski School, an all-day ($67) or half-day ($57) program that includes downhill lessons, a lift ticket, and rental equipment; children are grouped by age and ability. Licensed day care is available for infants (tel. 209/258–8783) and (in a separate facility) nonskiing children ages 2 to 6 who are out of diapers ($55 all day or $45 half day). At Kirkwood's Learn-to-Ski Center first-timer ski packages with four hours of lessons, lift ticket, and rental equipment cost $45, while Learn to Snowboard packages are $60. (Kirkwood's freestyle terrain park has quarter pipes, tabletop jumps, and a snake—all the things to keep boarders happy.) Kirkwood's Nordic Ski Center offers lessons plus three separate trail systems that wind through mountains, meadows, and forests; a trail for kids, the "Kiddie Kilometer," has life-size cutouts of forest animals along the way.

🏨 *Kirkwood Ski Resort, Box 1, Kirkwood 95646, tel. 209/258–6000, snow phone 209/258–3000, ski hot line 415/989–7669, fax 209/258–8899. Hwy. 88, 60 mi east of Jackson. Facilities: lodging, 2 day lodges, general store, rentals, lessons, children's programs, child care, food concessions. All-day lift tickets: $45 ages 25–59, $35 ages 13–24, $7 ages 6–12, under 6 free. Half-day, multi-day, senior, and seasonal discounts. Nordic-trail passes: $15 adults, $11 ages 13–18, $5 ages 7–12. AE, DC, MC, V. Open mid-Nov.–May, daily 9–4.*

Mammoth Mountain and June Mountain

(👫 **ALL**) Everything about Mammoth Mountain lives up to its name: big mountain, big ski area, big crowds, big prices. Mammoth is one of the busiest ski areas in the state, with packed slopes on weekends and holidays. This is the favorite Sierra getaway for Southern Californians, and no wonder: The Mammoth Lakes region (see Chapter 18) is a gorgeous alpine resort area, much less developed than Lake Tahoe, and convenient to the southern part of the state with access on U.S. Highway 395, which skirts the eastern Sierra. (It's not so convenient for San Francisco Bay Area residents, for whom the only direct auto route to the eastern Sierra goes through Yosemite's Tioga Pass, which closes in winter.) On an average day, Mammoth grooms more acreage than any other ski area in the country, and it has 30 lifts in operation. With a base elevation of nearly 8,000 feet and a summit of more than 11,000 feet, Mammoth usually gets plenty of snow, extending its typical season into June. Mammoth's nearby twin resort, June Mountain (13 miles north on Highway 395 at June Lake), is much smaller, but its runs are popular with beginning and advanced skiers; June is good for families

seeking a less crowded, more intimate resort area. June Mountain is also well known for its snowboarding terrain, including beginning and expert runs; rental equipment and lessons are available. The Mammoth Ski School offers all sorts of instruction; its Woollywood Children's Ski and Snowboard School, for ages 4 to 6 and 7 to 12, costs $75 all day including lunch; half day is $34. Children's private lessons cost from $55 to $75, and $10 for an additional child. For nonskiers, Small World Child Care (at Mammoth Mountain Inn across from the Main Lodge) provides supervised care for infants and toddlers up to 24 months ($56 all day, $40 half day) or for ages 2 to 12 ($49 all day, $35 half day); reservations required (call 760/934–0646). June Mountain also has a Children's Ski School for ages 3 to 6 and 7 to 12 and a day-care center, at the base of the mountain ($41 all day, $30 half day); call 760/648–7609 for reservations. Mammoth and June also offer cross-country skiing, sledding, and tobogganing, and at Mammoth you can also snowmobile, go sleigh riding or dogsledding, or even ride in a hot-air balloon. Nonskiers can take a ride on the scenic Mammoth Gondola ($10 adults, $5 children), which goes to the top of the mountain. The Mammoth Mountain Inn (tel. 800/228–4947) is the top choice for lodgings and restaurants, but the towns of Mammoth Lakes and June Lake also contain a wide range of motels and condominiums (see Chapter 18), many connected to the ski areas by free shuttle services.

🏨 *Mammoth Mountain Ski Area, Box 24, Mammoth Lakes 93546, tel. 760/934–0745 or 888/462–6668, snow phone 760/934–2571 or 888/766–9778, fax 760/934–0603. Facilities: 3 day lodges, rentals, lessons, food concessions. All-day (8:30–4) lift tickets: $49 adults, $37 ages 13–18, $25 ages 7–12, ages 6 and under free. Afternoon, night, beginner, springtime, and multiday discounts. AE, D, MC, V. Open Nov.–June, daily 8:30–4, weekends and holidays 8:30 AM–9 PM. June Mountain, Box 146, June Lake 93529, tel. 760/648–*

7733 or 888/586–3668, fax 760/648–7367.
Facilities: day lodge, rentals, classes, day care,
food concessions. All-day lift tickets: $40
adults, $30 teens, $20 ages 7–12, ages 6
and under free. Senior, multiday discounts.
Open weekdays 8:30–4, weekends and
holidays 8–4.

Northstar-at-Tahoe

(✖✖ 2–15) In a largely undeveloped area 6
miles north of Lake Tahoe, Northstar, a golf
and tennis resort in summer (see Chapter
12), becomes in winter a ski haven that's
consistently rated among the top family ski
areas in the West. This resort has it all:
downhill skiing with terrain for all abilities,
cross-country trails, snowboarding, an excellent ski school with top children's programs
and day care, sleigh rides, lodging, restaurants, a recreation center, and other facilities. You can spend your entire vacation at
Northstar and never have to leave. For
downhill skiers, the resort has 63 runs,
recreational ski racing, 2,400 tree-lined acres
of terrain (most of it beginning or intermediate), 12 lifts, and a vertical drop of nearly
2,300 feet from the top of 8,600-foot
Mount Pluto. For cross-country skiers and
snowshoers, Northstar provides nearly 40
miles of groomed and track trails and services for all ability levels. Snowboarders are
welcome on Northstar's mountain as well
as its 75-yard-long, 45-foot-wide half-pipe
course (for doing skateboard-style tricks on
snow). Kids ages 5 to 12 can learn to ski or
snowboard in the Starkids program ($69 all
day, $59 half day), while toilet-trained
youngsters ages 2 to 6 are eligible for
Minors' Camp licensed day care ($51 all day,
$31 half day; call 530/562–2278 for reserva-
tions). Learn-to-ski options for kids 3 to 6
can be added to Minors' Camp for an additional fee; for this, kids are divided into
those with no experience, and 5- to 6-year-
olds with some experience. Kids are transported to the learning area on the "Magic
Carpet" surface lift, and parents are provided pagers while they're skiing elsewhere
if they need to check in. If parents want to

switch off skiing and taking care of the kids,
they can buy a "Parents' Predicament" ticket
for $48, allowing mom to ski in the morning
and dad in the afternoon, or vice versa. An
Introduction to Skiing package costs $43 for
ages 5 to 12 and $54 to $69 for kids 13 and
up, depending on experience level. First
Tracks, an introductory cross-country program for ages 5 to 12, is offered weekends
and holidays for $25; Introduction to Snow-
boarding costs $54 for ages 5 to 12, $54 to
$69 for kids 13 and up. Skiers and boarders
of intermediate ability, age 13 and up, can
take free group "skill improvement" lessons
daily here. Northstar also offers free skiing
for families who book lodgings at the resort
for selected days during the winter season.
Most of Northstar is privately owned, but
about half of the units are available for rent;
you can stay in condominiums or houses,
both with kitchens, or in hotel-type units at
the base village, near the resort's major
restaurants and shops and the recreation
center, which guests can use at no extra
charge. Free shuttles transport guests from
outlying lodgings to the base village. Non-
skiers of all ages can ride the gondola up the
mountain for $5.
🏠 *Northstar-at-Tahoe, Box 129, Truckee*
96160, tel. 530/562–1010, snow phone 530/
562–1330, accommodations 800/466–6784,
fax 530/562–2215. 6 mi north of Lake Tahoe
and 6 mi south of Truckee on Hwy. 267. Facili-
ties: lodging, day lodge, lessons, rentals, shuttle
service, recreation center, sleigh rides, horse-
back riding, children's programs, child care,
food concessions. All-day lift tickets: $48 ages
23–59, $38 ages 13–22, $10 ages 5–12.
Afternoon, multiday, and senior discounts.
Nordic-trail passes: $17 adults, $10 ages 5–
12. AE, D, MC, V. Open Thanksgiving–mid-
Apr., daily 8:30–4.

Royal Gorge

(✖✖ 4–15) Royal Gorge, on Donner Summit (7,000 feet) near Lake Tahoe, is North
America's largest cross-country ski resort,
with 88 trails and some 200 miles of
groomed track covering more than 9,000

acres of terrain. Whether that's a plus or a minus depends entirely on your perspective. Our family found it a bit overwhelming the day we skied here, but friends of ours with two young boys ski at Royal Gorge often and consider it their favorite spot. (The sheer size of the place may simply take getting used to.) In any event, there are plenty of trails here for every level of ability, more than 75% of them for beginners and intermediates; the advanced trails, be forewarned, are not for the faint of heart. Royal Gorge even includes four surface lifts, something rarely seen at a cross-country area: These allow skiers to enjoy scenic outlying trails without continually climbing steep hills (a boon to youngsters and out-of-shape parents). The rustic Wilderness Lodge, in the heart of the resort's track system—you arrive by means of a 3-mile sleigh ride—is a treat for families with children ages 5 and up. Rooms are furnished with double or bunk beds, with bathrooms down the hall, and there's a hot tub and sauna; ask about weekend and midweek packages. The Royal Gorge Ski School offers a variety of lessons for all skill levels, including a Ski-Able program for skiers with disabilities. Pee-Wee Snow School offers lessons for ages 4 to 12, available weekends and some holiday periods ($20–$45), and Learn to Ski Special Packages are offered daily ($42 adults, $25 ages 10–16).

🏠 *Royal Gorge, 9411 Hillside Dr., Box 1100, Soda Springs 95728, tel. 530/426–3871; outside Northern CA, 800/500–3871; fax 530/426–9221. Off I-80 at Soda Springs/Norden exit. Facilities: 2 trailside lodges, day lodge, rentals, lessons, 10 warming huts, food concessions. Nordic-trail passes: $13.50–$21.50 adults, $8.50 ages 12–16, ages 11 and under free. Twilight and multiday discounts. MC, V. Open mid-Nov.–late May, weekdays 9–5:30, weekends and holidays 8:30–5.*

Squaw Valley USA

(👫 **ALL**) Squaw Valley, which gained worldwide fame as the site of the 1960 Winter Olympics, is the one Lake Tahoe ski resort you should see, even if you don't plan to ski here. Whenever we visit Tahoe, our family rides the scenic cable car to the spectacular 8,200-foot High Camp Bath & Tennis Club, where we ice-skate outdoors at the Olympic Ice Pavilion, the world's highest—and possibly most beautiful—Olympic-size skating rink, open daily year-round. Meanwhile, new skiers can test their fledgling skills on gentle slopes in the same area—one of the few resorts where beginners can start out on the *top* of a mountain. High Camp also has six tennis courts (two playable in winter), a swimming lagoon and spa, an 80-foot bungee tower, six sundecks, and three restaurants. Don't miss this spot. Another mid-mountain complex, Gold Coast, is the site of Squaw's snowboard park and half pipe; you can get there by gondola from High Camp, or from the Base Village by the new high-speed Funitel. If you do ski Squaw, you'll find one of the largest facilities in the country, spread over six Sierra peaks with 4,000 acres of terrain served by 30 lifts. Seventy percent of the open bowl terrain is geared for beginners and intermediates; advanced skiers can set out on miles of wilderness runs. For family skiers, there's Children's World (tel. 530/581–7225), a supervised ski playground for ages 4 to 12—complete with its own ski hill, school, and facilities ($60 all day, $45 half day; rentals $13 extra). Toddlers (2 to 3 years of age) can stay here, too, at a licensed day-care center ($60 all day, $45 half day, reservations required; call 530/581–7280). At Squaw Valley's regular Ski and Snowboard School group and private lessons are available for skiers and boarders of varying abilities, ages 13 and up. Squaw's ski season runs until late May or even longer, and in the future the resort hopes to keep one run open year-round through the magic of snowmaking. Stay-and-ski packages are available at several resorts, inns, condominiums, and hostels in the immediate area, whose accommodations range from luxurious to basic.

🏠 *Squaw Valley USA, 1960 Squaw Valley Rd., Box 2007, Olympic Valley 96146, tel.*

530/583–6985, snow phone 530/583–6955, central reservations 888/766–9321 or 530/ 583–5585, fax 530/581–7106. Off Hwy. 89 between Truckee and Tahoe City. Facilities: mountaintop sports center, cable car, lessons, rentals, children's program, child care, food concessions. All-day lift tickets: $49 adults, $5 under 13; night skiing: $20 adults, $5 under 13; half-day and multiday discounts. Nonskier cable-car rides: $14 adults, $5 under 13; with skate pass, $5 additional per person. AE, D, MC, V. Open Nov.–May, weekdays 9–4 (mid-Dec.–mid-Apr., 9–9), weekends and holidays 8:30 AM–9 PM.

Los Angeles and Environs

Bear Mountain Ski Resort

(👫 **4–15**) With a peak elevation of 8,805 feet (and a 1,665-foot vertical drop), Bear Mountain is Southern California's highest ski resort—and one of the region's best all-around family ski areas. Its 195 developed acres (and 500 additional off-trail acres for the adventurous) extend over four separate peaks in the San Bernardino Mountains, with 75% of its 32 runs suitable for novices and intermediates. Children under 6 ski or snowboard for free, and kids ages 4 to 12 can take skiing or snowboarding lessons at the Magic Minors' Camp for $70 all day, $60 half day; prices include rental equipment, and, for the all-day program, lunch. Kids age 3 can take a half-day lesson. Another entice-ment is a trailside theme park where kids can ski in and among a replica of a log fort, a Western town facade, a tepee, a mine shaft, and a bear cave. There's an Introduction to Skiing/Snowboarding Program for new beginners ages 13 and up ($49), where beginners learn on their own practice area. Group lessons for more advanced skiers cost $69. The resort also has its own race-course, where you can race on your own for $1 a run; racing clinics cost $68. Bear

Mountain allows snowboarding on all of its runs, and snowboarders have the use of separate terrain parks and half pipes. Snow-shoes and snowblades are also available. For people with disabilities Bear Mountain has a Handicap Ski School, the only one of its kind in the region.

🏔 *Bear Mountain Ski Resort, 43101 Gold-mine Dr., Box 6812, Big Bear Lake 92315, tel. 909/585–2519, snow phone 800/232–7686, fax 909/585–6805. 2 mi southeast of Big Bear on Moonridge Rd.; follow Hwy. 38 from Redlands to Hwy. 18. Facilities: lessons, rentals, children's school, food concessions, video arcade. All-day lift tickets: $30 adults and $45 (holiday), $30 ages 13–22 and $35 (holiday), $10 ages 6–12, 5 and under free. Half-day and multiday discounts. AE, D, MC, V. Open Nov.–late Apr., weekdays 8–4, weekends and holidays 7:30–4.*

Mountain High Resort

(👫 **4–15**) Mountain High, which changed ownership in 1997, is the second-largest ski area in Southern California and the sixth largest in the state based on number of vis-its. The resort has upgraded and expanded many of its facilities to handle the increased skier and snowboarding traffic. One of its big selling points is that it's easily accessible by major roads from the Los Angeles area and can be reached from many communi-ties in less than an hour, with no mountain driving. With temperatures up to 50° cooler than in the L.A. basin, you could go from a warm morning swim in the ocean to a crisp afternoon's skiing on the same day. Moun-tain High is also the only local resort to offer daily night skiing—on a clear night you can see a glittering array of lights from L.A. in one direction and distant sparkles from high-desert cities in the other. In the San Gabriel Mountains, it has a summit 8,200 feet high, providing a vertical drop of 1,600 feet to the ski area base. The area has 220 skiable acres, with 50 runs totaling more than 19 miles; beginner and intermediate runs make up 60% of the total. The ski area is set on two mountains, East and West, connected by free daytime shuttle service. At the Children's Ski Academy, skiers ages 4 to 8 and boarders ages 7 to 8 can learn for $30 a half day, $70 a full day. Children ages 9 to 12 and beginners 13 and up can choose Guaranteed Learn-to-Ski or Learn-to-Snowboard packages; prices for each are $45 for the adults, $35 for the kids, including rentals, lesson, and lift ticket. Mountain High's creative new ticketing policy allows skiers or boarders to purchase Flex Tickets (sold in blocks of four, eight, or 14 hours) or Point Tickets (sold by the run)—and which don't all have to be used on one day, a potential money-saver for visitors who want to ski a few hours or runs at a time.

🏔 *Mountain High Resort, 24510 Hwy. 2, Box 3010, Wrightwood 92397, tel. 760/249–5808, snow phone 888/754–7878, fax 760/249–3155. 3 mi past Wrightwood on Hwy. 2 via Hwy. 138. Facilities: rentals, lessons, food concessions. 8-hour Flex lift tickets: $35 adults, $29 ages 13–22, $10 ages 7–12, ages 6 and under free. Half-day, extended day, and night discounts. MC, V. Open Nov.–Apr., weekdays 8–5, weekends and holidays 7:30–5; night skiing daily 3:30–10.*

Snow Summit Mountain Resort

(🕯 2–15) Though relatively small in size, Snow Summit does the highest volume business of any ski resort in Southern California. It's never overly crowded here, though, because the resort limits the number of lift tickets sold. (Advance reservations are essential for most Saturdays and holiday periods.) Lines are also kept short by a well-organized system of 12 lifts designed to disperse skiers throughout the resort. With an 8,200-foot summit and 1,200-foot vertical

drop, Snow Summit offers terrain for all abilities; most runs are low-intermediate to intermediate, along with long, gentle slopes for beginners and wild, challenging drops for advanced skiers and snowboarders. Snowboarding is very popular here, as is night skiing—and Snow Summit's rates and family services are among the best. Its Family Park contains five low-intermediate upper-mountain runs for skiers and boarders. More flashy snowboarders can show off their moves at two half pipes and several freestyle parks. At the Children's Ski/Snowboard School kids ages 8 to 12 can get a "Beginner's Special" (lift ticket and lesson) for $25, plus $9 for ski rental or $16 for snowboard rental. Younger siblings ages 5 to 7 can join the Little Bear Ski/Snowboard School for ski and snowboard classes ($25 for 2 hours, $45 for 4 hours); those ages 4 to 7 can opt for the Little Bear Camp (day care and one or two ski lessons) for $35 to $65; and kids ages 2 to 7 can play at the Little Bear Care Center all day ($40) or a half-day ($25). Two-hour "Family Private" lessons (for parents and their kids) cost $100.

🏔 *Snow Summit Mountain Resort, 880 Summit Blvd., Box 77, Big Bear Lake 92315, tel. 909/866–5766, ski reservations 909/866–5841, snow phone 909/866–4621, Big Bear central lodging reservations 909/866–7000, fax 909/866–3201. Hwy. 38 from Redlands, then Hwy. 18 to Big Bear, 100 mi east of Los Angeles; or Hwys. 30, 330, and 18 off I–10 or I–215. Facilities: day lodge, rentals, lessons, children's programs and day care, food concessions. All-day lift tickets: $32 adults, $10 ages 7–12, ages 6 and under free. Half-day, half-night, and night and discounts. AE, D, MC, V. Open Nov.–Apr., Mon.–Thurs. 8–4:30, Fri. 8–6; weekends and holidays, 7:30–6 (night skiing Fri.–Sat. and holidays, 3–9:30).*

SADDLE UP, DIVE IN, TEE OFF, LOUNGE AROUND

12

FAMILY RESORTS, GUEST RANCHES, LODGES, AND INNS

Swimming, horseback riding, hiking, fishing, tennis, golf, windsurfing, barbecues, ranch-style feasts, and endless hours of fun and relaxation—all these activities and more attract families to child-friendly resorts, guest ranches, lodges, and inns around California. (You'll find other resorts detailed in Part III of this book as well.) Many of them offer an outstanding feature: special children's programs that keep kids happy and busy while parents play or relax on their own. Children's programs differ markedly in approach, however, so don't hesitate to ask detailed questions about them before you send in your deposit. Here are some points to consider:

• How much supervision is provided? A good rule of thumb is that there should be at least one staff member for every eight to 10 children; a ratio of 1:5 is excellent. If you're leaving little ones in the hands of an undermanned staff, at least make sure the facility is properly enclosed. There's nothing worse than arriving at pickup time to discover that your child has wandered off and no one noticed (yes, this has happened to some parents).

• What kinds of activities are available? Look for a mix of indoor and outdoor, quiet and active pursuits—arts and crafts in the morning, say, with swimming parties and group hikes in the afternoon.

• Are activities divided by age group? Ideally, separate activities should be available for preschoolers, 6- to 9-year-olds, preteens, and teens.

• Does the program depend on how many kids sign up? If your two children are among five sign-ups and the minimum number is six, you could find yourself pulling child-care duty.

• Is the program included in the rates, or does it cost extra? Are discounts available for more than one child in a family?

• How flexible are the hours? If your kids want to join in for a while, then leave to go swimming with their family, are they allowed to do so? Some children may not do well in a rigidly scheduled all-day program.

Many of these places book up well in advance, especially at peak vacation times, so try to make reservations well ahead of time. Weekly rates are generally a better deal than daily rates, and you'll want to factor in whether a property includes meals and/or activities in its room rates. The following price categories have been used: $$$—over $150; $$—$100–$150; $—under $100. All prices are for a standard room for a family of four, per night, excluding local taxes.

You may want to prepare your child for the possibility that the resort or ranch where you're staying will have no TV or telephone in the room—many don't. But if plenty of other activities are going on, TV probably won't be missed.

Northern Forests and Lakes

Coffee Creek Ranch

After a mountainous drive along Trinity (Clair Engle) Lake, about 70 miles northwest of Redding, kids arrive at Coffee Creek to find the names and ages of all arriving children posted in front—so they can start to look for playmates right away. It's one of many ways the staff helps families feel welcome at this onetime miners' boardinghouse at the edge of the remote and beautiful Trinity Alps Wilderness. In warm weather you can ride horses, swim in a heated pool or various swimming holes, fish in the lake or creek, or go canoeing in the pond. Archery, riflery, square and line dancing, gold panning, barbecues, hayrides, evening bonfires—plus that traditional kids' favorite, rock sliding into the creek—are other popular activities. When snows come, you can go cross-country skiing, snowshoeing, ice fishing, or sledding. The well-organized summertime kids' programs provide supervised play for the under-3s at the Kiddie Korral; free pony rides, arts and crafts, stories, and lawn games for 3- to 7-year-olds; a horsemanship program and fishing for ages 8 to 12; and for ages 13 to 17, camp-outs, all-day hikes, and roping and riflery instruction. You'll stay in one- and two-bedroom cabins nestled among pine and apple trees, most with theme furnishings—cowboys, Indians, birds, or forest animals, which can get a bit corny—and wood-burning stoves or

heaters. Most guests stay for a week or more; high season is mid-June to early September, when you'll pay about $3,100 per week for two parents and two kids ages 3 through 12 (teens cost more, but kids under 3—and cribs—are free except for child care from mid-June to mid-August). Meals, served family style and included in the rates, always offer fresh-baked breads and fresh fruits and vegetables.

🏠 *HC2 Box 4940, Trinity Center 96091, tel. 800/624–4480 or 530/266–3343, fax 530/ 266–3597. Hwy. 299 from Redding, then follow signs for Hwy. 3 north past Trinity Center to Coffee Creek Rd.; turn left to reach ranch. 14 cabins. Facilities: dining room, heated pool, hot tub, exercise room, cross-country skiing, horseback riding ($30 for 2-hr ride, $60 for all-day ride; minimum age 5). Children's programs: 2 and under ($250/wk); ages 3–7, 8– 12, 13–17 included in room rates, horseback rides extra; baby-sitting (by arrangement). AE, D, MC, V. $$$ (3 meals/day included).*

Drakesbad Guest Ranch

I learned about Drakesbad from well-traveled friends who returned from this secluded, century-old ranch exclaiming about one of the most memorable family vacations they'd ever taken. If you want to get away from it all, this is the place. Drakesbad doesn't even have direct-dial telephone service, and most of the rooms don't have electricity; they're lighted by kerosene lamps. But they are clean and comfortable, and include furnace heat and either half or full bath. Though Drakesbad is located within

Lassen Volcanic National Park (see Chapter 8), I wouldn't recommend using it as a base for exploring the park; the city of Redding is more convenient for that, as the ranch is in an out-of-the-way area. Instead, focus on activities available here: hiking, excellent trout fishing, horseback riding, and swimming or soaking in a pool filled with natural hot-spring water. Games include horseshoes, table tennis, volleyball, croquet, and badminton. For children there are free supervised activities three afternoons a week, but it's all pretty informal. Kids can make friends with the horses by feeding them carrots, then head on out to campfires under the stars. Reading and games around the lodge fireplace are other nightly entertainments (it's pretty quiet here). The altitude is 5,700 feet, so you may run into chilly weather, possibly even snow on the ground in June; July and August are usually warm during the day, with cool evenings. Except for a Wednesday-night cookout, dinner is served at the tables in the dining room, while breakfast and lunch are buffet style (sack lunches are provided for day hikes and trail rides). Some of the dinner dishes are more innovative than typical ranch-style fare, so if your kids have special requests, let the chefs know in advance and they'll try to accommodate.

🏠 *June 1–early Oct.: Drakesbad Guest Ranch, Chester 96020 (ask AT&T long-distance operator for Drakesbad Toll Station No. 2 via Susanville in area code 530). Oct.–May: 2150 N. Main St., Suite 5, Red Bluff 96080, tel. 530/529–1512, fax 530/529–4511. 17 mi northwest of Chester; turn north on Feather River Rd. and follow signs to Drakesbad. 19 rooms. Facilities: dining room, pool, horseback riding ($24 1st hr, $18/hr thereafter); no phones, no TV; children's activities. Call for local baby-sitters. MC, V. Closed early Oct.–May. $$$ (3 meals/day included).*

Highland Ranch

After driving 4 miles of narrow uphill twists and turns, on a road just past Hendy Woods State Park, guests arrive at a knoll overlooking a 100-year-old, oak-shaded ranch house, a handful of cabins, some fishing ponds, tennis courts, a small pool, a barn and riding ring, and hammocks strung beneath ancient redwood trees. This is 250-acre Highland Ranch, a haven where families can get some exercise and fresh air, good food, and peace and quiet enough to possibly unnerve big-city dwellers. The six fir plywood-lined cabins (divided into 11 rooms) are fairly rustic but all have private baths and fireplaces and come with porches or decks from which to watch deer or the jackrabbits that sometimes bound across the landscape. Given the hefty prices, though ($220 per adult per day, $150 per day for a child 11 and under; infants free, with cribs available), most families come here for the activities, which are included in the rates (some equipment does cost extra). You can go horseback riding—each rider has his or her own saddle for the length of the stay (parents shouldn't expect young, inexperienced riders to go galloping off into the sunset, however). Other activities include swimming, tennis, hiking, clay-pigeon shooting (for older kids only), horseshoes, boccie, and fishing for bass or perch. Food—three hearty ranch-style meals daily are included, along with all beverages—is a big part of the experience here. The only TV set is in the main ranch house. There's a two-night minimum stay.

🏠 *Box 150, Philo, CA 95466, tel. 707/895–3600, fax 707/895–3702. Call for directions. 11 cabin rooms. Facilities: fireplace, deck, phone in rooms, cribs available; pool, 2 tennis courts (racquets provided), fishing, horseback riding, hiking, horseshoes, boccie, trampoline, clay-pigeon shooting. AE, MC, V. $$$$ (3 meals/day included).*

Konocti Harbor Resort and Spa

Next to a full-service marina on the shores of Clear Lake (about 30 miles north of the Napa-Sonoma Wine Country), this resort draws families with a wide range of outdoor and entertainment interests. You can fish here, go boating and waterskiing, tour the lake in an 80-passenger paddle wheeler, swim at two pools, play tennis and miniature golf (with real golf nearby), visit the health spa, or attend open-air concerts by the lake headlined by country-western, blues, and pop music stars. Kids can head for the Konocti Kids Camp ($20 per session, ages 4–13), which runs daily from mid-June to Labor Day and year-round on concert nights and offers games, swimming, arts and crafts, movies, and minigolf. (Most other major activities cost extra here, too.) Or they can try out the playground, the video arcade, and sand volleyball courts. The resort, spread over 120 acres, is so big it even has its own shuttle service to get around. Accommodations range from standard rooms to beach cottages and apartment suites, some with lake views. Kids 12 and under stay free in their parents' room. *8727 Soda Bay Rd., Kelseyville 95451, tel. 707/279–4281 or 800/862–4930, fax 707/ 279–8575. 149 rooms, 93 suites. Facilities: restaurant, snack bars, 2 pools, 2 wading pools, marina, tennis, 18-hole minigolf, volleyball, video arcade, spa, health club, children's program, baby-sitting. AE, D, DC, MC, V. $–$$$ (no meals included).*

Lost Whale Inn

The Lost Whale is a rarity: a bed-and-breakfast that truly welcomes children. On a bluff overlooking the ocean, a few miles north of the fishing village of Trinidad, it's a picture-perfect little hostelry for families. While parents soak in the ocean views from the deck, backyard, or outdoor hot tub, kids can pick berries, explore a playhouse and playground, feed the goats and ducks down the street, play with toys and games—even contribute stories to an ongoing book being compiled, the *Legend of the Lost Whale*. Speaking of whales, you might spot some swimming past during the winter–spring migrating season, and at most times of year here you can fall asleep to the barking of sea lions. The spacious, modern rooms and suites have wood-plank flooring, skylights, and private baths;

some have ocean views and sleeping lofts, which kids especially like. Breakfast is served family style. The inn has its own beach, but it's a long, steep climb down, and children should not go there unattended; the beach is too rocky for comfortable sunbathing, but the views of sea lions are terrific. When you're here don't miss visiting beautiful Patrick's Point State Park, right up the road, or Redwood National Park, 20 miles north (see Chapter 8). *3452 Patrick's Point Dr., Trinidad 95570, tel. 707/677–3425 or 800/677–7859, fax 707/677–0284. Hwy. 101 5 mi north from Trinidad, turn onto Patrick's Point Dr. exit and go 1 mi. 8 rooms. Facilities: hot tub, children's playground; no TV, no restaurant. 2-night minimum stay. AE, D, MC, V. $$–$$$ (breakfast and beverages included).*

Railroad Park Resort

With its Caboose Motel, cabins, campground, and rail-car restaurant, Railroad Park offers a colorful, year-round base for exploring the surrounding countryside, including the adjacent Castle Crags State Park (see Chapter 7) and towering Mount Shasta, 9 miles north. Hiking, fishing (in the Sacramento River), and wintertime skiing are all close by. The motel (composed of former freight cabooses) is arranged around a swimming pool, hot tub, and wooden deck; each caboose has a different interior decor, with a private bath and TV. Rates are based on double occupancy; extra persons (including kids) are $8 each. Some cabins have kitchens. The RV park/campground, along a creek, has a swimming hole, a convenience store, and hot showers. The restaurant, built from nine vintage train cars and decorated with railroad relics, is just like eating in a dining car, without the motion. Children's plates are available. *100 Railroad Park Rd., Dunsmuir 96025, tel. 530/235–4440 or (in CA) 800/974– 7245, fax 530/235–4470; campground tel. 530/235–0420. Take Railroad Park exit off I– 5. 23 rooms, 4 cabins, 60 campsites. Facilities: restaurant, pool, hot tub. AE, D, DC, MC, V. $*

Spanish Springs Ranch

Spanish Springs is an authentic working cattle ranch in northeastern California, a rugged 70,000-acre spread where you can ride horses, explore high desert mountains and canyons, fish for trout in reservoirs and lakes, and watch for pronghorn antelope, giant buffalo, or wild mustangs on the open range; at the other end of the spectrum are more resort-type activities, like guided nature walks, arts-and-crafts classes, volleyball, shuffleboard, and horseshoes. Kids can visit the petting zoo and children's playground and participate in "dudeos"—rodeos for dudes—which provide a chance to try new skills such as "mutton busting" (riding sheep) and goat-tying. Horse-drawn hayrides, pony-cart rides, cookouts, campfires, and western barbecues are scheduled throughout spring and summer; sleigh rides take off in winter. If you like to rough it, several outlying ranches contain remote sites with few modern amenities, mainly for people who want to do a lot of horseback riding. The main ranch fits the classic "dude" ranch mold, with accommodations ranging from duplexes and modern suites with kitchens to rustic log cabins and a bunkhouse (private bedrooms for parents, plus boys' and girls' dormitory-style bunk rooms, with separate shared baths for men and women). Meals are served family style in the dining room and included in the rates; supervised kids' activities in summer are also included. Discounted weekend packages are offered between October and May.

🏠 *Mailing address: 801 A St., San Rafael 94901, tel. 530/234–2150, 800/272–8282, or 800/560–1900, fax 530/234–2153 or 415/456–4073. Off Hwy. 395, 6 mi south of Ravendale. 4 cabins, 16 suites, 6 duplexes, bunkhouse (112 beds total). Facilities: dining room, heated pool, archery, cross-country skiing, ice-skating, sleigh rides, sledding, horseback riding, skeet shooting, tennis. Children's programs: free supervised activities daily on drop-in basis, June 15–Labor Day, divided by age groups. AE, D, MC, V. $$$ (3 meals/day included).*

Trinity Alps Resort

Trinity Alps Resort doesn't look like it's changed much in its 70-year history: Rustic cabins are scattered among pine trees, overlooking the Stuart Fork River and the Trinity Alps. Some organized activities are available here—trail rides, bonfires, sports tournaments, talent shows, square dancing, movies, bingo games, sing-alongs—but mostly it's a place to do things together as a family. You can go swimming or tubing in the river, hike, picnic, fish, pan for gold, or play tennis, badminton, basketball, volleyball, horseshoes, and table tennis. Or relax and loaf a bit; the day we were there I found a couple of people snoozing in a hammock and a family drifting down the river in an inner tube. Cabins have one or two bedrooms (you're asked to bring your own bedding and towels), a sleeping veranda overlooking the river, a bathroom or two, a fully equipped kitchen, and an outside barbecue, so you can save money by cooking some or most of your meals here. (A general store sells basics, but if you want fresh produce and meat, bring it with you.) When you want to "dine out," you can stroll to the resort's family-style restaurant, which has a pleasant outdoor patio overlooking the river. During the busiest months, from June to August, the minimum stay is one week; in May and September a three-night minimum applies. Ask about special all-inclusive vacations in May and September, which include horseback riding and meals in the cabin price.

🏠 *1750 Trinity Alps Rd., Trinity Center 96091, tel. and fax 530/286–2205. 43 cabins. Facilities: restaurant, bar, tennis, horseback riding (from $18 for 1 hr to $60 for ½ day). Children's programs: baby-sitting by arrangement. No credit cards. Closed Oct.– mid-May. $*

Sierra and the Gold Country

Camp Richardson Resort

Spread over 80 acres at Camp Richardson, an old logging camp, this historic resort is 7 miles from the casinos of State Line, Nevada, but "100 years away in atmosphere," as the management puts it. No glitz—just sandy beaches, pine forests, year-round recreation, and comfortable lodgings. The longest continuously operating Lake Tahoe resort (it's been open since 1926), Camp Richardson Resort is the type of place generations of families return to year after year, for good reason. It's a wonderful family bargain, too: You can stay in a lodge room with two double beds for $79 to $90 a night in summer, from $59 to $69 a night in winter; beachfront cabins big enough for a family of four start at $595 a week in summer, while ski cabins go for $100 to $115 a night in winter (there are also three tent or RV campgrounds). Next to the beach is a full-service marina (tel. 530/542–6570), where you can rent kayaks, paddle boats, and power boats or sign up for water-ski lessons, jet skiing, parasailing, and fishing charters. Camp Richardson has a mountain-bike and in-line skate rental shop (tel. 530/542–6584)—a mostly level 3½-mile bike path skirts the lake—and a stable for renting horses. Or you can fish, hike, ski, or go white-water rafting nearby. (See Chapter 18 for more on Lake Tahoe attractions.) From June 15 to September 15, cabins are available on a weekly basis only and should be reserved by the previous October. Some cabins have woodstoves and fireplaces. The Beacon (tel. 530/541–0603), a good restaurant with views of the lake, serves burgers, steak, pasta, and fresh seafood.
fifi 1900 Jameson Beach Rd., Box 9028, South Lake Tahoe 96158, tel. 530/541–1801 or 800/544–1801, fax 530/541–1802. Off Hwy. 89 (Emerald Bay Rd.). 38 cabins (only 17 open in winter), 29 lodge rooms, 7 hotel rooms, 330 campsites. Facilities: restaurant, delicatessen, water sports, horseback riding, tennis, cross-country skiing, children's playground; no phones or TVs in cabins. AE, MC, V. $

Greenhorn Creek Guest Ranch

In the lush Feather River country about 65 miles north of Lake Tahoe, Greenhorn Creek is a homey, family-oriented guest ranch nearly surrounded by national forest lands. The emphasis here is on a wealth of organized activities and group participation. Daily guided two-hour trail rides (for ages 7 and up) along mountain creeks and through evergreen forests are included in the rates; there are separate rides for beginners and experienced. Other popular activities include nature walks, hayrides, hiking, fishing for rainbow trout or kokanee salmon, swimming in a heated pool or at a "swimming hole," horseshoes, volleyball, badminton, and table tennis. A petting farm with baby animals—goats, chickens, rabbits, and pigs—is always a hit with kids. Guests are rounded up regularly for events like the weekly frog race and end-of-the-week minirodeo. Evenings bring barbecues and cookouts, bonfires with campfire singing and marshmallow roasting, talent shows, and square dancing lessons. The Wee Wranglers, an organized program for kids ages 3 to 6, keeps the young set busy in the Kiddie Corral—where pony rides are among the activities—while older siblings take trail rides. The accommodations are in rustic but comfortable one- and two-room cabins with private baths, or in lodge rooms big enough for three, with adjoining rooms available. All meals are included in the rates.
fifi 2116 Greenhorn Ranch Rd., Quincy 95971, tel. 530/283–0930 or 800/334–6939, fax 530/283–4401. Hwy. 89 north to Graeagle, then Hwy. 70 to ranch turnoff at Spring Garden. 16 cabins, 11 lodge rooms. Facilities: dining room, pool, hot tub, exercise room, horseback riding (minimum age 7); nearby golf, tennis, hiking, fishing, boating, sailing, rafting, waterskiing (most at extra cost).

Children's programs: supervised activities, included in rates. MC, V. Closed Dec.–Mar. $$$

($20/day), children's program. Baby-sitting by arrangement. AE, D, MC, V. $$–$$$

Northstar-at-Tahoe

Best known as a winter ski resort (see Chapter 11), this 2,500-acre forested retreat 6 miles from Lake Tahoe is a top warm-weather resort as well. The list of activities is impressive: mountain biking, horseback and pony riding for all ages and abilities, swimming at two outdoor heated pools, tennis, golf, guided nature hiking, fly-fishing, and an Adventure Park. The latter includes a 25-foot climbing wall (where all ages can practice rock climbing), an orienteering course (for practicing compass-reading and navigation skills, also suitable for all ages) and—for ages 10 and up—an adult ropes course (an obstacle course using ropes, cables, mountaineering gear, and tall fir trees). There's also a junior ropes course for kids age 4 to 13, where parents help a bit. Most of these activities require extra fees, as does Minors' Camp, Northstar's licensed child-care facility for toilet-trained kids ages 2 to 10; it runs from 9 to 5, except Sunday, from mid-June through August. Minors' Camp organized activities include nature walks, art projects, and field trips. Morning sessions cost $26, full days cost $43; both include lunch; a one-time ½-day session is included with lodging. Room choices at Northstar include condos, hotel-type rooms, and rental homes; except for lodge rooms, all units have kitchens and fireplaces. Summer season here is from June to October, though some activities end by Labor Day. A two-night minimum stay is required.

🏠 *Box 129, Truckee 96160, tel. 530/562–1010 or 800/466–6784, fax 530/562–2215. Off Hwy. 267, 6 mi north of Lake Tahoe and 6 mi south of Truckee. 30 lodge rooms, 200 condos, 20 homes. Facilities: 2 restaurants, delicatessen, 2 pools, 4 hot tubs, 2 saunas, horseback riding ($20 for 1 hr, $35 for 2 hrs), pony rides ($5 for 15 min), golf (18 holes/$70), 10 tennis courts, mountain-bike rentals ($10–$32), ropes courses ($12–$40), climbing wall*

Resort at Squaw Creek

At the base of onetime Olympic site Squaw Valley USA, 6 miles northwest of Lake Tahoe, this luxurious year-round resort manages to accommodate business conferences while keeping a prime focus on families. In winter, you can ski out of your room onto alpine trails (there's an on-site rental shop), go sleighing or ice-skating, or ride the cable car to the downhill ski slopes at Squaw Valley (see Chapter 11). In warm weather, families can swim in an outdoor pool complex with a 120-foot water slide; there's a wading pool with its own sand beach for little ones. Other activities (most of which require additional fees) include golf, tennis, mountain biking, fly-fishing, and nearby horseback riding. The year-round Mountain Buddies children's program (ages 3 to 13) includes indoor and outdoor camp-style activities (hiking, biking, swimming, arts and crafts) in morning, afternoon, and evening sessions; each session costs between $30 and $35 (more with meals); the fee for the whole day is $65. Reservations are recommended. Guest rooms and suites are spacious, with a rugged ski-lodge look, and all have in-room movies, refrigerators, and valley or forest views. Some suites have fireplaces and kitchens.

🏠 *400 Squaw Creek Rd., Box 3333, Olympic Valley 96146, tel. 530/583–6300 or 800/327–3353, fax 530/581–6632. 205 rooms, 200 suites. Facilities: 5 restaurants, 3 pools, 4 hot tubs, mountain biking (rentals $15/hr, $35 all day), health spa, fitness center, golf (18 holes/$40–$110), 2 tennis courts ($12/hr), video arcade, children's program, evening baby-sitting. AE, D, DC, MC, V. $$$*

Sorensen's Resort

A charming, hospitable all-season resort, Sorensen's sits on the site of an old wagon-train trail about 25 miles south of Lake

Tahoe in secluded Hope Valley. Lodging is in log or cedar cabins and houses nestled among pine trees with views of high mountain meadows; when you're here, you feel like you're hours rather than minutes away from the commercial buildup of South Lake Tahoe. In warm months, you're close to horseback riding, fishing (including a kids' pond stocked with trout), river rafting, and hot springs; hiking trails lead off into the forests, with occasional guided hikes offered at discounts to Sorensen's guests. In winter, a cross-country ski center operates at the resort, offering rentals, ski tours, and lessons for ages 6 and up. About 6 miles of trail are groomed. Accommodations, all connected by a sprawling series of paths, range from rustic to semi-luxurious. About two-thirds of the cabins are big enough for a family of four or more, with some sleeping up to six or 10. Most have kitchens or kitchenettes (the three that don't are B&B units); the majority also include wood-burning stoves. The cabins vary widely in style, cost, and age as well as size; you may want to ask about the availability of the Norway House (a replica of a 13th-century sod-roof log cabin) or Saint Nick's, which has a Christmas theme. Rates also vary dramatically by season here, making this either a bargain (in fall or late spring) or a luxury (in winter and summer); expect two-night minimum stays on weekends and three- to four-night minimums in some holiday periods. Families can save money by cooking some or most of their meals in their cabins, but there's a good on-premises restaurant (open for three meals a day) serving pastas, fresh fish, and barbecued chicken and steak. It has an outdoor deck for summer dining.

🏨 *14255 Hwy. 88, Hope Valley 96120, tel. 530/694–2203 or 800/423–9949; no fax. East of junction of Hwys. 88 and 89. 27 cabins, 3 houses. Facilities: restaurant, cross-country skiing, kitchens, children's play area and fishing pond. MC, V. $–$$$ (breakfast included in 3 B&B units).*

Tenaya Lodge at Yosemite

Two miles from the southern entrance of Yosemite National Park, the Tenaya Lodge has so many attractions of its own that families may be tempted to put off the visit to Yosemite for another day, so they can stick around the resort. The enticements include two swimming pools (one indoor, one out), table tennis, croquet, volleyball, board games, mountain-bike rentals, and family hikes to waterfalls and through sugar-pine forests (including nighttime flashlight hikes). You can fish, swim, or boat at nearby Bass Lake, rent horses from a local stable, or go on wagon rides or rock-climbing expeditions. Summer is the high season, but in winter you can ski at Yosemite's Badger Pass ski area (see Chapter 11) or rent cross-country skis, including kids' sizes, at the lodge; sledding, snowshoeing, and sleigh riding are other winter options. Our family also found Tenaya to be a convenient base for riding the Yosemite Mountain Sugar Pine Railroad and visiting Yosemite's Glacier Point and the Wawona Big Trees (see Chapter 8 for all). The kids' program, Camp Tenaya—which operates daily in summer and only on Friday and Saturday the rest of the year—offers nature walks, crafts projects, Native American theme games, movies, and water play for kids age 5 to 12. Lodge rooms are modern and include cable TV. The attractive restaurant has a kids' menu, and on many summer evenings families can go on special Western-style campfire cookouts.

🏨 *1122 Hwy. 41, Fish Camp 93623, tel. 209/683–6555 or 800/635–5807, fax 209/683–0249. 244 rooms (includes 15 suites). Facilities: restaurant, delicatessen, 2 pools, 2 hot tubs, spa, fitness center, sauna, steam room, cross-country skiing; fishing, horseback riding, and downhill skiing nearby. Children's program: $35 (includes lunch). Baby-sitting by arrangement. AE, D, DC, MC, V. $$$*

San Francisco and the Bay Area

Chanslor Guest Ranch

The Chanslor is one of the few guest ranches in the state located on the coast—in this case, the rugged, scenic Sonoma coast on the northern end of Bodega Bay, across the road from Salmon Creek Beach, about 65 miles north of the Golden Gate Bridge. Horses, sheep, and cattle graze on the hillsides of this historic 400-acre working ranch, while its outlying reaches harbor coyotes, bobcats, eagles, and a saltwater marsh with rare birds. Horseback riding (minimum age 7), hay wagon rides, pony rides, hiking, and fishing are favorite activities here. Riding is a large part of the fun, so kids under 7 may not have as good a time as older kids, though there's a petting zoo with llama, donkeys, goats, pigs, ponies, and ducks. A suite in the Ranch House (combining two rooms) has a total of three beds; the Loft is a modern two-room suite with a fireplace, balconies, and a private bath; no children under 10 are allowed in the Loft. If you have your own horses, you can board them at the ranch.

🏠 2660 Hwy. 1, Box 1510, Bodega Bay 94923, tel. 707/875–2721, fax 707/875–2785. 1 room, 2 suites. Facilities: horseback riding (guided trail rides $25–$50; pony rides $10; riding lessons $40/hr.). MC, V. $–$$ (Continental breakfast included).

Claremont Resort, Spa and Tennis Club

The Claremont, the Bay Area's only urban resort, has been compared to a sparkling white wedding cake resting in the Oakland-Berkeley hills. The refurbished 1915 Victorian-style structure gleams inside and out. With its castlelike towers and turrets, and 22 landscaped acres, it's only slightly less dramatic a sight than San Diego's Hotel del Coronado (see below). Rooms come in all shapes and sizes. Grael and Lia (who've spent a lot of time in cookie-cutter hotel rooms) loved the cozy, atticlike shape of our minisuite, with its slanted ceiling (it lay just below the roof), cubbyholes, and dormer windows facing out on a panorama of San Francisco Bay. Along with its renovations, the Claremont has grown from mere hotel into an elegant spa and sports haven as well. Our kids could spend all day in the Olympic-size outdoor pool, one of two pools on premises. The resort also contains extensive European-style spa facilities, with health and beauty treatments of all kinds, and 10 tennis courts. Though there are no children's programs, kids 17 and under stay free in their parents' room.

🏠 41 Tunnel Rd. (Ashby and Domingo Aves.), Berkeley 94705, tel. 510/843–3000 or 800/551–7266, fax 510/848–6208. 204 rooms and 35 suites. Facilities: restaurant, 2 pools, hot tub, spa, saunas, health and fitness center. AE, D, DC, MC, V. $$$

Manka's Inverness Lodge

Near the southern reaches of the gorgeous Point Reyes National Seashore (see Chapter 8), Manka's is a onetime hunting lodge (dating from 1917) set in the hills above the village of Inverness. You can stay in the old lodge itself, in a cottage or cabin, or in a motel-type annex next to the lodge, all of which are known for their quirky hunting decor and tendency to attract eccentric guests. For a really unusual place to stay, ask about the Chicken Ranch, a two-bedroom guest house 1 mile away; built as a hunting cabin in the 1850s it sits right on Tomales Bay. The Boathouse, a two-unit house also off the grounds, is also right on the water. In the lodge the nicest rooms are those with decks overlooking Tomales Bay. The cabins (warm and rustic with buffalo robe motifs) have fireplaces. The menu at Manka's superlative restaurant typically includes grilled game, fresh local seafood, soups, greens, and terrific desserts like wild berry pies. The chefs will prepare child-size portions and will cook special dishes upon request.

🏠 Box 1110, Inverness 94937, tel. 415/ 669–1034, fax 415/669–1598. From Sir Francis Drake Blvd., turn left on Argyle St., in north Inverness. 4 lodge rooms, 2 cabins, 4 motel units, 1 suite, 2 houses. Facilities: restaurant, some fireplaces, some TVs. AE, MC, V. $$–$$$

Central Coast and Valley

Alisal Guest Ranch and Resort

Forget images of dust and dirty jeans at this luxurious guest ranch and working cattle ranch. At the Alisal, spread over 10,000 choice acres of the beautiful Santa Ynez Valley, your family can ride horses across rolling hills topped by sycamores, golf at two championship 18-hole courses, or sail, windsurf, or fish on a 90-acre private lake. You may even run into movie stars here or catch a glimpse of former President Reagan's ranch over the hill. Yet for all its luxury, the Alisal is a family-oriented place, with an excellent children's program for all ages—including special outings for teens and a dinnertime Kiddie Korral for ages 3 to 5. Arts and crafts, horseback riding, hayrides, nature walks, a petting zoo, swimming and pool games, fishing, archery, mountain biking, movies, scavenger hunts, bingo, sing-alongs, pizza parties, barbecues, races, games and contests, storytelling, and western dancing are all on the docket from mid-June to Labor Day and during school holiday periods; arts-and-crafts sessions are available year-round. When the kids put on talent shows and minirodeos, the entire ranch is likely to turn out to watch them perform. Some children's activities are included in the rates; others are priced individually. Except for warm-weather family barbecues, dinner at the Alisal is a more formal occasion than at many guest ranches; it's a four-course meal, men are required to wear jackets, and children are not permitted to wear jeans, shorts, or T-shirts. Accommodations are in

73 ranch-style studios or two-room cottages, all with wood-burning fireplaces and refrigerators. A two-night minimum stay is required. 🏠 1054 Alisal Rd., Solvang 93463, tel. 805/ 688–6411 or 800/425–4725, fax 805/688– 2510. 2 mi from Solvang, off Hwy. 246. 36 studio rooms and 37 suites. Facilities: restaurant, pool, daily trail rides ($50 for 2 hrs, minimum age 7), 7 tennis courts ($12/hr), 2 golf courses (minimum age 7), private lake; no phones or TVs in suites. Children's programs for all ages. AE, DC, MC, V. $$$ (2 meals included)

Miramar Resort Hotel

When you have kids in tow few things are more convenient than being able to walk from your room right to the beach. The Miramar is the only resort in Santa Barbara where you can do exactly that, and you don't have to pay a bundle for the privilege. Miramar's amenities read like those of a much more expensive destination: a private beach on the Pacific, two heated swimming pools, tennis courts, a fully equipped exercise gym, and 15 acres of landscaped gardens. One warning: Trains pass right through the property—and what's fun to watch during the day can get awfully noisy late at night (they stop around 11 PM and start up again around 7 AM). Accommodations are in motel-type rooms and suites with private patios or balconies, overlooking either the ocean or one of the pools; or in cottages with up to four bedrooms, some with parlors, fireplaces, and kitchenettes, set amid gardens and lawns. Between May and October there's a two-night minimum stay on weekends (three nights for holiday weekends). Of the two eating places, a beachside snack bar in a converted railcar diner is a special favorite of kids. 🏠 1555 S. Jameson La., Santa Barbara 93108, tel. 805/969–2203; in CA, 800/ 322–6983; fax 805/969–3163. 3 mi south of Santa Barbara on U.S. 101 at San Ysidro turnoff. 201 rooms, 9 suites. Facilities: restaurant, snack bar, 2 pools, hot tub, 4 tennis courts, exercise gym, saunas, children's play-

ground. Baby-sitters' names provided. AE, MC, V. $–$$

Ojai Valley Inn

The Spanish-style town of Ojai, set in a valley with mountain views 30 miles east of Santa Barbara, is an escape for Hollywood stars—and the luxurious hacienda-style Ojai Valley Inn could easily pass as a romantic resort for grown-ups. Instead, it actively courts the family trade, with Camp Ojai, an excellent year-round children's program, and half-price deals on meals for kids in its restaurants. About half of each Camp Ojai day is spent at Rancho dos Rios, an 800-acre ranch about a mile from the inn, where kids can watch horses and visit a petting zoo with a miniature horse (28 inches tall!), pygmy goats, cuddly rabbits, and a potbellied pig. The ranch also offers families guided trail rides through oak woodlands and secluded meadows; mounts and rides are available for all levels, minimum age 8, with pony rides for younger kids. Besides golf and tennis, guided hikes and mountain-bike rides are available, too. With the exception of some complimentary bikes, all activities cost extra. Most of the rooms have private patios or balconies, some have fireplaces, and all are stocked with top-end hotel amenities such as TV movies, video games, hair dryers, minibars, and robes.

🏨 *Country Club Rd., Ojai 93023, tel. 805/ 646–5511 or 800/422–6524, fax 805/646– 7969. 188 rooms, 15 suites and 4 cottages. Facilities: 2 restaurants, 3 heated pools, fitness center, trail rides ($40), pony rides ($5), 18-hole golf course, 8 tennis courts, croquet, playground. Children's programs: year-round supervised activities for ages 3–12 ($70/day, $55 for ½-day or evening session; includes meal). AE, D, DC, MC, V. $$$*

Quarter Circle U Rankin Ranch

A working cattle ranch for more than 130 years—it's one of the oldest and largest (31,000 acres) family-owned ranches in California—the Rankin Ranch has been accommodating guests for more than 30 years. Besides horseback riding in the Tehachapi Mountains and valley meadows (minimum age 6; kids under 12 have their own rides), activities here include hay wagon rides, tennis, barbecues, swimming in the pool, trout fishing—catch some for your breakfast— horseshoes, and a supervised children's program for ages 4 to 11 (kids under 4 must be in their parents' care). The children's program runs from mid-June to Labor Day and during some spring holiday periods. From 9 to 3:30, and again at 5:30 PM (so parents can participate in the pre-dinner Patio Party), counselors lead arts and crafts projects, nature hikes, scavenger hunts, swim meets, miniboat races, and talent shows. After hiking to a creek, kids can try grinding wild rye on a grinding rock as Paiute Indians did more than a century ago. There's also a petting farm where kids can help bottle-feed baby calves and lambs, and a lake with a water slide. All activities (among them horseback rides and the supervised kids' program) and three meals a day are included in the rates. Accommodations are in good-size duplex cabins with private baths, carpeting, and picture windows. Children's rates apply even if the kids occupy a separate room from parents. The ranch is open from the week before Easter till early October.

🏨 *Box 36, Caliente 93518, tel. 661/867– 2511, fax 661/867–0105. Off Hwy. 58, 42 mi northeast of Bakersfield; call for directions. 6 cabins (12 rooms). Facilities: horseback rides, pool, tennis, archery, volleyball, horseshoes, children's program. MC, V. $$$ (3 meals included)*

Los Angeles and Environs

Disneyland Resort

The Disneyland Resort—made up of the Disneyland Hotel and the Disneyland Pacific Hotel—would be a delightful family resort even without the great theme park right outside. At buffet-style Goofy's Kitchen in the Disneyland Hotel, Disney characters stroll from table to table meeting the kids. There's an inland marina where children can ride pedal boats or pilot remote-control tugboats, and a white sandy beach for building sand castles. Garden paths wind amid waterfalls and streams and past pools filled with brightly colored koi fish. A family arcade includes dozens of video games. And the nightly entertainment spotlights Fantasy Waters, a spectacle of choreographed fountains and lighting effects set to music. (While most of these amenities are at the Disneyland Hotel, guests of both hotels have access to facilities at each; a walkway connects the two.) No wonder some small children think they're already in the Magic Kingdom when they arrive with their parents for check-in at this 65-acre resort complex, linked directly via monorail to Disneyland. You can stay more cheaply at other hotels in the area (though special packages are available here, too), but if you're centering a vacation around Disneyland (see Chapter 9), staying a monorail ride away is a terrific convenience. You can come back for a swim and a nap and an early dinner in late afternoon, and return to the park refreshed for the evening. And on four to six mornings a week, every guest receives a bonus: a voucher good for early admission to Disneyland—1½ hours before the general public—so you can hit some popular rides and attractions before the crowds arrive. Children 17 and under stay free with parent at both hotels, and cribs are free.

🏨 *Disneyland Hotel: 1150 W. Cerritos Ave., Anaheim 92802, tel. 714/778–6600 or 714/956–6400, fax 714/956–6582. Disneyland Pacific Hotel: 1717 S. West St., Anaheim 92802, tel. 714/999–0990 or 714/956–6400. 1,136 rooms and suites (Disneyland Hotel); 502 rooms and suites (Disneyland Pacific Hotel). Combined facilities: 17 restaurants and lounges, marina, 5 pools, 2 hot tubs, 10 tennis courts, 2 fitness centers, 3 games arcades. Baby-sitting referrals. AE, D, DC, MC, V. $$$ (no meals included)*

Lake Arrowhead Resort

This has long been *the* resort at Lake Arrowhead (see Chapter 18), with a prime lakeside location (next to Lake Arrowhead Village), a small private beach, a fishing dock, tennis courts, and an excellent supervised activities program for children ages 4 to 12—with the one drawback that activities aren't separated by age. The Jr. Mountaineers runs daily from Memorial Day to Labor Day and on weekends and most holidays the rest of the year, with early morning fishing beginning at 7 and, on Friday and Saturday night, pizza, movies, games, and beach sing-alongs going till 10. Most kids, though, opt for regular morning and/or afternoon sessions that run from 9 to 4:30 and include beach games, nature hikes, arts and crafts, duck feeding, and trips to the local children's museum. The fees range from $10 for the fishing trips to $35 for combined morning and afternoon sessions, which include two meals (additional children in a family usually get a discount). The Children's Lending Desk, meanwhile, provides games, books, and videos, and kids can order pizza and popcorn from room service. Kids also enjoy the big outdoor pool overlooking the lake; two hot tubs are nearby, one just for kids. And there are mountain bikes for rent. Rooms here are big and many have their own balconies overlooking the lake; some have fireplaces. There are also lakeside units and suites with kitchens, living rooms, and multiple bedrooms, some with lofts and whirlpool baths. These are expensive but very nice—much like having your own vacation home. Kids stay free in their parents' room.

🏨 *27984 Hwy. 189, Box 1699, Lake Arrowhead 92352, tel. 909/336–1511 or 800/800–6792, fax 909/336–1378. 177 rooms and suites. Facilities: 2 restaurants, heated pool, 2 hot tubs, saunas, health club, children's program. AE, D, DC, MC, V. $$–$$$ (no meals included)*

Ritz-Carlton Laguna Niguel

On a 150-foot bluff overlooking the Pacific halfway between Los Angeles and San Diego (about 2 miles from Dana Point Harbor), this Orange County resort consistently wins awards as tops in the area. For families it offers a complete package (albeit at luxury prices): beach, oceanfront golf, tennis, two outdoor heated swimming pools, fitness center, beach volleyball, lawn croquet, complimentary in-room movies, and the Ritz Kids program. The latter, for kids ages 4 to 12, includes pool games, arts and crafts, koi fish and seagull feeding, sandcastle building, and seaside walks. Saturday nights are Kids Night Out, when dinner, movies and popcorn, and games entertain the youngsters. Once you pay a $15 resort fee, which provides access to all activities at the Ritz, the kids' program is complimentary. Like other Ritz-Carltons, Laguna Niguel's walls are lined with fine artworks, its hallways lighted with crystal chandeliers; yet somehow this elegant atmosphere doesn't intimidate (the main reason, I think, is that service is always so friendly). If you really want to do up the luxury bit, ask for one of the private Club Rooms; for an additional fee, you get use of a private lounge with complimentary concierge and food and drink service throughout much of the day (we've seen lots of families taking advantage of this). All rooms, however, have luxuries like marble bathrooms and private balconies, many with oceanfront views. The resort goes all out at winter holiday time; the 50-foot Christmas tree (with 350,000 lights), the immense gingerbread castle in the lobby, and the Holiday Magic (making ornaments and stockings) and Breakfast With Santa programs (for 5- to 12-year-olds) all make for seasonal enchantment.
🏨 One Ritz-Carlton Dr., Dana Point 92629, tel. 949/240–2000 or 800/241–3333, fax 949/240–0829. 362 rooms and 31 suites. Facilities: 3 restaurants, 2 heated pools, hot tubs, saunas, adjacent golf course, 4 tennis courts, volleyball, croquet, fitness center, chil-

dren's program. AE, D, DC, MC, V. $$$ (no meals included)

San Diego and the Southern Deserts

Furnace Creek Inn and Ranch Resort

Furnace Creek is an oasis in the middle of Death Valley National Park, the major non-camping lodging in this magnificent desert park (see Chapter 8). Attractions include refreshing dips in swimming pools fed by 84° natural spring water, golf at the lowest elevation course in the country, tennis (including lighted courts for cooler evening games), and guided horseback rides gentle enough for kids as young as 6 ($25 for one hour, $40 for two hours). There are actually two separate resorts here under the same ownership: Furnace Creek Inn and Furnace Creek Ranch, separated by state Highway 190 (a bit less than a mile's drive from each other). Beautifully landscaped Furnace Creek Inn is quiet and formal, the type of place that serves daily afternoon tea and requires men to wear jackets at dinner in the main Dining Room. Furnace Creek Ranch, considerably less formal and less expensive, attracts more families, who stay in rustic cottages or deluxe motel and poolside rooms (motel and poolside rooms have TVs and refrigerators, cottages do not). The Ranch's casual-dress eateries include a steak house, an ice-cream shop, and an international food court. The riding stables are located here—because of Death Valley's extreme heat they're closed in summer—along with a children's playground, basketball and volleyball courts, horseshoe pits, and a museum with displays on local history. From October to April is the most pleasant time to visit, but if you're willing to endure the heat (over 100° on many days), you can get some good deals here in summer.

🏨 Box 1, Death Valley 92328, tel. 760/786–2345, fax 760/786–2514. 290 rooms. Facilities: 10 restaurants, 2 pools, golf (18 holes), 6 tennis courts, horseback riding. AE, D, DC, MC, V. $–$$$ (2 meals included in inn rates)

Hotel del Coronado

One of America's most famous hotels, this National Historic Landmark built in 1888 has hosted 13 U.S. presidents and numerous celebrities. Its ornate gingerbread architecture—with a castlelike turret, red shingled roofs, and gleaming white wood—has served as backdrop for Hollywood movies such as Some Like It Hot, and was said to have inspired Wizard of Oz author L. Frank Baum's vision of the Emerald City. The "Del" is also the premier landmark in beautiful Coronado, and is said to be the largest beach resort on the West Coast. All kinds of activities are available to kids and their parents from mid-June till Labor Day. You can rent beach cruisers, mountain bikes, kids' bikes, tandems, and boogieboards, take surfing lessons, go kayaking in the bay, or play water volleyball in the pool. There's also a structured program for kids ages 4 to 12. Called Tent City Kids—it's headquartered in a striped canvas tent—it takes place daily in summer and during major school holidays both in the daytime and in the evenings. Each of 17 three-hour sessions during the week has a different theme, such as a scavenger hunt or a pirate night or a "water Olympics" under the stars. Including either lunch or dinner, the cost is $24 per session ($20 for additional siblings). Kids ages 3 or 4 can participate in a separate program called Tent City Tykes, and there are also special activities for teens such as swimming, tennis, or rollerblading. The fine family programs include ice-cream socials and evening sailing trips. Rooms in the original five-story structure range from quite small to oversized, while those in the two newer sections are fairly standard.

🏨 1500 Orange Ave., Coronado 92118, tel. 619/435–6611 or 800/468–3533, fax 619/522–8238. 691 rooms. Facilities: 3 restaurants, 2 pools, spa, sauna, beach, tennis, bike rentals. Children's programs. AE, D, DC, MC, V. $$$ (no meals included).

La Costa Resort and Spa

This is one of the finest golf and tennis resorts and luxury spas in the world, with two championship golf courses; a golf school; grass, clay, and composite tennis courts; and a huge spa with whirlpool baths, saunas, exercise gyms, fitness classes, and jogging track, plus massage, facials, and body treatments. While parents are playing and being pampered, kids ages 5 to 12 head for Camp La Costa for a full day (from 10 to 5; cost $40, which includes lunch) of fun such as golf and tennis, swimming, arts and crafts, kite flying, or touring a nearby fire station. On Friday and Saturday evening Camp La Costa Nightclub ($30) presents a predinner mixer with appetizers, followed by dinner, and then activities such as scavenger hunts, charades, story hour, and breaking a piñata. The ratio of staff to kids is about 1:5, and, while there are no set divisions by age, counselors try to tailor activities to the ages present. The guest rooms are downright luxurious, with private safes, hair dryers, and minibars. Special package deals allow unlimited use of golf, tennis, the spa, or a combination of the three (call for specifics). Children under 18 stay for no extra charge in the same room with their parents; cribs are also free.

🏨 Costa del Mar Rd., Carlsbad 92009, tel. 760/438–9111 or 800/854–5000, fax 760/931–7585. I–5 to La Costa Ave. exit. 423 rooms, 55 suites. Facilities: 5 restaurants, 2 18-hole golf courses ($110 greens fee), 21 tennis courts ($16/hr), 5 pools, health spa; children's programs. Baby-sitting arranged through concierge. AE, D, DC, MC, V. $$$ (no meals included).

Rancho Bernardo Inn

Set amid gardens and pines with views of the San Pasqual Mountains 25 miles north of downtown San Diego, this golf and tennis haven is particularly appealing to families during the month of August and during holidays throughout the year, when Camp RBI is in action. This nonstop, all-day (from 9 to 9) program has one counselor for every five children, with staffers trained in CPR, first aid, and water safety. The program schedule changes daily, and kids ages 5 to 17 (who are divided into younger and older groups) can choose a half- or full-day program, or stay only a couple of hours. The younger kids may go swimming or on scavenger hunts, make movies or ice-cream sundaes, fly kites, do arts-and-crafts projects, play miniature golf or other games, or attend casino parties or carnivals. The older kids help plan their own activities, such as going to the beach or playing golf or tennis. Activities often reflect a theme such as Wild West Day, Movie Day, or Earth Day. Family cookouts and other theme dinners for parents and kids are held periodically. But even when Camp RBI is not in session, Rancho Bernardo Inn is geared to active families, with swimming, golf, tennis, and a fitness center and spa (adults only) offering workout equipment, saunas, and massage. All these require additional fees, but some special packages include them in room rates. The best deal for families is the $288-a-night "Family Entertainment" package, which includes room, box lunch, an in-room movie, and tickets for four to the San Diego Zoo, San Diego Wild Animal Park, or Sea World (see Chapters 6 and 9). Rooms have refrigerators, wall safes, TVs, in-room movies, and mountain or golf course views. The high season is from January to June.

⋔ *17550 Bernardo Oaks Dr., San Diego 92128, tel. 760/675–8500 or 800/542–6096, fax 760/675–8437. 229 rooms and 58 suites. Facilities: 2 restaurants, 2 outdoor pools, 7 hot tubs, golf (45 holes), 12 tennis courts ($15/hr), bike rentals, game room, fitness center. Children's programs: supervised activities during Aug., spring break, winter holidays, and holiday weekends (July 4, Labor Day, Thanksgiving) ($25/day, $20/half day, with discounts for siblings; optional lunch $6.50, dinner*

$8); baby-sitting for children under 5 arranged through concierge. AE, D, DC, MC, V. $$–$$$ (no meals included)

San Diego Paradise Point Resort

Set on a 44-acre island in Mission Bay, complete with five swimming pools, six tennis courts, and its own sandy beaches, this resort has been a family favorite for years. The cottage-style rooms and suites all have patios and a tropical, airy feel; some have bay views and kitchens. But as nice as our room was, when we stayed here we didn't spend much time in it; there was too much to do outside. Lia and Grael sampled all five pools, and we all enjoyed walking around the beautifully landscaped gardens, lagoons, and botanical trails. Among many activities available, the Kids' Camp for ages 4 to 12 offers organized afternoon and evening sessions ($10 each, including a snack) from mid-June to Labor Day and on holiday weekends. Teens and other members of the family can participate in tennis and golf tournaments. Of the resort's three restaurants, the casual Village Cafe (with a children's menu) is the best for families.

⋔ *1404 W. Vacation Rd., San Diego 92109, tel. 619/274–4630 or 800/344–2626, fax 619/581–5977. 462 rooms, including 103 suites. Facilities: 3 restaurants, pool bar, 5 pools, whirlpool, sauna, fitness room, bicycle and boat rentals, 6 tennis courts ($10/hr), putting course, croquet, volleyball, sailing, children's program. AE, D, DC, MC, V. $$$*

Westin Mission Hills

This enormous Moroccan-style resort spreads across the desert like an oasis, with palms, fountains, gardens, lagoons, three pools, cascading waterfalls, and the lush greens of two golf courses. The ultimate oasis for kids, though, is the 60-foot S-curved water slide that slips into a lagoon-like swimming pool. (In summer children can win prizes in the Biggest Splash Contest in the Las Brisas pool, which holds 330,000 gallons of water.) Kids can also rent bikes and play shuffleboard, croquet, sand volleyball, or other games. "Cactus Kids," Mission Hills' supervised activities program for ages 4 to 12, operates daily from Memorial Day to Labor Day and from Friday to Sunday the rest of the year. Each four-hour morning or afternoon session costs $30 and includes pool games, arts and crafts, and putt-putt golf. The ratio of counselors to kids is about 1:5. Baby-sitting is also available. And there's more: Kids receive welcome gifts at check-in, and, in summer, families can get package deals that include free meals for kids 12 and under at the Bella Vista restaurant (where they can serve themselves from a buffet, or—the ultimate luxury—order from a special room service menu). Holidays throughout the year bring special activities such as cookie making, concerts, watermelon-eating contests, and pictures with Santa. High chairs, cribs, bottle warmers, bed rails, bicycle surreys, and jogging strollers are available on request. Rooms at the resort are nicely furnished in soft desert colors.

🏨 *Dinah Shore and Bob Hope Drs., Rancho Mirage 92270, tel. 760/328–5955 or 800/ 228–3000, fax 760/770–2199. 512 rooms. Facilities: 7 restaurants, 3 pools, 4 spas, 7 tennis courts, golf (36 holes), health club, croquet, volleyball, shuffleboard. Children's program, baby-sitting. AE, DC, MC, V. $$–$$$ (meals in one restaurant for kids under 12 included in summer)*

FAMILY CAMPS
THE NO-HASSLE OUTDOOR VACATION

13

Jessica goes horseback riding and plays volleyball with her newfound pals. Jeremy takes a sculpting class and practices archery. Meanwhile, Mom goes off hiking for the afternoon while Dad settles under a tree to read. When the dinner bell rings, they all meet to swap accounts of the day's events over barbecued chicken and salad. As darkness falls, the family sips hot cocoa or coffee together around a campfire, enjoying skits or a songfest. Then they retire to a cabin for the night.

It's camp time, family style—and it's become a popular way for families to vacation together. Kids can be with other kids, parents with other adults; everyone can be as active or inactive as he or she chooses. It's camping without the cooking and cleaning up; even better, it's vacationing without having to find (and pay for) a host of hotels, restaurants, and entertainments—at most camps, lodging, meals, and activities are all included in the rates.

California has dozens of family camps, most set amid spectacular mountain, forest, or coastal scenery. Some camps are simply places to have fun in the great outdoors and escape temporarily from the pressures of urban living. Others add a layer of music, religion, or academic and social programs. Many of the camps are affiliated with university alumni associations, church groups, or cities and towns, yet even these camps typically welcome all comers; you don't have to be a member or resident to attend any of the camps described in this chapter.

Our own family camp experience came when our daughter Lia was 7 and son Grael was 10. In the fresh alpine air of Montecito-Sequoia, near Sequoia National Park, Lia learned new swimming strokes, Grael loved sliding down a slippery rock into a secluded mountain pool, my wife, Catharine, and I took a flashlight night hike up a mountain (while staff members checked on the kids in the cabin), and we all went canoeing. We had a blast.

Family camps aren't for everyone, it's true. You'll be roughing it to some degree, probably joining in some ritual hoopla, and possibly sharing a dining table or bathhouse with people you've never met before. If such things bother you, nix the idea of a camp vacation. Many families, however, find that camps offer the right mix of togetherness and individual freedom. Single parents especially seem to welcome the chance to relax and spend time with other adults while having someone else watch the kids.

If a family camp vacation appeals to you, call to sign up as far in advance as possible. For price comparison purposes, each camp is rated according to a rough estimated cost for a week's stay for a family of four. Keep in mind that the younger your kids are, the less you're likely to have to pay. On the other hand, if you want to stay for less than a set time, which is usually a week, those camps that do allow stays of a night or two tend to charge the short-term campers more per day. Nonresidents of a town that runs a camp can also expect to pay a bit more. Almost all camp rates include meals; those that don't are noted. Some camps charge extra for certain activities; these are also noted. The price categories are: $$$—over $1,500; $$—$1,000–$1,500; $—under $1,000.

All of the following camps operate in summer only, and some—which are kids-only camps for much of the season—have only limited sessions for families. Each camp included in the chapter is suitable for all ages.

Northern Forests and Lakes

Emandal

At Emandal, a working ranch that doubles as a camp in summer, "city folks" can escape to the country for a different kind of family vacation. If your kids have never spent time on a farm, this is a good place to introduce them to sheep, cows, pigs, pickle-making, and lazy days by the river. Nestled amid oaks and firs in the scenic Eel River valley in Mendocino County, the camp has 17 redwood cabins with electricity but cold water only (bathrooms and hot showers are nearby). Meals, served family-style in the dining hall, emphasize farm-grown meat, eggs, fruit, vegetables, and freshly baked breads. Emandal is far less structured than most family camps, with no daily schedule of planned activities; families here are encouraged to spend time together in an unstructured environment. You can swim in the Eel River at one of several swimming holes, collect driftwood, hunt rocks, and sunbathe. A lake for kayaking and canoeing is nearby, and the wooded hills around the farm are etched with hiking trails. If you wish, you can pitch in with some of the daily farm chores: kids, especially, might enjoy feeding chickens,

gathering eggs, and picking berries. At night, campers sit around the campfire to sing, play games, tell stories, perform skits—or simply stargaze.

🏠 16500 Hearst Post Office Rd., Willits 95490, tel. 707/459–5439 or 800/262–9597, fax 707/459–1808. Camp: 16 mi northeast of Willits; call for directions. Four to five 1-wk sessions Aug. and early Sept., plus 2- to 3-day seasonal weekends (call for weekend dates and rates). $$–$$$

Sierra and the Gold Country

Berkeley Tuolomne Family Camp

Beside the south fork of the Tuolomne River near Yosemite National Park (see Chapter 8), this camp—run by the city of Berkeley but open to nonresidents—is an affordable way for a family to enjoy a mountain vacation. Don't look for fancy amenities—only the basics amid scenic splendor. There's no pressure here to always be "doing something." Most campers do head for a swimming hole complete with sandy beach and—most kids' favorite—rocks to jump or slide off. Other active pursuits include archery, hiking, and volleyball. On most mornings, afternoons, and evenings, staff members supervise one- to two-hour Kiddie Kamps for ages 2 to 4 in a fenced-in play area. Staffers also lead weekday Children's Hours (once in morning, once in late afternoon) for ages 5 to 12, and arts and crafts projects for all ages. Kids ages 5 to 12 can also participate in the Tuolomne Rangers program at the camp's Nature Center, and families can enjoy group nature hikes, including some to Yosemite. Nighttime brings campfire programs, talent shows, bingo, naturalist talks, and theme dances. The 73 rustic and cozy tent cabins come with beds (bring your own bedding), dressers, and decks. Only the wheelchair-accessible cabins have plumbing and electricity, but community bathrooms with hot showers, toilets, and laundry facilities are close by. Meals are family-style in a lodge overlooking the river; vegetarian entrées are available. You can request bag lunches for picnics.

🏠 *2180 Milvia St., Berkeley 94704, tel. 510/644–6520, no fax. Camp: on Hwy. 120, 7 mi west of Yosemite National Park. Late June–late Aug. Daily stays possible; discounts for 5 or more days. Nonresidents apply after mid-Feb. $$*

Camp Concord

Flexibility is the key word here. Running at the same time as a children's camp program, the Family Camp here (operated by the Bay Area city of Concord but open to nonresidents, who pay a bit more) offers families the option of letting their 8- to 14-year-olds join in the Children's Camp activities or take part in the kids' activities organized for the Family Camp. The latter includes a twice-daily Kids Hour (ages 4 to 10) with nature hikes, crafts, and other programs, or teen activities such as miniature golf and night hikes. Campers can also swim, fish, canoe, hike, play volleyball, practice archery, and go on day trips. There's no additional charge for any activities except horseback riding. Nestled in a forest near Lake Tahoe, the

camp has comfortable private cabins with electricity and bunk and double beds; hot showers, flush toilets, and laundry facilities are nearby (bring your own bedding). Three cafeteria-style meals are served daily in the main lodge, or you can get a bag lunch for a picnic. Evening baby-sitting is also available at extra charge.

🏠 *Mailing address: 1948 Colfax St., Concord 94520, tel. 925/671–3273, fax 925/671–3412. Camp: off Hwy. 89 near Camp Richardson, about 3 mi west of South Lake Tahoe. Late June–mid-Aug. Daily stays possible; discounts for 4 or more days. No cut-off date for nonresident applications. $*

Camp Mather

Camp Mather, a city of San Francisco–run camp that sits at elevation 4,500 feet near the northwest entrance to Yosemite National Park (see Chapter 8), is best for families who aren't seeking a highly structured environment. Fewer organized activities are offered here than at the typical family camp, and meal tickets must be purchased separately ($152 per week ages 13 and older; $91 ages 6 to 2, $85 ages 2 to 5, under 2 free). The camp is usually booked up by the end of April each year (about ⅔ of the camp's population consists of non–San Francisco residents savvy enough to snap up spaces as soon as they become available, in mid-April; nonresidents pay a bit extra). Camp Mather's rustic cabins, containing up to six cotlike twin beds (bring your own bedding, including air mattresses for extra comfort), have electricity but no running water. Bathhouses with hot showers are separate; coin-operated laundry facilities are nearby. For the 20 tent sites (about half the cost of a cabin), campers must bring their own tents. Meals are served cafeteria-style in a dining hall. Don't be surprised if you see bears wandering around at night—but don't try to befriend them. You can swim in the camp pool or at Birch Lake (both have lifeguards) and play tennis, badminton, table tennis (bring your own racquets and paddles), horseshoes, volleyball, and softball. Children can participate in organized programs—arts and crafts, nature walks, and outdoor games. There's also a playground. In the evenings staff and campers join forces for talent shows, dances, campfire songs, bingo games, and ice-cream parties.

🏠 *Mailing address: San Francisco Recreation and Parks Dept., McLaren Lodge, Golden Gate Park, 501 Stanyan St., San Francisco 94117, tel. 415/831–2715, no fax. Camp: off Rte. 120 before northwest entrance to Yosemite National Park. Mid-June–late Aug. Nonresidents apply after mid-Apr. Meals not included. $*

Camp Sacramento

Nestled along the South Fork of the American River in a pine forest at 6,500 feet, 17 miles from Lake Tahoe, Camp Sacramento (operated by the city of Sacramento) offers families a rustic but relaxing mountain vacation. Residents and nonresidents of Sacramento are welcome; nonresidents pay a bit more. Lodging is in 58 rustic cabins equipped with electric lights and simple furnishings. You must bring your own bedding, and the cabins have no heat, running water, or electrical outlets. Hot showers and electrical outlets are available in modern bathhouses; laundry facilities are also available. The meals are served cafeteria-style, except for periodic barbecues or sack lunches for picnics. Each week, the camp distributes a daily schedule of organized activities for all ages. Supervised activities for children, divided into age groups (3–5, 6–9, 10–12, and teens), include nature programs, hikes, crafts projects, volleyball, basketball, horseshoes, softball, table tennis, campfires, dances, movies, and talent shows. Teens also can go bike riding at Tahoe or on overnight campouts. Adults can play in sports tournaments, go on organized hikes, learn tie-dyeing or batiking, or practice archery. Baby-sitting for tots is available by arrangement.

🏠 *Mailing address: 4623 T St., Sacramento 95819, tel. 916/277–6098, fax 916/454–3956. Camp (tel. 530/659–7202, fax 530/ 659–7037, June–Aug.): off Hwy. 50, 1 mi east of Twin Bridges. 61-wk sessions early July–late Aug.; 6 3-day sessions late June–late Aug. Daily stays possible; call previous Wed. for availability. No cut-off date for nonresident applications. $–$$.*

Feather River Vacation Camp

Run by the city of Oakland but open to nonresidents, this camp is a good budget choice for families willing to rough it a bit. In the scenic Plumas National Forest in the northern Sierra, the camp offers a wide range of activities: swimming in Spanish Creek, fishing, hiking, nature walks, archery, dancing, games, talent shows, arts and crafts, volleyball, horseback riding, and an outdoor adventure ropes obstacle course (the latter two at extra cost). Organized excursions may set out to explore local gold mines, fishing holes, or an Indian sweat lodge. During certain weeks, the camp offers specialty theme programs: storytelling, folk dancing, chamber music. The only daily age-specific activity here is the Tot Lot: two hours of child care offered up to three times a day for 2½- to 5-year-olds. But ask about special weeks when boys and girls age 7–12 can learn basic camping skills, and kids ages 8 to 12 and 11 to 15, respectively, can study visual and performing arts, with end-of-the-week showcases. Another week brings a three-day pack-out trip for teens ages 13 to 16. Campers here stay in rustic wooden cabins, with cots and mattresses, or in tents with floors; none of these has heat or plumbing (some do have electricity). Community shower rooms, rest rooms, and coin-laundry facilities are provided. Meals are served family-style in the dining hall, except for periodic barbecues and buffets.

🏠 *Mailing address: Office of Parks and Recreation, 1520 Lakeside Dr., Oakland, tel. 510/238–3791, fax 510/238–2224. Camp (tel. 530/283–2290): off Hwy. 70, 5 mi south of Quincy. Late June–mid-Aug. Daily stays possible; discounts for 4 or more days. No cut-off date for nonresidents. $*

Lair of the Golden Bear

Run by the University of California–Berkeley Alumni Association, this mountain retreat in the Gold Country is open to all association members and their families. You can join the association for $40, whether or not you attended the university, but if you aren't an alum—and many campers aren't—you may have to acquire some instant school spirit. The two camps here, Blue and Gold (the Cal school colors, of course), accommodate about 300 campers each in rustic tent cabins, with wooden floors and sides and a canvas top. Campers sleep on metal-frame beds with mattresses and must bring their own bedding. The cabins have electricity but no plumbing; modern bathhouses are scattered throughout the camp, and coin-operated washing machines (no dryers) are available. Meals are served family-style in the dining hall. Staff counselors (mostly Cal students) lead a host of organized activities for everyone age 2 and up; kids are divided into six age groups that meet two or three times a day. While the 2- to 4-year-olds enjoy arts and crafts, games, music, nature activities, and play equipment in the Kub Korral, there may be pool games and short hikes for 5- to 7-year-olds; nature projects and fishing for 8- and 9-year-olds; water games, softball, and arts and crafts for preteens (10–12); and dancing and longer hikes for teens (13–14 and 15–17). Adults can play tennis, volleyball, and horseshoes or attend lectures by university faculty members. In the evenings, families unite once again for dancing, bingo, games, and staff shows.

🏠 *Mailing address: Lair Reservations, 1 Alumni House, Berkeley 94720, tel. 510/642-0221 or 888/225-2586, fax 510/642-6252. Camp: off Rte. 108, 30 mi northeast of Sonora, near Pinecrest. 11 1-wk sessions, mid-June–late Aug.; one 3-day mini-wk, mid-June. $$*

Montecito-Sequoia High Sierra Family Camp

California's best-known family camp—it regularly draws vacationers from across the United States and other countries—sits at 7,500 feet in Sequoia National Forest between Kings Canyon and Sequoia national parks, amid giant trees and with views of snowcapped peaks. Most families who come here are active types, usually itching to learn waterskiing or sailing or to join group hikes or art projects. The daily schedule is crammed with activities. Activities for kids are divided into six different age groups, from 2-year-olds to teens. In general, kids ages 2 to 7 can enjoy swimming, pony rides, kiddie Olympics, goodie bakes, story time, and the like—while ages 8 to adult can choose among activities such as swimming (in heated pool or cool lake), canoeing, sailing, tennis, archery, riflery, volleyball, arts and crafts, fishing, improv theater, and nature hikes. Instruction is offered to all levels. Waterskiing and horseback riding require additional fees. Each week has a theme night such as Hello, Hollywood, or 70s Disco Night when campers are invited to dress in costume and participate in contests and parties. Other evenings are filled with campfire sing-alongs, night hikes, variety shows, and skits. Accommodations range from lodge rooms with private baths to cabins with nearby community bathhouses; rates vary according to the type of lodging. Cabins have electricity, beds, and bunks (bring your own bedding), but no running water or toilets. Breakfast is cafeteria style, while lunch and dinner are served buffet style; some nights bring special barbecue dinners, and you can request a sack lunch for an out-of-camp excursion. A snack bar is open 24 hours.

🏠 *Mailing address: 1485 Redwood Dr., Los Altos 94024, tel. 650/967-8612 or 800/227-9900, fax 650/967-0540. Camp: off Generals Hwy., 10 mi south of southeast entrance to Kings Canyon National Park. 10 1-wk sessions and 3 4-day sessions, mid-June–early Sept. $$$*

Pacific Family Camp

For an outdoor vacation without having to rough it you can sign up at this luxurious camp at the Feather River Inn (a conference center most of the year) in the northern reaches of the Sierra. Run by the University of the Pacific Alumni Association—but open to the public (with an extra fee)—the 4,500-foot-elevation camp has pine-shaded grounds with a 9-hole golf course, a heated pool, a gym, tennis courts, horseshoe pits, outdoor volleyball courts, and fishing ponds. Accommodations are in cabins and alpine chalets, all with private baths and outdoor porches. Meals are served buffet style. Each weeklong session includes organized programs for children of all ages—arranged in nine age groups from infants to teens—as well as separate activities for adults. The under 5s have supervised sessions each morning; baby-sitters are available afternoons and evenings for an extra fee. The other kids meet with their age groups both mornings and afternoons. Staff counselors, mostly college students, lead arts and crafts projects and take kids on nature walks, swimming, tubing, or on out-of-camp excursions. Parents can compete in volleyball and horseshoes, take golf lessons (for an extra fee), hike, or learn to paint watercolors and throw a pot (though not at each other). Families reunite at campfires, square dances, a family Olympics, and the weekly talent show—or can swim, fish, play table tennis, and eat together anytime.

🏠 *Mailing address: University of the Pacific Alumni Association, 3601 Pacific Ave., Stockton 95211, tel. 209/946–2391. Camp (tel. 530/ 836–6908): Feather River Inn Rd., Blairsden, off Hwys. 89 and 70, about 50 mi northwest of Truckee. 5 1-wk sessions, early July–early Aug. $$–$$$*

San Jose Family Camp

In a mountain retreat near the west gate of Yosemite National Park, the San Jose Family Camp, run by the city of San Jose, offers so many activities that you may feel guilty relaxing. A small dam upstream from the dining hall creates a swimming hole in the Tuolomne River, complete with sandy beach, diving area, and roped-off shallows for small children and novice swimmers. Nature-oriented crafts programs, for both kids and adults, and organized hikes and excursions in and out of camp are scheduled daily. Mornings, afternoons, and evenings, young children can scurry off to the supervised playground at Fort Tuolomne or their own kiddie campfire area on Miners Island. Teens can opt for overnight camp-outs. Softball, volleyball, basketball, shuffleboard, fishing, panning for gold, and archery are all on tap. Each evening brings a different program of campfires, night hikes, skits, talent shows, and socials. This camp is not structured in weekly sessions; families of campers come and go throughout the week, staying an average of four nights each. More than 60 wood-frame, canvas-covered tent cabins are tucked among pine and oak trees. Cots sleep up to six people per cabin (bring your own bedding), and each cabin has an outdoor porch. Some have electrical outlets ($2.50 extra), but bathhouses provide hot showers, toilets, electricity, and washbasins. Meals are served in a dining hall overlooking the Tuolomne River; breakfast and lunch are cafeteria style, dinner is family style. Sack lunches are provided for picnics away from camp.

🏠 *Mailing address: 1300 Senter Rd., San Jose 95112, tel. 408/277–4666, fax 408/277– 3270. Camp: 11401 Cherry Lake Rd., Groveland, off Hwy. 120. Mid-June–late Aug. Daily stays; early summer midweek discounts. $–$$*

Silver Lake Camp

Half a mile from Silver Lake in Amador County, the Silver Lake Camp—run by the city of Stockton but open to nonresidents— sits 7,200 feet high in the Sierra. This isn't a camp where parents can drop their kids off with counselors and forget about them; there are a few supervised programs for children on the daily posted schedule, and limited baby-sitting services are available for a small charge, but in general parents are expected to supervise their kids. There's plenty to keep everyone busy: fishing and swimming in the lake, arts and crafts, nature hikes, volleyball, horseshoes, shuffleboard, basketball, table tennis, softball, a weekly variety show, barbecues, and nightly campfire programs. Campers stay in 45 rustic wooden cabins each with one double bed and two sets of bunk beds. Bring your own bedding. If your child needs a crib, bring that, too. Cabins have generator-supplied electricity; a modern central bathhouse has attached laundry facilities. Meals are served cafeteria style in the main lodge, and a camp store sells snacks.

🏠 *Mailing address: City of Stockton Parks and Recreation, 6 E. Lindsay St., Stockton 95202, tel. 209/937–8371, no fax; camp, after mid-July, tel. 209/258–9886 or 209/258–8810. Camp: Plasses Rd. at Silver Lake, Hwy. 88, 60 mi northeast of Jackson. Mid-July–early Aug. Daily stays. $*

Skylake Yosemite Camp

A children's camp for most of the summer, Skylake offers short sessions of family camping at the beginning and end of the season. The longtime privately owned camp is on Sierra National Forest land overlooking Bass Lake about 15 miles south of the Wawona (southern) entrance to Yosemite National Park. At 3,600 feet elevation, and with breezes blowing off the lake, the site avoids the worst of Central Valley summer heat; nights tend to be cool. The lake water, however, is warm enough for swimming and water sports, which are mainstays of the activity schedule. At the lakeside beach, campers can swim, boat, kayak, canoe, sail, waterski (for an extra fee), and windsurf. In the camp area, crafts, archery, tennis, table tennis, badminton, softball, volleyball, horseshoes, horseback riding (one free ride for all), and a ropes obstacle course are available. Activities aren't supervised; parents are responsible for their kids. Each night brings a campfire with marshmallow toasting, and sometimes singing and skits. After young kids go to bed, parents can play cards and table games or read in the lodge. Campers stay in 34 rustic screened cabins, which each sleep up to eight and have no electricity; bring your own flashlights and sleeping bags, and shower at a nearby bathhouse. Meals are served buffet style in the camp dining hall, and dinners are preceded by a social hour with snacks and ice provided (bring your own drinks). Children 4 and under stay for free. Reserve early.

🏠 *Mailing address: Skylake Yosemite Camp, 37976 Rd. 222, #25, Wishon 93669, tel. 209/642–3720, fax 209/642–3395. Camp: east of Rte. 41 on Rd. 222, 15 mi south of Yosemite. 2-, 3-, and 6-night sessions, late May–mid-June and mid-Aug.–late Sept. $$*

Central Coast and Valley

Family Vacation Center at UC Santa Barbara

During most of the year the San Rafael Residence Hall houses University of California–Santa Barbara students. For two months each summer, however, the hall—on a bluff overlooking the Pacific Ocean—becomes a family camp run by the UCSB Alumni Association. (Everyone is welcome to attend; Alumni Association members receive a discount.) No rugged camping here: Families stay in fully furnished suites that include living rooms with a refrigerator, two to four bedrooms, private baths, even daily maid service. Three full-course buffet meals a day are served, including choices of entrées, salad bars, fresh fruit, baked goods, and ice cream sundaes. Parents can entrust their children to daily organized programs from 9 to 9, with breaks at mealtimes. Kids are divided into eight age groups, from infant to college age. For 1-month-olds to 3-year-olds comprehensive care ranges from outdoor play to crafts, storytelling, creative movement, and snacks. Kids ages 4 to 12 swim, hike, do crafts, play group games, and hold beach barbecues. Teens stay busy with bicycling, tennis, dancing, movies, softball, and an overnight campout. For adults (or the whole family) there are sports tournaments, golf lessons, tennis clinics (ask about special weeks emphasizing either golf or tennis), trips to the beach (a short walk away), faculty seminars, and museums.

🏠 *Family Vacation Center, UCSB Alumni Association Center, Santa Barbara 93106, tel. 805/893–3123, fax 805/893–4918. 8 1-wk sessions, July–Aug. Discounts for members of any UC alumni association. $$$*

SCamp

SCamp, at the River Way Ranch Camp in the foothills of Kings Canyon National Park, is run by the University of Southern California Alumni Association. Nonalums are welcome—you don't even have to join the alumni association to attend the camp—but take warning: You'll probably encounter lots of "Trojan spirit" and hoopla. Even so, this camp may be worth putting up with all that. The ranch is situated amid oaks and sycamores, near a creek and a lake. Meals are served buffet style on a patio overlooking the lake, and accommodations are luxurious: 50 guest rooms (some holding up to eight people) come with air-conditioning, wall-to-wall carpeting, and private baths. Some fully furnished platform cabins are also available at a lower rate. Children are divided into nine age groups—from tiniest tots to teens—for supervised activities. Those up to age 8 have a structured schedule; ages 9 and up have free choice. Campers can dip into the lake for swimming, waterskiing, sailing, kayaking, and canoeing. Horseback options include trail riding and pony rides, while kids who prefer motorized horsepower can try go-carts or minibikes. Arts and crafts and a farm-animal petting zoo also occupy younger kids; parents can attend lectures by faculty speakers. Special events include overnight camp-outs, carnivals, theme nights, talent shows, dances, campfires, and a Parents Night Out. Except for designated activity and social hours, child care costs extra.

🏠 *6450 Elwood Rd., Sanger 93657, tel. 209/787–2551 or 800/821–2801, fax 209/787–2556. 3 1-wk sessions, Aug. $$$*

Los Angeles and Environs

Los Angeles Metropolitan YMCA Camps

Los Angeles area YMCAs sponsor several different family camps each year, at locations ranging from the greater L.A. area to Mammoth Lakes in the southern Sierra. One of the main locations, YMCA Camp Harold F. Whittle at Big Bear Lake in the San Bernardino Mountains, offers family cabins and activities such as horseback riding, arts and crafts, folk and square dancing, hiking, backpacking, water sports, rock climbing, windsurfing, bicycling, nature study, sailing, archery, field trips, a rope obstacle course, and volleyball. Though YMCA camps typically include some religious emphasis, they are open to all. Most hold family camp at various times during the school year, primarily on weekends and during school vacations. Call for information on dates, prices, and locations for all area Y's, or sign up at your local Y.

🏠 *Los Angeles Metropolitan YMCA Camps, tel. 909/866–3000, fax 909/866–5065. Various sessions, Sept.–May. $*

San Diego and the Southern Deserts

Idyllwild Arts Family Camp

Families can appreciate the arts along with the outdoors during two one-week summer sessions at Idyllwild Arts, a school of music, theater, painting, and applied arts. The camp perches at 5,500 feet on the western slopes of the San Jacinto Mountains, surrounded by

alpine forests, meadows, and creeks, about 2½ hours from either San Diego or Los Angeles. Each session is limited to 20 families, who can spend their days in classes and activities such as hiking and rock climbing, swimming and dancing. Children under 3 remain under their parents' supervision; toilet-trained 3- to 4-year-olds have supervised morning sessions of short hikes, crafts, and games, and group baby-sitting is available in the evenings. For older kids—grouped by age—counselors lead arts and crafts, theater games, nature outings, sports, and swimming. Adults can spend their days and evenings on organized hikes or in dancing classes, at concerts or lectures, or reading and relaxing, by the pool or under a tree. Music and arts faculties are the camp's real strength; it has indoor and outdoor theaters, art studios, dance studios, and piano practice rooms. Classes are available in painting, ceramics, batik, jewelry-making, photography, woodcarving, and tie-dyeing. In addition, you'll find traditional camp activities like campfires, games, and a weekly family talent show, presented toward the end of the week. Families stay in a modern residence hall, which has one- or two-bedroom lodgings that have private bathrooms with showers and daily maid service. Meals are served in a dining hall.
🏠 *Box 38, Idyllwild 92549, tel. 909/659–2171, ext. 365, or 213/622–0355, fax 909/659–5463 or 213/622–6185. Two 1-wk sessions, late June–early July. $$$*

PART III

PLACES

Major Cities and Family-Friendly Resort Areas

SAN FRANCISCO

14

CABLE CARS, CHINATOWN, THE BAY, AND THE GOLDEN GATE

S an Francisco is among the world's most cosmopolitan cities, and just like adults, kids can easily fall in love with it. Start with exotic attractions like the cable cars and Chinatown, and continue to other famed, kid-friendly sites like Golden Gate Park, the Golden Gate Bridge, Fisherman's Wharf, Alcatraz Island, and the zoo. Then there are the little things that captivate young imaginations: some of the world's steepest and most crooked streets; glass elevators that whisk you way above the city; kites shaped like fish or butterflies flapping in the bay breezes. Although both my children were born and reared here, they never tire of playing "tourist" in their home town.

Older kids may appreciate how a visit to San Francisco brings a taste of traveling the globe. Within a few blocks of our house, for example, we can visit restaurants from a dozen Asian cultures alone. We sometimes hear more Russian and Cantonese spoken on the streets here than English.

Keep one thing in mind when you're visiting San Francisco in summer: It can get cold. When the fog blankets the bay, you won't want to be caught shivering in shorts and T-shirts—pack some warm clothes. (May and September are often the city's warmest months.)

The Basics

Resources

Contact the **San Francisco Convention & Visitors Bureau** (tel. 415/391–2000 or 415/391–2001 for 24-hour recorded information; website www.sfvisitor.org) for information about attractions and lodging. For a visitors' information packet, including *The Lodging Guide* and its quarterly general guide *The San Francisco Book*, which includes up-to-date information on kids' activities, send $3 to the SFCVB, Box 429097, San Francisco 94142. You can also receive information via the Fast Fax system at 800/220–

5747 or 617/960–9216 outside the U.S. or Canada. When you arrive, stop at the bureau's **Visitor Information Center** on the lower level in Hallidie Plaza (900 Market Street at Powell) downtown. Along with brochures and maps, you can pick up hotel coupons and discount transit passes. The center is open weekdays from 9 to 5:30, Saturday from 9 to 3, and Sunday from 10 to 2. For **city-wide hotel reservations,** call 888/782–9673.

The **Oakland Convention and Visitors Bureau** (550 10th St., Suite 214, Oakland 94607, tel. 510/839–9000 or 800/262–5526) provides information about the East Bay; the **Marin County Convention & Visi-**

tors **Bureau** (Avenue of the Flags, San Rafael 94903, tel. 415/472–7470) provides information about North Bay communities; and the **San Jose Convention and Visitors Bureau** (333 W. San Carlos St., Suite 1000, San Jose 95110, tel. 408/295–9600 or 800/726–5673) covers South Bay attractions.

Parent's Press (1454 6th St., Berkeley 94710, tel. 510/524–1602), *San Francisco Peninsula Parent* (1480 Rollins Rd., Burlingame 94010, tel. 650/342–9203), sister publications *Bay Area Parent* and *Valley Parent* (401 Alberto Way, Suite A, Los Gatos, CA 95032, tel. 408/358–1414) are free monthly publications listing events and activities for kids and families; they're available at many libraries, YMCAs, and kids' stores.

Getting in and out of San Francisco

BY AIR. San Francisco International Airport (tel. 650/761–0800), 15 miles south of downtown off U.S. 101, is served by all major airlines and car-rental agencies. The **SFO Airporter** (tel. 415/495–8404) runs every 10 to 20 minutes from 5 AM to 11 PM, leaving from the lower level outside the baggage claim area and taking passengers to various downtown hotels. The fare is $10 one-way. For $12 per person, **Super-Shuttle** (tel. 415/558–8500) will take you from the airport to anywhere within the San Francisco city limits. A number of other door-to-door shuttle services also operate at the airport. **Taxis** to or from downtown take 20 to 30 minutes and average $30.

Oakland International Airport (1 Airport Dr., off I–880, tel. 510/577–4000) lies across the bay to the east. To reach downtown San Francisco from the Oakland airport, use BART (see Getting Around, *below*).

BY CAR. I–80 finishes its westward journey from New York at the Bay Bridge, which links Oakland to San Francisco. U.S. 101 and coastal Highway 1 connect San Francisco to points north and south. The fastest route to

and from Los Angeles and San Diego is I–5 (reached via I–580 in Oakland).

BY TRAIN. Amtrak (tel. 800/872–7245) trains (the California *Zephyr,* from Chicago via Denver; and the *Coast Starlight,* from Los Angeles or Seattle) stop in Emeryville, near Oakland; buses connect to downtown San Francisco.

BY BUS. Greyhound (tel. 800/231–2222) serves San Francisco from the Transbay Terminal at 1st and Mission streets.

Getting Around San Francisco

BY CAR. Because San Francisco is so compact, it's entirely possible—and often preferable—to get around the city either on foot or via the extensive public transportation system (see *below*). Hills, one-way streets, traffic, and a shortage of parking can make driving in this city difficult. If you arrive without a car, though, consider renting one for a day or two for scenic excursions.

Major streets in town include Van Ness Avenue, which runs from the Civic Center north to the bay, connecting via Lombard Street to the Golden Gate Bridge; Geary Street (which becomes Geary Boulevard west of downtown), which runs west from downtown to the ocean, passing near Golden Gate Park; The Embarcadero, which runs along the waterfront; Market Street, which runs from The Embarcadero to the Castro district; and 19th Avenue/Park Presidio (Highway 1), which leads south from the Golden Gate Bridge through Golden Gate Park.

BY BUS AND STREETCAR. The San Francisco Municipal Railway System, or **Muni** (tel. 415/673–6864), includes buses and trolleys, surface and below-surface streetcars, and cable cars. Service runs 24 hours and links most areas of the city. Fares (except for cable cars; see *below*) are $1 for adults, 35¢ for ages 5 to 17; exact fare is required. Unlimited-ride Muni passports ($6 one day,

$10 three days, $15 seven days) may be purchased at the Visitor Information Center in Hallidie Plaza and other locations.

Golden Gate Transit (tel. 415/923–2000) runs the weekend Bus 63 from the Golden Gate Bridge Plaza to several popular sightseeing spots in Marin County including Stinson Beach (see Beaches, *below*); some sights are visited only in certain seasons. Fares vary according to destination.

BY CABLE CAR. San Francisco's cable cars are open-air National Historic Landmarks that *move,* and a must for every sightseer. Kids are usually fascinated to watch the gripman in action—there's real skill in keeping these antique conveyances on track—and to hear the bells clang, brakes screech, and cables hum. There are three lines, connecting the most frequented tourist areas. The **Powell-Mason** and the **Powell-Hyde** lines begin at Powell and Market streets, climb over Nob and Russian hills, and terminate at Fisherman's Wharf. The Powell-Hyde Line, which ends at pretty Victorian Park (Hyde and Bay Sts.) has the better scenery and more thrills as it plunges down steeply toward the bay; the Powell-Mason Line stops three blocks short of the Wharf, turning around at Bay and Taylor streets in a blighted area. The **California Street Line** runs east–west from California and Market streets near The Embarcadero to Van Ness Avenue, climbing over Nob Hill.

Cable cars are often crowded, and long lines form at the turnarounds, where passengers gather to make sure of getting seats. But you don't have to board at turnarounds; cars stop every other block or so along the routes (look for maroon-and-white signs) to let off and pick up passengers. If you board en route, approach the car quickly as it pauses, wedge into an available space, and hold on tight. (If you have small children, make sure they're safely inside, holding on, before the car starts to move.) One-way fares are $2 (under 5 free); operators will make change if necessary. Some terminals have self-service ticket machines.

BY BART. **Bay Area Rapid Transit** (tel. 650/992–2278) sends air-conditioned, high-speed underground trains to Oakland and other East Bay cities, as well as south to Colma. Wall maps in the stations list destinations and fares ($1.10–$4.70). Trains run weekdays from 4 AM to midnight, Saturday from 6 AM to midnight, Sunday from 8 AM to midnight.

BY TAXI. Rates are high in the city, though most rides are short. It's hard to hail a passing cab, especially on weekends, so use the nearest hotel taxi stand, or phone a cab company such as **Yellow Cab** (tel. 415/626–2345) or **Luxor** (tel. 415/282–4141).

BY FERRY. **Golden Gate Ferry** boats (tel. 415/923–2000) depart from the Ferry Building, Embarcadero at Market St., for Sausalito, a Mediterranean-style village in Marin County ($4.70 adults, $3.50 ages 6–11, ages 5 and under free, with special weekend family fares). They also go to Larkspur in the North Bay. **Blue and Gold Fleet** ferries, based at Pier 39 and Pier 41, Fisherman's Wharf (tel. 415/773–1188 for schedules, 415/705–5555 for tickets) travel to Alcatraz (see Historic Sites, *below*), the seaside towns of Sausalito and Tiburon in the North Bay, Angel Island (see Parks, *below*), Muir Woods (see Chapter 7), and Alameda/Oakland and Vallejo (home of the Six Flags Marine World Theme Park; see Chapter 9) in the East Bay.

Family-Friendly Tours

Gray Line Cable Car Tours offers 1½- and 2½-hour loop tours on motorized cable cars (with wheels) that go to the Presidio, Japantown, and Golden Gate Bridge. Leave from Union Square, Pier 39, or the Embarcadero Center, then get off and reboard at various stops if you wish. *Tel. 415/558–9400. Fare: $16–$22 adults, $8–$11 ages 5–11.*

One-hour narrated bay cruises—passing by Alcatraz and under the Golden Gate Bridge—are offered by the **Blue & Gold Fleet** (Pier 39's West Marina, tel. 415/705–5555) and **Red & White Fleet** (Pier 43½, tel. 415/447–0597). Fares: $17 adults, $13 ages 12–18, $9 ages 5–11; ages 4 and under are free.

The tall ship *Hawaiian Chieftain,* a replica of an 18th-century trading vessel, sails the bay from April to October (and in winter, sails along the California coast and in the Sacramento Delta). The best sailings for families are the four-hour Saturday Adventure Sails, when kids and their parents can lend a hand with the lines. The boat leaves from Sausalito's Marina Plaza Harbor off Marinship Way. Buffet lunch on board is included.
🏠 *3020 Bridgeway, Suite 266, Sausalito, tel. 415/331–3214. Fare: $40 per adult, $25 per child. Reservations required.*

Hornblower Dining Yachts operates weekday lunch (call for schedule) and weekend brunch cruises on the bay, serving bountiful meals aboard elegant boats. Kids are encouraged to visit the pilot house.
🏠 *Pier 33, tel. 415/788–8866. Fare: $32 (weekday) and $39.50–$44 (weekend) adults; ages 4–12 are half price.*

Many individuals, groups, and companies operate walking tours. **City Guides** (tel. 415/557–4266) offers free walking tours of ethnic neighborhoods or on topics like Gold Rush San Francisco. **Friends of Recreation and Parks** (tel. 415/221–1311) gives free guided walking tours of Golden Gate Park on weekends from May to October. **Javawalk** (tel. 415/673–9255) combines walking and local history with samples of North Beach coffeehouse culture. The **Wok Wiz** (tel. 415/981–8989) provides both glimpses and tastes of Chinatown. Let the guides know you're bringing children.

Whale-watching tours run from October to May during the annual gray whale migrations along the coast (prime months are January and March). **Five Star Charters** (tel. 415/381–9503) and **Oceanic Society Expeditions** (tel. 415/474–3385) in San Francisco operate excellent trips. Half-day and full-day adult fares range from $32 to $62; children under 13 are discounted up to half price.

Pit Stops

A French company has installed self-cleaning pay toilets (25¢) around the city, at busy locations such as downtown and Fisherman's Wharf. Watch for the dark green Parisian-style structures with city maps on the sides. Otherwise, head for rest rooms in major department stores (such as **Macy's** on Union Square and **Nordstrom** in the San Francisco Centre), at shopping complexes such as **Ghirardelli Square, The Cannery,** and **Pier 39,** and in big hotels such as the **Grand Hyatt** and **Westin St. Francis** on Union Square. At 3rd and Mission streets there are rest rooms at **Yerba Buena Gardens** (near Moscone Center). Golden Gate Park has a barely adequate supply, but all the museums there are well equipped.

Baby-Sitters

Check first with your hotel concierge or manager—many major hotels can arrange on-site baby-sitting. Otherwise, call **Bay Area Child Care** (tel. 650/991–7474), which will send bonded, CPR-certified sitters to your hotel room, days or evenings.

Emergencies

Police, fire, or **ambulance** can be reached by dialing 911. The **Poison Control Center** number is 800/523–2222. **San Francisco General Hospital** (1001 Potrero Ave., tel. 415/206–8000) and the **Medical Center at the University of California, San Francisco** (500 Parnassus Ave., tel. 415/476–1000) have 24-hour emergency rooms.

Several **Walgreens Drug Stores** have 24-hour pharmacies: Try 500 Geary Street near Union Square (tel. 415/673–8411), 135 Powell St. near Market St. (tel. 415/391–7222), or 3201 Divisadero Street at Lombard Street (tel. 415/931–6417).

Telephone Area Codes

Area codes 415 (San Francisco and Marin counties) and 408 (the San Jose area) are both due to split in 1999. Neither the new area codes nor their geographic regions were available at press time.

Scoping out San Francisco

The Union Square area, the heart of downtown, makes a handy starting point. Northeast of Union Square lie, in geographical order, vibrant Chinatown, Italian-flavored North Beach, and Fisherman's Wharf. Just southeast of Union Square is the South of Market district, the hot new scene for restaurants and nightlife. Heading west on Market Street brings you to the Civic Center area, and northwest of that, the beautiful Marina District borders the bay, with the Golden Gate Bridge and Golden Gate Park farther west. East of Golden Gate Park is the Haight-Ashbury neighborhood, center of 1960s flower power. Twin Peaks, which provides a spectacular overview of the city, rises just south of the Haight. Top attractions are covered at length in various chapters in Part II; we've simply cross-referenced them here.

Historic Sites

(👫 3–15) Alcatraz Island (see Chapter 4), site of the former maximum-security prison in the middle of the bay, makes an eerie, fascinating sightseeing stop.
🏠 Pier 41, Fisherman's Wharf, tel. 415/705–1042 (park information); 415/773–1188 (boat schedules and information); 415/705–5555 or 800/426–8687 (credit-card ticket orders).

(👫 3–15) If the most hands-on activity your kids have gotten lately is hitting the button on the remote control, take them to Ardenwood Historic Farm. This East Bay farm, right out of the pastoral 19th century, gives urban kids a real change of pace. They can watch demonstrations of horseshoe hammering, hay harvesting, and biscuit bak-

ing, then try their hands at pumping water, cranking an old clothes wringer, and feeding livestock. Short train and wagon rides add to the fun.
🏠 34600 Ardenwood Blvd., Fremont, tel. 510/796–0663. Admission: $6 adults, $4 over age 64, $3.50 ages 4–17, ages 3 and under free. Open Apr.–mid-Nov., Thurs.–Sun. 10–4.

(👫 ALL) The Cliff House (see Chapter 4), perched above the Pacific at Ocean Beach, combines spectacular views with an old-time game arcade and restaurant.
🏠 1090 Point Lobos Ave., tel. 415/386–3330.

(👫 ALL) Coit Tower (see Chapter 4) has panoramic views of the city and bay.
🏠 Top of Telegraph Hill, tel. 415/362–0808.

(👫 ALL) The Ferry Building, whose 230-foot clock tower was once the tallest structure west of the Mississippi, anchors a beautiful waterfront promenade called Herb Caen Way in honor of the city's late, legendary newspaper columnist. Bring a stroller, in-line skates, or a picnic lunch; some bay ferries embark from here, too. The Ferry Building also houses the International Children's Art Museum (see below). Across The Embarcadero, at Justin Herman Plaza, the modernistic Vaillancourt Fountain is a virtual magnet for kids, who love to scamper behind its falling waters.
🏠 Embarcadero at foot of Market St.

(👫 ALL) Fisherman's Wharf remains by far the city's most heavily visited site. The historic waterfront district runs for eight or nine blocks from Aquatic Park to Pier 39, often overwhelmed with schlocky souvenir stands and mediocre seafood restaurants. Still, the bay and boats are near at hand, and it's a colorful, noisy, active place, which most kids like. Try to get here by mid-morning to beat the worst of the crush. Worth seeing are the Hyde Street Pier, with its collection of historic ships (see below); the USS Pompanito (Pier 45, tel. 415/775–1943; $7 ages 13 and up, $4 ages 6–12, open daily 9–6), a restored World War II submarine; Richard

Henry Dana Street (the former "Fish Alley"), where you can still glimpse the real working wharf; and the bubbling **crab pots** on Jefferson Street, where you can stop for an overpriced crab or shrimp cocktail. More commercial attractions, which have nothing to do with fishermen, include **The Wax Museum** (145 Jefferson St., tel. 415/885–4975; $9.95 adults, $6.95 ages 13–17, $4.95 ages 6–12, under 6 free; open Sun.–Thurs. 9 AM–10 PM, Fri.–Sat. 9 AM–11 PM), with some 270 wax figures from King Tut to Eddie Murphy, as well as a Chamber of Horrors with occupants ranging from Dracula to Al Capone; and **Ripley's Believe It or Not** (175 Jefferson St., tel. 415/771–6188; $8.50 adults, $7 ages 13–17, $5.25 ages 5–12, under 5 free, open daily Memorial Day–Labor Day, 9 AM–11 PM, rest of year 10–10, open every Fri.–Sat. until midnight), exhibiting such oddities as a shrunken human torso, an 8-foot-long cable car built from matchsticks, and a portrait of Rudolph Valentino made from dryer lint. There's usually a delightful collection of street performers—jugglers, musicians, magicians—doing their things around the Wharf, either on the streets or at the area's four main shopping centers: **Ghirardelli Square, the Cannery, Pier 39**, and the **Anchorage** (see Shops, *below*). To eat in the area, try **McCormick and Kuleto's Seafood Restaurant** in Ghirardelli Square (tel. 415/929–1730) for fish and terrific bay views; Alioto's #8 (tel. 415/673–0183), which has old-time atmosphere and excellent fish; **A. Sabella's** (2766 Taylor St., tel. 415/771–4416) for seafood and pasta with an extensive children's menu; or the prison-cell themed **Alcatraz Cafe and Grill** at Pier 39 (tel. 415/434–1818) for seafood, burgers, and pizza.

🏠 *Bounded by Aquatic Park, North Point, Powell St., and Pier 39.*

(👫 **6 – 15**) **Fort Point**—built during the Civil War to help protect San Francisco from sea attack and now part of Presidio National Park (see *below*)— has brick walls, cannons, barracks, and a dramatic view of the Golden Gate Bridge, which runs literally

overhead. Head for the top of the fort for some of the best bridge and bay views anywhere; there are usually windsurfers braving the waves or freighters passing beneath the Golden Gate. Rangers give daily cannon-loading demonstrations, a complex, fascinating process.

🏠 *Marina Blvd. toward Golden Gate Bridge, turn at Fort Point sign, tel. 415/556–1693. Admission free. Open Wed.–Sun. 10–5.*

(👫 **ALL**) **The Golden Gate Bridge** (see Chapter 4), the world's most photographed span, is a thrill to drive or walk across.

🏠 *Hwy. 1 or 101 north to bridge. Car toll $3 (southbound only).*

(👫 **3 – 15**) **The Hyde Street Pier,** part of the **San Francisco Maritime National Historic Park**—the country's only floating national park—lets kids on board the world's largest fleet of historic ships (by tonnage). Our favorite is the *Balclutha,* an 1886 square-rigged sailing vessel that navigated Cape Horn 17 times. Other ships on permanent display are the *C.A. Thayer,* a three-masted schooner; the bay's oldest ferry, the paddle-wheel *Eureka*; the *Hercules,* a steam-powered ocean tug; and the century-old scow schooner *Alma.* Special family events—sail-raisings, sea chanty songfests, evening concerts—are held here periodically.

🏠 *Foot of Hyde St., tel. 415/556–3002 or for tickets, 415/556–0859. Admission: $4 adults, $2 ages 12–17; ages 11 and under free; family tickets $10. Open daily 9:30–5.*

(👫 **3 – 15**) The Liberty Ship **SS *Jeremiah O'Brien*,** which in 1994 sailed round trip to Europe to celebrate the 50th anniversary of D-Day, is available for shipboard tours unless it's making one of its periodic voyages. It's the only one of more than 2,500 World War II Liberty Ships to remain in its original condition.

🏠 *Pier 32, tel. 415/441–3101. Admission: $5 adults, $3 ages 6–18, under 6 free. Open daily 9–4.*

(👫 **ALL**) **Lombard Street** is a must on every driving itinerary. The 1000 block, commonly known as the "crookedest street in the world," has eight snakelike curves winding slowly down from Russian Hill—built to allow cars to negotiate its steep grade. Two blocks away is one of the city's two steepest streets, which run straight downhill: Filbert Street between Hyde and Leavenworth streets (31.5% grade). Like Lombard Street, you can drive down it, but not up.

🏠 *Lombard St. between Hyde and Leavenworth Sts.*

(👫 **6–15**) **Mission Dolores** (see Chapter 4), San Francisco's oldest building, has a fascinating old cemetery next to the chapel.

🏠 *16th and Dolores Sts., tel. 415/621–8203.*

(👫 **ALL**) **The Palace of Fine Arts,** a neoclassical Beaux Arts beauty built for the 1915 Panama-Pacific Exhibition, rises alongside a lovely tree-shaded lagoon in the Marina District. Kids can feed the ducks, then proceed inside to the **Exploratorium,** an outstanding hands-on science museum (see Museums, *below,* and Chapter 5).

🏠 *Baker St. off Marina Blvd.*

(👫 **3–15**) **The Sutro Baths,** below the Cliff House (see *above*), were once the largest indoor saltwater baths in the world. Today you can walk along the foundations (watch young kids carefully), gaze out at the Seal Rocks and the ocean, and set out on coastal hiking trails.

🏠 *Point Lobos Ave., below Cliff House, tel. 415/556–0560.*

Museums

(👫 **2–12**) **The Bay Area Discovery Museum** (see Chapter 5), across the Golden Gate Bridge in Marin County, is one of the top children's museums in the state.

🏠 *Fort Baker, 557 E. McReynolds Rd., Sausalito, tel. 415/487–4398.*

(👫 **3–15**) **The Cable Car Museum** (see Chapter 5) is where kids can discover the secrets of what makes the cable cars go.

🏠 *1201 Mason St., tel. 415/474–1887.*

(👫 **3–15**) **The California Academy of Sciences** (see Chapter 5), one of the world's largest natural science complexes, contains a natural history museum, an aquarium (see Aquariums, Zoos, and Wildlife, *below*), and a planetarium.

🏠 *Golden Gate Park, tel. 415/750–7145.*

(👫 **6–15**) **The California Palace of the Legion of Honor** (see Chapter 5) showcases European art in a gleaming, palacelike museum.

🏠 *Legion of Honor Dr., Lincoln Park, off 34th Ave. and Clement St., tel. 415/863–3330.*

(👫 **ALL**) **The Cartoon Art Museum** displays cartoons (from political cartoons to comic books to animation drawings) dating back to the early 18th century. Kids can look for original *Peanuts, Calvin and Hobbes,* or *Batman* strips and view animation cels from Bugs Bunny cartoons or from the Disney films ***Pinocchio, Snow White,*** and ***101 Dalmatians.***

🏠 *814 Mission St., tel. 415/227–8666. Admission: $5 adults, $3 students, $2 ages 6–12, ages 5 and under free. Open Wed.–Fri. 11–5, Sat. 10–5, Sun. 1–5.*

(👫 **6–15**) **The Chabot Observatory and Science Center,** which opens in the summer of 1999 in the Oakland hills, will contain the country's largest public telescope, a state-of-the-art planetarium, and an Omnimax theater. You'll also find hands-on science exhibits, a Virtual Science Center multimedia and online education facility, and a 6-acre environmental education area and nature trail.

🏠 *10902 Skyline Blvd., Oakland, tel. 510/530–3480. Call for admission prices and hrs.*

(👫 **3–15**) **Coyote Point Museum for Environmental Education** has live animals in realistic habitats: river otters, burrowing owls, porcupines, badgers, skunks, birds of prey, toads, kingsnakes, lizards, bobcats—even lowly banana slugs. Located in a bayside park about 2 miles south of San Francisco airport (see Parks, *below*), the museum also contains computer games and displays that illustrate the redwood forests, grasslands, and other major ecosystems of the Bay Area.

🏛 *1651 Coyote Point Dr., San Mateo, tel. 650/342–7755. Admission: $3 adults, $2 ages 13–17, $1 ages 4–12; free 1st Wed. of month; park admission, $4. Open Tues.–Sat 10–5, Sun. noon–5.*

👥 2 – 15 **The Exploratorium** (see Chapter 5), one of the world's top science museums, contains 650 hands-on exhibits.
🏛 *3601 Lyon St., tel. 415/561–0360.*

👥 6 – 15 **Fort Mason Center** (tel. 415/ 979–3010), the hub of the Golden Gate National Recreation Area, contains several small museums: the **Mexican Museum** (Bldg. D., tel. 415/441–0404; $3 adults, $2 students, under 10 free) has the country's top collection of Mexican art; the **Museo Italo Americano** (Bldg. C, tel. 415/673–2200; $2 adults, $1 students, ages 12 and under free) exhibits the works of Italian-American artists; and the **San Francisco Craft and Folk Art Museum** (Bldg. A north, tel. 415/ 775–0990; $3 adults, $1 ages 12–17) displays American folk art and crafts.
🏛 *Marina Blvd. and Buchanan St.*

👥 3 – 15 **The International Children's Art Museum,** which opened in 1995, was the first in the country devoted to children's art from around the world. You'll see only a small part of the museum's collection on display; it includes more than 4,000 artworks from more than 100 countries. Kids who come here can create their own art as well; one room, the Studio, has art supplies out every day, and, on Saturdays, drop-in art workshops. Some of the work may then be displayed at the museum.
🏛 *World Trade Center, Suite 103, Ferry Building, The Embarcadero, tel. 415/772– 9977. Admission: $1 adults, 50¢ ages 18 and under. Open Mon.–Fri. 11–5, Sat. 10–4.*

👥 3 – 15 **The Lawrence Hall of Science** (see Chapter 5) across the bay is another museum loaded with interactive displays.
🏛 *Centennial Dr., Berkeley, tel. 510/642– 5132.*

👥 2 – 15 **The Lindsay Museum** (see Chapter 5) displays local animals being treated for injuries in creative settings resembling their natural habitats.
🏛 *Larkey Park, 1931 1st Ave., Walnut Creek, tel. 925/935–1978.*

👥 6 – 15 **The M.H. de Young Memorial Museum** (tel. 415/863–3330) and the adjacent **Asian Art Museum** (tel. 415/379– 8801) are two of the city's top art museums, focusing in turn on American art and Asian art (see Chapter 5).
🏛 *Tea Garden Dr., off 8th Ave. and John F. Kennedy Dr., Golden Gate Park.*

👥 3 – 15 **The Museum of Children's Art,** near Jack London Square in Oakland, is similar to San Francisco's International Children's Art Museum (see *above*), letting kids see art created by children, both local and from abroad. The museum has plenty of art supplies on hand so that kids can produce their own minimasterpieces.
🏛 *560 2nd St., Oakland, tel. 510/465– 8770. Admission free; kids' open studios, $3. Open Mon.–Sat. 10–5, Sun. noon–5.*

👥 6 – 15 **The National Maritime Museum,** whose art deco structure itself resembles a ship, displays an extensive collection of ship models, relics, photos, and maps that chronicle West Coast maritime history.
🏛 *Aquatic Park at foot of Polk St., tel. 415/ 556–3002. Admission free (donations accepted). Open daily 10–5.*

👥 6 – 15 **The Oakland Museum of California** (see Chapter 5) contains comprehensive displays on California history, art, and ecology.
🏛 *1000 Oak St., Oakland, tel. 510/238– 2200 or 888/625–6873.*

👥 3 – 15 **The Randall Museum,** overlooking the city in Corona Heights Park, is a small children's museum chock full of intriguing hands-on nature and science exhibits, plus Saturday drop-in art workshops, and a live animal room where kids can see owls, snakes, and raccoons up close. Young kids especially like the petting corral, where they can stroke rabbits and ducks.

🏛 *199 Museum Way, tel. 415/554–9600. Admission free. Open Tues.–Sat 10–5.*

(👫 8 – 15) The **San Francisco Bay Model** is a 1½-acre, three-dimensional scale model of San Francisco Bay (operated by the U.S. Army Corps of Engineers), which looks something like a cross between a science experiment and a huge work of modern art. Hands-on exhibits and videos help explain the bay's natural history, wildlife, and geology, and you can walk around on ramps to survey the "lay of the land." The most interesting time to view the model is when simulated bay tides are flowing over it; call for times.

🏛 *2100 Bridgeway, Sausalito, tel. 415/332–3871. Admission free. Open Tues.–Fri. 9–4, Sat. 10–6.*

(👫 6 – 15) The **San Francisco Fire Department Museum** displays a collection of horse-drawn fire wagons and early fire engines, along with other vintage equipment (pumps, buckets, uniforms) and historic photographs.

🏛 *655 Presidio Ave., tel. 415/558–3546 or 415/563–4630. Admission free. Open Thurs.–Sun. 1–4.*

(👫 9 – 15) The **San Francisco Museum of Modern Art** (see Chapter 5) showcases contemporary painting and sculpture in its spectacular quarters near Yerba Buena Gardens.

🏛 *151 3rd St., tel. 415/357–4000.*

(👫 6 – 15) The **Wells Fargo History Museum,** in a downtown bank, displays gold nuggets and other Gold Rush mementos, and contains a re-created Wells Fargo office and a century-old stagecoach that once carried passengers from St. Louis to San Francisco. On the upper floor, kids can climb on a cutaway stagecoach seat and play driver.

🏛 *420 Montgomery St., tel. 415/396–2619. Admission free. Open weekdays 9–5. Closed bank holidays.*

Aquariums, Zoos, and Wildlife

(👫👫 10 – 15) The **Farallon National Wildlife Refuge** (see Chapter 6), on the offshore Farallon Islands, offers sightings by boat of seabirds, sea lions, dolphins, and whales.

🏛 *Oceanic Society Expeditions, tel. 415/474–3385.*

(👫👫 3 – 15) The **Marine Mammal Center** in the Marin Headlands lets kids visit rescued sea lions, seals, and sea otters who are injured, sick, or orphaned. Displays focus on marine life and ecology.

🏛 *Marin Headlands, about a 10-min drive north and west of Golden Gate Bridge (call for directions), tel. 415/289–7325. Admission free. Open daily 10–4.*

(👫👫 ALL) The **Oakland Zoo** (see Chapter 6) presents siamangs, giraffes, and elephants in naturalistic habitats. There's also a Children's Zoo, a minitrain, and a carousel.

🏛 *Golf Links Rd., Knowland Park, Oakland, tel. 510/632–9525.*

(👫👫 6 – 15) The **Richardson Bay Audubon Center** is an 11-acre bird and wildlife sanctuary situated along 900 acres of tidal wetlands in Marin County. The best months for viewing migrating birds are October through March. Stop at center headquarters for free self-guided nature trail maps.

🏛 *376 Greenwood Beach Rd., Tiburon (call for directions), tel. 415/388–2524. Admission: $2 adults, $1 under 16. Open Wed.–Sun. 9–5.*

(👫👫 6 – 15) The **San Francisco Bay National Wildlife Refuge** (see Chapter 6) has 25 miles of shoreline for spotting migratory birds and harbor seals.

🏛 *South of Dumbarton Bridge toll plaza, Fremont, tel. 510/792–0222.*

(👫👫 ALL) The **San Francisco Zoo** (see Chapter 6) is the largest in Northern California, with an excellent Children's Zoo and Primate Discovery Center.

🏛 *Sloat Blvd. and 45th Ave., tel. 415/753–7080.*

👫 ALL The **Steinhart Aquarium** (see Chapter 6), part of the California Academy of Sciences complex (see Museums, *above*), is one of the state's top aquariums.
🏨 *Golden Gate Park, tel. 415/750–7145.*

👫 ALL **UnderWater World** at Pier 39 (see Chapter 6) takes visitors for diver's-eye views of sharks, rays, and other local aquatic life.
🏨 *Beach St. and The Embarcadero, tel. 415/ 623–5300 or 888/732–3483.*

Ethnic Neighborhoods

👫 ALL **Chinatown,** one of the largest Chinese communities outside Asia, can be a magical place for kids: neon signs, pagoda roofs, dragon-entwined lampposts, and shops packed with strange-looking herbs. Chinatown today is a colorful jumble of restaurants, teahouses, temples, souvenir shops, and produce markets. See the area on foot (don't drive—the streets are crowded and parking is very tight). Beyond the dragon-crowned gate on Bush Street is Grant Avenue, the main thoroughfare, lined with bazaars, restaurants, and curio shops. Stockton Street, parallel to Grant, is where most Chinese shop for produce and fresh fish. Along narrow streets like Hang Ah, Spofford Lane, and Ross Alley you can hear the click of mah-jongg tiles, the whir of sewing machines, and the clinking of tea-cups. Don't miss the **Golden Gate Fortune Cookie Factory** (see Serendipities, *below*). At any of the numerous herb shops in the area kids can ogle dried lizards and other exotic herbs and medicinals. You can also visit the oldest Buddhist temple in the United States, the **Tin How Temple** (125 Waverly Pl., open daily 10–4). **The Chinese Culture Center** in the Holiday Inn at 750 Kearny Street (tel. 415/986–1822, admission free, open Tues.–Sun. 10–4) presents small exhibitions; it's fun to walk over Kearny via the footbridge. At **Portsmouth Square,** across from the Holiday Inn, old men play cards while children romp in the playground. Hungry? Pick up a snack of almond cookies

or steamed pork buns at a Chinese bakery, or stop for dim sum (filled dumplings and other small dishes, chosen from carts that are wheeled from table to table) at **New Asia** (772 Pacific Ave., tel. 415/391–6666) or **Pearl City** (641 Jackson St., tel. 415/398–8383). For a full dinner, try the Cantonese seafood at the **Great Eastern Restaurant** (649 Jackson St., tel. 415/986–2500). During **Chinese New Year** (usually in February), don't miss the spectacular Chinese New Year Parade (see Chapter 3).
🏨 *Bounded by Bush, Broadway, Stockton, and Kearny Sts, tel. 415/982–6306.*

👫 ALL **Japantown** is the focal point for San Francisco's 12,000 citizens of Japanese descent, who first settled this area after the 1906 earthquake. Its commercial heart is the **Japan Center,** a three-block complex of shops, restaurants, hotels, movie theaters, a bowling alley, and more. This place is fun for kids to wander around, eyeing the plastic food displays in restaurant windows or shopping for CDs. If you're hungry, stop for noodles at **Mifune** (Kintetsu Mall, 1737 Post St., tel. 415/922–0337), which has children's plates; or at **Isobune Sushi** (Kintetsu Mall, 1737 Post St., tel. 415/563–1030), where you can pluck the sushi of your choice from little boats as they float around the counter (but make sure your kids eat what they pluck). Highlight of the year is the **Cherry Blossom Festival** every April (see Chapter 3).
🏨 *Bounded by Geary Blvd. and Fillmore, Laguna, and Bush Sts., tel. 415/922–6776.*

👫 ALL The **Mission District,** the heavily Hispanic, often sunny area lying south of Civic Center and east of Twin Peaks (Mission and 24th streets are the main thoroughfares), moves primarily to a Latin beat. The burrito and taco are king, salsa music is everywhere, and streets are lined with Mexican and Salvadoran restaurants, bakeries, and shops—as well as the city's oldest and most atmospheric soda fountain, the **St. Francis Fountain and Candy Store,** at 2801 24th St., tel. 415/ 826–4200. Sights include historic **Mission Dolores** (see Historic Sites, *above*) and hundreds of brilliantly colored outdoor murals. The best mural-viewing is at little **Balmy Alley** off 24th Street between Harrison and Treat streets, where dozens of them adorn walls, garage doors, and fences (for a guided tour or walking map of the murals, call 415/ 285–2287). Annual Mission District highlights include the **Cinco de Mayo** festival in early May and, Memorial Day weekend, the colorful **Carnaval** parade (see Chapter 3). 🏠 *Bounded by Potrero Ave. and 16th, Dolores, Cesar Chavez (Army) Sts.*

(👫 **ALL**) **North Beach** hasn't been a beach for more than a century; thanks to landfill, it now rests in a valley between Russian and Telegraph hills, Chinatown and Fisherman's Wharf. Italian fishermen settled here in the late 19th century to be near what were then the docks, and Italian remains the dominant ethnic flavor. Family-style restaurants, pizza parlors, Italian delis, and colorful Washington Square (see Parks, *below*) lure families here, and lively, cosmopolitan North Beach contains more cafés, restaurants, and nightspots per square inch than any other part of the city. The corner of Broadway and Columbus is the major intersection. 🏠 *Bounded by Broadway, Kearny, Francisco, and Taylor Sts.*

Parks, Gardens, and Playgrounds

Angel Island State Park, the bay's largest island, is a forested gem right in the middle of this huge urban area. The fun begins with a 40-minute ferry ride to the island (boats leave from San Francisco's Pier 41; the round-trip fare is $10 for adults, $9 for ages 12 to 18, $5.50 for ages 5 to 11). You can also leave weekends from Tiburon in the North Bay (21 Main St., tel. 415/435–2131; $6 adults, $4 ages 5 to 11, ages 4 and under [one per adult] free, $1 per bike), which is a shorter boat ride. All ferry tickets include the park admission fee. A former Civil War fort and immigration station, Angel Island was once known as the "Ellis Island of the

West." You can visit long-abandoned barracks where Asian immigrants were detained for months, even years during the early 20th century; in all, 100 historic structures remain on the island. Near the ferry dock is a grassy cove with a small beach, and picnic areas; many families simply spread out blankets here and enjoy the day. But the island contains miles of hiking and biking trails, including the paved 5-mile Perimeter Road, which has views of some of the island's old gun mounts and historic structures. Allow 2½ hours to hike it, or take the 50-minute narrated tram ride along part of the road. You can also bike it; either bring your own bikes, or, from April to October, rent them on the island for $10 per hour or $25 per day. The North Ridge Trail and the Sunset Trail take hikers to the heights of the island, for panoramic bay views (allow 2½ hours round-trip for this fairly steep climb). Angel island also has nine hike-in campsites (tel. 800/444–7275 for reservations; $7– $11 per night). *Box 866, Tiburon 94920, tel. 415/435–1915 or 415/705–5555 (ferry). Open daily 8 AM–sunset.*

Aquatic Park, below the National Maritime Museum (see Museums, *above*), is a good place to escape the hubbub of nearby Fisherman's Wharf. Kids can wade in the water at a small, sandy beach; the Municipal Pier beckons anglers and provides great bay views; and the gorgeous Golden Gate Promenade sets off on a 3-mile paved trail to the Golden Gate Bridge. *Foot of Polk St., tel. 415/556—3002.*

Coyote Point Park, south of San Francisco in San Mateo, is a popular all-purpose family destination, with hiking trails, picnic areas, playgrounds, a marina, a summer swimming beach, and a highly regarded nature museum (see Museums, *above*). *Bay side of Hwy. 101, San Mateo, tel. 650/573–2592. Park admission: $4/car.*

The Filbert and Greenwich Street Steps, which together form a little-known but classic corner of San Francisco, parallel each other as they lead down toward the bay from the east side of Telegraph Hill. The steep steps are flanked by gardens and secluded homes and provide great views. Going up can be a chore; going down is much easier. *Filbert St. and Greenwich St. between Montgomery and Sansome Sts.*

The Golden Gate National Recreation Area (GGNRA; see Chapter 8) includes Alcatraz, Fort Point, the Cliff House, the Golden Gate Promenade, the Marin Headlands, and much more. *Information center, Fort Mason, Bldg. 201, tel. 415/556–0560.*

Golden Gate Park, one of America's most beautiful urban parks (not to be confused with the GGNRA, *above*), is a "don't miss" family attraction. Allot at least a full day here if you can. Pick up a park map at **McLaren Lodge** (Stanyan and Fell Sts., open weekdays 8–5), where you can also get a Golden Gate Park Explorer Pass ($12.50 per person) for adult admission to several museums and the Japanese Tea Garden, plus other discounts. Most attractions are clustered in the eastern half of the 3-mile-long park, including some of the city's top museums—the **Asian Art Museum, the de Young,** and **the California Academy of Sciences** (see Museums, *above*). Down the road from the museums on Tea Garden Drive is the lovely **Japanese Tea Garden** (tel. 415/752–1171; $3.50 adults, $1.25 ages 6–12, under 6 free, open daily), with arched bridges, koi fish ponds, a Zen garden, a bronze Buddha, a towering red pagoda, and a pavilion that serves tea and fortune cookies (the fortune cookie was reputedly invented here). Across the road from it is **Strybing Arboretum and Botanical Gardens** (tel. 415/661–1316; admission free, open daily), where flowers, redwoods, cacti, and other flora from around the world can be found; don't miss the duck pond near the entrance. Up Martin Luther King Jr. Drive is pretty **Stow Lake** (tel. 415/752–0347), where you can rent boats, feed ducks, and picnic. Cross footbridges to hilly Strawberry Island, in the middle of the lake, and hike to the top for great city views; you can peer over the crest of Huntington Falls, which plunge 125 feet from the hilltop into the

lake. Other attractions nearby include the **Rhododendron Dell,** which blazes with color in spring, and the **Conservatory of Flowers,** a Victorian greenhouse closed for several years due to severe wind damage; renovations may take years, but the outdoor flower gardens are kept up. In the southeast corner, the **Children's Playground** (off Kezar or Bowling Green Dr.) has loads of swings, slides, and climbing structures, and the adjacent 1912 **Herschell-Spillman Carousel** ($1 a ride for adults, 25¢ ages 12 and under) has 62 hand-carved animals—not only horses but zebras, roosters, and frogs. The park's western half is more woodsy and pastoral; toward the ocean (along Kennedy Dr.) you can visit a herd of bison, and hike, bike, or stroll along quiet tree-lined trails. *Bounded by Fulton and Stanyan Sts., Lincoln Way, and Great Hwy., tel. 415/831–2700.*

Huntington Park, on the top of Nob Hill, has a well-kept playground for small children. *California and Taylor Sts.*

Julius Kahn Playground is a cypress-shaded park on the edge of the Presidio, with climbing structures, slides, tennis courts, a softball field, and plenty of green grass for picnics. *W. Pacific Ave. and Spruce St.*

Lafayette Park in upscale Pacific Heights contains four square blocks of grass perfect for sunbathing and Frisbee tossing. There's a small playground here for kids. *Bounded by Gough, Sacramento, Washington, and Laguna Sts.*

Lakeside Park is a "must" stop for families in the East Bay. The 120-acre park is surrounded on three sides by Lake Merritt, a natural saltwater lake that was the country's first state game refuge. Playgrounds, gardens, waterfowl feeding areas, and the delightful Children's Fairyland theme park (see Chapter 9) provide fun; you can also rent small boats. *Grand and Bellevue Aves., Oakland, tel. 510/444–3807.*

The Marina Green is one of San Francisco's prettiest parks, a wide stretch of grass and bayside walkways that's popular with kite-flyers, joggers, Rollerbladers, bicyclists, sun-bathers, and volleyball players. It borders a marina harboring hundreds of pleasure boats. *Marina Blvd. between Baker and Buchanan Sts.*

Muir Woods (see Chapter 7), 12 miles north of the Golden Gate Bridge, is the state's most heavily visited redwood park. *North on U.S. 101 to Hwy. 1, Hwy. 1 to Panoramic Hwy., Panoramic Hwy. to Muir Woods Rd., tel. 415/388–2595.*

Point Reyes National Seashore (see Chapter 8) has great hiking, wildlife viewing, secluded beaches, a replica of an Indian village, and close-up views of an earthquake fault. *Hwy. 1 north to Sir Francis Drake Hwy., then Bear Valley Rd., tel. 415/663–1092.*

The Presidio, a longtime military base occupying a choice site overlooking the Golden Gate, is now a national park. Full conversion to park uses will take several more years, but the Presidio already contains miles of hiking and biking roads and trails, winding through cypress and eucalyptus groves, along coastal bluffs, and past historic buildings and defense installations (for one of them, Fort Point, see Historic Sites, *above*). At the Presidio Army Museum (Lincoln Blvd. and Funston Ave., tel. 415/561–4331; admission free, open Wed.–Sun 10–4), you can see two cottages that housed homeless survivors of the 1906 earthquake. An off-beat site that might interest kids is the **Pet Cemetery** near the stables, where Presidio families buried their cats and dogs; follow Lincoln Boulevard to McDowell Street. *Entrances at Lombard and Lyon, Presidio and Pacific, Arguello and West Pacific, and many coastal points, tel. 415/556–0560.*

Tilden Park is the East Bay's answer to Golden Gate Park, with an abundance of recreation and picnic areas amid its 2,000 acres of grassy lawns, rolling hills and eucalyptus groves. For kids, there's a 1911 carousel, ponies, and a miniature steam train to ride. At the **Little Farm** kids can pet and feed pygmy goats, sheep, and rabbits. **Lake Anza** has a sandy beach that's very popular for swimming in summer; the beach area and the water are generally sun-warmed but sheltered from the wind by hills. Tilden also has numerous woodsy hiking trails; the park's Environmental Education Center has hiking and nature programs for kids year-round. *Grizzly Peak Blvd. to Canyon Dr., Shasta Rd., or South Park Dr., Berkeley, tel. 510/562–7275.*

Washington Square, a green plaza in the heart of North Beach (see Ethnic Neighborhoods, *above*), is crowned at one end by beautiful Sts. Peter and Paul Church. On sunny Sunday afternoons families spread out blankets on the grass and let the kids run around while parents read the paper with a café latte. *Bounded by Powell, Union, Stockton, and Filbert Sts.*

Yerba Buena Gardens, a showplace park in the South of Market area, is a place to relax among well-tended flower gardens, green grass, and cafés. The Martin Luther King Jr. Memorial Fountain includes a 50-foot-wide, 20-foot-high waterfall that kids can scamper behind. *Bounded by Mission, 3rd, 4th, and Folsom Sts.*

The long-awaited **Rooftop@Yerba Buena Gardens** opened in 1998 atop the roof of Moscone Convention Center. The area has something for almost every kid (and parents, too), ranging from rides and sports to educational activities. A 1906-vintage Looff carousel ($1 per ride, open Wed.–Sun. noon–6), which whirled at San Francisco's long-defunct Playland-at-the-Beach, has been restored and is whirling once again. The Zeum (tel. 415/777–2800, admission $7 adults, $5 ages 5–18, under 5 free, open Wed.–Fri. noon–6, Sat.–Sun, 11–5), a high-tech arts studio, offers hands-on experiences in the visual, media, and performing arts. There's also an NHL-size public Ice Skating Center with city skyline views (see Sports, *below*), a bowling alley, a child development center (for neighborhood kids only), and 3 acres of landscaped grounds. *4th, Howard, and Folsom Sts.*

Beaches

Don't come to San Francisco for swimming—the water is cold and often rough—but the city's beaches are fine for sand play, sunbathing (when it's not foggy), splashing along shore, picnicking, and watching the waves come in. Cross a bridge to Marin County or the East Bay for sunnier skies and warmer, calmer waters. Here are some of the area's best for families:

Baker Beach, a mile-long, secluded stretch of sand with wonderful views of the Marin Headlands and Golden Gate Bridge, is popular for sand play, sunbathing, picnicking, and surf fishing. The surf is rough and swimming is dangerous here. *Lincoln Blvd. to Bowley St. and Gibson Rd., tel. 415/556–0560. Rest rooms, changing rooms.*

China Beach, on a secluded cove in the exclusive Sea Cliff area southwest of Baker Beach, is one of the few places in San Francisco where the surf is usually gentle enough for swimming. *End of Sea Cliff Ave., off 25th Ave., tel. 415/556–8371. Showers, changing rooms, sundeck; lifeguards mid-Apr.–mid-Oct.*

Crown Beach requires a trip to Alameda in the East Bay, but it's worth it to find a safe, warm stretch of sandy beach for swimming in the bay. The water near the shore is shallow enough for young kids to wade in, and there's grass for picnics and barbecues. *1231 McKay St., Alameda, tel. 510/635–0135. Parking: $3.*

Heart's Desire Beach is one of our family's favorites. This secluded, wind-sheltered sandy cove near Point Reyes National Seashore has generally calm bay waters, lagoons for wading, picnic tables, and hiking trails. *Tomales Bay State Park, Sir Francis Drake Blvd. to Pierce Point Rd., then 1.3 mi to park entrance, tel. 415/669–1140. Parking: $5. Rest rooms, changing rooms.*

McNear's Beach on San Pablo Bay in Marin County is very popular for families with young children. A sandy beach, a swimming pool with lifeguards, picnic sites, plenty of grass, a fishing pier, and snack bar are among the draws. *Hwy. 101 to Central San Rafael exit, then east on 2nd St., which becomes San Pedro Rd., to Cantera Way, tel. 415/499–6387. Admission: $7 per car weekends, $5 weekdays.*

Ocean Beach stretches for 3 miles along the ocean edge of the city, across the Great Highway from Golden Gate Park. Expert surfers ride the waves here below the Cliff House, but swimming can be treacherous. Bicyclists and joggers love the long stretch of sidewalk along the beach. In summer Ocean Beach is often foggy, windy, and chilly. *Great Hwy. between Cliff House and Sloat Blvd., tel. 415/556–8371.*

Stinson Beach, along the Marin County coast below Mount Tamalpais, is usually packed on sunny summer weekends, when San Francisco may be fogged in. Three-mile-long, white-sand Stinson is often suitable for both swimming and surfing, though average water temperatures are a brisk 58°F. *U.S. 101 north to Hwy. 1, then drive about 15 mi, tel. 415/868–0942. Rest rooms, changing rooms, snack bar, picnic areas; lifeguards late May–mid-Sept.*

Serendipities

(👫 **ALL**) A California sea lion colony that took up residence on K-dock, on the northwest side of Pier 39 has been delighting onlookers for more than a decade. The number of pinnipeds ranges from 10 to 600, depending on time of year; winter is best, summer slimmest); free guided talks are given on weekends from noon to 4 PM by docents from Marin County's Marine Mammal Center.

(👫 **3–15**) The Golden Gate Fortune Cookie Factory (56 Ross Alley, tel. 415/781–3956) in Chinatown lets kids watch the dough being folded into cookies—and discover the secret of how the fortunes get inside. You can buy some cookies to munch on, but take heed: Some bags contain X-rated fortunes.

👫 3–15 **San Francisco Fountain,** on the front steps of the Grand Hyatt Hotel (345 Stockton St., Union Square), depicts landmarks kids may already have seen around the city—Chinatown, the Golden Gate Bridge, the cable car turnaround—plus Snoopy on his doghouse, Superman flying, and characters from the Wizard of Oz. Dozens of children helped sculptor Ruth Asawa complete the work, which was originally molded from bread dough.

👫 ALL **Spreckels Lake,** toward the western end of Golden Gate Park (Spreckels Lake Dr. off 36th Ave.), is where a local club sails elaborate model boats, fashioned after battleships or historic boats like the *Bounty* or the *African Queen.* Sunday has the most action; powerboats get the nod in the morning, sailboats in the afternoon. Kids may spot turtles in the lake here, too.

👫 3–15 **The Wave Organ,** an unusual structure in the Marina, creates "natural music" made by waves as they funnel through pipes from the breakwater into the bay. Come at high tide for the best effect. There are lots of rocks for kids to climb on while parents relax on the stone steps and enjoy views of yachts and the city skyline. 🏠 *Eastern tip of breakwater that forms Marina Small Craft Harbor; follow path past St. Francis Yacht Club.*

👫 3–15 Outside glass elevators at the **Westin St. Francis Hotel** (see Where to Stay, *below*) zoom nonstop to the 32nd floor, offering great views of San Francisco and plenty of thrills for kids (the elevators are fast—and the trip down is really a rush). Head for the "Tower Elevators" for one of the great free rides in the city. 🏠 *335 Powell St., tel. 415/397–7000.*

Sports

Big Leagues

3Com Park at Candlestick Point will be home to the **San Francisco Giants** baseball team

(tel. 415/467–8000) until they move into new Pacific Bell Park along the bay at China Basin in the year 2000. 3Com is also home to the **San Francisco 49ers** football team (tel. 415/468–2249), who will move to a new stadium early in the 21st century. The **Oakland A's** (tel. 510/638–0500) play baseball and the **Oakland Raiders** (tel. 510/615–1888 or 510/ 762–2277 for tickets) play football at the Oakland Coliseum; the **Golden State Warriors** (tel. 510/762–2277 for tickets) play basketball at the Oakland Coliseum Arena. The **San Jose Sharks** (tel. 408/287–7070) play hockey at the San Jose Arena.

Outdoor and Indoor Action

BICYCLING. Despite all its hills, San Francisco provides good bike routes, even for beginners. Start at **Golden Gate Park,** where John F. Kennedy Drive is off-limits to cars on Sunday, providing miles of wide road for cycling. (Watch out for Rollerbladers.) On other days, plenty of roads in the park get little traffic, especially near the ocean. We like to ride down to **Ocean Beach** (see Beaches, *above*), where a wide 3-mile sidewalk fronts the sands and a bike trail runs along the eastern side of the Great Highway. Past Sloat Boulevard, the trail leads to **Lake Merced,** which is circled by a 5-mile sidewalk. Rent bikes near Golden Gate Park at **Park Cyclery** (1749 Waller St., tel. 415/ 751–7368) or **Golden Gate Park Skate and Bike** (3038 Fulton St., tel. 415/668–1117).

Other great places to ride in the city include the flat sidewalks of the **Marina Green** and **Golden Gate Promenade**; for a hillier challenge tackle the **Presidio,** which has 15 miles of bike routes winding through the forests. (See Parks, *above*.) Rent bikes near Marina Green at **American Bicycle Rental** (2715 Hyde St., tel. 415/931–0234). Our favorite biking expedition is across the **Golden Gate Bridge,** an unforgettable 1.7-mile ride. (The east walkway is open to cyclists on weekdays, the west walkway on weekends.) If we're really feeling energetic, we continue to Sausalito in Marin County (follow the bike lane at the end of the Vista Point parking lot to Alexander Ave., which winds into Sausalito). Kids should be experienced riders for this one because they'll be sharing the road with cars.

For mountain bikers, the ultimate test is **Mount Tamalpais State Park** (see Chapter 10 for details).

For information about bike routes, contact the **San Francisco Recreation and Park Department** (tel. 415/831–2700).

BOATING. **Stow Lake** (tel. 415/752–0347) in Golden Gate Park has rowboat, pedal boat, and electric boat rentals. The lake is open daily for boating; call for seasonal hours. Also within the city, **Lake Merced,** bounded by Lake Merced Boulevard, John Muir Drive, and Skyline Boulevard, has rowboat and pedal boat rentals (tel. 415/753–1101). Oakland's **Lake Merritt** (tel. 510/444–3807) is the East Bay small-boating capital, with excellent learn-to-sail lessons, plus rentals of paddleboats and rowboats.

San Francisco Bay offers year-round sailing; see Chapter 10 for details.

FISHING. The best lake fishing within the city limits is at **Lake Merced** (bounded by Lake Merced Blvd., John Muir Dr., and Skyline Blvd.), where the waters are stocked with trout. The Lake Merced Boating and Fishing Co. (tel. 415/753–1101) rents equipment. The best fishing in the Bay Area, though, is at the East Bay's **San Pablo Reservoir** (San Pablo Dam Rd. between the towns of El Sobrante and Orinda, tel. 510/223–1661), a large lake stocked with hundreds of thousands of trout and catfish each year. You can fish from shore or rent a boat and equipment; fishing licenses are available.

You can cast a line from the **San Francisco Municipal Pier** at Aquatic Park (see Parks, *above*); or at the **Golden Gate Park Fly-Casting Pools,** west of the bison paddock near Kennedy Drive.

For information on deep-sea fishing, see Chapter 10.

GOLF. The 9-hole, par-3 course in **Golden Gate Park** (47th Ave. at Fulton St., tel. 415/751–8987) is great for beginners; it's first-come, first-served. **Lincoln Park** (34th Ave. and Clement St., tel. 415/221–9911) is one of the most beautiful public golf courses anywhere, 18 holes that lie along the Golden Gate.

HIKING. Within the city, the **Presidio** (see Parks, *above*) is laced with more than 10 miles of hiking trails through forests and along creeks and coastal bluffs. The **Golden Gate National Recreation Area** (see Parks, *above,* and Chapter 8) also contains wonderful hiking trails above the water all the way from the Golden Gate Bridge to Land's End; ask for information at Fort Mason Center or the Cliff House. **Angel Island** and **Point Reyes National Seashore** (see Parks, *above*) are great hiking spots outside the city.

Mount Tamalpais State Park is the best hiking spot in the Bay Area; dozens of trails lead to redwoods, waterfalls, and panoramic views. We like to picnic on the south side of the mountain, overlooking San Francisco and the Golden Gate, then drive up to the East Peak parking lot ($5) and hike the easy Verna Dunshee Trail, which loops the 2,600-foot peak and has wonderful views of the entire Bay Area and beyond. A snack bar, rest rooms, and visitors center are at the trailhead. *U.S. 101 north to Shoreline Hwy., exit at Panoramic Hwy. and follow signs, tel. 415/388–2070.*

HORSEBACK RIDING. Golden Gate Park contains 12 miles of equestrian trails, and **Golden Gate Park Stables** (Kennedy Dr. and 36th Ave., near the Polo Field, tel. 415/668–7360) offers lessons, guided one-hour trail rides, and pony rides (ages 1 and up). Outside the city, two jointly run stables along Highway 1 a mile north of Half Moon Bay (south of San Francisco) have rentals for beach rides: **Friendly Acres Ranch** (2150 N. Cabrillo Hwy.) and **Sea Horse Ranch** (1828 N. Cabrillo Hwy.); tel. 650/726–8550 for both. Near Point Reyes in Marin County, try **Five Brooks** (Hwy. 1, Olema, tel. 415/663–1570).

ICE SKATING. The Ice Skating Center at Yerba Buena Gardens (750 Folsom St., between 3rd and 4th Sts., tel. 415/777–3727) is San Francisco's only public rink open year-round (from 1 to 5 daily). The fee is $6 for adults, $4.50 for kids, skate rentals are $2.50 additional. **Berkeley Iceland** (2727 Milvia St., Berkeley, tel. 510/843–8800), **Oakland Ice Center** (519 18th St., Oakland, tel. 510/268–9000), and **Belmont Iceland** (815 Old County Rd., Belmont, tel. 650/592–0532) are other large Bay Area rinks open year-round. Outdoor ice rinks are open seasonally in winter at the Embarcadero Center and at Union Square.

KAYAKING. See Chapter 10.

KITE-FLYING. The top spot for kite-flying in the city is the **Marina Green** (see Parks, above). You can buy exotic kites from around the world at **Kite Flite** (Pier 39, tel. 415/956–3181).

ROLLERBLADING. Throngs of in-line skaters join the bicyclists in **Golden Gate Park,** especially on Sunday, when Kennedy Drive is closed to cars. At 6th Avenue and Fulton Street there's a flat, multipurpose paved area where flashy skaters gather to do jumps and tricks to music. Rent equipment at **Skates on Haight** (1818 Haight St., near Stanyan St. entrance, tel. 415/752–8375) or **Golden Gate Park Skate and Bike** (3038 Fulton St., tel. 415/668–1117). A good area for beginners is the **Marina Green,** which offers an easy, flat, 1½-mile round-trip with gorgeous bay views; **Marina Skate and Snowboard** (2271 Chestnut St., tel. 415/567–8400) rents skates and protective gear.

SURFING. See Chapter 10.

SWIMMING. In the East Bay there's good summertime swimming at **Lake Temescal** (Hwys. 13 and 24, tel. 510/635–0135), where you'll find a sandy beach, warm water, and a roped-off area for kids. The city of San Francisco (tel. 415/831–2700) runs one outdoor swimming pool—the **Mission Pool** (19th St. at Linda St., open summers only)—and eight indoor pools, including the popular **Rossi Pool** (Arguello Blvd. and Anza St.) and **Sava Pool** (19th Ave. at Wawona St.)

TENNIS. The city maintains 130 free tennis courts; the largest set, with six courts, is at **Dolores Park** (18th and Dolores Sts.) in the Mission District. **Golden Gate Park** has 21 public courts, where 90 minutes' play costs $4–$6; call 415/753–7001 for weekend and evening reservations.

WINDSURFING. Brightly colored sailboards dot the bay off **Crissy Beach** near the Golden Gate Bridge, but the big waves here are strictly for experts. Beginners can learn on mild **Lake Merced** (tel. 415/753–1101) or at Oakland's **Lake Merritt** (tel. 510/444–3807). Alameda's **Crown Beach** (see Beaches, above) is a popular East Bay spot for windsurfing. **Lake Del Valle,** in Del Valle Regional Park south of Livermore (call for directions, tel. 925/373–0332, parking $4 per car), is one of the top spots in the Bay Area for water sports; besides windsurfing, this reservoir has fishing, boating, and summertime swimming at two lifeguarded beaches.

Shops

The Fisherman's Wharf area is host to four major shopping centers: Pier 39, Ghirardelli Square, The Cannery, and The Anchorage. All have pay parking garages (Wharf traffic is brutal) and all keep kids entertained with performers such as magicians, musicians, and jugglers, starting around noon.

Pier 39 (Embarcadero, near foot of Powell St., tel. 415/981–7437) is one of San Francisco's top attractions in its own right. Among the 100 or so shops are those selling puppets and other toys, kites, San Francisco memorabilia, and chocolate. Shops open daily at 10:30 AM. The 1,000-foot pier also has wonderful bay views, a resident herd of sea lions (see Serendipities, *above*), a double-deck carousel, turbo rides, a games arcade (see Entertainments, *below*), and the UnderWater World aquarium (see Aquariums, *above*, and Chapter 6). Finding a place to eat isn't a problem: Try the Alcatraz Cafe and Grill (tel. 415/434–1818), the historic Eagle Cafe (tel. 415/433–3689), or a number of snack shops such as the Burger Cafe or the Boudin Sourdough French Bread outlet. Restaurants open at 11:30 AM daily. Originally a chocolate factory, **Ghirardelli Square** (Northpoint and Larkin Sts., tel. 415/775–5500) entices kids with the Ghirardelli Chocolate Manufactory (tel. 415/474–3938), where the soda fountain turns out bounteous ice cream/chocolate concoctions. **The Cannery** (Leavenworth, Beach, Hyde, and Jefferson Sts., tel. 415/771–3112) began life as the world's largest fruit-canning plant; among its stores is a branch of Basic Brown Bear (see *below*). **The Anchorage** is at Leavenworth and Jones streets (tel. 415/775–6000).

In **Chinatown**, wander down Grant Avenue and along the side streets and stop at any number of shops displaying baskets filled with toys and other inexpensive Chinese imports. **The Japan Center**, west of downtown, has a number of stores carrying flyingfish kites, miniature notepads, and other colorful items from Japan. See Ethnic Neighborhoods, *above*.

At the **San Francisco Shopping Centre** (865 Market St., across from Powell St. cable-car turnaround, tel. 415/495–5656), most kids love to ride the multistory circular escalators; shops include Nordstrom and the Warner Bros. Studio Store.

Across the street from the San Francisco Shopping Centre, there's a **Gap Kids** branch (890 Market St., tel. 415/421–4906). Nearby is a bustling **F.A.O. Schwarz** toy store (48 Stockton St., tel. 415/394–8700). A huge **Disney Store** (400 Post St., tel. 415/391–6866), and next to it a **Borders Books and Music** store (Post and Powell sts., tel. 415/399–1633), are both on Union Square.

A favorite stop for San Francisco teens and preteens is the **Esprit** outlet (499 Illinois St. at 16th St., tel. 415/957–2550), with discounted sportswear. Not far away is the **Basic Brown Bear Factory and Store** (444 De Haro St., tel. 415/626–0781), where kids can watch toy bears being made and then stuff one of their own to take home, at factory prices; call for tour times. In the Beach Chalet out by the ocean, a branch of **The City Store** (1000 Great Highway, tel. 415/831–4758) sells authentic San Francisco memorabilia—you might take home a brick from Lombard Street or a piece of cable from the city's cable car system.

Eats

San Francisco is one of the world's great restaurant cities, with more restaurants per capita than any other in the United States. With that kind of competition, restaurants need to be good to survive, and many of the best are inexpensive-to-moderately priced neighborhood establishments that appeal to families. Besides sampling some of the best Chinese food this side of Hong Kong, you can introduce your kids to cuisines they may not be familiar with; Grael and Lia's favorites include Burmese, Peruvian, and Vietnamese. But there are good burger places, pizza parlors, and Mexican restaurants as well. For restaurants in Chinatown and Japantown, see Ethnic Neighborhoods, *above*. For restaurants in the Fisherman's Wharf-Pier 39 areas, see Historic Sites, *above*, and Shops, *above*. But to savor the most genuine flavors of San Francisco, venture beyond the tourist areas and into the neighborhoods, where, as a general rule, the food is better, the prices are lower, and the service is friendlier.

Downtown/Union Square

John's Grill. Best known as the restaurant where Sam Spade (Dashiell Hammett's fictional detective in *The Maltese Falcon*) dined nightly on chops, John's—here since 1908—is a good place to soak up some local atmosphere, with dark paneled walls, antiques, and photos of old San Francisco. The menu is classic American, with some Italian flavor: steaks, chops, seafood, pastas. *63 Ellis St., tel. 415/986–0069. Reservations accepted. Dress: casual but neat. AE, D, DC, MC, V. No Sun. lunch. $$$*

Sears Fine Foods. This landmark near Union Square has been feeding hungry visitors breakfast and lunch for decades. (No, there's no connection to Sears department stores.) The house specialty is the plate of 18 Swedish pancakes—small, delicate, and delicious. Also popular is the sourdough French toast, served with strawberry preserves. For lunch are salads (Caesar, Chinese chicken), soups, and sandwiches. Sears is crowded, but service is friendly and efficient. *439 Powell St., tel. 415/986–1160. No reservations. Dress: casual. No credit cards. No dinner. $*

South of Market

Chevy's. This Mexican minichain has hit on a formula that works: Serve dishes made with fresh ingredients in a bright, festive atmosphere. Our kids love this place, starting with "El Machino," a machine that produces freshly made flour tortillas. Chips and salsa are also made fresh; while munching, kids can color the children's menu. Kids' meals include a choice of soft or crisp chicken or beef taco, cheese quesadillas, bean and cheese burrito, or a flauta with an ice cream cone for dessert. This location, near Yerba Buena Gardens and the Moscone Center, has indoor and outdoor seating. *4th and Howard Sts., tel. 415/543–8060. Children's menu. Reservations accepted. Dress: casual. AE, MC, V. $$*

Max's Diner. This attractive art deco–style diner promises "everything you always wanted to eat," and though the menu isn't quite that comprehensive, most everything that we've tried here has been on the mark. Food is freshly made, and portions are big. With young children you can go two ways:

the children's menu—which includes little hamburgers, spaghetti, grilled cheese, turkey sandwich, and fried chicken (followed by a treat "if you finish your lunch or dinner—or try real hard")—or appetizers, such as a basket of three "sliders" (small hamburgers) with crisp french fries or killer onion rings, washed down by thick milk shakes. The regular menu also has New York deli–style sandwiches (big, juicy Reubens are the specialty), blue-plate and low-fat specials, pastas, salads, all-day breakfast, seafood or chicken dinners, and a slew of baked desserts. All are consumed to the beat of '50s, '60s, or big band music on the jukebox. *3rd and Folsom Sts., tel. 415/546–6297. Children's menu. No reservations. Dress: casual. AE, D, DC, MC, V. $–$$*

Civic Center/Van Ness

The Golden Turtle. We've rarely had a bad Vietnamese meal anywhere in San Francisco, but the Golden Turtle is consistently among the best, with excellent food in classy (though not overly formal) surroundings. You walk past a goldfish pond into an attractive wood-paneled room decorated with hand carvings, gnarled tree branches, and a fish tank. Ingredients in the food often balance sweet with spicy, hot with cold, soft with crunchy. Our kids especially love the delicate, crisp imperial rolls (deep-fried rice paper stuffed with pork, prawn, and crab) and fresh lemonade. Other dishes we like include the hot-and-sour shrimp soup (which is somewhat spicy), the charbroiled shrimp sticks, the beef salad, the five spices roast chicken, and for dessert, bananas flambé. *2211 Van Ness Ave., tel. 415/441–4419. Reservations accepted. Dress: casual but neat. AE, MC, V. Closed Mon. $$*

Hard Rock Cafe. Take heart—that line out the door may well be for souvenir T-shirts rather than for table seating at this branch of the international chain. Even if you have to wait it should be worth it, especially if you have teenagers in tow. This is the place to check out teen culture by the Bay, and it's all done to a rock beat that drowns out most conversation (don't come here with a headache). The Hard Rock also serves up some of the best burgers in town along with barbecued chicken and ribs, and a Caesar salad with grilled chicken that has lately won Lia over from the burgers. *1699 Van Ness Ave., tel. 415/885–1699. No reservations. Dress: casual. AE, D, DC, MC, V. $–$$*

North Beach

Capp's Corner. One of North Beach's old family-style trattorias, this landmark eatery is still thriving: The food is better than ever, prices are at bargain level, and crowds continue to fill its narrowly spaced tables, sitting elbow-to-elbow with fellow diners. Even before you order, a tureen of minestrone is brought to the table, which cures any urgent cases of the munchies. Next comes salad, also served in a big bowl family-style, then pasta, main courses and vegetables, and dessert. Main courses include roast chicken, fresh fish of the day, or veal chop; main-course pastas are less expensive. *1600 Powell St., tel. 415/989–2589. Reservations advised. Dress: casual. AE, D, DC, MC, V. No weekend lunch. $$–$$$*

Stinking Rose. Don't even think of coming here unless everyone in the family likes garlic—the motto is "We season our garlic with food," and 1½ tons of garlic are consumed here each month, plus 3,000 after-dinner mints. A toy train transports garlic, and two rooms are lined floor-to-ceiling with wonderful cartoon murals depicting garlic-bulb people. When it's time to eat, start with the *bagna calda* (soft, roasted garlic cloves in olive oil, to be spread on bread). The juicy, 40-clove garlic chicken sandwiches—not nearly as strong as the name implies—are Grael's favorite, and Lia loves the pizettes (appetizer pizzas) with garlic sausage. For adult appetites, the 40-clove roast chicken with garlic mashed potatoes is ideal. And for dessert? Garlic ice cream, of course (or lemon sorbet or tiramisu). *325 Columbus Ave., tel. 415/781–*

7673. Reservations advised. Dress: casual. AE, DC, MC, V. $$

Tommaso's. Like Capp's, Tommaso's is a vintage slice of North Beach. You descend into a fairly small, dark, rustic dining room with booths lining the walls. Try to get here before 6:30 PM, as there's often a line and the waiting area gets stuffy. The pizza, baked in a wood-burning oven, is crisp, cheesy, and delicious; the calzone, which is like a folded-over pocket pizza, is equally good. Tommaso's also serves Neapolitan-style spaghetti and other types of pasta, some good side salads and vegetables, and a selection of veal and chicken dishes. *1042 Kearny St., tel. 415/398–9696. No reservations. Dress: casual. MC, V. No lunch. Closed Mon. $$*

Mo's. Though it does serve some other sandwiches, Mo's is best known for its thick, juicy hamburgers. Most young kids may have a hard time working their way through the seven ounces of beef, so you might consider splitting an order. Burger toppings range from bacon and barbecue sauce to various cheeses and mushrooms. There are alternatives here: chicken sandwiches, even vegetarian items. But most everyone comes for the burgers, which many consider the best in town. The decor is black and white tile and chrome. *1322 Grant Ave., tel. 415/788–3779. No reservations. Dress: casual. MC, V. $*

Embarcadero

Il Fornaio. Long a favorite Italian restaurant among San Francisco's trendy young adults, this stylish trattoria (Italian tiles, white marble, blond hardwood) also has a children's menu. Rotisserie-roasted meats and poultry, mesquite-grilled fish, regional pastas, pizzas from a wood-burning oven, and breads baked fresh on premises are the specialties. Kids can choose from among small pizzas, pastas with cheese, tomato, or meat sauces, and traditional kids' menu items like hamburgers and chicken tenders, all printed up on a place mat to color. Il Fornaio has sister locations in Marin County, the South Bay, and on the Peninsula; the one in Burlingame

(327 Lorton Ave., tel. 415/375–8000) is handy to the San Francisco airport. *1265 Battery St., tel. 415/986–0100. Children's menu. Reservations advised. Dress: casual but neat. AE, DC, MC, V. $$$*

Chevy's. This is another branch of the popular Mexican minichain, with both indoor and outdoor seating. (See South of Market, above.) *2 Embarcadero Center, tel. 415/391–2323. Children's menu. Reservations accepted. Dress: casual. AE, MC, V. $$*

Golden Gate Park Area

Mels Drive-In. No other restaurant lights up my daughter Lia's eyes like Mels. Part of it is the '50s ambience: the oldies on the jukebox, the booths, the gum-chewing waitresses, the chrome-and-Formica decor—all straight out of the movie *American Graffiti* (in which the original Mels played a featured role). The kids' menu comes with crayons, and kids' meals (burger, hot dog, grilled cheese, chicken, or fish, served with fountain treats like milk shakes and cherry Cokes) are served in a toy Corvette that can be taken home. The regular menu includes the "Famous Melburger," a classic ½-pounder, plus a variety of hot and cold sandwiches, salads, blue-plate specials, and thick milk shakes, root-beer floats, and sundaes. *3355 Geary Blvd., tel. 415/387–2244. Children's menu. No reservations. Dress: casual. No credit cards. $–$$*

PJ's Oyster Bed. This is where San Franciscans come to eat seafood, and it's one of our family's favorites. PJ's has a relaxed, kid-friendly atmosphere, with lazily rotating ceiling fans, though it's fairly small and does get crowded. Several crayon-decorated children's menus are tacked up near the cash register. The children's menu includes fried shrimp, grilled sole, or a hamburger. Both our kids, however, are partial to the Dungeness crab (in season) from the regular menu. All the seafood here, whether fish or shellfish, is impeccably fresh and beautifully prepared. *737 Irving St., tel. 415/566–7775. Children's menu. Reservations advised. Dress: casual. AE, D, DC, MC, V. $$–$$$*

The Beach Chalet. Housed on the upper floor of a 1925 structure designed by architect Willis Polk, which had been mostly unoccupied for two decades, the Beach Chalet opened as a restaurant, brew-pub, and Golden Gate Park visitors center in 1997 and has been drawing big crowds since. A big attraction is the views looking out over Ocean Beach—sunsets are especially nice. The menu is mostly American and eclectic, ranging from meat and seafood to pasta to sandwiches to vegetarian dishes; take note that beers are consumed in large quantities. Children's menu items are $5 each and include hot dog and fries, grilled cheese sandwich with tossed salad, and macaroni and cheese. *1000 Great Hwy., tel. 415/386–8439. Children's menu. Reservations recommended. Dress: casual but neat. MC, V. $$.*

Ton Kiang. In the Richmond District (just north of Golden Gate Park, where many Chinese live), Ton Kiang draws large families who chow down on the delicious "Hakka" food. Hakka is a lightly seasoned cuisine of South China, much like Cantonese but with some exotic specialties like the delicious steamed salt-baked chicken, which isn't salty but moist and delectable. Along with the chicken, seafood is the star here: panfried rock cod, crab sautéed with ginger and scallion, and clay-pot Hakka casseroles (tofu with seafood, oysters with roast pork). For lunch, come for the exceptional dim sum—dumplings and other "little bites," served daily until 3 PM. *5821 Geary Blvd., tel. 415/387–8273; 3148 Geary Blvd., tel. 415/752–4440. Reservations advised. Dress: casual. MC, V. $–$$*

Marina District

Mels Drive-In. This is a clone of the Mels on Geary Blvd. (see Golden Gate Park Area, above), except for a different physical layout. *2165 Lombard St., tel. 415/921–3039. Children's menu. No reservations. Dress: casual. No credit cards. $–$$*

Mission District

La Taqueria. People come from all over town to feast on the tacos and burritos at La Taqueria, on a palm-lined stretch of Mission Street. This is a casual place, where you order at the counter, but it's attractively decorated with colorful tile, Mexican murals, wooden tables, and upbeat music on the jukebox. Everything is scrupulously clean, and the food is fresh-tasting and delicious. There are only three choices here: burritos, soft tacos, and quesadillas. The burritos and tacos are stuffed with *carne asada* (grilled beef), *carnitas* (stewed pork), *chorizo* (spicy Mexican sausage), *pollo* (chicken), or beans and cheese. The quesadillas, or "cheese treats," might be a good choice for young ones. Don't miss the refreshing fresh fruit drinks, which might include strawberry, pineapple, and mango. *2889 Mission St., tel. 415/285–7117. No reservations. Dress: casual. No credit cards. $*

Where to Stay

The customary places for families to stay in San Francisco are downtown (around Union Square), the Embarcadero, and Fisherman's Wharf, within walking distance of restaurants, sights, and cable cars. These hotels tend to be more expensive than those in other areas of town, however, and they're in heavily trafficked, congested areas. To get a little more space, consider the avenues way out near the Pacific Ocean (prices are lower there, too). There's also a utilitarian motel row along Lombard Street in the Marina District, which is a good place to try if others are filled. Choices include the **Marina Motel** (2576 Lombard St., tel. 415/921–9406); the **Surf Motel** (2265 Lombard, tel. 415/922–1950); and the **Town House Motel** (1650 Lombard St., tel. 415/885–5163 or 800/255–1516). If you'd like to stay at a bed-and-breakfast, contact **Bed & Breakfast California** (tel. 650/696–1690), a free service that matches families to suitable accommodations. Note that many San Francisco hotels do not have swimming pools. Price ranges below do not include 14% city hotel tax.

The Clift. Hotelier Ian Schrager has added a touch of postmodern panache to the always-elegant Clift, set in the heart of the theater district. The Clift maintains impeccable service, old-style grandeur, and a huge welcome mat for families. The Clift provides a "childproof" room equipped with nightlights, faucet protectors, and covers on all the electrical outlets. Children find small-size robes to use during their stay, plus a miniature table, chair, and bathtub stool; cookies and milk at bedtime; and age-appropriate entertainments (from toddler toys to books to video games). On request, the hotel also provides cribs, rollaways, high chairs, baby blankets, bottles and bottle warmers, diapers, strollers, and wipes; there's a baby-sitting service, 24-hour on-call pediatrician, a children's menu in the classy French Room restaurant, and kids' room service menus. Rooms are large and freshly decorated; upper floors (the Clift is 17 stories high) provide views. *495 Geary St., 94102, tel. 415/775–4700 or 800/652–5438, fax 415/441–4621. 298 rooms, 31 suites. Facilities: restaurant, exercise room, children's amenities. AE, DC, MC, V. $$$*

Hyatt Regency. One of the best things about the Hyatt Regency is its location, in the Embarcadero Center near the waterfront. The dramatic 17-story atrium lobby has trees and plants, an indoor fountain, and inside glass elevators that kids love to ride. Rooms have refrigerators and views of the bay or downtown San Francisco, and many have balconies. Children under 18 stay free with their parents; for parents seeking privacy, the Family Plan allows children to stay in a connecting room at a 50% discount. *5 Embarcadero Center, 94111, tel. 415/788–1234 or 800/233–1234, fax 415/398–2567. 759 rooms, 44 suites. Facilities: 2 restaurants, exercise room, parking (fee). AE, D, DC, MC, V. $$$*

San Francisco Marriott. Known locally as the "Jukebox" because of its fan-shape mirrored windows that resemble an old-fashioned platter spinner, the Marriott is a huge business-oriented hotel that's making a genuine attempt to lure families. Local schoolkids designed the children's menu (both food and artwork) for the hotel's mezzanine restaurant, Allie's American Grille, and the results are "way cool," as one child put it. Rooms are standard business-type but most enjoy nice views of the city. Few kids can resist the intriguing sculpture fountain (with paper-thin sheets of water) in the lobby. *55 4th St., 94103, tel. 415/896-1600 or 800/ 228-9290, fax 415/896-6177. 1,366 rooms and 134 suites. Facilities: 3 restaurants, pool, spa, saunas, health club, in-room movies. AE, D, DC, MC, V. $$$*

Sheraton Fisherman's Wharf. Just a block or so from the waterfront, the Sheraton provides a number of good features for families: a heated outdoor pool, TVs with movie channels, underground parking (for a fee), and, during July and August, a Kids' Koncierge service that offers suggestions and maps for kids' activities in the area. Most rooms are of decent size; don't expect great views, though—the hotel is only four stories high. Children 17 or under stay free with parents; connecting rooms are available. Keep in mind that you're paying a lot for location here; similar accommodations cost much less away from the Wharf. *2500 Mason St., 94133, tel. 415/362-5500 or 800/325-3535, fax 415/956-5275. 525 rooms. Facilities: restaurant, pool. AE, D, DC, MC, V. $$$*

Westin St. Francis. One of the great landmark hotels of San Francisco, on Union Square with cable cars clanging by, the St. Francis is the very picture of a world-class big-city hotel. Emperors, queens, and presidents have stayed here, and the St. Francis is the world's only hotel that *washes* its coins (legal money-laundering). My kids like to come in to gape at the stylish marble lobby, then ride the outside glass elevators that

zoom up to the 32nd floor and down (see Serendipities, *above*). Rooms are luxurious, though those in the original building are fairly small; those in the modern tower are larger and have brighter, lacquered furniture. The hotel's restaurants have children's menus, and recent summers have featured a kids-eat-free policy. There's no extra charge for kids 18 and under staying with parents; if an additional room is rented, single rates apply on both. *335 Powell St., 94102, tel. 415/397-7000 or 800/228-3000, fax 415/ 774-0124. 1,116 rooms and 83 suites. Facilities: 3 restaurants, exercise room. AE, D, DC, MC, V. $$$*

The Commodore. This hotel, primarily oriented to the "adventurous" tourist rather than the business traveler, is one of the best accommodations values in the city—and the staff goes out of its way to be helpful to visitors. The Commodore believes that one of its missions is to introduce its guests to the "hidden sights, sounds, and tastes of San Francisco"—they've even worked up two dozen detailed tip sheets on restaurants, unusual tours, top views, and, yes, kids' activities. It's also a cheerful place to stay. The hotel has a whimsical nautical motif—be sure to check out the attached Titanic Café—and the rooms are all named and themed after San Francisco landmarks. No cookie-cutter rooms, these—each is different and quite spacious, considering the budget price. (All are clean and comfortable.) The Commodore is three blocks west of Union Square. *825 Sutter St., San Francisco 94109, tel. 415/923-6800 or 800/338- 6848, fax 415/923-6804. 113 rooms, 2 suites. Facilities: restaurant, laundry service, parking (fee). AE, D, DC, MC, V. $$-$$$*

The Mansions. Owner Bob Pritikin has played host to celebrities at his Mansions Hotel, and some of the rooms here are downright opulent, but this is a place that should delight kids. Start with the unusual motif. Pritikin, an ad man in his other life, is a natural showman, and curios (such as a collection of ugly ties), murals, assorted objects, sculptures, and pig paintings—yes, paintings of pigs—are everywhere. Pritikin himself dresses in sequined jacket and plays the saw every weekend at the "magic extravaganzas" staged here each night after dinner (the shows are free for guests). There's also a resident ghost named Claudia, which you might expect in a twin-turreted Queen Anne Victorian that dates from 1887. Breakfast is included in the rates. *2220 Sacramento St., 94115, tel. 415/929–9444 or 800/826–9398, fax 415/567–9391. 26 rooms. Facilities: restaurant, full breakfast. AE, DC, MC, V. $$–$$$*

Travelodge at the Wharf. Across the street from the Sheraton (but closer to the bay), the four-story Travelodge is known for being family-oriented, with comparatively reasonable rates and bay views. The higher-priced rooms on the two upper floors have balconies that provide unobstructed views of Alcatraz and overlook a landscaped courtyard and heated outdoor pool. The rooms are simply but brightly furnished; some have refrigerators. The pool area connects to the '50s-style Johnny Rockets diner, which has good burgers and fries; you can eat poolside. Children under 18 stay free with parents. *250 Beach St., 94133, tel. 415/392–6700 or 800/578–7878, fax 415/986–7853. 246 rooms, 4 suites. Facilities: 3 restaurants, pool, parking (fee). AE, D, DC, MC, V. $$–$$$*

Marina Inn. Only a few blocks from the Marina Green, this four-story inn provides European-style bed-and-breakfast accommodations at reasonable prices—and is family-friendly to boot. The rooms are done up English country-style, with pine poster beds, comforters, and cable TV. Breakfast is served in the sitting room, as are afternoon cookies and beverages; chocolates appear on your pillows at night. Families may want to opt for the junior suites, which contain one queen bed and a daybed. *3110 Octavia St., at Lombard St., 94123, tel. 415/928–1000 or 800/274–1420, fax 415/928–5909. 40 rooms. Continental breakfast. AE, MC, V. $–$$.*

Seal Rock Inn. This attractive motel has a wonderful location near the Cliff House and Land's End; you can hear sea lions barking and ocean surf crashing nearby. Rooms are good-size and have ocean views; some have fireplaces or kitchenettes, and connecting rooms are available. There's a small outdoor swimming pool, too, though the weather can get foggy and brisk here in summer. *545 Point Lobos Ave., 94121, tel. 415/752–8000, fax 415/752–6034. 27 rooms. Facilities: restaurant (breakfast and lunch only), pool, free parking. AE, DC, MC, V. $*

Entertainments

Dance

(**👫 5–15**) **The Oakland Ballet** (tel. 510/452–9288) also presents an annual Nutcracker performance.

(**👫 5–15**) **The San Francisco Ballet** (tel. 415/865–2000) draws kids to its annual holiday Nutcracker ballet.

(**👫 6–15**) **The San Francisco Ethnic Dance Festival** (tel. 415/474–3914) each June hosts dance troupes representing ethnic cultures from around the world.

Movies

For first-run films in San Francisco head to the **AMC Kabuki 8 Theatres** in the Japan Center (Post and Fillmore Sts., tel. 415/931–9800), the **AMC 1000 Van Ness** (1000 Van Ness Ave., tel. 415/922–4262), and the **United Artists Galaxy** (Van Ness Ave. and Sutter St., tel. 415/474–8700). The showplace theater in the East Bay is the **Grand Lake** (Grand Ave., Oakland, tel. 510/452–3556).

Music

(**👫 6–15**) **The Golden Gate International Children's Choral Festival,** presented on odd-numbered years in June, draws children's choirs from around the world. The public can attend the opening and closing concerts in the East Bay as well as various free performances by individual choirs around the Bay Area during festival week.

(**ii 6–15**) **The San Francisco Symphony** (tel. 415/864-6000) stages an annual Music for Families series of weekend concerts, as well as a Concerts for Kids series on some weekday mornings.

(**ii 3–15**) **The Stern Grove Midsummer Music Festival** (tel. 415/252–6252) is the nation's oldest free outdoor concert series, and a great family favorite.
🏠 *Piedmont Choirs, 401A Highland Ave. Piedmont 94611, tel. 510/547–4441. Admission: $8 adults, $5 under 13.*

Theater

Try the **Palo Alto Children's Theater** (tel. 650/329–2216); the **New Conservatory Children's Theatre Company** (tel. 415/861–8972) and **Young Performers Theatre** (tel. 415/346–5550), both in San Francisco; the summertime **Make*A*Circus** (tel. 415/242–1414); and Sunday matinees of San Francisco's longest-running musical revue, **Beach Blanket Babylon** (tel. 415/421–4222).

(**ii 6–15**) **The Center for the Arts** at Yerba Buena Gardens (3rd and Howard Sts., tel. 415/978–2787) offers theater, music, and dance presentations; call for the current schedule.

(**ii 6–15**) **The San Francisco Shakespeare Festival** brings free Shakespeare productions to public parks around the Bay Area, and picnicking with the Bard is encouraged. Staging one or two plays each season, the troupe starts either in Oakland's Lakeside Park (at Lake Merritt) or Cupertino's Memorial Park in July, switches to the other in August, and beginning on Labor Day weekend finishes its run in San Francisco, next to the Conservatory of Flowers on Kennedy Drive in Golden Gate Park.
🏠 *Tel. 415/422–2222. Admission free.*

Theme and Amusement Parks and Arcades

(**ii 1–9**) **Children's Fairyland** (see Chapter 9) is a place of small-child enchantment that is said to have inspired Disneyland.
🏠 *Lakeside Park, Oakland, tel. 510/238–6876.*

(**ii 2–12**) **The Discovery Zone Fun Center** is an indoor playground where kids can exercise while having fun: crawling through tunnels, bouncing in ball bins, whooshing down slides, climbing "mountains," and playing skill games for prizes.
🏠 *El Camino Real and Littlefield St., Target Shopping Center, Redwood City, tel. 650/568–4386. Admission: adults free, $5.99 ages 3–12, $3.99 ages 2–3.*

(**ii 1–12**) **The Jungle** bills itself as the West Coast's largest indoor play facility, where kids can slide, bounce, hide, frolic in a ball pond, climb nets, and generally cut loose. Parents play free; everyone needs to wear socks.
🏠 *555 9th St., tel. 415/552–4386. Admission: $3.95–$6.95 ages 3–12, $4.95 under 3. Open Sun.–Thurs. 10-8, Fri.–Sat. 9–9.*

(**ii ALL**) **Metreon,** a Sony Entertainment Center, opened in Yerba Buena Gardens (see Parks, *above*) in spring 1999. Metreon brings the first IMAX theater to San Francisco, complete with an 80-by-100-foot screen and 3-D capability. The complex also includes 15 regular movie screens, as well as shops and themed restaurants. Three interactive attractions are based on literary works by author-artist Maurice Sendak (*Where the Wild Things Are* and *In the Night Kitchen*), French graphic novelist Jean Giraud "Moebius" (*The Airtight Garage*), and author-architect David Macauley (*The Way Things Work*). In the *Where the Wild Things Are* play space, kids (and adventurous parents) will encounter goblins, a hall of mirrors, and a 17-foot-tall Wild Thing. The Airtight Garage area contains three electronic and virtual-reality games, including a "cap-

ture-the-flag"–type game, a demolition derby, and a "virtual" bowling alley. And in the *The Way Things Work* area, visitors view a three-screen, three-dimensional show illustrating how mechanical things work—and sometimes go awry, with bubbles, smoke, and unexpected blasts of air and water.
🏛 *4th and Mission Sts., tel. 415/537–3400. Call for prices and hrs.*

(👫 6–15) **Paramount's Great America** (see Chapter 9) is the Bay Area's top spot for thrill rides.
🏛 *Great America Pkwy., Santa Clara, tel. 408/988–1776.*

(👫 ALL) **Pier 39** (see Shops, *above*) features a number of rides and entertainments including a double-deck Venetian Carousel; an arcade with video games and bumper cars; a midway with skill games for young kids; Turbo Ride, a motion-simulated adventure ride; and the Pier 39 Cinemax Theatre, showing *The Great San Francisco Adventure*.
🏛 *The Embarcadero at Powell St., tel. 415/ 981–7437.*

(👫 ALL) **Six Flags Marine World Theme Park** (see Chapter 9) combines animal and sea shows with rides and environmental education.
🏛 *Marine World Pkwy., Vallejo, tel. 707/ 643–6722 or 707/644–4000.*

For Parents Only

San Francisco's potpourri of evening entertainment runs the gamut from sophisticated cabarets to bawdy bistros, with hotel lounges, discos, comedy clubs, and music clubs in between. The **South of Market** area has the trendiest nightspots—for blues, jazz, and rock, try **Slim's** (333 11th St., tel. 415/522–0333); for casual lively jazz, it's the **Cafe du Nord** (2170 Market St., tel. 415/861–5016). Nob Hill has the best nighttime view in town from the **Top of the Mark** (Mark Hopkins Hotel, 999 California St., tel. 415/392–3434). For an eclectic music nightclub try the **Great American Music Hall** (859 O'Farrell St., tel. 415/885–0750).

LOS ANGELES

15

THEME PARKS, MOVIE STARS, MUSEUMS, AND SURF

L ong America's dream factory, Los Angeles was shaken in the 1990s by a series of highly publicized nightmares. But just as images of eternal sunshine, surfers, and movie stars never told the whole L.A. story before, neither do the past decade's earthquakes, floods, fires, and sensational murder trials paint the whole picture now. The City of Angels has shown remarkable resiliency, absorbing blow after blow like a veteran fighter: The downtown area and the public transit system continue to be revitalized, folks still flock to beaches and parks, and Hollywood makes movies about it all. For children, the attractions of the Los Angeles area are as stellar as ever: world-class theme parks and museums, wide beaches, minitrain rides, drive-ins and diners, Hollywood glitz, historic sites from the not-*too*-dusty past, an abundance of outdoor sports, and nearly year-round mild weather. It's as if this city and its environs had been custom-built for kids.

The five counties of greater L.A. have a larger population than all but three states—yet when we travel to the area, we often find ourselves ranging over much of it: from Anaheim to Hollywood, Pasadena to Santa Monica, Newport Beach to Malibu, Beverly Hills to Long Beach. Assuming that you'll do the same, this chapter doesn't confine itself to Los Angeles proper, but covers Orange County, the San Fernando Valley, and other widespread points that many have simply come to refer to as "L.A." You can't do it all, of course—but you and your kids can have a lot of fun trying.

The Basics

Resources

The **Los Angeles Convention and Visitors Bureau** (633 W. 5th St., Suite 6000, Los Angeles 90071, tel. 213/624–7300) provides tourist information about the region. The bureau also runs a 24-hour multilingual events hot line; call 213/689–8822. For Orange County, the best source is the **Anaheim/Orange County Visitor and**

Convention Bureau (800 W. Katella Ave., Box 4270, Anaheim 92803, tel. 714/765–8888). You may also want to contact the **Beverly Hills Visitors Bureau** (239 S. Beverly Dr., Beverly Hills 90212, tel. 310/271–8174 or 800/345–2210); the **Long Beach Area Convention and Visitors Bureau** (1 World Trade Center, Suite 300, Long Beach 90831, tel. 562/436–3645 or 800/452–7829); the **Santa Monica Visitor Center** (1400 Ocean Ave., Santa Monica 90401, tel. 310/393–7593); and the **Pasadena Convention and Visitors Bureau**

(171 S. Los Robles Ave., Pasadena 91101, tel. 626/795–9311).

When you arrive, stop by the **Downtown Los Angeles Visitor Information Center** (685 S. Figueroa St., open weekdays 8–5, Sat. 8:30–5), or the **Hollywood Visitor Information Center** (6541 Hollywood Blvd., open Mon.–Sat. 9–5).

L.A. Parent (443 E. Irving Dr., Suite D, Burbank 91504, tel. 818/846–0400) is a monthly newspaper filled with events listings and resources, available free at libraries, supermarkets, museums, and toy stores.

Getting in and out of Los Angeles

BY AIR. Los Angeles International Airport (tel. 310/646–5252 or 310/646–5260), usually referred to as LAX, is the largest airport in the area, served by more than 85 major airlines including American, Continental, Delta, Northwest, Southwest, TWA, United, and US Airways. **SuperShuttle** (tel. 310/782–6600 or 323/775–6600) is one of several 24-hour-a-day door-to-door shuttle services; the trip to downtown hotels costs about $12 a person. **Shuttle One** (tel. 310/670–6666) provides door-to-door service and low rates ($10) to hotels in the Disneyland/Anaheim area. The **Airport Coach** (tel. 714/938–8900 or 800/772–5299) provides regular service between LAX and the Pasadena and Anaheim areas. **Taxis** charge a flat fee of $30 to downtown L.A. (if arranged in advance).

Other airports in greater L.A. may actually be more convenient than LAX for your destination: There's the **Burbank/Pasadena/Glendale Airport** (tel. 818/840–8847) in the San Fernando Valley; **Ontario International Airport** (tel. 909/937–2700), about 35 miles east of downtown L.A., which serves the San Bernardino–Riverside area; and Orange County's **John Wayne Airport** (tel. 949/252–5006).

BY CAR. Los Angeles is at the western terminus of I–10, a major east–west highway

that runs all the way to Florida. Interstate 5, which runs north–south through California, leads north to San Francisco (about 400 miles away) and south to San Diego (about 100 miles away). More scenic (but slower) routes from San Francisco include Highway 101 and coastal Highway 1. Interstate 15, angling southwest from Las Vegas, swings through the San Bernardino area before heading to San Diego.

BY TRAIN. Amtrak (tel. 800/872–7245) connects Los Angeles to the Bay Area, Portland, and Seattle via the *Coast Starlight.* The *Southwest Chief* travels between Los Angeles and Chicago, and the *Sunset Limited* runs from Los Angeles to New Orleans and Florida. There is also frequent daily service to San Diego and Santa Barbara. The Los Angeles train terminal is the landmark Union Station at 800 N. Alameda Street, tel. 213/683–6979.

BY BUS. Greyhound (tel. 800/231–2222) serves Los Angeles from cities all across the country; the terminal is at 1716 E. 7th Street.

Getting Around Los Angeles

BY CAR. Although L.A. is improving its public transit system, a car remains a must here. You will inevitably encounter heavy traffic on the freeways, especially during rush hours (7–9 AM and 3–7 PM). At these times, boulevards such as Wilshire or Pico may be faster than I–10, which runs west to Santa Monica and the coast; and La Cienega Boulevard is often the quickest route north from the airport to Beverly Hills and West Hollywood. Be sure to carry a good, detailed road map, and turn on your car radio—many stations give frequent traffic reports.

BY BUS. A ride on **Metropolitan Transit Authority** (tel. 213/626–4455) buses costs $1.35, plus 25¢ for each transfer. DASH (Downtown Area Short Hop) minibuses travel in a loop around the downtown area, stopping every two blocks or so; you pay 25¢ every time you get on, no matter how far you go. DASH runs weekdays from 6 AM to 7 PM. Long Beach runs a free downtown shuttle called the Runabout, serving most area attractions including the Queen Mary Seaport.

BY LIGHT RAIL. The **Metrorail Blue Line** (tel. 213/626–4455) runs daily 5 AM and 10 PM from downtown Los Angeles (corner of Flower and 7th Sts.) to Long Beach (corner of 1st St. and Long Beach Ave.), with 18 stops en route, most in Long Beach. The 20-mile **Metrorail Green Line** connects beach communities between Redondo Beach and Norwalk. The **Metrolink** (tel. 213/808–5465) connects the Inland Empire and Ventura County with Orange County on weekdays, with limited Saturday service.

BY SUBWAY. The **Metro Red Line** (tel. 213/626–4455) runs from Union Station downtown to Wilshire Blvd. and Western Avenue via Hollywood.

BY TAXI. Don't expect to be able to hail a cab on the street in Los Angeles. If you need one, call **Independent Cab Co.** (tel. 213/385–8294) or **United Independent Taxi** (tel. 323/653–5050). The metered rate is $1.90 to start plus $1.60 per mile.

Family-Friendly Tours

Maps for self-guided tours of movie stars' homes are sold on many street corners in Hollywood and West Hollywood (double-check the date before you buy). We bought one for $2 and took the kids on a spin through Beverly Hills and some of the winding canyon roads to the north; we got thoroughly lost a few times, but had a memorable few hours hunting for the homes (or ex-homes) of celebrities like Steve Martin, Lucille Ball, and Elvis. Are the maps reliable? Who knows—but we certainly saw some nice houses.

Hornblower Dining Yachts sails from Marina del Rey (13755 Fiji Way, tel. 310/

301–9900) and Newport Beach (tel. 949/631–2469). We enjoyed a Sunday brunch cruise in Marina del Rey, complete with heaping platters of food, cooling breezes, calm waters, and nice views of the boats and beaches as we sailed slowly past. Rates for brunch cruises are $39.95 adults, $20 ages 4 to 12. Hornblower also operates 45-minute narrated harbor tours of Marina del Rey (May–Sept., daily; Oct.–Apr., weekends only); tickets are $8 adults, $4 ages 4 to 12.

Whale-watching cruises leave from various points around Los Angeles, mid-December through April. Try **Spirit Cruises and Whale Watch** (San Pedro Harbor, tel. 310/548–8080); the **Charter Connection** (Marina del Rey, tel. 310/827–4105); **Redondo Sport Fishing** (King Harbor in Redondo Beach, tel. 310/372–2111); **Newport Landing Sportfishing** (Newport Beach/Balboa Pavilion, tel. 949/675–0550); **Long Beach Sportfishing** (2nd St. Harbor, Long Beach, tel. 562/432–8993); **Belmont Pier Sportfishing** (Belmont Pier, Long Beach, tel. 562/434–6781); and **Dana Wharf Sportfishing** (Dana Point Marina, tel. 949/496–5794). Cruises last from 1½ to four hours and cost from $10 to $15 for adults, and from $6 to $10 for children. Check with individual companies on exact rates, times, and recommended minimum ages.

Older children may enjoy **gondola cruises** through the canals of Naples Island, Long Beach; the one-hour Italian-style cruises can accommodate up to six people. Hors d'oeuvres, ice, and glasses are provided; bring your own beverages. The price is $55 for the first couple, $10 for each additional person. Contact **Gondola Getaway** (5437 E. Ocean Blvd., Long Beach, tel. 562/433–9595; open 10 AM–midnight). To sail on an authentic **tall ship,** the Californian, and perhaps help to raise a sail, call 800/432–2201 in Long Beach for sailing dates and rates.

The **NBC Television Studio Tour** offers behind-the-scenes glimpses of TV show sets, wardrobe and makeup departments, and maybe a star or two at work. Your kids may get a chance to see themselves "fly" on video—even "disappear" on screen—as tour guides demonstrate special effects. All ages are welcome, but because the tour requires about an hour of walking and listening, kids who are school age are the most likely to enjoy it. You can also pick up tickets here to see tapings of live shows, though most have minimum ages ranging between 10 and 16. *3000 W. Alameda Ave., Burbank, tel. 818/840–3537. Admission: $7 adults, $3.75 ages 5–12. Tours weekdays 9–3.*

Southwest, Delta, Alaska, and other airlines all have offered L.A. packages including hotel, rental car, and passport to Disneyland; call individual airlines for details. For information about family-oriented tour agencies that arrange other package trips to the Los Angeles area, see Chapter 2.

Pit Stops

One hazard of freeway driving is a lack of rest rooms along the highway; it can get to be a real problem if you're stuck in traffic, so urge your kids to visit the bathroom before you climb in and buckle up. Fortunately, L.A.'s theme parks, museums, major shopping malls, and most of its beaches are well equipped with rest rooms. Downtown, in Hollywood or Beverly Hills look for big hotels, which almost always have rest rooms in the lobbies.

Baby-Sitters

Check first with your hotel concierge; many top hotels can arrange for on-site baby-sitting. Otherwise, **Sitters Unlimited** (tel. 800/328–1191) has franchises in Los Angeles and Orange counties.

Emergencies

Police, fire, or **ambulance** can be reached by dialing 911. Cedars-Sinai Medical Center (8700 Beverly Blvd., tel. 310/855–5000) and Queen of Angels Hollywood Presbyterian

Medical Center (1300 N. Vermont Ave., tel. 213/413–3000) are among the many hospitals with 24-hour emergency rooms.

Many **Sav-On Drug Stores** throughout the Los Angeles area operate 24 hours. **Thrifty** is another big drugstore chain with numerous locations and varying hours.

Telephone Area Codes

In 1999 the 310 area code will receive an overlay, meaning that only new numbers will be given the new code, 494. However, if you're dialing a 310 number from another 310 number, you'll have to dial 1+310 first. The new 909 region area code and the area it will cover, scheduled for the year 2000, was not available at press time.

Scoping out Los Angeles

Always try to plan your schedule before setting out to explore Los Angeles with kids, and don't try to cover too much in one day—or one visit. Think of the region as a collection of destinations, each to be visited separately. To help you organize your visit, we've subdivided Los Angeles into eight major districts: **Downtown,** site of high-rise office buildings, ethnic neighborhoods, and historic areas; to the northwest, **Hollywood** and its associated movie sites (though most studios have moved elsewhere); the **Westside,** west of downtown, including affluent Beverly Hills and West Hollywood; farther west, the **coastal communities** of Malibu, Santa Monica, Venice, and Marina del Rey; to the south, the communities around the **Long Beach** area; **Griffith Park** and **the Valleys,** north of Hollywood (the San Fernando Valley includes Burbank, the Santa Clarita Valley is home to Six Flags California amusement park, and the San Gabriel Valley contains Pasadena); **Orange County,** southeast of downtown; and the **Inland Empire** of San Bernardino and Riverside, to the east. Distances are substantial; Santa Monica, for instance, is 15 miles from downtown, Anaheim is about 25 miles, Pasadena and Universal City are 9 miles. Allow plenty of time for travel and for rest breaks.

Major attractions that are covered at length in Part II of this book are merely cross-referenced here; though the write-ups are short, these are the top sights.

Historic Sites

DOWNTOWN

(**5 – 15**) The **Central Library,** a classic 1926 Egyptian-style structure, has become a tourist attraction since its renovation after a 1986 fire. There's a 1½-acre garden outside and a children's Story Theater inside.
630 W. 5th St., tel. 213/228–7000. Admission free. Open Mon.–Thurs. 10–8; Fri.– Sat. 10–6, Sun. 1–5.

(**6 – 15**) El Pueblo de Los Angeles Historic Monument (see Chapter 4) includes Mexican-flavored Olvera Street and the city's oldest buildings.
Bounded by Alameda, Arcadia, Spring, and Macy Sts., tel. 213/628–1274.

(**6 – 15**) Watts Towers (see Chapter 4), masterpieces of folk-art sculpture, are worth driving off the beaten tourist track to find, but will be closed for restoration until sometime in the year 2000.
1765 E. 107th St., tel. 213/485–1795.

HOLLYWOOD

(**ALL**) The **Capitol Records Building,** built in the shape of a stack of 45-rpm records, is a Hollywood landmark and a classic example of '50s chic. Drive by to show your kids what shape music used to come in before cassettes and CDs.
1750 N. Vine St., tel. 213/462–6252.

(**ALL**) The **Hollywood Sign** may be the easiest site to view in the entire state, but no visit would be complete without

it. Simply stand on Hollywood Boulevard and look north, up into the hills—the 50-foot-tall letters should be visible atop Mount Lee, unless there's an attack of killer smog. (The sign originally spelled "Hollywoodland" to advertise a housing development, but the "land" part was removed in 1949.)

(**ALL**) The **Hollywood Walk of Fame** (see Chapter 4) honors Hollywood celebs with sidewalk stars.
Hollywood Blvd. between Gower St. and Sycamore Ave.; Vine St. between Yucca and Sunset Blvd., tel. 213/469–8311.

(**ALL**) **Mann's Chinese Theatre** (see Chapter 4) displays in cement the handprints (and footprints, pawprints, gunprints, and so on) of past and present Hollywood stars.
6925 Hollywood Blvd., tel. 213/464–8111.

WESTSIDE

(**ALL**) **The La Brea Tar Pits** (see Chapter 4) contain the world's richest known deposits of Ice Age fossils.
Hancock Park, 5801 Wilshire Blvd., Los Angeles, tel. 323/934–7243.

COASTAL COMMUNITIES

(**ALL**) **The Santa Monica Pier** (see Amusement Parks, *below*), the West Coast's oldest pleasure pier, dates from 1908. It juts into the ocean next to lovely Santa Monica beach. Don't miss the 1922-vintage indoor Looff carousel (open July– early Sept., Tues.–Sun. 10–9; otherwise weekends 10–5; tickets 50¢), featured in numerous Hollywood movies, including *The Sting.* Nearby is Pacific Park, a full-scale amusement park on the pier (see Chapter 9). You can fish from the end of the pier as well, or eat in one of many snack bars or restaurants.
End of Colorado Blvd. at Ocean Ave., Santa Monica, tel. 310/393–7593. Admission to pier free. Pier open daily.

LONG BEACH AREA

👫 ALL   The *Queen Mary* (see Chapter 4), once one of the world's great ocean liners, is docked for public viewing.
🏛 *Queen Mary Seaport, 1126 Queen's Hwy., end of Long Beach Fwy. (I–710), Long Beach, tel. 562/435–3511 or 800/437–2934.*

GRIFFITH PARK AND THE VALLEYS

👫 9 – 15 Like many other Los Angeles structures, the historic Gamble House has a movie tie-in: It was "Doc's" house in *Back to the Future*. If your kids have seen that film, use this to lure them inside, where you can expose them to superb examples of the Craftsman architectural movement; the furniture, stained glass, rugs, and other details are magnificent.
🏛 *4 Westmoreland Pl., tel. 626/793–3334. Admission: $5 adults, $3 students; under 12 free. Open Thurs.–Sun. noon–3; 1-hr tours every 20 min.*

ORANGE COUNTY

👫 3 – 15 The Crystal Cathedral, televangelist Robert Schuller's church, is spectacularly constructed from more than 10,000 panes of glass, resembling a sparkling four-pointed star. If you're in town at the right time, consider attending one of its annual pageants, the "Glory of Christmas" and the "Glory of Easter," each featuring live animals, flying angels, and other special effects.
🏛 *12141 Lewis St., Garden Grove, tel. 714/971–4013. Donation requested. Guided tours Mon.–Sat. 9–3:30; call for schedule. Pageant reservations tel. 714/544–5679.*

Museums

DOWNTOWN

👫 3 – 15 The California Afro-American Museum, a bright, airy facility in Exposition Park, mounts changing exhibitions of artworks, photographs, and historical displays by and about African-Americans.

🏛 *600 State Dr., Exposition Park, tel. 213/744–7432. Admission free. Open Tues.–Sun. 10–5.*

👫 3 – 15 The California Science Center (see Chapter 5) contains fascinating interactive exhibits about life on earth and technology, as well as an IMAX theater.
🏛 *700 State Dr., Exposition Park, tel. 213/744–7400 or 213/744–2014.*

👫 3 – 12 The Los Angeles Children's Museum (see Chapter 5) is a colorfully designed setting for children to learn about life in the city via hands-on exhibits and projects.
🏛 *310 N. Main St., tel. 213/687–8800.*

👫 6 – 15 The Museum of Contemporary Art displays artworks dating from 1940 to the present. Kids may enjoy the bright colors and geometric shapes of Jackson Pollock and other top painters, as well as some of the rooms devoted to unusual conceptual art pieces.
🏛 *250 S. Grand Ave., tel. 213/626–6222. Admission: $6 adults, $4 students over 11, ages 12 and under free; free for all Thurs. 5–8 PM. Open Tues.–Wed. and Fri.–Sun. 11–5; Thurs. 11–8.*

👫 2 – 15 The Natural History Museum of Los Angeles County (see Chapter 5) is loaded with displays of dinosaurs, insects, gems, fossils, reptiles, and other creatures.
🏛 *900 Exposition Blvd., Exposition Park, tel. 213/763–3466.*

👫 5 – 15 The Wells Fargo History Museum contains memorabilia of more than a century of western history, such as a 100-year-old stagecoach, a 2-pound gold nugget, and a replica of a 19th-century Wells Fargo agent's office.
🏛 *333 S. Grand Ave., tel. 213/253–7166. Admission free. Open weekdays (except bank holidays) 9–5.*

WESTSIDE

👫 3 – 15 The Carole and Barry Kaye Museum of Miniatures displays what's said to be the world's largest collection of contemporary miniature houses and dioramas. From antique automobiles to an old-time soda shop, antebellum mansions to medieval abbeys, first ladies to jazz stars, everything and everyone is re-created on a scale of ½ or less—a tiny yet intricately detailed fantasy world that should appeal to kids. Watch for the complete tea set that sits on a quarter and the tobacco pipe that can't be seen without a magnifying glass. The Petite Elite Shop and Doll Gallery is attached.

🏛 *5900 Wilshire Blvd., Los Angeles, tel. 323/ 937–6464. Admission: $7.50 adults, $5 students ages 12–21, $3 ages 3–12. Open Tues.–Sat. 10–5, Sun. 11–5.*

👫 6–15 The Craft and Folk Art Museum showcases art, textiles, and masks from around the world. The museum's annual International Festival of Masks, held at nearby Hancock Park on a mid-October weekend, is capped by a colorful parade.

🏛 *5800 Wilshire Blvd., Los Angeles, tel. 323/ 937–4230. Admission: $4 adults, $2.50 students, under 12 free. Open Tues.–Sun. 11–5.*

👫 3–15 The George C. Page Museum of La Brea Discoveries (see Chapter 5) is the place to see fossils from the adjacent La Brea Tar Pits (see Historic Sites, above).

🏛 *Hancock Park, 5801 Wilshire Blvd., Los Angeles, tel. 323/934–7243.*

👫 6–15 The J. Paul Getty Museum at the Getty Center (see Chapter 5), a truly great art collection, welcomes children to its galleries in the new Getty Center in the Brentwood Hills.

🏛 *1200 Getty Center Dr., Brentwood, tel. 310/440–7300.*

👫 6–15 The Los Angeles County Museum of Art (see Chapter 5) is the largest art museum in the western United States.

🏛 *5905 Wilshire Blvd., Los Angeles, tel. 323/ 857–6000.*

👫 9–15 The Museum of Tolerance (see Chapter 5) teaches kids (and parents)

about racial tolerance and the lessons of the Holocaust.

🏛 *9786 W. Pico Blvd., Los Angeles, tel. 310/ 553–9036.*

👫 3–15 The Petersen Automotive Museum (see Chapter 5) chronicles L.A.'s car culture in imaginative settings, showcasing more than 200 rare and classic autos and other vehicles.

🏛 *6060 Wilshire Blvd., Los Angeles, tel. 323/ 930–2277.*

👫 4–15 The Skirball Cultural Center and museum presents exhibits on the experience of Jewish immigration, including benches from Ellis Island and a Hanukkah lamp whose eight branches are all fashioned after the Statue of Liberty. At the interactive Discovery Center, kids can participate in an outdoor simulated archaeological dig.

🏛 *2701 N. Sepulveda Blvd., tel. 310/440–4500. Admission: $8 adults, $6 students, under 12 free. Open Tues.–Sat noon–5, Sun. 11–5.*

👫 6–15 The Southwest Museum at LACMA West (see Chapter 5) is an expansion of Highland Park's Southwest Museum (see *below*) into space shared with the Los Angeles County Museum of Art (see *above*) in the onetime May Co. department store building. The Southwest specializes in Native American art and artifacts.

🏛 *6067 Wilshire Blvd. at Fairfax Ave., tel. 323/933–4510.*

HOLLYWOOD

👫 6–15 The Hollywood Entertainment Museum. This museum takes you behind the scenes of Hollywood entertainment—TV, movies, radio, and recording. You can see original sets and props such as the bar from the TV series *Cheers* and the "beaming up" mechanism from *Star Trek*, visit a re-created back lot, play with some interactive computer exhibits, tour a screening room and film editor's room, and find out what a foley artist does. Artifacts from the old Max Factor Makeup Museum, now closed, have also surfaced here.

🏨 *7021 Hollywood Blvd., tel. 323/465–7900. Admission: $7.50 adults, $4.50 students, $4 ages 5–12, under 5 free. Open daily 10–6.*

👫 6–15 **The Hollywood Guinness World of Records** and nearby **Hollywood Wax Museum** can be viewed separately or on one combination ticket. The Guinness museum documents thousands of world sports, space, animal, and other records with videos, pictures, and life-size replicas (the world's tallest man, the world's longest neck). The wax museum (less classy than Orange County's Movieland Wax Museum, see *below*) immortalizes the likes of Rambo, Hulk Hogan, and Michael J. Fox in wax.
🏨 *6764 and 6767 Hollywood Blvd., tel. 323/463–6433 (Guinness), 323/462–8860 (Wax). Admission to each: $9.95 adults, $6.95 ages 6–12; combination ticket $14.95 adults, $8.95 ages 6–12. Open Sun.–Thurs. 10 AM–midnight, Fri.–Sat. 10 AM–2 AM.*

👫 3–15 **Ripley's Believe It or Not** devotes itself to "fact stranger than fiction": paintings created entirely from dryer lint or cobwebs, a Fiji "mermaid," a shrunken head, and an eight-legged pig. Sure, it's schlocky, but it's also oddly fascinating. Some exhibits require reading small print, so you may have to answer a lot of questions from curious little ones. Buena Park has a similar museum (see Orange County Museums, *below*).
🏨 *6780 Hollywood Blvd., tel. 213/466–6335. Admission: $8.95 adults, $5.95 ages 5–12. Open Mon.–Thurs. 10 AM–11 PM, Fri.–Sun. 10 AM–midnight.*

COASTAL COMMUNITIES

👫 3–15 **Angel's Attic,** set in Santa Monica's oldest house (a beautiful Queen Anne Victorian), displays an enchanting collection of antique dolls, dollhouses, and miniatures. (Curious tots may be frustrated that they can't touch, so consider waiting till they're older; strollers aren't permitted.) "Santa's Workshop" is on display from November to January.

🏨 *516 Colorado Ave., Santa Monica, tel. 310/394–8331. Admission: $6.50 adults, $3.50 under 12. Open Thurs.–Sun. 12:30–4:30.*

👫 6–15 **The Museum of Flying** is designed to show kids that there's more to flying than pilots, with interactive exhibits on aircraft design, maintenance, and other aspects of aviation. But kids can still climb into cockpits and listen on headphones to real communications with Santa Monica Airport's control tower. Forty planes and helicopters are on display, and children can build model planes and gliders in museum workshops.
🏨 *2772 Douglas Loop, Santa Monica, tel. 310/392–8822. Admission: $7 adults, $3 ages 3–17. Open Wed.–Sun. 10–5.*

LONG BEACH AREA

👫 3–15 **The Lomita Railroad Museum,** set in a replica of a century-old train station, houses one of the largest collections of railroad memorabilia in the West. Kids can climb aboard a real steam engine and a caboose.
🏨 *2137 250th St., Lomita, tel. 310/326–6255. Take Harbor Fwy. (Hwy. 110) south to Pacific Coast Hwy. exit, go west to Narbonne Ave.; turn right to 250th St. Admission: $1 adults, 50¢ ages 5–12. Open Wed.–Sun. 10–5.*

GRIFFITH PARK AND THE VALLEYS

👫 3–15 **The Autry Museum of Western Heritage** (see Chapter 5) introduces kids to the colorful characters who forged the West.
🏨 *4700 Western Heritage Way, Griffith Park, tel. 323/667–2000.*

👫 3–15 **Griffith Observatory Hall of Science** (see Chapter 5) presents interactive astronomy exhibits, planetarium shows, and a telescope for night viewing.
🏨 *2800 E. Observatory Rd., Griffith Park, tel. 323/664–1191.*

👫 3–15 **The Huntington Library, Art Collections, and Botanical Gardens** (see

Chapter 5) contains a remarkable assortment of artworks, manuscripts, and exotic flora (see also Parks and Gardens, *below*).
🏛 *1151 Oxford Rd., San Marino, tel. 626/405–2141.*

(👫 1–12) Kidspace (see Chapter 5) is one of the L.A. area's superb children's museums.
🏛 *390 S. El Molino Ave., Pasadena, tel. 626/449–9143.*

(👫 6–15) The Norton Simon Museum (see Chapter 5) houses a world-class art collection ranging from Old Masters to modernists.
🏛 *411 W. Colorado Blvd., Pasadena, tel. 626/449–6840.*

(👫 6–15) The Pacific Asia Museum, which resembles a Chinese palace, showcases magnificent arts and crafts from Asia and the Pacific islands. The courtyard garden is a peaceful place to sit and relax. The third Saturday of each month is "Family Free Day."
🏛 *46 N. Los Robles Ave., Pasadena, tel. 626/449–2742. Admission: $5 adults, $3 students, under 12 free. Open Wed.–Sun. 10–5.*

(👫 6–15) The Southwest Museum (see Chapter 5) brings Native American cultures alive for children.
🏛 *234 Museum Dr., Highland Park, Los Angeles, tel. 323/221–2164.*

ORANGE COUNTY

(👫 6–15) The Bowers Museum of Cultural Art and Kidseum (see Chapter 5), Orange County's largest museum, houses a first-rate collection of artwork plus a children's museum where kids can learn about the cultures of the Pacific Rim.
🏛 *1802–2002 N. Main St., Santa Ana, tel. 714/567–3600 (Bowers) and 714/480–1520 (Kidseum).*

(👫 ALL) The Children's Museum at La Habra (see Chapter 5) lets kids dig for dinosaurs or "drive" a real bus.
🏛 *301 S. Euclid St., La Habra, tel. 562/905–9693.*

(👫 ALL) The Discovery Museum of Orange County helps make the history of Southern California come alive. Kids (and adults) can play a pump organ, talk on a hand-cranked telephone, look through a stereoscope, try on Victorian clothing, churn butter, and wash clothes on a scrub board. Restored houses, gardens, a blacksmith shop (with demonstrations the third Sunday of each month), seasonal family festivals and teas, and educational workshops for kids are all part of the action on this 11-acre site.
🏛 *3101 W. Harvard St., Santa Ana, tel. 714/540–0404. Admission: $4 adults, $3 ages 12 and under. Open Wed.–Fri. 1–5, Sun. 11–3.*

(👫 ALL) The Discovery Science Center, a spin-off of the Discovery Museum of Orange Co. (see *above*), opened at the end of 1998 and contains 100 hands-on, interactive exhibits for children and their parents. The 55,000-square-foot facility includes indoor and outdoor exhibits, all designed to spark kids' curiosity about science, math, and technology. Themed areas include "Dynamic Earth," "Human Perception," and "The Computer Lab." A 3-D laser theater costs an extra $2.
🏛 *2500 N. Main St., Santa Ana, tel. 714/542–2823. Admission: $8 ages 18–54, $6 ages 55 and up, $6 ages 3–17, ages 2 and under free. Open daily 10–5.*

(👫 6–15) The International Surfing Museum showcases 80 years' worth of surfing memorabilia.
🏛 *411 Olive St., Huntington Beach, tel. 714/960–3483. Admission: $2 adults, $1 students, under 6 free. Open Wed.–Mon. noon–5.*

(👫 6–15) The Movieland Wax Museum elevates a kitschy genre into something resembling art; this is one of the world's top wax museums, with 250 major stars (Whoopi Goldberg, Tom Cruise, Madonna, plus lots of old-timers) depicted. The effects in the gruesome "Chamber of Horrors" could be scary for little kids (you can detour around it). Discounted combination tickets are available with the nearby Ripley's Believe It or Not (see *below*).

🏠 *7711 Beach Blvd., Buena Park, tel. 714/ 522–1154. Admission: $12.95 adults, $10.55 ages 55 and up, $6.95 ages 4–11. Open Mon.–Fri. 10–6, Sat.–Sun. 9–7.*

(👫 3–15) **Ripley's Believe It or Not** is similar to the museum of the same name in Hollywood (see Hollywood, *above*). Discounted combination tickets are available with the nearby Movieland Wax Museum (see *above*).

🏠 *7850 Beach Blvd., Buena Park, tel. 714/ 522–7045. Admission: $8.95 adults, $6.95 ages 55 and up, $5.25 ages 4–11. Open Mon.–Fri. 11–5, Sat.–Sun. 10–6.*

INLAND EMPIRE

(👫 ALL) **The Orange Empire Railway Museum,** a sprawling outdoor complex south of Riverside, is loaded with old locomotives and trolley cars from Los Angeles' long-gone (and lately lamented) Red Line. The best days to come are on weekends and major holidays, when the museum gets its historic trolleys, and sometimes its trains, up and running. You can ride the trolleys or trains all day for $7 adults, $5 ages 5–11.

🏠 *2201 S. A St., Perris, tel. 909/657–2605. Admission free (except trolley or train rides). Open daily 9–5.*

(👫 1–12) **A Special Place Children's Hands-On Museum** allows kids with and without disabilities to participate side-by-side: They dress up for stage shows, learn history at old school desks, play with shadows or in a mini–health clinic, or experiment with wheelchairs and crutches in the Disability Awareness area. The museum also has an aquarium, turtles, and birds.

🏠 *1003 E. Highland Ave., San Bernardino, tel. 909/881–1201. Admission $2, ages 2 and under free. Open Mon. 1–5, Tues.–Thurs. 9–1, Fri. 9–5, Sat. 11–3.*

Theme and Amusement Parks

L.A. is the West Coast's theme park capital. Allow at least one whole day each for the majors, and start early to get through the gate ahead of the crowds.

(👫 2–10) **Adventure City** is a colorful park built for kids, who can spin, twirl, and zoom through their first "thrill" rides in a relaxed, nonthreatening atmosphere (as parents watch and applaud). Everything in this city is scaled to kids. They can ride a mini–Ferris wheel, roller coaster, and vintage carousel, play engineer on a little train, fly their own planes, ride a fire truck, and get bumper to bumper in freeway traffic (it's fun for them). Besides the rides—which kids can take over and over as part of the admission price—a petting farm, face painting, puppet shows, games, and snack carts provide plenty of action. The park is in the Hobby City complex on the edge of Anaheim (see Shops, *below*).

🏠 *10120 S. Beach Blvd., Stanton, tel. 714/ 236–9300. Admission: $10.95 (discounts for limited rides). Call for hrs.*

(👫 3–15) **Balboa Fun Zone** at the pier in Newport Beach contains a Ferris wheel, video games, kiddie rides, and arcades. Admission is free; rides and games are priced separately.

🏠 *Balboa Blvd., Newport Beach, tel. 949/ 673–0408. Call for hrs.*

(👫 2–9) **Club Disney** is more a play area with a Disney-movie theme than a theme park; kids can play multimedia computer games at the Chat Hat, wander the Maddening Maze, experiment in the Wizard's Lab, and climb to the Lion King Clubhouse.

🏠 *The Promenade at Westlake, Thousand Oaks, tel. 888/258–2347. Admission: $8. Open daily; call for hrs.*

(👫 ALL) **Disneyland** (see Chapter 9) remains California's top attraction for kids and families.

🏨 *1313 Harbor Blvd., Anaheim, tel. 714/ 781–4565.*

(👭 ALL) **Knott's Berry Farm** (see Chapter 9) combines attractions for preschoolers (Camp Snoopy) with spine-tingling thrill rides for teens and entertainments for all ages.
🏨 *8039 Beach Blvd., Buena Park, tel. 714/ 220–5200.*

(👭 ALL) **Pacific Park** at Santa Monica Pier (see Chapter 9) has 12 pay-as-you-go rides for all ages, including a roller coaster and a giant Ferris wheel with ocean views.
🏨 *End of Colorado Blvd. at Ocean Ave., Santa Monica, tel. 310/260–8744.*

(👭 2 – 15) **Raging Waters** (see Chapter 9) is the Los Angeles area's top water park.
🏨 *111 Raging Waters Dr., San Dimas, tel. 909/592–6453 or 909/592–8181.*

(👭 3 – 15) **Six Flags California** (see Chapter 9) combines thrill rides at Magic Mountain with water rides at the adjacent and separately priced Hurricane Harbor.
🏨 *26101 Magic Mountain Pkwy., off I–5, Valencia, tel. 661/225–4100.*

(👭 3 – 15) **Universal Studios Hollywood** (see Chapter 9), set at the world's largest film studio, provides an action-packed assortment of movie-theme rides, shows, and behind-the-scenes tours.
🏨 *Universal City Plaza, Universal City, tel. 818/622–3801.*

(👭 3 – 15) **Wild Rivers** (see Chapter 9) offers a truly wild collection of water-theme rides and attractions.
🏨 *8770 Irvine Center Dr., Irvine, tel. 949/ 768–9453.*

Aquariums, Zoos, and Wildlife

LONG BEACH AREA

(👭 2 – 15) **The Cabrillo Marine Aquarium** (see Chapter 6) presents the world's largest collection of Southern California

marine life. From March to August each year thousands of grunion (small silver fish) wash up on L.A.–area beaches to spawn and lay their eggs; the aquarium has entertaining educational programs about grunion during most of the runs.
🏨 *3720 Stephen White Dr., San Pedro, tel. 310/548–7562.*

(👭 3 – 15) **The Long Beach Aquarium of the Pacific** (see Chapter 6), across the harbor from the *Queen Mary* (see *above*), focuses on the marine life of the Pacific.
🏨 *100 Aquarium Way, Long Beach, tel. 562/ 590–3100 or 888/826–7257.*

GRIFFITH PARK AND THE VALLEYS

(👭 ALL) **The Los Angeles Zoo** (see Chapter 6) houses a children's zoo and more than 1,200 rare animals.
🏨 *5333 Zoo Dr., Griffith Park, Los Angeles, tel. 323/644–6400.*

ORANGE COUNTY

(👭 6 – 15) **The Bolsa Chica Ecological Reserve,** a restored salt marsh near Huntington Beach, is one of the best places in Southern California to see migrating birds. Kids may spot great blue herons, black-bellied plovers, snowy egrets, loons, and sandpipers (or 300 other species of birds). A 1½-mile loop trail meanders through the reserve; early morning and evening are the best times to come. Free 1½-hour guided tours are offered the first Saturday of each month at 9 AM, year-round.
🏨 *Off Pacific Coast Hwy. between Warner Ave. and Golden West St., Huntington Beach, tel. 714/897–7003. Admission free. Open daily.*

(👭 3 – 15) **The Orange County Marine Institute** contains aquariums and touch tanks and offers tours of tide pools around Dana Point. You can even ride on a research vessel, the RV/Marine Explorer, to see offshore sea lions ($20 adults, $14 ages 12 and under.)
🏨 *24200 Dana Point Harbor Dr., Dana Point, tel. 949/496–2274. Admission: donation requested. Open daily 10–4:30.*

ALL The **Santa Ana Zoo** at Prentice Park displays more than 250 animals; a highlight is the Amazon's Edge, a primate exhibit with howler monkeys and capybaras. At the children's zoo children can feed ducks and pet kids.

1801 E. Chestnut Ave. and 1st St., Santa Ana, tel. 714/836–4000. Admission: $4 adults, $2 ages 3–12. Open daily 10–5.

6–15 The **Upper Newport Bay Ecological Reserve,** Southern California's largest estuary, provides a yearly temporary home for 200 species of migratory birds. You can hike and ride bikes on trails past the wetlands.

Shellmaker Rd., Newport Beach, tel. 949/ 640–6746. Take Pacific Coast Hwy. to Jamboree Blvd., follow Jamboree to Backbay Dr., then onto Shellmaker Rd. Admission free. Open dawn–dusk.

Ethnic Neighborhoods

DOWNTOWN. Chinatown, in downtown L.A., lacks the neon glow and bustling street life of its San Francisco counterpart, but kids can still catch glimpses of authentic Asian life here, where more than 15,000 Chinese and Southeast Asian (mostly Vietnamese) Americans live. Heart of the action is a six-block stretch of North Broadway, where you can stop for a meal (see Eats, *below*) or browse through the exotic herb shops. Giant dragons snake down North Broadway to celebrate the Chinese New Year every February. *Bordered by Yale, Bernard, and Ord Sts., and Alameda Ave., tel. 213/617–0396.*

Little Tokyo, the cultural focal point for L.A.'s Japanese-American community (North America's largest), is more compact and colorful than Chinatown. My kids like to wander around its pedestrian malls, which are lined with restaurants and shops. A commemorative time line tells the story of six decades of Japanese-American life in the United States, leading up to World War II. Nisei Week is celebrated every August with traditional drums, dancing, a carnival, and a

parade; Children's Day, a two-day festival each May (see Chapter 3), brings family entertainments. *Bounded by 1st, San Pedro, 3rd, and Los Angeles Sts., tel. 213/620–0570.*

Olvera Street, the heart of El Pueblo de Los Angeles Historic Monument (see Historic Sites, *above*) provides an entertaining glimpse into Mexican culture. At the Plaza between Main and Los Angeles streets you're likely to see mariachis and folkloric dance troupes performing on weekends. At Easter time you can watch the Blessing of the Animals (see Chapter 3), and at Christmastime (nightly December 16–24) there's Las Posadas, a parade of merchants and visitors led by children dressed as angels. Other festivities take place around Cinco de Mayo (May 5) and Mexican Independence Day (Sept. 16). *Tel. 213/628–7833 or 213/628–1274.*

Parks, Gardens, and Playgrounds

WESTSIDE. Roxbury Park has a playground with innovative wooden structures, one for younger kids and one for older kids. There are tables or grassy areas for picnics. *471 S. Roxbury Dr., at Olympic Blvd., Beverly Hills, tel. 310/550–4761.*

COASTAL COMMUNITIES. Burton W. Chace County Park is a cool and breezy spot to watch the boats come and go in Marina del Rey, the world's largest manmade pleasure-craft harbor. Surrounded on three sides by water and moored boats, this 6-acre patch of green is also great for picnicking. *End of Mindanao Way, Marina del Rey.*

Palisades Park, a narrow ribbon of green on a bluff overlooking the Pacific, usually bustles with cyclists, skaters, joggers, walkers, Frisbee throwers, and sunbathers. It's a good place to take a baby for a scenic walk in a stroller. You may also see a movie crew at work (the park's a popular filming spot). *Colorado Ave. to just north of San Vicente Blvd., Santa Monica.*

Will Rogers State Historic Park, dedicated to the famous cowboy/humorist of the 1920s and '30s, has broad lawns for picnicking, hiking trails (with panoramic views of ocean and mountains), and free polo matches on weekends (call for polo schedule). You can also view the two-story ranch house where Rogers once lived. *1501 Rogers State Park Rd., Pacific Palisades, tel. 310/454–8212. Admission free; parking $6. Open daily 8–sunset.*

LONG BEACH AREA. El Dorado Regional Park and Nature Center, a huge park divided into east and west sections, has broad shady lawns for picnicking, duck ponds, walking and cycling paths, and lakes stocked for fishing. The Nature Center is a wildlife and native plant sanctuary in El Dorado East, laced with hiking trails. *7550 E. Spring St., Long Beach, tel. 562/570–3145.*

GRIFFITH PARK AND THE VALLEYS. Griffith Park, the country's largest urban park, can easily absorb a family for several days. Though not as pretty and much more spread out than San Diego's Balboa Park and San Francisco's Golden Gate Park, Griffith nonetheless has plenty to keep kids happy: playgrounds; train, pony, and carousel rides; bike lanes, horse trails, biking trails; tennis, golf, and much more. The Los Angeles Zoo is here (see Zoos, *above*), as well as the Griffith Observatory Hall of Science and the Autry Museum of Western Heritage (see Museums, *above*). So is Travel Town (5500 Zoo Dr., tel. 323/662–9678; admission free; open weekdays 10–4, weekends 10–5), a mostly outdoor museum where you can see 16 steam locomotives, vintage railroad cars, classic autos, old fire engines, and old planes. One treat for kids is the miniature railroad that toots around Travel Town every few minutes; tickets are $1.75 adults, $1.25 ages 19 months–13 years. There are also pony rides here ($1.50) for children from 1 year of age to those weighing up to 100 pounds. A larger pony ride concession on Crystal Springs Drive (tel. 323/664–3266, entrance

near I–5 and Los Feliz Blvd.) has different speeds of ponies for toddlers, preschoolers, and school-age kids (rides cost $1.50). Another miniature train ($1.75 adults, $1.25 ages 19 months–13 years) operates near here. Up the street is a vintage merry-go-round (see Serendipities, *below*). *Griffith Park Ranger Station, 4730 Crystal Springs Dr., tel. 323/665–5188.*

The **Descanso Gardens,** once part of a vast Spanish rancho, now displays acres of camellias, azaleas, roses, and live oaks. Easy walking trails and trams cross the grounds, and there's a teahouse with pools, waterfalls, and a Zen garden where you can stop for refreshments. *1418 Descanso Dr., La Canada, tel. 818/952–4400. Admission: $5 adults, $3 students, $1 ages 5–12; half-price 3rd Tues. of each month. Open daily 9–4:30.*

The **Huntington Botanical Gardens** at the Huntington Library (see Museums, *above,* and Chapter 5) present 15 garden environments from around the world, from jungles to deserts. *1151 Oxford Rd., San Marino, tel. 626/405–2141.*

The **Placerita Canyon Nature Center** is where gold was first discovered in California, in 1842 (surprisingly, predating the Mother Lode by six years). The site is near the "Oak of the Golden Dream," where a shepherd's dream is said to have led to the discovery. Eight miles of hiking trails lead through this wildlife preserve, including a ½-mile trail to the oak and another ½-mile ecology trail. The Nature Center has exhibits on local animals, plants, and rocks. *19152 Placerita Canyon Rd. (off Hwy. 14), Newhall, tel. 661/259–7721. Admission free; parking $3. Open daily 9–5.*

The **Santa Monica Mountains National Recreation Area** (see Chapter 8) encompasses canyons, waterfalls, meadows, oak groves, beaches, and lagoons, remarkably close to the L.A. urban sprawl. *30401 Agoura Rd., Suite 100, Agoura Hills, tel. 818/597–9192.*

William S. Hart County Park is an authentic cowboy ranch once owned by old-time Western actor William S. Hart; there are hiking trails, flat lawns for picnicking, and a small museum. Hart's house is filled with cowboy art and memorabilia. *24151 N. San Fernando Rd., Newhall, tel. 661/259–0855. Admission free. House open Wed.–Fri. 10–12:30, weekends 11–3:30, tours every ½ hr. Park open 7 AM–sunset.*

ORANGE COUNTY. Huntington Central Park, a 350-acre park in Huntington Beach, delights kids with playgrounds, a lake with ducks, a nature center and trails, fishing, horseback riding, picnicking, a library with children's programs, and great hide-and-seek spots along the bank of the lake. At Adventure Playground (tel. 714/842–7442; admission: $2; open summer only), where there's a Tom Sawyer pond with rafts, hammers, and saws to build things, plus a mud slide, a tire swing, and a bridge, kids can—and usually do—get very muddy (wear old sneakers and clothing). It's best for kids ages 6–12. *Talbert Ave. and Central Park Dr., Huntington Beach, tel. 714/960–8847.*

Beaches

From Malibu to Orange County, the Los Angeles area has miles of beaches suited for swimming, surfing, or exploring. The Pacific Coast Highway—PCH for short—runs along the coast. Los Angeles County–run beaches (and state beaches operated by the county) all have year-round lifeguards and many have showers, rest rooms, and public parking available for a fee (for further information, call 310/305–9546). All state, county, and city beaches in Orange County allow swimming, but watch for potentially strong undertow; try to swim near a staffed lifeguard stand. Most Orange County public beaches have fire pits, volleyball courts, showers, and rest rooms.

COASTAL COMMUNITIES. Manhattan County Beach offers 44 acres of sand and plenty of opportunities for swimming, diving,

surfing, and fishing. *West of Strand, Manhattan Beach, tel. 310/372–2166. Lifeguards, snack bar.*

Mother's Beach, as Marina Beach in Marina del Rey is called locally, is very popular with families; nestled between the sleek sloops and singles condos, this tiny crescent of man-made beach provides a wonderfully protected environment for very young children, with virtually no waves. *Admiralty Way and Via Marina, Marina del Rey, tel. 310/305–9545. Lifeguards, rest rooms, playground.*

Paradise Cove is a sandy, secluded family beach with a pier and equipment rentals. *28128 PCH, Malibu, tel. 310/457–2511. Lifeguards summers only; rest rooms.*

Redondo County Beach is wide, sandy, and usually packed with families in summer. At the northern end, the Redondo Pier has restaurants, shops, excursion boats, boat launching ramps, pier fishing, and summer rock and jazz concerts. *Foot of Torrance Blvd., Redondo Beach, tel. 310/372–2166. Lifeguards, showers, snack bars, volleyball.*

Santa Monica State Beach, the widest expanse of sand on the Pacific Coast, is one of L.A.'s most popular beaches, with plenty of families in evidence. Adjacent to historic Santa Monica Pier (see both Historic Sites and Theme Parks, *above*), the beach has a playground, volleyball courts, facilities for people with disabilities, and nearby bike paths. Make sure young kids don't swim too close to the pier. *West of PCH, Santa Monica, tel. 310/394–3266. Lifeguards.*

Surfrider Beach/Malibu Lagoon State Beach, north of Malibu Pier, are adjoining beaches, the first run by the county, the second by the state. The area has steady 3- to 5-foot waves that attract a host of longboard surfers. (The International Surfing Contest is often held at Surfrider in September.) Water runoff from Malibu Canyon forms a natural lagoon that's a sanctuary for shorebirds, and there are nature trails and good picnic spots. *23200 block of PCH, Mal-*

ibu, tel. 310/457–2527 (Surfrider), 818/880–0350 (Malibu Lagoon). Parking: $6 (Malibu Lagoon). Lifeguards, rest rooms.

Topanga Canyon State Beach is a surfing favorite, where dolphins sometimes swim close enough to shore to startle sunbathers. 18700 block of PCH, Malibu, tel. 310/456–8800. Lifeguards, snack bar.

Venice Municipal Beach is a must-see, even if you don't plan to swim. The surf and sands are similar to nearby Santa Monica State Beach (see above), but the main attractions are along the boardwalk: Rollerbladers—some who dance and do tricks—and cyclists zip by (watch small kids when crossing the bike path); magicians, acrobats, and rappers perform; muscle builders flex and strain while lifting weights; street artists create sidewalk masterpieces; street merchants push body oils. Teens usually love the scene. Lots of food stands and cafés sell snacks, and you can picnic on the grass. The best action is on Sunday afternoon. Ocean Front Walk, Venice. Lifeguards, rest rooms.

Will Rogers State Beach is wide, sandy, and several miles long, with separate areas for swimming and surfing. 14800 PCH, Pacific Palisades, tel. 310/454–8212. Lifeguards, rest rooms.

Zuma Beach County Park is Malibu's largest and sandiest beach, a favorite of surfers. 30050 PCH, Malibu, tel. 310/457–9891. Lifeguards, showers, snack bar, playground, volleyball.

LONG BEACH AREA. Mother's Beach, on Alamitos Bay, is protected by a breakwater, so the water is calm and ideal for young children. An adjacent park has play equipment. 54th and Bayshore, Long Beach.

Belmont Shore, south of downtown Long Beach, offers 3 miles of sandy beach divided by the Belmont Pier. 1st St. and Alamitos, extending to 72nd Pl., Long Beach.

ORANGE COUNTY. Corona del Mar Beach, backed by cliffs, is an exceptionally

beautiful beach where kids can explore tide pools (don't miss those at adjacent Little Corona Beach, as well), a cave, and a rock pier that juts into the ocean. Off Hwy. 1, south of Newport Beach, tel. 949/675–8420. Lifeguards, rest rooms, snack bars, volleyball, barbecue pits.

Crystal Cove State Park, a hidden treasure with 3½ miles of unspoiled beach, offers some of the best tidepooling in Southern California. Kids can look for sea stars, crabs, and lobsters on the rocks; rangers conduct nature walks on Saturday mornings. Midway between Corona del Mar and Laguna Beach, tel. 949/494–3539. Admission: $6 per car.

Dana Point, a natural harbor backed by high bluffs, draws many families. There's a sheltered beach for swimming (the calm waters are good for kids), tide pools, a marine institute (see Aquariums, above), a pier with boat rentals, and a replica of the schooner Pilgrim to tour (tel. 949/496–2274; donation requested; open Sun. 10–2:30). Parklands, bike and walking trails, and a collection of upscale restaurants, shops, and hotels are nearby. Dana Point Harbor Dr., off Hwy. 1 south of Laguna Beach, tel. 949/661–7013. Lifeguards in summer; rest rooms, picnic areas.

Doheny State Beach Park, with a mile of sandy beach just south of Dana Point, attracts families who love to swim in the warm waters and camp, picnic, fish, and go tidepooling. This is also one of Southern California's best surfing spots for beginners. The visitors center contains five aquariums and a simulated tide pool. Dana Point Harbor Dr., off PCH in Dana Point, tel. 949/496–6172 or 949/492–0802. Lifeguards, rest rooms, picnic areas.

Huntington State Beach and **Bolsa Chica State Beach,** connected by a long bike path that's great for kids, contain miles of white sand. Huntington Beach, especially, is a huge surfing area; the U.S. Open Surfing Championships are held at Huntington City Beach (tel. 714/536–5281) annually in August, and a surfing museum is in town (see Museums, *above*). The waves can be towering. The Bolsa Chica wetlands (see Aquariums, Zoos, and Wildlife, *above*) and 1,800-foot-long Huntington Pier (California's longest fishing pier) are adjacent to the beaches. *PCH opposite Magnolia Ave., Huntington Beach, tel. 714/536–1454 or 714/848–1566. Lifeguards, rest rooms, snack bar, changing rooms.*

Laguna Beach's Main Beach Park, in the center of town, has nonstop action. For young kids, it's a great seaside playground; for teens, it's a place to play volleyball and basketball. *End of Broadway at PCH, Laguna Beach, tel. 949/494–1018. Lifeguards, picnic spots, showers, rest rooms.*

Newport Beach is the quintessential upscale beach town, with miles of wide sands; waters for surfing, fishing, and swimming; and an island-dotted yacht harbor. Gondola cruises are available from Gondola Company of Newport (3400 Via Oporto, tel. 949/675–1212). The Newport Pier juts out into the ocean near 20th Street, where fishermen hawk their catch on the beach nearby on weekday mornings; on weekends, rollerbladers, skaters, cyclists, and skateboarders weave among the pedestrians. At Balboa Pier, another 1½ miles south, you can fish off the pier without a license or ride bikes on a trail along the beach, then visit the Victorian 1906 Balboa Pavilion, where whale-watching cruises leave in winter and boats sail for Catalina Island (see Chapter 17) year-round. The Balboa Fun Zone (see Theme and Amusement Parks, *above*) is near here, and there are also kayak rentals (Adventures at Sea, tel. 800/229–2412; or Balboa Boat Rentals, tel. 949/673–7200) and sportfishing trips (Davey's Locker, tel. 949/673–1434). *Tel. 949/722–1611. Lifeguards, rest rooms.*

Newport Dunes Aquatic Park is a lagoon with sandy beaches and shallow, calm waters, perfect for younger children; pedalboat, sailboat, and kayak rentals are available. In the middle of the lagoon is a pirate-themed playground and a big blue Fiberglas whale named Moe B. that kids can swim to and climb on. *1131 Backbay Dr., off Jamboree Blvd. and PCH, Newport Beach, tel. 949/729–3863. Lifeguards, rest rooms.*

Wood's Cove, quieter than Laguna's Main Beach, is surrounded by high cliffs and has lots of rocks to climb; kids may startle crabs lurking in the rocks. *Off PCH at Diamond St., Laguna Beach, tel. 949/494–1018. Lifeguards, rest rooms.*

Serendipities

HOLLYWOOD

At the **Junior Arts Center at Barnsdall Art Park,** kids can take low-priced arts and crafts classes year-round; and, on periodic Sundays, parents can join kids at free workshops for art projects supervised by local artists. *4800 Hollywood Blvd., Hollywood, tel. 213/485–4474. Classes priced individually. Open Tues.–Sun. 12:30–5.*

DOWNTOWN

The Angels Flight Railway, a Victorian-era funicular, takes riders on a 70-second climb up or down a 298-foot incline via two wooden cable railway cars—the world's shortest railway. Start at Hill Street between 3rd and 4th streets and ride up to Olive Street and California Plaza. *Tel. 213/626–1901. Admission: 25¢ one way. Open daily 6:30 AM–10 PM.*

COASTAL COMMUNITIES

(**ALL**) The Del Rey Lagoon (6660 Esplanade) along Playa del Rey, which stretches south from Marina del Rey, has a grassy pond that's home to dozens of ducks, and kids can bring bread to feed the quackers. The white sandy beach nearby has lifeguards, barbecue pits, and picnic tables.

(**3 – 15**) Leo Carrillo State Beach, tucked along a rough and mountainous stretch of coastline, has intriguing rock formations with secret coves, sea caves, and tunnels to explore; low tide brings spectacular tide pools, where kids can comb for anemones, crabs, and sea stars. Kids can also watch for whales, dolphins, and sea lions swimming in kelp beds offshore.

🏨 *35000 block of PCH, Malibu, tel. 818/ 880–0350. Day use: $6 per car.*

(👫 **ALL**) Third Street Promenade, a pedestrian-only shopping street in Santa Monica, comes alive most evenings with street entertainers—magicians, jugglers, dancers. This is a great place to bring kids; there are whimsically sculpted dinosaurs to see and good places to snack (try Benita's Frites, a Belgian-style french-fry stand at 1439 Third Street Promenade, tel. 310/ 458–2889).

GRIFFITH PARK AND THE VALLEYS

(👫 **ALL**) The Griffith Park Merry-Go-Round, built in 1926, has four rows of hand-carved jumping horses on which kids can take a melodic ride.

🏨 *Tel. 323/665–3051. Admission: $1. Open June–Aug. and Easter and Christmas vacations, daily 11–5; rest of year, weekends 11–5.*

(👫 **ALL**) Universal CityWalk lets kids ice-skate at a temporary outdoor rink in winter; in summer they can dash through a fountain. This pedestrian-only walkway, outside the entrance to Universal Studios Hollywood (see Theme Parks, *above*, and Chapter 9), was built to resemble surrealistic versions of famous L.A. streets like Sunset Strip and Melrose Avenue. A wonderful, safe environment to bring kids, it has colorful shops (see Shops, *below*), great outdoor eating places (see Eats, *below*), street performers, and movie theaters. The Museum of Neon Art adds to the color with exhibits of historic signs. And the Emaginator (tel. 818/752–3388, admission $5, no one under 42 inches admitted) is a cinematic thrill ride in theater-style seats.

🏨 *Take Universal Center or Lankershim Blvd. exits off Hollywood Fwy. (Hwy. 101), Universal City, tel. 818/622–4455.*

Sports

Big Leagues

Dodger Stadium (1000 Elysian Park Ave., exit off I–110, the Pasadena Fwy.) is the home of the **Los Angeles Dodgers** (tel. 323/224–1400) of baseball's National League; the **Anaheim Angels** (tel. 714/634–2000) of the American League play at Edison International Field of Anaheim (off I–5). The National Basketball Association's **Los Angeles Clippers** play at the L.A. Sports Arena (3939 S. Figueroa, Los Angeles, tel. 213/745–0500), while the NBA's **Los Angeles Lakers** play at the Great Western Forum (3900 W. Manchester, Inglewood, tel. 310/419–3100). The Forum is also home to the **Los Angeles Kings** hockey team (tel. 310/419–3160). (Both the Lakers and Kings are slated to move into the luxurious new Staples Center next to the Los Angeles Convention Center in the fall of 1999.) The NHL's **Mighty Ducks** play at The Pond in Anaheim (tel. 714/704–2700).

Outdoor Action

For additional information, contact the **Los Angeles Department of Recreation and Parks** (200 N. Main St., Suite 1380, City Hall East, Los Angeles, 90012, tel. 213/485–5515).

BICYCLING AND ROLLERBLADING. The **L.A. County Parks and Recreation Department** (433 S. Vermont Ave., 4th floor, Los Angeles, 90020, tel. 213/738–2961) has bike trail maps. The most famous—and probably most beautiful—trail in the city is the **South Bay Bike Path,** which runs 22 miles along the Pacific Ocean from Pacific Palisades south to Redondo Beach. The most crowded areas are along the Santa Monica and Venice beaches; the Venice Beach section is the unofficial in-line skating capital of the city, possibly the world. Rent skates at **Skatey's** (102 Washington Blvd., Venice, tel. 310/823–7971), bikes at **Venice Pier Bike Shop** (21

Washington Blvd., Venice, tel. 310/301–4011) or other rental stands along the beaches. The 4½-mile **Griffith Park Bikeway** follows a marked lane on Crystal Springs Drive south to Los Feliz Boulevard, passing the zoo and Travel Town along the way. Long Beach has a 5-mile coastline bike path. Rent bikes at the Bike Station (1st St. and the Promenade, Long Beach, tel. 562/436–2453).

The Santa Ana River Bike Trail in Orange County follows the river for 22 miles from Yorba Regional Park south to the Pacific Coast Highway, then connects to the 10-mile Bolsa Chica Bike Path, running along Bolsa Chica and Huntington state beaches (see Beaches, *above*); both are separate from traffic. More than 75% of the streets in the town of Huntington Beach have bike lanes; Newport Beach and Laguna Beach have more good trails. Rent bikes at **Team Bicycle Rentals** (8464 Indianapolis St., Huntington Beach, tel. 714/969–5480), **Rainbow Bicycles** (485 N. Coast Hwy., Laguna Beach, tel. 949/494–5806), or **Oceanfront Wheel Works** (Balboa Pier, Main St., Newport Beach, tel. 949/723–6510).

Mountain bicyclists like to head to the Santa Monica Mountains (see Parks, *above*).

BOATING. The biggest boating town of all is **Newport Beach,** where you can rent sailboats and small motorboats at the **Balboa Boat Co.** in the harbor (tel. 949/673–7200); rented boats are not allowed out of the bay. At Dana Point Harbor in Dana Point, rent sailboats and powerboats at **Embarcadero Marina** (tel. 949/496–6177).

FISHING. Shore fishing and surf casting are excellent on many of the beaches, such as **Doheny State Beach** and **Manhattan State Beach** (see Beaches, *above*) and **Las Tunas State Beach** (19444 PCH, Malibu, tel. 310/457–9891). Pier fishing is popular at the **Malibu, Santa Monica, Newport Beach,** and **Redondo Beach** piers, all have bait-and-tackle shops nearby. The lakes in Long Beach's **El Dorado Regional Park** (see Parks,

above) are stocked with catfish, carp, and trout.

For boat excursions in search of sea bass, rock cod, halibut, bonita, and yellowtail, try the **Redondo Sport Fishing Company** (233 N. Harbor Dr., Redondo Beach, tel. 310/372–2111); **Marina del Rey Sportfishing** (13759 Fiji Way, tel. 310/822–3625); or **Dana Wharf Sportfishing** (Dana Point marina, tel. 949/496–5794).

GOLF. Young golfers can tee up for 18 holes at **Harding Golf Course** or **Wilson Golf Course,** both at 4730 Crystal Springs Drive in Griffith Park (tel. 323/663–2555); for a more challenging course try the park's 9-hole **Roosevelt Course** (2650 N. Vermont Ave., tel. 323/665–2011). Another course in the Griffith park vicinity—good for beginners—is the 9-hole **Los Feliz Pitch 'n' Putt** (3207 Los Feliz Blvd., tel. 323/663–7758).

HIKING. For families with young children **Nursery Nature Walks** offers dozens of leisurely, safe walks each month at sites such as Malibu Lagoon, Topanga State Park, and Will Rogers State Park. The walks are two hours or less, with many stops to smell the plants, hug the trees, and discover the wonders of the outdoors. Some trails are stroller accessible. Walks are geared for newborns through 8-year-olds. *1440 Harvard St., Santa Monica, tel. 310/998–1151. $5 donation requested per family.*

William O. Douglas Outdoor Classroom (tel. 310/858–3834 or 310/858–3090) offers free hikes for kids (from babies through school-age) at Franklin Canyon Ranch (2600 Franklin Canyon Dr., Beverly Hills) in the Santa Monica Mountains. Reserve in advance.

Will Rogers State Historic Park and **Griffith Park** (see Parks, *above*) have several good trails for kids. One Griffith Park trail leaves from the Observatory parking lot and offers great city vistas; another runs through Fern Dell (off Fern Dell Dr., reached from Los Feliz Blvd.), shaded by thousands of ferns.

To get away from it all, we like to hike in the **Santa Monica Mountains National Recreation Area** (see Parks, *above*, and Chapter 8). The **National Park Service** (tel. 818/597–9192) can tell you about various free guided hikes led daily by park rangers and docents.

For further information on hiking in the area, contact the Sierra Club (343 Wilshire Blvd., Suite 320, Los Angeles 90010, tel. 213/387–4287).

HORSEBACK RIDING. The Griffith Park area has more than 50 miles of bridle trails; contact **Bar "S" Stables** (1850 Riverside Dr., Glendale, tel. 818/242–8443) or the **Griffith Park Horse Rentals Los Angeles Equestrian Center** (480 Riverside Dr., Burbank, tel. 818/840–8401).

KAYAKING. For kayaking off the Malibu and Newport coasts, see Chapter 10.

SNORKELING. Snorkeling off **Leo Carrillo State Beach** (see Serendipities, *above*) is considered some of the best along the Pacific Coast. **Corona del Mar,** with two colorful coral reefs and no boats allowed, and **Laguna Beach,** a marine preserve, also are good spots. **New England Divers** (2936 S. Clark Ave., Long Beach, tel. 562/421–8939) and **Dive & Surf** (504 N. Broadway, Redondo Beach, tel. 310/372–8423) rent equipment.

SURFING AND BOOGIEBOARDING. Top surfing beaches include **Huntington State Beach, Doheny State Beach** (good for beginners), **Surfrider Beach, Topanga Canyon State Beach,** and **Zuma Beach County Park** (see Beaches, *above*). "The Wedge" at **Newport Beach** is one of the most famous surfing spots in the world—but don't try it unless you're an expert. Rental stands are found at all beaches. **Hobie's Sports** has locations in Dana Point (tel. 949/496–2366) and Laguna Beach (tel.

949/497–3304); in Malibu try **Malibu Ocean Sports** (south of Malibu Pier, tel. 310/456–6302), where you can also get lessons.

TENNIS. **Lincoln Park** (Lincoln and Wilshire Blvds., Santa Monica), **Griffith Park** (Riverside Dr. and Los Feliz Blvd.), and **Barrington Park** (Barrington Ave. just south of Sunset Blvd. in L.A.) all have well-maintained, lighted public courts; each charges an hourly fee.

WINDSURFING. Marina del Rey, Malibu, Long Beach, and Dana Point are among the best places for windsurfing. **Malibu Ocean Sports** (see Surfing, *above*) offers lessons.

Shops

L.A. is a big shopping town. Our kids especially like **Universal CityWalk** (tel. 818/622–4455; see Serendipities, *above*), where Grael's favorite stop is Wizardz Wonderz, a great magic shop; other shops include Things From Another World for comics and replicas of dinosaurs and space aliens; and The Nature Company, which has a rain-forest motif.

Another good place for kids is **Olvera Street** (tel. 213/628–1274) in downtown L.A., where colorful Mexican-style stands line the street (see Ethnic Neighborhoods, *above*). Also downtown, the block-long **Grand Central Market** (317 S. Broadway, tel. 213/624–2378) is the city's most bustling market, filled with exotic produce stands and ethnic fast food booths. Don't confuse it with **Farmers Market** (6333 W. 3rd St. at Fairfax Ave., tel. 213/933–9211), a few blocks from the Hancock Park museums, which contains not only produce stands but dozens of shops, delis, and eateries, many with outdoor dining. It's next to CBS-TV studios, so you may spot stars munching donuts or Caesar salads.

Santa Monica Place (3rd and Broadway, Santa Monica, tel. 310/394–5451) contains many children's stores, including toy and clothing chains such as Imaginarium, Gap Kids, and Gymboree. In summer, Friday mornings at 11, there's a live half-hour show, A Kids' World, on Level 3, which introduces younger children to world cultures through music and folklore.

Take teens window shopping on **Rodeo Drive** (tel. 310/271–8126) in Beverly Hills— L.A.'s ritziest, most famous shopping street, with the toney likes of Polo/Ralph Lauren, Cartier, Tiffany, and Chanel wedged into 2½ blocks between Wilshire and Santa Monica boulevards. Both teens and preteens should enjoy the scene along **Melrose Avenue** between Fairfax and La Brea avenues, site of a long string of funky, eccentric, trendy boutiques. Check out **Time After Time** (7425 Melrose Ave., tel. 323/653-8463) for vintage clothing and **Wasteland** (7428 Melrose Ave., tel. 323/653–3028), for reasonably priced retro clothing. **Fantasies Come True** (8012 Melrose Ave., tel. 213/655–2636) is filled with Walt Disney memorabilia, and **Wound and Wound** (7374 Melrose, tel. 323/653-6703) stocks loads of windup toys, robots, and rubber animals.

Children's Book World (10580½ Pico Blvd., West Los Angeles, tel. 310/559–2665) is a large, airy space filled with a tempting selection.

In Orange County, head for the huge **South Coast Plaza** (3333 Bristol St., Costa Mesa, tel. 714/435–2000), which includes an F.A.O. Schwarz toy store, The Disney Store, and Sesame Street General Store. **Hobby City** (1238 S. Beach Blvd., Anaheim, tel. 714/527–2323) sells dolls, miniatures, baseball cards, and trains, and has a Doll and Toy Museum; doll-lovers can also check out **Doll City U.S.A.** (2080 S. Harbor Blvd., Anaheim, tel. 714/750–3585).

In the Inland Empire, **Ontario Mills** (1 Mills Circle, Ontario, tel. 909/484–8300) stakes a claim to being the nation's largest shopping mall. Besides nearly 200 outlet shops, it contains a huge food court and a 30-screen

movie theater. You might also want to visit **American Wilderness Experience,** which provides an ersatz look at the animals and habitats of five California environments; or the **Sega Game Works,** which offers an interactive play area.

Eats

Los Angeles is one of America's premier dining cities, filled with trendy restaurants— not all receptive to children. Still, even some trendy spots offer children's menus, high chairs, and booster seats, and there are plenty of diners, ethnic restaurants, and classic L.A. dining spots that do cater to families. Keep in mind: If the kids are hungry, it's best to choose a restaurant near where you are, and go early to avoid a long wait.

Beverly Hills and the Westside

The Hard Rock Cafe. This branch of the international chain is a great place to star watch; teens can also observe local teen culture, absorb blasts of rock music, and gape at a remarkable assortment of rock memorabilia. You'll spot the 1959 green Cadillac plunging through the roof outside—and, in all likelihood, a line out the door. The food is consistently good (burgers, salads, barbecued chicken and ribs) served with efficiency considering the ever-present noise and crowds. Hard Rock also has a branch in Newport Beach (see *below*). *8600 Beverly Blvd., in the Beverly Center, West Hollywood, tel. 310/276–7605. Children's menu. No reservations. Dress: casual. AE, D, DC, MC, V. $$*

Dive! You might expect a theatrical setting from a restaurant whose name ends with an exclamation point and which was developed by Steven Spielberg, and you won't be disappointed at Dive! Eating at this Century City spot is something like going on a simulated submarine ride at a theme park. Try to land a table near a porthole, but if you can't, you'll still be part of the experience when the entire "submarine"—that's the ambience here—goes on a "dive." The specialty, natch, is submarine sandwiches. The s'mores make a nice dessert, even without a campfire to eat them around. Expect a wait at peak hours. *10250 Santa Monica Blvd., Los Angeles, tel. 310/788–3483. No reservations. Dress: casual. AE, D, DC, MC, V. $–$$*

Ed Debevic's. A '50s-style diner with attitude, Ed Debevic's is a raucous place with rock oldies on the jukebox and waitresses who sit at your table when you order. The decor is gleaming chrome and Formica, with mottos posted to keep you amused if you have to wait for a table: "Eat and Get Out," "Good Food, Fresh Service," and "We Are Not Responsible for Children Trampled in the Aisles." But it's all in good fun (I think), just like the food: tasty burgers, onion rings, chili fries, and shakes from the old-fashioned soda fountain (plus other sandwiches, blue-plate dinners, soup and salad buffet, and all-day breakfast). *134 N. La Cienega Blvd., Beverly Hills, tel. 310/659–1952. No reservations. Dress: casual. AE, D, DC, MC, V. $–$$*

The Apple Pan. When only a burger and fries will do, and you want them done right, head for The Apple Pan, a Westside fixture for decades. At this small diner, everyone sits at a U-shape counter that surrounds an open kitchen on three sides. Chances are you'll have to wait, but service is fast and the cooks put on a good show. What will it be—steakburger or steakburger with cheese? And if you really want to go wild, how about a tuna salad or ham-and-swiss sandwich? That about covers the menu, except for great fries and big slices of apple pie (with or without ice cream). Most items are served on paper plates or in paper cups. *10801 W. Pico Blvd., West Los Angeles, tel. 310/475–3585. No reservations. Dress: casual. No credit cards. $*

Hollywood

Hollywood Hills Coffee Shop. Believe it or not, this unpretentious place has become a spot for star-watching. Is that Brad Pitt digging into an omelet? Jennifer Aniston sampling the huevos rancheros? Breakfast is served all day at this café that was used as a setting in the film *Swingers* and has been drawing celebs since. But whether the stars are out, the Mexican-accented American food is terrific. (You don't have to have breakfast; there are regular meat and seafood entrées at lunch and dinner; on the dinner-only children's menu are macaroni and cheese, grilled-cheese sandwiches, and burgers.) You might have to wait in line, but it's worth it: The person behind you might be Sandra Bullock. *6145 Franklin Ave., Hollywood, tel. 323/467–7678. Children's menu (at dinner). No reservations. Dress: casual. MC, V. $–$$*

Roscoe's House of Chicken 'n' Waffles. You want fried chicken? You want waffles? You want both fried chicken with waffles? This longtime Hollywood favorite is the place to come for good, inexpensive down-home Southern cooking served in casual surroundings. The restaurant hasn't a children's menu, how many children don't like, well, chicken or waffles? *1514 N. Gower St., tel. 323/466–9329. No reservations. Dress: casual. AE, D, DC, MC, V. $.*

Downtown

La Golondrina. This Mexican restaurant serves good food at reasonable prices, but the real reason to come is the location in the heart of Olvera Street. In the city's historic first brick building, La Golondrina has indoor and outdoor seating; we like the front patio, where you can watch the street action and hear mariachis play on weekends. Enchiladas, tostadas, tacos, and other Mexican dishes are served, along with combination plates including taquitos, flautas, and chile. House specialties include fajitas, chiles relleno, and charbroiled fresh fish. The *niños*

menu includes a burrito, taquitos with gua-
camole, or a *hamburguesa* and fries. *W–17
Olvera St., tel. 213/628–4349. Children's
menu. Reservations advised. Dress: casual to
dressy casual. AE, D, DC, MC, V. $$*

Mon Kee's Sea Food Restaurant. This
bustling, rather plain two-room restaurant
has long served some of the best Chinese
food in the city. The specialty is Hong Kong–
style fresh seafood: steamed fish, crab with
ginger and green onion, stir-fried shrimp
with snow peas. Everyone shares dishes,
Chinese-style, so there's no need for a chil-
dren's menu. (If your kids are uncertain
about the seafood, order some of the chow
mein, or some Chinese-style crisp fried
chicken.) The one downside is that Mon
Kee's is on a rather dark, sparsely traveled
street, two blocks from the brighter lights of
North Broadway, but there's often a line of
other prospective diners waiting outside for
company. Mon Kee's also has a location in
Manhattan County Beach (see *above*). *679
N. Spring St., Los Angeles, tel. 213/628–6717.
Reservations accepted. Dress: casual. AE, DC,
MC, V. $$*

Philippe the Original. This downtown landmark (since 1908) draws customers of
every description for casual, cheap, delicious
food. Philippe is credited with inventing the
French dip sandwich, and that's what almost
everyone orders. It comes in five varieties:
pork, beef, ham, lamb, or turkey, all dipped
in natural juices and served on French rolls
(you can add cheese, and hot mustard is on
the tables). Pickles, coleslaw, deli salads, and
desserts (ice cream, baked apple) are available on the side. The sandwiches are small
enough for a child to finish easily. We like to
come here for a quick lunch or afternoon
snack—this isn't the place for a relaxing dinner. (You order at a counter and wait to pick
up your food, then sit on stools at long, family-style tables.) Philippe's serves breakfast—
and one of America's last dime cups of coffee. Free parking is available. *1001 N.
Alameda St., tel. 213/628–3781. No reservations. Dress: casual. No credit cards. $*

Malibu/Pacific Palisades

Gladstone's 4 Fish. The self-proclaimed
most popular restaurant on the Pacific coast,
Gladstone's accommodates many people
between its sprawling indoor dining area
and big outdoor deck, but you'll probably
still have to wait if you arrive right at meal-
time. On the outdoor deck you sit on
wooden benches at concrete tables that
overlook the beach, so the kids can always
scamper down to the sand if they get restless. Come hungry—portions are huge.
(Ask to split portions for kids.) The specialty
is seafood, naturally, much of it mesquite-
broiled. You can get fish chowder, seafood
salads, a classy tuna sandwich with fresh
potato chips, or an enormous hamburger
for lunch; the fish or shellfish dinners come
broiled, fried, or steamed. The fish is good,
but more to the point, this is a classic L.A.
scene. *17300 PCH (at Sunset Blvd.), tel. 310/
573–0212. Reservations accepted. Dress:
casual. AE, DC, MC, V. $$–$$$*

Pasadena

Souplantation. This noisy, bustling, but
pleasant restaurant is one of the best food
deals in greater L.A. Customers serve themselves cafeteria-style from an all-you-can-eat
salad bar and a soup bar with six different
choices. There's a selection of muffins, corn
bread, and focaccia, and the desserts include
soft ice cream, fruit, and bakery items. Hungry teens and adults can really load up here
at lunch for $6.99 each; kids ages 6 to 12 eat
for $3.99; and kids 3 to 5 eat for 99¢. After
4 PM and on weekends the prices rise, but
only a dollar or so. No sharing is allowed,
and all food must be eaten on premises.
Souplantation also has several branches in
Orange County (see *below*). *201 S. Lake
Ave., Pasadena, tel. 626/577–4797. No reservations. Dress: casual. D, MC, V. $–$$*

Santa Monica

I Cugini. If I had to choose one restaurant
for a special meal out with the kids in L.A., it

would be this Italian trattoria. Everything about I Cugini is buonissimo—the decor (high ceilings, marble tables, a screened patio with ocean views), the accommodating way kids are treated, and the food, which is simply superb. You can comfortably bring young kids here for an early dinner—the Kids' Menu includes spaghetti with meat, butter, or tomato sauces, or pizza. Children also get a menu to color and a box of crayons. Parents, meanwhile, can feast on great roast chicken, grilled seafood, huge panini (Italian sandwiches), wonderful fresh salads and pastas, wood-fired gourmet pizzas, or brunch items like French toast with smoked bacon or a wild mushroom omelet. All breads are baked on the premises and taste so good you could make a meal of them (but don't stop there). *1501 Ocean Ave., Santa Monica, tel. 310/451–4595. Children's menu. Reservations advised. Dress: casual but neat. AE, D, DC, MC, V. $$$*

Gaucho Grill. Here is one of our favorite restaurants on Santa Monica's Third Street Promenade, where Argentinian specialties include several types of grilled chicken and steak, all reasonably priced. You can get grilled, marinated chicken on the bone or boneless; and short ribs or rib-eye and sirloin steaks, all served with curlicue fries. You can also choose from salads (including grilled chicken salad), or chicken and steak sandwiches. Inside, the restaurant has brick walls, beamed ceilings, and wooden tables; outside, there are some smallish tables along the Promenade. Either way, the setting is busy, rather noisy, and fun. Gaucho Grill also has locations in Hollywood, Studio City, Brentwood, and Glendale (call for locations). *1253 Third Street Promenade, Santa Monica, tel. 310/394–4966. Reservations for 5 or more only. Dress: casual. AE, DC, MC, V. $$*

Wolfgang Puck Cafe. (See Universal City, below.) *1323 Montana Ave., Santa Monica, tel. 310/393–0290. Reservations accepted. Dress: casual. AE, DC, MC, V. $$*

Universal City

The Hard Rock Cafe Hollywood. (See Beverly Hills and the Westside, above.) This two-story branch on Universal's CityWalk beckons with a 65-foot neon guitar out front. *1000 Universal Center Dr., tel. 818/622–7625. Children's menu. No reservations. Dress: casual. AE, D, DC, MC, V. $$*

Marvel Mania Hollywood. OK, so this is another gimmicky theme restaurant, but it is Hollywood, so relax and enjoy it. This is the only full-service restaurant within Universal Studios Hollywood (see Chapter 9), and it can also be entered from Universal CityWalk. Once inside, you've entered the world of Spiderman, the Fantastic Four, The Incredible Hulk, Silver Surfer, and Captain America—and there's no escape from them (even in the rest rooms!). Expect flashing lights, sirens, and other special effects, including the "Morph Wall," a 20-ft-by-20-ft video screen that emits vapors while broadcasting animated Marvel comic shows. And what of the food? Well, how about Mutant Chicken Wings, Pulse-Pounding Pizzas, Hulk Smashed Potatoes, Super Hero Burgers, and Sinister Six Layer Cake? A kids' menu (and you thought the preceding was the kids' menu?) includes Defender Tenders, Dare Dogs, and the Wolverine Chocolate Chip Claw. *1000 Universal City Dr., Universal City, tel. 818/762–7835. Children's menu. Reservations accepted. Dress: casual. AE, D, DC, MC, V. $$*

Wolfgang Puck Cafe. Just because you have kids along doesn't mean you can't sample the creations of L.A.'s most famous chef, Wolfgang Puck (the genius behind Spago and other restaurants)—and at very reasonable prices. This attractive café on Universal's CityWalk serves up specialty pizzas (including herb sausage, spicy chicken, marinated shrimp, smoked salmon, and four-cheese toppings), freshly made salads, pastas, and delicious rotisserie chicken (try the rosemary half chicken with garlic mashed potatoes). You can sit inside, with its open kitchen and multicolored tile floors and walls, or on the front patio with umbrella-shaded tables and great people-watching. There are also branches in Santa Monica (see *above*) and Costa Mesa (see *below*). *1000 Universal Center Dr., Universal City, tel. 818/985–9653. No reservations. Dress: casual. AE, DC, MC, V. $$*

Orange County

Besides the listings *below*, try the dinner theater shows at **Medieval Times** or **Wild Bill's** in Buena Park (see *Theater, below*). At Disneyland, head to **Goofy's Kitchen** at the Disneyland Resort (see Where to Stay, *below*).

The Hard Rock Cafe. (See Beverly Hills and the Westside, *above*). *451 Newport Center Dr., Newport Beach, tel. 949/640–8844. Children's menu. No reservations. Dress: casual. AE, D, DC, MC, V. $$*

Mrs. Knott's Chicken Dinner Restaurant. Since 1934, when Mrs. Walter Knott started frying chickens for patrons of her husband's fledgling Knott's Berry Farm amusement park, this restaurant has been dishing out huge portions of poultry to steady crowds of customers. You can get fried chicken and eggs for breakfast, and after 11 AM, four-piece chicken dinners (fried, broiled, or with dumplings) that also include appetizer or soup, salad, vegetable, biscuits, dessert, and nonalcoholic beverages. It's a lot of food; you can order a smaller version for lunch, or a chicken sandwich or salad. The Snoopy-theme Children's Menu, suitable for coloring, offers kid-size chicken delights. Though it's adjacent to Knott's Berry Farm, you can eat here without going to the theme park. *8039 Beach Blvd., Buena Park, tel. 714/827–1776. Children's menu. No reservations. Dress: casual. AE, D, DC, MC, V. $$*

Wolfgang Puck Cafe. (See Universal City, *above*.) *South Coast Plaza, 3333 Bear St., Costa Mesa, tel. 714/546–9653. No reservations. Dress: casual. AE, DC, MC, V. $$*

Souplantation. (See Pasadena, *above*.) *1555 Adams Ave., Costa Mesa, tel. 714/556–1903,* *and other locations. No reservations. Dress: casual. D, DC, MC, V. $–$$*

Where to Stay

Los Angeles is spread out, so it's a good idea to choose a hotel based on its location. The Santa Monica, Marina del Rey, and Beverly Hills areas lie along or near the beaches; Universal City is convenient for Universal Studios Hollywood and the San Fernando Valley; downtown L.A. has big-city lights and bustle; and Anaheim is the place to be for Disneyland and other Orange County attractions. Many hotels charge for parking, sometimes a substantial amount, and bed taxes range from 12% to L.A.'s 14%.

Anaheim Hilton and Towers. A short, complimentary shuttle ride from Disneyland, this 14-story luxury hotel—Orange County's largest—makes a good effort to compete with the Disneyland Resort for families' affections. There's a free summer day-care center ("Vacation Station") for children ages 5 to 13; kids check in at their own registration desk and receive a Family Fun Kit with suggestions of things to do and coupons good for cookies and milk and other goodies; and during their stay kids can check out toys, video and other games, and books from a lending desk. Kids can also take behind-the-scenes tours of the hotel, which is virtually a self-contained city—it even has its own post office. The Anaheim Convention Center is only 50 feet from the front door (handy for parents attending conventions, but increasing the crowds and noise in the three-story lobby, especially at breakfast time). Children of any age stay free with their parents. *777 Convention Way, Anaheim 92802, tel. 714/750–4321, 800/222–9923 or 800/932–3322. 1,576 rooms and 96 suites. Facilities: 4 restaurants, 2 pools, 5 hot tubs, sauna, fitness center. AE, D, DC, MC, V. $$$*

Disneyland Resort. (See Chapter 12.) This luxury family resort with two hotels is a monorail ride away from Disneyland. *1150*

W. Cerritos Ave., Anaheim 92802, tel. 714/ 956–6400. $$$

Loews Santa Monica Beach Hotel. Santa Monica is one of the nicest places for families to stay in the L.A. area, and Loews is the nicest family-oriented hotel there. In fact, it's as much a city resort as a hotel. The location couldn't be better—right on the beach, two blocks from the Santa Monica Pier and three blocks from the Third Street Promenade. The design is dramatic—a five-story glass atrium rises over the lobby, the glass-domed swimming pool ranges both indoors and outdoors, and the deck off the pool provides sweeping views of the ocean. Rooms are California casual, with wicker furniture and colors of sand and sky; most have ocean views. Kids ages 5 to 12 can head for the "Splash Club," which offers supervised activities mornings and evenings ($5 per one-hour session). The fun may include building sand castles, running relays on the beach, making videos (starring themselves), fashioning puppets and masks, diving for treasure in the pool, and painting T-shirts. Kids can also check out books, video games, and board games. The hotel provides complimentary cribs with musical mobiles, playpens, car seats, and childproofing kits for use during the family's stay. Kids under 18 stay free in their parents' room, or in a connecting room for 50% off in summer. 1700 Ocean Ave., Santa Monica 90401, tel. 310/ 458–6700 or 800/235-6397, fax 310/458– 6761. 350 rooms, including 31 suites. Facilities: 2 restaurants, pool, hot tub, health club, bike and skate rentals, children's program. AE, D, DC, MC, V. $$$

Marina del Rey Hotel. When you gaze out from this attractive deluxe hotel overlooking the world's largest man-made marina, it's almost easy to forget that you're only minutes from LAX and a huge urban area. The hotel faces the marina's main channel, with great views of the boats and water. Guest rooms (contemporary with nautical touches) are good size, with divided bathrooms (sink separate), plus balconies and

patios; many have harbor views. It's a very relaxing place to stay, and you may even see a wedding being held in the beautiful gazebo area in front of the water. We had almost a front-row view from our balcony, and I had to make sure Lia didn't catch the bouquet! 13534 Bali Way, Marina del Rey 90292, tel. 310/301–1000 or 800/882–4000, fax 310/ 301–8167. 157 rooms. Facilities: restaurant, pool, free airport transport, free parking. AE, DC, MC, V. $$$

Sunset Marquis. Once known as one of L.A.'s top "rock-'n'-roll hotels"—it's right off the Sunset Strip—the Sunset Marquis is now going for the family trade (including pop stars who now have kids and have mellowed). Guests stay in hotel rooms (all suites) and adjacent Spanish-style villas, surrounded by lush gardens, pools, and a waterfall. The patio restaurant has a dinosaur-decorated children's menu that includes pizza and burgers. And here's a gimmick guaranteed to please most any kid: The hotel has a bunny hutch, and children of villa guests are invited to choose and name a pet to play with during their stay. 1200 N. Alta Loma Rd., West Hollywood 90069, tel. 310/657–1333 or 800/858–9758, fax 310/ 652–5300. 114 suites, 12 villas. Facilities: restaurant, pool, sauna, exercise room, refrigerators. AE, DC, MC, V. $$$

Waterfront Hilton Beach Resort. This resort on the Orange County coast overlooks some 8 miles of white sandy beaches, and every guest room has a view of the surf from its own private balcony. (Note, however, that the resort is across the highway from the beach; you can cross at a signal light.) A big draw for families in summer (and some weekends the rest of the year) is the resort's Dolphin Youth Club for ages 5 to 12, most of it complimentary. The program includes supervised activities such as poolside games, arts and crafts, and movies; Thursday to Sunday evening sessions, including a meal, are $5. The Dolphin Club operates in conjunction with Hilton's Vacation Station program, which provides welcome gifts for kids and free use of toys and games, including video games. Swimming (at an ocean-view pool), bike riding, Rollerblading, kite-flying, tennis, beach cookouts, and surfing are all available in or around the resort. *21100 Pacific Coast Hwy., Huntington Beach 92648, tel. 714/960–7873 or 800/822–7873, fax 714/960–2642. 290 rooms including 24 suites. Facilities: restaurant, pool, hot tub, health club, children's program. AE, D, DC, MC, V. $$$*

Westin Bonaventure. Oh, to be a kid exploring the Westin Bonaventure. Not that I'm suggesting you turn kids loose in this 35-story, futuristic complex—even the manager describes it as "perhaps overwhelming" at first—but what fun a kid *could* have. The hotel's five circular glass towers, each with its own outside glass elevators (seen in several movies), and its wild multistory lobby with inventive architecture have made the Bonaventure a sightseeing stop even for people not staying here. The lower floors are circled with some 40 shops and restaurants, including all manner of casual ethnic eateries. You can swim surrounded by skyscrapers at the outdoor pool off the fourth floor. Some standard rooms are smallish, but many have wonderful views, and the hotel recently converted one of its towers to all suites. Children age 18 and under stay free with their parents. *404 S. Figueroa St., Los Angeles 90071, tel. 213/624–1000 or 800/228–3000, fax 213/612–4797. 1,368 rooms including 157 suites. Facilities: 17 restaurants, pool, tennis, health club. AE, D, DC, MC, V. $$$*

Holiday Inn Select Beverly Hills. This recently renovated 12-story hotel provides convenient location and some nice amenities at a price less than more toney properties nearby. There's an outdoor pool, a restaurant suitable for family dining, complimentary membership at a Family Fitness Center up the street, and a full-time, friendly concierge to answer questions and solve problems. Rooms, especially the suites, are spacious, and some have excellent views of the surroundings. *1150 S. Beverly Dr., Los Angeles 90035, tel. 310/553–6561 or 800/465–4329, fax 310/277–4469. 260 rooms, 12 suites. Facilities: restaurant, pool. AE, D, DC, MC, V. $$–$$$*

Mission Inn. If your travels take you to the Riverside area (55 miles east of L.A.)—or if you merely want to stay in a memorable historic inn in the Los Angeles area—consider this National Historic Landmark, which covers an entire city block. The Mission Inn should delight kids with its striking, eclectic, way-out architecture: gargoyles, flying buttresses, domes, a bell tower, clock towers, courtyards, patios, fountains, and a five-story circular rotunda (the look has been compared to a Spanish palace, with Moorish, Italian, even Japanese touches). The inn, a favorite of several U.S. presidents from McKinley to Reagan—Richard and Pat Nixon were married here, as were Humphrey Bogart and Bette Davis (though not to each other), received extensive renovations in the early 1990s. The heated outdoor Olympic-size pool and in-room movies are likely to keep kids busy. Many rooms have unusual features, such as domed ceilings, wrought-iron balconies, tile floors, wall niches, and stained-glass windows. *3649 Mission Inn Ave., Riverside 92501, tel. 909/784–0300, fax 909/683–1342. 236 rooms, including 33 suites. Facilities: 2 restaurants, pool, spa, health club. AE, DC, MC, V. $$–$$$*

Sheraton Universal. If you'd like to be first in line at Universal Studios Hollywood—and maybe spot some movie and TV stars in your hotel lobby—head for the Sheraton Universal, a 21-story hotel within walking distance (or a free tram ride) of the Universal Studios Tour and Universal CityWalk. The comfortable rooms, decorated in soft natural tones, have floor-to-ceiling windows that open; upper-story rooms have great views. Ask about special package deals that include passes to the Universal Studios tour. Kids under 16 stay free with parents. *333 Universal Terrace Pkwy., Universal City 91608, tel. 818/980–1212 or 800/325–3535, fax*

818/985–4980. 442 rooms, 20 suites. Facilities: restaurant, pool, health club, self and valet parking (fee). AE, D, DC, MC, V. $$–$$$

Hotel Queen Mary. It's exciting for most kids just to visit the *Queen Mary* (see Historic Sites, *above*, and Chapter 4), once the world's largest luxury liner, now docked permanently in Long Beach; but to stay on the *Queen* is an unforgettable experience. The ship has 365 of its original but recently renovated first-class staterooms available for stays. While the rooms are smallish for a hotel, they're good size for a ship and bespeak the elegance of a bygone era: the craftsmanship, right down to the original bathroom fixtures, is exceptional. If you stay here—as we did—you can take all the time you need to explore the ship. You can also book adjoining rooms. The Promenade Café serves casual family meals. *1150 Queen's Hwy., Pier H, Long Beach 90802, tel. 562/435–3511. 300 rooms. Facilities: 2 restaurants, deli. AE, MC, V. $$*

Pacific Shore Hotel. Across the street from the beach, this eight-story Santa Monica hotel offers good value for families. The rooms are modern and spacious, and many have ocean views. There's a big outdoor pool in back, with a terrace and poolside food and drink service, and the staff is quite friendly. Children under 12 stay free with their parents. *1819 Ocean Ave., Santa Monica 90401, tel. 310/451–8711 or 800/622–8711, fax 310/394–6657. 168 room. Facilities: restaurant, pool, hot tub, free parking. AE, D, DC, MC, V. $–$$*

Peacock Suites Hotel. Two blocks from Disneyland, with complimentary shuttle service to the theme park, this all-suites hotel provides a less expensive alternative to the Disneyland Resort or Anaheim Hilton (see *above*). The two-room suites have refrigerators and microwaves. Complimentary Continental breakfast is served. *1745 Anaheim Blvd., Anaheim 92802, tel. 714/535–8255 or 800/522–6410, fax 714/535–8914. 140 suites. Facilities: kitchenettes, pool, spa, health club, game area. AE, D, DC, MC, V. $–$$*

Best Western Royal Palace. This smallish hotel is right off I–405 (the San Diego Freeway), making it convenient to ocean beaches, LAX, and Beverly Hills; each is within 8 or 10 miles. Kids should like the outdoor pool, and there's also an indoor hot tub. Suites have microwaves and refrigerators, as well as love seats. Complimentary Continental breakfast is served. *2528 S. Sepulveda Blvd., West Los Angeles 90064, tel. 310/477–9066 or 800/528–1234, fax 310/478–4133. 23 rooms, 32 suites. Facilities: pool, hot tub, laundry, free parking. AE, D, DC, MC, V. $*

Entertainments

Arcades

Play arcade games or minigolf and ride go-carts or bumper boats at **Golf N' Stuff Family Fun Center** (10555 E. Firestone Blvd., tel. 562/868–9956) in Norwalk. Rides cost $1 to $5; it's open daily from 10 AM, closing at 10 PM Monday–Thursday and at 1 AM Friday–Sunday.

Dance

Check out **Dance Kaleidoscope Festival** (tel. 323/343–6610), with special Saturday shows for kids.

Movies

Mann's Chinese Theatre (6925 Hollywood Blvd., tel. 323/464–8111) and **El Capitan** (6838 Hollywood Blvd., tel. 323/467–7674) are classic venues for movie watching. More modern spots for first-run films include the **Loews Cineplex Universal City Cinema** (Universal Center Dr., Universal City, tel. 818/508–0588), one of the world's largest movie complexes; the **AMC Santa Monica 7** (1310 3rd St., Third Street Promenade, Santa Monica, tel. 310/395–3030); and the **Mann's Westwood** (1050 Gayley Ave., Westwood, tel. 310/208–7664). The **IMAX**

Theater (tel. 213/744–2014) next to the California Science Center (see Chapter 5) shows sensational nature and science movies on a seven-story screen. The **Pacific Cinerama Dome** (6360 Hollywood Blvd., Hollywood, tel. 323/466–3401) shows Cinerama films on a giant screen.

Music

Look for the **Los Angeles Philharmonic** (tel. 213/850–2000) kids' concerts series; the six-week summer performance series **Open House at the Hollywood Bowl** (tel. 323/850–2000); Orange County's springtime arts festival **Imagination Celebration** (tel. 714/556–2121) and kids' concerts by the **Pacific Symphony Orchestra** (tel. 714/755–5788); and the outdoor family concerts at the **Redlands Bowl Summer Music Festival** (tel. 909/793–7316).

(**ALL**) **Sunday Concerts in the Park** is a series of free summer afternoon concerts held at the Peter Strauss Ranch in the Santa Monica Mountains National Recreation Area (see Parks, *above*). An annual Mother's Day concert kicks off the season, which typically presents an assortment of folk, bluegrass, mariachi, and ethnic dance performers.
🏠 *Visitor Center, 30401 Agoura Rd., Agoura Hills 91301, tel. 818/597–9192.*

TV and Movie Tapings

For free tickets to tapings, call **ABC-TV** at 818/506–0067 or 818/506–0043; **CBS-TV** at 213/852–2458; **NBC-TV** at 818/840–3537; and **Paramount Pictures** at 213/956–5575. Free TV show tickets are also often available outside Mann's Chinese Theatre in Hollywood, at Universal Studios Hollywood, and along Ocean Front Walk on Venice Beach. Or call **Television Tickets** (tel. 213/467–4697) or **Audiences Unlimited** (tel. 818/506–0067), which also distribute free tickets. Keep in mind that many shows do not admit children under 10, while others have minimum ages ranging up to 18.

Theater

(**ALL**) The **Bob Baker Marionette Theater** presents classic marionette theater where kids get to sit up close to the stage and refreshments are served afterward. Don't let the fairly bleak downtown location keep you away.
🏠 *1345 W. 1st St., Los Angeles, tel. 213/250–9995. Admission: $10. Tues.–Fri. 10:30 AM, weekends 2:30 PM.*

(**6–15**) The **Shakespeare Festival/LA** stages free or low-cost productions at various locations around Los Angeles County, including Descanso Gardens in LaCanada and Citicorp Plaza downtown (canned food is collected for the poor in lieu of admission at most performances).
🏠 *411 W. 5th St., Suite 815, Los Angeles 90013, tel. 213/489–1121. Call for schedule.*

(**ALL**) The **Hollywood Children's Festival of the Arts,** held annually at Barnsdall Art Park (see Serendipities, *above*), presents various entertainments: puppets, storytelling, magic tricks, ethnic dance, and music (such as sing-alongs and mariachi).
🏠 *4800 Hollywood Blvd., Los Angeles, tel. 213/485–4474. A Sun. in mid-Aug.; call for date, time, and admission.*

(**ALL**) The **Theater Arts Festival for Youth** (TAFFY), held annually at the Peter Strauss Ranch in the Santa Monica Mountains National Recreation Area (see Parks, *above*), presents professional theater, along with music, ethnic dance, puppetry, juggling, storytelling, and mime. Food, face painting, arts displays, and hands-on crafts round out the festivities.
🏠 *30000 Mulholland Hwy., Agoura 91301, tel. 818/998–2339 or 818/597–9192. Oct. Admission: $10 adults, $9 ages 3–12, under 3 free.*

(**9–15**) The **California Youth Theater,** on the Paramount Studios lot, stages four shows a year, such as *Godspell, Oliver!,* or *Children of a Lesser God.* Young people ages

12 to 25 receive theatrical instruction, then display their talents in plays and musicals around the L.A. area.

🏠 *517 Westmount Dr., Los Angeles 90048, tel. 310/657–3270. Call for schedule.*

(👫 3 – 15) The **Laguna Playhouse's Moulton Theater** has a special children's theater with changing fare.

🏠 *606 Laguna Canyon Rd., Laguna Beach, tel. 949/494–0743.*

Other performances for kids and families are staged by the **Glendale Centre Theatre** (tel. 818/244–8481), the **Louis B. Mayer Theatre at the Los Angeles Children's Museum** (tel. 213/687–8800), the **Santa Monica Playhouse** (tel. 310/394–9779), and **Storybook Theater** (tel. 818/761–2203).

Kids can have their first dinner-theater experiences at two Buena Park establishments tailor-made for families: **Medieval Times Dinner and Tournament** (tel. 714/521–4740) and **Wild Bill's Wild West Dinner Extravaganza** (tel. 714/522–6414).

For Parents Only

Nightlife in L.A. includes trendy rock clubs, smooth country-and-western establishments, intimate jazz spots, and comedy clubs. The fabled Sunset Strip (Sunset Boulevard from West Hollywood to Beverly Hills) has a wide assortment; **Westwood,** the area around UCLA, comes alive at night with rock and new wave clubs. The **San Fernando** and **San Gabriel valleys** are scattered with jazz clubs, discos, and comedy clubs.

SAN DIEGO
SUNSHINE, BEACHES, PARKS, AND WILDLIFE

San Diego may be the most child-friendly city in the country, offering a rare combination of urban activities in a beautiful, relaxed setting. Though it's the nation's sixth-largest city, it never seems overly crowded, the pace tends to be on the slow side (except for skateboarders and jet-skiers), the streets are generally clean, and usually you can even find a parking space. All this in a climate meteorologists have described as nearly perfect: Daytime temperatures average 70∞F year-round, and sunshine is the norm. Many of the things kids like most—beaches, parks, exotic animals, outdoor sports—are abundant, and even toddlers can enjoy themselves here. Our family has visited San Diego nearly every year since the kids were tiny, and we never tire of it. The exceptional San Diego Zoo and Wild Animal Park, museum-rich Balboa Park, the recreational mecca Mission Bay, and miles of beautiful beaches add up to a superb place to visit.

The Basics

Resources

Several weeks before you go, contact the **San Diego Convention & Visitors Bureau** (401 B St., Suite 1400, Dept. 700, San Diego 92101, tel. 619/232–3101) for a copy of the *San Diego Official Visitors Guide,* a book full of information on accommodations, restaurants, attractions, and special events. Request a free "Sunny Money Super Savings" coupon booklet (available Apr.–Dec.), containing discounts at area attractions, hotels, restaurants, and shops. Information is available on the Web at http://www.sandiego.org. When you arrive, stop at the downtown **International Visitor Information Center** (Horton Plaza, 1st Ave. and F St., tel. 619/236–1212; open Mon.–Sat. 8:30–5; also June–Aug., Sun. 11–5) for maps, brochures, and advice. At the **San Diego Visitor Information Center** (2688 E. Mission Bay Dr., off I-5, tel. 619/276–8200; open daily 9–

5:30) you can make lodging reservations. For information about Coronado, contact the **Coronado Visitors Bureau** (1047 B Ave., Coronado 92118, tel. 619/437–8788 or 800/622–8300). For more about attractions north of the city, contact the **San Diego North Convention & Visitors Bureau** (720 N. Broadway, Escondido 92025, tel. 760/745–4741 or 800/848–3336).

San Diego Family Magazine, a monthly publication, carries listings of events and resources; it's available by mail (Box 23960, San Diego 92193, tel. 619/685–6970) for $16 a year, or pick up a free copy once you're in San Diego, at area McDonald's franchises, Blockbuster video stores, drugstores, libraries, and other outlets.

Getting in and out of San Diego

BY AIR. San Diego International Airport (tel. 619/231–7361), about 3 miles northwest of downtown, is one of the most convenient urban airports anywhere. The rest rooms have diaper-changing facilities. The airport, which has two terminals (East and West), is fairly compact; pizza, burgers, and frozen yogurt are among the snack options. Major domestic airlines serving San Diego include Alaska, American, Continental, Delta, Northwest, Southwest, TWA, United, and US Airways.

How to get into downtown: If you rent a car at the airport, follow Harbor Drive to downtown (it's about a five-minute drive). **San Diego Transit** (tel. 619/233–3004) Route 2 buses leave for downtown from the front of East Terminal's US Airways section; the fare is $1.50. Taxis charge from $7 to $9 to most center-city hotels. **Cloud 9 Shuttle** (tel. 619/278–8877 or 800/974–8885) and **Airport Shuttle** (tel. 619/234–4403 or 888/254–0333) provide door-to-door transportation anywhere in the San Diego area 24 hours a day, at set rates that can be lower than taxis if you're traveling more than a short distance. Flag a shuttle outside either terminal; to return to the airport, call for a reservation. Many hotels and resorts offer guests complimentary airport transportation.

BY CAR. Most car travelers arrive and depart via one of three interstate highways. Interstate 5 is the fastest route from Los Angeles (120 miles north) and San Francisco. Interstate 15 connects San Diego with the San Bernardino–Riverside–Ontario areas east of Los Angeles, as well as Las Vegas. Interstate 8 is an east–west highway leading to and from Yuma, Arizona, and points east.

BY TRAIN. San Diego's **Amtrak** station, the historic Santa Fe Depot (1050 Kettner Blvd. near Broadway, tel. 619/239–9021), is close to the harbor downtown, with convenient connections to the San Diego Trolley (see below). Amtrak (tel. 800/872–7245) runs frequent daily service to Los Angeles (three-hours), and stops at beach communities in northern San Diego County.

BY BUS. Greyhound/Trailways (tel. 619/239–8082 or 800/231–2222) operates 26 buses a day between San Diego's downtown terminal (120 West Broadway) and Los Angeles, connecting to all major U.S. cities.

Getting Around San Diego

BY CAR. Except at rush hours, streets and freeways are remarkably uncrowded. Interstate 5, which runs north–south, and I–8, which runs east–west, intersect just north of Old Town; I–15 (another north–south route) and I–8 cross each other near Qualcomm Stadium; and I–5 and I–15 meet south of downtown. To reach scenic Coronado, take the sweeping 2.2-mile Coronado Bridge ($1, free with two or more passengers).

BY LIGHT TRAIN AND BUS. The bright red cars of the **San Diego Trolley** (tel. 619/231–8549 or 619/233–3004) circle downtown every 15 minutes daily and connect it to Old Town, the eastern suburbs, and to Tijuana, Mexico. An extension to the Blue Line goes to Mission Valley and Qualcomm Stadium, home of the Padres and Chargers (see Sports, below). Buy tickets before boarding, using the sidewalk vending machines at each stop (fare: $1–$2.25, ages 4 and under free). **Coaster** (tel. 800/262–7837) weekday commuter trains run north up the coast from Old Town to the beach towns of Del Mar, Solana Beach, Encinitas, Carlsbad, and Oceanside; there's also limited service on Saturdays. **San Diego Transit** (tel. 619/233–3004 or 619/685–4900) buses offer service throughout the region; most buses to major attractions leave from 1st, 4th, or 5th avenues and Broadway downtown. A one-day ($5) or four-day ($12) Day Tripper Pass lets you ride on all municipal buses, trolleys, and ferries. You can buy passes at The Transit Store (102 Broadway at 1st Ave.), downtown.

BY TAXI. **Taxi companies** include Yellow Cab (tel. 619/234–6161), Orange Cab (tel. 619/291–3333), Coronado Cab (tel. 619/435–6211), and La Jolla Cab (tel. 619/453–

4222). The average rate is $2 for the first mile, $1.40 for each additional mile.

BY FERRY. The **San Diego-Coronado Ferry** (tel. 619/234–4111) leaves from the Broadway Pier (1050 N. Harbor Dr. and Broadway) daily on the hour, 9 to 9 (10 PM Friday and Saturday). A one-way crossing ($2; $2.50 with bicycle) takes 15 minutes. (Once on Coronado, you can take a bus or Electric Shuttle to the Hotel del Coronado and the beach.) Ferries return to San Diego every hour on the half-hour, from 9:30 to 9:30 (10:30 PM on Friday and Saturday). The **San Diego Water Taxi** (tel. 619/235–8294) ferries passengers around the bay from 10 to 10 daily, with fares ranging from $5 to $20.

Family-Friendly Tours

Kids can quickly tune out adult "talking heads" on standard bus tours, but substitute a horse-drawn carriage, a boat, or a trolley, and their attentiveness often picks up.

Cinderella Carriage Co. drives scenic horse-drawn carriage rides for four to nine people along San Diego's waterfront or through the historic Gaslamp Quarter downtown. *801 W. Market St., San Diego 92101, tel. 619/239–8080. Cost for 4 people: $45 for ½ hr, $60 for 45 min, $80 for 1 hr. Tours daily noon–11.*

Old Town Trolley Tours are narrated sightseeing tours of San Diego on orange and green trackless trolley cars. A nice feature for families is that you can get off (and later reboard) if you wish to walk around places such as Old Town, the harbor, Coronado, and Balboa Park. A complete circuit takes two hours. *Tel. 619/298–8687. Cost: $20 adults, $8 ages 4–12. Tours daily 9–4.*

San Diego Harbor Excursion and **Hornblower Invader Cruises** run frequent daily, narrated, one- or two-hour cruises through San Diego Harbor, departing from the Broadway Pier. For younger children, I'd recommend the one-hour tour, which provides views of the U.S. Navy fleet, aircraft carriers,

shipyards, and the Coronado Bridge. (The two-hour tour adds Point Loma.) No reservations are needed for harbor tours. Both also offer narrated whale-watching tours, daily mid-December to mid-March; the tours are 3 to 3½ hours long (small children may get bored between whale sightings), and reservations are recommended. Both vessels have snack bars and rest rooms aboard; bring jackets, even on sunny days. *San Diego Harbor Excursions: 1050 N. Harbor Dr., tel. 619/234–4111 or 800/442–7847. Hornblower Invader Cruises: 1066 N. Harbor Dr., tel. 619/234–8687. Cost: 1-hr cruise $12 adults, $6 ages 4–12; 2-hr cruise $17 adults, $8.50 ages 4–12; whale-watching cruise $19.50 adults, $9.75 ages 4–12, 3 and under free.*

Other local companies offering whale-watching excursions are **H&M Landing** (2803 Emerson St., San Diego, tel. 619/222–1144) and **Point Loma Sportfishing** (1403 Scott St., San Diego, tel. 619/223–1627).

Pit Stops

It's not always easy to find a public bathroom downtown, so when nature calls, head for the Horton Plaza shopping complex (between Broadway and G St. and 1st and 4th Aves.), which has several sets of rest rooms. If you're in Balboa Park, run for the Visitors Center or the nearest museum. Near the harbor, scout out the rest rooms with diaper-changing facilities at Seaport Village. The major tourist attractions in the city are all well equipped with rest rooms, most with diaper-changing facilities, and the major beaches all have public rest rooms.

Baby-Sitters

Ask your hotel concierge about child care available at the hotel or from bonded local agencies such as Marion's Child Care (tel. 619/582–5029).

Emergencies

Police, ambulance, and **fire departments** can all be reached by dialing 911. For the

Poison Control Center, call 800/876–4766. Hotel Docs (tel. 619/275–2663) offers 24-hour medical services to San Diego hotels. Sharp Memorial Hospital (7901 Frost St., tel. 619/541–3411), Mercy Hospital and Medical Center (4077 5th Ave., tel. 619/294–8111), and UCSD Medical Center (200 W. Arbor Dr., Hillcrest, tel. 619/543–6222) have 24-hour emergency rooms.

The Rite-Aid (550 Robinson Ave., tel. 619/291–3703) drugstore near Balboa Park is open 24 hours.

Telephone Area Codes

The 619 area code is scheduled for a split in 1999. The new number and locations were not available at press time.

Scoping out San Diego

San Diego is in many ways a collection of separate neighborhoods and communities. The revitalized downtown and harbor areas are the heart of the city. Balboa Park, site of the San Diego Zoo, lies just northeast of downtown. Old Town, San Diego's historic birthplace, is about 4 miles northwest of downtown. Mission Valley lies northeast of Old Town, and the Mission Bay area (including Sea World and several top beaches) is northwest. A few miles north of Mission Bay along the coast is La Jolla, a picturesque seaside community. Coronado is a peninsula that extends into San Diego Bay west and south of downtown. The Mexican border is a half hour or so south of downtown by car.

The top attractions are covered at length in various chapters in Part II; we've simply cross-referenced them here. Many of San Diego's best attractions are free—the beaches, Balboa Park, much of Old Town—but others can be costly, like the zoo, Wild Animal Park, Sea World, and harbor excursions. To save money on these, pay a visit to Arts Tix, a discount ticket service in Horton

Plaza at Broadway Circle (tel. 619/497–5000; open Tues.–Thurs. 11–6, Fri.–Sat. 10–6).

Historic Sites

3 – 15 Cabrillo National Monument (see Chapter 4) on the tip of Point Loma honors the European discovery of California here in 1542. But the real attractions are the panoramic views (you can see all the way to Mexico on a clear day), plus tide pools and seasonal whale-watching (see Serendipities, *below*).
Point Loma (via Catalina Blvd.), tel. 619/557–5450.

6 – 15 The Gaslamp Quarter is a 16½-block, historic downtown district that contains renovated Victorian-era architecture, shops, and a variety of good restaurants.
Bounded by 4th Ave., 6th Ave., L St., and Broadway, tel. 619/233–5227.

6 – 15 Hotel del Coronado (see Chapter 12; see also Where to Stay, *below*) is a gingerbread Victorian hotel that's become a National Historic Landmark. Historical tours ($10) take place from Wednesday to Sunday at 10 AM and 11 AM.
1500 Orange Ave., Coronado, tel. 619/435–6611.

6 – 15 Mission San Diego de Alcala, founded by Father Junipero Serra in 1769, was the first outpost of the Spanish colonial government in what is now California, and the first of the state's 21 historic missions. This beautifully restored "Mother of Missions" was originally built on Presidio Hill and moved to its present site six years later. Children can see the mission bells in the tower, throw coins into the wishing well in the flower-filled garden, and wander through one of the oldest graveyards in California.
10818 San Diego Mission Rd., tel. 619/281–8449. Admission: $2 adults, $1 students, 50¢ under 12. Open daily 9–5.

3 – 15 Old Town State Historic Park (see Chapter 4) encompasses several

restored sites in California's first European settlement, at the foot of Presidio Hill.
🏛 *North of downtown at Juan St., near intersection of I–5 and I–8, tel. 619/220–5422.*

Museums

BALBOA PARK. Most San Diego museums are found in Balboa Park (see Parks, *below*), where you can take a quick break at a playground or picnic area if your kids tire. Parents with children old enough for serious museum-hopping may want to purchase a Passport to Balboa Park ($21), good for admission to 12 museums in one week. (You can buy it at the Balboa Park Visitors Center or at any participating museum.) On Tuesday the museums offer free admission on a rotating basis; ask at the Visitors Center for a schedule.

(🕇🕇 3 – 15) The **Mingei International Museum of World Folk Art** presents the "arts of the people" from around the world—costumes, jewelry, furnishings, and everyday objects made beautiful, including frequent doll and toy displays.
🏛 *1439 El Prado, tel. 619/239–0003. Admission: $5 adults, $2 ages 5–12. Open daily 10–4.*

(🕇🕇 ALL) Reuben H. Fleet Science Center (see Chapter 5) combines a fascinating hands-on Science Center with an Omnimax theater.
🏛 *1875 El Prado, tel. 619/238–1233.*

(🕇🕇 ALL) The **San Diego Aerospace Museum** (see Chapter 5) presents colorful displays depicting the history of aviation and aviators.
🏛 *2001 Pan American Plaza, tel. 619/234–8291.*

(🕇🕇 3 – 15) The **San Diego Automotive Museum** displays more than 60 classic and vintage cars, ranging from "horseless carriages" to sleek Aston Martins and Lamborghinis and a rare 1948 Tucker.
🏛 *2080 Pan American Plaza, tel. 619/231–2886. Admission: $6 adults, $2 ages 6–16. Open daily 10–5:30.*

(🕇🕇 3 – 15) The **San Diego Hall of Champions Sports Museum** showcases uniforms, photographs, posters, and memorabilia honoring San Diego's star athletes. Videos of funny sports "bloopers" should amuse even the non-sports fan.
🏛 *Casa de Balboa, El Prado, tel. 619/234–2544. Admission: $3 adults, $1 ages 6–17. Open daily 10–4:30.*

(🕇🕇 ALL) The **San Diego Model Railroad Museum** so entranced our then 11-year-old son, Grael, on his first visit that he didn't want to leave. This is one of the world's largest collections of minigauge railways, with working scale models of four historic California trains running their routes, complete with authentic landscaping, flashing lights, and tooting whistles. On one interactive exhibit, kids can work the throttles to speed up or slow down the trains. Local model railroad buffs are often on hand to answer kids' questions.
🏛 *1649 El Prado, tel. 619/696–0199. Admission: $3 adults, $2.50 students, under 15 free. Open Tues.–Fri. 11–4, weekends 11–5.*

(🕇🕇 6 – 15) The **San Diego Museum of Art** showcases an excellent collection of European paintings and Asian artworks. Look for the superb full-color Family Gallery Guides that "Bring Baroque to Life" and propel youngsters on a "Rocket to the Renaissance." The museum hosts periodic Family Days featuring art projects or storytelling; call 619/696–1956 for a schedule.
🏛 *1450 El Prado, tel. 619/232–7931. Admission: $7–$8 adults, $2 ages 6–17. Open Tues.–Sun. 10–4:30.*

(🕇🕇 3 – 15) The **San Diego Museum of Man** (see Chapter 5), an anthropology museum focusing on the native cultures of the Americas, displays ritual masks, colorful costumes, and other fascinating items.
🏛 *1350 El Prado, tel. 619/239–2001.*

(🕇🕇 ALL) The **San Diego Natural History Museum** is small compared to its counterparts in Los Angeles and San Francisco, but the dinosaur skeletons, Insect Zoo (where kids can watch live honeybees and other displays at kids' eye level), Hall of Mineralogy, desert ecology exhibits, and exhibits on threatened and endangered species make this worth a stop. Museum volunteers lead free family nature walks in areas around San Diego County; call for a schedule.

🏛 *1788 El Prado, tel. 619/232–3821. Admission: $6 adults, $3 ages 6–17. Open daily 9:30–5:30.*

(👫 **6–15**) The **Timken Art Gallery** is a privately owned little jewel of a museum that displays a beautiful collection of Russian icons plus paintings by European masters. It's tiny, so this may be just the place to launch your child on the road to high art.

🏛 *1500 El Prado, tel. 619/239–5548. Admission free. Open Oct.–Aug., Tues.–Sat. 10–4:30. Closed Sept.*

Museums Outside Balboa Park

(👫 **1–12**) The **Carlsbad Children's Museum,** in northern San Diego County, contains hands-on exhibits that are fun and intriguing for kids. Kids' Marketplace, a scaled-down grocery store, helps teach about recycling; Castle Play lets kids dress up as king, princess, or knight in a replica of a medieval castle; Mirror Magic presents mirror tic-tac-toe and the workings of a kaleidoscope; Step to the Music matches floor lights to different tones; and Little People's Corner is for toddlers.

🏛 *300 Carlsbad Village Dr., Suite 103, Carlsbad, tel. 760/720–0737. Admission: $3.50; under 2 free. Open Labor Day–June, Tues.–Thurs. noon–5, Fri.–Sat. 10–5, Sun. noon–5; July–Labor Day, daily 10–5.*

(👫 **1–12**) The **Children's Museum of San Diego/Museo de los Niños of San Diego** (see Chapter 5) is for kids and parents, where touching and exploration are encouraged.

🏛 *200 W. Island Ave., tel. 619/233–5437.*

(👫 **3–15**) The **Firehouse Museum** displays antique fire-fighting memorabilia from around the world (including a 150-year-old hand-drawn pumper cart) in San Diego's oldest firehouse, downtown.

🏛 *1572 Columbia St., at Cedar St., tel. 619/232–3473. Admission $2 adults, $1 ages 13–17, under 13 free. Open Thurs.–Fri. 10–2, Sat.–Sun 10–4.*

(👫 **3–15**) The **Maritime Museum** is a floating collection of three historic ships berthed in the harbor. The magnificent *Star of India,* an 1863 windjammer, is the world's oldest iron sailing ship still afloat; kids like to scamper around the deck. Also here for touring are the *Berkeley,* a classy 1898 steam ferryboat from San Francisco, and the *Medea,* a 1904 Scottish yacht.

🏛 *1306 N. Harbor Dr., tel. 619/234–9153. Admission: $5 adults, $4 ages 13–17, $2 ages 6–12. Open daily 9–8.*

Aquariums, Zoos, and Wildlife

(👫 **2–15**) The **Birch Aquarium at Scripps** (see Chapter 6) is a sparkling facility with more than 30 aquarium tanks and an outdoor tide pool.

🏛 *2300 Expedition Way, La Jolla, tel. 619/534–3474.*

(👫 **3–15**) The **Chula Vista Nature Center,** a living wetland museum in a national wildlife refuge, lets kids feed and pet sharks and bat rays, and watch flocks of migratory birds from a lookout. From the San Diego Trolley's "E" Street Station, catch a shuttle.

🏛 *1000 Gunpowder Pt. Dr., Chula Vista, tel. 619/422–2473. Admission: $3.50 adults, $1 ages 6–17, 5 and under free. Open Sept.–May, Tues.–Sun. 10–5; June–Aug., daily 10–5.*

(👫 **2–15**) The **San Diego Wild Animal Park** (see Chapter 6) is a fascinating 2,100-acre wildlife preserve dedicated to protecting endangered species.

🏛 *15500 San Pasqual Valley Rd., Escondido, tel. 619/234–6541.*

(👫 **ALL**) The **San Diego Zoo** (see Chapter 6), is the city's indispensable stop for families.

🏛 *Zoo Dr., Balboa Park, tel. 619/234–3153 or 619/231–1515.*

👫 ALL   **Sea World** (see Chapter 9) is one of the world's largest marine-life parks, with fabulous marine exhibits and the long-time hit Shamu Show.
🏛 *1720 S. Shores Rd., Mission Bay, tel. 619/ 226–3901.*

Parks and Gardens

To reach the San Diego County Department of Parks and Recreation, call 619/694–3049.

Balboa Park, the recreational and cultural heart of the city, is a top draw for almost every family visiting San Diego. Besides the San Diego Zoo and more than a dozen museums (see *above*), the lush 1,400-acre park includes five theaters, three playgrounds, beautifully landscaped gardens, plenty of shady trees, and acres of grass for playing and picnicking. El Prado, the park's main thoroughfare, is lined with Moorish-style museums and theaters, some dating from the Panama-California Exposition of 1915. The **Balboa Park Visitors Center** (House of Hospitality Building, 1549 El Prado, tel. 619/239–0512, open daily 9–4) provides information, and a free daily tram service carries passengers around the park (9:30–5:30 in summer and 10–4 in winter). A miniature train ($3 adults, $2.50 students, ages 15 and under free) loops for ½ mile through eucalyptus groves near the zoo; on the nearby 1910 carousel ($1.25), grabbing the brass ring wins a free ride; and the adjacent butterfly rides are for kids age 5 and under; all run from 11 to 5:30 daily mid-June to Labor Day, and on weekends and school holidays only the rest of the year. *Hwy. 163 or Park Blvd. to El Prado.*

Children's Park, part of the Martin Luther King Jr. Promenade, is a new downtown park across from the San Diego Convention Center and near the San Diego Children's Museum (see Museums, *above*). It has grassy knolls, trees, lighted pathways, and a pond with a spray fountain.

Embarcadero Marina Park North is one spot we're drawn to every time we visit San Diego. Blessed with wonderful views of the harbor, this 8-acre grassy point is a favorite of kite flyers, skaters, and picnickers. *End of Kettner Blvd., beyond Seaport Village.*

Mission Bay Park exemplifies San Diego's commitment to outdoor life: Not content with miles of beautiful natural coastline, the city transformed a swamp into a 4,600-acre aquatic sports center, the world's largest. You can swim, sail, windsurf, kayak, waterski, and fish here, mostly in areas designated for one sport only—so swimmers won't collide with powerboats and anglers don't tangle lines with waterskiers. Boats and equipment are available for rent at several marinas. On land, there are picnic areas, children's playgrounds, and plenty of space for bike riding, in-line skating, and kite flying. Mission Bay is also the home of Sea World (see *above*) and several top resorts. *Follow I–8 to Mission Bay Dr. or Ingraham St., or I–5 to Mission Bay exits.*

Mission Trails Regional Park, 8 miles north of downtown, is one of California's largest urban parks. Within its 5,800 acres are 35 miles of trails for hiking, mountain biking, and horseback riding. Trails range from easy (including some paved for wheelchair and stroller access) to challenging; one of the latter, which leads to San Diego's highest point (1,600 feet), offers a 360-degree view. You can also fish in two lakes or visit the historic Old Mission Dam (dating from 1810) on the San Diego River. *1 Father Junipero Serra Trail, tel. 619/668–3275. Visitors Center open daily 9–5.*

Presidio Park, site of the first European settlement in California, occupies a hill overlooking Old Town (see Historic Sites, *above*) and is a wonderful scenic spot for a picnic. *Follow Taylor St. and Presidio Dr. uphill from Old Town.*

Scripps Memorial Park offers wonderful coastal walkways perfect for strolling with a baby, plus green grass and thatched huts ideal for picnics by the sea. *La Jolla Cove and Coast Blvd., La Jolla.*

Torrey Pines State Reserve, along the coast north of La Jolla, is one of our favorite hiking spots. This 1,000-acre wilderness is the last remaining mainland preserve of the beautiful, gnarled Torrey Pine. Some trails (consult with rangers) are suitable for young children—strollers are permitted—but make sure kids don't stray near the cliffs. The ocean and forest views are terrific, and one steep trail leads down to a secluded stretch of Torrey Pines State Beach (see Beaches, below). *12000 N. Torrey Pines Rd. (south of Del Mar; watch for signs near beach), tel. 619/ 755–2063. Admission: $4 per car. Open daily 9–sunset.*

Beaches

The San Diego area offers more than 70 miles of beaches, from Oceanside to the Mexican border—and all are open and free to the public.

Children's Pool Beach, south of La Jolla Cove, is a small and popular curve of sand where the shallow waters are protected by a concrete seawall. Kids can swim and explore tide pools, but watch for slippery rocks. *Follow La Jolla Blvd. north to Coast Blvd. Rest rooms; lifeguards year-round.*

Coronado Beach—San Diego's widest—is a long strand of clean, sugary-white, oceanfront sand that runs in front of the Hotel del Coronado (see Where to Stay, *below*). The surf is often gentle enough for swimming, and, though popular with families, the beach seldom seems too crowded. *From Coronado Bridge, turn left on Orange Ave. and follow signs. Changing rooms, showers; lifeguards in summer.*

La Jolla Cove is a tiny, exceptionally pretty beach tucked into a sheltered cove along La Jolla's rocky coast. Tide pools invite exploration, and large grassy areas offer nearby picnicking. It's a popular snorkeling and diving area, part of the San Diego–La Jolla Underwater Park. *Follow Coast Blvd. north to Scripps Park. Changing rooms, lifeguards.*

La Jolla Shores Beach is a popular family beach north of La Jolla Cove; there are great tide pools, the surf is often calm enough for small kids to swim, and there's plenty of space for picnics. *Follow La Jolla Shores Dr. to Ave. de la Playa. Lifeguards in summer.*

Mission Beach is San Diego's longest stretch of sand. Adjacent to Mission Bay Park (see Parks, *above*), it's often very crowded, especially with teenagers who like to stroll, skate, and bike along the boardwalk (watch out from behind). While you'll see lots of families on the beach, expect ocean surf—kids who can swim well can rent boogieboards to ride the waves—along with blaring music and boisterous volleyball games. *Exit I–5 at Garnet Ave. then west to Mission Blvd.; turn south for parking. Changing rooms, showers, lifeguards.*

Ocean Beach, south of Mission Beach (but separated by Mission Bay Channel), is a favorite of surfers and volleyball players. *Off I–8 and Sunset Cliffs Blvd. Changing rooms, showers, lifeguards.*

Pacific Beach, essentially a northern continuation of Mission Beach and equally popular, has its own boardwalk and pier. Bikes, skates, and boogieboards are available for rent. *Exit I–5 at Garnet Ave., then head west to Mission Blvd.; turn north for street parking. Lifeguards, changing rooms, showers.*

Silver Strand State Beach extends along the long, narrow sandbar that connects Coronado to the mainland at Imperial Beach. This clean, seashell-strewn beach with picnic areas is a favorite of families for its shallow, calm waters; you can swim in either the bay or the ocean. *Palm Ave. exit from I–5, then west to Hwy. 75; turn right and follow signs.*

Tel. 619/435–5184. Parking: $4 per car. Rest rooms, lifeguards.

Torrey Pines State Beach, part of the Torrey Pines State Reserve (see Parks, *above*), is one of San Diego's prettiest beaches and, beyond the lifeguard towers, one of the most secluded. For swimming, stick to the lifeguard area—the surf can be rough. *N. Torrey Pines Rd., south of Del Mar; watch for signs near beach, tel. 619/755–2063. Parking: $4 per car. Rest room, lifeguards.*

Serendipities

(☗ ALL) **Bonita Cove** in Mission Bay Park (see Parks, *above*) is one of the best places to spend a relaxed day with small children. Kids can romp in the playground, swim in calm waters, and enjoy a picnic on the grassy knolls. It's also within a short walk of Belmont Park (see Amusement Parks, *below*) and Mission Beach (see Beaches, *above*).

(☗ 2–9) The **Broadway Flying Horses Carousel** (tel. 619/234–6133) at Seaport Village (see Shopping, *below*), is a true classic, created at Coney Island in 1890 with hand-carved horses. Rides are $1 (2- to 3-year-olds free with parent). The carousel spins at a good clip, so parents should ride with small children. Other vintage carousels can be found at Balboa Park (see Parks, *above*) and Belmont Park (see Amusement Parks, *below*).

(☗ ALL) The **Lily Pond** (tel. 619/234–8901) in front of the Botanical Building on El Prado in Balboa Park is stocked with beautiful koi goldfish that delight many small—and older—children.

(☗ 3–15) **Naval Ship Open Houses,** held on most Saturdays and Sundays at the Broadway Pier (on Harbor Dr.), offer kids a chance to board and tour a destroyer, an aircraft carrier, or a submarine. It's best to call first, though, because the schedule can be erratic.
🏢 *Tel. 619/532–1431. Admission free. Open most weekends 1–4.*

(☗ ALL) The **Skyfari** aerial tram at the San Diego Zoo (see Zoos, *above*) provides dramatic bird's-eye views of buffalo, tigers, and gorillas from over the treetops for $1 a ride.

(☗ 6–15) **Tide pools** at Cabrillo National Monument on Point Loma (see Chapter 4 and Historic Sites, *above*) teem with sea stars, crabs, mussels, and anemones. Best viewing is fall through spring during low tides (check with rangers). Make sure that kids wear shoes with rubber soles that grip; the rocks can be slippery. The tide pools are at the foot of the western cliffs below the monument. Also at Point Loma, **whale-watching** from 400 feet above sea level can provide thrills between December and March each year, when California gray whales migrate south to Baja California. Peak viewing is mid-January, when up to 200 whales a day have been sighted offshore (watch for the spouts). A glassed-in observatory provides protection from the wind; bring binoculars.
🏢 *Point Loma, tel. 619/557–5450. Admission: $5 per car. Open daily 9–5:15; summer hrs may be extended.*

Sports

Big Leagues and the Olympics

Qualcomm Stadium (9449 Friars Rd., tel. 619/525–8266) is home to the **San Diego Chargers** football team (tel. 619/280–2121) and the **San Diego Padres** baseball team (tel. 619/283–4494 for general information or 619/297–2373 for tickets).

(☗ ALL) The **Arco Olympic Training Center,** the country's first warm-weather, year-round, multisport Olympic training complex (the others are in upstate New York and Colorado), is located on the shores of Lower Otay Reservoir in Chula Vista, south of San Diego. Visitors can take a narrated 1½-mile tour with views of the athletic facilities and dorms and glimpse Olympic hopefuls as they train in sports such as track and field, tennis, archery, canoe/kayaking, rowing, cycling, and soccer. The tour begins with a short film and ends, perhaps not surprisingly, with a chance to buy Olympic merchandise.

🏛 *1750 Wueste Rd., Chula Vista, tel. 619/ 482–6222 or 619/481–6103. Admission free. Hourly tours Mon.–Sat. 9–4, Sun. noon–4.*

Outdoor Action

BICYCLING. San Diego is a wonderful city for biking, and many streets and highways have specially marked bike lanes. For an area bike map, call 619/231–2453. The most popular route is along the **Mission Beach** and **Pacific Beach boardwalks**; they become very crowded on weekends and are primarily suited for older kids. Also try the paths around nearby **Mission Bay Park.** You can rent bikes in Mission Beach at **Hamel's Action Sports Center** (704 Ventura Pl., tel. 619/488–5050) and in Pacific Beach at **Aquarius Surf 'n Skate** (747 Pacific Beach Dr., tel. 619/488–9733).

The longest bike path (8 miles), along **Silver Strand** in Coronado, is ideal for young children because it's flat and quiet; bring bikes over on the Coronado Ferry (50\ extra) or rent them at the Ferry Landing Marketplace at **Bikes and Beyond** (tel. 619/435–7180). For biking on the waterfront bike path along the Embarcadero, rent at **Bike Tours San Diego** (509 5th Ave., tel. 619/238-2444), where bikes are $15 per day.

FISHING. San Diego is one of the best places for fishing along the Pacific Coast (see Chapter 10). Off San Diego's piers you can fish for free (for yellowtail, perch, and bonita) and don't need a license. **Ocean Beach Pier** and **Crystal Pier** at Pacific Beach and the piers at **Shelter Island,** the **Coronado Ferry Landing, Imperial Beach,** and **Oceanside** are all good, and most have bait-and-tackle

shops. To fish directly from the shore adults require a license from the state Department of Fish and Game (available at bait-and-tackle stores); children under 16 do not.

Several companies offer half-day or daylong sportfishing expeditions in search of marlin and bass; see Chapter 10.

GOLF. For the junior golfers in your family, the **Mission Bay Golf Course** (2702 N. Mission Bay Dr., tel. 619/490–3370) is a convenient and fairly easy (par 3 and 4) 18-hole public course; it also has a driving range and is lighted for night play. **Torrey Pines Municipal Golf Course** (11480 N. Torrey Pines Rd., La Jolla, tel. 619/452–3226 or 800/985–4653) is one of the best public courses in the country, with 36 holes, a driving range, and spectacular views of the Pacific.

HOT-AIR BALLOONING. You can take your family up, up, and away over the Del Mar coast, for beautiful views and peaceful (if expensive) adventure. Among many local companies are **A Skysurfer Balloon Co.** (tel. 619/481–6800 or 800/660–6809), and **California Dreamin' Balloon Adventures** (tel. 760/438–9550 or 800/373–3359).

KITE-FLYING. **Mission Bay Park** is one of the best and breeziest places for unfurling a kite. Head for the grassy open fields in the Tecolote Shores area near I–5 and Sea World Drive. **Embarcadero Marina Park North** (adjacent to Seaport Village) also offers excellent kite-flying. You can buy kites at **Kite Flite** (tel. 619/234–5483) in Seaport Village or at **Kite Country** (tel. 619/233–9495) in Horton Plaza.

ROLLERBLADING, ROLLER SKATING, AND SKATEBOARDING. The best skating for younger children is along the sidewalks of **Mission Bay** (see Parks, *above*). The **Mission Beach** and **Pacific Beach boardwalks** (which get very crowded with skaters, boarders, bikers, and strollers) are popular with teens. Rent skates or boards at **Hamel's Action Sports Center** in Mission Beach (tel. 619/ 488–5050), and at **Aquarius Surf 'n Skate**

(tel. 619/488–9733) in Pacific Beach. On Coronado rent at **Bikes & Beyond** (Ferry Landing Marketplace, tel. 619/435–7180). Near the waterfront downtown try **Bike Tours San Diego** (tel. 619/238–2444).

SAILING. San Diego is a sailing paradise, and **Mission Bay** is the top spot for it (see Chapter 10). You can rent a sailboat and get instruction (for kids and adults) at **Mission Bay Sportcenter** (1010 Santa Clara Pl., tel. 619/488–1004) or at **Seaforth Mission Bay Boat Rental** (1641 Quivira Rd., tel. 619/223–1681).

SNORKELING. La Jolla Cove (see Beaches, *above*) offers protected underwater reefs and some of the clearest waters on the California coast. Rent snorkel gear at **Mitch's** in La Jolla (631 Pearl St., tel. 619/459–5933).

SURFING. Thanks to wet suits, you can surf year-round off San Diego, and most public beaches have separate areas for surfers. Good spots for beginners include **Mission Beach** and **Pacific Beach**. Experienced surfers like the area near the pier at **Ocean Beach** and celebrated **Windansea Beach** in La Jolla. Rent boards at **Hamel's** in Mission Beach (tel. 619/488–5050), **Star Surfing Company** in Pacific Beach (tel. 619/273–7827), or **Mitch's** in La Jolla (631 Pearl St., tel. 619/459–5933).

TENNIS. We often play at **Morley Field** in Balboa Park (tel. 619/295–9278), which has 25 courts, 19 lighted ($4-per-person fee per court).

WATERSKIING. Mission Bay's 1½-mile course is one of the most popular waterskiing runs in Southern California. Rent boats and equipment at **Seaforth Mission Bay Boat Rentals** (1641 Quivira Rd., tel. 619/223–1681).

WINDSURFING. Mission Bay offers the smooth waters and light breezes ideal for this sport; for details, see Chapter 10.

Shops

Some of San Diego's leading shopping complexes double as sightseeing attractions—they're interesting even for kids who hate being dragged on shopping expeditions.

The **Bazaar del Mundo** (Juan St., Old Town, tel. 619/296–3161) is a festively decorated, open-air, Spanish-style marketplace. Geppetto's carries domestic and imported children's toys and clothing; Artes de Mexico features folk art, crafts, and clothing from Mexico. When tummies rumble, treat the kids to a *churro* (a Mexican pastry) and Mexican hot chocolate at La Panaderia. Spanish and Mexican dancers and mariachi bands entertain on weekend afternoons.

Stretching over seven blocks of downtown, **Horton Plaza** (bounded by Broadway, G St., 1st Ave., and 4th Ave., tel. 619/238–1596) is a colorful, multilevel complex of diverse architectural styles. Street musicians and jugglers frequently perform, and the views from the top level are terrific, but keep track of the kids—it's easy to get lost in the jumble of levels and ramps. There are more than 150 shops and stores, plus myriad places to snack. A free shopping shuttle picks up and drops off passengers from various downtown locations.

Built to resemble a turn-of-the-century fishing village, **Seaport Village** (West Harbor Dr. at Kettner Blvd., tel. 619/235–4014) consists of 60 shops on the waterfront. A wooden boardwalk leads along the water, and the Broadway Flying Horses Carousel (see Serendipities, *above*) and various street performers keep kids entertained.

The **White Rabbit** (7755 Girard Ave., La Jolla, tel. 619/454–3518) is the best children's bookstore in the San Diego area, carrying thousands of books for tots through junior-high age.

Eats

Most kids like Mexican food, which is abundant in San Diego. But food choices have broadened considerably in recent years, with good Italian and Asian restaurants springing up, and old standards—seafood and burger places and family diners—improving. Prices remain generally reasonable, with some true bargains still to be found. For an explanation of price categories, see How to Use This Book.

Our favorite picnic spots include Scripps Park in La Jolla, Embarcadero Marina Park North along the waterfront, Presidio Park above Old Town, Mission Bay Park, and Balboa Park (see Parks, *above,* for details).

Harbor/Downtown

Bayou Bar and Grill. My kids love the shrimp and sausage po'boy sandwiches at this Cajun/Creole restaurant in the Gaslamp Quarter. Inside, ceiling fans create a New Orleans atmosphere, but on warm evenings we like to sit outside at umbrella-shaded tables on the sidewalk. Younger kids could easily split one po'boy (served with red beans and rice), or request appetizer-size portions of entrées such as barbecue shrimp, red beans and rice with Andouille sausage, and seafood gumbo. Don't miss dessert here: The Cajun velvet pie (peanut butter mousse) and Creole pecan pie are yummy. *329 Market St., tel. 619/696–8747. Reservations advised weekends. Dress: casual. AE, D, DC, MC, V. $$–$$$*

The Panda Inn. San Diego's most popular Chinese restaurant affords harbor views from its glassed-in veranda. Almost everything on the extensive menu is good, but if your kids aren't accustomed to spicy foods, avoid the Szechuan items (or ask the servers to tone down the heat). Mu shu pork—shredded meat and vegetables that you wrap in thin pancakes—is a dish kids have fun with, and the seafood dishes are always fresh. *506 Horton Plaza, tel. 619/233–7800. Dress: casual but neat. AE, D, DC, MC, V. $$*

San Diego Pier Cafe. We've been eating at this Seaport Village stalwart for years, and the food and views keep bringing us back. Built around an old boathouse on the end of a short pier on the bay, it has indoor and outdoor seating with views of the Coronado Bridge and passing pelicans. We especially like the breakfasts here: waffles, pancakes, omelets, eggs Benedict, even oatmeal, usually served with delicious muffins and fresh fruit. For lunch and dinner, you can get fresh seafood, clam chowder, fish-and-chips, fish tacos, or fried calamari; the children's menu includes cheeseburgers and fish-and-chips. *885 W. Harbor Dr., tel. 619/239–3968. Children's menu. Dress: casual. AE, D, MC, V. $–$$*

El Indio Shop. More than a taco stand, this has been a San Diego tradition since 1940 and now has two city locations. The newer branch in the Gaslamp Quarter is more accessible to tourists, but the original one on India Street, which has spotless indoor seating or outdoor patio seating across the street, is more authentic. We almost always end up ordering the moist, delicious burritos—the *carne asada* (grilled beef) and chicken burritos are especially good—along with some cheese enchiladas. Miniburritos are available for smaller appetites. Also great for kids are the shredded beef and chicken *taquitos* (little tacos), a house specialty, along with homemade tortillas, which you can watch being made, and wonderfully crisp chips. *3695 India St., tel. 619/299–0333; 409 F St., tel. 619/239–8151. No reservations. Dress: casual. MC, V. $*

Old Spaghetti Factory. You can find better pasta in San Diego, but for lots of food at budget prices in a colorful setting it's hard to beat this chain restaurant in the Gaslamp Quarter. Arrive early or expect a wait. The outlandish decor (including a real trolley car, where you can sit and eat, plus antiques galore) will keep the kids busy gaping. Complete meals include spaghetti with a choice of sauces (or lasagna, ravioli, or chicken), plus salad, bread, drink, and spumoni ice cream; Junior Meals (smaller portions) are even cheaper. *275 5th Ave., at K St., tel. 619/ 233–4323. Children's menu. No reservations Mon.–Thurs. Dress: casual. MC, V. $*

Mission Bay

Guava Beach Bar and Grill. This spot reminds us of some of the seaside eateries we've enjoyed in Mexico, with ceiling fans, music, palm trees, and a casual beach atmosphere. Butcher-block paper and markers are provided for young diners. The menu combines Mexican (tacos, chiles rellenos, Baja-style lobster) and Caribbean (swordfish with fruit salsa) cooking with traditional American fare like hamburgers and mashed potatoes, and somehow it all works. The children's menu lists macaroni and cheese, meat loaf, and chicken strips. *3714 Mission Blvd., tel. 619/488–6688. Children's menu. Dress: casual. AE, MC, V. $$*

Old Town

Casa de Pico. It always seems like fiesta time at this lively Mexican restaurant in Old Town's Bazaar del Mundo; mariachi bands and folkloric dancers often entertain. We like to sit outside at one of the umbrella-shaded tables in the flower-filled courtyard, but the interior adobe-style dining rooms are festive, too. Food is classic Tex-Mex: *carne asada* (grilled meat) burritos, chicken or beef fajitas, cheese enchiladas, tamales, tacos, flautas. Kids' plates offer smaller versions of each, plus *taquitos* (little tacos) and quesadillas. Try to get here early for dinner or anytime on weekends—it's very popular. *2754 Calhoun St., tel. 619/296–3267. Children's menu. No reservations. Dress: casual. AE, D, DC, MC, V. $–$$*

Perry's. Locals stream in here for tasty, big, inexpensive breakfasts and lunches (expect a wait, especially on weekends). In addition to the typical egg dishes, Perry's serves up Mexican breakfasts (*huevos rancheros*, burrito *con*

huevos) and frittatas (Italian omelets), served with potatoes or fruit. For lunch the choices include burgers, sandwiches, Mexican dishes (such as tacos and enchiladas), and salads. The children's menu offers junior pancakes, French toast, grilled cheese sandwiches, hot dogs, and hamburgers. Perry's has a sister restaurant in suburban El Cajon. *4610 Pacific Hwy., tel. 619/291–7121; 475 N. Magnolia Ave., El Cajon, tel. 619/440–5724. Children's menu. No reservations. Dress: casual. D, MC, V. No dinner. $*

Balboa Park/Hillcrest

The Corvette Diner. Wild '50s decor, rock music, chrome, flashing neon, gum-popping waitresses, a real Corvette, and an old-fashioned soda fountain set the scene here. The menu is pure diner: burgers, onion rings, chicken-fried steak, and blue-plate specials, plus root-beer floats and other great fountain drinks. The kids' menu (age 12 and younger) adds spaghetti and meat sauce, chicken fingers, corn dogs, grilled cheese, and peanut butter and jelly, all with ice-cream bars. A DJ spins platters in the evenings, and a magician performs on some nights. It's the most entertaining place in town for a family meal. *3946 5th Ave., tel. 619/542–1001. Children's menu. No reservations. Dress: casual. AE, D, DC, MC, V. $–$$*

Chicken Pie Shop of San Diego. Though now in a relatively new location, this place has been serving up "real home cooking" to a cross section of families for what seems like forever, according to one regular. Expect big portions and fast service of basics like chicken pies, chopped steak, fried chicken, fish fillets, and roast beef. Don't come here looking for atmosphere; think of it as a refueling stop. *2633 El Cajon Blvd., tel. 619/295–0156. No reservations. Dress: casual. No credit cards. $*

Mission Valley

Prego. This has become one of our favorite restaurants for a special meal with the kids.

You forget you're in a shopping center as soon as you enter; with fountains, olive trees, open rotisseries, and a walled courtyard for patio dining, it seems much like Italy. So does the food: antipasti, pastas, gourmet pizzas, fresh-grilled fish, and spit-roasted meats (try the chicken breast with garlic, rosemary, and grilled polenta). Our kids like the angel-hair pasta with tomato, garlic, and basil, and the spaghetti with clams. Prego isn't overly fancy, but it's probably best suited for kids age 6 and up. Come in the early evening, before the "trendy" crowd arrives. *1370 Frazee Rd., Hazard Center, Mission Valley, tel. 619/294–4700. Reservations advised. Dress: casual but neat. AE, DC, MC, V. No weekend lunch. $$–$$$*

Point Loma

Pizza Nova. Among the many designer/ gourmet pizza places in San Diego, this local minichain with four locations is one of the best, especially for families. Wary of lox and goat cheese pizza, duck sausage pizza, or Mexican lime chicken pizza? Never fear—kids can still get child-size plain cheese or pepperoni. Pastas are also available, as are soups and salads, and "banana rama" (bananas, sweet cream, mascarpone, and puff pastry) for dessert. *3955 5th Ave., tel. 619/296–6682; 5120 N. Harbor Dr., tel. 619/226–0268; 5500 Grossmont Center Dr., tel. 619/589–7222; 945 Loma Santa Fe, Solano Beach, tel. 619/259–0666. Children's menu. Dress: casual. AE, D, DC, MC, V. $$*

La Jolla

Hard Rock Cafe. Our kids never seem to tire of the rock-and-roll atmosphere at these chain restaurants (don't expect to carry on a conversation over the din). And the food is surprisingly good: the ⅓-pound burgers, ribs and chicken combo, and Caesar salad with grilled sliced chicken breast are our kids' favorites. Regular portions are big, but there's a children's menu with grilled

cheese sandwiches, burgers, chicken fingers, and kid-size shakes and desserts. Although prices are reasonable, your bill may increase by the cost of a T-shirt or two. *909 Prospect St., La Jolla, tel. 619/454–5101. Children's menu. No reservations weekends. Dress: casual. AE, DC, MC, V. $–$$*

Where to Stay

Location is so important in spread-out San Diego that many lodgings put their general region—Old Town, Mission Bay, Harbor View—right in their name (sometimes they stretch the geography a bit, too). Mission Bay and the beaches are the top areas for families, though we also like the harbor/Embarcadero area. (The rest of downtown gets awfully deserted at night.) Old Town is another good family choice. Hotel Circle in Mission Valley—a cluster of mostly moderately priced hotels—lacks charm and scenery, but it's convenient to most attractions. Try the **Ramada Hotel Circle** (2151 Hotel Circle S, San Diego 92108, tel. 619/ 291–6500 or 800/405–9102); **Quality Resort** (875 Hotel Circle S, San Diego 92108, tel. 619/298–8281 or 800/362– 7871); or **Days Inn Hotel Circle** (543 Hotel Circle South, San Diego 92108, tel. 619/ 297–8800 or 800/345–9995).

Summer is high season for rates and occupancy; try to book as far in advance as possible. There's a surplus of hotel rooms in San Diego, so you can usually find hotels offering special rates (or deals such as free tickets to Sea World), especially in winter. **San Diego Hotel Reservations** (tel. 619/627–9300 or 800/728–3227) books accommodations, at no charge, at more than 200 resorts and hotels in the area; ask them about preferred rates and specials, too. Several lodgings listed include kitchens or kitchenettes, which can save money on food. For an explanation of price categories, see How to Use This Book. Rates do not include the 10.5% city tax added to each hotel bill.

Loews Coronado Bay Resort. Set on a private 15-acre peninsula off Silver Strand Beach (see Beaches, *above*), this Coronado resort is a beauty. All the rooms have balconies with water views (of the Pacific, San Diego Bay, or the resort's own marina). Loads of activities are available. The "Commodore Kids Club," for kids ages 4 to 12, has its own clubhouse and offers arts and crafts, nature hikes, kite-flying, pool games, sand-castle building, beach play, and G-rated videos. In summer, kids can also learn to swim, snorkel, or play tennis, and, during the holiday season, make ornaments. Other enticements for families include baby-proofing room safety kits, and some free meals for kids as long as they're with paying adults. *4000 Coronado Bay Rd., Coronado 92118, tel. 619/424–4000 or 800/815–6397, fax 619/424–4400. 403 rooms, 37 suites. Facilities: 3 restaurants, 3 pools, 2 hot tubs, 5 tennis courts, sailboat and bike rentals, health club. Children's program: $30 full day (9–4), $17 ½ day; siblings half price; Thurs.–Sat. evening $12. AE, D, DC, MC, V. $$$*

Holiday Inn on the Bay. During our stay we had a magnificent view from our balcony of San Diego Bay. The comfortable, good-size rooms have all been renovated, and the lobby area has a tropical look. Our kids loved to ride in the outside glass elevators. Children under 12 stay free in their parents' room, and in summer kids eat free at the hotel's restaurant when they order from the children's menu. *1355 N. Harbor Dr., San Diego 92101, tel. 619/232–3861 or 800/877–8920, fax 619/232–4924. 584 rooms, 16 suites. Facilities: restaurant, outdoor pool, hot tub, exercise room, free airport and Amtrak transfers, laundry facilities. AE, D, DC, MC, V. $$–$$$*

Hotel del Coronado (see Chapter 12) is one of America's most famous and picturesque hotels, as well as a top beach resort with excellent children's programs in summer. *1500 Orange Ave., San Diego 92118, tel. 619/435–6611 or 800/468–3533, fax 619/522–8238. $$–$$$*

San Diego Hilton Beach and Tennis Resort. With its location in Mission Bay Park (see Parks and Gardens, *above*), this Hilton resort is primed for active families: surrounded by sea and sand, it offers swimming in a huge pool (or splashing in a wading pool), proximity to the ocean at Mission Beach, sailing or windsurfing from a private dock, tennis, and bike rentals. The Kids Klub, for ages 6 to 12, presents supervised activities such as pool play, treasure hunts, arts and crafts, fish feeding, face painting, and cartoon watching. Most activities are free. Rooms offer views of Mission Bay or the landscaped grounds (complete with ponds and Japanese bridges) and have refrigerators, private terraces or patios, and in-room movies. Children of any age stay free in their parents' room. *1775 E. Mission Bay Dr., San Diego 92109, tel. 619/276–4010 or 800/221-2424, fax 619/275–7991. 337 rooms, 20 suites. Facilities: 2 restaurants, 2 pools, 2 hot tubs, water sport rentals, 5 tennis courts, bike rentals, exercise room, playground, free parking, children's program. AE, D, DC, MC, V. $$–$$$*

San Diego Paradise Point Resort (see Chapter 12). On a 44-acre island in Mission Bay, this longtime family favorite has five swimming pools and summertime kids' programs. *1404 W. Vacation Rd., San Diego 92109, tel. 619/274–4630 or 800/344-2626, fax 619/581–5977. $$–$$$*

Blue Sea Lodge. This Best Western property is great for families who want the convenience of being able to walk directly onto the beach—in this case, popular Pacific Beach. Steps beyond the lodge lie the ocean and the boardwalk, where kids can bike or skate. About half the rooms have full kitchens, and all have balconies or patios, many with ocean views. Some of the rooms are on the small size, but six roomy oceanfront suites are available. There's a small oceanfront heated pool and hot tub, and a free Continental breakfast is served each morning. Children 12 and under stay free with parents. The lodge is near at least 10 restaurants. *707 Pacific Beach Dr., San Diego 92109, tel. 619/488–4700 or 800/258–3732, fax 619/488–7276. 94 rooms, 6 suites. Facilities: free Continental breakfast, heated pool, hot tub. AE, D, DC, MC, V. $$*

Embassy Suites San Diego Bay. This all-suite chain offers an unbeatable deal for families, and this branch provides a good location near the Embarcadero. Everyone in our family loves the spacious suites, with big living rooms and bedrooms; parents have privacy, and kids can have their pick of TVs. Each suite includes a microwave and a refrigerator, and all open onto the hotel's dramatic 12-story garden atrium; some offer spectacular harbor views as well. Our kids also like riding in the glass elevators for the indoor views. A cooked-to-order breakfast is complimentary, as are afternoon cocktails and snacks. Children 12 and under stay free in the same suite with parents. *601 Pacific Hwy., at Harbor Dr., San Diego 92101, tel. 619/239–2400 or 800/362–2779, fax 619/239–1520. 337 suites. Facilities: restaurant, free breakfast, indoor pool, sauna, health club, video games, airport and Amtrak transfers, laundry facilities. AE, D, DC, MC, V. $$*

Hacienda Hotel Old Town. Another Best Western hotel, this beautifully landscaped hacienda-style inn is perched on a quiet, terraced hillside overlooking Old Town. The tile-roof, white adobe architecture (courtyards, fountains, and patios), and the room décor are right out of the Southwest. All rooms are studio-size junior suites—one bedroom with a queen bed or two and a small sitting area with a sofa bed—each with a refrigerator, microwave, and VCR (ask at the front desk for videos). Some connecting rooms are available for larger families. Kids 16 and under stay free in a room with their parents; cribs are free. The Acapulco (Mexican) restaurant on the premises is convenient for breakfast, with patio dining overlooking Old Town and the bay. *4041 Harney St., at Juan St., San Diego 92110, tel. 619/298–4707 or 800/888–1991, fax 619/298–4771. 168 rooms. Facilities: restaurant, heated*

outdoor pool, hot tub, exercise room, laundry facilities, free indoor parking, free airport transfer. AE, D, DC, MC, V. $$*

La Jolla Cove Suites. Overlooking beautiful La Jolla Cove, this motel is right across from Scripps Park, La Jolla Cove beach, snorkeling, tide pools, and, a few blocks away, Children's Pool Beach. The studio-size rooms are too small for most families, though; suites—each with a kitchenette or full-size kitchen, and TV in every room—are the ticket here (summer prices for suites are slightly above the $$ price category). Stay in a suite with a balcony, and you'll have spacious accommodation with magnificent views and ocean breezes at lower rates than some of the more fashionable nearby lodgings. You can use your kitchen to fix picnics for the beach. *1155 S. Coast Blvd., La Jolla 92037, tel. 619/459–2621 or 800/248–2683, fax 619/454–3522. 43 rooms, 73 suites. Facilities: pool, hot tub, solarium, sundeck, laundry room, free parking. AE, D, DC, MC, V. $$*

Old Town Inn. The setting—along Pacific Highway near Old Town—won't win any scenery awards, but the location is central to most San Diego attractions, the rooms are amply sized (most with queen-size beds), the staff is friendly, and the prices are budget level. Children under 12 stay free. (Ask about special rates if you're staying a week or more, especially out of season.) About half the rooms here are in older but refurbished bungalow-style units, while the others are in a newer building and cost a bit more. Both sections have some rooms with kitchenettes. There are also two family-size suites. *4444 Pacific Hwy., San Diego 92110, tel. 619/260–8024 or 800/225–9610, fax 619/296–0524. 81 rooms, 2 suites. Facilities: some kitchenettes, laundry facilities. AE, D, MC, V. $*

Surfer Motor Lodge. Another good value at Pacific Beach, this motel has plain but comfortable rooms, several with balconies and fine ocean views. Choose among double-doubles (with two double beds), kitch-enette units, and two-family units that sleep up to six people; three connecting units are also available. The real attraction here is proximity to the beach, with swimming, surf-ing, biking, skating, fishing, and sand just out-side. The attached World Famous Restau-rant has a beach terrace, or you can head to one of several other (equally or more famous) restaurants nearby. *711 Pacific Beach Dr., San Diego 92109, tel. 619/483–7070 or 800/787–3373, fax 619/274–1670. 52 rooms. Facilities: restaurant, pool, free park-ing. AE, DC, MC, V. $*

Entertainments

For half-price day-of-performance (and full-price advance sale) tickets to theater, music, and dance events, call **Arts Tix** (tel. 619/497–5000), or visit the downtown ticket booth at Broadway Circle in Horton Plaza (open Tues.–Thurs. 11–6, Fri.–Sat. 10–6).

Amusement, Theme, and Water Parks and Arcades

(👫 ALL) **Belmont Park,** a free-admis-sion amusement park along Mission Beach, allows kids who are at least 50 inches tall to ride on the Giant Dipper ($3), a restored vintage wooden roller coaster that zooms over 13 hills. Children of any size can ride the Liberty Carousel ($1.50) or take a dip in the Plunge, the largest indoor swimming pool in Southern California ($2.50 adults, $2.25 under 17). Pirate's Cove Family Play-land, an indoor fun center designed for kids ages 3 to 12, has brightly colored tunnels, slides, and an obstacle course. *3146 Mission Blvd. at W. Mission Bay Dr., tel. 619/491–2988. Open daily.*

(👫 ALL) **Family Fun Centers**—with miniature golf, go-carts, batting cages, bumper boats, battle tanks, and an arcade

center—have four locations in the San Diego area. *6999 Clairemont Mesa Blvd., San Diego, tel. 619/560–4211; 830 Dan Way, Escon-dido, tel. 619/741–1326; 1525 W. Vista Way, Vista, tel. 619/945–9474; 1155 Graves Ave., El Cajon, tel. 619/593–1155.*

(👫 2–12) **Legoland California** (see Chapter 9) is a colorful new theme park inspired by Legos, the toy building bricks. *One Lego Dr., Carlsbad, tel. 760/918–5300.*

(👫 ALL) **Time Out Family Amusement Center** (tel. 619/233–5277), a video arcade, is at Seaport Village.

(👫 6–15) **Ultrazone** is a multilevel laser tag arena located in a shopping center; if you have restless teens, it stays open till 2 AM on Friday and Saturday. *3146 Sports Arena Blvd., San Diego, tel. 619/221–0100. Admission: $6.50 per person per game; $5 per person per game ages 11 and under weekends before 2 PM and every-one after midnight. Open daily; call for hrs.*

(👫 2–15) The **Wave Water Park** in Vista, north of San Diego, has four water slides, a river for tubing, a competition pool, and a children's play area (for kids up to 48 inches tall), among other water attractions. *161 Recreation Dr., Vista, tel. 760/940–9283. Admission: $9.25 ages 7–59, $6.25 ages 3–6 and 60 up, ages 2 and under free. Adult spectator admission $2.25. Open early June–Labor Day, daily 10:30–5:30, rest of Sept. weekends 11–5.*

(👫 2–15) **White Water Canyon,** a big new water park south of San Diego in Chula Vista, contains 16 water slides, a wave pool, a play structure for kids, and a river for tubing, plus a ball park, a volleyball pit, and picnic facilities. *2052 Otay Valley Rd., Chula Vista, tel. 619/661–7373. Admission: $20.99 adults, $14.99 children under 48″, ages 2 and under free. Open May–Sept., daily 10–6.*

Dance

👫 5 – 15 The California Ballet (tel. 619/
560–5676) stages an annual *Nutcracker* at
the San Diego Civic Theatre and at the
Poway Center for the Performing Arts in
suburban Poway.

👫 5 – 15 The San Diego Civic Youth
Ballet (Casa del Prado Theatre, Balboa
Park, tel. 619/233–3060) stages ballets in
spring and at Christmas, starring dancers
ages 4 to 19.

Movies

👫 5 – 15 The Reuben H. Fleet Science
Center in Balboa Park (see Museums,
above) offers a *really* big screen experience
at its Omnimax theater, which has a giant
dome screen, a special camera, and 152
speakers that give viewers the sensation of
traveling in a spaceship. The noise and special effects might frighten small children, but
most post-toddlers think those are the best
parts.

👫 ALL UA Horton Plaza (475 Horton Plaza, tel. 619/234–4661) and Mann
Hazard Center 7 (7510 Hazard Center Dr.,
tel. 619/291–7777) in Mission Valley both
show first-run movies on multiple screens.
The Mann Cinema 21 (1440 Hotel Circle
North, tel. 619/291–2121) offers an old-
fashioned big-screen experience.

Music

👫 6 – 15 The La Jolla Chamber Music
Society (Sherwood Auditorium, 700
Prospect St., La Jolla, tel. 619/459–3728)
stages a Discovery series for rising young
stars at 3 PM on selected Sundays from
September to May.

👫 ALL La Jolla Concerts by the Sea
(tel. 619/645–8115) presents free summertime music at Scripps Park on Sunday from
2 to 4 PM.

👫 ALL Twilight in the Park Summer
Concerts (tel. 619/239–0512 or 619/235–

1105) take place at the Spreckels Organ
Pavilion in Balboa Park from Tuesday to
Thursday at 6:15 PM.

Theater

👫 3 – 12 Christian Community Youth
Theater (tel. 619/588–0206), a nondenomi-
national theater program, stages 15 productions by and for youths in various locations
around San Diego County; shows have
included *Cinderella* and *Man of La Mancha*.

👫 ALL Fern Street Circus (tel. 619/
235–9756) presents an entertaining mix of
acrobatics, music, and other circus antics,
with performers ages 3 to 70. Call for a
schedule.

👫 6 – 15 Lamb's Players Theater (1142
Orange Ave., Coronado, tel. 619/437–
0600) stages several shows a year suitable
for families and children, such as *My Fair
Lady* and *The Secret Garden*. The troupe's
holiday shows are especially popular.

👫 2 – 10 Marie Hitchcock Puppet Theater (tel. 619/685–5045) at the Palisades
area in Balboa Park is where puppetry
groups perform such shows as *Rumplestilt-
skin*. Shows ($2 adults, $1.50 ages 2–14)
take place from Wednesday to Sunday year-
round; call for times.

👫 6 – 15 The Old Globe Theatre
(Simon Edison Centre for the Performing
Arts, Balboa Park, tel. 619/239–2255 or
619/231–1941) stages an outdoor summer
Shakespeare festival that's ideal for introduc-
ing kids to the Bard.

👫 3 – 12 The San Diego Actors Theatre (tel. 619/268–4494) sponsors the
"Children's Classics" series of fairy tales
and children's stories adapted for the stage
such as the *Mad Hatter's Tea Party, Little
Red Riding Hood,* and *Rapunzel*. The productions are held on selected Saturday
mornings throughout the year at two locations: the Better Worlde Galeria (4010
Goldfinch St., Mission Hills, tel. 619/260–

8007) and L'Auberge Del Mar Garden
Amphitheater (1540 Camino Del Mar, tel.
619/259–1515).

(🕇🕇 3–15) **San Diego Junior Theatre**
(Casa del Prado, Balboa Park, tel. 619/239–
8355) presents student actors ages 8 to
18, in shows such as *Little Women* and
Peter Pan.

(🕇🕇 3–15) **Starlight Musical Theatre** (tel.
619/544–7800) puts on summer outdoor
musicals in Balboa Park's Starlight Bowl.

For Parents Only

San Diego, which used to lock up early, now
comes alive after dark. The quintessential
nightspots in the city are the discos, jazz
clubs, and bars downtown in the restored
Victorian-era Gaslamp Quarter and at
Pacific and Mission beaches. For a quieter
evening, the piano bars at the Hotel del
Coronado (1500 Orange Ave., Coronado,
tel. 619/435–6611) and the downtown
Westgate Hotel (1055 2nd Ave., tel. 619/
238–1818) are both mellow and elegant.

BY THE SEA

olden beaches, salt air, blue sea: classic California images, and, for many families, vital ingredients for any Golden State vacation. From the redwood-lined headlands of the north to the sun-splashed sands of the south, California's coastline offers nearly 1,000 miles of natural majesty and seaside pleasure. (Don't overlook the beaches in the San Francisco, Los Angeles/Orange County, or San Diego areas, either: you'll find those detailed in Chapters 14, 15, and 16.) So pack your swimsuits and get ready for a splash in the surf, California-style.

Mendocino/Fort Bragg

In a sparsely settled region where only 10 towns have more than 700 people, Mendocino (population 1,000) and nearby Fort Bragg (with 6,000 or so residents) are the centers of tourism along the North Coast. Yet the two towns still have a relaxed feel. Picturesque Mendocino, perched on a bluff high above the ocean, began as a lumber town but has evolved into an artists' colony; the long-running TV series *Murder She Wrote* used it as a stand-in for the Maine fishing village where Angela Lansbury's character was supposed to live (her TV home, an inn known as "Blair House," is one block north of the post office). Longtime lumber town Fort Bragg is considerably less scenic but more family-oriented than artsy Mendocino, with lots of family lodgings, restaurants, and attractions. But the real glory of the Mendocino/Fort Bragg area for families is its redwood parks and its wild beaches, ideal for spreading out a picnic, searching for tide pools, combing for treasures, watching for wildlife, and playing Frisbee.

The Basics

RESOURCES. Fort Bragg–Mendocino Coast Chamber of Commerce (332 N.

Main St., Box 1141, Fort Bragg 95437, tel. 707/961–6300 or 800/726–2780). **Redwood Empire Association** (2801 Leavenworth St., 2nd Fl., at The Cannery, San Francisco 94133, tel. 415/394–5991 or 888/678–8502, open daily 9–5).

GETTING IN AND OUT OF MENDOCINO/FORT BRAGG. By Air: San Francisco International Airport (see Chapter 14) is about 170 miles south of Mendocino; United Express (tel. 800/241–6522) flies to the small Arcata/Eureka Airport, 140 miles north of Mendocino).

By Car: Mendocino and Fort Bragg, 8 miles north, both lie along coastal Highway 1. The most scenic drive from San Francisco is north via Highway 1, but it can take a full day. To get here in under four hours, take Highway 101 north from San Francisco to Route 128 in Cloverdale, which joins Highway 1 south of Mendocino. From Eureka, you can drive south along the Avenue of the Giants (see Chapter 7) to Highway 1.

By Train: One of the most exciting ways to get to Fort Bragg is by rail through the redwoods on the **Skunk Train,** which connects to Willits (along Highway 101 about 40 miles away). See Scoping out Mendocino/Fort Bragg, *below.*

By Bus: Greyhound (tel. 800/231–2222) from San Francisco has a daily run to Willits, where you can connect next day to the Skunk Train. **Mendocino Stage** (tel. 707/ 964–0167) operates van service between Mendocino and Fort Bragg several times daily, for $2.50 adults, and $1.25 for children under 12, one-way.

FAMILY-FRIENDLY TOURS. The **Mendocino Carriage Co.** (Lansing and Little Lake Sts., Mendocino, tel. 800/399–1454) conducts horse-drawn carriage tours year-round, weather permitting. You can negotiate with your driver over length and cost, but figure about $35 for a 30-minute ride.

Whale-watching tours leave from Noyo Harbor, south of downtown Fort Bragg, from December to April. **Misty II Charters Sportfishing** (N. Harbor Dr., tel. 707/964–7161) offers two-hour tours for $25 per person. Others to try are **Tally Ho** (N. Harbor Dr., tel. 707/964–2079) and **Telstar Charters** (N. Harbor Dr., tel. 707/964–8770).

Scoping out Mendocino/Fort Bragg

(†ï ALL) The Skunk Train—formally known as the California Western Railroad—is a former logging train so called because of its once-stinky gas engines (they're now steam- or diesel-powered). Chugging along the Noyo River through towering redwoods, the train climbs 1,700 feet over 30 bridges and trestles, around nearly 400 switchbacks and curves, and through two pitch-black tunnels. For children who tend to get restless on long rides I'd recommend the half-day trips: you board at the depot in Fort Bragg, ride 22 miles to Northspur (a camp in the redwoods), have a snack or picnic (the train stops here for ½ hour), and return to Fort Bragg, all within about 3½ hours. A full-day trip takes you all the way to Willits (40 miles) and returns the same or next day. The narration is full of redwood country lore. You can sit indoors, stand in an open observation car, or even ride up front with the conductor.

Make reservations well ahead, especially on weekends.

♠ *100 Laurel St. Depot, Box 907, Fort Bragg 95437, tel. 707/964–6371 or 800/777–5865. Fare: $26 adults ($21 for ½ day), $12 ages 5–11 ($10 for ½ day), under 5 free unless occupying a seat. Family fare: $49–$79, for 2 adults and 1–4 children, ½ day. Runs daily starting at 9:20.*

(†ï ALL) **MacKerricher State Park,** a gorgeous 8-mile stretch of rocky coast, contains black-sand beaches where kids can watch harbor seals and search tide pools for hermit crabs (ours found hundreds of them). You can also fish for trout or boat on freshwater Lake Cleone. Between March and June, don't miss the harbor seal rookery at Laguna Point, where mother seals give birth on the rocks and beaches. During whale migration (from November to March) the headland—with a stroller-accessible boardwalk—is an excellent vantage point. The park has 152 campsites.

♠ *Hwy. 1, 3 mi north of Fort Bragg, tel. 707/ 937–5804, camping 800/444–7275. Day use admission free. Camping: $14–$18.*

(†ï ALL) The **Mendocino Coast Botanical Gardens,** 1½ miles south of Fort Bragg, is a wonderful formal garden that kids can enjoy, with 47 acres of trails (many stroller-accessible) leading past rhododendrons, fuchsias, and heathers, through pine forests, and along ocean bluffs.

♠ *18220 N. Hwy. 1, Fort Bragg, tel. 707/ 964–4352. Admission: $5 adults, $3 ages 13–18, $1 ages 6–12. Open Mar.–Oct., daily 9–5; Nov.–Feb., daily 9–4.*

(†ï ALL) **Jughandle State Reserve** is best known for its Ecological Staircase Trail, a three-hour round-trip hike that climbs from windswept headlands 2½ miles into the forest. You'll pass through fir, pine, redwood, and, at the end, a pygmy forest. The beautiful 0.8-mile headlands loop is suitable for younger hikers. Picnic tables are at the trailhead.

♠ *Hwy. 1, 3 mi south of Fort Bragg, tel. 707/ 937–5804. Admission free.*

ALL **Russian Gulch State Park** contains 3 superb miles of forested hiking trails and a sandy beach. At the headland you can see ocean waves surging in the Devil's Punchbowl—a "blowhole" caused by the collapse of a sea tunnel. For a great day hike follow the Fern Canyon Trail and then take the loop trail to Russian Gulch Falls; paved for the first 2½ miles, the trail follows a stream along a canyon before climbing to a cascading waterfall. The park has 30 developed campsites.
🏠 *Hwy. 1, 2 mi north of Mendocino, tel. 707/937–5804. Admission: $5 per car. Camping: $14–$18.*

6–15 **Ford House,** built in 1854, offers one big attraction for kids: a scale model of Mendocino as it looked in the 1890s (the town once had a 12-seat outhouse). The house is the visitors center for **Mendocino Headlands State Park** (tel. 707/937–5804), which nearly surrounds Mendocino; the park includes 3 miles of easy hiking trails along the bluffs. Watch for otters and, in winter, migrating whales.
🏠 *Main St., Mendocino, tel. 707/937–5397. Admission free. Open daily 11–4.*

3–15 **The Kelley House Museum** contains photos of Mendocino from the 1800s, plus changing exhibits. Even if you don't go in, drop by to see the gardens and duck pond outside.
🏠 *Main St., Mendocino, tel. 707/937–5791. Admission: $1, under 12 free. Open June–Sept., daily 1–4; Oct.–May, Fri.–Mon. 1–4.*

ALL **Van Damme State Park** has a beautiful beach, good for beachcombing, picnicking, or watching abalone divers (April–November). Inland are 10 miles of forest and canyon trails. A paved trail for mountain bikes runs along luxuriant Fern Canyon, and a self-guided stroller- and wheelchair-accessible Discovery Trail leads through a pygmy forest of dwarf cypresses and pines. You can either hike to the Discovery Trail or drive 3½ miles to the parking lot via Little River Airport Road, which is off Highway 1. The park has 74 developed campsites and 10 hike-in campsites.
🏠 *Hwy. 1, 3 mi south of Mendocino at Little River, tel. 707/937–5804. Admission: $5 per car. Camping: $8–$18.*

BEACHES. Never let children go unattended on the beaches and bluffs, and don't turn your back on the powerful ocean waves. Rocks along shore can be slippery, so wear shoes that grip when you explore tide pools. **Big River Beach** is a good place for sunning, picnicking, and beach play. Follow a trail from Mendocino's Main Street down the bluffs to the beach.

Glass Beach in Fort Bragg (access from the west end of Elm Street) is the place to search for wave-polished shards of pottery and glassware. Farther north is **Pudding Creek Beach,** with little dunes to explore. It's under a trestle bridge off Highway 1 at the south end of MacKerricher State Park (see *above*). **Ten Mile Beach** at MacKerricher, complete with dunes, tide pools, black sand, and harbor seals on offshore rocks, is our favorite beach in the area.

Sports and Action

BICYCLING. MacKerricher, Russian Gulch, and Van Damme state parks have paved trails along coastal streams and through redwood and fern canyons (see *above*). Road biking is popular in Mendocino. Rent road or mountain bikes (limited children's sizes available) at **Catch a Canoe & Bicycles, Too!** (Stanford Inn by the Sea, Hwy. 1 at Comptche-Ukiah Rd., Mendocino, tel. 707/937–0273).

CANOEING AND KAYAKING. See Chapter 10.

FISHING. Fish for rockfish from the beaches at Russian Gulch State Park or at Mendocino Headlands State Park. For tackle rentals and bait visit **Noyo Fishing Center** (32450 N. Harbor Dr., Fort Bragg, tel. 707/964–7609) or **North Coast**

Angler (1260 N. Main St., Fort Bragg, tel. 707/964–8931).

For sportfishing, see Chapter 10.

HORSEBACK RIDING. **Ricochet Ridge Ranch** (24201 N. Hwy. 1, Fort Bragg, tel. 707/964–7669), about 3 miles north of town, offers 1½-hour guided group trail rides four times daily along Ten Mile Beach; riders must be 6 or older. The cost is $35 per person; call for reservations.

Shops

For the Shell of It (344 N. Main St., Fort Bragg, tel. 707/961–0461) carries sea shells, gems, rocks, and other items.

Try a waffle cone from the **Mendocino Ice Cream Co.** on Main Street, next to the Mendocino Hotel (tel. 707/937–5884).

The **Village Toy Store** (10450 Lansing St., Mendocino, tel. 707/937–4633) carries toys and kites from around the world.

Eats

Cafe Beaujolais. We first brought the kids here when both the restaurant—located in a Victorian farmhouse surrounded by gardens—and the kids were relatively new. Now, foodies come here from all over to sample some of the finest and freshest cuisine in Northern California, and dinner is a candlelight affair, with no children's menu. Well-behaved kids age 7 and up, however, are welcome, and the chef will try to accommodate young tastes—say, by preparing pasta with cheese or butter. *961 Ukiah St., Mendocino, tel. 707/937–5614. Reservations advised. Dress: casual but neat. No credit cards. No breakfast or lunch. $$$*

Wharf Restaurant and Lounge. At this wonderful location at Noyo Harbor you can take in views of fishing boats, a trestle bridge, and, in the evenings, often-glorious sunsets. And the food does justice to the views. Seafood is featured, naturally: Lia loved her fried calamari, Grael his salmon.

Portions are large, but at dinner kids can order from a children's menu that includes fish-and-chips, cheeseburgers, or chicken. On the regular menu, steaks and chicken are also available at dinner, soups and sandwiches for lunch. *780 N. Harbor Dr., Fort Bragg, tel. 707/964–4283. Children's menu (dinner). Reservations advised. Dress: casual but neat. MC, V. $$–$$$*

Egghead Omelettes. Friendly, cozy, and clean, this eatery has old-fashioned wooden booths and a Wizard of Oz theme that should delight younger kids. (The walls are lined with movie posters, and you follow a "yellow brick road" to the rest room out back.) My kids thought their omelets were the best they'd ever had: You can choose from more than 40 types, or opt for light, fluffy pancakes, all in large portions (small children may want to split an order). At lunch you can also have hamburgers, soups and salads, and "sandwitches." Egghead is a handy block away from the Skunk Train depot. *326 N. Main St., Fort Bragg, tel. 707/964–5005. No reservations. Dress: casual. MC, V. No dinner. $–$$*

Mendocino Bakery and Cafe. This cafeteria-style establishment is great for a casual meal. For breakfast try a freshly baked Danish or a burrito; for lunch or dinner there's pizza, soups, sandwiches, salads, or special entrées. Sit indoors or on a large outdoor deck. *10485 Lansing St., Mendocino, tel. 707/937–0836. No reservations. Dress: casual. No credit cards. $*

FOR PICNICS. Pick up fixings at **Tote Fete** (10450 Lansing St., Mendocino, tel. 707/937–3383).

Where to Stay

Mendocino contains many B&Bs and historic inns that aren't well suited for children; the motels in Fort Bragg are often a better bet for families. If you reserve well in advance, however, you can find good family accommodations in both towns. **Mendocino Coast Accommodations** (tel. 707/937–

5033) is a reservations service. **Mendocino Coast Reservations** (1000 Main St., Box 1143, Mendocino 95460, tel. 707/937–5033 or 800/262–7801) handles vacation rentals. Camping is available at MacKerricher, Russian Gulch, and Van Damme state parks (see *above*); call 800/444-7275 for reservations.

The Little River Inn. Overlooking the ocean and adjacent to Van Damme State Park (see *above*), this family-friendly resort south of Mendocino has a 9-hole golf course, two lighted tennis courts, and flower gardens. All the rooms have ocean views. The original Victorian inn (with four rooms) dates from 1853, and there are also three cottages, some motel-type units, and other more luxurious rooms. Some rooms have fireplaces and decks overlooking the Pacific, and all have TVs. The inn's restaurant serves breakfast, dinner, and Sunday brunch, and children are always welcome; kids' plates are half-price. Children under 12 stay free. *7751 N. Hwy 1, Box B, Little River, 95456, tel. 707/ 937–5942 or 888/466–5683; fax 707/937– 3944. 65 units. Facilities: restaurant, golf, tennis. MC, V. $–$$$*

The Harbor Lite Lodge. Overlooking the Noyo River and the fishing village at Noyo Harbor, this is a motel, nothing fancy, but the rooms are spacious and nicely furnished. Some deluxe units have wood-burning stoves and refrigerators, and many rooms have balconies with views of the harbor, river, and fishing fleet. *120 N. Harbor Dr., Fort Bragg 95437, tel. 707/964–0221 or 800/ 643–2700. 79 rooms. Facilities: sauna. AE, D, DC, MC, V. $–$$*

McElroy's Inn. Family-friendly McElroy's is built around an old water tower. Ask about the loft room (which has ocean views) or the two-room minisuites, one of which has a fireplace. None of the rooms have TVs or phones. *998 Main St., Box 1881, Mendocino 95460, tel. 707/937–1734. 4 units. Facilities: some minirefrigerators, 1 fireplace. No credit cards. $–$$*

The Seabird Lodge. Kids can enjoy the indoor heated pool, hot tub, and HBO movies on TV at this better-than-average motel. The spacious rooms have refrigerators, and a few have balconies or kitchens. The motel runs a free shuttle to the Skunk Train depot (ask about special two-night Skunk Train packages). Kids under 12 stay free. *191 South St., Fort Bragg 95437, tel. 707/964–4731 or 800/345–0022, fax 707/ 961–1779. 65 units. Facilities: adjacent restaurant, pool, hot tub. AE, D, DC, MC, V. $*

Entertainments

FOR PARENTS ONLY. The North Coast is not the place to come for swinging nightlife, but the **Caspar Inn** (Caspar St. at Hwy. 1, tel. 707/964–5565), between Mendocino and Fort Bragg, presents live music nightly, from folk to jazz to ska.

Santa Cruz

At the northern tip of Monterey Bay "where the redwoods meet the sea," Santa Cruz is a casual resort town with great weather. Like Santa Barbara, Santa Cruz faces south, and gets many more warm, sunny summer days than Monterey or San Francisco. Though near the Bay Area, Santa Cruz has a touch of Southern California in it, with golden sands, comparatively warm waters, superlative surfing, and the Santa Cruz Beach Boardwalk, the West Coast's largest seaside amusement park. Nearby are other beach towns such as Capitola and Aptos to the south, and the town of Felton and the redwood-forested Santa Cruz mountains to the north.

The Basics

RESOURCES. Santa Cruz County Conference and Visitors Council (701 Front St., Santa Cruz 95060, tel. 831/425–1234 or 800/833–3494). An information kiosk on

Ocean St. (between Water St. and Soquel Ave.) is open daily in summer from 10 to 4.

GETTING IN AND OUT OF SANTA CRUZ. By Air: The closest major airport is **San Jose International** (tel. 408/277–4759), 35 miles northeast of Santa Cruz on Highway 17. Major domestic airlines plus regional carriers serve the airport. The **Santa Cruz Airporter** (tel. 831/423–1214 or 800/497–4997) and **ABC Transportation** (tel. 831/464–8893 or 800/734–4313) offer ground transportation from the airport, as well as from San Francisco International.

By Car: Santa Cruz is 75 miles south of San Francisco. The most scenic route is Highway 1 down the coast; on sunny weekends traffic can be very slow, but allow about 1½ hours for the drive in normal traffic. The best alternative is to take I–280 south to Highway 17, which heads west over the mountains to Santa Cruz.

By Train: Amtrak (tel. 800/872–7245) *Coast Starlight* trains, which operate between Los Angeles and Seattle, stop in San Jose (connect to Santa Cruz by bus).

By Bus: From San Francisco and San Jose, **Greyhound** (tel. 800/231–2222) serves Santa Cruz several times daily. Municipal bus service is provided by the **Santa Cruz Metropolitan Transit District** (tel. 831/425–8600).

FAMILY-FRIENDLY TOURS. C. Stagnaro (tel. 831/423–2010) at the Santa Cruz Municipal Wharf operates seasonal bay cruises and whale-watching tours. One-hour bay cruises depart daily from Memorial Day to Labor Day and cost $6 per person. Whale-watching trips (three hours long) depart from December to April and cost from $17 to $20 for adults, $13 to $14 for children under 14.

Scoping out Santa Cruz

ALL The Santa Cruz Beach Boardwalk (see Chapter 9) is one of the great family attractions on the central coast.
400 Beach St., tel. 831/426–7433.

ALL The Santa Cruz Municipal Wharf, down the beach from the Boardwalk, is lined with shops, fish markets, and seafood restaurants. We love to walk here at night, when the lights of the Boardwalk are aglitter, or in early morning when the air is cool. The wharf is ½ mile long; you can also drive out most of the way. The barking sea lions that hang around the pilings at the end are always entertaining.
Front and Beach Sts., tel. 831/429–3628.

3 – 15 The Santa Cruz City Museum of Natural History focuses on the area's geology, flora, and fauna, with a touch tide pool for inquisitive young hands, plus Ohlone Indian relics and a beehive. But the big hit with many kids is the climbable, full-size cement gray whale outside.
1305 E. Cliff Dr., tel. 831/429–3773. Admission: $2 adults, $1 students, 50¢ ages 11 and under. Open Tues.–Sun. 10–5.

6 – 15 The Santa Cruz Surfing Museum is a tiny collection of vintage surfboards, photos, and videos displayed in the Mark Abbott Memorial Lighthouse, which occupies a beautiful spot on the coast. A colony of sea lions holds court offshore on Seal Rock and, appropriately, surfers ply the waves right off Lighthouse Point at renowned Steamers Lane.
W. Cliff Dr., tel. 831/429–3429. Admission free. Open Wed.–Mon. noon–4.

3 – 15 The Joseph M. Long Marine Laboratory and Aquarium, near Natural Bridges State Beach, lets kids handle hermit crabs, anemones, and sea stars in a touch tank and see sea lions, dolphins, and an 86-foot-long blue whale skeleton.
West end of Delaware Ave., tel. 831/459–4308. Admission: $2 adults, $1 students, ages 16 and under free. Open Tues.–Sun. 1–4.

ALL The Capitola Wharf, more than 125 years old, is a rustic reminder of the days when Capitola was the state's first seaside resort. You can fish here (no license required), shop, or eat seafood.

🏕 *Adjacent to beach, Capitola, tel. 831/ 462–2208.*

👫 **6 – 15** **Wilder Ranch State Park,** 2 miles north of Santa Cruz, is a ranch and dairy where kids can tour barns and chicken coops and see live animals (goats, sheep, horses, turkeys). Docents wear late–19th-century costumes and give blacksmithing, butter churning, and other demonstrations on some weekends. Bring a picnic lunch and take a hike along the 2-mile Old Cove Landing Trail to the sea, where you may spot harbor seals or cormorants. This is also a popular mountain biking area.
🏕 *1401 Old Coast Rd., off Hwy. 1, tel. 831/ 426–0505 or 831/423–9703. Parking: $6. Open June–Labor Day daily 8–5; rest of year, Wed.–Sun. 10–4.*

👫 **ALL** **Felton Covered Bridge Park,** 7 miles north of Santa Cruz, contains the tallest covered bridge in the United States. Built in 1892 and later reconstructed, it's one of the few covered bridges left in the state. A park with picnic tables and a children's playground adjoins the bridge.
🏕 *Graham Hill Rd., Felton, tel. 831/454– 7956. Open daily 7–sunset.*

👫 **ALL** **The Roaring Camp & Big Trees Narrow Gauge Railroad** takes passengers on a 6-mile, 1¼-hour steam-train ride from Felton through the redwoods to the summit of Bear Mountain and back. You'll pass along hairpin switchbacks and over bridge trestles while climbing some of the steepest grades in North America. Atop Bear Mountain the train stops at a pretty redwood grove. You can picnic here and take a later train back—but make sure space is available, or you may have to hike back down. From late May to September a standard-gauge steam train, the **Santa Cruz, Big Trees, and Pacific Railway Co.,** makes an 8-mile trip from the Santa Cruz Beach Boardwalk over the mountains and through the San Lorenzo River Gorge to Roaring Camp, a re-creation of a frontier logging camp complete with an old-time general store, picnic areas, and chuck-wagon barbecues.

🏕 *Graham Hill Rd., Felton, tel. 831/335– 4400. Roaring Camp & Big Trees fare: $13.50 adults, $9.50 ages 3–12, under 3 free (on lap). Santa Cruz, Big Trees, and Pacific fare: $15 adults, $11 ages 3–12. Parking: $5. Open daily except Dec. 25. Santa Cruz, Big Trees, and Pacific runs Apr.–Nov.*

👫 **3 – 15** **The Mystery Spot,** in the redwoods 3 miles north of downtown Santa Cruz, is a place where the laws of gravity seem to go haywire (balls appear to roll uphill) and you'll find yourself leaning at precarious angles—unable to stand up straight. Your children may even appear taller than you. But are these "mysterious natural phenomena" (as guides claim) or merely clever hillside carpentry?
🏕 *1953 Branciforte Dr., tel. 831/423–8897. Admission: $4 adults, $2 ages 5–11, under 5 free. Open Sept.–May, daily 9–5; June–Aug., daily 9–8.*

BEACHES. Capitola City Beach, a cliff-sheltered mile-long beach at the mouth of Soquel Creek in Capitola by the Sea, is one of the best family beaches in the area. Ocean waters are generally warm and calm enough for swimming. Besides swimming, this beach is popular for surfing, windsurfing, sand-castle building, kite-flying, and volleyball. The Esplanade along the beach is lined with outdoor restaurants and shops, and the historic Capitola Wharf (see *above*) is nearby. *Tel. 831/475–6522. Lifeguards in summer.*

Cowell Beach, to the right of the Santa Cruz Municipal Wharf as you face the Pacific, offers calm, warm ocean waters. *Tel. 831/429–3747. Lifeguards.*

Main Beach is a beautiful, nearly mile-long stretch of sand in front of the Boardwalk. You can sun, swim, and rent beach equipment here. *Beach St., tel. 831/426–7433. Lifeguards in summer; rest rooms.*

Natural Bridges State Beach has a natural sandstone arch carved by crashing surf and one of the largest monarch butterfly colonies on the West Coast (see Chapter

7). The surf is too strong for swimming. *2531 W. Cliff Dr., tel. 831/423–4609. Day-use parking: $6. Hiking trails, fishing, picnic areas, rest rooms. Open 8 AM–sunset.*

New Brighton State Beach offers uncrowded white sand, swimming, surf fishing, picnicking, and campsites. *State Park Dr., off Park Ave., near Capitola, tel. 831/475–4850. Day use parking: $6 per car. Rest rooms.*

Pleasure Point Beach is a favorite of surfers. Rocky paths lead to the beach, and a trail along the cliffs offers bay views. *E. Cliff Dr. and Pleasure Point Dr., tel. 831/454–7956.*

Rio Del Mar State Beach, popular for swimming, biking, and barbecuing, contains explorable tide pools. *Rio Del Mar Blvd., Aptos, tel. 831/429–2850. Day-use fee: $6 per car. Lifeguards in summer.*

Santa Cruz Harbor Beach offers swimming, sunbathing, and beach equipment rentals. *End of 5th Ave. at E. Cliff Dr., tel. 831/475–6161. Rest rooms, snack bars; lifeguards in summer.*

Seabright Beach—long, sandy, and beautiful—is near the Yacht Harbor. *East Cliff Dr. at Seabright, tel. 831/429–2850. Lifeguards in summer; rest rooms.*

Seacliff State Beach is sunny, with picnic tables, barbecue pits, campsites, and pier fishing from a cement-hulled ship. *State Park Dr., Aptos, tel. 831/685–6500. Seacliff exit off Hwy. 1. Day-use parking: $6 per car. Lifeguards in summer; rest rooms.*

Twin Lakes State Beach, one of the area's warmest beaches, is at the opening of Schwann Lagoon. The lagoon leads back to a wild bird sanctuary and is ideal for boating and for novice windsurfers. *E. Cliff Dr. and 7th Ave., tel. 831/429–2850. Lifeguards in summer; rest rooms.*

Sports and Action

BICYCLING AND ROLLERBLADING. The scenic **West Cliff Drive Bikepath** winds

about 2 miles along the headlands from west of the Municipal Wharf to Natural Bridges State Beach. Past the first hill, the going is flat and easy. You'll pass surfers, joggers, and sea lions, and have unobstructed views of the coast. For great mountain biking trails head to Forest of Nisene Marks State Park (see Hiking, *below*) or Wilder Ranch State Park (see *above*).

Rent touring or mountain bikes at the **Bicycle Rental Center** (131 Center St., tel. 831/426–8687). Rent skates from **Go Skate Surf and Sport** (601 Beach St., tel. 831/425–8578).

For indoor roller skating try the **Santa Cruz Roller Rink** (1606 Seabright Ave., tel. 831/423–0844); open daily.

BOATING. **Chardonnay II Sailing Charters** (Yacht Harbor, FF Dock, tel. 831/423–1213) conducts sailing excursions on Monterey Bay aboard a 70-foot yacht. **Pacific Yachting Sailing School and Charters** (790 Mariner Parkway, tel. 831/423–7245) takes passengers on excursions and offers lessons.

FISHING. Try pier fishing (no license required) at the end of the **Municipal Wharf** in Santa Cruz and at the **Capitola Wharf** in Capitola. Catches include rock cod, ling cod, halibut, and salmon. Visit **Capitola Boat and Bait** (1400 Wharf Rd., Capitola, tel. 831/462–2208) or any of the bait shops on the Santa Cruz Municipal Wharf. **C. Stagnaro** (tel. 831/423–2010) operates deep-sea rock cod fishing trips ($32–$36 adults, $25–$29 under 16) from the Santa Cruz wharf. Salmon trips ($44–$45 per person, any age), leave at 6 AM from March to November.

You can rent a boat and fish on the lake at **Loch Lomond Recreation Area** (tel. 831/335–7424), in the Santa Cruz Mountains redwoods northeast of Felton. Call for directions.

HIKING. **Big Basin State Park,** about 23 miles north of Santa Cruz (follow Rtes. 9 and 236 north) contains 50 miles of hiking trails leading from stands of giant ancient redwoods to fern canyons and waterfalls. You can camp here (147 sites) or stay in one of 36 tent cabins. *21600 Big Basin Way, Boulder Creek, tel. 831/338–8860, camping 800/444–7275, tent cabins 800/874–8368. Day-use fee: $6 per car. Camping: $14–$18; tent cabins $40–$42.*

Henry Cowell Redwoods State Park has a flat, easy, self-guiding 0.8-mile loop, the Redwood Grove Trail. Kids love to crawl into the hollowed-out Fremont Tree (bring a flashlight). A 4-mile round-trip hike via several connecting trails leads to a central observation deck; maps are for sale at the park's nature center. The park has 112 developed campsites and you can swim, fish, or picnic here. *101 N. Big Trees Park Rd., off Graham Hill Rd., Felton, tel. 831/335–4598, camping 800/444–7275. Day-use parking: $6 per car. Camping: $14–$18.*

The Forest of Nisene Marks State Park in Aptos—the epicenter of the 1989 earthquake that toppled buildings and flattened freeways in San Francisco—has hiking and biking trails and picnic areas among the redwoods. *Aptos Creek Rd., Aptos, tel. 831/763–7063.*

KAYAKING. You can go sea kayaking on guided tours or on your own in Monterey Bay. For tours and lessons appropriate for beginners, call **Kayak Connection** (413 Lake Ave., tel. 831/479–1121). For peaceful kayaking or canoeing head to Schwann Lagoon by Twin Lakes Beach (E. Cliff Dr., tel. 831/429–2850).

SKATEBOARDING. **Derby Park** in Santa Cruz (Woodlawn Way and San Jose St., off W. Cliff Dr., 831/429–3777) has its own skateboard course, plus play structures for younger siblings.

WATER SPORTS. For details about surfing in Santa Cruz, see Chapter 10. With lots of waves, the windsurfing in Santa Cruz is generally not for beginners, but **Cowell Beach** and **Schwann Lagoon** are good for novices. **Capitola Beach** is popular for advanced sail-

boarders. **Club Ed** at Cowell Beach (tel. 831/459–9283 or 800/287–7873) rents sailboards for windsurfers.

Eats

India Joze. With exotic and delicious dishes ranging from East Indian and Southeast Asian to Mediterranean and Middle Eastern, the menu here appeals most to kids with adventurous appetites. The dessert selection is fantastic. Of the small children's menu (offered at dinner), Lia has sampled the charbroiled chicken skewers and approved. The dining area is light and airy, and there's a garden patio as well. *1001 Center St., tel. 831/427–3554. Children's menu. Reservations accepted. Dress: casual but neat. AE, D, DC, MC, V. $$–$$$*

Riva Fish House. One of a string of seafood restaurants on the Municipal Wharf, Riva serves high-quality but reasonably priced family dinners. The atmosphere is informal, and many tables have views of the water (but get here early for those). Snapper, tuna, prawns, squid, scallops, and other seafood items are broiled, sautéed, grilled, or fried; portions are generous, especially considering the low prices. *Santa Cruz Municipal Wharf, tel. 831/429–1223. No reservations. Dress: casual but neat. No credit cards. $$*

Dolphin Restaurant. On a scenic site at the end of the Municipal Wharf, this small, casual restaurant has pleasant decor: Booths have bay views, ceiling fans whir, walls are the color of driftwood. The Dolphin serves good breakfasts—hotcakes, French toast, omelets, cereals—plus seafood lunches and dinners. Typical fare is clam chowder, seafood sandwiches, salads, and fried squid or shrimp; you can also get pasta or burgers. A kids' menu includes a corn dog, a hot dog, a grilled cheese sandwich, fish-and-chips, and spaghetti. *Santa Cruz Municipal Wharf, tel. 831/426–5830. Children's menu. No reservations. Dress: casual. MC, V. $–$$*

The Pontiac Grill. At this '50s-style diner, you'll find vinyl booths (each with a mini-jukebox) and car themes: Kids' place mats have old Pontiacs to color, and the menu uses terms like "spare parts" (side orders) and "first gears" (appetizers). Besides classic American dishes like meat loaf, barbecued beef ribs, and Southern fried chicken, the emphasis here is on burgers—14 different varieties—plus fries, onion rings, and shakes. The kids' menu includes a choice of hot dog, burger, or grilled cheese served in a cardboard classic car. *429 Front St., tel. 831/427–2290. Children's menu. Reservations for 6 or more only. Dress: casual. MC, V. $*

FOR PICNICS.   Pick up sandwiches and other items to go at **Zoccoli's Deli** (1534 Pacific Ave., tel. 831/423–1711).

Where to Stay

Inn at Manresa Beach. Set amid rolling hills near Manresa Beach, this 1867 mansion is about 10 miles south of Santa Cruz. Most of the nature-theme rooms at this B&B can be converted into suites by opening or closing off the cleverly placed doors. Children of any age are welcome—the owners have young kids themselves. Bring your tennis racquets; two clay courts await. The full breakfast includes a cooked-to-order entrée. *1258 San Andreas Rd., La Selva Beach 95076, tel. 831/728–1000 or 888/523–2244, fax 831/728–8294. 9 rooms. Facilities: tennis, croquet, volleyball. AE, D, MC, V. $$$*

Capitola Venetian Hotel. With a beach location—within easy walking distance of Soquel Creek, Capitola Wharf, and numerous restaurants—this photogenic sand-colored stucco hotel (along with adjoining multihued condos) displays 1920s charm. The units are best described as little apartments; all have kitchenettes, and some have fireplaces and views of the water. This hotel is very popular with families, so reserve months ahead for summer stays. *1500 Wharf Rd., Capitola 95010, tel. 831/476–6471 or 800/332–2780, fax 831/475–3897. 20 units. AE, D, MC, V. $$–$$$*

WestCoast Santa Cruz Hotel. This beachfront resort opens right onto Cowell Beach; if it's too cold to swim in the ocean, you can head for the heated swimming pool and hot tub. Every room has an oceanfront balcony or patio, plus minirefrigerators and VCRs. Children under 12 stay free with parents. *175 W. Cliff Dr., Santa Cruz 95060, tel. 831/426–4330 or 800/662–3838, fax 831/427–2025. 147 rooms, 16 suites. Facilities: 2 restaurants, pool, sauna, hot tub. AE, D, DC, MC, V. $$–$$$*

Ocean Pacific Lodge. You can save money by staying a few blocks from the beach at this modern multistory motel where the amenities include an outdoor heated pool and hot tub, TVs with VCRs, free Continental breakfast, and, in some rooms, refrigerators and microwaves. Rates are reasonable in the off-season but zoom up in summer. *120 Washington St., Santa Cruz 95060, tel. 831/457–1234 or 800/995–0289, fax 831/457–0861. 44 rooms, 13 suites. Facilities: heated pool, hot tub, VCRs, some kitchenettes, some in-room whirlpool baths, exercise room. AE, D, DC, MC, V. $–$$*

Entertainments

For movies in downtown Santa Cruz head for the **Del Mar Theatre** (1124 Pacific Ave., tel. 831/425–0616). Check out the annual summertime **Cabrillo Music Festival** (tel. 831/429–3444). **Shakespeare Santa Cruz** (tel. 831/459–2121) presents its annual six-week summer festival at the University of California–Santa Cruz, with most performances in an outdoor wooded glen.

FOR PARENTS ONLY

The Catalyst (1011 Pacific Ave., tel. 831/423–1336) nightclub hosts rock and blues acts. **Palookaville** (1133 Pacific Ave., tel. 831/454–0600) presents nationally known and local musicians. **Moe's Alley** (1535 Commercial Way, tel. 831/479–1854) has live blues and dancing nightly.

Monterey/Carmel

On the wooded Monterey Peninsula 120 miles south of San Francisco and 340 miles north of Los Angeles, the resort towns of Monterey and Carmel (officially Carmel-by-the-Sea) draw families year-round. The attractions include seaside sports, wildlife, sea life, history—Monterey was the capital of Spanish Alta California—and rugged, often breathtaking, coastal scenery. Monterey is the hub of the region, with a population of about 30,000 and a wealth of lodgings and restaurants. In a day you can explore Monterey and adjacent Pacific Grove, a community of ornate Victorian mansions, rocky shoreline, and monarch butterfly groves. With two days you can add Pebble Beach—famous for golf courses, palatial homes, and spectacular coastline—and Carmel, known for its art galleries, shops, upscale accommodations, and beautiful beaches. Carmel is not as intrinsically appealing to most kids as it is to adults, but it does have small-town charm. On weekends, however, the crowds and traffic here can be brutal.

The Basics

RESOURCES. Carmel Visitors Center (Box 4444, Carmel 93921, tel. 831/624–2522 or 800/550–4333). **Monterey Peninsula Chamber of Commerce and Visitors & Convention Bureau** (Box 1770, 380 Alvarado St., Monterey 93942, tel. 831/649–1770 or 800/555–9283). **Pacific Grove Chamber of Commerce** (584 Central Ave., Box 167, Pacific Grove 93940, tel. 831/373–3305).

GETTING IN AND OUT OF MONTEREY/CARMEL. By Air: The **Monterey Peninsula Airport** (200 Fred Kane Dr., off Hwy. 68, Monterey, tel. 831/648–7000), 3 miles from downtown Monterey, has direct service to and from San Francisco, Los Angeles, and San Jose on American Eagle, SkyWest-Delta, United and United Express, and US Airways Express.

By Car: The drive south from San Francisco to Monterey can be made comfortably in 2½ to 3 hours; you'll need most of a day to drive up from Los Angeles. The most scenic route is Highway 1 along the coast. U.S. 101 runs inland; take Highway 68 west to Monterey. From San Francisco, another freeway route is I–280 south to Highway 17, which connects to Highway 1 in Santa Cruz.

By Train: Amtrak (tel. 800/872–7245) *Coast Starlight* trains, which operate between Los Angeles and Seattle via Oakland, stop in nearby Salinas; the connection to Monterey is by Amtrak bus.

By Bus: Greyhound (tel. 800/231–2222) stops in Monterey. **Monterey-Salinas Transit** (tel. 831/424–7695) provides frequent bus service (day passes: $3–$6) from Salinas to Monterey, stopping in the towns in between. The WAVE shuttle-bus service ($1 a day) along the Monterey waterfront makes stops downtown and in Pacific Grove; the shuttles run between 9 and 6:30 from Memorial Day to Labor Day.

FAMILY-FRIENDLY TOURS. Glass Bottom Boat Sea Life Tours (90 Fisherman's Wharf, tel. 831/372–7150) conducts 25-minute harbor tours in a glass-bottom boat for $6 adults, $5 ages 11 and under. Two-hour whale-watching cruises are offered from mid-December through March by **Monterey Sport Fishing and Cruises** (Fisherman's Wharf, tel. 831/372–2203; $15 adults, $12 ages 11 and under). From July to September the company offers three-hour tours for $25 adults, $20 ages 11 and under.

BABY-SITTING. The staff members of **Time...Out!** (tel. 831/375–9269) are bonded, trained in CPR, and speak numerous languages.

Scoping out Monterey/Carmel

(**ALL**) The **Monterey Bay Aquarium** (see Chapter 6) is the area's premier family attraction, with touch pools, a bat ray pet-

ting tank, a giant kelp forest, and a wing that showcases life in the open ocean.
🏠 *886 Cannery Row, Monterey, tel. 831/ 648–4888.*

(👫 **ALL**) **Cannery Row** (see Chapter 4), immortalized by author John Steinbeck, is a once-thriving sardine canning area that's been converted to shops, restaurants, and hotels.
🏠 *Along Monterey Bay from aquarium to Coast Guard pier, tel. 831/373–1902.*

(👫 **6 – 15**) **Steinbeck's Spirit of Monterey Wax Museum** on Cannery Row depicts the story of Monterey in wax. It's fun and informative, an easy way to absorb some history.
🏠 *700 Cannery Row, Monterey, tel. 831/ 375–3770. Admission: $5.95 adults, $4.95 students and ages 55 and up, $2.95 ages 6– 13. Open Memorial Day–Labor Day, daily 9– 9; rest of year, Mon.–Thurs. noon–6, Fri. and Sun. 10–8, Sat. 10–10.*

(👫 **ALL**) **The Edgewater Packing Company** (640 Wave St., Monterey, tel. 831/ 649–1899), right above Cannery Row, is one of those tacky tourist magnets that most kids (mine included) can't seem to resist. Lia declared the antique carousel the fastest she'd ever ridden; dozens of electronic and video games attracted Grael; and an old-fashioned ice-cream parlor kept their parents happy.

(👫 **ALL**) **Fisherman's Wharf** in Monterey is now primarily for tourists rather than fishermen, but this old wood-planked pier— its origins date from 1846—retains the sights and smells of the sea along with its many restaurants, shops, and tour boats. To my mind, it's more appealing than its larger and more famous counterpart in San Francisco. The barking sea lions at the end of the pier are favorites of kids. You can grab some take-out seafood or board a harbor cruise here.
🏠 *Across from Custom House Plaza on waterfront, Monterey, tel. 831/373–0600.*

(👫 **6 – 15**) **The Maritime Museum** in Custom House Plaza offers exhibits on seafaring—everything from the Spanish colonizers

to the sardine fishing of Steinbeck's day. A free 20-minute film about early Monterey shows several times daily in the theater.
🏠 *Stanton Center, Monterey, tel. 831/375– 2553. Admission: $3 adults, $2 ages 13–18, ages 12 and under free. Open daily 10–5.*

(👫 **6 – 15**) **Monterey State Historic Park** (see Chapter 4) encompasses most of old Monterey; you can take a self-guided walking tour (pick up a brochure at Stanton Center) of historic buildings and adobes.
🏠 *Custom House Plaza, Monterey, tel. 831/ 649–7118.*

(👫 **ALL**) **El Estero Park** makes a great stop for families after a morning's sightseeing (it's not far from the waterfront). Rent a paddleboat ($7 for ½ hour, $11 for 1 hour) and watch ducks on Lake El Estero, then head for the innovative Dennis the Menace Playground, designed by Dennis's creator, cartoonist Hank Ketcham. Kids can climb on a real, full-size steam-train engine, scurry around a hedge maze, and cross a suspension bridge.
🏠 *Del Monte Ave. between Camino El Estero and Camino Aguajito, Monterey, tel. 831/375–1484 (paddleboat rentals).*

(👫 **3 – 15**) **The Pacific Grove Museum of Natural History** may be overshadowed by the nearby Monterey Bay Aquarium, but see both if you can—this is a good complement to the big aquarium. In front, a life-size bronze whale named Sandy attracts kids who love to climb on its back. Inside are exhibits on local tide pools, seabirds, geology, and butterfly preserves.
🏠 *165 Forest Ave., Pacific Grove, tel. 831/ 648–3116. Admission free. Open Tues.–Sun. 10–5.*

(👫 **ALL**) **The Monarch Grove Sanctuary,** in the Monterey pines adjacent to Pacific Grove's Butterfly Grove Inn (1073 Lighthouse Ave.), is home to thousands of migrating monarch butterflies from October to March; they cluster in the trees when the air is cold and flutter around when it's warm. In some years the monarchs flock instead to nearby Washington Park, at Alder and Spruce streets. In either location it's a dazzling sight.

🏠 *Enter from Ridge Rd. off Lighthouse Ave., Pacific Grove. Open daily sunrise–sunset.*

(👫 **6 – 15**) **Point Piños Lighthouse,** the West Coast's oldest lighthouse still in operation—it's been going since 1855—stands at the tip of the Monterey Peninsula. The lighthouse has been refurnished in late–19th-century style; docents dressed in period costume relate the structure's history.

🏠 *Lighthouse Ave. off Asilomar Blvd., Pacific Grove, tel. 831/648–3116. Admission free. Open Thurs.–Sun. 1–4.*

(👫 **6 – 15**) **Carmel Mission** (see Chapter 4) is the most authentically restored and probably most beautiful of the state's 21 historic Franciscan missions.

🏠 *3080 Rio Rd., Carmel, tel. 831/624–3600.*

(👫 **3 – 15**) **Point Lobos State Reserve** (see Chapter 8) is a wonderful spot to view sea otters, sea lions, and harbor seals.

🏠 *Hwy. 1, 3 mi south of Carmel, tel. 831/624–4909.*

(👫 **ALL**) **The 17-Mile Drive,** a private toll road, is one of the most beautiful scenic drives in all of California, passing rugged coastline and wind-bent Monterey cypress and pine trees, as well as fabulous homes, golf courses, and resorts. The best views are along a 6-mile coastal stretch from Spanish Bay to Pebble Beach. You can stop to hike, sit on the beach, let the kids clamber over rocks, and view wildlife or sunsets. (Benches and rest rooms are placed strategically at major stops.) Don't miss Seal and Bird Rocks, where sea lions, harbor seals, and seabirds hang out, or the Lone Cypress, the landmark tree at the tip of a rocky point.

🏠 *Toll entrances from Hwy. 1, Carmel, and Pacific Grove. Admission: $7.25 per car. Open daily sunrise–sunset.*

(👫 **ALL**) **The Poor Man's 17-Mile Drive,** so called because there are no gates or entrance fees (and it's only about 4 miles

long), follows the Pacific Grove coastline from just beyond the Monterey Bay Aquarium to Asilomar Beach, past gabled Victorian inns and rocky coves. The scenery rivals that of Pebble Beach, and, if you get out to walk, you're almost certain to see sea lions, harbor seals, and sea otters.

🏠 *From Ocean View Blvd. and 3rd St. to Sunset Dr., Pacific Grove.*

BEACHES. Because of the generally cool weather here (especially in summer), the local waters are chilly. Surf can also be very hazardous; be aware of riptides when children are playing near shore. Enjoy the beaches for walking, picnicking, and exploring tide pools; a few, however, do have shallow areas where wading or light swimming is possible.

Asilomar State Beach is a long, stunning stretch of preserved dune areas, golden sands, rocky shoreline, and tide pools. Stick to beach walks and picnicking here; the surf can be treacherous. *Follow Ocean View Blvd. to Sunset Dr., Pacific Grove.*

Carmel City Beach may be the area's most beautiful, with powdery white sands, breezes good for kite-flying, and beautiful sunsets. The surf is often unsafe for swimming, though, and the beach can get very crowded. *Foot of Ocean Ave., Carmel, tel. 831/624–3543. Rest rooms.*

Carmel River State Beach is a quiet, rugged beach flanked by dunes. It lies alongside a shallow lagoon at the mouth of the river, which offers reasonably warm and calm waters and tide pools to explore. (In late summer bacteria sometimes reach hazardous levels, so check before swimming.) At the adjacent **Carmel River Bird Sanctuary** you may spot pelicans, sandpipers, herons, and egrets in the marshes. *Follow Scenic Rd. south from Carmel, tel. 831/624–4909. Rest rooms.*

Lovers Point, the most dramatic spot along the "Poor Man's 17-Mile Drive" (see *above*), has twin coves with pretty beaches where kids can play in the usually gentle surf, and you can rent kayaks (also watch for scuba divers). Grael and Lia love to scramble over the huge rocks that jut out over the bay here. The grassy park above the coves has picnic tables and rest rooms. *Ocean View Blvd. at Forest Ave., Pacific Grove.*

Monterey State Beach (tel. 831/384–7695), which starts east of Monterey's Municipal Pier (Wharf No. 2), is really three separate beaches that extend to the nearby town of Seaside. The waters here are often calm enough for wading or swimming, and you may see kayakers. *Rest rooms, lifeguards.*

Sports and Action

BICYCLING AND ROLLERBLADING. The **Monterey Peninsula Recreation Trail** and **17-Mile Drive** have superb biking (see Chapter 10) and skating. **On the Beach Surf Shop** (693 Lighthouse Ave., Monterey, tel. 831/646–9283) rents skates.

FISHING. Try pier fishing from the **Monterey Municipal Pier** (Wharf No. 2), tel. 831/646–3950. Rent tackle from **Randy's Fishing Trips** (tel. 831/372–7440) on Fisherman's Wharf. No license is needed. From Fisherman's Wharf, deep-sea fishing charters go out into Monterey Bay and Carmel Bay for rockfish, salmon, and albacore; contact **Monterey Sport Fishing and Cruises** (tel. 831/372–2203 or 800/200-2203); **Sam's Fishing Fleet** (tel. 831/372–0577); and **Randy's Fishing Trips** (see *above*). Children 15 and under don't need a license.

GOLF. The Monterey Peninsula is one of the golf capitals of the world. Greens fees can be astronomical, however, at some of the most famous courses. The **Old Del Monte Golf Course** (1300 Sylvan Rd., Monterey, tel. 831/373–2700) is an 18-hole public course with greens fees ranging from $15 to $75.

HORSEBACK RIDING. Our family enjoyed a beautiful ride along the coast and through the Del Monte Forest at Pebble Beach; contact **Pebble Beach Equestrian Center** (Por-

tola Rd., Pebble Beach, tel. 831/624–2756). The minimum age is 6.

Carmel Valley is another good area for horseback riding; try the **Holman Ranch** (tel. 831/659–2640) for guided trail rides over country hills. Children's pony rides are also available.

KAYAKING. Monterey Bay is one of the West Coast's top spots for sea kayaking; see Chapter 10.

SURFING AND BOOGIEBOARDING. Surfing is popular off Asilomar State Beach in Pacific Grove and off Carmel Beach; if you aren't experienced, these aren't the places to learn. Rent surfboards, wet suits, and boogieboards at **On the Beach Surf Shop** (693 Lighthouse Ave., Monterey, tel. 831/646–9283; also at Ocean and Mission Sts., Carmel, tel. 831/624–7282).

Shops

The **American Tin Cannery** (125 Ocean View Blvd., Pacific Grove, tel. 831/372–1442) contains more than 45 discount factory outlets; it's one block from the Monterey Bay Aquarium.

Thinker Toys (7th and San Carlos Sts., Carmel, tel. 831/624–0441) has puppets, puzzles, games, trains, and dolls. **The Mischievous Rabbit** (Lincoln and Ocean Sts., Carmel Bay Company Courtyard, Carmel, tel. 831/624–6854) features Beatrix Potter–illustrated items: stuffed animals, music boxes, books, tapes, infant clothing.

Eats

Abalonetti Seafood Trattoria. This is our top choice among the seafood restaurants at Fisherman's Wharf: Kids are given coloring books when they sit down, the bay views are great, and the food is consistently good. Calamari is the specialty here—you can have it fried, baked, stuffed, or pounded, breaded, and sautéed like abalone. If squid isn't your dream dish, choose from a selection of Italian dishes such as seafood pasta and wood-fired pizza. The children's menu includes pizza, pasta, hamburgers, and fish-and-chips, or kids can get half-orders of regular dishes. Right next to the full-service restaurant, Abalonetti's casual deli serves Italian antipasti items, pizza, and wonderful fried calamari—a great place to snack. *57 Fisherman's Wharf, Monterey, tel. 831/373–1851. Children's menu. Reservations accepted. Dress: casual. AE, D, DC, MC, V. $$–$$$*

The Fishwife. If you're looking for family-friendly seafood away from the tourist hordes, head for this casual restaurant near Asilomar Beach in Pacific Grove. It's known for its excellent values—most entrées are under $10 (and child's plates are half that). Some dishes have a Latin accent—you might find black beans as a side dish, or prawns sautéed Belize style—and the fish is well prepared. Grilled snapper and sole are among the specialties, and frying is done with a light touch. Seafood pastas are also served. Seafood sandwiches and salads are featured at lunch. *1996½ Sunset Dr., Pacific Grove, tel. 831/375–7107. Children's menu. Reservations advised. Dress: casual. AE, D, MC, V. Closed Tues. $$*

The Hog's Breath Inn. With its oddball name and its celebrity part-owner (Carmel's own Clint Eastwood), this restaurant was bound to be popular, but we've returned for the food and lively atmosphere. It has roaring fireplaces and rustic decor; you can eat indoors or on an outdoor heated patio under an oak tree. Sometimes we order a Dirty Harry Burger or a Sudden Impact (Polish sausage) sandwich, but we usually go for the fresh seafood, nicely grilled. Expect hearty portions (though kids can order smaller portions) and a long wait at dinnertime. *San Carlos St. between 5th and 6th Sts., Carmel, tel. 831/625–1044. No reservations. Dress: casual. AE, DC, MC, V. $$*

Pasta Mia Trattoria. This excellent Italian restaurant is set in a century-old Victorian building; families come here for an early dinner after visiting the aquarium. The tables are set with butcher paper, perfect for kids to crayon on. Start with a delicious antipasti assortment, then move on to pastas, meat, or seafood dishes. The kitchen will fix half-portions of any dish for kids. Lia enjoyed her half order of linguine with meat sauce, while Grael still talks about his polenta and Italian sausages. *481 Lighthouse Ave., Pacific Grove, tel. 831/375–7709. Reservations accepted. Dress: casual but neat. MC, V. No lunch. $$*

The Tinnery. Across the street from beautiful Lovers Point, this is among our favorite eating places in the area, especially for breakfast—fresh-squeezed orange juice, followed by pancakes or omelets. The contemporary decor is casual, and picture windows yield views of Monterey Bay. You can get burgers or other sandwiches for lunch; dinner menus tend toward Continental seafood and meat dishes. *631 Ocean View Blvd., Pacific Grove, tel. 831/646–1040. Children's menu. No reservations. Dress: casual but neat. AE, D, DC, MC, V. $$*

FOR PICNICS. Pick up picnic supplies at the **Mediterranean Market** (Ocean Ave. and Mission St., Carmel, tel. 831/624–2022); the **5th Avenue Deli** (5th Ave. between Dolores and San Carlos Sts., Carmel, tel. 831/625–2688); or **Nielsen Bros. Market** (San Carlos and 7th Sts., Carmel, tel. 831/624–6441). Prime spots are Carmel Beach, Point Lobos State Reserve, and Monterey's El Estero Park.

Where to Stay

The Highlands Inn. On a pine-covered cliff overlooking one of the most dramatic vistas on the California coast, this landmark inn has hosted presidents, princes, movie stars, and honeymooners—along with many families. When kids reach their rooms, they receive milk and cookies and goody bags. It's hard to leave your room here: with a fire roaring, you can gaze out at jagged rocks and ocean waters and hear waves crashing and sea lions barking below. Binoculars are provided to watch for passing whales. Most units are suites with fully equipped kitchens. Ask about midweek specials from November to June. *Box 1700, Carmel 93921 (off Hwy. 1, 4 mi south of Carmel), tel. 831/624–3801 or 800/682–4811 (in CA), fax 831/626–1574. 40 rooms, 102 suites. Facilities: 2 restaurants, pool, hot tubs. Baby-sitting by arrangement. AE, D, DC, MC, V. $$$*

The Hyatt Regency Monterey. Surrounded by flower gardens (complete with strutting peacocks), this luxurious resort is next to the Old Del Monte Golf Course, where guests get a discount. Camp Hyatt ($10 per hour; $5 each additional child from family), an excellent children's program that includes arts and crafts, swimming, tennis lessons, games, cooking classes, and picnics, operates daily from Memorial Day to Labor Day. Kids also like to hang out at the resort's sports bar, which has food, sports on TV, and electronic games. Kids under 18 stay free with parents. *1 Old Golf Course Rd., Monterey 93940, tel. 831/372–1234 or 800/824–2196 (in CA), fax 831/372–4277. 535 rooms, 40 suites. Facilities: 2 restaurants, 2 pools, 2 hot tubs, exercise room, golf (18 holes), tennis, children's program. AE, D, DC, MC, V. $$$*

La Playa. Carmel's prettiest hotel is built on a hillside lush with flowers, two blocks from the beach. Five roomy, secluded cottages nestled among pine, oak, and cypress trees a half block from the Mediterranean-style hotel come with fireplaces, full kitchens, and private patios. Book the cottages well in advance for summer months. Children under 12 stay free. *Box 900, Camino Real and 8th Sts., Carmel-by-the-Sea 93921, tel. 831/624–6476 or 800/582–8900, fax 831/624–7966. 75 rooms, 5 cottages. Facilities: restaurant, heated pool. AE, DC, MC, V. $$$*

Lighthouse Lodge and Suites. We love the quiet, woodsy setting of this resort near Asilomar State Beach. There are two separate complexes here: lodge and suites. The suites are larger and come with more amenities (fireplaces, kitchens, Jacuzzi baths),

but lodge rooms, which are considerably less expensive, are also spacious, and they open onto a year-round heated pool and hot tub. A complimentary hot buffet breakfast sets everyone up for the day. *1150 and 1249 Lighthouse Ave., Pacific Grove 93950, tel. 831/655–2111 or 800/858–1249, fax 831/655–4922. 68 rooms, 31 suites. Facilities: heated pool, hot tub, sauna, full breakfast. AE, D, DC, MC, V. $–$$$*

Pacific Grove Motel. This is one of the best bargains on the Monterey Peninsula, with family-size rooms starting as low as $64. You'll feel like you're way off the tourist track—it's set in the woodsy part of Pacific Grove, where deer often roam—yet it's only a short drive from Monterey, or 17-Mile Drive. Some units have connecting rooms and enclosed rear terraces. Amenities include a barbecue area and a small children's playground. *Lighthouse Ave. at Grove Acre, Pacific Grove 93950, tel. 831/372–3218 or 800/858–8997, fax 831/372–8842. 30 rooms. Facilities: heated pool, hot tub, refrigerators, playground. AE, D, MC, V. $*

Entertainments

Catch first-run movies at **Galaxy 6 Cinemas** (280 Del Monte Center, Monterey, tel. 831/655–4617) or **Lighthouse Cinemas** (525 Lighthouse Ave., Pacific Grove, tel. 831/655–4617).

Look for the annual **Carmel Bach Festival** (tel. 831/624–2046) in July and August; melodramas performed at **California's First Theatre** (tel. 831/375–4916); and free family shows midsummer at the **Monterey Bay Theatrefest** (tel. 831/622–0700).

FOR PARENTS ONLY. Head to Monterey's Cannery Row area for nightlife. **Kalisa's** (851 Cannery Row, tel. 831/372–3621) is a freewheeling café with a potpourri of entertainment—belly dancing, flamenco, jazz, folk dancing, or magic. **Doc's Nightclub** (95 Prescott St., tel. 831/649–4241) hosts rock bands nightly. **Planet Gemini** (625 Cannery

Row, tel. 831/373–1449) presents comedy shows on most nights, followed by dancing to live rock music. The **Monterey Plaza Hotel** (400 Cannery Row, tel. 831/646–1700) has piano music in a romantic setting overlooking the bay at its Duck Club.

Santa Barbara

If Santa Barbara isn't the perfect family beach resort, it comes awfully close. Start with miles of idyllic beaches, lapped by water warm enough—and surf calm enough—for swimming much of the year. Throw in abundant waterside sports and a climate that's mild and sunny year-round. The pace is generally easy and relaxed; the setting and architecture are Mediterranean to match the climate; restaurants and accommodations are excellent; and there's even plenty of history and culture to soak up between swims.

The Basics

RESOURCES. Santa Barbara Beachfront Visitors Information Center (1 Santa Barbara St. at Cabrillo Blvd., tel. 805/965–3021). **Santa Barbara Conference and Visitors Bureau** (12 E. Carrillo St., 93101, tel. 805/966–9222 or 800/927–4688).

GETTING IN AND OUT OF SANTA BARBARA. By Air: The Santa Barbara Municipal Airport (500 Fowler Rd., tel. 805/683–4011) is 8 miles from downtown. Carriers flying here include American/American Eagle, SkyWest/Delta, United/United Express, and US Airways Express. **Santa Barbara Airbus Express** (tel. 805/964–7759 or 800/733–6354) runs between the Santa Barbara airport and Los Angeles International Airport (see Chapter 15); it also connects Santa Barbara with Burbank's airport. **Metropolitan Transit District** (tel. 805/683–3702) Bus 11 runs from the Santa Barbara airport to downtown. **SuperRide Air-**

port Shuttle (tel. 805/683–9636) provides door-to-door van service from the airport to local destinations.

By Car: Santa Barbara is 90 miles north of Los Angeles, a two-hour drive on Highway 101. It's 330 miles south of San Francisco—follow either Highway 1 along the coast (the dramatic drive via Big Sur) or Highway 101, a faster, less scenic alternative. Allow a day or more for this drive.

By Train: Amtrak (tel. 800/872–7245) *Coast Starlight* (which operates between Los Angeles and Seattle via Oakland) and *San Diegan* (which operates between Santa Barbara and San Diego via Los Angeles) trains serve Santa Barbara. The depot is at 209 State Street.

By Bus: Greyhound (tel. 800/231–2222) serves Santa Barbara from Los Angeles and San Francisco. The station is at 34 W. Carrillo St. **Downtown-Waterfront Electric Shuttle**'s battery-powered buses run between the harbor, Stearns Wharf, and East Beach and the zoo, and also from Stearns Wharf to downtown and to Montecito. Rides are 25¢ each (under 5 free). **Santa Barbara Metropolitan Transit District** buses (tel. 805/683–3702, fare 75¢ serve Santa Barbara, Goleta, and Carpinteria.

FAMILY-FRIENDLY TOURS. For families with children old enough to walk for 12 blocks (or young enough to ride in a stroller), ask at the beachfront visitors information center (see Resources, *above*) for a free guide to the downtown "Red Tile Walking Tour," which passes several of the town's top historic and cultural sites.

The **Santa Barbara Trolley Co.** (tel. 805/965–0353) traverses a 90-minute narrated circuit, departing from Stearns Wharf five times daily from 10 to 5:30, with stops at State Street, Mission Santa Barbara, the County Courthouse, shops, and hotels, as well as the adjoining community of Montecito. You can stop along the route and pick up another trolley when you're ready to continue. The fare is $5 adults, $3 under 12.

Captain Don's (125 Harbor Way, Bldg. 3, tel. 805/969–5217) 30-minute cruises ($5 per person) aboard the *Harbour Queen* travel along the coast, daily from mid-June to mid-September and on weekends and holidays the rest of the year. Captain Don's runs blue-whale-watching expeditions from July to September.

For two-hour gray-whale-watching tours ($24 adults, $14 under 13) from December to May, contact the **Sea Landing Aquatic Center** (tel. 805/963–3564) or the **Sailing Center of Santa Barbara** (tel. 805/962–2826 or 800/350–9090).

On the two-hour coastline sailing tours of **Sunset Kidd's** (near the breakwater, tel. 805/962–8222; $25 per person), you might see dolphins, sea lions, or whales.

BABY-SITTING. Some hotels will arrange baby-sitting for guests; check with your concierge or manager. Or call the **Children's Resource and Referral Center** (tel. 805/962–8988), **Child's Play** (tel. 805/966–6767), or **Grandmothers Only Babysitting Service** (tel. 805/685–4450).

Scoping out Santa Barbara

(**ÅŸ ALL**) **Stearns Wharf,** the oldest working pier on the West Coast (dating from 1879 and recently reconstructed), survived a fire in late 1998 and remains a must. There are a few restaurants and shops, but the three-block-long wooden wharf is less commercialized than the wharves in San Francisco and Monterey, with plenty of space for strolling, fishing, and taking in the fine open views of ocean.
🏛 *Foot of State St., at Cabrillo Blvd., Santa Barbara. Admission free.*

(**ÅŸ ALL**) **The Sea Center** at Stearns Wharf, a branch of the Museum of Natural History (see *below*), presents exhibits on marine life, including life-size models of whales and dolphins, six aquariums, remains of shipwrecks, and interactive computer and video displays. But the top draw for kids is

the outdoor Touch Tank, where they can handle anemones, crabs, and sea stars.
🏛 *211 Stearns Wharf, tel. 805/962–0885. Admission: $2 adults, $1.50 ages 13–17 and over 62, $1 ages 3–12, under 3 free. Open June–Labor Day, daily 10–5; rest of year, weekdays noon–5 and weekends and some holidays 10–5; touch tank open Thurs.–Tues. noon–4.*

(**ÅŸ ALL**) The Moreton Bay Fig Tree (see Chapter 7) is an eye-catching natural wonder in the middle of the city.
🏛 *Chapala and Montecito Sts., 1 block south of Hwy. 101, tel. 805/965–3023.*

(**ÅŸ ALL**) The Santa Barbara Zoological Gardens (see Chapter 6) provides natural habitats for its animals; it's small enough that even a young child won't feel overwhelmed.
🏛 *500 Niños Dr., tel. 805/962–5339.*

(**ÅŸ ALL**) The Andrée Clark Bird Refuge, a peaceful freshwater lagoon adjoining the zoo, attracts more than 200 species of birds. A nature trail flat enough for strollers winds through the refuge.
🏛 *1400 E. Cabrillo Blvd.*

(**ÅŸ 6–15**) El Presidio de Santa Barbara State Historic Park, dating from 1782, was Santa Barbara's birthplace and one of four military strongholds established by the Spanish along the coast of California. The guardhouse, El Cuartel, is the second-oldest adobe in the state.
🏛 *123 E. Cañon Perdido St., tel. 805/965–0093. Admission free. Open daily 10:30–4:30.*

(**ÅŸ 3–15**) The Santa Barbara County Courthouse is an architectural treat. My children were amazed that this 1929 Spanish-Moorish "palace," as they called it, is actually a courthouse, with Moorish tiles, tiled floors, arched doorways, porticos, and tropical gardens. Don't miss the Board of Supervisors Assembly Room on the second floor, decorated with historical murals and a vaulted ceiling. Take the elevator to the deck of the 80-foot-high clock tower (open until 4:45 PM) for a terrific panorama.

🏡 *1100 block of Anacapa St., tel. 805/962–6464. Admission free. Open weekdays 8–5, weekends and holidays 9–5. Free 1-hr guided tours Mon.–Sat. 2 PM, also Wed. and Fri. 10:30 AM.*

(👫 6 – 15) The Santa Barbara Historical Museum is a surprising find, filled with colorful exhibits, such as Spanish fans, antique dolls, turn-of-the-century costumes, silver saddles, and a Chinese temple.
🏡 *136 E. De la Guerra St., tel. 805/966–1601. Admission free (donations accepted). Open Tues.–Sat. 10–5, Sun. noon–5. Guided tours Wed., Sat., and Sun. 1:30.*

(👫 6 – 15) The Santa Barbara Museum of Art has a good collection of European paintings, but the highlight for us in this small museum was the collection of Asian art and artifacts, including Tibetan, Chinese, and Japanese pieces. (Don't miss the striking Japanese horned helmet and suit of armor.)
🏡 *1130 State St., tel. 805/963–4364. Admission: $4 adults, $1.50 students and ages 6–17; free Thurs. and 1st Sun. of month. Open Tues., Wed., Fri., and Sat. 11–5; Thurs. 11–9; Sun. noon–5.*

(👫 6 – 15) Mission Santa Barbara (see Chapter 4) is Santa Barbara's most famous landmark.
🏡 *Laguna St., tel. 805/682–4713.*

(👫 3 – 15) The Santa Barbara Museum of Natural History, two blocks north of the Mission, has its first star attraction right outside the doors: the massive skeleton of a 72-foot blue whale, which kids can touch (but not climb on). Inside, they can see swarms of live honeybees, listen to a rattlesnake, and learn about the birds and mammals of the offshore Channel Islands and the Mojave Desert. Watch for listings of kids' activities and special events. Behind the museum, there's a small park with little trails to hike.
🏡 *2559 Puesta del Sol Rd., tel. 805/682–4711. Admission: $5 adults, $4 ages 13–17, $3 ages 2–12, free to all 1st Sun. of month. Open Mon.–Sat. 9–5, Sun. and most holidays 10–5.*

(👫 3 – 15) The Santa Barbara Botanic Garden, about 1½ miles north of the Mission along some winding roads, is a bit tricky to find but provides the best family hiking in the city: 5 miles of trails meander through 65 acres of native California trees, including a rare (for this far south) grove of redwoods and plants such as wildflowers and cacti. (The trails are easy, but too hilly for strollers.) The creek trail crosses a dam built by Mission Indians and padres in 1807.
🏡 *1212 Mission Canyon Rd., tel. 805/682–4726. Admission: $3 adults, $2 ages 12–17, $1 ages 5–12, under 5 free. Open Mar.–Oct. weekdays 9–5, weekends 9–6; Nov.–Feb. weekdays 9–4, weekends 9–5.*

BEACHES AND PARKS. Alameda Park is the site of Kids' World Playground, a maze of fantasy climbing structures, turrets, slides, and tunnels built by local parents. *Santa Barbara St. near Micheltorena St.*

Arroyo Burro Beach, in an isolated area west of the harbor, is a beautiful swath of sand backed by cliffs. Attractions include a lagoon, a good beachside restaurant, tide pools, pelicans and other birds to watch—and sometimes offshore whales, sea lions, or dolphins. *2981 Cliff Dr. at Las Positas Rd., tel. 805/687–3714. Rest rooms, picnic area; lifeguards in summer.*

Carpinteria State Beach, 12 miles south of Santa Barbara, is long, wide, and sandy. With shallow waters and few riptides, it's the area's safest swimming beach, but it's often crowded and has limited parking. There are tide pools to explore and 262 developed campsites. *Follow Palm Ave. or Linden Ave., Carpinteria, tel. 805/684–2811. Rest rooms, picnic area; lifeguards in summer. Day use fee: $5 per car. Camping (tel. 800/444–7275): $17–$23 per night.*

East Beach is Santa Barbara's most popular beach: long, wide, and white-sand beautiful (it shows up on many "best beaches in the world" lists). Volleyball courts, a bike path, an outdoor café, and a play area in the sand with slides, swings, and a jungle gym all draw the crowds. *E. Cabrillo Blvd., east of Stearns Wharf. Picnic areas, changing rooms; lifeguards in summer.*

Goleta Beach Park, north of Santa Barbara, has easy surf good for families with young children and beginning surfers. There are volleyball courts, as well as boating and fishing off Goleta Beach Pier. *5990 Sandspit Rd., Goleta, tel. 805/967–1300. Picnic area, lifeguards in summer.*

Leadbetter Beach, right past the breakwater, is big, broad, and sandy, with a landscaped park and a snack bar. It's known for good surfing and windsurfing. Shoreline Park, which overlooks the beach on Shoreline Drive, offers bluff-top views of the Pacific, a children's play area, and good kite flying. *Shoreline Dr. and Loma Alta Dr. Picnic area; lifeguards in summer.*

Rincon Beach Park, south of Carpinteria Beach, is known for great waves, surfing, and surf fishing. *Bates Rd. and Hwy. 101, Carpinteria, tel. 805/654–3951. Lifeguards in summer.*

West Beach is on the other side of Stearns Wharf from East Beach. The waters are often calm, and there are adjoining park areas. *W. Cabrillo Blvd. between Stearns Wharf and harbor. Picnic areas, bike paths; lifeguards in summer.*

Sports and Action

BICYCLING AND ROLLERBLADING. The level, two-lane **Cabrillo Bike Lane** (see Chapter 10) is a great route along the waterfront. You can rent bikes or Rollerblades at **Beach Rentals** (22 State St., tel. 805/966–6733 or 805/966–2282), or at **Cycles 4 Rent** (101 State St. and two other locations, tel. 805/652–0462).

BOATING. The **Sailing Center of Santa Barbara** (Santa Barbara Harbor, at the launching ramp, tel. 805/962–2826 or 800/350–9090) offers sailing instruction and also rents and charters sailboats.

FISHING. Fish for bass or halibut from **Stearns Wharf** or **Goleta Beach Pier;** no license is required. For surf fishing, no license is required for kids under 16. Try **Carpinteria Beach, Arroyo Burro Beach,** or **Goleta Beach Park.**

Fully equipped boats leave the harbor for full- and half-day sportfishing trips from **Sea Landing Aquatic Center** (Cabrillo Blvd. at Bath, tel. 805/963–3564). Kids under 16 don't need a license, but adults do (one-day licenses are available).

KAYAKING. Sea kayaking is available along the coast; see Chapter 10.

KITE FLYING. Breezes are good at Shoreline Park and Chase Palm Park. Buy kites at **Come Fly a Kite** (1228 State St., tel. 805/966–2694).

WATER SPORTS. Beginning surfers can try Leadbetter Beach, while experienced surfers should head for Rincon Point, where the surf is high. Others to try are Arroyo Burro and Goleta beaches (see Beaches, *above*). Rent surfboards, boogieboards, and wet suits from **Sundance Ocean Sports** (809 State St., tel. 805/966–2474).

Waterskiers favor the waters at the east end of Stearns Wharf off East Beach. Rent skis at **Oceanwear Sports** (22 State St., tel. 805/966–6733).

West Beach or Goleta Beach Park are good for beginning windsurfers; Leadbetter Beach offers some of the best windsurfing in town. Rent sailboards or sign up for lessons at **Sundance Ocean Sports** (2026 Cliff Dr., tel. 805/966–2474).

Shops

The **Paseo Nuevo** (State St. and De La Guerra St., tel. 805/963–2202), a very attractive open-air mall downtown, is the best area in the city to take kids shopping. We wandered in for ice cream (there are several cafés) and stayed to browse. Department stores include The Gap, Nordstrom, and Macy's; specialty shops include the Sesame Street General Store, The Nature Company, and Stampa Barbara (with thousands of clever rubber stamps).

Kernohan's Toys (1324 State St., tel. 805/ 962–2695) sells stuffed animals, dolls, games, and creative toys.

Eats

Keeper's Lighthouse. As we ate seafood here, we sat out on the deck, admiring views of the Pacific (too bad busy Cabrillo Boulevard lies between the restaurant and the ocean). We liked the spicy seafood chili, steamed clams, and grilled fresh fish. The children's menu, for ages 12 and under, includes fish-and-chips, chicken breast, and grilled fish on a skewer; the menu comes with crayons for coloring. *15 E. Cabrillo Blvd., Santa Barbara, tel. 805/965–1174. Children's menu. Reservations accepted. Dress: casual. AE, DC, MC, V. $$*

Palazzio Trattoria. The motto at this attractive restaurant is "People generally don't leave here hungry." Indeed. Servers continually bring freshly baked garlic rolls to your table, and most entrées are so big that two people can split one. The first-rate food is mostly pasta (six different shapes and sizes, served with various sauces) and a few specialties (try the roasted rosemary chicken). Children are welcome and respected here: Crayons are brought to the table, and the "Young Person's Menu"—with kid-size pasta, soups, salads, and desserts—invites kids to visit the kitchen. *1151 Coast Village Rd., Montecito, tel. 805/969–8565. Children's menu. Reservations accepted. Dress: casual but neat. MC, V. No Sun. lunch. $$*

Hola! Amigos Restaurante Cantina. Across Cabrillo Boulevard from the beach, this colorful Mexican restaurant with adobe-style architecture and ceiling fans is big and noisy. The menu is classic Tex-Mex, starring fajitas, tacos, tostadas, and enchiladas. The kids' menu includes *taquitos* (small tacos), quesadillas, tacos, burritos, and hamburgers. *29*

E. Cabrillo Blvd., tel. 805/963–1968. Children's menu. Reservations accepted. Dress: casual. AE, D, DC, MC, V. $–$$

Be Bop Burgers. Here's one of those '50s diners that serves up a fantasy version of the era along with burgers and shakes. After pulling your car into your "Ricky Nelson" or "Beach Boys" parking space, you take a seat at a gleaming booth inside, peruse the rock and TV memorabilia, and listen to oldies (there's a live DJ at night). Besides burgers, typical fare includes "Rock 'n Roll (onion) Rings," "Surf City Sodas," or "La Bamba Chili." A kids' menu has hot dogs, grilled cheese, and peanut butter and jelly sandwiches. *111 State St., Santa Barbara, tel. 805/ 966–1956. Children's menu. No reservations. Dress: casual. D, MC, V. $*

La Super-Rica. For a quick, tasty lunch it's hard to beat this little taco joint whose reputation far exceeds its humble neighborhood (Julia Child was a longtime patron). Order at the window, then sit at a wooden table on a semicovered patio to eat the delicious soft-sided steak, pork, chicken, or chorizo (Mexican sausage) tacos. Everything is cheap, authentic—and good. *622 N. Milpas St., tel. 805/963–4940. No reservations. Dress: casual. No credit cards. $*

Where to Stay

The city has two free accommodations reservation services: **Hot Spots** (36 State St., tel. 805/564–1637 or 800/793–7666), which provides general visitors information and doubles as an espresso bar, and **Coastal Escapes** (tel. 800/292–2222). For summer weekends, especially, book rooms well in advance; some hotels require two-night stays at peak times.

Fess Parker's Doubletree Resort. Yes, it's *the* Fess Parker of Davy Crockett fame. His resort is something of a showplace, with an enormous (almost ostentatious) lobby and Spanish-style stucco architecture that occupies a long, prime stretch of beachfront. Every room is spacious and has a patio or balcony, with a view of either the ocean, a garden courtyard, or mountains (you save money facing the mountains). Children under 18 sharing with an adult stay free. *633 E. Cabrillo Blvd., Santa Barbara 93103, tel. 805/564–4333 or 800/879–2929, fax 805/962–8198. 336 rooms, 24 suites. Facilities: 2 restaurants, pool, hot tub, sauna, tennis, exercise room, bike rentals. AE, DC, MC, V. $$$*

The Four Seasons Biltmore. This luxurious Spanish-style estate, on 19 lush acres overlooking the Pacific, has attracted movie stars and other celebrities for some 70 years. All rooms and cottages have VCRs; the light, airy cottage suites include patios and fireplaces. Kids For All Seasons, a complimentary children's program, offers kids ages 5 to 12 supervised activities daily in summer and on Saturdays the rest of the year. Upon check-in, depending on age, kids receive milk and cookies and other amenities. A schedule of planned activities has a different theme each day. Evening movies are also provided. Beach-cruiser bicycles are complimentary for all guests. Children 17 and under stay free with their parents. *1260 Channel Dr., Montecito 93108, tel. 805/969–2261 or 800/332–3442, fax 805/969—5715. 200 rooms and 17 suites. Facilities: 2 restaurants, pool, hot tub, sauna, health club, tennis, croquet, shuffleboard, children's program. AE, DC, MC, V. $$$*

The San Ysidro Ranch. In the foothills above Montecito, with fine views of both the Pacific Ocean and the Santa Ynez Mountains, this resort once won an award as the "most romantic country hideaway in the world." John and Jacqueline Kennedy honeymooned here, and Hollywood stars have flocked here for escape. Yet the ranch welcomes children. At Camp SYR, a complimentary program that runs daily in summer, kids ages 5 to 12 are offered a full schedule of activities including hikes, games, picnic lunches, treasure hunts, and kite flying. Children's menus are available in the restaurant. Comfortable cottages have fireplaces, VCRs,

and private decks. Two-night minimum stays are required on weekends, and three- to four-night minimums on holidays. *900 San Ysidro La., Montecito 93108, tel. 805/969–5046 or 800/368–6788, fax 805/565–1995. 42 rooms and suites in 21 cottages. Facilities: restaurant, heated pool, tennis, fitness center, children's program. AE, MC, V. $$$*

The Upham. This friendly B&B in downtown Santa Barbara is 14 blocks from the beach but very near Alameda Park, which has a kids' playground. You can stay in the original Victorian-style building (the hotel dates from 1871) or in one of five garden cottages; the latter are ideal for families and have porches or patios, with some fireplaces. The rates include a Continental breakfast buffet (muffins, pastries, breads, cereals, fruits), wine and cheese (lemonade for kids) in the afternoon, and cookies and milk at night. Children 12 and under stay free with parents. *1404 De la Vina St., Santa Barbara 93101, tel. 805/962–0058 or 800/727–0876, fax 805/963–2825. 46 rooms, 4 suites. Facilities: free buffet breakfast. AE, D, DC, MC, V. $$–$$$*

The Cabrillo Inn. Across from East Beach and near the zoo (ask at the front desk for discount zoo passes), this motel has spacious rooms, each with either a partial or full view of the ocean (selecting a partial view can save money). *931 E. Cabrillo Blvd., Santa Barbara 93103, tel. 805/966–1641 or 800/648–6708, fax 805/965–1623. 40 units. Facilities: free Continental breakfast, 2 pools, in-room refrigerators. AE, D, MC, V. $–$$*

The Inn by the Harbor. It's actually two blocks from the harbor, but you can save money by walking the distance. We found this motel very comfortable, and the two-queen suites, which include kitchenettes, are a great deal for families. Children under 3 stay free and the rates include a Continental breakfast. *433 W. Montecito St., Santa Barbara 93101, tel. 805/963–7851 or 800/626–1986, fax 805/962–9428. 33 rooms, 10 suites. Facilities: pool, hot tub. AE, D, DC, MC, V. $–$$*

The Miramar Resort Hotel. This longtime family favorite resort (see Chapter 12) is directly on the beach. *1555 S. Jameson La., Santa Barbara 93108, tel. 805/969–2203 or 800/322–6983, fax 805/969–3163. $–$$*

Entertainments

The **Santa Barbara Youth Symphony** (tel. 805/967–0781) is a hit with local families. The **Granada Theatre** (1216 State St., tel. 805/966–2324) and **Lobero Theatre** (33 E. Canon Perdido St., tel. 805/963–0761) present music, theater, and dance.

FOR PARENTS ONLY. Most major hotels present entertainment nightly during the summer and on weekends all year. The free weekly *Santa Barbara Independent* newspaper carries nightlife listings.

Catalina Island

Santa Catalina may be only 22 miles across the sea from Los Angeles, but it's far removed from the mainland's urban sprawl. The third largest of the Channel Island chain and the only one with a resident population, Santa Catalina is almost two separate destinations. One is the Mediterranean-style resort town of Avalon, built on a crescent-shape cove, with a yacht-dotted harbor and numerous hotels, restaurants, and shops. With its pedestrian-only street running along the bay and few motor vehicles anywhere, the town is safe for young children to walk around. Most of the island, however, is rugged and mountainous; the two highest peaks are over 2,000 feet high. Eighty-six percent of the 21-mile-long island is a nature preserve, owned and managed by the Santa Catalina Island Conservancy. Catalina's only other real settlement besides Avalon is the rustic village of Two Harbors, set on a narrow (½-mile-wide) isthmus separating Catalina's southern and northern coasts. Catalina can be a pleasant day trip, but stay longer to explore the still-wild interior and to soak up Catalina's fascinating history.

The Basics

RESOURCES. The **Catalina Island Visitors Bureau** (Box 217, at foot of Green Pleasure Pier, Avalon 90704, tel. 310/510–1520) publishes an annual Visitors Guide. You can also get information from the **Santa Catalina Island Company Visitors Information Center** (Box 737, Avalon 90704, corner of Crescent and Catalina Aves., across from Pleasure Pier, tel. 310/510–2500 or 800/ 322–3434) and **Two Harbors Visitors Information** (tel. 310/510—7265 or 888/ 510–7979).

GETTING IN AND OUT OF CATALINA. By Boat: Catalina Express (tel. 310/519– 1212 or 800/618–5533) runs frequent high-speed ferries from the Queen Mary Seaport in Long Beach to Avalon in 55 minutes and from San Pedro to Avalon in 75 minutes (there's also 90-minute service to Two Harbors). Round-trip fares are $36 adults, $27 ages 2–11; $2 infants. You can sit on deck, as we did, or inside in airplane-type reclining seats. **Catalina Cruises** (tel. 800/228–2546), leaving from downtown Long Beach, offers two-hour crossings in 700-passenger vessels; round-trip fares are $23 adults, $19 ages 2– 11, $2 infants. From Balboa Pavilion in Newport Beach, **Catalina Passenger Service** (tel. 714/673–5245) operates one daily catamaran crossing (departs at 9), which takes 75 minutes (returns at 4:30). These trips cost $33 round-trip for adults, $16.50 for ages 3 to 12, $2 ages 2 and under; reservations required. Reservations are highly recommended for all boats in summer.

By Air: Island Express (tel. 310/510–2525) flies by jet helicopter from San Pedro and Long Beach to the Catalina Heliport, ¼ mile from Avalon. The trip takes 15 minutes and costs $66 one-way, $121 round-trip. **Island Hopper/Catalina Airlines** (tel. 619/279– 4595 or 800/339–0359) flies five-passenger planes to Catalina from San Diego's Montgomery Field three times daily in summer. Fares range from $75 to $100 one-way, depending on the number of passengers. Planes arrive at Catalina's Airport-in-the-Sky (tel. 310/510–0143), at an elevation of 1,600 feet in the island's interior.

By Car: You can't take a car to or rent a car on the island. Taxi service is provided by **Catalina Cab Company** (tel. 310/510–0025). Golf carts are permitted on most town streets, but not in the interior. **Island Rentals** (125 Pebbly Beach Rd., Avalon, tel. 310/510–1456) rents golf carts for $30 an hour. **Cartopia** (615 Crescent St., tel. 310/510–2493) has similar rates.

By Bus: The **Catalina Safari Shuttle Bus** (tel. 310/510–7265 or 888/510–7979) has scheduled bus transportation (one-way fare: $18 adults, $13 ages 2–11) between Avalon and Two Harbors with stops at campgrounds, beaches, picnic spots, trails, and the airport. Tickets can be purchased at the Safari office on Island Plaza in Avalon or at the Visitors' Services Office at the base of the pier in Two Harbors.

FAMILY-FRIENDLY TOURS. The **Santa Catalina Island Company** (Box 737, Avalon 90704, tel. 310/510–8687 or 800/322–3434), which owns most of the island not managed by the Santa Catalina Island Conservancy, runs a number of well-organized Discovery Tours (see Scoping out Catalina, *below,* for details). The basic 50-minute **Avalon Scenic Tour** costs $8.50 adults, $4.25 ages 2 to 11. Tickets for all tours are available at the Discovery Tours Center across from the Pleasure Pier or at any Santa Catalina Island ticket booth.

Catalina Adventure Tours (Box 797, Avalon 90704, tel. 310/510–2888 or 310/510–0409) runs glass-bottom boat tours, city tours, a Botanical Garden tour, coastal cruises, and a two-hour Adventure Tour of the interior. **Island Tram Tours** (tel. 310/510–2000) conducts 40-minute narrated city/harbor tours in open-air trams, departing from the boat terminal. And **Catalina Safari Tours** (tel. 310/510—7265 or 888/510–7979) runs an inland adventure tour out of Two Harbors.

The **Catalina Express Coastal Shuttle** (tel. 310/519–1212 or 800/618–5533) runs narrated 45-minute boat trips (round-trip $36 adults, $27 ages 2–11, $2 infants) between Avalon and Two Harbors from June to September.

Scoping out Catalina

I usually don't like taking bus tours with children, but in Catalina doing so is virtually a necessity if you want to see more of the island than the area around Avalon. The **Santa Catalina Island Company** (see Family-Friendly Tours, *above*) operates all the tours below; ask about money-saving combinations that include both land and sea tours.

(9–15) The Casino is Catalina's most famous landmark. This Art Deco structure on the bay never hosted a blackjack or roulette game; its name comes from the Italian for "place of gathering or entertainment." A 40-minute guided **Casino Tour** ($8.50 adults, $4.25 ages 2–11) includes views of the stylish Avalon Theatre and the world's largest circular ballroom. The Casino also houses the **Catalina Island Museum** (tel. 310/510–2414; open daily 10:30–4; admission $1.50 ages 12 and up, free with Casino tour), which has exhibits on the island's cultural and natural history, spanning 7,000 years.

(6–15) The Wrigley Memorial and Botanical Garden harbors 38 acres of plants native to Catalina, along with cacti and succulents. A mammoth concrete monument to chewing gum magnate William Wrigley, Jr.—who once owned most of the island and helped develop it as a resort in the 1920s—stands at the head of Avalon Canyon. The memorial and gardens are 1½ miles from town; shuttle service is available from Island Plaza downtown, or you can see the garden as part of a combined city tour ($17 adults, $8.50 ages 2–11).
1400 Avalon Canyon Rd., Avalon, tel. 310/510–2288. Admission: $1. Open daily 8–5.

👫 ALL Glass-Bottom Boat Tours pass through the crystal-clear waters of Avalon Bay and the giant kelp beds of Lover's Cove Marine Preserve. On our trip, we saw bright orange garibaldi fish, checkered calico bass, bat rays, small sharks, and a playful sea lion who swam right beneath the glass. Boat-crew members feed the fish, so the marine life tends to congregate along the route. On nighttime tours, underwater lights attract nocturnal fish. 🏨 *Admission: $8.50 adults, $4.25 ages 2–11. Year-round; 40 min.*

👫 3–15 The Flying Fish Boat Trip takes to the water during the evening in search of the island's flying fish, which soar at speeds up to 40 mph and are said to be the world's largest. (Sometimes they jump right in the tour boats.) 🏨 *Admission: $8.50 adults, $4.25 ages 2–11. Apr.–mid-Oct.; 55 min.*

👫 3–15 The Seal Rocks Cruise visits the natural habitat of migratory sea lions, who can be seen swimming and sunning here. 🏨 *Admission: $8.50 adults, $4.25 ages 2–11. Apr.–mid-Oct.; 55 min.*

👫 3–15 The Skyline Drive Tour is a two-hour narrated trip that's a good choice for families with younger children. The first 3½ miles (10 minutes) of the ride is very steep and curvy, with spectacular views of Avalon as you climb into the hills; at one point there's a 1,000-foot drop-off. (Ride up front for special thrills.) Later, kids can keep watch for bison, wild boar, goats, mule deer, bald eagles, or herons. (The bison were brought here in 1924 for a movie and have since multiplied thirtyfold.) The tours stop at the Airport-in-the-Sky, where the Island Conservancy has set up an interesting Nature Center. 🏨 *Admission: $17 adults, $8.50 ages 2–11. Year-round.*

👫 9–15 The Inland Motor Tour adds to the Skyline Drive tour an Arabian horse show at a ranch and views of Little Harbor and the southern coastline. It's long—about four hours—so think carefully before bringing the young and the restless. 🏨 *Admission: $29.50 adults, $14.75 ages 2–11. Year-round.*

👫 6–15 The Sundown Isthmus Cruise heads to scenic Two Harbors at twilight; make sure kids are old enough to last through the 4½-hour trip. 🏨 *Admission: $30 adults, $15 ages 2–11. Apr.–Oct.*

👫 3–15 Undersea Tours use semi-submersible vessels to go below the water's surface to view Catalina's Undersea Gardens, including a kelp forest, both during the day and at night. Though these 40-minute rides are a bit glitzier—and considerably more expensive—than glass-bottom boats, you don't see all that much more. 🏨 *Admission: $22 adults, $11 ages 2–11. Year-round.*

BEACHES. Crescent Beach is steps from much of the action in Avalon. The beach lies along the bay, so the waves are usually gentle enough for small children. If you come to Catalina for the day, you can rent a locker near the ferry dock and change clothes in the rest rooms on the Pleasure Pier; public showers (open 7–5) are along nearby Casino Way. Crescent Beach is small and narrow, so you'll need to get here early if you want to stake out a spot on the sand in summer. *Tel. 310/510–1520. Lifeguards in summer.*

Descanso Beach is the site of a private beach club about a five-minute walk beyond the Casino on Descanso Bay. The beach here is bigger and less crowded than Crescent Beach, and there's a playground area, volleyball, and horseshoes; beach rentals—including kayaks and snorkels—are available (tel. 310/510–1226). You aren't permitted to bring your own food or coolers here, but there's a seaside café and cantina, and cookouts are held summer evenings. *Tel. 310/510–7400. Day-use fee: $1.50 per person. Lifeguards in summer; rest rooms, showers,* *changing rooms. Open daily in summer, weekends in spring and fall.*

Little Harbor, which faces the Pacific on Catalina's south shore, has two palm-fringed sandy beaches, one with usually calm water good for swimming and snorkeling, the other with ocean surf. You can boogieboard, fish, sunbathe, or hike here. A campground is nearby.

Two Harbors Beach, which is bigger than Avalon's, is good for sunning, swimming, picnicking, and shell collecting. *Tel. 310/510–7265. Rest rooms.*

Sports and Action

BICYCLING. You can bicycle in and around Avalon and Two Harbors easily; rent from **Brown's Bikes** (near the ferry dock, 107 Pebbly Beach Rd., Avalon, (tel. 310/510–0986). To bike in the island's interior you need a permit ($75 per family, good for one year) from **Santa Catalina Island Conservancy** (Box 2739, Avalon 90704, tel. 310/510–2595). Permits can be purchased at Brown's Bikes, at the Conservancy's office (125 Claressa Ave., Avalon), at the tower at the Airport-in-the-Sky, or at the Two Harbors Visitors Services Office. Only mountain bikes are permitted in the interior, and bikers must remain on marked trails and roadways. If you bring your own bikes to Catalina, there's a $6 round-trip charge on Catalina Express boats.

BOATING. Rent motorboats ($22–$30 per hour), pedal boats ($10 per hour), or rowboats ($10 per hour) from April to October at **Joe's Rent-A-Boat** on the Green Pleasure Pier (tel. 310/510–0455).

DIVING AND SNORKELING. For snorkeling head to **Lover's Cove** or **Little Casino Reef** at Casino Point in Avalon; in Two Harbors try **Emerald Bay.** Noncertified divers (ages 12 and up) can try scuba, assisted by a trained instructor-guide. Near Avalon you can dive at the **Underwater Marine Park**

near the Casino or at **Descanso Beach** (tel. 310/510–1226). In the Two Harbors area try **Emerald Cove, Ship Rock, Bird Rock Reef,** or **Blue Caverns.** For snorkeling or scuba rentals, lessons, and tours try **Catalina Divers Supply** (tel. 310/510–0330 or 800/353–0330), with locations at Casino Point, the Pleasure Pier, and Lover's Cove. Other snorkeling outfitters in Avalon include **Descanso Beach Ocean Sports** (tel. 310/510–1226) and **Joe's Rent-A-Boat** (tel. 310/510–0455). In Two Harbors visit the **West End Dive Center** (tel. 310/510—7265 or 888/510–7979), which operates scuba and snorkel boat trips.

FISHING. You can fish from the Green Pleasure Pier without a license. Rent tackle from **Joe's Rent-A-Boat** on the Pier (tel. 310/510–0455). **Catalina Island Sportfishing** (tel. 310/510–7265) runs full- and half-day fishing trips year-round, leaving from Two Harbors.

GOLF. The **Catalina Visitors Golf Course** (tel. 310/510–0530) has nine holes, open to the public.

HIKING. With young children, it's probably best to do your hiking around Avalon (the area up behind the Wrigley Memorial is nice) and the isthmus at Two Harbors, where there are some short trails. If your children are at least 9 and your family is ready for some strenuous hiking, try some of the island's many interior trails. You'll need a free permit from the **Santa Catalina Island Conservancy;** pick them up at the Conservancy's office at 125 Claressa Avenue in Avalon (tel. 310/510–2595), the **Airport-in-the-Sky** (tel. 310/510–0143), or the **Catalina Cove and Camp Agency** in Two Harbors (tel. 310/510–0303). Carry food and water on your hikes, and don't approach any of the island wildlife.

HORSEBACK RIDING. Catalina Stables (600 Avalon Canyon Rd., tel. 310/510–0478) conducts year-round guided trail rides in the hills and canyons near Avalon. The minimum age is 8.

KAYAKING. For details on sea kayaking, see Chapter 10.

MINIATURE GOLF. You can play 18 holes at **Miniature Golf Gardens** (Sumner Ave. at Island Plaza, tel. 310/510–1200; Memorial Day–Sept., daily 9–9; Oct.–Memorial Day, weekends 10–5).

RAFTING. **Catalina Ocean Rafting** (103 Pebbly Beach Rd., Avalon, tel. 310/510–0211 or 800/990–7238) operates half-day, full-day, and two-day island rafting trips. You can see secluded coves, sea caves, and beaches, and go snorkeling at Emerald Bay and Two Harbors. These trips are recommended for ages 5 and up only.

Shops

The **Catalina Cookie Company** in the Metropole Market Place (tel. 310/510–2447) bakes and sells delicious brownies and chocolate-chip cookies. **Catalina Kids** (201 Crescent Ave., tel. 310/510–1559) carries beachwear for infants through teens, plus toys. **Island Toy Shop** (119 Claressa Ave., tel. 310/510–1869) is well stocked with games, beach toys, books, and dolls.

Eats

Ristorante Villa Portofino. This northern Italian spot is best for a special dinner with older kids; the atmosphere—white tablecloths, soft music, candles on the table—isn't stuffy, but a crying baby or wriggling toddler would definitely stand out. Pastas (such as *cappellini* with fresh tomatoes, basil, and garlic) are excellent, as are the antipasti. Chicken, beef, and veal dishes are served with pasta and vegetables. The dessert tray groans with wonderfully rich cakes. The kitchen will prepare half orders for kids. *101 Crescent Ave., Avalon, tel. 310/510–0508. Reservations accepted. Dress: casual but neat. AE, MC, V. Closed Jan. and Feb.; closed Wed. and Thurs. in Nov., Dec., and Mar. No breakfast or lunch. $$$*

Antonio's Pizzeria. Though it's also Italian, this place is the spiritual opposite of the Villa Portofino—so casual it redefines the term. Peanut shells litter the floor and the walls are covered with wooden and neon signs; ceiling fans revolve and oldies music plays. Kids can make noise or spill food here and no one will notice. If the weather's nice and there's room, sit outside on a deck overlooking the water. Cuisine is Sicilian and hearty, while portions are huge and sometimes messy (our meatball-and-mushroom and sausage-and-peppers sandwiches quickly spilled all over the plate). Pizza is the big favorite with kids here anyway; burgers and fish-and-chips are also on the menu. Seafood, pastas, chicken, and steaks are among dinner items, and breakfast is also served. *230 Crescent Ave., Avalon, tel. 310/510–0008. No reservations. Dress: casual. MC, V. $$*

The Pancake Cottage. Here's a good place to go for breakfast or lunch in downtown Avalon, especially if you want to catch an early boat back to the mainland. This homey, friendly place serves breakfasts from 6:30 AM until 2 PM closing time, with pancakes the specialty: up to 10 varieties, at least when fresh strawberries and peaches are in season. (Chocolate-chip pancakes are on the menu, too.) And there are myriad other choices: waffles, French toast, more than 100 omelet combinations, cereals, and giant muffins. "Kiddie's Plates" (for under age 10) feature pancakes or French toast. Lunches include numerous sandwiches, chili, Mexican entrées, and salads. *118 Catalina St., Avalon, tel. 310/510–0726. Children's menu. No reservations. Dress: casual. No credit cards. No dinner. $–$$*

FOR PICNICS. For beach picnic supplies stop at **Fred & Sally's Market** (117 Catalina Ave., tel. 310/510–1199).

Where to Stay

Summer is high season on Catalina, where hotel rates are higher and advance booking is essential. After Labor Day and before

Memorial Day, however, many hotels offer packages that include transportation from the mainland and/or sightseeing tours. **Catalina Island Accommodations** (tel. 310/510–3000) runs a reservations service for hotels and condos in different price ranges.

The Hotel Villa Portofino. A few steps from the beach, this hotel could have been lifted right out of Italy. Many rooms have ocean views, all have cable TV, and some have refrigerators or fireplaces. Adjoining suites and multiple rooms are available with no extra charge for up to two kids. Guests can use a private sundeck, as well as towels and chairs for the beach. The in-house restaurant is the Ristorante Villa Portofino (see Eats, *above*). *Box 127, 111 Crescent Ave., Avalon 90704, tel. 310/510–0555 or 888/510–5555, fax 310/510–0839. 30 rooms, 4 suites. Facilities: restaurant, free Continental breakfast. AE, D, DC, MC, V. $$–$$$*

The Pavilion Lodge. This is one of the best motels in Avalon. The location couldn't be better—on Crescent Avenue, close to the beach and boat landings (complimentary baggage service provided). The rooms are spacious and comfortable, and cable TVs show free movies. Some rooms connect to form family suites. The central courtyard is surrounded by green grass for the kids to run on, and lawn chairs for parents to sit. Kids under 12 aren't charged when staying in their parents' room. Ask about package deals that include boat trips and Catalina tours. *Box 737, 513 Crescent Ave., Avalon 90704, tel. 310/510–2500 or 800/446–0271, fax 310/510–7254. 73 rooms. Facilities: in-room refrigerators, free Continental breakfast. AE, D, MC, V. $–$$$*

CAMPING. The camping nearest to Avalon (1½ miles from the boat landing) is at **Hermit Gulch Campground** (tel. 310/510–8368), which has 68 sites, indoor hot showers, flush toilets, barbecue stands, and tent, tepee, and equipment rentals. Sites are $7.50 per night per person, ages 6 and under free. Reservations are required in July and August. For camping elsewhere on the island, contact **Catalina Camping Reservations** (Box 5044, Two Harbors 90704, tel. 310/510–2500 or 888/510-7979). One of the nicest campgrounds is at Two Harbors, near the beach about ¼ mile from town; another beautiful one is at Little Harbor (reached by Safari Shuttle bus from Avalon or Two Harbors). Black Jack campground, in the island's interior near the airport, is reached by Safari Shuttle bus and then a 1.3-mile hike. Parson's Landing is a remote campground on the island's northwest shore, accessible by trail or by boat and then a 1¼-mile hike.

Entertainments

The **Avalon Theatre** in the Casino building plays first-run films, often accompanied by pipe-organ performances. Movies are shown in the evenings year-round; for shows and times, call 310/510–0179. The **Mardi Gras Arcade** (Metropole Market Place, tel. 310/510–0967) includes video games, Skeeball, and pinball. More video games and Skeeball are found at the **Avalon Arcade** (601 Crescent Ave., tel. 310/510–0291).

FOR PARENTS ONLY. The **Catalina Comedy Club** (Glenmore Plaza Hotel, 12 Sumner St., tel. 310/510–0017) is a cocktail lounge with stand-up comics. Each night at about 9 or 10 PM the **El Galleon Restaurant** (411 Crescent Ave., tel. 310/510–1188) and **Antonio's Pizzeria** (see Eats, *above*) welcome karaoke singers and other live entertainment.

Mountain and Inland Resorts ▐18

Though many non-Californians picture the Golden State as one endless beach, there are plenty of inland landscapes as well: cool forests, shimmering alpine lakes, rugged mountain peaks, sun-soaked vineyards, and desert sands. Resorts such as Lake Tahoe, Palm Springs, and the Wine Country north of San Francisco are world-renowned; Mammoth Lakes in the eastern Sierra and Big Bear and Arrowhead lakes in the San Bernardino Mountains are lesser known but just as appealing for kids and parents who love the outdoors. Each of these classic destinations can be enjoyed year-round, with every season bringing new adventures for young explorers.

Lake Tahoe

Mark Twain once called it "the fairest picture the whole earth affords"—a crystal-clear, deep-blue lake set at 6,200 feet in the Sierra Nevada, surrounded by forests and snowcapped mountain peaks. Lake Tahoe is North America's largest alpine lake: 22 miles long, 12 miles wide, 72 miles around, with an average depth of nearly 1,000 feet, and water that's an astonishing 99.7% pure. Since Twain first set eyes on Tahoe, the lake has been transformed into a year-round playground. The Tahoe area contains the largest concentration of ski resorts in the country (see Chapter 11), and with nearly 300 days of sunshine annually, the lake entices visitors all year with water sports, hiking, camping, fishing, bicycling, and horseback riding.

About two-thirds of the lake is in California and one-third is in Nevada, where high-rise casinos dominate the resort scene. (If you want to visit casinos, keep in mind that children aren't allowed in the gambling areas, though most have game arcades and some offer special kids' activities all day.) Each shore of the lake has its own "personality": the commercial hub along the southeast shore, centered on South Lake Tahoe, California, and Stateline, Nevada; the somewhat quieter and more rustic north shore; and on the west and east shores, woodsy trails, quiet beaches, and unobstructed lake views. We've visited in every season and stayed along every shore, and our children never tire of discovering new wonders at their favorite mountain lake.

The Basics

RESOURCES. **Lake Tahoe Visitors Authority** (for south shore: 1156 Ski Run Blvd., South Lake Tahoe 96150, tel. 530/544–5050 or 800/288–2463). **North Lake Tahoe Resorts Association** (for north shore: Box 5578, Tahoe City 96145, tel. 530/583–3494 or 800/824–6348). **Truckee-Donner Chamber of Commerce** (12036 Donner Pass Rd., Box 2757, Truckee 96160, tel. 530/587–2757). **U.S. Forest Service Lake Tahoe Visitors Center** (Rte. 89 west of Tallac Historic Site on south shore, tel. 530/573–2674; open June 15–Sept., daily 8–5:30; Memorial Day–mid-June and in Oct., weekends 8–5:30).

GETTING IN AND OUT OF LAKE TAHOE. **By Air: Lake Tahoe Airport** (tel. 530/542–6180), on Route 50, 3 miles south of the lake, is served by Boone Air from San Francisco, Los Angeles, and San Diego. Nevada's **Reno-Tahoe International Airport** (tel.

702/328–6400), the closest major airport (50 minutes from north Tahoe), is served by a number of national and regional airlines including American, United, and TWA. **Sierra Shuttle Service** (tel. 530/550–1777 or 888/417–8427) provides shuttle service to and from the airport. **Tahoe Casino Express** (tel. 702/785–2424 or 800/446–6128) runs 14 daily round-trip coaches from Reno Airport to South Lake Tahoe; the cost is $17 one-way, $30 round-trip; children under 12 ride free.

By Car: Lake Tahoe is about 200 miles northeast of San Francisco, a four- to five-hour drive. The major route is I–80 via Sacramento, which cuts through the Sierra Nevada about 14 miles north of the lake; from there routes 89 and 267 reach the north shore. U.S. 50 from Sacramento is a more direct route to the south shore. From Los Angeles, a drive of about 475 miles, follow Route 14 and U.S. 395 north, then head west on U.S. 50 to the south shore. For the north shore take routes 89 or 28 north from U.S. 50.

A scenic 72-mile highway (Rte. 89 on the southwest and west shores, Rte. 28 on the north and northeast shores, and U.S. 50 on the southeast) circles the lake. Allow at least three hours for a nonstop drive. Some stretches (especially around Emerald Bay) involve sharp winding curves.

By Train: Amtrak (tel. 800/872–7245) trains from the Oakland area, Sacramento, or Reno stop in Truckee, 14 miles north of Tahoe City on the north shore. Call 530/581–3922 for information on connections to Lake Tahoe.

By Bus: Greyhound (tel. 530/587–3822) stops in Truckee and South Lake Tahoe from San Francisco and Sacramento. The **South Tahoe Area Ground Express** (STAGE) and **Bus Plus** (tel. 530/573–2080) run 24 hours a day along U.S. 50 and the neighborhoods of South Lake Tahoe; June through Labor Day, STAGE runs a daily beach shuttle (called The Trolley) from

South Lake Tahoe to Camp Richardson and to Zephyr Cove, Nevada. On the lake's west and north shores, **Tahoe Area Transit** (TART, tel. 530/581–6365 or 800/736–6365) runs between Sugar Pine Point State Park (from Meeks Bay in summer) and Incline Village daily from 6:30 to 6:30, and from Tahoe City to Truckee; the fares are $1. The Tahoe City Trolley, serving downtown Tahoe City and adjacent recreation centers (10–5 daily, free); and the Truckee Trolley, serving downtown Truckee and Donner Lake (7:30–7:30 daily, $1), operate from late June to Labor Day only.

FAMILY-FRIENDLY TOURS. Hornblower's *Tahoe Queen* (Ski Run Marina, South Lake Tahoe, tel. 530/541–3364 or 800/238–2463), a 500-passenger paddle wheeler with a glass-bottom viewing area, sails on 2¼-hour narrated cruises to Emerald Bay ($16 adults, $8 under 12). During much of ski season, the boat also serves as a ski shuttle between the south and north shores of the lake; fares, including hotel transfers and lift ticket, are $75 adults, $50 ages 11 and under. The *MS Dixie II* (tel. 702/588–3508 or 702/882–0786), a 570-passenger paddle wheeler that also has glass-bottom viewing, sails on two-hour narrated cruises from Zephyr Cove, Nevada, to Emerald Bay, year-round ($16 adults, $5 ages 3–11). The 150-passenger paddle wheeler *Tahoe Gal* (tel. 530/583–0141 or 800/218–2464) takes two-hour historic and scenic cruises along the west shore and 3¼-hour cruises to Emerald Bay year-round, departing from Tahoe City ($15–$19 adults, $5–$8 ages 3–12).

BABY-SITTING. For a list of baby-sitters on the north shore, call the North Lake Tahoe Resorts Association (tel. 800/824–6348).

Scoping out Lake Tahoe

Attractions are arranged in rough geographic order, starting in South Lake Tahoe and continuing clockwise (west, north, then east) around the lake, to Nevada.

👫 3–15 The Heavenly Aerial Tram climbs on a five-minute, mile-long journey up to 8,250 feet at the Heavenly Ski Resort (see Chapter 11). The views of snowcapped Sierra peaks and the shimmering blue lake below are stunning. The Monument Peak Restaurant serves lunch, dinner, and Sunday brunch (lunch only in winter) with the panorama. Dinner-and-tram packages are available. The 2-mile Tahoe Vista Trail—suitable for youngsters—circles the summit; in summer you can explore on your own or take guided interpretive hikes.
🏔 *Follow Ski Run Blvd., then signs to Heavenly resort, South Lake Tahoe, tel. 702/586–7000 or 530/541–1330. Fare: $12 adults, $6 under 12. Open June–Oct., daily 9–9; Nov.–May, daily 9–3:30. Closed 1 or 2 wks for maintenance fall and spring.*

👫 6–15 The Tallac Historic Site on the south shore showcases three opulent summer estates—the Pope, Baldwin, and Valhalla—dating from the 1890s to 1930s. At the Baldwin Estate, don't miss the 1920-vintage room with period furnishings. The annual Great Gatsby Festival is held here in late August, when the 1920s flower again, complete with vintage clothing, music, cars, and kids' games. Surrounding the site is the Pope-Baldwin Recreation Area, which contains several easy trails (see Hiking, *below*), beaches for swimming, picnic areas among pines, and the U.S. Forest Service's Visitor Center (see Resources, *above*).
🏔 *Hwy. 89, 3 mi northwest of South Lake Tahoe, tel. 530/541–5227 or 530/573–2600. Admission: call for tour fees. Parking for Pope and Baldwin beaches: $3. Historic site open Memorial Day–mid-Oct.; call for tour hrs. Recreation area open year-round.*

👫 ALL Emerald Bay State Park (see Chapter 8), our pick for Tahoe's most beautiful spot, has scenery, hiking, a small beach, and, open for summer touring, **Vikingsholm,** a 38-room replica of a medieval Scandinavian castle.
🏔 *Hwy. 89 at Emerald Bay, tel. 530/525–7277 or 530/525–7232.*

👫 ALL D. L. Bliss State Park (see Chapter 8) is one of Tahoe's nicest, with great hiking, camping, and a sandy beach.
🏔 *Hwy. 89 between Emerald Bay and Meeks Bay, tel. 530/525–7277 or 530/525–7232.*

👫 ALL Sugar Pine Point State Park, Tahoe's largest, has sandy beaches, year-round camping amid cool forests, and a fishing pier. Kids 9 and up might enjoy touring the **Ehrman Mansion,** a stately, three-story summer estate set within the park. Free tours of the mansion, which was built in 1903 and is furnished in period style, are given between July and Labor Day, six times daily from 11 to 4.
🏔 *Hwy. 89, 1 mi north of Meeks Bay, tel. 530/525–7232 year-round or 530/525–7982 during summer. Park day-use fee: $5. Camping (175 sites): $14–$18 per night.*

👫 3–15 Fanny Bridge spans Lake Tahoe's only outlet, the Truckee River. One glance will tell you how the bridge acquired its name—all those people lined up with their backsides to the road, peering over the side for glimpses of giant trout. Bring some bread so the kids can feed the fish.
🏔 *Hwys. 89 and 28, Tahoe City.*

👫 6–15 The Gatekeeper's Log Cabin Museum offers one of the best records of the area's past, displaying Washoe and Paiute baskets and clothing as well as pioneer settlers' memorabilia. The surrounding park, which has nice picnic facilities, is open from mid-May through September.
🏔 *130 W. Lake Blvd., Tahoe City, tel. 530/583–1762. Admission free. Museum open May–Sept., daily 11–5.*

👫 9–15 The Watson Cabin Museum, Tahoe City's oldest building, dating from 1909, is furnished in period style.
🏔 *560 N. Lake Tahoe Blvd., Tahoe City, tel. 530/583–8717. Admission free. Open mid-June–Labor Day, daily noon–4.*

👫 3–15 The Squaw Valley Cable Car takes you on a 2,000-foot ride up to the

8,200-foot High Camp Bath and Tennis Club, site of the world's highest ice-skating rink (see Chapter 11), open year-round. Other High Camp recreation includes swimming, biking, hiking, tennis, and volleyball.
🔼 *Off Hwy. 89, 6 mi northwest of Tahoe City, tel. 530/583–6985. Cable car fare: $14 adults, $5 under 13. Open daily late June–mid-Sept., 8:30 AM–9:20 PM; mid-Sept.–late June, 8:30–4.*

(👫 **6–15**) **Truckee,** an old mining, logging, and railroad town northwest of Lake Tahoe, has a historic downtown section that retains much of its original look. Take the kids to see the Old Jail (one of the West's oldest) and other sites along Commercial Row, where there are also shops and restaurants to try out. Pick up a walking tour map at the Visitors Center (12036 Donner Pass Rd.).
🔼 *14 mi northwest of Tahoe City via Hwy. 89 (or Hwy. 267 from Kings Beach), tel. 530/ 587–2757.*

(👫 **1–12**) **The Sierra Nevada Children's Museum** allows kids to dress up in space suits and enter a spaceship, shop at a simulated store for kids, do arts-and-crafts projects, and explore changing interactive exhibits.
🔼 *11400 Donner Pass Rd., Truckee, tel. 530/ 587–5437. Admission: $3 ages 2 and over. Open Wed.–Sat. 10–4.*

(👫 **ALL**) **Donner Memorial State Park** honors the infamous Donner Party expedition, which resorted to cannibalism to survive the harsh winter of 1846–47. The Emigrant Trail Museum (open Sept.–May, daily 9–4; June–Aug., daily 9–5; admission $2 adults, $1 ages 6–12) documents the history with exhibits and a movie, and the park offers hiking, picnicking, camping (Memorial Day–Oct.; tel. 530/582–7894) and lakeside fishing and boating.
🔼 *Donner Pass Rd. (off I–80) 2 mi west of Truckee at Donner Lake, tel. 530/525–7232 or 530/582–7892. Park admission: $5 per car.*

(👫 **6–15**) **The Cal-Neva Resort** hotel and casino on the lake's northeastern shore straddles two states: The California-Nevada line runs right through the lobby. The quiet California side displays a nice collection of Washoe Indian artifacts; the Nevada side is a noisy whirl of slot machines and gaming tables and, for kids, a video arcade. Our kids like to stand with one foot in each state; in the outdoor pool, guests can swim from one state to the other.
🔼 *2 Stateline Rd. (Hwy. 28), Crystal Bay, NV, tel. 702/832–4000.*

(👫 **3–15**) **The Ponderosa Ranch**—you'll need to cross into Nevada for this one—appeals even to kids who have never seen *Bonanza* in reruns. At this ranch where the TV show was set, they can explore a replica of a Western town and ranch house, visit Hoss's "Mystery Mine," pet farm animals, and try their skill in a shooting gallery. For an extra $2 early risers can join hay-wagon breakfast rides, which leave from 8 to 9:30 daily Memorial Day to Labor Day. Summer also brings gold panning and free pony rides for young kids.
🔼 *Hwy. 28 south of Incline Village, NV, tel. 702/831–0691. Admission: $9.50 adults, $5.50 ages 5–11. Park open mid-Apr.–Oct., daily 9:30–5; limited hrs and activities rest of year, weather permitting; call for schedule and discount rates.*

BEACHES. Kids and polar bears may want to swim anytime, but most sane people wait till August.

El Dorado, Connelly, and **Regan** are three adjacent public beaches in South Lake Tahoe. El Dorado is the largest, but Regan has a children's playground. *Lakeview Ave. off Hwy. 50, South Lake Tahoe, tel. 530/544–4366.*

Camp Richardson Beach, convenient to South Lake Tahoe, has a marina with watersports rentals and a lakefront restaurant. *Hwy. 89 at Camp Richardson, tel. 530/542– 6570. Parking: $3. Rest rooms.*

Pope, Baldwin, and **Kiva** are three of the nicest beaches along the south shore. They're located in the Pope-Baldwin Recreation Area adjacent to the Tallac Historic

Site (see Scoping out Lake Tahoe, *above*). *Hwy. 89, 3 mi northwest of South Lake Tahoe, tel. 530/573–2600. Parking: $3.*

West End Beach, at the west end of Donner Lake, is another of our favorite family swimming places, with a sandy beach, a roped-off shallow area for tots, a children's playground, paddleboat rentals, fishing areas, tennis courts, and volleyball. *Donner Pass Rd. from I–80. Admission: $2.50 adults, $1.50 ages 2–18. Lifeguards during summer; picnic areas, rest rooms.*

The Kings Beach State Recreation Area on the north shore contains a 2,900-foot-long beach, a swimming area, a playground, picnic facilities, and water-sports (boats, canoes, kayaks, waterskis) rentals. *Hwy. 28, Kings Beach, tel. 530/546–7248; sports rentals, 530/546–2782. Parking: $5. Rest rooms.*

The North Tahoe Beach Center, a popular spot on a pretty stretch of the north shore, has an enclosed swim area, 26-foot glass-enclosed hot tub, four sand volleyball courts, a barbecue and picnic area, windsurfing, boat rentals, a fitness center, a sauna, a snack bar, and a clubhouse with games. *Hwys. 28 and 267, Kings Beach, tel. 530/546–2566. Admission: $7 adults, $3.50 under 12. Rest rooms.*

Sand Harbor Beach, a mile-long crescent of golden sand in Nevada's Lake Tahoe State Park, is well worth a trip across the state line. Kids can climb rocks and plunge into crisp, shallow waters. Get here early on summer weekends, when parking lots often fill up by 11 AM. *Hwy. 28 south of Incline Village, NV, tel. 702/831–0494. Day-use fee: $6 per car. Lifeguards during summer; picnic areas, rest rooms.*

Sports and Action

BICYCLING AND ROLLERBLADING. For details on mountain biking here, see Chapter 10. Stop at the Forest Service Lake Tahoe visitors center (see Resources, *above*) for trail maps ($3).

For road biking on the south shore follow the paved **City of South Lake Tahoe Bike Path,** which runs from El Dorado Beach to Pope Beach on the south shore. Then connect to the nearly flat 3½-mile paved **Pope-Baldwin Bike Path,** which runs from Pope to Baldwin beaches, paralleling Highway 89 along the lake; this path is also good for skaters. Rent bikes on the south shore at **Anderson's Bicycle Rental** (645 Emerald Bay Rd. at Hwy. 89, South Lake Tahoe, tel. 530/541–0500), which is located near the bike trail, or **Sierra Cycle Works** (3430 Hwy. 50, tel. 530/541–7505). Rent skates at **Lakeview Sports** (3131 Hwy. 50, South Lake Tahoe, tel. 530/544–0183).

On the north shore, the scenic and mostly flat **Truckee River Bicycle Trail** runs along the river 4½ miles from Tahoe City to Midway Bridge. The **West Shore Bike Path** runs along the lake from Tahoe City 9 miles south to Sugar Pine Point; some of the path runs along the shoulder of the highway and some terrain is steep, so this one is better for older kids. A great side trip off this path is to **Blackwood Canyon,** where a relatively flat road through the forest leads to a bridge over Blackwood Creek (off Hwy. 89, south of Sunnyside). All these trails are good for both cyclists and skaters. Another trail runs from Tahoe City 2½ miles northeast to **Dollar Point;** this one is mostly flat the first 2 miles. Rent bikes at **Cyclepaths** (1785 W. Lake Blvd., Tahoe Park, tel. 530/581–1171); or **Mountain Cyclery** (255 N. Lake Blvd., Tahoe City, tel. 530/581–5861; 8299 N. Lake Blvd., Kings Beach, tel. 530/546–3535). Rent skates at **Porter's Ski and Sport** (501 N. Lake Blvd., Tahoe City, tel. 530/583–2314); **Tahoe Gear** (5095 W. Lake Blvd., Homewood, tel. 530/525–5233); or **Cyclepaths** (see *above*).

BOATING, KAYAKING, AND CANOEING. For information about sailboats, powerboats, and kayaks, see Chapter 10. To canoe on Lake Tahoe, rent from **Tahoe Paddle & Oar** in Kings Beach on the north shore (tel. 530/581–3029); **Tahoe Water Adventures**

in Tahoe City (120 Grove St., tel. 530/583–3225); or, on the west shore, **Meeks Bay Marina** (Hwy. 89, 10 mi south of Tahoe City, tel. 530/525–7242).

CLIMBING AND ORIENTEERING. **Northstar's Adventure Park** (tel. 530/562–2285) offers an outdoor climbing wall for all ages. Other summer options at Northstar-at-Tahoe (see Chapter 12) are ropes challenge courses for ages 4 to 9 and 10 and up, and a mid-mountain orienteering course teaching map and compass reading. **Squaw Valley USA** (tel. 530/583–7673) has a 30-foot indoor rock-climbing wall, open every afternoon.

FISHING. Lake Tahoe, which never freezes, is open for fishing year-round. Licenses are available at local sporting goods stores; kids under 16 don't need a license. Prime catches include six kinds of trout plus kokanee salmon. You can fish from the lake shore at **Dollar Point** northeast of Tahoe City, along the **west shore** below Tahoe City, and at **Sand Harbor** and **Cave Rock** on the east shore. You can fish of the pier at **Sugar Pine Point State Park** when the water level is high enough. The **Truckee River** between Tahoe City and Truckee offers good trout fishing. For easy no-limit trout fishing from Memorial Day to Labor Day visit the **Tahoe Trout Farm** (Blue Lake Ave. off Hwy. 50, tel. 530/541–1491), where no license is needed. Admission, bait, and tackle are free; pay only for the fish you catch.

For half-day and all-day sportfishing trips in search of trout and salmon, contact **Tahoe Sportfishing Co.** (900 Ski Run Blvd., at Ski Run Marina, South Lake Tahoe, tel. 530/541–5448 or, in CA, 800/696–7797), the **Kingfish** (tel. 530/525–5360) in Homewood, or the **Big Mack** (tel. 530/546–4444 or 800/877–1462) in Carnelian Bay.

GOLF. The nine-hole **Bijou Municipal Course** (3464 Fairway Ave., South Lake Tahoe, tel. 530/542–6097) is good for beginners.

HIKING. Self-guided nature trails around the Forest Service visitors center (tel. 530/573–2600) at the **Pope-Baldwin Recreation Area** are wonderful for small children. The ⅛-mile Smokey's Trail has a safe campfire construction theme; the ¼-mile Tallac Historic Site trail leads to three historic estates (see Scoping out Lake Tahoe, *above*); the ½-mile Rainbow Trail along Taylor Creek leads to the Stream Profile Chamber, where kids can watch trout (and kokanee salmon spawning in the fall) through the floor-to-ceiling windows of an underwater viewing chamber; and the ⅜-mile Lake of the Sky Trail leads to Tahoe's south shore. A fairly flat 1-mile trail leads from the visitors center to gorgeous Fallen Leaf Lake, with views of Mount Tallac looming above.

The 4-mile Rubicon Trail (see Chapter 8) is my pick for the lake's most beautiful trail. Hugging the shoreline from **D. L. Bliss State Park** to **Emerald Bay,** it's rugged and moderately strenuous.

The **Tahoe Rim Trail** (tel. 702/588–0686) is a nearly complete 170-mile hiking path around the lake with high-elevation views. You can gain access to it at several points. Grades are generally moderate, but kids should be strong hikers to attempt sections of this trail.

HORSEBACK RIDING. Camp **Richardson Corral** (Hwy. 89 at Fallen Leaf Rd., Camp Richardson, tel. 530/541–3113) offers guided trail rides (including breakfast and evening barbecue rides), wagon rides, and pack trips from mid-May through September. **Northstar Stables** (910 Northstar Dr. off Hwy. 267, 6 miles north of lake, tel. 530/562–1230) offers trail rides, pony rides, hayrides, and pack trips from Memorial Day through September. **Squaw Valley Stables** (1525 Squaw Valley Rd., Olympic Valley, tel. 530/583–7433) offers summertime guided trail rides and pony rides.

HOT-AIR BALLOONING. Soar over the Sierra with **Mountain High Balloons** (tel. 530/587–6922 or 888/462–2683), or **Lake**

Tahoe Balloons (tel. 530/544–1221 or 800/872–9294). Both offer ½-hour and one-hour rides, with rates starting at $85 to $99. Mountain High flies from spring through fall and has no set minimum age for passengers; Lake Tahoe Balloons flies year-round, weather permitting, and has a minimum age of 7.

ICE SKATING. Skate daily at the Olympic-size rink at Squaw Valley's **High Camp Bath & Tennis Club** (tel. 530/583–6985). The **South Lake Tahoe Ice Center** (1176 Rufus Allen Blvd., South Lake Tahoe, tel. 530/542–4700) is open daily and welcomes skaters of all abilities.

MINIATURE GOLF. Magic Carpet Miniature Golf (5167 N. Lake Blvd., Carnelian Bay, tel. 530/546–4279; 2455 U.S. 50, South Lake Tahoe, tel. 530/541–3787) has locations on both the north and the south shores. **Lake Tahoe Mini-Golf** (3196 N. Lake Blvd., tel. 530/546–3196) is in Kings Beach. **Fantasy Kingdom** (Hwy. 50, 530/544–3833) is in South Lake Tahoe.

PLAYGROUNDS. Some of the best playgrounds in the Tahoe area are at **Regan Beach** (Lakeview Ave. off Hwy. 50, South Lake Tahoe, tel. 530/544–4366); **Kilner Park** (Hwy. 89, south of Sunnyside, tel. 530/583–3796); **Commons Beach** (Hwy. 28, Tahoe City, tel. 530/583–5544); and **North Tahoe Regional Park** (National Ave., 1 mi north of Hwy. 28, Tahoe Vista, tel. 530/546–7248).

RAFTING AND TUBING. In nondrought years, when the water level is high enough, rafting and tubing are popular on the **Truckee River,** starting at Tahoe City. These runs are fine for kids as young as 4—no white water here. Rent rafts and tubes at the **Truckee River Rafting Center** (205 River Rd., Tahoe City, tel. 530/583–7238 or 888/584–7238) or **Tahoe Raft and Gas** (Hwy. 89 and 28, Tahoe City, tel. 530/581–0123).

WATERSKIING. Rent water skis at **Porter's Ski and Sport** (501 N. Lake Blvd., Tahoe City, tel. 530/583–2314) or **Kings Beach Aqua Sports** (tel. 530/546–2782) at Kings Beach State Recreation Area. Take lessons at **La Pointe Watersports Center** (Tahoe City Marina, tel. 530/581–2066).

Eats

Besides the restaurants detailed below, you may want to check out the all-you-can-eat buffets at the casinos in Stateline, Nevada (which start a few yards from California). **Harrah's Forest Buffet** (tel. 702/588–6611) and **Harvey's Garden Buffet** (tel. 702/588–2411) are two of the best; they're open daily for breakfast, lunch/brunch, and dinner.

Tahoe House. This is our favorite place for a special family dinner at the lake. Brick walls, tablecloths, and candles make for a nice atmosphere. The big draw is the Swiss-German food: Wiener schnitzel, roast duckling, raclette. There's also California cuisine such as seafood specials, pastas, and wonderful appetizers like grilled polenta and crab cakes. Besides Wiener schnitzel, the children's menu includes fried chicken, spaghetti, and a small steak. All desserts are made in-house; few can resist the Sacher torte or the tiramisu. *625 W. Lake Blvd. (Hwy. 89, ½ mi south of intersection with Hwy. 28), Tahoe City, tel. 530/583–1377. Children's menu. Reservations advised. Dress: casual but neat. AE, D, DC, MC, V. $$$*

Lanza's. A classic family-style Italian restaurant with red-checked tablecloths, low lighting, and pine-paneled walls, Lanza's is bustling, noisy, and popular. The excellent food centers around pasta, chicken, veal, and Sicilian-style pizza. Kids can also choose from a children's menu (complete with puzzles and pictures to color) that includes spaghetti with meat sauce, ravioli, and other pasta dishes. *7739 N. Lake Blvd., Kings Beach, tel. 530/546–2434. Children's menu. No reservations. Dress: casual. MC, V. No lunch. $$–$$$*

Passaretti's. This casual knotty-pine Italian restaurant sticks to a simple formula: Serve plenty of good food at low cost. The soup and salad bar, for instance, costs $7.95 for unlimited visits. Among the main courses are old standards like chicken parmigiana or cacciatore, veal marsala, clams marinara, cannelloni, and filet mignon. Seven shapes of pasta are served with a choice of 11 different sauces. The children's menu includes spaghetti, manicotti, macaroni and cheese, and chicken strips. *1181 Emerald Bay Rd., tel. 530/541–3433. Children's menu. Reservations advised. Dress: casual. AE, MC, V. $$*

Heidi's. Promising the "best breakfast you'll ever have"—only a slight exaggeration—Heidi's certainly helps convince my kids to roll out of bed. The Swiss chalet–style decor fits well at alpine Lake Tahoe. The only problem is choosing from the huge, appealing menu (servers bring crayons to the table so kids can color). For breakfast choose from scrumptious Belgian waffles, crepes, omelets, pancakes, and French toast. Heidi's also serves lunch: hot and cold sandwiches, burgers, and salads. *3485 Hwy. 50, South Lake Tahoe, tel. 530/544–8113. Children's menu. No reservations. Dress: casual. MC, V. No dinner. $–$$*

Log Cabin Caffe. This local favorite is one of the top family breakfast spots in Tahoe. Tabletops are decorated with children's drawings, and your own budding young artist's work may be added to the decor if the staff, which provides crayons and paper, likes it. Breakfast choices, served all day, include waffles with fresh fruit, omelets, huevos rancheros, and eggs Benedict. Lunch features hot and cold sandwiches and burgers. Kids' lunch choices include a hamburger, "Mickey's grilled cheese and chips," or an "Elmer Fudd" (peanut-butter-and-jelly and chips). *8692 N. Lake Blvd., Kings Beach, tel. 530/546–7109. Children's menu. No reservations. Dress: casual. MC, V. No dinner. $–$$*

Where to Stay

Summer and ski season bring the highest prices at Lake Tahoe. Holiday periods require reservations well in advance. For reservations on the south shore, call 800/288–2463; for north shore reservations, call

800/824–6348. Ask about Family Adventure Packages, which include lodging, dining, and choice of recreational activities for four people over four nights.

Resort at Squaw Creek (see Chapter 12). A year-round resort at the base of beautiful Squaw Valley USA, Squaw Creek offers numerous family activities plus a children's program. *400 Squaw Creek Rd., Box 3333, Olympic Valley 96146, tel. 530/583–6300 or 800/327–3353, fax 530/581–6632. $$$*

Embassy Suites Resort. Adjacent to the Nevada state line in South Lake Tahoe, this nine-story, all-suites hotel is a great choice for families: near casinos and bright lights, but still in nongambling California. The spacious suites each have a bedroom (one king or two double beds and a TV), a large living room (sofa bed, armchair, TV and VCR, desk), and a galley kitchen with refrigerator and microwave. If you have young children, ask about childproof suites. My kids love to ride in the glass-walled elevators that overlook the three-level garden atrium. Children 12 and under stay free with parents. *4130 Lake Tahoe Blvd., South Lake Tahoe 96150, tel. 530/544–5400 or 800/362–2779, fax 530/544–4900. 400 suites. Facilities: 2 restaurants, deli, complimentary buffet breakfast, pool, fitness center, hot tub, sauna, coin laundry. AE, D, DC, MC, V. $$–$$$*

Inn by the Lake. Across U.S. 50 from a sandy beach, this luxury motel has good-size rooms with balconies, many with lake views. Seven suites are especially well suited to families, with living rooms that include couches and refrigerators; each room has its own TV, and the tub has a whirlpool bath. Videos and games are kept at the front desk for kids, and complimentary bicycles (suitable for ages 10 and up) are available for the bike path along the beach. Children under 12 sharing their parents' room stay free, and a complimentary Continental breakfast is served. *3300 Lake Tahoe Blvd., South Lake Tahoe 96150, tel. 530/542–0330 or 800/877–1466, fax 530/541–6596. 93 rooms, 7 suites. Facilities: Pool, hot tubs, sauna, croquet,* coin laundry, free shuttle to casinos and ski resorts. AE, D, DC, MC, V. $$–$$$

Northstar-at-Tahoe (see Chapters 11 and 12). This is one of Tahoe's top year-round family resorts, with organized children's programs and plenty of recreation. *Off Rte. 267, 6 mi north of lake, Box 129, Truckee 96160, tel. 530/562–1010 or 800/466–6784, fax 530/562–2215. $$–$$$*

Lakeland Village Beach and Ski Resort. On a sandy beach on the southern shores of Lake Tahoe, Lakeland Village provides the convenience of being near the lights and activity of South Lake Tahoe with a remarkably peaceful setting. We enjoyed our stay here in a modern condo unit that included full kitchen, fireplace, and a sleeping loft that the kids made a beeline for. Some units have four bedrooms, big enough for possibly two families to share (most of these units have multinight minimums). *3535 Lake Tahoe Blvd., South Lake Tahoe 96150, tel. 530/544–1685 or 800/822–5969, fax 530/544–0193. 212 rooms, 32 suites. Facilities: pool, tennis, hot tub, sauna, children's playground, horseshoes. Babysitting by reservation. AE, MC, V. $–$$$*

Camp Richardson Resort (see Chapter 12). A longtime family favorite along the south shore, this rustic resort is one of the top bargains at Tahoe. *Hwy. 89, Box 9028, South Lake Tahoe 96158, tel. 530/541–1801 or 800/544–1801, fax 530/541–1802. $–$$*

Falcon Lodge and Suites. This is another good family motel along the north shore, with a sandy beach, a pool, and a sundeck. You can get two- and three-bedroom family units here as well as regular rooms with double or queen beds. Some rooms have kitchens or microwaves; between October and May, the rates include a Continental breakfast. *8258 N. Lake Blvd., Kings Beach 96143, tel. 530/546–2583, fax 530/546–8680. 31 units. Facilities: Pool, beach, hot tub, coin laundry. AE, MC, V. $–$$*

Cedar Glen Lodge. A children's playground and grassy area for barbecuing first attracted us to this family-oriented motel nestled in

pine and cedar trees along the north shore. Motel units and cottages are available; most have refrigerators, many have kitchenettes, and the rates include a Continental breakfast. A heated swimming pool is open in summer, a spa and sauna year-round; a sandy beach lies across the highway. *6589 N. Lake Blvd., Box 188, Tahoe Vista 96148, tel. 530/546–4281 or 800/341–8000, fax 530/546–2250. 31 units. Facilities: Pool, hot tub, sauna. AE, D, MC, V. $*

Lazy S Lodge. The Lazy S contains motel units and cottages in a woodsy setting along the south shore, a few miles west (and away from the clamor) of downtown South Lake Tahoe. The rustic cottages include kitchenettes, dining rooms, and fireplaces; some motel units also have kitchenettes; and everyone has access to picnic tables and barbecues on the tree-shaded lawns. There's a heated pool (in summer) and a hot tub year-round, and the lodge is near biking and hiking trails, ski areas, and riding stables. *609 Emerald Bay Rd. (Hwy. 89), South Lake Tahoe 96150, tel. 530/541–0230 or 800/862–8881, fax 530/541–2503. 21 units. Facilities: pool, hot tub, picnic area, kitchenettes, fireplaces, courtesy shuttle to casinos (summer). AE, D, MC, V. $*

CAMPING. The campgrounds at **D. L. Bliss State Park** (168 sites), **Donner Memorial State Park** (154 sites), and **Emerald Bay State Park** (100 sites), all open from May to October, are especially nice; the campground at **Sugar Pine Point State Park** (175 sites) stays open all year. (See Scoping out Lake Tahoe, *above,* for more information on the parks.) You can also camp at South Lake Tahoe's **El Dorado Campground** (1150 Rufus Allen Blvd., tel. 530/542–6096, open Apr.–Oct.), adjacent to public beaches and a swimming pool.

Entertainments

AMUSEMENTS. Lake Tahoe Amusement Park (Hwy. 50, South Lake Tahoe, tel. 530/541–1300) includes rides, slides, a minitrain, and a raceway.

ARCADES. Besides the obvious attractions for adults, many Nevada-side casinos have arcades to entertain the kids. Among them are **Harvey's Resort Casino** (tel. 702/588–2411), **Horizon Casino Resort** (tel. 702/588–6211), and **Caesar's Lake Tahoe** (tel. 702/588–3515) in Stateline; and the **Cal-Neva Resort** (tel. 702/832–4000, **Tahoe Biltmore Lodge and Casino** (tel. 702/831–0660), and the **Crystal Bay Club** (tel. 702/831–0512), all in Crystal Bay.

MOVIES. In north Tahoe catch a flick at the **Cobblestone Theatre** (Cobblestone Center, Tahoe City, tel. 530/546–5951) or the **Brockway Theatre** (8707 N. Lake Blvd., Kings Beach, tel. 530/546–5951). In south Tahoe head for the **New Lakeside Cinema** (1043 Emerald Bay Rd., tel. 530/541–2121) or the **New Tahoe Cinema** (1054 Emerald Bay Rd., tel. 530/541–8406).

MUSIC, DANCE, THEATER. The annual **Valhalla Summer Arts and Music Festival** (tel. 530/541–4975) takes place in July and August at the Tallac Historic Site on the south shore. The annual **Lake Tahoe Summer Music Festival** and **Tahoe Mountain Musicals** are held under the stars each summer. **Shakespeare at Sand Harbor** (tel. 800/747–4697) presents the Bard each August in a natural sand amphitheater at Nevada's Sand Harbor State Park on Highway 28.

FOR PARENTS ONLY. Major nighttime entertainment is found at the big showrooms in Nevada casinos. The top venues are **Circus Maximus** at Caesar's Tahoe (tel. 702/588–3515), the **Emerald Theater** at Harvey's (tel. 702/588–2411), the **South Shore Room** at Harrah's (tel. 702/588–6611), and Horizon's **Grande Lake Theater** (tel. 702/588–6211).

The Wine Country

This bucolic region of hillside vineyards, old stone wineries, and small Victorian towns, only an hour's drive north of San Francisco,

can prove as enchanting to children as to adults. Because driving can be slow around here, it's usually best for one trip to choose either the upscale Napa Valley, the more rustic Sonoma Valley, or the woodsy Russian River area. In Calistoga, at the northern end of the Napa Valley, resorts focus around swimming pools fed by hot springs; the town of Sonoma has historic sites and a wonderful town plaza; and Healdsburg, along the Russian River, is a center for outdoor activities. Although summer is the most popular season here, the mild Mediterranean climate makes the Wine Country a good year-round destination. Autumn—when grapes are being harvested and the air turns crisp—is the nicest time of all.

The Basics

RESOURCES. Napa Valley Conference and Visitors Bureau (1310 Napa Town Center, Napa 94559, tel. 707/226–7459). **Sonoma County Convention and Visitors Bureau** (5000 Roberts Lake Rd., Suite A, Rohnert Park 94928, tel. 707/586–8100 or 800/326–7666; for lodgings reservations, tel. 800/576–6662). **Sonoma Valley Visitors Bureau** (10 E. Spain St., Sonoma 95476, tel. 707/996–1090). **Russian River Chamber of Commerce** (16200 1st St., Guerneville 95446, tel. 707/869–9000).

GETTING IN AND OUT OF WINE COUNTRY. By Air: San Francisco International and **Oakland International** (see Chapter 14) are the major airports closest to the Wine Country. The **Sonoma Airporter** (tel. 707/938–4246 or 800/611–4246) provides daily door-to-door service between San Francisco International and Sonoma. The **Sonoma County Airport**, near Santa Rosa, is served by United Express, which connects with San Francisco.

By Car: From San Francisco, follow U.S. 101 north across the Golden Gate Bridge. For the Russian River area stay on 101 north for about 55 miles to Healdsburg. To reach the Sonoma Valley, which starts about 35 miles from San Francisco, take Route 37 east from 101, then follow routes 121 and 12. To reach the Napa Valley, about 45 miles from San Francisco, follow Route 37 east to Route 29 in Vallejo, then go north. If you want to drive through beautiful uncongested countryside, head for the Silverado Trail, which parallels Route 29 for the length of the Napa Valley only a few miles to the east.

By Bus and Train: Golden Gate Transit (tel. 415/332–6600 or 707/544–1323) runs buses between San Francisco and Sonoma daily. **Amtrak** (tel. 800/872–7245) runs connecting bus service from Oakland to Santa Rosa, Napa, and Sonoma. **Sonoma County Transit** (tel. 707/576–7433) and **Napa Valley Transit** (tel. 707/255–7631 or 800/696–6443) provide bus transportation between Wine Country towns.

FAMILY-FRIENDLY TOURS. The restored vintage **Napa Valley Wine Train** (1275 McKinstry St., Napa, tel. 707/253–2111 or 800/427–4124) makes three-hour runs between Napa and St. Helena. Brunch, lunch, and dinner rides are offered, with rates ranging from $56.50 to $69.50 for adults and $12.50 to $16.50 for kids age 12 and under; children pay extra, however, for food ordered off a special children's menu. For the train ride only, with an à la carte menu available, adult tickets in a special deli car are $27.50. Reservations are required. Among special trips are murder mystery dinner theaters, an Easter Bunny train, a Santa Claus express, and a Halloween ghost train.

Scoping out the Wine Country

Attractions are arranged in geographical order, beginning with Sonoma County and then moving east to the Napa Valley.

(**ALL**) **Sonoma Plaza** is the largest—and probably the prettiest—town square in the state. Whenever we visit Sonoma, we spread out a blanket on the tree-shaded grass and have a picnic. There are two chil-

dren's playgrounds, a duck pond, and nearby places to buy picnic food and ice cream.
Bounded by Spain St., Napa St., and E. and W. 1st Sts.

(**9–15**) **Sonoma State Historic Park** (see Chapter 4) includes the Sonoma Mission and the home of General Mariano Vallejo.
Spain St., Sonoma, tel. 707/938–1519.

(**ALL**) **Sonoma Traintown** offers rides on scaled-down steam trains winding for 20 minutes through a forested park—passing waterfalls, crossing trestles, and stopping at a little petting farm, where kids can feed sheep, goats, and a llama.
20264 Broadway (Hwy. 12), 1 mi south of Sonoma Plaza, tel. 707/938–3912. Admission: $3.50 adults, $2.50 ages 16 months–16 years. Open mid-June–Labor Day, daily 10–5; Sept.–mid-June, Fri., weekends and holidays (except Christmas) 10–5.

(**3–15**) **Buena Vista** is California's oldest premium winery, and one of the most beautiful. We love its big picnic area, with tree-shaded tables lined up along a woodsy creek. Picnic supplies are for sale, and self-guided tours are offered.
18000 Old Winery Rd., Sonoma, tel. 707/938–1266. Open daily 10:30–4:30.

(**3–15**) **Jack London State Historic Park** (see Chapter 4), where the author of *The Call of the Wild* lived, worked, and died, is a great spot to hike and picnic.
2400 London Ranch Rd., Glen Ellen, tel. 707/938–5216.

(**9–15**) **The Luther Burbank Home and Gardens** (see Chapter 4) displays the handiwork—including unusual plant species—of the famed botanist.
Sonoma and Santa Rosa Aves., Santa Rosa, tel. 707/524–5445.

(**ALL**) **Howarth Memorial Park** has a special kids' area with a playground, pony rides, summertime petting zoo, merry-go-round, and miniature train. Families can also rent rowboats, paddleboats, and small sailboats ($7 per hour) for use on Lake Ralphine, or fish, play tennis, and hike.

🏕 *Summerfield Rd. off Sonoma Ave., Santa Rosa, tel. 707/543–3292. Amusements: $1– $1.50 each. Park open daily. Children's area open mid-June–Aug., Tues.–Sun. 11–5; Feb.– mid-June, Sept., and Oct., weekends 11–5.*

(👫 6–15) **Safari West** gives kids a chance to imagine themselves on an African safari, viewing giraffes, gazelles, zebras, and some 400 other exotic animals on a 240-acre wildlife preserve. Tours, which last about three hours, are given three times daily from April to October, and twice daily the rest of the year. Reservations are required.

🏕 *3115 Porter Creek Rd., Santa Rosa, tel. 707/579–2551. Call for directions. Admission: $48 adults, $24 under 17, ages 2 and under free. Open daily, weather permitting.*

(👫 3–15) **Windsor Waterworks and Slides,** in the Russian River area, lets kids cool off on four water slides (including a kiddie slide) and in swimming and wading pools. There's also a picnic area, volleyball court, and an arcade.

🏕 *8225 Conde La., Windsor, tel. 707/838– 7760. Admission: $13.25; adults may pay $7.25 for pools only. Open May–mid-June, weekends 10–7; mid-June–early Sept., daily 11–7.*

(👫 9–15) **The Silverado Museum** is dedicated to the life and works of Robert Louis Stevenson, author of *Treasure Island* and *Silverado Squatters.*

🏕 *1490 Library La., St. Helena, tel. 707/ 963–3757. Admission free. Open Tues.–Sun. noon–4.*

(👫 ALL) **V. Sattui** winery has a big, grassy picnic area filled with tree-shaded tables. The extensive deli sells cheeses, meats, and breads. You can taste in this stone winery, but not tour. Arrive early to get a good picnic spot.

🏕 *Hwy. 29 and White La., St. Helena, tel. 707/963–7774. Open daily 9–5.*

(👫 6–15) **Bale Grist Mill State Historic Park** centers on a restored 1848 flour mill

where a 36-foot waterwheel powers the heavy grindstones. On weekends a miller gives tours and demonstrations; everyone can sample the freshly milled grains.

🏕 *Hwy. 29, 3 mi north of St. Helena, tel. 707/963–2236. Day-use fee: $2 adults, $1 ages 6–17. Open mid-June–mid-Sept., daily 10–5; mid-Sept.–mid-June, weekends and holidays 10–5.*

(👫 3–15) **Old Faithful Geyser** (see Chapter 7) erupts every 40 minutes in a tower of steam and vapor.

🏕 *1299 Tubbs La., Calistoga, tel. 707/942– 6463.*

(👫 ALL) **The Petrified Forest** is a wonderland of huge stone logs created by ancient volcanic eruptions (see Chapter 7).

🏕 *4100 Petrified Forest Rd., 5 mi west of Calistoga, tel. 707/942–6667.*

(👫 3–15) **Sterling Vineyards** is fun to reach; SkyTram cars make a four-minute climb up to this white stucco winery, perched on a hilltop. You can take a self-guided tour, picnic on the terrace, and gaze out over the Napa Valley.

🏕 *1111 Dunaweal La., Calistoga, tel. 707/ 942–3344. Tram fee: $6 adults, $3 ages 3– 18. Open daily 10:30–4:30.*

(👫 6–15) **The Sharpsteen Museum,** tucked away on a Calistoga side street, is worth hunting out for its detailed diorama depicting Calistoga in its 19th-century heyday as a luxury spa; doll-like figures, dressed in the finery of the day, parade about with parasols and play croquet. A restored stagecoach also recalls the days when the wealthy rode up from San Francisco to "take the waters."

🏕 *1311 Washington St., Calistoga, tel. 707/ 942–5911. Admission free. Open May–Oct., daily 10–4; Nov.–Apr., daily noon–4.*

(👫 6–15) **Robert Louis Stevenson State Park,** where the author and his wife spent their 1880 honeymoon in a cabin on the slopes of Mount St. Helena, is cool, woodsy, and mostly undeveloped. A steep trail leads up to the old cabin site and beyond.

🏃 *Hwy. 29, about 7 mi north of Calistoga, tel. 707/942–4575. Admission free. Open daily 8 AM–sunset.*

Sports and Action

BICYCLING. Scenic country lanes ideal for road or mountain biking honeycomb the Napa and Sonoma valleys. The area around Calistoga in the upper Napa Valley is especially fine; ask for suggestions at bike rental shops. Experienced bicyclists love the **Silverado Trail** through the Napa Valley, but kids should be old and steady enough to ride on a highway. The town of Sonoma has paved bike paths that run by General Vallejo's home and other historic sites. In Sonoma rent bikes at the **Sonoma Valley Cyclery** (1061 Broadway, Sonoma, tel. 707/935–3377) or the **Good Time Bicycle Co.** (18503 Hwy. 12, Sonoma, tel. 707/938–0453 or 888/525–0453. In the Napa Valley rent at the **St. Helena Cyclery** (1156 Main St., St. Helena, tel. 707/963–7736).

CANOEING. The **Russian River,** which winds through much of the northern Sonoma Wine Country, offers great canoeing (see Chapter 10).

HIKING. One of the best hikes in Wine Country is the mile-long, gradual uphill trek to the ruins of Wolf House in **Jack London State Historic Park** (see Scoping out the Wine Country, *above*). **Armstrong Redwoods State Reserve** (Armstrong Woods Rd., 2 mi north of Guerneville, tel. 707/869–2015; parking fee $5), the best place in Wine Country to see virgin redwoods, has great easy trails: the ½-mile Pioneer Trail and the adjoining ¾-mile Luther Burbank Circle. **Bothe-Napa Valley State Park** (3801 Hwy. 29, 4 mi north of St. Helena, tel. 707/942–4575; day use fee $5 per car) also has hiking trails through redwoods, and a mile-long "History Trail" between Bothe-Napa Valley and **Bale Grist Mill State Historic Park** (see Scoping out the Wine Country, *above*), which is good for all ages. Energetic families with older children may want to tackle the

5-mile trail to the top of Mount St. Helena in **Robert Louis Stevenson State Park** (see Scoping out the Wine Country, *above*); the reward is views of the Napa Valley and distant mountain peaks.

HORSEBACK RIDING. The **Sonoma Cattle Company** (tel. 707/996–8566) offers guided trail rides year-round through Jack London State Historic Park (see Scoping out the Wine Country, *above*), Bothe-Napa Valley State Park (see *above*), and mountainous Sugarloaf Ridge State Park, between the Napa and Sonoma valleys. Riders must be at least 8. In the Russian River area you can take two-hour or half-day trail rides at the **Armstrong Woods Pack Station** (tel. 707/887–2939) in Armstrong Redwoods State Reserve. Rates range from $40 to $50. Riders without experience must be at least 8 years old; reservations are required.

HOT-AIR BALLOONING. The Napa Valley is a popular area for hot-air ballooning; see Chapter 10 for details. In the Sonoma Valley try **Air Flambuoyant** in Santa Rosa (tel. 707/838–8500 or 800/456–4711), which has a minimum passenger age of 5, or **Aerostat Adventures,** also in Santa Rosa (tel. 707/579–0183 or 800/579–0183). Both charge $175 for adults, $125 up to age 12.

ICE SKATING. The beautiful **Redwood Empire Ice Arena** (1667 W. Steele La., Santa Rosa, tel. (707/546–7147) is owned by cartoonist Charles Schulz, creator of *Peanuts.* The arena is open for public skating each afternoon and evening; hours vary, so call for times. It's closed to skaters during December for an ice show.

SWIMMING. For lake swimming head for **Lake Berryessa,** a man-made lake 25 miles northeast of Napa (take Hwy. 128 east from Hwy. 29; tel. 707/966–1419); or man-made **Lake Sonoma,** in the far northern reaches of the Wine Country (take Canyon Rd. or Dry Creek Rd. from Hwy. 101; tel. 707/433–9483). To swim in the Russian River try **Monte Rio Beach** in Monte Rio; **Johnson's Beach** or **Midway Beach** in Guerneville; or

Healdsburg Veterans Memorial Beach along Old Redwood Highway in Healdsburg. The hot-water pools (including a toddler wading pool) at **Morton's Warm Springs** (1651 Warm Springs Rd., off Hwy. 12, Kenwood, tel. 707/833–5511) are open from May to September. The hot pools at **Indian Springs Resort** (see Where to Stay, *below*) and the **Calistoga Spa Hot Springs** (1006 Washington St., Calistoga, tel. 707/942–6269) are open to the public.

Shops

The **Snoopy Gallery and Gift Shop** (tel. 707/546–3385) at the Redwood Empire Ice Arena (see Sports and Action, *above*) offers the world's largest selection of *Peanuts* merchandise.

One of the more atmospheric shopping centers in the area is a converted brick winery called **Vintage 1870** (Washington St., Yountville, off Rte. 29, tel. 707/944–2451). Sure to attract kids are Gillespie's, which sells ice cream and chocolate candy treats, and the Toy Cellar.

Eats

Ristorante Piatti. The northern Italian cooking is first-rate at this minichain with branches in the Sonoma and Napa valleys, and the decor is right out of Tuscany, open and rustic, with partially shaded outdoor dining patios. At the Yountville branch, we sat next to a 2-year-old boy who thoroughly enjoyed his "Bambini" pasta (with butter and cheese). The kitchen will also fix simple sauces (plain tomato sauce without garlic, for instance) for children. Parents and older kids can enjoy wood-fired pizzas, fresh salads, inventive sandwiches, house-made pastas, and grilled and roasted meats. *405 1st St. W, Sonoma, tel. 707/996–2351; 6480 Washington St., Yountville, tel. 707/944–2070. Reservations advised. Dress: casual but neat. AE, MC, V. $$–$$$*

Compadres Bar and Grill. When it's warm in the Napa Valley, we like to eat outdoors, and this lively Mexican restaurant has a large patio with shaded tables that overlook a green, rolling lawn. Inside, with ceiling fans and brick walls, Compadres has the feel of an old baronial mansion, which the place was. Tex-Mex standards—enchiladas, fajitas, tacos, burritos—are on the menu, along with specialties like *chile colorado* (Mexican stew) and an assortment of international quesadillas. Portions are very large. The children's menu includes a taco, a burrito, a Tijuana burger, or nachos. *6539 Washington St., Yountville, tel. 707/944–2406. Children's menu. Reservations advised. Dress: casual. AE, MC, V. $$*

The Diner. Though small and unpretentious-looking—a roadside diner with a counter, booths, and tables—this is one of the best-known and most popular eating spots in the Napa Valley. Breakfast, especially, draws big crowds, with dishes such as German potato pancakes, Southern-style cornmeal pancakes, breakfast burrito, and omelets. Lunch and dinner bring burgers and sandwiches plus Mexican specialties and American "home-style" meals. The children's menu includes grilled cheese, tacos, and roast chicken. *6476 Washington St., Yountville, tel. 707/944–2626. Children's menu. Reservations for 6 or more. Dress: casual. No credit cards. Closed Mon. $$*

The Spot. Everyone in the family should be able to find something to like at this colorful, informal diner: Burgers, pizza, a salad bar, a pasta bar, Mexican items, and dishes for kids are among the offerings. The Spot's old-fashioned soda fountain complements its '50s decor of pink plastic tablecloths, ceiling fans, pictures of rock-and-roll idols, and oldies on the jukebox. *Hwy. 29, 1 mi south of St. Helena, tel. 707/963–2844. Children's menu. No reservations. Dress: casual. MC, V. $*

FOR PICNICS. In Sonoma we always stop at the bustling **Sonoma Cheese Factory** (2 West Spain St., tel. 707/996–1931), for Sonoma jack cheese, sandwiches, and salads. Two exceptional Italian-style delis are **Lo Spuntino** (400 First St., Sonoma, tel. 707/

935–5656) and, in the Napa Valley, **Genova** (1500 Trancas Rd., Napa, tel. 707/253–8686).

Where to Stay

Meadowood Resort. On 250 wooded acres off Napa Valley's Silverado Trail, Meadowood provides a green, cooling retreat for active families. A rambling, New England–style country lodge and cozy bungalow suites nestle on the hillside. Furnishings are luxurious, and many units have fireplaces. The resort is noted for its outstanding croquet lawn. *900 Meadowood La., St. Helena 94574, tel. 707/963–3646 or 800/458–8080, fax 707/963–5863. 38 rooms, 48 suites. Facilities: 2 restaurants, 9-hole golf course, 2 heated pools, hot tub, sauna, children's playground, croquet, tennis courts, hiking trails, baby-sitting through concierge. AE, D, DC, MC, V. $$$*

Indian Springs Resort and Spa. Robert Louis Stevenson is said to have vacationed at this historic spa in 1880; today, families can stay in white wooden cottages and enjoy swimming in a wonderful Olympic-size outdoor mineral-water pool, built in 1913 and naturally heated by underground geysers. The homey cottages have kitchens, patios, and fireplaces; they are surrounded by wide lawns equipped with barbecues, lawn chairs, and hammocks. Parents can also take mud baths here—a unique experience—with real volcanic ash. *1712 Lincoln Ave., Calistoga, tel. 707/942–4913, fax 707/942–4919. 17 cottages. Facilities: pool, children's playground, croquet, tennis court, shuffleboard, surrey bicycles. MC, V. $$–$$$*

Best Western Sonoma Valley Inn. A block west of Sonoma Plaza, this good-size motel blends in with the early California feel of the town, with balconies, handcrafted furniture, and a courtyard that holds a heated pool and hot tub. Rooms have refrigerators and most have fireplaces. Free Continental breakfast is delivered to your room. Children under 12 stay free with parents. *550*

2nd St. W, Sonoma 95476, tel. 707/938–9200 or 800/334–5784, fax 707/938–0935. 72 rooms. Facilities: Pool, hot tub, free laundry. AE, D, DC, MC, V. $–$$

Napa Valley Railway Inn. Though billing itself as the "Napa Valley's most romantic inn," the Railway Inn can appeal to kids as much as to cooing couples. Nine restored vintage railroad cars sit on two tracks as though they were trains waiting at "Yountville Station"; each is a lodging unit, with one or two queen beds, TVs, big windows, and skylights. Views include vineyards and, from some cars, the passing Napa Valley Wine Train. *6503 Washington St., Yountville 94599, tel. 707/944–2000, no fax. 9 rooms. MC, V. $–$$*

Entertainments

MOVIES. The **Sebastiani Theatre** (1st St. E, Sonoma, tel. 707/996–2020) and the **Raven Theatre** in Healdsburg (tel. 707/433–5448) show first-run films.

MUSIC, DANCE, THEATER. The **Luther Burbank Performing Arts Center** in Santa Rosa (tel. 707/546–3600) presents a full calendar of plays, concerts, and other performances. Healdsburg has **free concerts in Healdsburg Plaza** on Sunday afternoons in summer; for information call 707/433–6935 or, in CA, 800/648–9922. **Buena Vista Winery** (tel. 707/938–1266) hosts a Shakespeare Festival on summer Sunday evenings. The **Russian River Jazz Festival** brings jazz to Johnson's Beach in early September.

FOR PARENTS ONLY. Many of the larger hotels present live music on weekends, but the best Wine Country nightlife is often an elegant dinner served on a patio under the stars at one of the area's fine restaurants.

Mammoth Lakes

Only 45 miles from the eastern entrance to Yosemite lies one of the jewels of the eastern Sierra, Mammoth Lakes. At elevation 7,800 feet, surrounded by peaks more than

11,000 feet high, Mammoth is best known as a winter ski resort (see Chapter 11), and snow can fall as late as June. But for families who love to hike, fish, ride horses, go mountain biking, and explore lakes, rivers, forests, and waterfalls in a pristine environment, Mammoth Lakes beckons in warm-weather months, too. The town of Mammoth Lakes, which resembles an alpine village—even the local McDonald's is in a chalet—makes a good base for exploring the surrounding countryside.

The Basics

RESOURCES. Mammoth Lakes Visitors Bureau (Box 48, Mammoth Lakes 93546, tel. 760/934–2712 or 888/466–2666). **U.S. Forest Service Visitors Center** (Rte. 203 at Main St., tel. 760/924–5500).

GETTING IN AND OUT OF MAMMOTH LAKES. By Air: Mammoth Lakes Airport (tel. 760/934–3813), 6 miles south of town, is served by **Mountain Air Express** (tel. 562/595–1011 or 800/788–4247) from Long Beach. **Mammoth Shuttle** (tel. 760/934–3030) provides airport and ski-lift transport.

By Car: The main gateway to Mammoth Lakes from north or south is U.S. 395, one of California's most scenic highways. From San Francisco, take I–80 east to U.S. 395, then go south on 395. From Los Angeles, take Highway 14 or I–15 north to U.S. 395 and go north. Both drives are about 325 miles. The town of Mammoth Lakes is 3 miles west of U.S. 395 on Route 203.

In summer you can also reach U.S. 395 from San Francisco via Highway 120 and Yosemite's scenic Tioga Pass, a distance of about 270 miles.

Route 203 becomes Main Street in town. It later joins Minaret Road, which leads to Mammoth Mountain and Devil's Postpile National Monument. Main Street, in turn, becomes Lake Mary Road, which leads to the lakes of the Mammoth basin. Cars are not permitted on the road to Devil's Post-

pile in summer between 7:30 AM and 5:30 PM (see By Bus, *below*).

By Bus: Greyhound (tel. 800/231–2222) offers daily service from Los Angeles, and from San Francisco via Reno, Nevada.

A daytime **shuttle bus service** ($7 adults, $6 ages 5–11) runs from Mammoth Mountain Inn to campgrounds, trailheads, resorts, and Devil's Postpile National Monument (see Chapter 7), from 8 to 6:30, between late June and mid-September.

FAMILY-FRIENDLY TOURS. Sierra Meadows Ranch (Old Mammoth Rd. at Sherwin Creek Rd., tel. 760/934–6161) offers a variety of one-hour evening hayrides to the foot of the Sherwin Mountains and back; the cost is $15 to $20 adults, $10 to $15 ages 3 to 12.

BABY-SITTING. Small World Child Care (tel. 760/934–0646) provides licensed day care at Mammoth Mountain Inn for children up to age 12. Rates for kids 2 and above are $35 half-day, $49 full day; newborns up to age 2 are $40 to $56. (Reserve well in advance, especially for holiday periods.)

Scoping out Mammoth Lakes

(**3–15**) The Mammoth Mountain **Gondola** runs to the top of 11,000-foot Mammoth Mountain for views of the entire region. Board the gondola at the main lodge, across from the Mammoth Mountain Inn. *Tel. 760/934–0745. Fare: $10 adults, $5 ages 6–12. Open July 4–Oct., daily 9:30–5:30; Nov.–July 3, daily 8–4.*

(**3–15**) The **Minaret Vista**, a stop along Route 203 en route to Devil's Postpile, provides a beautiful view of the Ritter Range, including a series of jagged peaks known as the Minarets. You can follow a short self-guided nature trail here.

(**3–15**) Devil's Postpile National Monument (see Chapter 7) is about 13½ miles from Mammoth Lakes. Highlights are the Postpile itself and Rainbow Falls. Between 7:30 AM and 5:30 PM in summer you have to

take a shuttle bus, which leaves from Mammoth Mountain Inn. (See By Bus, *above*.)
🏔 *Follow Minaret Rd. (Rte. 203) from Mammoth Lakes, tel. 760/934–2289 (summer), 209/565–3341 (winter).*

👫 6 – 15 **Sotcher Lake,** our favorite lake in the Mammoth area, has a 1¼-mile nature hike circling the lake, passing by steep bluffs (watch young children) and through an eerily beautiful "ghost forest" of dead lodgepole pines. Parts of the trail may be wet and muddy, and you may have to climb over a few logs. Pick up a booklet at the trailhead.
🏔 *Off Red's Meadow Rd., off Rte. 203 past Devil's Postpile National Monument.*

👫 6 – 15 **The Inyo Craters,** two 500-year-old volcanic explosion pits that now hold small lakes, are reached by an easy ¼-mile hike.
🏔 *Minaret Rd. to Scenic Loop Rd.; watch for sign on west side of road.*

👫 ALL **Lake Mary Road,** the extension of Main Street, runs past several lakes. **Twin Lakes,** at 8,600 feet, come first, about 2½ miles from town; the Twin Falls Overlook reveals a 300-foot waterfall. Two miles farther is **Lake Mary,** the largest of the lakes near town. Just past Lake Mary on the same road is small and pretty **Lake Mamie**; park here for another view of the waterfall at Twin Lakes. **Lake George** (off Lake Mary Rd. to Crystal Crag Dr. and Lake George Rd.) has a wonderful alpine setting. At the end of Lake Mary Road, about 5 miles from town, is **Horseshoe Lake,** deep blue and framed by mountain peaks. It's a great picnicking and hiking spot, with a good ½-mile trail to **McLeod Lake.**

👫 3 – 15 **The Mammoth Consolidated Gold Mine,** the remains of a 1920s-era mining camp, can be viewed along a self-guided interpretive trail, negotiable by stroller.
🏔 *Trailhead at top of Coldwater Campground, near Lake Mary off Crystal Crag Dr. Admission free.*

👫 ALL **Convict Lake,** named for a group of escaped prisoners captured here

nearly 100 years ago, is set in a "bowl" with a spectacular mountain backdrop. The small lake is popular for hiking, camping, trout fishing, waterskiing, and boating; there's a full-service resort here as well.
🏔 *U.S. 395, 4 mi south of Mammoth Lakes, then follow Convict Lake Rd. 3 mi west.*

👫 3 – 15 **The Hot Creek Fish Hatchery,** about 7 miles from town, contains breeding ponds for most of the 5 million fish planted annually in the lakes and rivers of the eastern Sierra.
🏔 *U.S. 395 south to Hot Creek Fish Hatchery exit, then Owens River Rd., tel. 760/934–2664. Open daily 8–4, weather permitting.*

👫 3 – 15 **The Hot Creek Geologic Site,** created by an ancient volcano eruption, is a landscape of boiling hot springs, fumaroles, and occasional geysers about 10 miles from town. You can soak in the hot springs here in a lovely natural pool, at your own risk; prominent signs warn of scalding water and chemicals in the water, but dozens of people—including children of all ages—show up anyway to soak on nice weekends, and there are changing rooms at the parking lot. (Make sure your kids stay in the shallow waters and away from the sources of heat.) We loved it. Or you can simply walk along boardwalks through the steep canyon to view Hot Creek's steaming volcanic features. Fly-fishing for trout is popular upstream from the springs. In its setting surrounded by snowcapped peaks, this is one of the most beautiful spots in the Eastern Sierra.
🏔 *U.S. 395 south to Hot Creek Fish Hatchery exit, then Owens River Rd. (gravel rd last 3 mi), tel. 760/924–5500. Open daily sunrise–sunset.*

👫 ALL **Crowley Lake,** the region's largest, is a man-made reservoir that offers boating, waterskiing, camping, and some of the best trout fishing in the eastern Sierra.
🏔 *Off U.S. 395, about 13 mi south of Mammoth Lakes.*

👫 ALL **June Lake,** a well-developed ski resort area (see Chapter 11), is about 15 miles north of Mammoth Lakes. In summer you can swim at a beach here, fish, sail, windsurf, and hike; a scenic drive loops around June and three other lakes.

🚶 *U.S. 395 north from Mammoth Lakes then Rte. 158 west (June Lake Loop), tel. 760/ 648–7584.*

Sports and Action

BICYCLING. Mammoth Lakes is one of the centers of mountain biking in the state; see Chapter 10.

BOATING AND CANOEING. At **Lake Mary** you can rent motorboats, pontoon boats, paddleboats, or canoes at Barrett's Landing (tel. 760/934–5353) or Pokonobe Lodge (tel. 760/934–2437). **Lake Mamie** has rowboats for rent at Wildyrie Lodge (tel. 760/934–2444). **Lake George** rents boats at the dock (tel. 760/934–2261).

FISHING. The Mammoth area offers some of the best trout fishing in the state. See Chapter 10 for details.

HIKING. The U.S. Forest Service visitors center (see Resources, *above*) distributes a map that outlines good hikes in the area for kids and has information about permits for hiking in wilderness areas.

Our favorite hikes in this area are at Devil's Postpile, Sotcher Lake, and Horseshoe Lake (see Scoping out Mammoth Lakes, *above*). From **Lake George,** you can hike to **Barrett, T.J.,** and **Crystal** lakes, via rocky, rugged uphill climbs best suited for young mountain goats (or kids at least 6 years old).

HORSEBACK RIDING. Mammoth is a prime areas for horseback riding. See Chapter 10 for details.

ROLLERBLADING. Rent skates at **Sandy's Ski & Sports** (Main St. near Center St., Mammoth Lakes, tel. 760/934–7518) or at **Footloose Sports Center** (Canyon St. and Minaret Rd., tel. 760/934–2400).

WATERSKIING. Water-skiers head for Crowley Lake (June–July only) or to **Grant**

Lake in the June Lake Loop all summer. Rent skis from **Sandy's Ski & Sports** (Main St. near Center St., Mammoth Lakes, tel. 760/ 934–7518).

WINDSURFING. Go windsurfing at **June Lake, Grant Lake,** or **Horseshoe Lake.** Wet suits are essential, even in summer.

Eats

The Mogul. An old-fashioned steak house with a friendly atmosphere, this local favorite is tucked away on a quiet side street. The excellent beef is accompanied by potatoes and a visit to the salad bar. You can combine grilled chicken or charbroiled shrimp with your steak; everything is delicious. The Kid's Menu doesn't skimp on size: It includes a 7-ounce sirloin, a charbroiled chicken breast, a ⅓-pound hamburger, or a giant hot dog. *Mammoth Tavern Rd. off Old Mammoth Rd., tel. 760/934–3039. Children's menu. Reservations accepted. Dress: casual but neat. AE, D, MC, V. No lunch. $$$*

Nevados. Some of the best and most creative cuisine in town is served here, in a relaxing atmosphere (with jazz in the background). The decor is contemporary and attractive—white tablecloths and white walls with colorful prints. Menus change every night, but always include pasta (for example, linguine with shrimp, sun-dried tomatoes, and garlic); fresh seafood (like seared ahi tuna with Cajun spices); and grilled meats. Kids can order from the children's menu (which includes steak, shrimp, and pasta), ask for small portions of regular menu dishes, or make special requests. *Main St. and Minaret Rd., tel. 760/934–4466. Children's menu. Reservations advised. Dress: casual but neat. AE, D, DC, MC, V. Closed 1 wk in early June and from late Oct.–early Nov. $$$*

Berger's. Don't even think about coming to this bustling restaurant unless you're *hungry.* Berger's is known, appropriately enough, for burgers—and some of the biggest portions I've ever seen, anywhere. (A half side order of french fries was enough to feed two or three of us, and we love fries.) There are also other generously sized hot sandwiches and salads for lunch, and beef ribs, buffalo steak, broiled chicken, and a grilled vegetable plate for dinner. The children's menu is strictly for ages 12 and under. *Minaret Rd., tel. 760/934–6622. Children's menu. Reservations advised. Dress: casual. MC, V. No breakfast. Closed 4–6 wks in May and June and 4–6 wks in Oct. and Nov. $$*

Blondie's Kitchen and Waffle Shop. One of the best places in town for breakfast, Blondie's is another spot that serves up big portions—especially the "Dagwood" sizes. (As you might have guessed, this brightly decorated little café has a comic strip theme.) For breakfast (served all day) the Belgian waffles and four-egg omelets are excellent; or you can choose a "Dagwood's Pig Out" (biscuits and gravy) or "Blondie's Eat Healthy Plates" (oatmeal or granola). Among lunch items are burgers, salads, Dagwood sandwiches, or other sandwiches. *Main and Lupin Sts., tel. 760/934–4048. Children's menu. No reservations. Dress: casual. MC, V. No dinner. $–$$*

Where to Stay

The **Mammoth Reservations Bureau** (tel. 760/934–2528 or 800/527–6273) helps you book into local condo complexes. Stop by the **U.S. Forest Service visitors center** on Main Street (see Resources, *above*) for a list of campgrounds and any needed permits. Price categories below do not include Mammoth Lakes' 10% bed tax.

Snowcreek Resort. This 355-acre condominium community on the outskirts of Mammoth Lakes has a beautiful setting, complete with duck ponds, a golf course, and mountain peaks in the background. Accommodations range from one to four bedrooms; both standard and deluxe units are available. Units are spacious and comfortable, with full living and dining rooms, kitchens, fireplaces, and VCRs. One unit we saw had a child's bedroom decorated with

Mickey Mouse posters, stuffed animals on the twin beds, and a closet filled with games, while the kitchen came with full spice rack, espresso machine, and milk-shake maker. There's even an on-premises nursery with a beautifully equipped play area (cost is $1 per hour per child). *Box 1647, Old Mammoth Rd., Mammoth Lakes 93546, tel. 760/934–3333 or 800/544–6007, fax 760/934–1619. 150 units. Facilities: 2 pools, 5 hot tubs, 9 tennis courts, golf (18 holes), racquetball, fitness center, gym, day care. AE, MC, V. $$–$$$*

Tamarack Lodge Resort. Overlooking beautiful Twin Lakes, this year-round resort offers lodge rooms and housekeeping cabins in a quiet, woodsy setting. This is the place to stay if you want to commune with nature—there are no TVs, but you can fish in the lake, rent rowboats or canoes, watch birds, maybe even spot a bear or two. Cross-country ski trails pass right by, and rentals are available on site. The cozy cabins look rustic from the outside, but inside they are modern, neat, and clean, with knotty-pine kitchens and private baths; some have sitting rooms and fireplaces or wood-burning stoves. Cabins range in size from one to three bedrooms and have front porches with lake views. Most of the lodge rooms are too small for families with more than one child. The spacious lobby of the lodge has a fireplace, chairs, a toddler play area, and games for older kids. *Lake Mary Rd., off Hwy. 203, Box 69, Mammoth Lakes 93546, tel. 760/934–2442 or 800/237–6879, fax 760/934–2281. 11 rooms, 25 cabins. Facilities: restaurant, cross-country ski trails. D, MC, V. $$–$$$*

Mammoth Mountain Inn. Across from the ski lodge on the slopes of Mammoth Mountain, this year-round resort hotel is comfortable and convenient for families. You can stay here car-free: Someone from the inn will pick you up at the airport, a shuttle bus runs into town, and, in summer, shuttle service goes to Devil's Postpile National Monument. Mammoth Mountain itself offers mountain biking in summer, skiing in winter.

For the on-site children's activities program, Small World Child Care, for newborns to 12-year-olds (see Baby-sitting, *above*), reserve space when you book your room. Accommodations include standard hotel rooms and condo units. Condo units can sleep up to 13 people; they have lofts with twin beds (giving parents privacy downstairs) and full kitchens. *Minaret Rd., Box 353, Mammoth Lakes 93546, tel. 760/934–2581 or 800/228–4947, fax 760/934–0701. 124 rooms, 91 condo units. Facilities: 2 restaurants, 3 indoor hot tubs, video games, ski storage, playground area, child care. AE, MC, V. $–$$$*

The Sierra Lodge. This is one of the nicest motels in town. All rooms are spacious and include kitchenettes with microwaves and refrigerators; all are no-smoking. An outdoor hot tub can soothe muscles sore from hiking or horseback riding (or skiing in winter), and there's a covered parking garage with ski lockers for winter guests' equipment. Children under 12 stay free, and a complimentary Continental breakfast is served. Several restaurants are within easy walking distance, and there's free shuttle service to ski areas. *3540 Main St., Mammoth Lakes 93546, tel. 760/934–8881 or 800/356–5711 (So. Cal. only), fax 760/934–7231. 35 rooms. Facilities: Hot tub, some kitchenettes, ski storage. MC, V. $–$$*

Entertainments

MOVIES. The **Plaza Theatre** (Sherwin Plaza on Old Mammoth Rd., tel. 760/934–3131) and the **Bishop Twin Theater** (237 N. Main St., tel. 760/873–3575) are convenient to town.

MUSIC, DANCE, THEATER. The **Mammoth Lakes Jazz Jubilee** (tel. 760/934–2478 or 800/367–6572) takes place in July at various outdoor venues. **Mammoth Mountain Music** (tel. 760/934–0606 or 800/228–4947) presents summertime jazz, country-western, rock, and reggae concerts in the Yodler Pavilion at the Mammoth Mountain Ski Area; call for a schedule.

FOR PARENTS ONLY. **Whiskey Creek** (corner of Main and Minaret Sts., tel. 760/934–2555) presents live bands weekends year-round and most nights in winter, upstairs from the restaurant. **Goats Bar** (Mono and Main Sts., tel. 760/934–4629) is a neighborhood pub with darts and pool. **La Sierra's** (Main St. east of Minaret Rd., tel. 760/934–8083) hosts rock, country, and blues acts, plus Mammoth's largest dance floor.

Big Bear and Lake Arrowhead

Los Angeles residents who want to escape to the mountains don't have to travel far. Two man-made mountain lakes, Arrowhead and Big Bear, are within a two-hour drive of greater Los Angeles. Lake Arrowhead is a mile-high, forest-lined alpine gem, around which has grown a compact resort community. It's privately owned, so only property owners and guests at local lodgings can swim in or boat on the lake. Big Bear, at elevation 6,750 feet in a 7-mile-long valley, with surrounding peaks reaching nearly 9,000 feet, is a top ski resort area in winter (see Chapter 11) and, with 22 miles of shoreline and numerous marinas, is open for public recreation in summer. Big Bear Lake, on the southern shore (often called the "Village"), is the heart of the resort area; don't confuse it with the less interesting Big Bear City, at the far eastern end of the lake.

The Basics

RESOURCES. **Lake Arrowhead Communities Chamber of Commerce** (Lake Arrowhead Village, Bldg. F290, Box 219, Lake Arrowhead 92352, tel. 909/337–3715). **Big Bear Lake Resort Association** (630 Bartlett Rd., Box 1936, Big Bear Lake 92315, tel. 800/424–4232). **U.S. Forest Service:** at Lake Arrowhead (Hwy. 18, ¼ mi east of Arrowhead turnoff, tel. 909/337–2444) and at Big Bear (Hwy. 38, 3 mi east of Fawnskin on north shore of the lake, tel. 909/866–

3437). The Big Bear Discovery Center there has an observation deck and exhibits, and nature talks are given.

GETTING IN AND OUT OF BIG BEAR/LAKE ARROWHEAD. By Air: Ontario International (tel. 909/937–2700), the nearest major airport, is about a one-hour drive southwest of Lake Arrowhead and is served by all major domestic carriers.

By Car: Take I–10 east from Los Angeles to Highways 30 and 330, which connect at Running Springs to the **Rim of the World Scenic Byway** (Hwy. 18), hugging the edge of the San Bernardino Mountains. Lake Arrowhead is about 90 miles from L.A., Big Bear about 120 miles. When traffic is heavy, a less direct route—Highway 38 from Redlands, which reaches Big Bear first—is often faster. Lake Arrowhead and Big Bear are 30 miles apart along Highway 18.

By Bus: Rim of the World Transit (tel. 909/338–1113) provides local bus service in both Big Bear and Lake Arrowhead.

FAMILY-FRIENDLY TOURS. You can take narrated lake tours aboard picturesque paddle wheelers at both Arrowhead and Big Bear. The little **Lake Arrowhead Queen** offers 50-minute cruises, leaving daily from the waterfront marina in Lake Arrowhead Village (buy tickets at LeRoy's Sports, tel. 909/336–6992); fares are $10 adults, $6.50 ages 4 to 12. The **Big Bear Queen** (tel. 909/866–3218) departs from Big Bear Marina for 90-minute tours of Big Bear Lake, daily from May to October; the cost is $9.50 adults, $5 ages 3 to 12. **Big Bear Jeep Tours** (tel. 909/878–5337) offers 2- to 4½-hour off-road tours from May to October focusing on local flora, fauna, gold mines, history, and wildlife (you may see bears, eagles, bobcats). Rates range from $37.95 to $79.95. The **Time Bandit,** a one-third-scale reproduction of a 16th-century English galleon, cruises the lake. The fares are $12.95 adults, $9.95 ages 3 to 11, free ages 2 and under.

Scoping out Big Bear and Lake Arrowhead

(★★ 2–12) Lake Arrowhead Village, a tri-level shopping mall that's the resort's commercial center, has a prime location on the lake along with numerous shops and restaurants.

(★★ 1–12) The Lake Arrowhead Children's Museum is a tiny, inviting, hands-on museum where kids can climb through a maze like an ant, pretend they're camping out, put on a puppet show, or create recycled art. Toddlers have their own "Peter Pan" play area, complete with pirate ship.
🏠 Lake Arrowhead Village, tel. 909/336–3093. Admission: $3.50. Open Wed.–Mon. 10–5, weather permitting.

(★★ 3–15) Heaps Peak Arboretum contains an easy (though not stroller-accessible) 7/10-mile trail through 33 acres of native plants and trees, with mountain vistas and possible wildlife sightings.
🏠 Hwy. 18, 2½ mi east of Lake Arrowhead, tel. 909/337–2444.

(★★ ALL)

The National Children's Forest is a tiny (20-acre) forest dedicated to the efforts of many youngsters who helped replant here after a devastating 1970 forest fire. The forest has a paved ½-mile interpretive trail that's stroller- and wheelchair-accessible. This is a good place for kids to learn about forest ecology.
🏠 Keller Peak Rd. off Hwy. 18, about 12 mi east of Lake Arrowhead, tel. 909/337–2444. Open daily.

(★★ ALL) Lake Gregory, a county park near Crestline, offers warm-weather swimming, picnicking, rowboat rentals, and a 300-foot water slide from Memorial Day through Labor Day.
🏠 North on Lake Gregory Dr. from Hwy. 18, west of Lake Arrowhead, tel. 909/338–2233. Admission: $3.

☂☂ ALL) The Alpine Slide at Magic Mountain is a local family favorite. Kids pilot their own toboggans down a track, controlling the speed themselves (small kids can ride with parents). There's also a water slide in summer; tube sliding in the snow in winter; go-carts, and a video arcade.

🏠 *800 Wildrose La., ¼ mi west of Big Bear Lake, tel. 909/866–4626. Slide $3; $15 for 5 tickets; under 6 free with adult. Snowplay: $12. Go-carts: $3.50. Alpine slide open mid-June–mid-Sept., daily 10–6; late Sept.–early June, weekdays 10–4, weekends 10–dusk. Snowplay daily in winter, 10–4. Water slide open mid-June–mid-Sept., daily 10–4.*

☂☂ 3 – 15) The Scenic Sky Chair at Snow Summit Mountain Resort (see Chapter 11) takes a mile-long, 20-minute ride to the top of the mountain, for panoramic views of Big Bear Lake. At the 8,200-foot summit you can hike, mountain bike, or have lunch at the outdoor View Haus Barbecue.

🏠 *Tel. 909/866–5766. Round-trip fare (or one-way trip with bicycle): $7 adults, $3 ages 7–12. All-day pass with bike: $19 adults, $8 ages 3–12 (half day: $14 adults, $6 ages 7–12). Open mid-May–mid-June and mid-Sept.–start of ski season, weekends 8–4; mid-June–mid-Sept., daily 8–4.*

☂☂ ALL) Moonridge Animal Park is a small zoo in a pine forest setting across from the Bear Mountain Ski Resort (see Chapter 11). It showcases species native to the San Bernardino Mountains: wolves, mountain lions, coyotes, foxes, eagles, grizzly bears, and a rare display of plains bison. Orphaned and injured wildlife are cared for here, too.

🏠 *Moonridge Rd., Big Bear Lake, tel. 909/866–0183. Admission: $2.50 ages 11 and up, $1.50 ages 3–10, ages 2 and under free. Open late May–Oct., daily 10–4.*

☂☂ 3 – 15) The Stanfield Marsh Waterfowl Preserve is the place to spot waterbirds and possibly, November through February, a wintering bald eagle.

🏠 *North Shore Dr., east of Stanfield Cutoff Rd. at eastern end of Big Bear Lake, tel. 909/866–7000.*

Sports and Action

BICYCLING. In the Arrowhead area, mountain bikers can use all Forest Service hiking trails except those in Heaps Peak Arboretum, the National Children's Forest, and the Pacific Crest Trail; get information from the U.S. Forest Service (see Resources, *above*). Rent mountain bikes at the **Lake Arrowhead Resort** (tel. 909/336–1511; see Where to Stay, *below*) or at **Snow Valley Ski Resort** (Hwy. 18, Running Springs, tel. 909/867–2751).

Big Bear is Southern California's top spot for mountain biking (see Chapter 10). For road biking the scenic 2-mile paved **Alpine Pedal Path** runs along the mostly undeveloped north shore of Big Bear Lake. Rent bikes at **Big Bear Bikes** (41810 Big Bear Blvd., Big Bear Lake, tel. 909/866–2224).

BOATING. Big Bear Lake is popular for sailboaters and powerboaters; see Chapter 10. At Lake Arrowhead, only property owners and lodging guests can launch private boats, but you can rent rowboats and pedal boats in summer at nearby **Green Valley Lake** (go north on Green Valley Rd., 7½ mi past Heaps Peak Arboretum, tel. 909/867–2009). You can also rent boats at the marina at **Silverwood Lake State Recreation Area** (at Crestline, go north from Hwy. 18 on Hwy. 138, tel. 760/389–2303).

FISHING. **Lake Arrowhead Resort** (see Where to Stay, *below,* and Chapter 12), has a fishing dock for guest use. Otherwise, anglers will have to head for **Lake Gregory** (see Scoping out Big Bear and Lake Arrowhead, *above*), **Green Valley Lake** (see Boating, *above*), or **Silverwood Lake** (see Boating, *above*).

Trout, bass, bluegill, perch, and catfish are prime catches in Big Bear Lake; get licenses and permits and rent boats and equipment at several lakeside marinas, including **Pleasure Point Landing** (tel. 909/866–2455). You can fish without a license at **Alpine Lakes Trout Fishing** (tel. 909/866–4532, see Chapter 10). The Big Bear area has several fishing competitions just for kids; ask at any marina for details.

HIKING. In the Big Bear area, most children should be able to handle the **Woodland Trail,** a mostly level 1½-mile loop on the north shore. On the south shore, the **Champion Lodgepole Pine Trail** and the **Bluff Mesa Trail** form an easy, connected 0.7-mile walk through lodgepole and Jeffrey pines. You can also gain access to the **Pacific Crest National Scenic Trail,** which runs for 39 miles through the Big Bear district, offering magnificent vistas. Ask for directions for these trails at the Forest Service ranger station (see Resources, *above*).

HORSEBACK RIDING. For guided trail rides, call **Snow Valley Riding Stables** (tel. 909/867–4048) near Running Springs; **Baldwin Lake Stables** (tel. 909/585–6482) east of Big Bear City; or **Magic Mountain Stables** (tel. 909/878–4677), next to the Alpine Slide. Most have minimum age requirements for trail rides, so check in advance.

ICE SKATING. The **Ice-A-Plex Ice Castle** (27307 Hwy. 189, Blue Jay, tel. 909/337–5283) is a beautiful open-sided Olympic-size rink in the forest, west of Lake Arrowhead. Admission is $6 for adults, $5 for ages 12 and under; a Sunday Family Pass costs $17 for two adults and two kids. Skate rentals are $2 extra. Call for public hours.

SWIMMING. Big Bear's sandy **Swim Beach** (Meadow Park, tel. 909/866–0130) is exclusively for swimming—no boats—and has lifeguards in summer.

WATER SPORTS. At Lake Arrowhead the **McKenzie Waterski School** (tel. 909/337–3814) rents waterskiing boats with driver. **Holloway's Marina** (tel. 909/866–5706) provides waterskiing lessons on Big Bear Lake. For water-ski rentals visit **Pine Knot**

Landing (tel. 909/866–2628) or **Skyline Ski & Sports** (653 Pine Knot Blvd., Big Bear Lake, tel. 909/866–3500).

For windsurfing at Big Bear try **Holloway's Marina** (tel. 909/866–5706) or **Pleasure Point Landing** (tel. 909/866–2445).

Shops

Visit **What in the World** (Lake Arrowhead Village, tel. 909/337–5080) for nature, science, and environmental items. The **North Pole Fudge Company** (618 Pine Knot Blvd., Big Bear Lake, tel. 909/866–7622) serves up more than 20 flavors of fudge, plus hand-dipped ice-cream bars, ice-cream sodas, and hot-fudge sundaes. **Teddy Bear Miniatures and Dolls** (583 Pine Knot Blvd., Big Bear Lake, tel. 909/866–2811) carries a delightful selection of dolls, dollhouses, teddy bears, miniatures, and toys.

Eats

Mozart's. For lunch at Mozart's you can have an Asian chicken salad, a duck salad with mango and papaya, or a tri-tip wrap in a tortilla. At dinner there's rack of pork or wild game such as quail and pheasant. The children's menu includes chicken tenders, butter noodles, and a kid-sized pizza. In warm weather you can eat outside on the patio. *40701 Village Dr., Big Bear Lake, tel. 909/866–9497. Children's menu. Reservations accepted. Dress: casual but neat. AE, D, DC, MC, V. $$–$$$*

Woody's Boat House. With indoor and outdoor dining overlooking the lake, Woody's has an airy, comfortable setting. The menu is pretty standard—beef, seafood, and salad bar—but the food is perfectly fine. Deep-fried ice cream is a guilty pleasure for dessert. *28200 Hwy. 189, Lake Arrowhead Village, tel. 909/337–2628. Children's menu. Reservations advised on weekends. Dress: casual. AE, D, MC, V. $$–$$$*

The Belgian Waffle Works. Right on the lake in Lake Arrowhead Village, this small café has attractive Victorian decor, but we like the outdoor patio (kids can feed the ducks). Belgian waffles (served with fruit, eggs, or bacon) are the delectable specialty, available until late afternoon. Lunch adds sandwiches, hamburgers, and salads. Dinner choices include fish, pasta, or fried chicken. Try to get here early on summer weekends, when the wait can reach up to an hour. *Dockside at Lake Arrowhead, tel. 909/337–5222. Children's menu. Reservations accepted for 6 or more. Dress: casual. D, MC, V. Closes at 5 in winter. $–$$*

Teddy Bear Restaurant. Kids' colorings of teddy bears are part of the decor at this inexpensive family restaurant. For breakfast are omelets, waffles, and pancakes; the lunch options include hamburgers, chili, salads, and sandwiches; dinners run to steaks, seafood, and fried chicken. Weekly dinner specials such as grilled trout are reasonably priced. *583 Pine Knot Blvd., Big Bear Lake, tel. 909/ 866–5415. Children's menu. No reservations. Dress: casual. AE, MC, V. $–$$*

Where to Stay

For help with lodging reservations at Lake Arrowhead, contact the **Chamber of Commerce** (tel. 800/337–3716). At Big Bear, contact the **Big Bear Lake Resort Association** (tel. 909/866–6190).

Lake Arrowhead Resort (see Chapter 12). This is *the* resort at Lake Arrowhead, with a prime lakeside location and an extensive supervised activities program for kids. *27984 Hwy. 189, Box 1699, Lake Arrowhead 92352, tel. 909/336–1511 or 800/800–6792, fax 909/336–1378. $$$*

Arrowhead Tree Top Lodge. This attractive lodge nestled in a pine forest is south of Lake Arrowhead, within walking distance of Lake Arrowhead Village. Rooms have private patios; some have fireplaces. The suites have kitchens and hold up to six people. A heated pool attracts kids, who can also wander along a creek running through the woods. *Hwy. 173, Box 186, Lake Arrowhead 92352, tel. 909/337–2311 or 800/358–8733, fax*

909/337–1403. 14 rooms, 6 suites. Facilities: pool, barbecue area. AE, D, DC, MC, V. $–$$

Cozy Hollow Lodge. This tree-shaded lodge near the lake in Big Bear Lake Village quickly caught our eye because of its prominent children's play area in front. Of the cabins or lodge rooms, five are big enough to sleep from four to eight people. All family-size units have kitchens or kitchenettes, a fireplace, and a TV. Kids up to age 18 stay free with their parents. *40409 Big Bear Blvd., Box 1288, Big Bear Lake 92315, tel. 909/866–9694 or (in So. CA) 800/882–4480, fax 909/866–2692. 13 units. Facilities: children's play area, hot tub, barbecue. AE, D, DC, MC, V. $–$$*

Shore Acres Lodge. On Big Bear Lake's southern shore, far enough away from the Village to escape the crowds, stand 11 nicely furnished cabins, shaded by tall pines. The cabins have knotty pine interiors and TVs; some have fireplaces. Young kids go for the playground with swing set, and all ages go for the heated pool. There's also a hot tub, barbecues, and a private boat dock for guests—the lake fishing is said to be quite good here. *40432 Lakeview Dr., Box 110410, Big Bear Lake 92315, tel. 909/ 244–2327 or 800/524–6600, fax 909/866– 1580. 11 cabins. Facilities: pool, hot tub, volleyball, badminton, boat dock. AE, MC, V. $–$$*

CAMPING. For camping information, contact the U.S. Forest Service (tel. 909/337– 2444, Arrowhead; 909/866–3437, Big Bear). Big Bear's **Serrano Campground** (North Shore La. off Hwy. 38, 2 mi east of Fawnskin, open Apr.–Dec.) is one of the nicest facilities for families.

Entertainments

ARCADES. **Sportland Amusement Center** (672 Pine Knot Blvd., Big Bear Lake, tel. 909/ 866–4250) and **Super Bear Arcade** (Village Dr., Big Bear Lake, tel. 909/866–8620) offer arcade and video games.

MOVIES. **Blue Jay Cinema 4** (Hwy. 189 and North Bay Rd., Blue Jay, tel. 909/337–8404) has four theaters; the **Village Theaters** (Village Dr., Big Bear Lake, tel. 909/866–5115) has two screens.

FOR PARENTS ONLY. For nightlife head to Big Bear Lake Village. The **Tail of the Whale Lakeside Lounge** (350 Alden Rd., tel. 909/866–5514) presents local bands several evenings a week; the **Hayloft Saloon** (in the Bowling Barn, 40625 Lakeview Dr., tel. 909/878–2695) has live country-and-western music.

Palm Springs Desert Resorts

Until we visited, we thought of Palm Springs as a place where affluent adults lounged poolside at lavish resorts and played golf in the desert sun. But we were soon hooked on this gleaming oasis as a place where families can play together, too. There are plenty of moderately priced places to eat and stay, and, it turns out, many of the lavish resorts genuinely welcome children and families. The scenery is dramatic, the sunshine is seemingly endless (350 days a year), and the desert is a source of unfailing fascination.

"Palm Springs" is actually shorthand for several desert resort communities, including nearby Palm Desert, Indian Wells, Rancho Mirage, La Quinta, Cathedral City, and Indio, all strung along a 20-mile stretch of the Coachella Valley of the Sonoran Desert, bounded by mountain ranges on three sides. Except for Indio, another long-established community, Palm Springs itself is the only city with a real downtown and contains most of the attractions featured here; the newer resort communities are primarily known for their hotels, golf courses, and residential areas. Keep in mind that the desert can get awfully hot around midday—especially in summer, when temperatures often top 100°F (some attractions close down in summer). We like to eat an early breakfast and do our sightseeing first thing in the

morning, and again later in the afternoon. To cool off at midday ride the tram up to Mount San Jacinto (where temperatures are often 40 degrees cooler than on the valley floor), picnic in palm-shaded Indian canyons, or head for a swimming pool or water slide.

The Basics

RESOURCES. Palm Springs Desert Resorts Convention and Visitors Bureau (69–930 Hwy. 111, Suite 201, Rancho Mirage 92270, tel. 760/770–9000 or 800/417–3529). **Palm Springs Visitors Information Center** (2781 N. Palm Canyon Dr., Palm Springs 92262, tel. 760/778–8418 or 800/347–7746).

GETTING IN AND OUT OF PALM SPRINGS. By Air: Palm Springs Regional Airport (tel. 760/323–8161) is served by several airlines including Alaska, American/American Eagle, America West, Delta/Skywest, United/United Express, and US Airways Express. Many hotels provide shuttles to and from the airport. **Ontario International Airport** (tel. 909/937–2700) is about an hour's drive west of Palm Springs.

By Car: Palm Springs is 110 miles southeast of Los Angeles and 140 miles northeast of San Diego. From Los Angeles, take I–10 east to Highway 111, which becomes Palm Canyon Drive, Palm Springs' main thoroughfare and connecting route to other desert communities. From San Diego, I–15 north connects to I–60 and I–10 east, which lead to Highway 111. Although some areas such as Palm Canyon Drive in Palm Springs and El Paseo in Palm Desert are walkable, attractions are so spread out that a car is nearly essential here.

By Train: Amtrak (tel. 800/872–7245) *Sunset Limited* trains, which operate between Los Angeles and Florida, stop in Palm Springs, Palm Desert, and Indio.

By Bus: Greyhound (311 N. Indian Canyon Dr., tel. 760/325–2053) stops in Palm Springs. **SunBus** (tel. 760/343–3451) provides local service for the entire Coachella Valley; the **Palm Desert/Indian Wells Resort Express Shuttle** (tel. 760/346–6111) offers regular free service between major hotels and shopping centers.

FAMILY-FRIENDLY TOURS. **Desert Adventures** (67-555 E. Palm Canyon Dr., Suite A104, Cathedral City, tel. 760/324–5337 or 888/440–5337) takes to the wilds with two-to four-hour guided jeep tours of canyons, deserts, and mountains. We loved the two-hour "Santa Rosa Mountain Adventure" tour, which explored rugged high-desert roads as our guide regaled us with Native American lore and fascinating tidbits about desert geology, wildlife, and local history. Tours range from $69 to $99 for adults, $64 to $95 for ages 6 to 12; reservations are necessary. I'd recommend these tours for school-age kids only.

Kids can pretend they're pioneers on mule-drawn **Covered Wagon Tours** (Box 1106, La Quinta, tel. 760/347–2161 or 800/367–2161), two-hour desert rides followed by cookouts and sing-alongs back at camp. Tours are $55 with dinner, $30 without; ages 6 to 17 half fare. Reservations are required.

Scoping out the Palm Springs Area

🏃 3–15 The Palm Springs Aerial Tramway is one of the most exciting mountain cable car rides in the world, filled with dramatic scenery and enough thrills to match a roller coaster (most kids love it, but it might be scary for some parents). The 80-passenger tram cars start at about 2,600 feet and climb to 8,500 feet, rising from desert climate to alpine in 14 minutes, as canyons, waterfalls, and sharp rock formations pass below. Plan to spend some time on the mountain top, starting with the terrace overlook, which offers a panorama of the Coachella Valley. Stop at the visitors center, the theater (where a 20-minute film shows how the tramway was built), and, if you're hungry, the Alpine Restaurant; special

Ride 'n' Dine tickets allow you to eat dinner (4 PM–9 PM) for $3 to $4 more than the tram fare. And there's more: mule rides, 54 miles of hiking trails in adjacent **Mount San Jacinto State Park** (see Hiking, *below*), and, from mid-November to mid-April, cross-country skiing trails, sledding, and tubing. Bring jackets or sweatshirts for the mountaintop, even on the hottest days in Palm Springs.

🏔 *Tramway Rd. off Hwy. 111, north of Palm Springs (Valley Station is 3½ mi uphill), tel. 760/325–1391. Fare: $16.95 adults, $10.95 ages 5–12. Open weekdays 10–9 (daylight savings time), 10–8 (standard time); weekends and holidays 8 AM–9 PM. Closed 2 wks in Aug.*

🏃 3–15 The Indian Canyons, 5 miles south of downtown Palm Springs, are the ancestral homes of the Agua Caliente band of Cahuilla Native Americans, who prized the canyons for their lush oases—the largest natural fan-palm oases in North America—abundant water, and wildlife. They're still part of the Agua Caliente reservation (the tribe owns more than 40% of the Coachella Valley, including much of Palm Springs). Three canyons are open to visitors: 15-mile-long **Palm Canyon**, noted for its lush stands of palms; **Murray Canyon**, home of Peninsula bighorn sheep and wild ponies; and **Andreas Canyon**, with fan palms, unusual rock formations, a creek, and foot trails through the canyon. Both Palm and Andreas Canyons have picnic tables, and Palm Canyon also has a trading post that sells hiking maps, snacks, and Native American art and jewelry.

🏔 *End of S. Palm Canyon Dr., Palm Springs, tel. 760/325–5673. Admission: $5 adults, $1 ages 6–12. Open Sept.–Mar., daily 8–5; Apr.–Aug., daily 8–6.*

🏃 3–15 Moorten Botanical Garden, a "living museum" of the desert, is right up the road from the Indian Canyons. Nature trails lead past Joshua trees, agaves, chollas, giant saguaros, palms, and petrified logs—more than 3,000 plants from desert regions around the world.

🏠 *1701 S. Palm Canyon Dr., Palm Springs, tel. 760/327–6555. Admission: $2 adults, 75¢ ages 5–15. Open Mon.–Sat. 9–4:30, Sun. 10–4.*

👫 6–15 The Palm Springs Desert Museum (see Chapter 5) has natural science exhibits that provide a fascinating introduction to the desert.
🏠 *101 Museum Dr., Palm Springs, tel. 760/325–7186.*

👫 9–15 The Village Green Heritage Center illustrates Palm Springs' history with three historic buildings and a Native American museum. The 1885 mud-brick McCallum Adobe and the 1894 Miss Cornelia White's House (tel. 760/323–8297) contain pioneer-era memorabilia; the 1930s-vintage Ruddy's General Store Museum (tel. 760/327–2156) showcases products and music from that era. The Agua Caliente Cultural Museum Center (tel. 760/323–0151) contains Cahuilla artifacts.
🏠 *219–223 S. Palm Canyon Dr., Palm Springs. Admission: 50¢. Hrs vary among sites; limited summer hrs.*

👫 2–15 Oasis Waterpark (see Chapter 9) is one of Palm Springs' most popular spots on searing summer days.
🏠 *1500 Gene Autry Trail, Palm Springs, tel. 760/325–7873.*

👫 1–12 The Children's Discovery Museum of the Desert lets kids bake (and eat) goodies, grow produce, or try other hands-on activities such as sorting out skeleton bones or painting an old car. Toddlers have their own play areas. Adults must accompany children.
🏠 *71-701 Gerald Ford Dr., Rancho Mirage La., Rancho Mirage, tel. 760/321–0602. Admission: $1 adults, $2 under age 18. Call for hrs.*

👫 2–15 The Living Desert Wildlife and Botanical Park (see Chapter 6) helps kids truly appreciate the desert and its animals.
🏠 *47–900 Portola Ave., Palm Desert, tel. 760/346–5694.*

👫 ALL Joshua Tree National Park (see Chapter 8) is a stunning desert environment about 60 miles from Palm Springs.
🏠 *74485 National Park Dr., Twentynine Palms, tel. 760/367–5500.*

👫 6–15 Big Morongo Canyon Preserve, en route to the northern section of Joshua Tree National Park, is home to 200 species of birds plus bighorn sheep, bobcats, and, yes, snakes (which you're most likely to encounter during warm months). Several short loop trails lead through the preserve.
🏠 *East Dr. exit off Hwy. 62 in Morongo Valley, then follow signs, tel. 760/363–7190. Admission free. Open Wed.–Sun. 7:30 AM–sunset.*

👫 ALL The Cabazon Dinosaurs, an offbeat "roadside attraction," is almost bound to catch your kids' attention from the highway. Two huge sculpted dinosaurs—a 45-foot brontosaurus ("Dinney") and a 65-foot Tyrannosaurus ("Rex")—have been featured in TV commercials and movies. A dinosaur gift shop in Dinney's belly helps pay the bills.
🏠 *I-10 in Cabazon, about 15 mi west of Palm Springs, tel. 909/849–8309. Admission free. Open daily 9–dark.*

Sports and Action

BICYCLING. More than 35 miles of well-marked bike trails wind through Palm Springs. Contact the Palm Springs Recreation Department (401 S. Pavilion St., tel. 760/323–8272) for trail maps. Rent bikes at Palm Springs Cyclery (611 S. Palm Canyon Dr., Palm Springs, tel. 760/325–9319) or Mac's Bike Rental (70–053 Hwy. 111, Rancho Mirage, tel. 760/321–9444).

FISHING. Lake Cahuilla County Park is stocked with trout, bass, and bluegill. The fishing fee is $5 adults, $4 for ages 15 and under. There's night fishing on Friday and Saturday in summer. You can also swim, picnic, hike, and camp here. *East on Hwy. 111 from Palm Springs to Jefferson St., Indio, turn* *right and go about 6 mi, tel. 760/564–4712 or 800/234–7275. Day-use fee: $2 per person, ages 13 and up; $1 ages 12 and under.*

Whitewater Trout Company, where you're almost guaranteed to land a fish, is a good place to take kids if they're just learning; you can barbecue what you catch here. *West on I–10 to Whitewater exit, then follow Whitewater Canyon Rd. 5 mi, tel. 760/325–5570. Fee: $3 plus $2.72 per pound for fish caught (tackle and bait included). Open Wed.–Sun. 9–5.*

GOLF. The Palm Springs region, known as the "winter golf capital of the world," has more than 85 golf courses, many open to the public.

HIKING. In **Mount San Jacinto State Park and Wilderness,** a 10-minute walk from the Palm Springs Aerial Tramway station brings you to Long Valley, where you can pick up hiking information and permits at the ranger station (tel. 760/327–0222). Easy hikes include the 1½-mile Desert View Trail and a ⅔-mile nature trail; watch for deer, eagles, and mountain lion tracks. *Box 308, 25905 Hwy. 243, Idyllwild 92549, tel. 909/659–2607.*

HORSEBACK RIDING. At **Smoke Tree Stables** (2500 Toledo Ave., Palm Springs, tel. 760/327–1372), families can take guided rides over desert trails and through Indian Canyons. The minimum age for kids to ride by themselves is 5; younger kids can double up with parents. The **Ranch of the 7th Range** (58th Ave., behind PGA West, La Quinta, tel. 760/777–7777) also offers guided trail rides, as well as horse-drawn hayrides with western music and barbecues.

PLAYGROUNDS. Three Palm Springs city parks—**Demuth Park** (Mesquite Ave. and Mountain View Dr.), **Ruth Hardy Park** (700 Tamarisk Rd.), and **Sunrise Park** (Ramon Rd. and Sunrise Way)—have play areas, barbecues, and picnic facilities. *Tel. 760/323–8272.*

Eats

Blue Coyote Grill. This attractive restaurant owes as much to New Mexico as to old Mexico, serving up delicious Southwestern and Mexican cuisine. Inside, ceiling fans revolve, walls are whitewashed, and Indian weavings decorate the glassed tabletops. Outside, a patio attracts families on warm evenings. House specialties include charbroiled chicken breast with mild jalapeño cream sauce; lamb marinated in garlic and grapefruit juice; and grilled halibut marinated in olive oil, garlic, and onion. Tex-Mex standards like enchiladas, fajitas, and chiles rellenos are done with flair. Dinner for *"niños"* offers a choice of quesadillas, tacos, or burritos. *445 N. Palm Canyon Dr., Palm Springs, tel. 760/327–1196. Children's menu. Reservations for 6 or more. Dress: casual but neat. AE, DC, MC, V. $$–$$$*

Las Casuelas Terraza. One of five Las Casuelas restaurants in the Palm Springs area, Terraza is lively, colorful, and very popular—it transported us right back to Mexico. Inside is a maze of rooms with ceiling fans; outdoors is an inviting patio with fountains. The crowds and live music nightly make this a place to come when you don't mind noise. The menu includes fajitas, enchiladas, tostadas, and tacos, plus *carne asada* (charbroiled steak), *pollo asado* (marinated broiled chicken), and *camarones al mojo de ajo* (prawns sautéed in butter and garlic). Hamburgers, taco salads, and *platos de niños* (a quesadilla or bean burrito for kids) are also available. The original Las Casuelas, just down the street (368 N. Palm Canyon Dr., tel. 760/325–3213), is smaller and quieter. *222 S. Palm Canyon Dr., Palm Springs, tel. 760/325–2794. Children's menu. Reservations advised. Dress: casual but neat. AE, D, DC, MC, V. $$–$$$*

Tony's Pasta Mia. We were first attracted to Tony's by the sidewalk tables along Palm Canyon Drive—good for people-watching—and by the promise of $5.95 bowls of pasta. A dozen types (spaghetti, ravioli, rigatoni, linguine, and so on) are served with the sauce of your choice: meat, marinara, pesto, Alfredo, and more. Portions are large. Dinners include seafood, chicken, and veal dishes, served with soup, salad, pasta, and vegetables. *370 N. Palm Canyon Dr., Palm Springs, tel. 760/327–1773. Reservations accepted. Dress: casual but neat. AE, D, DC, MC, V. $$–$$$*

Elmer's Pancake and Steak House. A Palm Springs favorite, Elmer's serves breakfast all day (plus lunch and dinner) to an often packed house. Pancakes, waffles, crepes, and three-egg omelets are the breakfast specialties, with lots of varieties to choose from; the lunch menu includes various burgers and sandwiches, soups, salads. Dinner choices include steaks, seafood, and chicken. *1030 E. Palm Canyon Dr., Palm Springs, tel. 760/327–8419. Children's menu. No reservations. Dress: casual. AE, D, DC, MC, V. $–$$*

Where to Stay

Call the **Palm Springs Desert Resorts Convention and Visitors Bureau** (tel. 800/417–3529) or **Palm Springs Tourism** (800/347–7746) for help with hotel bookings and information. Palm Springs is known for its immense, glamorous, and expensive resorts, but several welcome children and rates often fall dramatically (by half or more) in summer. To stay in a condo or private home, contact the **Rental Connection** (tel. 760/320–7336 or 800/462–7256).

Marriott's Desert Springs Resort & Spa. With waterfalls, lagoons, and gondola-style boats to ferry guests around, this 400-acre resort is most often likened to a giant oasis in the desert. The Kids Klub, which operates year-round, provides supervised daytime activities—including arts and crafts, pool games, and movies—for children ages 5 to 12. The Kids Klub is centered at the 3,000-square-foot Springs Pool, which is surrounded by cabanas, palms, and lush landscaping. The five other swimming pools include one with its own beach. For parents and older kids there are two 18-hole golf courses and a putting course, plus tennis courts and a spa with gym and exercise pool. *74855 Country Club Dr., Palm Desert,*

92260, tel. 760/341–2211 or 800/331–3112, fax 760/341–1872. 832 rooms and 52 suites. Facilities: 10 restaurants, 6 pools, golf (36 holes), 20 tennis courts, spa, gym. Children's program: $35 full day (siblings $25), $21 half day. Baby-sitting through concierge. AE, D, DC, MC, V. $$$

Renaissance Esmeralda Resort. Surrounded by lakes and the Santa Rosa Mountains and shaded by palms, this is another lavish resort that caters to families. Kids can splash in a wading pool or a pool with a 10-foot waterfall and sandy beach, while parents and older kids play tennis, golf (two courses), beach volleyball, or lawn croquet. The Kids'Camp, open daily ($30 for 9 AM–1 PM session), offers supervised activities for ages 5 to 12. If you're willing to brave the summertime heat, ask about the Family Fun Package, which includes room, half-day enrollment in Kids'Camp, adult admission to the spa, and free breakfast for the kids—all for only $109 (midweek only). *44-400 Indian Wells La., Indian Wells, 92210, tel. 760/773–4444 or 800/408–3572, fax 760/773–9250. 560 rooms. 2 restaurants, 3 pools, wading pool, 2 hot tubs, sauna, 2 golf courses, putting green, 7 tennis courts, basketball, health club, volleyball, bicycle rentals, children's programs. AE, D, DC, MC, V. $$$*

Ritz Carlton Rancho Mirage. Tucked into a hillside in the Santa Rosa mountains, the Ritz is all gleaming marble and brass, with original artwork and plush carpeting. Rooms are enormous and outfitted with antiques, marble bathrooms, and often two TVs and phones. But kids are catered to, with an excellent supervised activities program, Ritz Kids, for ages 5 to 12. A Kids Night Out of dinner and movies is also available. And there's more: The concierge stocks children's books, coloring books, stuffed animals, and videos (plus strollers, playpens, and car seats), restaurants and room service have children's menus, and a huge outdoor pool beckons. *68–900 Frank Sinatra Dr., Rancho Mirage 92270, tel. 760/321–8282 or 800/241–3333, fax 760/321–6928. 221* rooms, 19 suites. Facilities: 3 restaurants, pool, hot tub, fitness center, 10 tennis courts, hiking trails, basketball, volleyball. Children's program ($25/day). AE, DC, MC, V. $$$

Westin Mission Hills (see Chapter 12). This enormous Moroccan-style resort with swimming pools and extensive kids' programs caters to families. Dinah Shore and Bob Hope Drs., Rancho Mirage, 92270, tel. 760/328–5955 or 800/228–3000, fax 760/321–2955. $$$

Quality Inn. With a central location on East Palm Canyon Drive, this upscale motel contains two-room family suites with king-size and sofa beds, plus two bathrooms and TVs. (Smaller standard rooms have two queen-size beds.) Most rooms have refrigerators. The grounds are spacious and parklike, and there are two outdoor pools—a children's wading pool and a larger pool surrounded by a sundeck and palm trees. Children 18 and under stay free with parents. 1269 E. Palm Canyon Dr., Palm Springs 92264, tel. 760/323–2775 or 800/228–5151, fax 760/323–4234. 100 rooms, 24 suites. Facilities: pool, hot tub. AE, D, DC, MC, V. $–$$

Vagabond Inn. Another centrally located motel, the Vagabond Inn offers good value for budget prices. Rooms are smallish but clean and comfortably furnished. (There's only one two-bedroom suite, so call way ahead for that.) You can rent refrigerators. Outside, there's a fairly large heated pool and hot tub; a poolside snack bar serves breakfast and lunch (a coffee shop is nearby, too). 1699 S. Palm Canyon Dr., Palm Springs 92264, tel. 760/325–7211 or 800/522–1555, fax 760/322–9269. 120 rooms, 1 suite. Facilities: pool, hot tub, saunas. AE, D, DC, MC, V. $

Entertainments

ARCADES AND AMUSEMENTS. At **Camelot Park** (67–700 E. Palm Canyon Dr., Cathedral City, tel. 760/321–9893), kids can play miniature golf and video games, ride go-carts and bumper boats, or take some cuts in the batting cage. You pay by the activity; the hours vary.

MOVIES. The **Town Center Cinema 10** (Palm Desert Town Center, tel. 760/322–3456), the **Courtyard 10** (777 Tahquitz Canyon Way, tel. 760/322–3456), and **Cinemark Movies 10** (34–491 Date Palm Dr., Cathedral City, tel. 760/324–7674) all have 10 screens.

MUSIC, DANCE, AND THEATER. The **McCallum Theatre for the Performing Arts** (Bob Hope Cultural Center, 73–000 Fred Waring Dr., Palm Desert, tel. 760/340–2787) sometimes stages family concerts. Palm Springs holds a fall **free concert series** in Sunrise Park on selected evenings.

FOR PARENTS ONLY. The **Fabulous Palm Springs Follies** (Plaza Theater, 128 S. Palm Canyon Dr., Palm Springs, tel. 760/327–0225), a vaudeville-style revue with performers over age 50, is the hottest show in the desert; reserve ahead. **Cecil's on Sunrise** (1775 E. Palm Canyon Dr., Palm Springs, tel. 760/320–4202) features dancing to Top-40 disco, while the **Cactus Corral** (67–501 E. Palm Canyon Dr., Cathedral City, tel. 760/321–8558) has dancing to live country music.

Northern Forests and Lakes

Sierra and the Gold Country